NEW TESTAMENT

Step into the Story of Scripture

the voice ™

NEW TESTAMENT

Step into the Story of Scripture

By
Ecclesia Bible Society

THOMAS NELSON
Since 1798

NASHVILLE   DALLAS   MEXICO CITY   RIO DE JANEIRO

Published in Nashville, Tennessee, by Thomas Nelson.
Thomas Nelson is a trademark of Thomas Nelson, Inc.

Published in association with Eames Literary Services, Nashville, Tennessee

Printed in the United States of America

11 12 13 14 15 16 17 18 19 20—8 7 6 5 4 3 2 1

Table of Contents

The Books of the New Testament

Contributors to *The Voice*

Editorial Review

Maleah Bell, B. C. Blackwell, Matthew Burleson, David B. Capes, James F. Couch, Jr., Amanda Haley, Kelly Hall, David Morgan, Merrie Noland, Chris Seay

Biblical Scholars

B. C. Blackwell, PhD; Joseph Blair, ThD; Darrell L. Bock, PhD; Beverly Burrow, PhD; David B. Capes, PhD; Alan Culpepper, PhD; Peter H. Davids, PhD; J. Andrew Dearman, PhD; Joseph Dodson, PhD; Brett Dutton, PhD; Dave Garber, PhD; Mark Gignilliat, PhD; Peter Rhea Jones, Sr., PhD; Sheri Klouda, PhD; Tremper Longman, PhD; Creig Marlowe, PhD; Troy Miller, PhD; David Morgan, PhD; Frank Patrick, PhD; Chuck Pitts, PhD; Brian Russell, PhD; Felisi Sorgwe, PhD; Kristin Swenson, PhD; Preben Vang, PhD; Nancy de Claissé Walford, PhD; Kenneth Waters, Sr., PhD; Jack Wisdom, JD

Contributing Writers

Ginny Allen, Lee Allen, Isaac Anderson, Eric Bryant, Beverly Burrow, David B. Capes, Cathy Capes, Daniel Capes, Don Chaffer, Lori Chaffer, Tara Leigh Cobble, R. Robert Creech, Greg Garrett, Christena Graves, Sara Groves, Charlie Hall, Amanda Haley, Kelly Hall, Greg Holder, Justin Hyde, Andrew Jones, E. Chad Karger, Tim Keel, Greg LaFollette, Katie Lerch, Evan Lauer, Paul Littleton, Todd Littleton, Phuc Luu, Christian McCabe, Brian McLaren, Donald Miller, Mike Morrell, Damien O'Farrell, Sean Palmer, Jonathan Hal Reynolds, Matthew Ronan, Chris Seay, Robbie Seay, Kerry Shook, Christopher R. Smith, Chuck Smith, Jr., Allison Smythe, Leonard Sweet, Kristin Swenson, Alison Thomas, Phyllis Tickle, Gideon Tsang, Matthew Paul Turner, Lauren Winner, Seth Woods, Dieter Zander

Other Contributors

Kipton Blue, Tyler Burkum, Steven Delopoulos, Jill Paquette DeZwaan, Marilyn Duncan, Brandon Graves, Andy Gullahorn, Steve Hindalong, Will Hunt, Kelly Jackson, Matthew P. Jones, Phil Keaggy, Russ Long, Maeve, Steve Mason, Sandra McCracken, Andrew Osenga, Kendall Payne, Rob Pepper, Holly Perry, U. J. Pesonen, Andrew Peterson, Jay Pfeifer, Jill Phillips, Robbie Seay Band, Jami Smith, Luke Sullivant, Amy Wallenbeck, Derek Webb, Matt Wertz

A Word from Ecclesia Bible Society

I speak for every artist, musician, editor, writer, and scholar involved in this project when I tell you that we are all honored to have a small part in the sacred work of translating the Scriptures. It has been an honor to have labored, studied, fasted, and prayed over the work that we believe God has placed before us. We have not taken the task lightly, and through the process we have been changed. We are thrilled to see the ways that God uses His Word to speak to His people and reveal Himself to those who have never heard His voice clearly.

As you engage in this story, you may experience a strange feeling that may be best described as a vague sense that you are being followed or pursued. If so, your instincts are correct. This pursuit is one of the distinguishing characteristics of the Christian faith. This is the story of God's relentless pursuit of us, and in the story we will begin to hear His footsteps following unfailingly behind us. Some religions invite seekers to study a new language before they can read their sacred text; then they are asked to chase after a god that dwells in the heavens. But those of us who walk in the path of Jesus are able to read the truth about God in our native tongue, and we experience the beauty of God who has drawn near to us in the person of Jesus. He continues to speak to us through His Spirit and the Scriptures as He has to other men and women, boys and girls, since the beginning of time.

We believe that as you read you will be able to experience God taking the broken pieces of your life and making you whole; your anger and resentment will be replaced with hope and grace; you will imagine a new way to live as a participant in God's redemptive work in this world.

I invite you to listen to **The Voice** with an open heart. You will hear God as He whispers of His love to you.

Chris Seay
President, Ecclesia Bible Society

Preface

Any literary project reflects the age in which it is written. **The Voice** is created for and by a church in great transition. Throughout the body of Christ, extensive discussions are ongoing about a variety of issues including style of worship, how we distinguish cultural expressions from genuine expressions of faith, what it means to live the gospel, and how we faithfully communicate the essential truth of historic Christianity. At the center of this discussion is the role of Scripture. Instead of furthering the division over culture and theology, it is time to bring the body of Christ together again around the Bible. Thomas Nelson Publishers and Ecclesia Bible Society together are developing Scripture products that foster spiritual growth and theological exploration out of a heart for worship and mission. We have dedicated ourselves to hearing and proclaiming God's voice through this project.

Previously most Bibles and biblical reference works were produced by professional scholars writing in academic settings. **The Voice** uniquely represents collaboration among scholars, pastors, writers, musicians, poets, and other artists. The goal is to create the finest Bible products to help believers experience the joy and wonder of God's revelation.

Uniqueness of *The Voice*

About 40 different human authors are believed to have been inspired by God to write the Scriptures. **The Voice** retains the unique literary perspective of the human writers. Most English translations attempt to even out the styles of the different authors in sentence structure and vocabulary. Instead, **The Voice** distinguishes the uniqueness of each author. The heart of the project is retelling the story of the Bible in a form as fluid as modern literary works, yet remaining painstakingly true to the original Greek, Hebrew, and Aramaic texts. Accomplished writers and biblical scholars are teamed up to create an English rendering that, while of great artistic value, is carefully aligned with the meaning inherent in the original language. Attention is paid to the use of idioms, artistic elements, confusion of pronouns, repetition of conjunctions, modern sentence structure, and the public reading of the passage.

To help the reader understand how the new rendering of a passage compares to the original texts, several indicators are embedded within the text.

- **Standard type** denotes the dynamic translation that is the base all the elements are built on. It translates the many imprecise words that English translations have borrowed in their renderings: Lord, Christ, baptism, angel, and apostle. The process for each book began as negotiation between a gifted writer and scholars working in the original language. After that first phase, a few selected scholars carefully read the manuscript, comparing it to the original language, and evaluated the faithfulness to the text and the theological nuances of the translation. At the same time a publishing team ran consistency checks, copyedited the manuscript, and compared the rendering with the major existing English translations. A final acceptance process included each of the three groups impacting the translation: biblical scholarship, English writing competence, and publishing expertise.

- **Italic type** indicates words not directly tied to the dynamic translation of the original language. These words bring out the nuance of the original, assist in completing ideas, and often provide readers with information that would have been obvious to the original audience. These additions are meant to help the modern reader better understand the text without having to stop and read footnotes or a study guide.
- **Delineated material** expands on the theme found in the text. This portion is not taken directly from the original language and is set apart in a second color or a colored line, dividing it from the Bible text. It may include cultural, historical, theological, or devotional thoughts.
- **Screenplay format** is used to identify dialogue and to avoid the endless repetition of conjunctions, articles, and certain verbs. The speaker is indicated, the dialogue is indented, and quotation marks are avoided. This helps greatly in immediate comprehension of the situation for the user and in intensifying the dramatic presence during the public reading of Scripture. Sometimes the original text includes interruptions in the dialogue to indicate the attitude of the speaker or to show who is being addressed. This is shown either as a stage direction immediately following the speaker's name or as part of the narrative section that immediately precedes the speaker's name.

We follow the standard conventions used in most translations regarding textual evidence. *The Voice* is based on the earliest and best manuscripts from the original languages (Greek, Hebrew, and Aramaic). When significant variations influence a reading, we follow the publishing standard by bracketing the passage and placing a note at the bottom of the page, while maintaining the traditional chapter and verse divisions. The footnotes reference quoted material and help the reader understand the translation for a particular word. Words that are borrowed from another language and words that are not common outside of the theological community (such as "baptism," "repentance," and "salvation") are given expanded translations derived from more common terminology. For clarity some pronouns are replaced with their antecedents. Because Greek word order and syntax differ significantly from English, we have followed standard translation practices and altered these elements when necessary to help the reader achieve clarity in understanding Scripture and its meaning.

Our purpose in using these literary devices is to reveal the beauty of the Scriptures and to assist the reader in clearly and quickly understanding the meaning of the text. We are constrained to be faithful to these ancient texts while giving the present reader a respectful and moving experience with the Word of God.

A Different Translation Process

The Voice Bible is a different sort of translation. It combines the relative strengths of scholars who are experts in the original languages (in the case of the New Testament, Greek) and modern writers, musicians, and poets who are skilled in their use of English, our target language. Our idea was to set up a collaborative process whereby scholars and writers could work together to create a translation that was faithful and accurate to the original languages while at the same time beautiful and readable to our English-speaking audience. In some cases scholars and writers worked closely together; in others they worked at some distance or even anonymously. Members of the translation team from Ecclesia Bible Society and Thomas Nelson coordinated the overall process.

Whenever people render one language into another (whether ancient or modern), they are involved in translation. There are levels of formality in the translation process. Generally, these are described on a continuum between formal and functional equivalence. But these approaches are not followed strictly by any Bible translation team, and most translations must mix formal with functional elements in order to communicate clearly. Realistically, languages are too complex and fluid to be reduced to a single approach in translation. A strictly formal translation process will result in an unreadable text that obscures the meaning of Scripture rather than making it accessible. A strictly functional translation process will result in a text that might communicate to a reader well what the original text means but not what the original says.

With *The Voice* Bible we acknowledge the difficulties translation teams face and offer what might be described as a mediating position between the extremes. We describe our approach as "contextual equivalence." Recognizing that context is the most important factor in determining the meaning of a word, sentence, paragraph, or narrative, we have sought to create a Bible translation that preserves both the linguistic and the literary features of the original biblical text. A "contextual equivalent" translation technique seeks to convey the original language accurately while rendering the literary structures and character of a text in readable and meaningful contemporary language. This particular translation approach keeps in mind the smaller parts and the larger whole. In endeavoring to translate sacred Scripture, *The Voice* captures uniquely the poetic imagery and literary artistry of the original in a way that is beautiful and meaningful.

Two other related descriptors are used to situate a Bible translation in the field. Some claim their translations are "word-for-word" in contrast to those that are "thought-for-thought." Word-for-word translations generally claim to be more literal and therefore superior to those that are thought-for-thought. The critique is sometimes made that thought-for-thought translations reflect the interpretive opinions of the translators and are influenced by the contemporary culture more than word-for-word translations. This critique is not necessarily relevant, for these translation endeavors—whether from the so-called "word-for-word" (formal) or "thought-for-thought" (functional) translation philosophies—are only different in degree, not in kind.

There are four primary objections to these claims. First, every translation is an interpretation. Anyone who has studied translation theory recognizes that it is impossible for translators to get outside their skins and objectively render a text. The Italians say it bluntly: *tradutorre, traditore*—"The translator is a traitor." Even if it were deemed useful to design a computer program to translate mechanically the Scriptures into English, human subjectivity and judgment would still come into play in various ways; for example, choosing which texts to translate and deciding which English word to use to translate a specific

Greek word. Subjectivity and interpretive opinions are impossible to avoid in the translation process and do not necessarily have a negative impact on a translation.

This leads to a second objection regarding the nature of words and thoughts. The strict distinction between "word" and "thought" must be questioned. After all, a word is merely an expressed thought, whether spoken or written. This becomes clear when dealing with people who are fluent in multiple languages. When they have a thought they wish to express, they must choose which language, then which word or words, then which word order. There may be line of distinction between a thought and a word, but it is not a hard and fast line; it is at best a dotted line.

Third, words generally do not have a single meaning; they have a range of meanings—what linguists refer to as a semantic field. Even the translators of the King James Bible recognized that words do not carry the same sense every time they occur in a text (see preface to the 1611 edition). So, for example, how should one translate the Greek noun *dikaiosunē?* In one place the word might mean "justice," in another "righteousness," in another "equity" or "integrity," yet in another something that is "true" or "right." One must understand the context in which a word is used in order to render carefully its meaning in another language. This context is not just semantic but also historical and social. For example, our use of "God's Anointed" or "the Anointed One" as a translation of the title "Christ"—and in selected places expanded to "God's Anointed, *the Liberating King*"—captures something of the historical and social reality behind Jesus' identity. He is God's Anointed King who comes to liberate His people from sin, addiction, disease, oppression, and death.

To press this point even further, words don't just *mean* things, they *do* things. Words have both meaning and function; they function within clauses, sentences, paragraphs, and stories in ways that are different from the definition a person might find in a dictionary or lexicon. Beyond this, however, words also function in various ways to elicit emotions, actions, and responses from those who hear them. In order to translate a text well, one must consider not only what words mean but what they do.

Fourth, a word-for-word correspondence is difficult to maintain because translators may need multiple words in one language to express the meaning of a single word in another. Take for instance the Greek word *sōthēsetai* (Romans 10:13). Because of the way the English language works, it takes no fewer than four words to translate this single Greek verb: "he/she will be saved." Again, the context will reveal who will be saved, what salvation entails, and when it is realized.

When all of these factors are taken into consideration, **The Voice** represents a hybrid of the word-for-word and thought-for-thought approaches. In some places **The Voice** follows a word-for-word translation; in others it expresses the meaning more in a thought-for-thought approach. This is necessitated contextually both by the original language and by our target language (English). Responsibility to render the biblical languages carefully and to create a readable translation for an audience is not an either/or pursuit; a "contextual equivalent" translation seeks to be faithful and realistic to both tasks.

Another issue **The Voice** project team had to address involved inclusive language. Generally speaking, we have made no attempt to make **The Voice** gender neutral or gender inclusive. We have tried to follow the sense of the text and have made translation decisions based on the context. When, for example, Paul reminded the *adelphoi* ("brothers") of Corinth of the content of the gospel (1 Corinthians 15:1-8), it is unlikely that he intended to include the "brothers" and exclude the "sisters." Since the apostle adopted typical letter-writing practices of his day, his manner of addressing the community was likely determined by cultural mores. In such cases, we have decided to render the text "brothers and sisters." However, in texts where it is clear that the admonition is addressed to one gender and not the other, we have taken seriously the historical situation and utilized the appropriate masculine or feminine nouns and pronouns. The warnings against loose women in Proverbs 5-7, for example, are clearly aimed at young men. Furthermore, Proverbs 31 does not describe a remarkable partner or spouse but a remarkable woman who happens to also be a wife. This perspective respects the particular situations that gave rise to the texts in their original historical settings and does not seek to exclude (or include for that matter) those not being directly addressed by the biblical writers. Commentaries and proper exegesis can make reasonable application of texts across gender lines in ways translations cannot.

Finally, although **The Voice** Bible represents a new approach to Bible translation, we have intentionally avoided the tendency to use trendy language. Our goal was to capture the beauty and brutal honesty of the Scriptures in language that is timeless and enduring. In the process, we have come to recognize our profound indebtedness to the various strands of Christian tradition that have made these texts available. We stand in gratitude to a multitude of saints who gave their lives to preserve and transmit the Scriptures in their original languages from one generation to the next. We acknowledge the significant contributions made by the Reformers and their followers (not to mention their predecessors) to give us a common language and scriptural heritage in the English-speaking world. Although we have not always tried to imitate them, we have always learned from them. Our hope and prayer is that a new generation of people will encounter the Scriptures through **The Voice** and step into the story of Scripture.

Christ in This Translation

In its original Greek language the New Testament refers to Jesus hundreds of times as *Christos*. Most English translations of Scripture render this "Christ," which is not a translation but a transliteration. The unfortunate effect of this decision is that most readers mistake "Christ" as a kind of second name for Jesus. In fact, *Christos* is not a name at all; it is a title. It is a Greek translation of the Hebrew title "Messiah." So when the New Testament writers call Jesus "(the) Christ," they are making a bold claim—one of the central claims of the Christian faith—that Jesus is the Messiah. While there was no single expectation about the Messiah in Jesus' day, many of his contemporaries would have recognized the Messiah to be God's agent who comes in the last days to redeem God's people and repair our broken world.

While we understand that no single English word or phrase captures the richness of the term "Messiah," we made a strategic decision in **The Voice** to translate *Christos* and not simply to transliterate it. The root idea of *Christos* is derived from a Greek verb meaning "to anoint (with oil)." The act of anointing someone with oil is a way of setting that person apart for God's use. When people are anointed—kings and priests, for example—oil is poured over their heads, signifying God's Spirit coming upon them and empowering them for the tasks ahead. This is why we have decided to translate *Christos* as "God's Anointed," "the Anointed," or "the Anointed One," depending on context and narrative flow.

But there is another aspect of *Christos* we need to highlight. You see, according to tradition, the Messiah is to be a son of David, and as such he has a royal function to continue David's dynasty and to reign over a newly constituted kingdom. In order to become king, a person must have God's anointing. So from time to time, as we translate *Christos* as "God's Anointed," we have added the explanatory phrase "the Liberating King" to remind us of the primary mission and of the reason God elects and empowers Jesus in the first place. Jesus comes as the King of a new kind of kingdom and exercises His royal power to rescue and liberate His creation. Now this liberation takes place on various levels, all of which are related.

Not long after Jesus begins his public ministry, he returns to the synagogue in Nazareth—where He had grown up—and reads the Scripture portion that day from Isaiah 61 (Luke 4:18-19):

> The Spirit of the Lord the Eternal One is on Me.
> *Why?* Because the Eternal designated Me
>   to be His representative to the poor, to preach good news to them.
> He sent Me to tell those who are held captive that they can now be set free,
>   and to tell the blind that they can now see.
> He sent me to liberate those held down by oppression.
> *In short, the Spirit is upon Me* to proclaim that now is the time;
>   this is the jubilee season of the Eternal One's grace.

From the way Jesus responds to the reading that day, it is clear that He understands His Spirit-enabled work to be about proclaiming the good news, releasing exiles and other political prisoners, healing the sick, and freeing the oppressed—in a word, "liberating" the poor, the captive, the sick, and the marginalized from whatever threatens them. But there is more. The Scriptures declare that Jesus comes to liberate those made in His image from the power and penalty of sin, which is the reason God's good creation is so fouled up and disordered in the first place. In fact Paul tells the Romans that all creation has been damaged by sin and longs for the day when God's children are revealed and set free from the power of sin and death. When that day comes, creation itself will be liberated from its own slavery to corruption (Romans 8:18-25). By translating *Christos* as "God's Anointed, *the Liberating King*" on occasion we are reminded of the title's true meaning and emphasizing an important truth—namely this: that the extent of Jesus' kingdom as God's Anointed and the reach of His liberating work extend beyond our hearts, beyond our politics, beyond our world.

Step into the Story of Scripture

A New Way to Process Ideas

Chris Seay's (president of Ecclesia Bible Society) vision for *The Voice* goes back more than 20 years to his early attempts to teach the whole biblical narrative as the story of God's redemptive work in God's Anointed, Jesus of Nazareth. Chris observed that the way this new generation processes ideas and information raises obstacles to traditional methods of teaching biblical content. His desire has grown to present the Bible in ways that overcome these obstacles to people coming to faith. Instead of primarily propositional-based thought patterns, people today are more likely to interact with events and individuals through complex observations involving emotions, cognitive processes, tactile experiences, and spiritual awareness. Hence, out of that early vision comes the need to present Scripture in a narrative form. The result is a retelling of the Scriptures: *The Voice,* not simply words, but also meaning and experience.

The Timeless Narrative

The Voice is a fresh expression of the timeless narrative known as the Bible. Stories of God's goodness that were told to each generation by their grandparents and tribal leaders were recorded and assembled to form the Christian Scriptures. Too often, the passion, grit, humor, and beauty have been lost in the translation process. *The Voice* seeks to recapture what was lost.

From these early explorations by Chris and others has come *The Voice:* a Scripture project to help readers step into the story of Scripture. Thomas Nelson Publishers and Ecclesia Bible Society have joined together to develop Scripture products and resources to foster spiritual growth and theological exploration out of a heart for the mission of the church and worship of God.

Communicating the Story

Putting the Bible into the language of modern readers is a painstaking process that involves correlating ancient languages and cultures with the English vernacular. Scripture is filled with passages intended to inspire, captivate, and depict beauty; but earlier translations have not always been successful in communicating the beauty, poetry, and story of Scripture. *The Voice* is a collage of compelling narrative, poetry, song, truth, and wisdom. *The Voice* will call you to step into the whole story of God with your whole heart, soul, and mind.

Four Ways to Step into the Story

We have become accustomed to reading a few verses of Scripture at a time. Because we seldom read entire books or even complete passages, we tend not to get the full benefit of the fullness of a passage. These four different plans for reading the New Testament will help you hear the voice of God and benefit from entering into the story.

Readings to Celebrate Advent

Advent is a season that varies in length each year depending upon which day of the week December 25 falls. The season begins on the 4th Sunday before Christmas Day. To find when to begin the Advent readings, find the year in the middle column and begin on the day to the right of the correct year. You will be starting on the first Sunday in the Advent season and will end on Christmas Eve.

November

2011	27	Hebrews 4:14-16
2016	28	Matthew 17:1-9
2015	29	Hebrews 5:1-10
2014	30	1 Timothy 1:15-17

December

2013	1	Luke 4:16-21
2012	2	Hebrews 2:1-9
2017	3	John 1:1-18
	4	Hebrews 1:1-14
	5	Philippians 2:1-11
	6	Luke 2:41-52
	7	Matthew 3:1-17
	8	Matthew 4:12-25
	9	John 5:17-24
	10	John 5:25-47
	11	Matthew 9:32-38
	12	Mark 8:27-38
	13	Mark 9:33-37
	14	Mark 10:13-31
	15	Luke 19:28-40
	16	Luke 12:49-53
	17	1 John 2:24-29
	18	Luke 1:8-23
	19	Matthew 1:18-23
	20	Luke 1:24-38
	21	Luke 1:39-56
	22	Luke 1:57-80
	23	Luke 2:1-20
	24	Matthew 2:1-11

Readings for Lent and Easter

Ash Wednesday	Philippians 1:27-30	Saturday	Luke 7:36-50
Thursday	2 Corinthians 1:3-7	**Fourth Sunday**	Mark 5:21-43
Friday	2 Corinthians 4:7-12	Monday	Acts 2:37-41
Saturday	Galatians 6:1-5	Tuesday	2 Timothy 2:8-13
First Sunday	Acts 5:40-42	Wednesday	2 Timothy 4:16-18
Monday	Philippians 3:7-11	Thursday	Acts 10:39-46
Tuesday	Acts 3:17-23	Friday	1 John 1:5-10
Wednesday	Mark 9:38-50	Saturday	Romans 3:21-28
Thursday	Luke 24:24-26	**Fifth Sunday**	James 5:13-18
Friday	Luke 24:46-49	Monday	Romans 5:1-11
Saturday	Hebrews 2:10-18	Tuesday	Romans 6:12-18
Second Sunday	Hebrews 4:6-10	Wednesday	Romans 7:7-14
Monday	Hebrews 9:23-28	Thursday	Romans 8:18-25
Tuesday	1 Thessalonians 4:1-8	Friday	John 12:1-7
Wednesday	Colossians 1:9-14	Saturday	John 12:23-36
Thursday	1 Peter 1:8-17		
Friday	1 Peter 2:21-25	**Palm Sunday**	Matthew 21:1-16
Saturday	1 Peter 3:8-18	Monday	Luke 22:39-62
Third Sunday	1 Peter 4:12-16	Tuesday	Luke 22:63-71
Monday	1 Peter 5:6-11	Wednesday	Luke 23:1-10
Tuesday	Matthew 6:1-13	Thursday	Mark 15:1-14
Wednesday	Matthew 18:15-22	Friday	John 19:1-37
Thursday	Ephesians 4:25-32	Saturday	John 19:38-42
Friday	Mark 11:19-26	**Easter Sunday**	John 20:1-31

Read the New Testament in 24 Weeks

Weeks 1–6

Week 1

Sunday	Matthew 1:1–2:23
Monday	Matthew 3:1–4:25
Tuesday	Matthew 5:1–7:29
Wednesday	Matthew 8:1–34
Thursday	Matthew 9:1–38
Friday	Matthew 10:1–42
Saturday	Matthew 11:1–30

Week 2

Sunday	Matthew 12:1–50
Monday	Matthew 13:1–58
Tuesday	Matthew 14:1–15:39
Wednesday	Matthew 16:1–17:27
Thursday	Matthew 18:1–19:30
Friday	Matthew 20:1–34
Saturday	Matthew 21:1–46

Week 3

Sunday	Matthew 22:1–46
Monday	Matthew 23:1–39
Tuesday	Matthew 24:1–51
Wednesday	Matthew 25:1–46
Thursday	Matthew 26:1–75
Friday	Matthew 27:1–66
Saturday	Matthew 28:1–20

Week 4

Sunday	Hebrews 1:1–2:18
Monday	Hebrews 3:1–5:14
Tuesday	Hebrews 6:1–7:28
Wednesday	Hebrews 8:1–9:28
Thursday	Hebrews 10:1–11:40
Friday	Hebrews 12:1–13:25
Saturday	Romans 1:1–32

Week 5

Sunday	Romans 2:1–3:31
Monday	Romans 4:1–5:21
Tuesday	Romans 6:1–7:25
Wednesday	Romans 8:1–39
Thursday	Romans 9:1–10:21
Friday	Romans 11:1–12:21
Saturday	Romans 13:1–14:23

Week 6

Sunday	Romans 15:1–16:27
Monday	Mark 1:1–45
Tuesday	Mark 2:1–28
Wednesday	Mark 3:1–35
Thursday	Mark 4:1–41
Friday	Mark 5:1–43
Saturday	Mark 6:1–56

Read the New Testament in 24 Weeks

Weeks 7–12

Week 7

Sunday	Mark 7:1-37
Monday	Mark 8:1-38
Tuesday	Mark 9:1-50
Wednesday	Mark 10:1-52
Thursday	Mark 11:1-33
Friday	Mark 12:1-44
Saturday	Mark 13:1-37

Week 8

Sunday	Mark 14:1-72
Monday	Mark 15:1–16:20
Tuesday	1 Corinthians 1:1-31
Wednesday	1 Corinthians 2:1–3:23
Thursday	1 Corinthians 4:1–6:20
Friday	1 Corinthians 7:1–8:13
Saturday	1 Corinthians 9:1–10:33

Week 9

Sunday	1 Corinthians 11:1–12:31
Monday	1 Corinthians 13:1–14:40
Tuesday	1 Corinthians 15:1-58
Wednesday	1 Corinthians 16:1-24
Thursday	2 Corinthians 1:1–2:17
Friday	2 Corinthians 3:1–4:18
Saturday	2 Corinthians 5:1–6:18

Week 10

Sunday	2 Corinthians 7:1–9:15
Monday	2 Corinthians 10:1–11:33
Tuesday	2 Corinthians 12:1–13:14
Wednesday	1 Peter 1:1–3:7
Thursday	1 Peter 3:8–5:14
Friday	2 Peter 1:1–3:18
Saturday	Luke 1:1-80

Week 11

Sunday	Luke 2:1-52
Monday	Luke 3:1-38
Tuesday	Luke 4:1-44
Wednesday	Luke 5:1-39
Thursday	Luke 6:1-49
Friday	Luke 7:1-50
Saturday	Luke 8:1-56

Week 12

Sunday	Luke 9:1-62
Monday	Luke 10:1-42
Tuesday	Luke 11:1-54
Wednesday	Luke 12:1-59
Thursday	Luke 13:1-35
Friday	Luke 14:1-35
Saturday	Luke 15:1–16:31

Read the New Testament in 24 Weeks

Weeks 13–18

Week 13

Sunday	Luke 17:1-37
Monday	Luke 18:1-43
Tuesday	Luke 19:1-48
Wednesday	Luke 20:1-47
Thursday	Luke 21:1-38
Friday	Luke 22:1-71
Saturday	Luke 23:1-56

Week 14

Sunday	Luke 24:1-53
Monday	Galatians 1:1-2:21
Tuesday	Galatians 3:1-4:31
Wednesday	Galatians 5:1-6:18
Thursday	Ephesians 1:1-2:22
Friday	Ephesians 3:1-4:32
Saturday	Ephesians 5:1-6:24

Week 15

Sunday	James 1:1-27
Monday	James 2:1-3:18
Tuesday	James 4:1-5:20
Wednesday	Acts 1:1-2:47
Thursday	Acts 3:1-4:37
Friday	Acts 5:1-6:15
Saturday	Acts 7:1-60

Week 16

Sunday	Acts 8:1-40
Monday	Acts 9:1-43
Tuesday	Acts 10:1-48
Wednesday	Acts 11:1-12:25
Thursday	Acts 13:1-52
Friday	Acts 14:1-15:41
Saturday	Acts 16:1-40

Week 17

Sunday	Acts 17:1-18:28
Monday	Acts 19:1-41
Tuesday	Acts 20:1-38
Wednesday	Acts 21:1-40
Thursday	Acts 22:1-23:35
Friday	Acts 24:1-25:27
Saturday	Acts 26:1-32

Week 18

Sunday	Acts 27:1-44
Monday	Acts 28:1-31
Tuesday	Philippians 1:1-2:30
Wednesday	Philippians 3:1-4:23
Thursday	Colossians 1:1-2:23
Friday	Colossians 3:1-4:18
Saturday	Titus 1:1-3:15

Read the New Testament in 24 Weeks

Weeks 19–24

Week 19

Sunday	Philemon 1-25
Monday	Jude 1-25
Tuesday	John 1:1-51
Wednesday	John 2:1-3:36
Thursday	John 4:1-54
Friday	John 5:1-47
Saturday	John 6:1-71

Week 20

Sunday	John 7:1-53
Monday	John 8:1-59
Tuesday	John 9:1-41
Wednesday	John 10:1-42
Thursday	John 11:1-57
Friday	John 12:1-50
Saturday	John 13:1-38

Week 21

Sunday	John 14:1-15:27
Monday	John 16:1-17:26
Tuesday	John 18:1-40
Wednesday	John 19:1-42
Thursday	John 20:1-21:25
Friday	1 Thessalonians 1:1-3:13
Saturday	1 Thessalonians 4:1-5:28

Week 22

Sunday	2 Thessalonians 1:1-3:18
Monday	1 Timothy 1:1-2:15
Tuesday	1 Timothy 3:1-4:16
Wednesday	1 Timothy 5:1-6:21
Thursday	2 Timothy 1:1-2:26
Friday	2 Timothy 3:1-4:22
Saturday	1 John 1:1-2:29

Week 23

Sunday	1 John 3:1-24
Monday	1 John 4:1-5:21
Tuesday	2 John 1-13
Wednesday	3 John 1-15
Thursday	Revelation 1:16-2:29
Friday	Revelation 3:1-4:11
Saturday	Revelation 5:1-6:17

Week 24

Sunday	Revelation 7:1-8:13
Monday	Revelation 9:1-11:19
Tuesday	Revelation 12:1-13:18
Wednesday	Revelation 14:1-16:21
Thursday	Revelation 17:1-18:24
Friday	Revelation 19:1-20:15
Saturday	Revelation 21:1-22:21

Daily Readings for Personal Growth

40 Days with God

Introduction to the New Testament

God's Covenants with His People

Covenants Are All Around Us

Our lives are filled with many different kinds of commitments or promises that may then be formalized into contracts. When couples exchange vows in a wedding, for example, they are entering into the covenant of marriage. Each person brings something to the relationship and can expect certain things in return. When someone buys or sells in the market, a covenant is made for goods or services. When a person goes to work for a company, covenants and contracts—some formal, others informal—are necessarily involved. When students receive a syllabus from an instructor, they are taking part in a covenant with their university. In every covenant, the agreeing parties bring something to the table. As we know from experience, different kinds of covenants have different kinds of expectations.

If we think about it, we realize that covenants are woven into the fabric of our everyday lives. Since so much of our lives are lived in covenant-making and covenant-keeping actions, the "covenant" became the perfect vehicle to carry God's plan to restore the broken world. The Christian Scriptures—both Old and New Testaments—bear witness to this covenant story.

But what is a "testament"? Simply put, a testament is a covenant, a contract, an agreement between two or more people or parties. So "testament" is a relational term; it implies that a relationship exists between at least two people. Often it is the act that establishes the relationship in the first place and makes the future possible.

The Story of God's Promises

The heart of the Christian Scriptures, both Old and New Testaments, is a narrative of God's covenants with and promises to His people and the world. Concerned with the proliferation of evil, sin, and its dire consequences on His creation, God decides that the best route to reclaim His broken creation is to reveal Himself to one person, and to another, and then to another, on the way to redeeming the entire world.

Part Two

The New Testament is part two of the Christian Scriptures. It consists of 27 books that were written originally in Greek within a generation or two of Jesus' death and resurrection. So while it may seem that you have in hand one book, it is not one book at all. The New Testament is a collection of books, the Book of books—Gospels, letters, a history, and an apocalypse—that tell us about the life of Jesus and the beginnings of the movement He founded. For most believers throughout history it has spoken as the norm for what they believe and how they live. So in that sense, it is the church's book. Here we find the beginnings of our own story.

The Foundation: Four Covenants

The first part of the Bible is the Old Testament. It essentially tells the story of four covenants that lay the foundation for the new covenant inaugurated in Jesus, our Liberating King. The first covenant involves God's promise to Noah, his family, and the world that He will never again destroy the earth with a flood. God places a rainbow in the sky as a sign of that promise. When God sees the rainbow, He remembers His covenant. After the floodwaters recede and the ark is resting on dry land, He instructs Noah and his family to populate the earth. This is the same command He gave the first man and woman in the garden. Creation starts over with Noah, his wife, and their children. Still it isn't long before sin's presence is once again felt in the world.

God makes a second covenant with a man named Abraham many generations after Noah's descendants have divided into nations and wandered far from their Creator. He brings to the table a number of promises for the wandering nomad and his family. He promises to give him a land, make him a great nation, give him a great name, and, perhaps most significantly, bless all the nations of the world through his descendants (Genesis 12:1-3). Abraham responds to God's call with faith and obedience. His journey is difficult; nevertheless, he continues in faith and becomes the father of a great nation. Abraham doesn't live long enough to see all of God's promises fulfilled. After Abraham's death, God renews this covenant with each successive heir. Abraham's grandson, Jacob, wrestles with God and struggles to remain faithful. Eventually, Abraham's descendants travel south to Egypt and become slaves in that land under Pharaoh's heel. The promise that Abraham would become a great nation seems all but impossible to generations of Hebrew slaves.

The third covenant in the Old Testament is between God and Israel, the descendants of Abraham. This covenant begins with a powerful act of deliverance when God rescues the Hebrew slaves from bondage in Egypt. The Eternal One answers the prayers of Abraham's hurting people, raising up Moses to demand from Pharaoh that the Hebrew people be set free. After a convincing display of power over the gods of Egypt and the waters of the sea, God instructs Moses to lead the former slaves to Mount Sinai. With the people camped at Sinai's base, Moses ascends the mountain to receive God's law, His blueprint for their lives and society. God promises to be with His people, protect and deliver them, and lead them into the promised land, a land flowing with milk and honey. In this covenant, the people of Israel pledge to obey and worship God alone, or else they will face harsh consequences. While obedience to God is guaranteed to bring blessing and prosperity in the land, disobedience brings adversity and the curse. Ultimately that will mean exile from the land of promise.

Centuries later, God comes to King David through the prophet Nathan to establish a fourth covenant. He promises David three things: David's son (Solomon) will build God a temple, his dynasty will continue forever, and God will relate to David's son as His own son (2 Samuel 7:12-16). God's covenant with David becomes the basis for what is known as the messianic promise. That is the expectation that one day one of David's descendants would be God's Anointed, the Liberating King. According to the prophets, the Liberating King would be God's agent to realize all of God's promises, renew the world, and bring salvation to the ends of the earth.

God's Anointed Fulfills the Covenants

These covenant promises and relationships compose the central story of the Old Testament, bearing witness to God's dealings with the world, His people, and finally all the nations. As God's plan and will unfold, each covenant brings the world nearer to God's kingdom, His ultimate rule over creation. These covenants become the basis for all the promises and hopes that are fulfilled in Jesus, who is God's Anointed, the Liberating King. That's why this collection of books known as the Old Testament is so important to early Christians. The followers of Jesus found His coming anticipated on almost every page. As you will see, the Old Testament stands in relationship to the New Testament as promise does to fulfillment, as foundation to temple, as classic to contemporary: You cannot have one without the other. The earlier covenants pave the way and make the last covenant, the new covenant, possible.

The New Covenant

The phrase "New Testament" goes back to the prophet Jeremiah. About 600 years before Jesus performed His first miracle, the prophet received a message from the Eternal One. In that oracle, he said that a day will come when God establishes a new covenant with His people. Unlike His earlier covenant, this time God will write His words upon the hearts of His people. The new covenant makes it possible for everyone to know the Eternal One and for forgiveness of sins to be extended to all (Jeremiah 31:31-34). Other prophets had seen and prophesied about how God would go about restoring His people and rescuing the world, but Jeremiah is known uniquely as the prophet of the new covenant.

Jesus knew these prophecies; so, on the night before He died, He ate with His disciples for the last time. He took the bread and wine, which commemorated God's deliverance of the Hebrew slaves, and offered them to His followers.

Then He took bread, gave thanks, broke it, and shared it with them.

Jesus: This is My body, My body given for you. Do this to remember Me.

And similarly, after the meal had been eaten, He took the cup.

Jesus: This cup, which is poured out for you, is the new covenant, made in My blood.

Luke 22:19-20

Reshaping the World

According to Jesus, the new covenant promised by Jeremiah—a covenant that would shake and radically shape the world—was being fulfilled through His death on the cross. God's plan to deal with sin and redeem creation reached its climax in the covenant established by Jesus, the Liberating King.

As you read through the New Testament, we invite you to enter into this story of beauty and grace. Unlike other stories you may hear, ancient or modern, this story is completely true.

David B. Capes, PhD

the Voice™

NEW TESTAMENT

Step into the Story of Scripture

MATTHEW

Royal lineage of Jesus of Nazareth

By Matthew, the apostle

All the Gospels are anonymous. But when early Christians began collecting them in the second century, they needed a way to distinguish each one from the others. So they gave them titles. The title "According to Matthew" is affixed to this Gospel because church tradition had credited it to Matthew, one of the twelve. It is fitting that Matthew's Gospel is the first book in the New Testament because it was the favorite Gospel of the early Christians. You see, the first disciples were all Jews; and Matthew sought to prove beyond any reasonable doubt that Jesus was the Messiah, the Anointed One, the Son of David, sent by God to rule His kingdom. So Matthew, more than the other Gospel writers, found Jesus' messiahship in strange and wonderful places where Jews would know to look: in genealogies, titles, numerology, and fulfilled prophecies.

Matthew wants his mainly Jewish audience, as God's chosen people, to consider how Jesus is the true son of Abraham, the ideal for Israel, even the perfect candidate to be the Anointed One. So he shows how Jesus identified with Israel—even with their spending time in exile in Egypt—and yet, unlike Israel, He did not fall into disobedience. As Matthew tells the story, Jesus has come to fill the Scripture full by His teachings and His example. In this way, Jesus is a new Moses, a new Lawgiver. But again, He is greater than Moses because He gives the law and writes it directly on the hearts of His disciples and of any who care to overhear the message of the kingdom of heaven. According to Matthew, five sermons of Jesus complete the picture of Jesus as Lawgiver. They don't replace the five books of Torah, but His words refine and complement God's instruction to the people of the new covenant.

For Matthew, Jesus is more than the Messiah, the fulfiller of prophecies, the true son of Abraham, and the new Moses who brings a new law: He is "God with us" who promises to be with us forever. That means that Jesus is no mere mortal: He is God in the flesh who saves us from our sins. The coming of Jesus into the world fulfills God's earlier promises to bring about redemption and a new creation. These images of Jesus that Matthew paints so beautifully fired the imaginations of Christians for centuries so that today, when we open our New Testaments, we find Matthew is first in line.

This is the story of Jesus the Son of David, the Anointed One, as told by Matthew, a disciple of the Lord. Now this account has been recorded for all those children of Abraham who have become followers of the true heir of the line of David so that they may know in whom they have believed. Because of the common Jewish heritage, Jesus of Nazareth can be understood—His miraculous healings, countless teachings filled with parables, righteous life, and lineage traced back to Abraham—as the One the prophets have spoken of since the early days.

This same Jesus is the One whom the Jews have been waiting for all these years. From the time when John was ritually cleansing people through baptism in the Jordan, as a sign of rethinking their lives of sin, to the wonderfully inspired teaching on the mountain in Galilee, throughout His parables, in His horrible death, and after His marvelous resurrection just days later, Jesus Himself is the King of the kingdom of heaven whom He taught about. There is no one like Jesus. The prophets of old looked for Him, David sang of Him, and Jewish leaders feared Him. He is the great King, the Teacher of wisdom, and the Prophet that Moses said was coming into the world.

The story begins with the lineage that establishes Jesus as the true Son of David.

---

1 This is the family history, the genealogy, of Jesus the Anointed, *the coming King. You will see in this history that* Jesus is descended from King David, and that He is also descended from Abraham.

It begins with Abraham, whom God called into a special, chosen, covenanted relationship, and who was the founding father of the nation of Israel.

[2] Abraham was the father of Isaac; Isaac was the father of Jacob; Jacob was the father of Judah and of Judah's 11 brothers; [3] Judah was the father of Perez and Zerah (and Perez and Zerah's mother was Tamar);

Tamar was Judah's widowed daughter-in-law; she dressed up like a prostitute and seduced her father-in-law, all so she could keep this very family line alive.

Perez was the father of Hezron; Hezron was the father of Ram; [4] Ram was the father of Amminadab; Amminadab was the father of Nahshon; Nahshon was the father of Salmon; [5] Salmon was the father of Boaz (and Boaz's mother was Rahab);

Rahab was a Canaanite prostitute who heroically hid Israelite spies from hostile authorities who wanted to kill them.

Boaz was the father of Obed (his mother was Ruth, *a Moabite woman who converted to the Hebrew faith*); Obed was the father of Jesse; [6] and Jesse was the father of David, who was the king *of the nation of Israel*. David was the father of Solomon (his mother *was Bathsheba, and she* was married to a man named Uriah);

V

Solomon's mother was Bathsheba, the wife of Uriah, a soldier in David's army. She was bathing in her courtyard one evening when David spied her and became interested in her. Later Bathsheba got pregnant during an adulterous liaison with David, so David had Uriah killed in battle and then married his widow. David and Bathsheba's first baby died, but later Bathsheba got pregnant again and gave birth to Solomon.

---

[7] Solomon was the father of Rehoboam; Rehoboam was the father of Abijah; Abijah was the father of Asa; [8] Asa was the father of Jehoshaphat; Jehoshaphat was the father of Joram; Joram was the father of Uzziah; [9] Uzziah was the father of Jotham; Jotham was the father of Ahaz; Ahaz was the father of Hezekiah; [10] Hezekiah was the father of Manasseh; Manasseh was the father of Amon; Amon was the father of Josiah; [11] Josiah was the father of Jeconiah and his brothers, and Josiah's family lived at the time *when God's chosen* people *of Israel* were deported *from the promised land* to Babylon.

¹²After the deportation to Babylon, Jeconiah had a son, Shealtiel. Shealtiel was the father of Zerubbabel; ¹³Zerubbabel was the father of Abiud; Abiud was the father of Eliakim; Eliakim was the father of Azor; ¹⁴Azor was the father of Zadok; Zadok was the father of Achim; Achim was the father of Eliud; ¹⁵Eliud was the father of Eleazar; Eleazar was the father of Matthan; Matthan was the father of Jacob; ¹⁶Jacob was the father of Joseph, who married a woman named Mary. It was Mary who gave birth to Jesus, and it is Jesus who is *the Savior,* the Anointed One.

¹⁷Abraham and David were linked with 14 generations, 14 generations link David to the Babylonian exile, and 14 more take us from the exile to the birth of the Anointed.

This long genealogy is given for a good reason: to show how this Jesus fulfills the prophecies that tell us the Anointed One will be a descendant of Abraham and of David.

Some of the women in Jesus' line are given to show how God is gracious to everyone, even to prostitutes and adulterers. Because some of the women listed weren't Israelites, but were strangers and foreigners, they foreshadow all the foreigners God will adopt into His church through Jesus. Some of the children in God's family are conceived under strange circumstances (like Tamar's twins being conceived as she played the harlot, and like King Solomon being born to adulterous parents). Now that it has been established this is an unusual family, what happens next shouldn't be a surprise—the conception of a baby under very strange circumstances.

---

¹⁸So here, *finally,* is the story of the birth of Jesus the Anointed* *(it is quite a remarkable story):*

Mary was engaged to marry Joseph, *son of David.* They hadn't married. And yet, some time well before their wedding date, Mary learned that she was pregnant by the Holy Spirit. ¹⁹Joseph, because he was kind and upstanding and honorable, wanted to spare Mary shame. He did not wish to cause her more embarrassment than necessary.

This is remarkable, because Mary has never had sex. She and Joseph have not even spent very much time alone, but they are pledged to each other and their wedding feast has been planned.

She has never even kissed a man. She is a virgin, yet she is pregnant. Miraculous! On the other hand, Joseph suspects that Mary has cheated on him and had sex with another man. He knows he will have to break their engagement, but he decides to do this quietly. Mary understands that it is God, in the Person of the Holy Spirit, who has made her pregnant.

---

²⁰Now when Joseph had decided to act on his instincts, a messenger of the Lord came to him in a dream.

Messenger of the Lord: Joseph, son of David, do not be afraid to wed Mary *and bring her into your home and family* as your wife. *She did not sneak off and sleep with someone else*—rather, she conceived the baby she now carries through the miraculous wonderworking of the Holy Spirit. ²¹She will have a son, and you will name Him Jesus, *which means "the Lord saves,"* because this Jesus is the person who will save *all of* His people from sin.

²⁴Joseph woke up from his dream and did exactly what the messenger had told him to do: he married Mary and brought her into his home as his wife ²⁵(though he did not consummate their marriage until after her son was born). *And when the baby was born,* Joseph named Him Jesus, *Savior.**

²²Years and years ago, *Isaiah,* a prophet of Israel, foretold the story *of Mary, Joseph, and Jesus:*

---

* 1:18 "Christ" and "Messiah" are translated as "Anointed" or "the Anointed One."   * 1:25 Verses 24 and 25 have been moved before verse 22 to help the reader understand the continuity of the passage.

²³A virgin will conceive and bear a Son,
  and His name will be Immanuel

(which is a Hebrew name that means "God
with us").*

V

Mary and Joseph name their
baby Jesus, but sometimes He is
referred to as Immanuel, because
by coming to dwell with us, living
and dying among us, He would be
able to save us from our sin.

2 Jesus was born in the town of Bethlehem, in the province of Judea, at the
time when King Herod reigned. *Not long
after Jesus was born,* magi, wise men or seers
from the East, made their way from the East
to Jerusalem. These wise men made inquiries.

These men from the East come looking
for the One who has been born who
will save His people from sin.

Wise Men: ²Where is this newborn, who is
the King of the Jews? When we were far
away in the East we saw His star, and we
have followed its glisten and gleam all this
way to worship Him.

³King Herod began to hear rumors of the wise
men's quest, and he, and all of his followers
in Jerusalem, were worried. ⁴So Herod called
all of the leading Jewish teachers, the chief
priests and head scribes, and he asked them
where *Hebrew tradition claimed* the long-
awaited Anointed One would be born.

Scribes and Priests: ⁵*An ancient Hebrew
prophet, Micah,* said this:

⁶But you, Bethlehem, in the land of Judah,
  are no poor relation—
For from your people will come a Ruler
  who will be the shepherd of My
  people Israel.*

V

From that prophecy we learn that
the Savior would be born in the
town of Bethlehem, in the province of Judea. This information in
hand, Herod orders the wise men
to come to his chambers in secret;

and when they arrive, Herod
quizzes them.

⁷Herod called the wise men to him, demanding to know the exact time the special star
had appeared to them. ⁸Then Herod sent
them to Bethlehem.

Herod: Go *to Bethlehem* and search high and
low for this *Savior* child; and as soon as you
know where He is, report it to me so that I
may go and worship Him.

⁹⁻¹⁰The wise men left Herod's *chambers* and
went on their way. The star they had first
seen in the East reappeared—*a miracle that,
of course,* overjoyed and enraptured the
wise men. The star led them to the house
where Jesus lay; ¹¹and as soon as the wise
men arrived, they saw Him with His mother
Mary, and they bowed down and worshiped
Him. They unpacked their satchels and gave
Jesus gifts of gold, frankincense, and myrrh.

V

These are exceptionally good gifts,
for gold is what is given a king, and
Jesus is the King of kings; incense
is what you expect to be given a
priest, and Jesus is the High Priest
of all high priests; myrrh ointment
is used to heal, and Jesus is a
healer. But myrrh is also used to
embalm corpses—and Jesus was
born to die.

¹²And then, *just as Joseph did a few months
before,* the wise men had a dream warning
them not to go back to Herod. *The wise men
heeded the dream. Ignoring Herod's instructions,* they returned to their homes in the
East by a different route.
    ¹³After the wise men left, a messenger of
the Lord appeared to Joseph in a dream.

Messenger of the Lord (*to Joseph*): Get up,
take the child and His mother, and head to
Egypt. Stay there until I tell you *it is safe
to leave.* For Herod *understands that Jesus
threatens him and all he stands for.* He is
planning to search for the child and kill
Him. *But you will be safe in Egypt.*

* 1:23 Isaiah 7:14   * 2:6 Micah 5:2

14So Joseph got up in the middle of the night; he bundled up Mary and Jesus, and they left for Egypt.*

16*After a few months had passed,* Herod realized he'd been tricked. The wise men *were not coming back.* Herod, *of course,* was furious. He simply ordered that all boys who lived in or near Bethlehem and were two years of age and younger be killed. *He knew the baby King was this age* because of what the wise men told him.

V

Herod knows ordinary babies will die in this purge, but he doesn't care—Herod is not so much cold-blooded as pragmatic, willing to do whatever is necessary to kill this new supposed King. And so all those other baby boys die. But, of course, Herod's plan ultimately fails. He doesn't know the baby Savior has been whisked to safety in Egypt.

17This *sad event* had long been foretold by the prophet Jeremiah:

18A voice will be heard in Ramah,
> weeping *and wailing* and mourning *out loud all day and night.*
The voice is Rachel's, weeping for her
> · children,
> her children who have been killed;
> she weeps, and she will not be
> comforted.*

15Joseph, Mary, and Jesus stayed *in Egypt* until Herod died. This fulfilled yet another prophecy. The prophet *Hosea* once wrote, "Out of Egypt I called My Son."

19And after Herod died, a messenger of the Lord appeared in a dream to Joseph in Egypt:

Messenger of the Lord: 20*You may go home now.* Take the child and His mother and go back to the land of Israel, for the people who were trying to take the child's life are now dead.

21So Joseph got up and took Mary and Jesus and returned to the land of Israel. 22Soon he learned that Archelaus, Herod's *oldest and notoriously brutal* son, was ruling Judea.

Archelaus might not be any friendlier than Herod had been. Joseph was simply afraid. He had another dream, and in this dream, he was warned *away from Judea;* so Joseph *decided* to settle *up north* in a district called Galilee, 23in a town called Nazareth. And this, too, fulfilled what the prophets have taught, "*The Savior* will be a Nazarene."

Nazarene means, "tender, green, or living branch." Jesus is the living Branch, the branch of David that extends the reach of the tree of Israel eventually to foreigners and outsiders.

3 Around the same time, a man called John* began to travel, preach, and ritually wash people through baptism in the wilderness of Judea. *John preached a stern but exciting message.*

John: 2Repent! For the kingdom of heaven is near.

3John's proclamation fulfilled a promise made by the *ancient* prophet Isaiah, who had said, "There will be a voice calling from the desert, saying,

> Prepare the road for the Eternal One's
> journey;
> *repair and* straighten out *every mile of*
> our God's highway."*

4John wore *wild* clothes made from camel hair with a leather belt around his waist—*the clothes of an outcast, a rebel.* He ate locusts and wild honey.

V

Sometimes when people see John they are reminded of the last time God's people had wandered in a wilderness—after the exodus from Egypt. John is all about wilderness. He preaches in the wilderness, and he wears clothes just like the prophet Elijah had worn. They think perhaps John is inaugurating a new exodus. Actually, that is a pretty good way to think of it. The Anointed One, whose way John

---

* 2:14 Verse 15 has been moved to follow verse 18 to help the reader understand the continuity of the passage.   * 2:18 Jeremiah 31:15
* 3:1 Literally, John who immersed, to show repentance
* 3:3 Isaiah 40:3

comes to prepare, will call humanity away from comfort and status; He will call His followers to challenge their assumptions and the things they take for granted.

⁵People from Jerusalem, all of Judea, and indeed from all around the river Jordan came to John. ⁶They confessed their sins, and they were baptized* by him in the Jordan.

But John is not exactly warm to all those who come to him seeking cleansing.

⁷He told some Pharisees and Sadducees who came for the ritual baptism,

John: *You children of serpents!* You brood of vipers! Did someone suggest you flee from the wrath that is upon us? ⁸⁻⁹*If you think that simply hopping in the Jordan will cleanse you, then you are sorely mistaken.* Your life must bear the fruits of turning toward righteousness. Nor are you correct if you think that being descended from Abraham is enough to make you holy and right with God. *Yes, the children of Abraham are God's chosen children,* but God can adopt as daughters and sons *anyone He likes—He can turn* these stones *into sons if He likes.*

To be made right with God, one must truly repent. It means to turn completely away from sin and completely toward God.

¹⁰Even now there is an ax poised at the root of every tree, and every tree that does not bear good fruit will be cut down and tossed into the fire. ¹¹I ritually cleanse you through baptism* as a mark of turning your life around. But someone is coming after me, someone whose sandals I am not fit to carry, someone who is more powerful than I. He will wash* you *not in water* but in fire and with the Holy Spirit. ¹²He carries a winnowing fork in His hand, and He will clear His threshing floor; He will gather up the good wheat in His barn, and He will burn the chaff with a fire that cannot be put out.

¹³And then, *the One of whom John spoke—the all-powerful* Jesus—came to the Jordan from

Galilee to be washed* by John. ¹⁴At first, John demurred.

John: I need to be cleansed* by You. Why do You come to me?

Jesus: ¹⁵It will be right, true, and faithful to God's chosen path for you to cleanse Me *with your hands in the Jordan River.*

John agreed, and he ritually cleansed Jesus, *dousing Him in the waters of the Jordan.* ¹⁶Jesus emerged from His baptism;* and at that moment heaven was opened, and Jesus saw the Spirit of God descending like a dove and coming upon Him, *alighting on His very body.*

Voice from Heaven: ¹⁷This is My Son, whom I love; *this is the Apple of My eye;* with Him I am well pleased.

4 The Spirit then led Jesus into the desert to be tempted by the devil. ²Jesus fasted for 40 days and 40 nights. After this fast, He was, *as you can imagine,* hungry. ³*But He was also curiously stronger,* when the tempter came to Jesus.

Devil: If You are the Son of God, tell these stones to become bread.

Jesus (*quoting Deuteronomy*): ⁴It is written, "Man does not live by bread alone. Rather, he lives on every word that comes from the mouth of the Eternal One."*

V

The point, of course, is not that Jesus couldn't have turned these stones to bread. A little later in the story He can make food appear when He needs to. But Jesus doesn't work miracles out of the blue, for no reason, for show or proof or spectacle. He works them in intimate, close places; He works them to meet people's needs and to show them the way to the Kingdom.

* 3:6 Literally, immersed, to show repentance　* 3:11 Literally, immerse, to show repentance　* 3:11 Literally, immerse, in a rite of initiation and purification　* 3:13 Literally, immersed, to show repentance　* 3:14 Literally, immersed, in a rite of initiation and purification　* 3:16 Literally, after being immersed, Jesus came up from the water.　* 4:4 Deuteronomy 8:3

⁵Then the devil took Jesus to the holy city, *Jerusalem,* and he had Jesus stand at the very highest point in the holy temple.

Devil: ⁶If You are the Son of God, jump! *And then we will see if You fulfill* the Scripture that says,

He will command His heavenly
    messengers concerning You,
and the messengers will buoy You in
    their hands
So that You will not *crash, or fall, or even
    graze* Your foot on a stone.*

Jesus: ⁷That is not the only thing Scripture says. It also says, "Do not put the Eternal One, your God, to the test."*

⁸And still the devil *subjected Jesus to a third test. He* took Jesus to the top of a very high mountain, and he showed Jesus all the kingdoms of the world in all their *splendor and* glory, *their power and pomp.*

Devil: ⁹If You bow down and worship me, I will give You all these kingdoms.

Jesus: ¹⁰Get away from Me, Satan. *I will not serve you. I will instead follow* Scripture, which tells us to "worship the Eternal One, your God, and serve only Him."*

¹¹Then the devil left Jesus. And heavenly messengers came and ministered to Him.
¹²*It was not long until powerful people put* John in prison. When Jesus learned this, He went back to Galilee. ¹³He moved from Nazareth to Capernaum, a town by the sea in the regions of Zebulun and Naphtali. ¹⁴He did this to fulfill one of the prophecies of Isaiah:

¹⁵In the land of Zebulun and the land of
    Naphtali,
    the road to the sea along the Jordan
      in Galilee, the land of the
      outsiders—
¹⁶*In these places,* the people who had been
    living in darkness
    saw a great light.
The light of life will overtake those who
    dwelt in the shadowy darkness of
    death.*

¹⁷From that time on, preaching was part of Jesus' work.

Jesus: Repent, for the kingdom of heaven is at hand.

By now Jesus desires a community around Him, friends and followers who help Him carry this urgent, precious message to people. His message is not dissimilar to John's: Turn away from sin; turn toward God. And so He calls a community to join Him. These first beloved followers are called "disciples," which means "apprentices." The first disciples are two brothers, Simon and Andrew. They are fishermen.

---

¹⁸*One day* Jesus was walking along the Sea of Galilee when He saw Simon (also called Peter) and Andrew throwing their nets into the water. They were, of course, fishermen.

Jesus: ¹⁹*Come,* follow Me, and I will make you fishers of men.

²⁰Immediately Peter and Andrew left their fishnets and followed Jesus.
²¹Going on from there, Jesus saw two more brothers, James the son of Zebedee and his brother John. *They, too, were fishermen.* They were in a boat with their father Zebedee getting their nets ready to fish. Jesus summoned them, *just as He had called to Peter and Andrew,* ²²and immediately they left their boat and their father to follow Jesus.
²³And so Jesus went throughout Galilee. He taught in the synagogues. He preached the good news of the Kingdom, and He healed people, ridding their bodies of sickness and disease. ²⁴Word spread all over Syria, as more and more sick people came to Him. The innumerable ill who came before Him had all sorts of diseases, they were in crippling pain; they were possessed by demons; they had seizures; they were paralyzed. But Jesus healed them *all.* ²⁵Large crowds from Galilee, from Jerusalem, from *the ten cities called* the Decapolis, from Judea, and from the region across the Jordan followed him.

* 4:6 Psalm 91:11-12 * 4:7 Deuteronomy 6:16 * 4:10 Deuteronomy 6:13 * 4:15-16 Isaiah 9:1-2

People talk about this Jesus, this Preacher and Healer. Word spreads of His charisma and wisdom and power and love. People who are too sick to walk persuade their friends and relatives to carry them to Jesus. These cripples and demonized and ill and paralytics come to Jesus, and He heals them, and they follow Him.

5 Now when He saw the crowds, He went up on a mountain (*as Moses had done before Him*) and He sat down (*as Jewish teachers of His day usually did*). His disciples gathered around Him.

There on the mountain Jesus teaches them all. And as He is teaching, crowds gather around and overhear His teachings, listen in, and are captivated. This, the Sermon on the Mount, is the first of the five Mosaic-like sermons in Matthew.

²And He began to teach them.

Jesus: ³Blessed are the spiritually poor—the kingdom of heaven is theirs.
⁴Blessed are those who mourn—they will be comforted.
⁵Blessed are the *meek and* gentle—they will inherit the earth.
⁶Blessed are those who hunger and thirst for righteousness—they will be filled.
⁷Blessed are the merciful—they will be shown mercy.
⁸Blessed are those who are pure in heart—they will see God.
⁹Blessed are the peacemakers—they will be called children of God.
¹⁰Blessed are those who are persecuted because of righteousness—the kingdom of heaven is theirs.

¹¹And blessed are you, *blessed are all of you,* when people persecute you or denigrate you or despise you or tell lies about you on My account. ¹²*But when this*

happens, rejoice. Be glad. Remember that God's prophets have been persecuted in the past. And know that in heaven, you have a great reward.

Salt draws out the good flavors subtly hidden in food and preserves what would otherwise spoil, as do those who claim to be children of God.

¹³You, *beloved,* are the salt of the earth. But if salt becomes bland and loses its saltiness, can anything make it salty again? *No.* It is useless. It is tossed out, thrown away, or trampled.
¹⁴And you, *beloved,* are the light of the world. A city built on a hilltop cannot be hidden. ¹⁵Similarly it would be silly to light a lamp and then hide it under a bowl. When someone lights a lamp, she puts it on a table or a desk or a chair, and the light illumines the entire house. ¹⁶*You are like that illuminating light.* Let your light shine everywhere you go, *that you may illumine creation,* so men and women everywhere may see your good actions, *may see creation at its fullest, may see your devotion to Me,* and may turn and praise your Father in heaven *because of it.*
¹⁷Do not think that I have come to overturn or do away with the law or the words of our prophets. *To the contrary:* I have not come to overturn them but to fulfill them.
¹⁸This, *beloved,* is the truth: until heaven and earth disappear, not one letter, not one pen stroke, will disappear from the sacred law—for everything, everything in the sacred law will be fulfilled and accomplished. ¹⁹Anyone who breaks even the smallest, most obscure commandment—not to mention teaches others to do the same—will be called small *and obscure* in the kingdom of heaven. Those who practice the law and teach others how to live the law will be called great in the kingdom of heaven. ²⁰For I tell you this: you will not enter the kingdom of heaven unless your righteousness goes deeper than the Pharisees', even more righteous than the most learned learner of the law.

Righteousness is the reason Jesus has come—to make the people righteous through and through. He then begins to interpret the law of Scripture for them with this in mind.

21As you know, long ago God instructed *Moses to tell* His people, "Do not murder;* those who murder will be judged *and punished.*" 22*But here is the even harder truth:* anyone who is angry with his brother will be judged for his anger. Anyone who *taunts his friend, speaks contemptuously toward him, or* calls him "Loser" or "Fool" or "Scum," will have to answer to the high court. And anyone who calls his brother a fool may find himself in the fires of hell.

23Therefore, if you are bringing an offering to God and you remember that your brother is angry at you or holds a grudge against you, 24then leave your gift before the altar, go to your brother, *repent and forgive one another,* be reconciled, and then return to the altar to offer your gift to God.

25If someone sues you, settle things with him quickly. Talk to him as you are walking to court; otherwise, he may turn matters over to the judge, and the judge may turn you over to an officer, and you may land in jail. 26I tell you this: you will not emerge from prison until you have paid your last penny.

27As you know, long ago God forbade His people to commit adultery.* 28*You may think you have abided by this Commandment, walked the straight and narrow,* but I tell you this: any man who looks at a woman with lust has already committed adultery in his heart. 29If your right eye leads you into sin, gouge it out and throw it *in the garbage—*for better you lose one part of your body than march your entire body *through the gates of sin and* into hell. 30And if your right hand leads you into sin, cut it off and throw it away—for better you lose one part of your body than march your entire body *through the gates of sin and* into hell.

31And here is something else: *you have read in Deuteronomy that* anyone who divorces his wife *must do so fairly—*he must give her the requisite certificate of divorce *and send her on her way, free and unfettered.** 32But I tell you this: unless your wife cheats on you, you must not divorce her, period. Nor are you to marry someone who has been married and divorces, for a divorced person who remarries commits adultery.

33You know that God expects us to abide by the oaths we swear and the promises we make. 34But I tell you this: do not ever swear an oath. *What is an oath?* You cannot say, "I swear by heaven"—*for heaven is not yours to swear by;* it is God's throne. 35And you cannot say, "I swear by this good earth," *for the earth is not yours to swear by;* it is God's footstool. And you cannot say, "I swear by *the holy city* Jerusalem," for *it is not yours to swear by;* it is the city *of God, the capital* of the King of kings. 36You cannot even say that you swear by your own head, *for God has dominion over your hands, your lips, your head.* It is He who determines if your hair be *straight or curly,* white or black; *it is He who rules over even this small scrap of creation.* 37*You need not swear an oath—*any impulse to do so is of evil. Simply let your "yes" be "yes," and let your "no" be "no."

38You know that *Hebrew Scripture* sets this standard *of justice and punishment:* take an eye for an eye and a tooth for a tooth.* 39But I say this, don't fight against the one who is working evil against you. If someone strikes you on the right cheek, you are to turn and offer him your left cheek. 40If someone connives to get your shirt, give him your jacket as well. 41If someone forces you to walk with him for a mile, walk with him for two instead. 42If someone asks you for something, give it to him. If someone wants to borrow something from you, do not turn away.

43You have been taught to love your neighbor and hate your enemy.* 44But I tell you this: love your enemies. Pray for those who torment you and persecute you—45in so doing, you become children of your Father in heaven. *He, after all, loves each of us—good and evil, kind and cruel.* He causes the sun to rise *and shine* on evil and good alike. He causes the rain *to water the fields* of the righteous and *the fields* of the sinner. 46It is easy to love those who love you—even a tax collector can love those who love him. 47And it is easy to greet your friends—even outsiders do that! 48*But you are called to something higher:* "Be perfect, as your Father in heaven is perfect."

Part of imitating the perfection of God is acting charitably and generously, doing good deeds, working for justice, and praying.

* 5:21 Exodus 20:13   * 5:27 Exodus 20:14   * 5:31 Deuteronomy 24:1   * 5:38 Exodus 21:24; Leviticus 24:20; Deuteronomy 19:21   * 5:43 Leviticus 19:18

6 Jesus: But when you do these righteous acts, *do not do them in front of spectators.* Don't do them where you can be seen, *let alone lauded,* by others. If you do, you will have no reward from your Father in heaven. [2]When you give to the poor, *do not boast about it,* announcing your donations with blaring trumpets as the play actors do. Do not brazenly give your charity in the synagogues and on the streets; *indeed, do not give at all* if you are giving because you want to be praised by your neighbors. Those people who give in order to reap praise have already received their reward. [3-4]When you give to the needy, do it in secret—even your left hand should not know what your right hand is doing. Then your Father, who sees in secret, will reward you.

[5]Likewise, when you pray, do not be as hypocrites who love to pray loudly at synagogue or on street corners—their concern is to be seen by men. They have already earned their reward. [6]When you pray, go into a private room, close the door, and pray unseen to your Father who is unseen. Then your Father, who sees in secret, will reward you. [7]And when you pray, do not go on and on, excessively and strangely like the outsiders; they think their verbosity will let them be heard *by their deities.* [8]Do not be like them. *Your prayers need not be labored or lengthy or grandiose*—for your Father knows what you need before you ever ask Him.

[9]Your prayers, rather, should be *simple,* like this:

Our Father in heaven,
   let Your name remain holy.
[10]Bring about Your kingdom.
   Manifest Your will here on earth,
      as it is manifest in heaven.
[11]Give us each day that day's bread—
      no more, no less—
[12]And forgive us our debts
   as we forgive those who owe us
      something.
[13]Lead us not into temptation,
   but deliver us from evil.
   [But let Your kingdom be,
   and let it be powerful
   and glorious forever. Amen.]*

Jesus says to declare forgiveness of those who have wronged us. This is because forgiveness of other people emulates God's forgiveness of us.

[14]If you forgive people when they sin against you, then your Father will forgive you *when you sin against Him and when you sin against your neighbor.* [15]But if you do not forgive your neighbors' sins, your Father will not forgive your sins.

[16]And when you fast, do not look miserable as *the actors and* hypocrites do when they are fasting—*they walk around town putting on airs about their suffering and weakness, complaining about how hungry they are.* So everyone will know they are fasting, they don't wash or anoint themselves with oil, *pink their cheeks, or wear comfortable shoes. Those who show off their piety,* they have already received their reward. [17]When you fast, wash your face and beautify yourself with oil, [18]so no one who looks at you will know about your discipline. Only your Father, who is unseen, will see your fast. And your Father, who sees in secret, will reward you.

[19]Some people store up treasures *in their homes* here on earth. *This is a shortsighted practice*—don't undertake it. Moths and rust will eat up any treasure you may store here. Thieves may break into *your homes* and steal *your precious trinkets.* [20]Instead, put up your treasures in heaven where moths do not attack, where rust does not corrode, and where thieves are barred at the door. [21]For where your treasure is, there your heart will be also.

[22]The eye is the lamp of the body. *You draw light into your body through your eyes, and light shines out to the world through your eyes.* So if your eye is well *and shows you what is true,* then your whole body will be filled with light. [23]But if your eye is clouded *or evil,* then your body will be filled with *evil and* dark clouds. And the darkness that takes over the body *of a child of God who has gone astray*—that is the deepest, darkest darkness there is.

V

When Jesus speaks of eyes and light, He means all people should keep their eyes on God because the eyes are the windows to the soul. Eyes should not focus on

6:13 Some early manuscripts omit this portion.

trash—pornography, filth, or expensive things. And this is what He means when He says, "Where your treasure is, there your heart will be also."

Jesus: [24]No one can serve two masters. *If you try, you will wind up loving the first master and hating the second, or vice versa.* People try to serve both God and money—but you can't. *You must choose one or the other.*

[25]Here is the bottom line: do not worry about your life. Don't worry about what you will eat or what you will drink. Don't worry about how you clothe your body. Living is about more than merely eating, and the body is about more than dressing up. [26]Look at the birds in the sky. They do not store food for winter. *They don't plant gardens.* They do not sow or reap—and yet, they are always fed because your heavenly Father feeds them. And you are even more precious to Him than a beautiful bird. *If He looks after them, of course He will look after you.* [27]*Worrying does not do any good;* who here can claim to add even an hour to his life by worrying?

[28]Nor should you worry about clothes. Consider the lilies of the field and how they grow. They do not work or weave or sew, *and yet their garments are stunning.* [29]Even King Solomon, dressed in his most regal garb, was not as lovely as these lilies. [30]*And think about grassy fields*—the grasses are here now, but they will be dead by winter. And yet God adorns them so radiantly. How much more will He clothe you, you of little faith, *you who have no trust?*

[31]So do not consume yourselves with questions: What will we eat? What will we drink? What will we wear? [32]Outsiders make themselves frantic over such questions; *they don't realize that* your heavenly Father knows exactly what you need. [33]Seek first the kingdom of God and His righteousness, and then all these things will be given to you *too.* [34]So do not worry about tomorrow. Let tomorrow worry about itself. Living faithfully is a large enough task for today.

7 **Jesus:** If you judge *other people,* then you will find that you, too, are being judged. [2]Indeed, you will be judged by

the very standards to which you hold other people.

So when someone is tempted to criticize his neighbor because her house isn't clean enough, she seems ill-tempered, or she is a bit flighty—he should remember those same standards and judgments will come back to him. No one should criticize his neighbor for being short-tempered one morning, when he is snippish and snappish and waspish all the time.

Jesus: [3]Why is it that you see the dust in your brother's or sister's eye, but you can't see what is in your own eye? [4]Don't ignore the wooden plank in your eye, while you criticize the speck of sawdust in your brother's eyelashes. [5]That type of criticism and judgment is a sham! Remove the plank from your own eye, and then perhaps you will be able to see clearly how to help your brother flush out his sawdust.

[6]Don't give precious things to dogs. Don't cast your pearls before swine. If you do, the pigs will trample the pearls with their *little pigs'* feet, and then they will turn back and attack you.

Now Jesus returns to prayer, an important and sometimes difficult topic. Here He gives the very essence of prayer.

[7]Just ask and it will be given to you; seek after it and you will find. *Continue to* knock and the door will be opened for you. [8]All who ask receive. Those who seek, find what they seek. And he who knocks, will have the door opened.

[9]Think of it this way: if your son asked you for bread, would you give him a stone? *Of course not—you would give him a loaf of bread.* [10]If your son asked for a fish, would you give him a snake? *No, to be sure, you would give him a fish—the best fish you could find.* [11]So if you, who are sinful, know how to give your children good gifts, how much more so does your Father in heaven, who is perfect, know how to give great gifts to His children! [12]This is what our Scriptures come to

teach: in everything, in every circumstance, do to others as you would have them do to you. ¹³*There are two paths before you; you may take only one path.* One doorway is narrow. *And one door is wide.* Go through the narrow door. For the wide door leads to a wide path, and the wide path is broad; the wide, broad path is easy, and the wide, broad, easy path has many, many people on it; but the wide, broad, easy, crowded path leads to death. ¹⁴Now then that narrow door leads to a narrow road that in turn leads to life. It is hard to find that road. Not many people manage it.

¹⁵Along the way, watch out for false prophets. They will come to you in sheep's clothing, but underneath *that quaint and innocent wool,* they are hungry wolves. ¹⁶But you will recognize them by their fruits. You don't find *sweet, delicious* grapes growing on thorny bushes, do you? You don't find *delectable* figs growing in the midst of *prickly* thistles. ¹⁷*People and their lives are like trees.* Good trees bear beautiful, tasty fruit, but bad trees bear ugly, bitter fruit. ¹⁸A good tree cannot bear ugly, bitter fruit; nor can a bad tree bear fruit that is beautiful and tasty. ¹⁹And what happens to the rotten trees? They are cut down. They are used for firewood. ²⁰*When a prophet comes to you and preaches this or that,* look for his fruits: *sweet or sour? rotten or ripe?*

²¹Not everyone who says to Me, "Lord, Lord," will enter the kingdom of heaven. *Simply calling Me "Lord" will not be enough.* Only those who do the will of My Father who is in heaven *will join Me in heaven.* ²²*At the end of time,* on that day *of judgment,* many will say to Me, "Lord, Lord, did we not prophesy in Your name? Did we not drive demons out *of the possessed* in Your name? Did we not perform miracles in Your name?" ²³But I will say to them, "I never knew you. And now, you must get away from Me, you evildoers!"

²⁴Those people who are listening to Me, those people who *hear what I say and* live according to My teachings—you are like a wise man who built his house on a rock, *on a firm foundation.* ²⁵*When storms hit,* rain pounded down and waters rose, *levies broke* and winds beat all the walls of that house. But the house did not fall because it was built upon rock. ²⁶Those of you who are listening and do not hear—you are like

a fool who builds a house on sand. ²⁷When a storm comes to his house, *what will happen*? The rain will fall, the waters will rise, the wind will blow, and his house will collapse with a great crash.

²⁸With that Jesus finished His teaching, and the crowds were amazed by all He had said. ²⁹But Jesus taught in His own name, on His own authority, not like the scribes.

This teaching is different. Usually rabbis cite generations of rabbis before them when making claims about the meaning of Hebrew Scriptures. Jesus honors the law, but He is clear—the law must be read in a new way.

8 Large crowds followed Jesus when He came down from the mountain. ²*And as Jesus was going along,* a leper approached Him and knelt down before Him.

Leper: Lord, if You wish to, *please* heal me and make me clean!

Jesus *(stretching out His hand)*: ³Of course I wish to. Be clean.

Immediately the man was healed.

Jesus: ⁴Don't tell anyone *what just happened.* Rather, go to the priest, show yourself to him, and give a wave offering as Moses commanded. Your actions will tell the story of what happened here today.

⁵Eventually Jesus came to *the little town of* Capernaum. In Capernaum a military officer came to Him and asked Him for help.

Officer: ⁶Lord, I have a servant who is lying at home in agony, paralyzed.

Jesus: ⁷I will come *to your house,* and I will heal him.

Officer: ⁸Lord, I don't deserve to have You in my house. *And, in truth, I know You don't need to be with my servant to heal him.* Just say the word, and he will be healed. ⁹That, after all, is how authority works. My troops obey me whether I am next to them or not—*similarly, this sickness will obey You.*

[10]Jesus was stunned by the depth of the officer's faith.

Jesus (to His followers): This is the plain truth: I have not met a single person in Israel with as much faith *as this officer*. [11]It will not be just the children of Abraham and Isaac and Jacob who celebrate at their heavenly banquet at the end of time. No, people will come from the East and the West—*and those who recognize Me, regardless of their lineage, will sit with Me at that feast*. [12]But those who have feigned their faith will be cast out into outer darkness where people weep and grind their teeth.

[13]Then Jesus turned to the Centurion.*

Jesus: You may go home. For it is as you say it is; it is as you believe.

And the officer's servant was healed, right then.

What happens next seems to embody the officer's wise opinion about authority: over and over Jesus shows just what His authority means.

[14]Jesus went to Peter's house, and there He saw Peter's mother-in-law lying in bed, sick and burning up with a fever. [15]Jesus touched her hand, and *then she was healed*—the fever vanished. She got up from bed and began to wait on Him. [16]Toward nighttime many people who were possessed by demons were brought to Jesus, and He said one word of command and drove the demons out, healing everyone who was sick. [17]These miraculous healings fulfilled what the prophet Isaiah had predicted:

He took our infirmities upon Himself,
and He bore our diseases.*

[18]Jesus saw that a crowd had gathered around Him, and He gave orders to go to the other side *of the sea*. [19]A scribe came up to Him.

Scribe: Teacher, I will follow You wherever You go.

Jesus: [20]Foxes have dens *in which to sleep*, and the birds have nests. But the Son of Man has no place to lay His head.

Disciple: [21]Jesus, before I do the things You've asked me to do, I must first bury my father.

Jesus: [22]Follow Me! And let the dead bury their own dead.

V

Does Jesus say, "Fair enough, you must of course bury your father. Just catch up with Me when you are done"? No. This is one of the strange and radical things Jesus brings about—our families are no longer our families. Our deepest bonds are not those of blood. Our family now is found in the bonds of fellowship made possible by this Jesus.

---

[23]And then Jesus got into a boat, and His disciples followed Him. [24]Out of nowhere, a vicious storm blew over the sea. Waves were lapping up over the boat, threatening to overtake it! Yet Jesus was asleep. [25]*Frightened (not to mention confused—how could anyone sleep through this?)*, the disciples woke Him up.

Disciples: Lord, save us! We're going to drown!

Jesus: [26]Please! What are you so afraid of, you of little faith?

Jesus got up, told the wind and the waves to calm down, and they did. The sea became still and calm *once again*. [27]The disciples were astonished.

Disciples: Who is this? What sort of man is He, that the sea and the winds listen to Him?

[28]Eventually Jesus came to the other side *of the sea*, to the region of the Gadarenes. There, two men *who lived* near the tombs and were possessed by demons came out *to the seaside* and met Jesus. They were flailing about, so violent that they obstructed the path of anyone who came their way.

Demons (*screaming at Jesus*): [29]Why are You here? Have You come to torture us even before the judgment day, O Son of God?

* 8:13 A Roman military officer in charge of about 100 foot soldiers
* 8:17 Isaiah 53:4

30A ways off, *though still visible,* was a large herd of pigs, eating.

Demons: 31If You cast us out *of the bodies of these two men,* do send us into that herd of pigs!

Jesus: 32*Very well then,* go!

And the demons flew out of the bodies *of the two flailing men,* they set upon the pigs, and every last pig rushed over a steep bank into the sea and drowned. 33The pig herders *(totally undone, as you can imagine)* took off; they headed straight for town, where they told everyone what they'd just seen—even about the demon-possessed men. 34And so the whole town came out to see Jesus for themselves. And when they saw Him, they begged Him to leave their area.

9 He got back in the boat, crossed *the sea,* and returned to His own town. 2When He got there, some men approached Him carrying a mat. On the mat was another man, a paralytic. *The men evidently believed that Jesus could heal the paralytic,* and Jesus saw their faith, how much faith they had in His authority and power.

Jesus: Rest assured, My son; your sins are forgiven.

3Now some scribes *and teachers of the law had been watching this whole scene.*

Scribes and Teachers *(to themselves)*: This man is blaspheming!

4*Though they had only spoken in low whispers among themselves,* Jesus knew their thoughts.

Jesus: Why do you hold such hardness and wickedness in your hearts? 5Look, is it easier to say, "Your sins are forgiven," or "Get up and walk"? 6To make clear that the Son of Man has the authority on earth to forgive sins (turning to the paralytic man *on the mat*), Get up, pick up your mat, and go home.

7And the man did. 8When the crowd saw this, they were amazed, *even a little scared,* and they praised God who had given humans the authority *to do such miraculous things.*

9Later Jesus was walking along and He saw a man named Matthew sitting in the tax collector's office.

Jesus *(to Matthew)*: Follow Me.

Matthew got up and followed Him.
10Once when He ate a meal at home with His disciples, a whole host of tax collectors and other sinners joined them. 11When the Pharisees saw this, they asked Jesus' disciples,

Pharisees: Why does your Teacher eat with tax collectors and sinners?

Jesus *(overhearing this)*: 12Look, who needs a doctor—healthy people or sick people? 13I am not here to attend to people who are already right with God; I am here to attend to sinners. *In the book of the prophet Hosea, we read,* "It is not sacrifice I want, but mercy."* Go and meditate on that for a while—*maybe you'll come to understand it.*

14And then some of the disciples of John came.

John's Disciples: *What's the story with fasting?* We fast and the Pharisees fast, but Your disciples do not fast!

Jesus: 15When you celebrate—as at a wedding when one's dearest friend is getting married—you do not fast. The time will come when the bridegroom will be taken from them. Then My friends and followers will fast. 16You would begin by washing and shrinking a patch you would use to mend a garment—otherwise, the patch would shrink later, pull away from the garment, and make the original tear even worse. 17You wouldn't pour new wine into old wineskins. If you did, the skins would burst, the wine would run out, and the wineskins would be ruined. No, you would pour new wine into new wineskins—and both the wine and the wineskins would be preserved.

18As He was saying these things, a certain official came before Jesus and knelt in front of Him.

Official: My daughter just died. Would You come and lay Your hands on her? Then, I know, she would live again.

* 9:13 Hosea 6:6

¹⁹Jesus got up, and He and His disciples went with the man. ²⁰⁻²¹*But as they were heading to the man's house,* a woman who had been hemorrhaging and bleeding for 12 years—*12 years!*—crept up behind Jesus.

> She evidently believes that if she so much as touches the fringes of His cloak, she will be healed.

And so she came up behind Him and touched His cloak. ²²Jesus turned around and saw her.

Jesus: Take heart, daughter. Your faith has healed you.

And indeed, from that moment, the woman was healed. ²³Then Jesus went to the official's house. He saw flute players and mourners.

Jesus (*to the crowd*): ²⁴Go away, *and do your ministering somewhere else.* This girl is not dead. She is merely asleep.

The crowd—*who knew with certainty that the girl was dead*—laughed at Him. ²⁵But they *obeyed Him and* left the house, *and once they were gone,* Jesus went to the girl. When He took her hand, she *opened her eyes and* stood up. ²⁶When the crowds outside learned that the girl was indeed alive, they spread throughout the town and the surrounding country telling everyone what had happened.
    ²⁷Jesus left the official's house. And as He was walking, two blind men began to follow Him.

Blind Men: Son of David! Have mercy on us!

²⁸Jesus went to their house, and the blind men sat in front of Him.

Jesus: Do you believe that I am able to do this?

Blind Men: Yes, Lord.

> Faith in Jesus and His power is essential for healing, so it isn't surprising that all it takes is Jesus' touch to heal these men.

Jesus (*touching their eyes*): ²⁹According to your faith, it will be done to you.

³⁰And they could see. Then Jesus spoke to them *as He had spoken to the leper.*

Jesus: Don't tell anyone about this.

³¹But when the men (*who could now see*) left, they told everyone in the area they met what had happened.
    ³²Later a man who was possessed by demons and could not talk was brought to Jesus. ³³Jesus drove out the demons, and the mute man spoke. The crowds were amazed.

Crowd: Nothing like this has ever been seen in Israel.

Pharisees: ³⁴It must be the prince of demons who gives Him the power to cast out demons.

³⁵Jesus went through many towns and villages. He taught in their synagogues. He preached the good news of the kingdom of God. He healed every disease and sickness. ³⁶Whenever crowds came to Him, He had compassion for them because they were so deeply distraught, malaised, and heartbroken. They seemed to Him like lost sheep without a shepherd. ³⁷*Jesus understood what an awesome task was before Him,* so He said to His disciples, "The harvest is plentiful but the workers are few. ³⁸Ask the Lord of the harvest to send more workers into His harvest field."

V

Matthew gives a summary of what Jesus has done—teaching, preaching, and healing—and why He has done it—because of His compassion. Jesus then calls His disciples to this same type of ministry. The following sermon that Jesus gives to His disciples is the second of the five main sermons in Matthew.

---

10 Jesus called His twelve disciples to Him. He endowed them with the authority to heal sickness and disease and to drive demons out of those who were possessed.

Up to this point, the disciples have been, mostly, following Jesus around, listening to Him teach, watching Him heal. And so now we call these twelve beloved men not merely "disciples," or "apprentices," but "apostles," which means "those who are sent as representatives, emissaries." Jesus is preparing to send them into the harvest field to do His Father's work.

---

²These are the names of the twelve apostles: Simon (who is called Peter, *which means "the rock"*) and his brother Andrew; James, son of Zebedee, and his brother John; ³Philip and Bartholomew; Thomas and Matthew (the tax collector); James, son of Alphaeus, and Thaddaeus; ⁴Simon the Zealot and Judas Iscariot (who would betray Him).

⁵Jesus sent out these twelve with clear instructions.

Jesus: Don't go to the outsiders or to the towns inhabited by Samaritans, *a people whose Jewish ancestors married Gentiles.* ⁶Go instead to find *and heal* the lost sheep of Israel. ⁷As you go, preach this message: "The kingdom of heaven is at hand." ⁸Heal the sick, raise the dead, and cleanse those who have leprosy. Drive out demons *from the possessed.* You received *these gifts* freely, so you should give *them* to others freely. ⁹Do not take money with you: don't take gold, silver, or even small, worthless change. ¹⁰Do not pack a bag with clothes. Do not take sandals or a walking stick. Be fed and sheltered by those who show you hospitality. ¹¹When you enter a town or village, look for someone who is trustworthy and stay at his house as long as you are visiting that town. ¹²When you enter this home, greet the household kindly. ¹³And if the home is indeed trustworthy, let your blessing of peace rest upon it; if not, keep your blessing to yourself. ¹⁴If someone is inhospitable to you or refuses to listen to your testimony, leave that house or town and shake the dust from your feet. ¹⁵This is the truth: Sodom and Gomorrah, *those ancient pits of inhospitality,* will fare better on judgment day than towns *who ignore you tomorrow or next week.*

¹⁶Listen: I am sending you out to be sheep among wolves. You must be as shrewd as serpents and as innocent as doves. ¹⁷You must be careful. You must be discerning. You must be on your guard. There will be men who try to hand you over to their town councils and have you flogged in their synagogues. ¹⁸Because of Me, naysayers and doubters will try to make an example out of you by trying you before rulers and kings. ¹⁹When this happens—*when you are arrested, dragged to court*—don't worry about what to say or how to say it. The words you should speak will be given to you. For at that moment, ²⁰it will not be you speaking; it will be the Spirit of your Father speaking through you.

²¹*Your task will be fraught with betrayal:* brother will betray brother, even to the point of death; fathers will betray their children, and children will rebel against their fathers, even to the point of death. ²²⁻²³When you are persecuted in one town, flee to the next town. This is the truth: you will not be able to witness to every town in Israel before the Son of Man comes. Everyone will hate you because of Me. But remember: the one who stays on the narrow path until the end will be saved.

²⁴A student is no greater than his teacher, and a servant is never greater than his master. ²⁵It is sufficient if the student is like his teacher and the servant like his master. If people call the head of a house "Beelzebul," *which means "devil,"* just imagine what they're calling the members of his household.

²⁶Do not be afraid of those *who may taunt or persecute you.* Everything they do—even if they think they are hiding behind closed doors—will come to light. All their secrets will eventually be made known. ²⁷And you should proclaim in the bright light of day everything that I have whispered to you in the dark. Whatever whispers you hear—shout them from the rooftops of houses.

²⁸Don't fear those who *aim to* kill just the body but are unable to touch the soul. The One to fear is He who can destroy you, soul and body, in the fires of hell. ²⁹Look, if you sold a few sparrows, *how much money would you get?* A copper coin apiece, perhaps? And yet your Father in heaven knows when those small sparrows fall to the ground. ³⁰⁻³¹You, beloved, are worth so much more than a whole flock of sparrows. God knows *everything about you,* even the number of hairs on your head. So do not fear.

³²*Whoever knows Me here on earth, I will know him in heaven.* And whoever proclaims faith in Me here on earth, I will proclaim *faith in* him before My Father in heaven. ³³But whoever disowns Me here, I will disown before My Father in heaven.

³⁴Do not imagine that I have come to bring peace to the earth. I did not come to bring peace, but a sword. ³⁵I have come to turn men against their fathers, daughters against their mothers, and daughters-in-law against their mothers-in-law. ³⁶You will find you have enemies even in your own household.* ³⁷If you love your father or mother more than you love Me, then you are not worthy of Me. If you love your son or daughter more than you love Me, then you are not worthy of Me. ³⁸If you refuse to take up your cross and follow Me *on the narrow road,* then you are not worthy of Me. ³⁹To find your life, you must lose your life—and whoever loses his life for My sake will find it.

Jesus calls His disciples to a radical commitment. Those who truly follow Jesus must be willing to follow Him to the point of death, just as He will later die for His commitment to God and others. Thus, whether they die literally or figuratively, His followers give up their lives for Him.

Jesus: ⁴⁰Anyone who welcomes you welcomes Me, and anyone who welcomes Me welcomes the One who sent Me. ⁴¹Anyone who welcomes a prophet and surrenders to his prophecy will receive a prophet's reward, and anyone who welcomes a righteous person and conforms to the righteousness that surrounds him and proceeds from him will receive a righteous man's reward. ⁴²And anyone who has given so much as a cup of cold water to one of the little ones, because he is My disciple, I tell you, that person will be well rewarded.

11 With that, Jesus finished instructing His disciples, and He went on to preach and teach in the towns *of Galilee.* ²John, meanwhile, was still in prison. But stories about the Anointed One's teachings and healing reached him.

Quite frankly, John is perplexed. He has been awaiting the Anointed, but he believes that person will be a great political ruler, a king, or a military hero. Jesus seems to be all about healing people and insisting that the poor and the meek are blessed.

So John sent his followers ³to question Jesus.

John's Followers: Are You the One we have been expecting as Savior for so long? *Are You the One Scripture promised would come?* Or should we expect someone else?

Jesus: ⁴Go back and tell John the things you have heard and the things you have seen. ⁵*Tell him you have seen* the blind receive sight, the lame walk, the lepers cured, the deaf hear, the dead raised, and the good news preached to the poor. ⁶Blessed are those who *understand what is afoot and stay on My narrow path.*

⁷John's disciples left, and Jesus began to speak to a crowd about John.

Jesus: What did you go into the desert to see? Did you expect to see a reed blowing around in the wind? ⁸No? Were you expecting to see a man dressed in the finest silks? No, of course not—you find silk in the sitting rooms of palaces and mansions, not in the middle of the wilderness. ⁹So what did you go out to see? A prophet? Yes. Yes, a prophet and more than a prophet. ¹⁰When you saw John, you saw the one whom the prophet *Malachi envisioned when he* said,

I will send My messenger ahead of You, and he will prepare the way for You.*

¹¹This is the truth: no one who has ever been born to a woman is greater than John the Baptist.* And yet the most insignificant person in the kingdom of heaven is greater than he. ¹²⁻¹³All of the prophets of old, all of the law—that was all prophecy leading up to the coming of John. *Now, that sort of prepares us for this very point,*

* 10:36 Micah 7:6 * 11:10 Malachi 3:1 * 11:11 Literally, John who immersed, to show repentance

right here and now. When John the Baptist* came, the kingdom of heaven began to break in upon us, and those in power are trying to clamp down on it—*why do you think John is in jail?* [14]If only you could see it—John is the Elijah, the prophet we were promised would come *and prepare the way.* [15]He who has ears *for the truth,* let him hear.

In this way, Jesus invites His followers to understand who John is, and, in turn, who He must be.

[16]What is this generation like? You are like children sitting in the marketplace and calling out, [17]"When we played the flute, you did not dance; and when we sang a dirge, you did not mourn." [18]*What I mean is this:* When John came, *he dressed in the clothes of a prophet, and* he did not eat and drink *like others but lived on honey and wild locusts.* And people wondered *if he was crazy,* if he had been possessed by a demon. [19]Then the Son of Man appeared—*He didn't fast, as John had,* but ate *with sinners* and drank *wine.* And the people said, "This man is a glutton! He's a drunk! And He hangs around with tax collectors and sinners, to boot." Well, Wisdom will be vindicated by her actions—*not by your opinions.*

[20]Then Jesus began to preach about the towns He'd visited. He'd performed some of His most fantastic miracles *in places like Chorazin and Bethsaida,* but still the people in those places hadn't turned to God.

Jesus: [21]Woe to you, Chorazin! And woe to you, Bethsaida! Had I gone to Tyre and Sidon and performed miracles there, they would have repented immediately, taking on sackcloth and ashes. [22]But I tell you this: the people from Tyre and Sidon will fare better on the day of judgment than you will. [23]And Capernaum! Do you think you will reign exalted in heaven? *No,* you'll rot in hell. Had I gone to Sodom and worked miracles there, *the people would have repented, and* Sodom would still be standing, *thriving, bustling.* [24]*Well, you know what happened to Sodom.* But know this—the people from Sodom will fare better on the day of judgment than you will.

[25]And then Jesus began to pray:

Jesus: I praise You, Father—Lord of heaven and earth. You have revealed Your truths to the lowly *and the ignorant, the children and the crippled, the lame and the mute.* You have hidden wisdom from those who pride themselves on being so wise and learned. [26]You did this, simply, because it pleased You. [27]The Father has handed over everything to My care. No one knows the Son except the Father, and no one knows the Father except the Son—and those to whom the Son wishes to reveal the Father. [28]Come to Me, all who are weary and burdened, and I will give you rest. [29]Put My yoke upon your shoulders—*it might appear heavy at first, but it is perfectly fitted to your curves.* Learn from Me, for I am gentle and humble of heart. *When you are yoked to Me,* your weary souls will find rest. [30]For My yoke is easy, and My burden is light.

12 The Sabbath came, and Jesus walked through a field. His disciples, who were hungry, began to pick some of the grain and eat it.

V

The Sabbath is a day of rest when one creates nothing, breaks nothing, gives nothing, makes no contracts, cuts no flowers, and boils no water; it is a day set aside by the Lord to remember the creative work of God, to experience the peace of the Lord, and to rest in the provision of God.

[2]When the Pharisees saw this, they reacted.

Pharisees: Look! Your disciples are breaking the law of the Sabbath!

Jesus: [3]Haven't you read what David did? When he and his friends were hungry, [4]they went into God's house and they ate the holy bread, even though neither David nor his friends, but only priests, were allowed that bread. [5]*Indeed,* have you not read that on the Sabbath priests themselves do work in the temple, breaking the Sabbath law yet remaining blameless?

---

* 11:12-13 Literally, John who immersed, to show repentance

6Listen, One who is greater than the temple is here.

7Do you not understand *what the prophet Hosea recorded*, "I desire mercy, not sacrifice"*? If you understood *that snippet of Scripture*, you would not condemn these innocent men *for ostensibly breaking the law of the Sabbath.* 8For the Son of Man *has not only the authority to heal and cast out demons, He also* has authority over the Sabbath.

9Jesus left the field and went to the synagogue, 10and there He met a man with a shriveled hand. The Pharisees wanted to set up Jesus.

Pharisees: Well, is it lawful to heal on the Sabbath too?

Jesus: 11Look, imagine that one of you has a sheep that falls into a ditch on the Sabbath—*what would you do?*

Jesus—who can see the Pharisees are testing Him and basically have missed the point—is growing a little testy. The Pharisees say nothing.

(to the Pharisees) You would dive in and rescue your sheep. 12Now what is more valuable, a person or a sheep? *So what do you think—should I heal this man on the Sabbath?* Isn't it lawful to do good deeds on the Sabbath? 13(to the man *with the shriveled hand)* Stretch out your hand.

As the man did so, his hand was completely healed, as good as new.

14The Pharisees went and mapped out plans to destroy Jesus.

15Jesus knew *that the Pharisees were plotting to kill Him* and left the area. Many people followed Him, and He healed them all, 16always insisting that they tell no one about Him. 17He did this in keeping with the prophecy Isaiah made so long ago:

18This is My servant, whom I have *well* chosen;
>> this is the One I love, the One in whom I delight.
> I will place My Spirit upon Him;
>> He will proclaim justice to all the world.
19He will not fight or shout
>> or talk loudly in the streets.

20He will not crush a reed under His heel
>> or blow out a smoldering candle
> until He has led justice *and righteousness* to final victory.
21All the world will find its hope in His name.*

22Some of the faithful brought Jesus a man who was possessed by a demon, who was blind and mute, and Jesus healed him. The man could see and talk, *and demons no longer crawled around in him.*

People *(astonished)*: 23Could this be the Son of David?

Pharisees: 24It is only through Beelzebul, the prince of demons, that this Jesus can cast out demons.

25Jesus knew what the Pharisees were thinking.

Jesus: That would be like a father splitting his own household down the middle or a king cutting his kingdom in half—the household and the kingdom would fall apart. 26So, too, if Satan *imbued people with the power to* drive out demons, Satan's kingdom would collapse. 27And you should think about this too: you have friends who drive out demons. If I am working as a tool of Beelzebul, whom are your people working for? 28When I come to you and drive out demons by the Spirit of your Father in heaven—*for the glory of your Father in heaven*—you should recognize and rejoice *that* the kingdom of God has come to you.

29Imagine you wanted to break into the house of your neighbor, a strong brawny man, and steal his furniture. First, you'd have to tie up your neighbor, *yes?* Once he was bound and tied, you could take whatever you wanted. 30*Similarly*—he who is not with Me is against Me, and he who is not doing the Father's work of gathering *up the flock* may as well be scattering *the flock.*

31-32It is one thing for you to speak ill of the Son of Man. People will be forgiven for every sin they commit and blasphemy they utter. *But those who call the work of God the work of Satan utterly remove themselves from God, and* those who blaspheme God's Spirit will not be forgiven, neither in this world nor in the world to come.

* 12:7 Hosea 6:6   * 12:18-21 Isaiah 42:1-4

33Good trees produce good fruits; bad trees produce bad fruits. You can always tell a tree by its fruits. 34You children of snakes, you who are evil—how could you possibly say anything good? For the mouth simply shapes the heart's impulses into words. 35And so the good man (who is filled with goodness) speaks good words, while the evil man (who is filled with evil) speaks evil words. 36I tell you this: on the day of judgment, people will be called to account for every careless word they have ever said. 37*The righteous* will be acquitted by their own words, and you *evildoers* will be condemned by your own words.

Scribes and Pharisees: 38Teacher, we want to see some miraculous sign from You.

Jesus: 39You wicked and promiscuous generation—you are looking for signs, *are you?* The only sign you will be given is the sign of the prophet Jonah. 40Jonah spent three days and three nights in the belly of a great fish, as the Son of Man will spend three days and three nights in the belly of the earth. 41One day, the people of Nineveh will rise up in judgment and will condemn your present generation—for the Ninevites turned from sin to God when they heard Jonah preach, and now One far greater than Jonah is here. 42The Queen of the South will also stand in judgment and condemn this generation—for she came from the ends of the earth to listen to Solomon's wisdom. And today One greater *and wiser* than Solomon is among you.

43*Let Me tell you what will happen to this wicked generation:* When an evil spirit comes out of a man, it rattles around through *deserts and other* dry places looking for a place to rest—but it does not find anywhere to rest. 44So the spirit says, "I will return to the house I left." And it returns to find that house unoccupied, tidy, swept, and sparkling clean. 45Well, then not only does one spirit set up shop in that sparkling house, but it brings seven even more wicked spirits along. And the poor man—the house—is worse off than he was before. This evil generation will suffer a similar fate.

46While Jesus was speaking to the crowd, His mother and brothers came up and wanted to speak to Him.

Someone in the Crowd: 47Your mother and brothers are waiting outside to speak to You.

Jesus: 48Who is My mother? And who are My brothers? 49(pointing to His disciples) These are My mother and brothers. 50Anyone who does the will of My Father in heaven is My mother and brother and sister.

13 That same day, Jesus left the house and went to sit by the sea. 2Large crowds gathered around Him, and He got into a boat on the sea and sat there. The crowd stood on the shore *waiting for His teaching.*

This next sermon series, the third of Jesus' five Mosaic-like sermons, is filled with parables or stories with a deeper meaning about the kingdom of heaven.

3And so Jesus began to teach. *On this day,* He spoke in parables. *Here is His first parable:*

Jesus: Once there was a sower who scattered seeds. 4One day he walked in a field scattering seeds as he went. Some seeds fell beside a road, and a flock of birds came and ate all those seeds. 5So the sower scattered seeds *in a field,* one with shallow soil and strewn with rocks. But the seeds grew quickly amid all the rocks, 6without rooting themselves in the shallow soil. Their roots got tangled up in all the stones. The sun scorched these seeds, and they died. 7And so the sower scattered seeds *near a path,* this one covered with thorny vines. *The seeds fared no better there*—the thorns choked them, *and they died.* 8*And so finally* the sower scattered his seeds in a patch *of* good earth. *At home in the good earth, the seeds grew and grew. Eventually* the seeds bore fruit, *and the fruit grew ripe and was harvested. The harvest was immense*—30, 60, 100 times what was sown.

9He who has ears to hear, let him hear.

Disciples: 10Why do You speak to the people in parables?

Jesus: 11The knowledge of the secrets of heaven has been given to you, but it has not been given to them. 12Those who have something will be given more—and they will have abundance. Those who have nothing will lose what they have—*they will be destitute.* [13]I teach in parables so the people may look but not see, listen but not hear or understand.* [14]They are fulfilling Isaiah's prophecy:

You will listen, but you will not
    understand;
    you will look, but you will not see.
[15]The people's hearts have turned to flab;
    their ears are clogged;
    their eyes are shut.
They will try to see, but they will not
    see;
    they will try to hear, but they will not
    hear;
    they will try to understand, but they
    will not comprehend.
*If they, with their blindness and deafness,
    so choose, then I will heal them.*

[16-17]Many holy prophets and righteous men and women *and people of prayer and doers of good* have wanted to see but did not see, and have wanted to hear but did not hear. Your eyes and ears are blessed. [18]This is what the parable of the sower means. [19]*It is about the kingdom of heaven.* When someone hears the story of the Kingdom and cannot understand it, the evil one comes and snatches away whatever *goodness and holiness* had been sown in the heart. This is like the seeds sown beside the road. [20-21]*You know* people who hear the word of God and receive it joyfully—but then, somehow, the word fails to take root in their hearts. It is temporary. As soon as there is trouble for those people, they trip: those people are the seeds strewn on the rocky soil. [22]And you know people who hear the word, but it is choked inside them because they constantly worry and prefer the wealth and pleasures of the world: *they prefer drunken dinner parties to prayer, power to piety, and riches to righteousness.* Those people are like the seeds sown among thorns. [23]The people who hear the word and receive it and grow in it—those are like the seeds sown on good soil. They produce a bumper crop, 30 or 60 or 100 times what was sown.

Our Father in heaven plants many seeds in order to ensure that some seeds bear fruit. The final harvest, however, is worth any amount of hard work.

[24]Jesus told them another parable.

Jesus: The kingdom of heaven is like this: Once there was a farmer who sowed good seeds in his field. [25]While the farmer's workers were sleeping, his enemy crept into the field and sowed weeds among all the wheat seeds. Then he snuck away again. [26]Eventually the crops grew—wheat, but also weeds. [27]So the farmer's workers said to him, "Sir, why didn't you sow good seeds in your field? Where did these weeds come from?"

[28]"My enemy must have done this," replied the farmer.

"Should we go pull up all the weeds?" asked his workers.

[29]"No," said the farmer. "*It's too risky.* As you pull up the weeds, you would probably pull up some wheat as well. [30]We'll let them both grow until harvesttime. I will tell the harvesters to collect the weeds and tie them in bundles to be burned, and only then to harvest the wheat and bring it to my barn."

[31]Jesus told them another parable.

Jesus: The kingdom of heaven is like a mustard seed, which a sower took and planted in his field. [32]Mustard seeds are minute, tiny—but the seeds grow into trees. Flocks of birds can come and build their nests in the branches.

[33]And Jesus told a *fourth* parable.

Jesus: *Imagine a woman preparing a loaf of bread.* The kingdom of heaven is like the leaven she folds into her dough. She kneads and kneads until the leaven is worked into all the dough.

Without the leaven, the dough remains flat. But the secret is the almost invisible leaven making her loaves fluff and rise.

[34]Jesus gave all these teachings to the crowd in parables. Indeed, He spoke only in parables [35]in fulfillment of the prophetic words *of the psalms:*

* 13:13 Psalm 78:2   * 13:14-15 Isaiah 6:9-10

I will open My mouth in parables;
I will tell them things that have been
hidden and obscure since the very
beginning of the world.*

³⁶Then Jesus left the crowds and returned to His house. His disciples followed Him.

Disciples: Explain to us the story You told about the weeds.

Jesus: ³⁷The one who sowed the good seed is the Son of Man. ³⁸The field is the world; the good seed represents the children of the Kingdom. The weeds—*who do you think the weeds are?* They are the children of the evil one, ³⁹and the enemy who threw the weeds among the wheat is the devil. The harvest is the end of the age, and the workers are God's heavenly messengers. ⁴⁰*In the parable*, I told you the weeds would be pulled up and burned—well, that is how it will be at the end of this age. ⁴¹The Son of Man will send His messengers out into the world, and they will root out from His kingdom everything that is poisonous, ugly, and malicious, and everyone who does evil. ⁴²They will throw all that wickedness into the fiery furnace where there will be weeping and grinding of teeth. ⁴³And the righteous will shine like the sun in their Father's kingdom. He who has ears to hear, let him hear.

⁴⁴The kingdom of heaven is like a treasure that is hidden in a field. A *crafty* man found the treasure buried there and buried it again *so no one would know where it was.* Thrilled, he went off and sold everything he had, and then he came back and bought the field *with the hidden treasure part of the bargain.*

⁴⁵Or the kingdom of heaven is like a jeweler on the lookout for the finest pearls. ⁴⁶When he found a pearl more beautiful and valuable than any jewel he had ever seen, the jeweler sold all he had and bought that pearl, *his pearl of great price.*

⁴⁷Or *think of it this way*: the kingdom of heaven is like a net that was cast into the sea, a net that caught a world of flickering fish. ⁴⁸When the net was full, the fishermen hauled it to shore. They separated the good fish from the bad, placing the good fish in a bucket and throwing out the inedible fish. ⁴⁹That is what the end of time will be like. The heavenly messengers will separate *the good from*

the bad*, the righteous from the wicked, the repentant from the prideful, the faithful from the hard-hearted.* ⁵⁰*The bad, the wicked, the prideful, and the hard-hearted* will be thrown into the fiery furnace where there will be weeping and grinding of teeth.

⁵¹Do you understand?

Disciples: Yes, *we understand.*

Jesus: ⁵²Every scribe *and teacher of the law* who has become a student of the ways of the Kingdom is like the head of the household who brings some new things and some old things, both out of the storeroom.

⁵³With that Jesus finished teaching His parables, and He moved on. ⁵⁴⁻⁵⁶He came to *Nazareth*, the town where He had grown up. He taught at the local synagogue, and the people were astonished.

People: *Is this our little Jesus? Is this Mary's son? Is this the carpenter's son? Is this Jesus, brother of James, Joseph, Simon, and Judas? Didn't we just see His sisters yesterday at the market?* Where did He learn all this? Whence His power?

⁵⁷They were offended by Him—*by His teachings, by who He was.*

Jesus: Prophets are respected—except in their hometowns and in their own households. *There the prophet is dishonored.*

⁵⁸Jesus didn't bother to work wondrous miracles there *in Nazareth* because the people did not believe.

14 At this time, the ruler *of Galilee* was Herod *Antipas.* He began to hear reports about all that Jesus was doing.

²*Like the people of Nazareth*, Herod wondered *where Jesus' power came from.*

Herod *(to his servants)*: He must be John the Baptist,* raised from the dead; thus his powers are at work in him.

Herod is concerned with the attention that John is receiving, but he doesn't

* 13:35 Psalm 78:2   * 14:2 Literally, John who immersed, to show repentance

want to be seen killing a holy man. And now, Jesus is creating an even greater problem.

3-5Herod's brother Philip had married a woman named Herodias, *who eventually married Herod.* John denounced Herod's marriage to her as adulterous. Herod was incensed (*not to mention a little fearful*) and wanted to kill John, but he knew the people considered John a prophet. Instead, he bound John and put him in jail.
    6-7*There John sat until* Herod's birthday. On that night, *Salome,* Herodias's daughter *by Philip,* came and danced for her stepfather and all his birthday guests. Herod so enjoyed her dancing that he vowed to give her whatever she wanted.

Salome (*after whispering with her mother*): 8Bring me the head of John the Baptist,* displayed on a platter.

This is not what Herod expected—he imagined his stepdaughter would ask for a necklace or maybe a slave.

9Herod still thought it unwise to kill John, but *because he had made such a show of his promise*—because he had actually sworn an oath and *because the scene was playing out* in front of *the watchful eyes* of so many guests— Herod felt bound *to give his stepdaughter what she wanted.* 10And so he sent orders to the prison to have John beheaded, 11and there was his head, displayed on a platter, given first to *Salome* and then passed on to her mother.
    12John's disciples went to the prison, got John's body, and buried him. Then they went to tell Jesus.
    13When Jesus learned what had happened, He got on a boat and went away to spend some time in a private place. The crowds, of course, followed Jesus on foot from their cities. 14*Though Jesus wanted solitude,* when He saw the crowds, He had compassion on them, and He healed the sick *and the lame.* 15At evening-time, Jesus' disciples came to Him.

Disciples: We're in a fairly remote place, and it is getting late; *the crowds will get hungry for supper.* Send them away so they have time to get back to the villages and get something to eat.

Jesus: 16They don't need to go back to the villages in order to eat supper. Give them something to eat here.

Disciples: 17*But we don't have enough food.* We only have five rounds *of flatbread* and two fish.

Jesus: 18Bring the bread and the fish to Me.

So the disciples brought Him the five rounds of flatbread and the two fish, 19and Jesus told the people to sit down on the grass. He took the bread and the fish, He looked up to heaven, He gave thanks, and then He broke the bread. Jesus gave the bread to the disciples, and the disciples gave the bread to the people; 20everyone ate and was satisfied. *When everyone had eaten,* the disciples picked up 12 baskets of *crusts and* broken pieces *of bread and crumbs.* 21There were 5,000 men there, not to mention all the women and children.
    22Immediately Jesus made the disciples get into the boat and go on to the other side of the sea while He dismissed the crowd. 23Then, after the crowd had gone, Jesus went up to a mountaintop alone (*as He had intended from the start*). As evening descended, He stood alone on the mountain, praying.

In the midst of the burdens of life and ministry, like when news of John's death reaches Him, Jesus seeks refreshment in solitary prayer.

24The boat was in the water, some distance from land, buffeted and pushed around by waves and wind. 25Deep in the night, *when He had concluded His prayers,* Jesus walked out on the water to His disciples *in their boat.* 26The disciples saw a figure moving toward them and were terrified.

Disciple: It's a ghost!

Another Disciple: A ghost? *What will we do?*

Jesus: 27Be still. It is I. You have nothing to fear.

Peter: 28Lord, if it is really You, then command me to meet You on the water.

Jesus: 29*Indeed,* come.

* 14:8 Literally, John who immersed, to show repentance

Peter stepped out of the boat onto the water and began walking toward Jesus. [30]But when he remembered how strong the wind was, his courage caught in his throat and he began to sink.

Peter: Master, save me!

[31]Immediately Jesus reached for Peter and caught him.

Jesus: O you of little faith. Why did you doubt *and dance back and forth between following* Me *and heeding fear?*

[32]Then Jesus and Peter climbed in the boat together, and the wind became still. [33]And the disciples worshiped Him.

Disciples: Truly You are the Son of God.

[34]All together, Jesus and the disciples crossed *to the other side of the sea.* They landed at Gennesaret, *an area famous for its princely gardens.* [35]The people of Gennesaret recognized Jesus, and they spread word of His arrival all over the countryside. People brought the sick *and wounded* to Him [36]and begged Him for permission to touch the fringes of His robe. Everyone who touched Him was healed.

15 Some Pharisees and scribes came from Jerusalem to ask Jesus a question.

Scribes and Pharisees: [2]The law of Moses has always held that one must ritually wash his hands before eating. Why don't Your disciples observe this tradition?

[3]Jesus turned the Pharisees' question back on them.

Jesus: Why do you violate God's command because of your tradition? [4]God said, "Honor your father and mother.* Anyone who curses his father or mother must be put to death."* [5-6]But you say that one need no longer honor his parents so long as he says to them, "What you might have gained from me, I now give to the glory of God." Haven't you let your tradition trump the word of God? [7]You hypocrites! Isaiah must have had you in mind when he prophesied,

[8]People honor Me with their lips,
   but their hearts are nowhere near Me.
[9]Because they elevate mere human ritual
   to the status of law,
      their worship of Me is a meaningless
      sham.*

[10](to the multitude) Hear and understand this: [11]What you put into your mouth cannot make you *clean or* unclean; it is what comes out of your mouth that can make you unclean.

[12]Later the disciples came to Him.

Disciples: Do You realize the Pharisees were shocked by what You said?

Jesus: [13]Every plant planted by someone other than My heavenly Father will be plucked up by the roots. [14]So let them be. They are blind guides. What happens when one blind person leads another? Both of them fall into a ditch.

Peter: [15]Explain that riddle to us.

Jesus: [16]Do you still not see? [17]Don't you understand that whatever you take in through your mouth makes its way to your stomach and eventually out *of the bowels* of your body? [18]But the things that come out of your mouth—*your curses, your fears, your denunciations*—these come from your heart, and it is the stirrings of your heart that can make you unclean. [19]For your heart harbors evil thoughts—fantasies of murder, adultery, and whoring; fantasies of stealing, lying, and slandering. [20]These make you unclean—not eating with a hand you've not ritually purified with a splash of water *and a prayer.*

[21]Jesus left that place and withdrew to Tyre and Sidon. [22]A Canaanite woman—*a non-Jew*—came to Him.

Canaanite Woman (*wailing*): Lord, Son of David, have mercy on me! My daughter is possessed by a demon. *Have mercy, Lord!*

[23]Jesus said nothing. *And the woman continued to wail.* His disciples came to Him.

Disciples: Do something—she keeps crying after us!

* 15:4 Exodus 20:12; Deuteronomy 5:16   * 15:4 Leviticus 20:9
* 15:8-9 Isaiah 29:13

Jesus: 24I was sent here only to gather up the lost sheep of Israel.

25The woman came up to Jesus and knelt before Him.

Canaanite Woman: Lord, help me!

Jesus: 26It is not right to waste the children's bread by feeding dogs.

Canaanite Woman: 27But, Lord, even dogs eat the crumbs that fall by the table as their master is eating.

28Jesus—*whose ancestors included Ruth and Rahab*—spoke *with kindness and insight.*

Jesus: Woman, you have great faith. And your request is done.

And her daughter was healed, right then and from then on.
29Jesus left and went to the Sea of Galilee. He went up on a mountaintop and sat down. 30Crowds thronged to Him there, bringing the lame, *the maimed,* the blind, the crippled, the mute, and many other *sick and broken* people. They laid them at His feet, and He healed them. 31The people saw the mute speaking, the lame walking, *the maimed made whole,* the crippled dancing, and the blind seeing; and the people were amazed, and they praised the God of Israel.

Jesus (to His disciples): 32We must take pity on these people for they have touched My heart; they have been with Me for three days, and they don't have any food. I don't want to send them home this hungry—they might collapse on the way!

Disciples: 33We'll never find enough food for all these people, out here in the middle of nowhere!

Jesus: 34How much bread do you have?

Disciples: Seven *rounds of flatbread* and a few small fish.

35He told the crowd to sit down. 36He took the bread and the fish, He gave thanks, and then He broke the bread and divided the fish. He gave the bread and fish to the disciples, the disciples distributed them to the people, 37and everyone ate and was satisfied.

When everyone had eaten, the disciples picked up seven baskets of *crusts and* broken pieces *and crumbs.*
38There were 4,000 men there, not to mention all the women and children. 39Then Jesus sent the crowd away. He got into the boat and went to Magadan.

16 They came to Him together, a band of Pharisees and a band of Sadducees, trying to trick and trap Him.

V

Now at this time in Judea, the Jews, the children of Israel, are a diverse bunch. One group of Jews, which Jesus has already encountered, is called the Pharisees. Another group of Jews is called the Sadducees. The two groups do not agree about how to read Scripture, they do not see eye-to-eye, and they do not get along. They rarely partner with each other, but here they are partnering—because they are so perplexed, befuddled, and panicked about this Jesus.

They asked Him for a sign from heaven.

Jesus: 2At evening time, you read the sky as a sign—you say, "The weather will be fine because the sky is shading red," 3and in the morning, *you read the sky as a sign, saying,* "The red, stormy sky tells me that today we will have storms." So you are skilled at interpreting the sky, but you cannot interpret the signs of the times? 4Only a cheating and evil generation *such as this* would beg for a miraculous sign *from heaven.* The only sign you will get will be the sign of Jonah.

And then Jesus left them and went away.
5When next the disciples crossed *the Sea of Galilee,* they forgot to bring any bread with them.

Jesus: 6Be careful; avoid the leaven of the Pharisees and Sadducees.

7The disciples *were not quite sure what Jesus meant, so they* discussed His warning among themselves.

Disciples: *He must mean not to buy any bread from a baker who associates with the Pharisees or Sadducees.* He must have given us this warning because we showed up here without any bread.

[8]Jesus knew what the disciples were saying among themselves, *and He took them to task.*

Jesus: You men of little faith, *do you really think that I care which baker you patronize? After spending so much time with Me, do you still not understand what I mean?* So you showed up without bread; why talk about it? [9-10]Don't you remember that we fed 5,000 men with five rounds of flatbread? Don't you remember that we fed 4,000 men with seven rounds of bread? Don't you remember, what excess, what abundance there was—*how many broken pieces and crusts you collected after everyone had eaten and was sated?* [11]So when I speak about leaven, I am not talking about what we will eat for dinner. I say again, avoid the leaven of the Pharisees and Sadducees.

[12]And then the disciples understood: Jesus was not talking about the bread you eat, *but about the food that feeds your soul. He was speaking in metaphor;* He was warning them against imbibing the teachings of the Pharisees and Sadducees.
[13]Jesus then went to Caesarea Philippi.

Jesus *(to His disciples)*: Who do people say the Son of Man is?

Disciples: [14]Some say John the Baptist.* And some say Elijah. And some say Jeremiah or one of the other prophets.

Jesus: [15]And you? Who do you say that I am?

Peter: [16]You are the Anointed One. You are the Son of the living God.

Jesus: [17]Simon, son of Jonah, your knowledge is a mark of blessing. For you didn't learn this truth from your friends or from teachers or from sages you've met on the way. You learned it from My Father in heaven. [18]This is why I have called you Peter *(rock)*: for on this rock I will build My church. The church will reign triumphant even at the gates of hell. [19]Peter, I give you the keys to the kingdom of heaven.

Whatever you bind on earth will be bound in heaven, and whatever you loose on earth will be loosed in heaven.

[20]And Jesus ordered His disciples *to keep these teachings secret.*

Jesus: You must tell no one that I am the Anointed.

[21]Then Jesus began to tell the disciples *about what would happen to Him. He said* He would have to go to Jerusalem. There the elders, chief priests, and scribes would meet Him; He would suffer at their hands; and He would be killed. But three days later, He would be raised *to new life.*
[22]*As Jesus spoke of the things to come,* Peter took Him aside. *Sad and confused, and maybe a little bit prideful,* Peter chastised Jesus.

Peter: No, Lord! Never! These things that You are saying—they will never happen to You!

Jesus *(turning to Peter)*: [23]Get away from Me, Satan!

This is the very thing He said to the devil during those wilderness temptations.

You are a stumbling block before Me! You are not thinking about God's story; you are thinking about *some distorted story of fallen, broken* people. [24](to His disciples) If you want to follow Me, you must deny yourself *the things you think you want.* You must pick up your cross and follow Me. [25]The person who wants to save his life must lose it, and she who loses her life for Me will find it. [26]Look, does it make sense to truly become successful, but then

* 16:14 Literally, John who immersed, to show repentance

to hand over your very soul? What is your soul really worth? [27]The Son of Man will come in His Father's glory, with His heavenly messengers, and then He will reward each person for what has been done. [28]I tell you this: some of you standing here, you will see the Son of Man come into His kingdom before you taste death.

V

Jesus is providing an entirely different perspective on success and happiness. The new Kingdom is breaking in, and the new community is coming together. This is the logic of that Kingdom and that community: to inhabit God's story, this is what must be done. To accrue fame and comfort and riches is counter to this new community. In the economics of this new community, real success is marked by a willingness to sacrifice one's very life to God, and the promised rewards are immense.

17 Six days later, Jesus went up to the top of a high mountain with Peter, James, and John. [2]There, *something spectacular happened:* Jesus' face began to glow and gleam and shine like the morning sun. His clothes gleamed too—bright white, like sunlight *mirroring off a snowfall.* He was, *in a word,* transfigured. [3]Suddenly there at the top of the mountain were Moses and Elijah, *those icons of the faith, beloved of God.* And they talked to Jesus.

Peter: [4]Lord, how amazing that we are here *to see these heroes of our faith, these men through whom God spoke.* Should I quickly build some shelter, three *small* tabernacles, for You, for Moses, and for Elijah?

[5]As Peter spoke, a bright cloud enveloped all of them.

Voice from the Cloud: This is My beloved Son. With Him I am well pleased. Listen to Him.

V

This is but an echo of the Voice that spoke at Jesus' ritual cleansing in baptism. It is an echo of what God said through Moses during his final sermon on the mount. God promised that although Moses could not enter the promised land, He would send His people another prophet. Moses' very last wish for his beloved people was that they would listen to this new prophet when He would come.

[6]This voice from heaven terrified the three disciples, and they fell prostrate on the ground. [7]But Jesus—*who was, by this time, used to His disciples being plagued by fear*—touched them.

Jesus: Get up. Don't be afraid.

[8]And when the disciples got up, they saw they were alone with their Lord.

[9]The four men hiked back down the mountain, and Jesus told His disciples to stay silent.

Jesus: Don't tell anyone what happened here, not until the Son of Man has been raised from the dead.

V

Why does Jesus often instruct His disciples to keep secrets? In this case, perhaps He does because He realizes they will not understand the meaning of the transfiguration until they live through that other hilltop event, the death of Jesus on the cross. Believers, like the disciples, will better understand this bath of light and revelation when they, too, come to Golgotha and the cross.

Disciples: [10]Master, why do the scribes teach that the prophet Elijah must come first?

Jesus: [11]*Scripture tells us clearly that indeed* Elijah will come to restore all things. [12]But see this: Elijah has come already. No one recognized him for who he was, so he was arrested and killed. *That is part of the preparation of which our Scripture speaks:* for the Son of Man, too, will be arrested and killed at the hands of people *who do not see Him for who He is.*

[13]And then the disciples realized the man they knew as John the Baptist* was the one Jesus was speaking of.

[14]*They had come down from the mountain, and as they headed toward town,* they came to a crowd. As they approached the crowd, a man rushed up to Jesus and knelt before Him.

Man from the Crowd: [15]Lord, have mercy on my son. He has seizures. Sometimes when they come on, my son falls into the fire or into a pond. *We are very concerned for him.* [16]I brought him to Your disciples, but they could not heal him.

Jesus: [17]This generation *is no better than the generation who wandered in the desert,* who lost faith and bowed down *to golden idols as soon as Moses disappeared upon Mount Sinai!* How long will I have to shepherd these unbelieving sheep? *(turning to the man)* Bring the boy to Me.

[18]*The man did, and* Jesus castigated the demon who had taken up residence in the boy. And the demon fled the boy's body *at the sound of Jesus' voice,* and the boy was healed from that moment on. *No more shaking. No more falling into fires.*

[19]*Later,* when they were away from the crowds, the disciples asked Jesus why they hadn't been able to drive out the demon themselves.

Jesus: [20]Because you have so little faith. I tell you this: *if you had even a faint spark of faith,* even faith as *tiny as* a mustard seed, you could say to this mountain, "Move from here to there," and *because of your faith,* the mountain would move. *If you had just a sliver of faith,* you would find nothing impossible. [[21]But this kind is not realized except through much prayer and fasting.]*

[22]Jesus and the disciples came to Galilee.

Jesus: The Son of Man is going to be betrayed into the hands of men. [23]They will kill Him, and on the third day, He will be resurrected, *vindicated, newly alive.*

The disciples were filled with grief.

[24]Then Jesus and His disciples went toward Capernaum, and when they arrived there, some people who had collected the two-drachma tax *that went for the upkeep of the temple* came up to Peter.

Temple Tax Collectors: Does your Teacher not pay the *temple* tax?

Peter: [25]He does pay the tax.

> Jesus knows that He and His followers are the true temple, and yet Jesus is canny. It is not quite time to shake the foundations of the temple or of the old way of doing things. And so He pays the tax and bides His time.

So when Peter came into the house where they were staying, Jesus explored the subject.

Jesus: Simon, what do you think? When kings collect taxes and duties and tolls, from whom do they collect? Do they levy taxes on their own people or on strangers and foreigners?

Peter: [26]The foreigners, my Lord.

Jesus: Well, then, we children of the King should be exempt from this two-drachma tax. [27]But all in all, it's better not to make any waves; *we'd better go on and pay the tax.* So do this: go out to the lake and throw out your line. And when you catch a fish, open its jaws and you will find a four-drachma coin. Take this to the tax collectors, and pay your taxes and Mine.

18 Around that same time, the disciples came to Jesus and questioned Him about the kingdom of heaven.

A Disciple: In the kingdom of heaven, who is the greatest?

> The disciples struggle with the concept of the kingdom of heaven.

---

* 17:13 Literally, John who immersed, to show repentance
* 17:21 The earliest manuscripts omit verse 21.

They do not yet understand that who is most important or most powerful is a contradiction in terms. This is the fourth of the five great sermons in Matthew.

---

²Jesus called over a little child. *He put His hand on the top of the child's head.*

Jesus: ³This is the truth: unless you change and become like little children, you will never enter the kingdom of heaven. ⁴In that kingdom, the most humble who are most like this child are the greatest. ⁵And whoever welcomes a child, *welcomes her* in My name, welcomes Me. ⁶And do not lead astray one of the weak and friendless who believes in Me. If you do, it would be better for you to be dragged down with a millstone and drowned in the bottom of the sea.

⁷Beware indeed of those in a world filled with obstacles and temptations *that cause people to turn away from Me.* Those temptations are woven into the fabric of a world *not yet redeemed,* but beware to anyone who lures righteous women and men off the narrow path. ⁸If your hand constantly grasps at the things of this world rather than serves the Kingdom— cut it off and throw it away. If your foot is always leading you to wander, then cut it off and throw it away; it is better for you to hobble, crippled, into *the kingdom of* life than to burn in hell with two hands and two feet. ⁹And if your eye always focuses on things that cause you to sin, then pull your eye out and throw it away. It is better for you to see *the kingdom of* life with one eye than to see the fires of hell with perfect sight.

¹⁰Make sure that you do not look down on the little ones, *on those who are further behind you on the path of righteousness.* For I tell you: they are watched over by those *most beloved* messengers who are always in the company of My Father in heaven. [¹¹The Son of Man has come to save all those who are lost.]* ¹²A shepherd in charge of 100 sheep notices that one of his sheep has gone astray. What do you think he should do? Should the shepherd leave the flock on the hills unguarded to search for the lost sheep? *God's shepherd goes to look for that one lost sheep,* ¹³and when he finds her, he

is happier about her return than he is about the 99 who stayed put. ¹⁴Your Father in heaven does not want a single one of the *tripped, waylaid, stumbling* little ones to be lost.

V

The wisdom of the world says the shepherd should forget that one missing sheep and chalk it up as a loss. In God's economy, each soul has its own value apart from all others. Jesus calls the people of His kingdom to help the weak and the friendless, the small and the frail, the mute and the poor, the ugly and the disfigured.

Jesus: ¹⁵This is what you do if one of your brothers or sisters sins against you: go to him, in private, and tell him just what you perceive the wrong to be. If he listens to you, you've won a brother. ¹⁶*But sometimes he will not listen.* And if he does not listen, go back, taking a friend or two friends with you (*for, as we have learned in Deuteronomy,* every matter of communal import should be testified to by two or three witnesses).* ¹⁷Then, if your brother or sister still refuses to heed, you are to share what you know with the entire church; and if your brother or sister still refuses to listen to the entire church, you are to cast out your unrepentant sibling and consider him no different from outsiders and tax collectors.

What God desires most is not the casting out of an unrepentant member, but loving chastisement for the sake of bringing the sinful back to God.

¹⁸Remember this: whatever you bind on earth will be bound in heaven, and whatever you loose on earth will be loosed in heaven. ¹⁹And this: if two *or three* of you come together as a community *and discern clearly* about anything, My Father in heaven will bless that discernment. ²⁰For when two or three gather together in My name, I am there in the midst of them.

* 18:11 The earliest manuscripts omit verse 11.   * 18:16 Deuteronomy 19:15

Peter: [21]Lord, when someone has sinned against me, how many times ought I forgive him? *Once? Twice?* As many as seven times?

Jesus: [22]You must forgive not seven times, but seventy times seven.

V

The response of Jesus is like the story of Lamech in Genesis. He was Adam and Eve's great-great-great-great-grandson who had two wives. One day he said to his wives, "Wives of Lamech, I need to tell you something! I killed a man who struck me. *Surely* Lamech *must be avenged* seventy-seven times" (Genesis 4:23-24). In this new Kingdom of forgiveness, we reverse and invert Lamech's plan. As Christians, we should forgive others' transgressions more readily than the world would avenge them.

Jesus: [23]If you want to understand the kingdom of heaven, think about a king who wanted to settle accounts with his servants. [24]Just as the king began to get his accounts in order, his assistants called his attention to a slave who owed a huge sum to him—what a laborer might make in 500 lifetimes.* [25]The slave, *maybe an embezzler,* had no way to make restitution, so the king ordered that he, his wife, their children, and everything the family owned be sold *on the auction block;* the proceeds from the slave sale would go toward paying back the king. [26]Upon hearing this judgment, the slave fell down, prostrated himself before the king, and begged for mercy: "Have mercy on me, and I will somehow pay you everything." [27]The king was moved by the pathos of the situation, so indeed he took pity on the servant, told him to stand up, and then forgave the debt.

[28]But the slave went and found a friend, another slave, who owed him about a hundred days' wages.* "Pay me back that money," shouted the slave, throttling his friend and shaking him with threats and violence. [29]The slave's friend fell down prostrate and begged for mercy: "Have mercy on me, and I will somehow pay you

everything." [30]But the first slave *cackled and was hard-hearted and* refused *to hear his friend's plea.* He found a magistrate and had his friend thrown into prison "where," he said, "you will sit until you can pay me back." [31]The other servants saw what was going on. They were upset, so they went to the king and told him everything that had happened.

[32]The king summoned the slave, *the one who had owed so much money, the one whose debt the king had forgiven. The king was livid.* "You slovenly scum," he said, *seething with anger.* "You begged me to forgive your debt, and I did. [33]*What would be the faithful response to such latitude and generosity?* Surely you should have shown the same charity to a friend who was in your debt."

[34]The king turned over the unmerciful slave to his brigade of torturers, *and they had their way with him* until he should pay his whole debt. [35]And that is what My Father in heaven will do to you, unless you forgive each of your brothers *and each of your sisters* from *the very cockles of* your heart.

19

After Jesus had finished His teaching about forgiveness, He left Galilee and He went to the section of Judea on the other side of the Jordan River. [2]Large crowds followed Him, *and when He got to Judea,* He set about healing them.

The religious leaders who are eyeing the crowds and watching the healings decide it is again time to try to trip up Jesus.

[3]So some Pharisees approached Jesus and asked Him this tricky question *about divorce:*

Pharisees: Is it ever lawful for a man to divorce his wife?

Jesus: [4]Haven't you read that in the beginning God created humanity male and female?* *Don't you remember what the story of our creation tells us about marriage?* [5]"For this reason, a man will leave his mother and father and cleave to his wife, and the two shall become one flesh."* [6]If a husband and wife are one flesh, *how can they divorce? Divorce would be a bloody*

---

* 18:24 Literally, 10,000 talents   * 18:28 Literally, denarii, Roman coins   * 19:4 Genesis 1:27   * 19:5 Genesis 2:24

amputation, would it not? "What God has brought together, let no man separate."

Pharisees: 7Why did Moses explain that if a man leaves his wife, then he must give her a certificate of divorce and send her away, free and clear of him?

Jesus: 8Moses permitted you to divorce your wives because your hearts were hard. *But divorce was an innovation, an accommodation to a fallen world.* There was no divorce at creation. 9Listen, friends: if you leave your wife, unless there is adultery, and then marry another woman, you yourself are committing adultery. *Only if there is adultery can you divorce your wife.*

Why? Because adultery itself is the divorce. Adultery is the thing that breaks the bond of marriage. Just as an excommunication merely recognizes the fact that someone has already been removed from the people, a divorce merely legalizes what harlotry has created. But should someone leave his wife for any other reason—because he has nothing to say to her, because she continually burns his food, because she is profligate with the household resources, because he simply cannot stand the sight of her—this is outside of the message Jesus offers here. If we behave as if a marriage has been undone— indeed, some may believe that a marriage has been undone—then we are deluding ourselves. In the eyes of God, the marriage bonds still hold a man to his wife.

Disciples: 10If this is how it is, then it is better to avoid marrying in the first place.

Jesus: 11Not everyone can hear this teaching, only those to whom it has been given. 12*Some people do not marry, of course.* Some people are eunuchs because they are born that way, others have been made eunuchs by men, and others have renounced marriage for the sake of the kingdom of heaven. Anyone who can embrace that call should do so.

13At this, some *of Jesus' followers* brought their children before Jesus; they wanted Him to place His hands on the children and pray *for them.* Some of the disciples, *mistakenly thinking that Jesus wouldn't want to be bothered with the likes of children,* began to rebuke the crowd.

Jesus: 14Let the little children come to Me; do not get in their way. For the kingdom of heaven belongs to children like these.

15He laid His hands on them, *He prayed with them,* and then He left that spot *and went elsewhere.* 16Then a *young* man came up to Jesus.

Young Man: Teacher, what good deed can I do to assure myself eternal life?

Jesus: 17Strange that you should ask Me what is good. There is only One who is good. If you want to participate in His *divine* life, obey the Commandments.

Young Man: 18Which Commandments *in particular?*

Jesus: *Well, to begin with,* do not murder, do not commit adultery, do not steal, do not give false testimony, 19honor your father and mother, and love your neighbor as yourself.*

Young Man: 20I've kept those Commandments faithfully. What else do I need to do?

Jesus can see the man wants to know how to participate in God's reality, and He knows his shoulders will sag under the weight of the next hard instruction.

Jesus: 21If you want to be perfect, go and sell all your possessions and give all your money to the poor; then you will have treasure in heaven. And then come, follow Me.

22The young man went away sad because he was very wealthy indeed.

Jesus: 23This is the truth: it is hard for a rich man to enter the kingdom of heaven. 24Yes, it is easier for a camel to go through the eye

* 19:19 Exodus 20:12-17; Deuteronomy 5:16-20; Leviticus 19:18

of a needle than for a rich man to enter the kingdom of God.

25The disciples, hearing this, were stunned.

Disciples: Who then can be saved?

Jesus: 26People cannot save themselves. But with God, all things are possible.

Peter: 27*You just told that man to leave everything and follow You.* Well, all of us have done just that. So what should we be expecting?

Jesus: 28I tell you this. When *creation is consummated and* all things are renewed, when the Son of Man sits on His throne in glory, you who have followed Me will also sit on thrones. There will be twelve thrones, and you will sit and judge the twelve tribes of Israel. 29You who have left your house and your fields, or your brothers and sisters, or your father and mother, or even your children in order to follow Me, *at that time when all is renewed, you will receive so much more*: you will receive 100 times what you gave up. You will inherit eternal life. 30Many of those who are the first will be last, and those who are the last will be first.

20 Jesus: The kingdom of heaven is like a wealthy landowner who got up early in the morning and went out, first thing, to hire workers to tend his vineyard. 2He agreed to pay them a day's wage* for the day's work. The workers headed to the vineyard *while the landowner headed home to deal with some paperwork.* 3About three hours later, he went back to the marketplace. He saw *some unemployed* men standing around with nothing to do.

Landowner: 4*Do you need some work?* Go over to my vineyard *and join the crew there.* I'll pay you well.

So off they went *to join the crew at the vineyard.* 5About three hours later, and then three hours after that, *the landowner went back to the market and saw another crew of men and hired them, too, sending them off to his vineyard and promising to pay them well.* 6Then finally late in the afternoon, *at the cusp of night,* the landowner walked again

through *the marketplace,* and he saw other *workers* still standing around.

Landowner: Why have you been standing here all day, doing nothing?

Workers: 7Because no one has hired us.

Landowner: Well, you should go over to my vineyard *and work.*

And off the workers went. 8When quitting time arrived, the landowner called to his foreman.

Landowner: Pay the workers their day's wages, beginning with the workers I hired most recently and ending with the workers who have been here all day.

9So the workers who had been hired just a short while before came to the foreman, and he paid them each a day's wage.* 10*Then other workers who had arrived during the day were paid, each of them a day's wage.* Finally, the workers who'd been toiling since early morning came thinking they'd be paid more, but the foreman paid each of them a day's wage.* 11As they received their pay, this last group of workers began to protest.

First Workers: 12*We've been here since the crack of dawn!* And you're paying us the exact same wage you paid the crew that just showed up. *We deserve more than they do.* We've been slogging in the heat of the sun all day—*these others haven't worked nearly as long as we have!*

13*The landowner heard these protests.*

Landowner (to a worker): Friend, no one has been wronged here today. *This isn't about what you deserve.* You agreed to work for a day's wage,* did you not? 14So take your money and go home. *I can give my money to whomever I please, and* it pleases me to pay everyone the same amount of money. 15Do you think I don't have the right to dispose of my money as I wish? Or does my generosity somehow prick at you?

16*And that is your picture:* The last will be first and the first will be last.

* 20:2 Literally, a denarius, a Roman coin   * 20:9 Literally, a denarius, a Roman coin   * 20:10 Literally, a denarius, a Roman coin
* 20:13 Literally, a denarius, a Roman coin

God's glory and kingdom are His, so He is free to lavish goodness on anyone He pleases. If someone feels jealous because her friend's husband seems nicer than her husband, or because another's brother works no harder than he does but somehow earns far more money, or because another's classmate who has the intelligence of a sponge always seems to get better grades, then God's generosity will indeed undo all we have come to know and expect.

17As Jesus was making His way to Jerusalem, He took His twelve disciples aside and *once again* told them *what was about to happen.*

Jesus: 18We are going to Jerusalem. The Son of Man will be betrayed to the chief priests and to the teachers of the law. He will be condemned to death, 19and the priests and teachers will turn Him over to the Romans, who will mock Him and flog Him and crucify Him. But on the third day, He will be raised from the dead *to new resurrected life.*

20*As Jesus was speaking about the things that were to come,* Zebedee's wife, whose sons were among Jesus' disciples, came to Jesus with her sons and knelt down before Him to ask a favor.

Jesus: 21What do you want?

Zebedee's Wife: When the kingdom of God is made manifest, I want one of my boys, *James and John*, to sit at Your right hand, and one to sit at Your left hand.

Apparently the wife of Zebedee secretly thinks her sons have worked harder and sacrificed more for Jesus than the other disciples, and she probably suspects that Jesus loves them best. She thinks He will at least do the right thing and reward their hardest work and most loyal service. She also hopes that if her sons are there on the nearest, closest thrones, she may

spend eternity near and close, too, clutching onto their coattails.

Jesus *(to all three)*: 22You don't understand what you are asking. Can you drink the cup I am going to drink? Can you be ritually washed in baptism just as I have been baptized?*

Zebedee Brothers: Of course!

Jesus: 23Yes, you will drink from My cup, and yes, you will be baptized* as I have been. But the thrones to My right and My left are not Mine to grant. My Father has already given those seats to those for whom they were created.

24The other ten disciples learned what the Zebedee brothers had asked of Jesus, and they were upset. 25So Jesus called the disciples together.

Jesus: Do you want the Kingdom run like the Romans run their kingdom? Their rulers have great power over the people, *but God the Father doesn't play by the Romans' rules.* 26*This is the Kingdom's logic:* whoever wants to become great must first make himself a servant; 27whoever wants to be first must bind himself as a slave—28just as the Son of Man did not come to be served, but to serve and to give His life as the ransom for many.

29So finally Jesus and His disciples left Jericho *and headed for Jerusalem*; and, *of course,* a large crowd followed them. 30Two blind men, sitting on the roadside, heard the crowd approaching with Jesus.

Two Blind Men: Lord, have mercy on us, Son of David!

31The crowd rebuked them and told them to be quiet, but they shouted louder.

Two Blind Men: Lord, Son of David, have mercy on us!

Jesus *(taking the two blind men aside)*: 32What is it that you want, *brothers?*

Two Blind Men: 33Lord, we want to see.

* 20:22 Literally, immersed, to show repentance   * 20:23 Literally, immersed, to show repentance

After a great parade, Jesus and His disciples walk into the temple area, and what He sees enrages Him. He sees moneychangers, buying and selling. He sees men sitting on benches, hawking doves to those who have come from the countryside to make a sacrifice. He sees that the salesmen and teachers have turned a sanctuary of worship into a place of spiritual prostitution. This is the place where Jesus came as a boy to sit with the great teachers. It is the place where His Father receives the offerings of His people. It is more than Jesus can take.

Can anyone be surprised at this other side to Jesus? He has turned out to be not just a kindly teacher; instead, He is the Anointed One, not to be taken lightly. In the midst of this scene filled with joy and chaos, there are extremes. Some are beginning to understand who this man from Galilee is—the Anointed—but the rulers are having great difficulty with the disruption to their orderly world.

34Jesus had compassion on them and touched their eyes. Immediately they could see, and so they followed Him.

21 Jesus, the disciples, and the great crowds were heading toward Jerusalem when they came to Bethphage on the Mount of Olives. Jesus stopped and beckoned to two of the disciples.

Jesus: 2Go to the village over there. There you'll find a donkey tied *to a post* and a foal beside it. Untie them and bring them to Me. 3If anyone tries to stop you, then tell him, "The Master needs these," and he will send the donkey and foal immediately.

4*He sent the disciples on ahead so His entry into Jerusalem could* fulfill what the prophet Zechariah had *long since* foretold:

5Tell this to Zion's daughter,
  "Look—your King is approaching,
  seated humbly on a donkey,
  a young foal, a beast of burden."*

6So the disciples went off and followed Jesus' instructions. 7They brought the donkey and foal *to Jesus*, they spread their cloaks on the animals, and Jesus sat down on them. 8The great crowd followed suit, laying their cloaks on the road. Others cut leafy branches from the trees and scattered those *before Jesus.* 9And the crowds went before Jesus, *walked alongside Him,* and processed behind—all singing.

Crowd: Hosanna, praises to the Son of David! Blessed is He who comes in the name of the Eternal One! Hosanna in the highest!*

The way Jesus enters the city on a lowly donkey, with crowds surrounding Him singing praises, surprises many within Jerusalem.

10*And that is how Jesus came into Jerusalem. The people noticed this strange parade. They wondered who this could be, this humble bearded man on a donkey who incited such songs.*

Crowd: 11This is Jesus, the prophet, from Nazareth in Galilee.

12Jesus came to the temple. He drove out all those who were buying and selling. He upended the moneychangers' tables and the dove-sellers' benches.

Jesus: 13It is written, "My house will be a house of prayer *for all people,*" but you have turned this house of prayer into a den of robbers.*

14Then the blind and the lame came to the temple, and Jesus healed them. 15Rings of children circled round and sang, "Hosanna to the Son of David." But the priests and scribes didn't understand. When they saw *the upturned tables, the walking paralytics, and the singing children,* they were *shocked,* indignant, *and angry, and they did not understand.*

Priests and Scribes: 16Do you hear what these children are saying?

Jesus: Yes. Haven't you read *your own psalter?* "From the mouths *and souls* of infants

* 21:5 Zechariah 9:9   * 21:9 Psalm 118:26   * 21:13 Isaiah 56:7; Jeremiah 7:11

and toddlers, *the most innocent,* You have decreed praises for Yourself."*

¹⁷At that, Jesus left *Jerusalem.* He went to Bethany, where He spent the night. ¹⁸The next morning, Jesus went back to the city. *It was early and* He was wanting breakfast, so ¹⁹He stopped at a lone fig tree by the road. The fig tree, *disappointingly,* had no figs, only leaves.

Jesus: May you never bear fruit again!

Immediately the tree shriveled up. ²⁰The disciples were amazed.

Disciples: How did that fig tree wither so quickly?

Jesus: ²¹I tell you this: if you have faith and do not doubt, then you will be able to wither a fig tree with one glance. You will be able to tell mountains to throw themselves into the ocean, and they will obey.

As Jesus says this, one or two disciples probably glance around the shadows of the early morning, confused and afraid. Jesus has just paraded into Jerusalem and upset the vendors and leaders with His bold talk. Now He is challenging His disciples to expect the physical creation to respond to their commands and faith. But Jesus isn't finished.

Jesus: ²²If you believe, whatever you ask for in prayer will be granted.

²³Jesus returned to the temple and began to teach. The chief priests and elders came to Him and wanted to know who had given Him permission to disturb the temple precincts and to teach *His crazy notions in this most sacred of spots.*

Chief Priests and Elders: Who gave You the authority to do these things?

Jesus: ²⁴I will answer your question if first you answer one of Mine: ²⁵You saw John ritually cleansing people through baptism* *for the redemption of their sins.* Did John's

cleansing come from heaven, or was he simply washing people of his own whim?

The elders knew that this question was tricky; there was no simple answer. If they acknowledged that John's ritual cleansing was from heaven, Jesus would ask why they had not accepted John's authority. ²⁶But if they said he had dipped people simply by his own accord, they would outrage the people who believed John was a prophet.

Chief Priests and Elders: ²⁷We don't know.

Jesus: Then neither will I tell you about the authority under which I am working. ²⁸*But I will tell you a story, and* you can tell Me what you make of it: There was a man who had two sons. He said to his first son,

   Father: Go and work in the vineyard today.

   First Son: ²⁹No, I will not.

   But later the first son changed his mind and went. ³⁰Then the father went to his second son.

   Father: Go and work in the vineyard today.

   Second Son: Of course, Father.

   But then he did not go. ³¹So which of the sons did what the father wanted?

Chief Priests and Elders (*answering at once*): The first.

Jesus: I tell you this: the tax collectors and prostitutes will enter the kingdom of God ahead of you. ³²John came to show you *the straight path,* the path to righteousness. You did not believe him, but the tax collectors and the prostitutes did. Even as you saw *the prostitutes and the tax collectors forgiven and washed clean, finding their footing on the straight path to righteousness,* still you did not change your ways and believe.
   ³³Here is another story: A landowner planted a vineyard, put a wall around it, fitted it with a winepress, and built a watchtower. Then he rented the vineyard and left

* 21:16 Psalm 8:2   * 21:25 Literally, immersing, an act of repentance

town. ³⁴When harvesttime came, the land-owner sent his servants to collect rent—in the form of grapes—*from his tenants*. ³⁵The tenants attacked these rent-collecting servants. They killed one, stoned another, and beat a third. ³⁶The *dismayed* landowner sent another band of servants *to try to collect his due*, a larger group of servants this time, but the tenants did the same thing—*capturing, beating, killing*. ³⁷Finally the landowner sent his son to the tenants, thinking, "They will at least respect my son." ³⁸*But the tenants knew the son was the best way to get to the landowner*, so when they saw the son approaching they said,

> Tenants: This is the landowner's heir apparent! Let's kill him and take his inheritance.

³⁹And so they did; they threw him out of the vineyard and killed him.
⁴⁰What do you think the landowner will do when he comes and sees those tenants?

Chief Priests and Elders: ⁴¹He will eviscerate them, *to be sure*! Then he will rent the vineyard to other tenants who will pay him at harvesttime.

Jesus: ⁴²I wonder if any of you has ever opened your own psalter:

> The stone that the builders rejected
>   has become the very stone that holds
>   together the entire foundation.
> This is the work of the Eternal One,
>   and it is marvelous in our eyes.*

⁴³Therefore, the kingdom of God will be taken away from you and given to people who will tend its *sweet* fruit *and who will give the Creator His due*. [⁴⁴He who falls on the stone will be broken to pieces, and he on whom the stone falls will be crushed.]*

V

Jesus has just confronted the spiritual leaders of the land with hard reality. They have two choices: they can believe Him and repent, or they can disbelieve Him and call His stories rabble-rousing and craziness. In their minds, the cost of believing is just too high. Everything they have—their positions and standings in the community, their worldviews, their own images of themselves—is at stake. But they can't openly condemn this popular teacher of the people.

---

⁴⁵And so the chief priests and the Pharisees, *the teachers and the elders*, knew that when Jesus told these stories He was speaking about them. ⁴⁶*Not believing*, they looked for a way to arrest Him—*a stealthy way, though*. They were afraid *to make too bold a move against Him* because all the people believed He was a prophet.

22

Jesus went on speaking in parables.

Jesus: ²The kingdom of heaven is like a king whose son was getting married. The king organized a great feast, *a huge wedding banquet*. ³*He invited everyone he knew. The day of the wedding arrived, and* the king sent his servants into town to track down his guests—but *when the servants approached them with the king's message*, they refused to come. ⁴So the king sent out another batch of servants.

> King: Tell those people I've invited to come to the wedding banquet! *Tell them* I have prepared a great feast! Everything is ready! The oxen and fattened cattle have all been butchered, *the wine is decanted, and the table is laid out just so.*

⁵*And off the servants went, and they carried the king's message to the errant guests*—who still paid not a whit of attention. One guest headed into his field *to work; another* sat at his desk to attend to his accounts. ⁶The rest of the guests actually turned on the servants, brutalizing them and killing them. ⁷*When he learned of this*, the king was furious. He sent his army to kill the murderers and burn their towns. ⁸*But there was, of course, still a wedding to celebrate*.

> King (to his remaining servants): The wedding banquet is ready, but those I invited didn't rise to the occasion. ⁹So

* 21:42 Psalm 118:22-23   * 21:44 Some manuscripts omit verse 44.

go into the streets and invite anyone you see; invite everyone you meet.

[10]And the servants did just that—they went into the streets and invited everyone they met, *rich and poor*, good and bad, *high and low, sick and well*. Everyone who was invited came, and the wedding hall practically burst with guests.

[11]The king looked around the wedding party *with glee*, but he spotted one man who was not dressed *appropriately. In fact, he was dressed rather plainly*, in clothes not at all fitting for a fine nuptial feast.

King: [12]Kind sir, how did you get in here without a proper suit of wedding clothes?

The man was speechless. *He had been invited in off the street, after all!* [13]*Getting no response*, the king told his servants,

King: Tie him up, and throw him out into the outer darkness, where there is weeping and grinding of teeth.

[14]For many are invited, but few are chosen.

[15]At that, the Pharisees left. They determined to trap this Jesus with His own words—*hang Him by His own rope, you might say.* [16]They sent a batch of students to Him, along with a group that was loyal to Herod.

Students: Teacher, we know You are a man of integrity and You tell the truth about the way of God. We know You don't cotton to public opinion. [17]*And that is why we trust You and want You to* settle something for us: should we, *God's chosen people*, pay taxes to Caesar or not?

[18]Jesus knew these men were out to trap Him.

Jesus: You hypocrites! Why do you show up here with such a transparent trick? [19]Bring Me a coin you would use to pay tax.

Someone handed Him a denarius.* [20]*Jesus fingered the coin.*

Jesus: Of whom is this a portrait, and who owns this inscription?

Students: [21]Caesar.

Jesus: Well then, render to Caesar what is Caesar's and to God what is God's.

[22]And those *who had come hoping to trick Jesus* were confounded and amazed. And they left Him and went away.

[23]That same day, a band of Sadducees—*a sect of Jewish aristocrats who, among other things,* did not expect a resurrection *or anticipate any sort of future life at all*—put their own question to Jesus.

Sadducees: [24]Teacher, *the law of* Moses teaches that if a *married* man dies with no children, then his brother must marry the widow and father children in his brother's name. [25]Now we knew a family of seven brothers. The eldest brother married and died, and since he had no children, the next brother married his widow. [26]*And shortly thereafter,* that second brother *died* and the next until there were seven marriages *with the same woman.* [27]Eventually the wife died. [28]So now, *Teacher*, whose wife will she be at the resurrection? *Will she have seven husbands,* since they were each married to her?

According to Deuteronomy 25:5-6, a family member is supposed to marry a relative's widow to carry on the deceased's family name. Each man in this story dies, having fathered no children; that poor widow keeps marrying these brothers, and they keep dying. So in heaven, who is the husband?

Jesus: [29]You know neither God's Scriptures nor God's power—and so your assumptions are all wrong. [30]At the resurrection, people will neither marry nor be given in marriage. They will be like the messengers of heaven.

In heaven all will be devoting themselves to praise. It will not be a simple continuation of life on earth.

[31]A key to this resurrected life can be found *in the words of Moses*, which you do claim to read: [32]"I am the God of Abraham, the

* 22:19 A Roman coin, equivalent to a day's wage

God of Isaac, and the God of Jacob."*
Our God is not the God of the dead.
He is the God of the living.

³³And again the crowd was amazed. They
were astonished at His teaching.

³⁴Hearing that Jesus had silenced the
Sadducees, *a group of* Pharisees met *to consider new questions that might trip up Jesus.*
³⁵A legal expert thought of one that would
certainly stump Him.

Pharisees: ³⁶Teacher, of all the laws, which
commandment is the greatest?

Jesus (*quoting Scripture*): ³⁷"Love the Eternal One your God with all your heart and
all your soul and all your mind."* ³⁸This
is the first and greatest commandment.
³⁹And the second is nearly as important,
"Love your neighbor as yourself."* ⁴⁰The
rest of the law, and all the teachings of
the prophets, are but variations on these
themes.

⁴¹Since the Pharisees were gathered together
there, Jesus *took the opportunity to* pose a
question of His own.

Jesus: ⁴²What do you think about the
Anointed One? Whose Son is He?

Pharisees: *But, of course,* He is the Son of
David.

Jesus: ⁴³Then how is it that David—*whose
words were surely shaped* by the Spirit—
calls Him "Lord"? *For in his psalms* David
writes,

⁴⁴The Master said to my master
　"Sit here at My right hand,
　in the place of honor and power,
　And I will gather Your enemies together,
　lead them in on hands and knees,
　and You will rest Your feet on their
　　backs."*

⁴⁵How can David call his own Son "Lord"?

⁴⁶No one had an answer to Jesus' question.
And from that day forward, no one asked
Him anything.

23 Jesus spoke to His disciples and
to the crowds that had gathered
around.

Jesus with the Pharisees listening uses them as an example of
the pious but truly unrighteous. He
calls the people to mind the Pharisees' words, not their examples,
because they talk about righteousness and faithfulness, but they are
a faithless and unrighteous crew.

Jesus: ²The Pharisees and the scribes
occupy the seat of Moses. ³So you should
do the things they tell you to do—but don't
do the things they do. ⁴They heap heavy
burdens upon their neighbors' backs, and
they prove unwilling to do anything to help
shoulder the load. ⁵They are interested,
above all, in presentation: they wrap their
heads and arms in the accoutrements of
prayer, they cloak themselves with flowing
tasseled prayer garments, ⁶they covet the
seats of honor at fine banquets and in the
synagogue, ⁷and they love it when people
recognize them in the marketplace, call
them "Teacher," and beam at them.

⁸But you: do not let anyone call you
"Rabbi," *that is, "Teacher."* For you are all
brothers, and you have only one teacher,
the Anointed One. ⁹Indeed, do not call
anyone on earth "Father," for you have only
one father, and He is in heaven. ¹⁰Neither
let anyone call you "leader," for you have
one leader—the Anointed One. ¹¹If you are
recognized at all, let it be for your service.
Delight in the one who calls you servant.
¹²For whoever exalts himself will be humbled, and whoever humbles himself will be
exalted.

¹³Woe to you, you teachers of the law
and Pharisees. *There is such a gulf between
what you say and what you do.* You will
stand before a crowd and lock the door
of the kingdom of heaven *right in front of
everyone*; you won't enter the Kingdom
yourselves, and you prevent others from
doing so.

[¹⁴Woe to you, you teachers of the law
and Pharisees. What you say is not what
you do. You steal the homes from under
the widows while you pretend to pray for
them. You will suffer great condemnation
for this.]*

¹⁵Woe to you Pharisees, woe to you who

* 22:32 Exodus 3:6　* 22:37 Deuteronomy 6:5　* 22:39 Leviticus
19:18　* 22:44 Psalm 110:1　* 23:14 The earliest manuscripts omit
verse 14.

teach the law, hypocrites! You traverse hills and mountains and seas to make one convert, and then when he does convert, you make him much more a son of hell than you are.

[16]Woe to you who are blind but deign to lead others. You say, "Swearing by the temple means nothing, but he who swears by the gold in the temple is bound by his oath." [17]Are you fools? You must be blind! For which is greater: the gold or the temple that makes the gold sacred? [18]You also say, "Swearing by the altar means nothing, but he who swears by the sacrifice on the altar is bound by his oath." [19]You must be blind! Which is greater: the sacrifice or the altar that makes it sacred? [20]So anyone who swears by the altar swears by it and by the sacrifices and gifts laid upon it. [21]And anyone who swears by the temple swears by it and by the God who sanctifies it. [22]And when you swear by heaven, you are swearing by God's throne and by Him who sits upon it.

[23]So woe to you, teachers of the law and Pharisees. You hypocrites! You tithe from *your luxuries and your spices, giving away a tenth of* your mint, your dill, and your cumin. But you have ignored the essentials of the law: justice, mercy, faithfulness. It is practice of the latter that makes sense of the former. [24]You *hypocritical,* blind leaders. You spoon a fly from your soup and swallow a camel.

[25]Woe to you, teachers of the law and Pharisees, you hypocrites! You remove fine layers of film and dust from the outside of a cup or bowl, but you leave the inside full of *greed and* covetousness and self-indulgence. [26]You blind Pharisee—can't you see that if you clean the inside of the cup, the outside will be clean too?

[27]Woe to you, teachers of the law and Pharisees, you hypocrites! You are like a grave that has been whitewashed. You look beautiful on the outside, but on the inside you are full of moldering bones and decaying rot. [28]You appear, at first blush, to be righteous, *selfless, and pure*; but on the inside you are *polluted,* sunk in hypocrisy *and confusion* and lawlessness.

[29]Woe to you, teachers of the law and Pharisees, you hypocrites! You build monuments to your dead, *you mouth pieties over the bodies of prophets,* you decorate the graves of your righteous ancestors. [30]And you say, "If we had lived when our forefathers lived, *we would have known better*—we would not have joined them when they rose up against the prophets." [31]*Even when you are preening,* you make plain that you descended from those who murdered our prophets. [32]So why don't you finish what your forefathers started? [33]You are children of vipers, you *belly-dragging* snakes. You won't escape the judgment of hell.

[34]That is why I am sending you prophets and wise men, teachers *of breadth and depth and substance.* You will kill some of them and crucify others. You will flog others in your synagogues. You will pursue them from town to town. [35]And on your heads, *stained through your hands and drenching your clothes, my friends,* will be all the righteous blood ever shed on this earth, from the blood of innocent Abel to the blood of Zechariah son of Berechiah whom you murdered *in the house of the Lord* between the sanctuary and the altar. [36]I tell you: this generation will bear the blood of all that has gone before.

[37]O Jerusalem, Jerusalem. You kill the prophets *whom God gives you*; you stone those God sends you. I have longed to gather your children the way a hen gathers her chicks under her wings, but you refuse to be gathered. [38]Surely you can see that God has already removed His blessing from the house *of Israel.* [39]I tell you this: you will not see Me again until you say, *with the psalmist,* "Anyone who comes in the name of the Eternal One will be blessed."*

24 Jesus left the temple. As He was walking away, His disciples came up to Him and asked what He thought about the temple buildings.

Jesus: [2]Look around you. All of it will become rubble. I tell you this: not one stone will be left standing.

[3]*Later,* as Jesus was sitting on the Mount of Olives, the disciples came to Him privately.

Disciples: *We don't understand Your predictions.* Tell us, when will these things happen: *When will the temple be destroyed?* What will be the sign that You are returning? How will we know that the end of the age is upon us?

* 23:39 Psalm 118:26

In this, the last of the five major sermons, Jesus focuses on prophetic and apocalyptic themes of judgment and the end times. The disciples have been listening to the prophetic judgment Jesus has issued on the religious leaders. They have images of collapsing temple buildings, of prophets pursued from town to town, of floggings, and of blood-soaked garments. They can imagine themselves blood-soaked. When will this all happen, and what does it mean?

Jesus: [4]Take care that you are not deceived. [5]For many will come in My name claiming they are the Anointed One, and many poor souls will be taken in. [6]You will hear of wars, and you will hear rumors of wars, but you should not panic. It is inevitable, *this violent breaking apart of the sinful world, but remember,* the wars are not the end. *The end is still unfolding.* [7]Nations will do battle with nations, and kingdoms will fight neighboring kingdoms, and there will be famines and earthquakes. [8]*But these are not the end.* These are the birth pangs, the beginning. *The end is still unfolding.*

[9]They will hand you over to your enemies, who will torture you and then kill you, and you will be hated by all nations because of Me. [10]And many *who have followed Me and claimed to love Me and sought God's kingdom* will turn away—*they will abandon the faith and* betray and hate one another. [11-12]The love that they had for one another will grow cold because few will obey the law. False prophets will appear, many will be taken in by them, and the only thing that will grow is wickedness. *There will be no end to the increase of wickedness.* [13]But those who do not waver from our path and do not follow those false prophets—those *among you* will be saved. [14]And this good news of God's kingdom will be preached throughout the whole world, a testimony to *all people and* all nations. Then, *beloved,* the end, *the consummation of all things,* will come.

[15]You will remember that the prophet Daniel predicted this—predicted the abomination that causes desolation*—when you see the prophesied desolation of the holy place. (Reader, take notice; it is important that you understand this.) [16]*When you see this,* let those in Judea flee to the mountains. [17]If you are *relaxing* on your rooftop *one evening and the signs of the temple's destructions come,* don't return to your house *to rescue a book or a pet or a scrap of clothing.* [18]If you are in the field *when the great destruction begins,* don't return home for a cloak. [19]Pregnant women and nursing mothers will have the worst of it. [20]*And as for you,* pray that your flight *to the hills* will not come on the Sabbath or in the cold of winter. [21]For the tribulation will be unparalleled—hardships of a magnitude that has not been seen since creation and that will not be seen again. [22]*Indeed the Lord God your merciful judge* will cut this time of trial short, and this will be done for the benefit of the elect *that some might indeed be saved*—for no one could survive *the depravity* for very long.

[23]*I cannot say this clearly enough: during this time,* someone will say to you, "Look, here is the Anointed One!" or *"Aren't you relieved? Haven't you seen the Savior down there, around the bend, over the hill and dale?"* Do not believe them. [24]False liberators and false prophets will appear, and *they will know a few tricks*—they will perform great miracles, *and they will make great promises.* If it were possible, they would even deceive God's elect. [25]But I am warning you ahead of time: *remember—do not fall for their lies or lines or promises.* [26]If someone says, "He's out there in the desert"—do not go. And if someone says, "He's here at our house, *at our table*"—do not believe him. [27]When the Son of Man comes, *He will be as visible* as lightning in the East is visible even in the West. [28]And where the carcass is, there will always be vultures.

[29]*And as the prophets have foretold it:* after the distress of those days,

The sun will grow dark,
   and the moon will be hidden.
The stars will fall from the sky,
   and all the powers in the heavens will
     be dislodged and shaken *from their places.**

[30]That is when the sign of the Son of Man will appear in the sky. All the nations of

* 24:15 Daniel 9:27; 11:31; 12:11   * 24:29 Isaiah 13:10; 34:4

the earth will mourn. They will see the Son of Man coming; they will see Him powerful and glorious, *riding on chariots* of clouds in the sky. [31]With a loud trumpet call, He will send out *battalions of* heavenly messengers; and they will gather His *beloved faithful* elect from the four corners of creation, from one end of heaven to the other.

[32]Now think of the fig tree. As soon as its twigs get tender *and greenish,* as soon as it begins to sprout leaves, you know to expect summer. [33]In the same way, when you see *the wars and the suffering and the false liberators and the desolations,* you will know the Son of Man is near—right at the door. [34]I tell you this: this generation will see all these things take place before it passes away. [35]*My words are always true and always here with you.* Heaven and earth will pass away, but My words will never pass away.

[36]No one knows the hour or the day, not even the messengers in heaven, not even the Son. Only the Father knows. [37]As it was at the time of Noah, so it will be with the coming of the Son of Man. [38]In the days before the flood, people *were busy making lives for themselves: they* were eating and drinking, marrying and giving in marriage, *making plans and having children and growing old,* until the day Noah entered the ark. [39]Those people *had no idea what was coming; they* knew nothing *about the floods* until the floods were upon them, sweeping them all away. That is how it will be with the coming of the Son of Man. [40]Two men will be plowing a field: one will be taken, and the other will be left *in the field.* [41]Two women will be *somewhere* grinding at a mill: one will be taken, and the other will be left *at the mill.*

[42]So keep watch. You don't know when your Lord will come. [43]But you should know this: If the owner of a house had known his house was about to be broken into, *he would have stayed up all night, vigilantly.* He would have kept watch, and he would have thwarted the thief. [44]So you must be ready because you know the Son of Man will come, but you can't know precisely when.

[45]The trustworthy servant is the one whom the master puts in charge of *all the servants of* his household; it is the trustworthy servant who *not only oversees all the work, but also* ensures the servants are properly fed and cared for. [46]*And it is, of course, crucial that a servant who is given such responsibility performs his responsibility to his master's standards*—so when the master returns he finds his trust has been rewarded. [47]For then the master will put that good servant in charge of all his possessions. [48]But imagine *that the master's trust was misplaced,* that the supposedly responsible servant is actually a thief who says to himself, "My master has been gone so long, *he is not possibly coming back."* [49]Then he beats his fellow servants and dines and drinks with drunkards. [50]*Well, when the master returns—as certainly he will—the servant will be caught unawares.* The master will return on a day and at an hour when he isn't expected. [51]And he will cut his worthless servant into pieces and throw him out *into darkness* with the hypocrites, where there is weeping and grinding of teeth.

25 **Jesus:** *Or picture* the kingdom of heaven *this way. It* will be like ten bridesmaids who each picked up a lantern and went out to meet a certain bridegroom. [2-4]Five of these women were sensible, *good with details,* and remembered to bring small flasks of oil for their lanterns. But five of them were flighty, *too caught up in the excitement of their jaunt,* and forgot to bring oil with them. [5]The bridegroom did not turn up right away. Indeed, all the women, *while waiting,* found themselves falling asleep. [6]And then in the middle of the night, they heard someone call, "The bridegroom is here, finally! Wake up and greet him!" [7]The women got up and trimmed the wicks of their lanterns *and prepared to go greet the groom.* [8]The five women who had no oil turned to their friends for help.

Ill-prepared Bridesmaids: Please give us some of your oil! Our lanterns are flickering and will go out soon.

[9]But the five women who'd come prepared with oil said they didn't have enough.

Prepared Bridesmaids: If we give you some of our oil, we'll all run out too soon! You'd better go wake up a dealer and buy your own supply.

[10]So the five *ill-prepared* women went in search of oil to buy, and while they were

gone, the groom arrived. The five who stood ready *with their lanterns* accompanied him to the wedding party, and *after they arrived,* the door was shut.

[11]Finally the rest of the women turned up *at the party.* They knocked on the door.

Ill-prepared Bridesmaids: Master, open up and let us in!

Bridegroom *(refusing):* [12]I certainly don't know you.

[13]So stay awake; you neither know the day nor hour [when the Son of Man will come].*

V

Jesus provides a picture of the coming reality of the kingdom of heaven. As they approach the time of His sacrifice, Jesus makes sure the disciples know that soon it will be too late; the door of opportunity will close, and for many the door will remain shut. He gives them another image of the same reality to bring the picture into focus. Once they were bridesmaids waiting for their bridegroom; now they are slaves waiting for their Master. This time they are given responsibilities that will be rewarded. The blessings of the Kingdom bring risks along with the benefits.

Jesus: [14]*This is how it will be.* It will be like a landowner who is going on a trip. He instructed his slaves about caring for his property. [15]He gave five talents to one slave, two to the next, and then one talent to the last slave—each according to his ability. Then the man left.

[16]Promptly the man who had been given five talents went out and bartered and sold and turned his five talents into ten. [17]And the one who had received two talents *went to the market and* turned his two into four. [18]And the slave who had received just one talent? He dug a hole in the ground and buried his master's money there.

[19]Eventually the master came back from his travels, *found his slaves,* and settled up with them. [20]The slave who had been given

five talents came forward and told his master how he'd turned five into ten; *then he handed the whole lot over to his master.*

Master: [21]Excellent. *You've proved yourself not only clever but loyal.* You've executed a rather small task masterfully, so now I am going to put you in charge of something larger. *But before you go back to work,* come join my great feast and celebration.

[22]Then the slave who had been given two talents came forward and told his master how he'd turned two into four, *and he handed all four talents to his master.*

Master: [23]Excellent. *You've proved yourself not only clever but loyal.* You've executed a rather small task masterfully, so now I am going to put you in charge of something larger. *But before you go back to work,* come join my great feast and celebration.

[24]Finally the man who had been given one talent came forward.

Servant: Master, I know you are a hard man, *difficult in every way. You can make a healthy sum when others would fail.* You profit when other people are doing the work. You grow rich on the backs of others. [25]So I was afraid, *dug a hole,* and hid the talent in the ground. Here it is. You can have it.

[26]*The master was furious.*

Master: You are a pathetic excuse for a servant! *You have disproved my trust in you and squandered my generosity.* You know I always make a profit! [27]You could have at least put this talent in the bank; then I could have earned a little interest on it! [28]Take that one talent away, and give it to the servant who doubled my money from five to ten.

[29]You see, everything was taken away from the man who had nothing, but the man who had something got even more. [30]And as for the slave who made no profit *but buried his talent in the ground*? His master ordered his slaves to tie him up and

* 25:13 The earliest manuscripts omit this portion.

throw him outside into the utter darkness where there is miserable mourning and great fear. ³¹When the Son of Man comes in all His majesty accompanied by throngs of heavenly messengers, His throne will be wondrous. ³²All the nations will assemble before Him, and He will judge them, distinguishing them from one another as a shepherd isolates the sheep from the goats. ³³He will put some, the sheep, at His right hand and some, the goats, at His left. ³⁴Then the King will say to those to His right,

King: Come here, *you beloved*, you people whom My Father has blessed. Claim your inheritance, the Kingdom prepared for you from the beginning of creation. ³⁵*You shall be richly rewarded*, for when I was hungry, you fed Me. And when I was thirsty, you gave Me something to drink. I was alone as a stranger, and you welcomed Me *into your homes and into your lives.* ³⁶I was naked, and you gave Me clothes to wear; I was sick, and you tended to My needs; I was in prison, and you comforted Me.

³⁷Even then the righteous *will not have achieved perfect understanding and will not recall these things.*

Righteous: Master, when did we find You hungry and give You food? When did we find You thirsty and slake Your thirst? ³⁸When did we find You a stranger and welcome You in, or find You naked and clothe You? ³⁹When did we find You sick *and nurse You to health*? When did we visit You when You were in prison?

King: ⁴⁰I tell you this: whenever you saw a brother *or sister hungry or cold*, whatever you did to the least of these, so you did to Me.

⁴¹At that He will turn to those on His left hand.

King: Get away from Me, *you despised* people whom My Father has cursed. *Claim your inheritance*—the pits of flaming hell where the devil and his minions suffer. ⁴²For I was starving, and you left Me with no food. When I was *dry and* thirsty, you left Me *to struggle with* nothing to drink. ⁴³When I was *alone as*

a stranger, you turned away from Me. When I was *pitifully* naked, you left Me unclothed. When I was sick, *you gave Me no care.* When I was in prison, you did not comfort Me.

Unrighteous: ⁴⁴Master, when did we see You hungry and thirsty? When did we see You friendless *or homeless or excluded*? When did we see You without clothes? When did we see You sick or in jail? *When did we see You in distress* and fail to respond?

King: ⁴⁵I tell you this: *whenever you saw a brother hungry or cold, when you saw a sister weak and without friends,* when you saw the least of these and ignored their suffering, so you ignored Me.

⁴⁶So these, *the goats*, will go off to everlasting punishment. But the beloved, *the sheep* (the righteous), will go into everlasting life.

26 And so this is what happened, *finally.* Jesus finished all His teaching, and He said to His disciples,

Jesus: ²The feast of Passover begins in two days. That is when the Son of Man is handed over to be crucified.

³*And almost as He spoke*, the chief priests were getting together with the elders at the home of the high priest, Caiaphas. ⁴They schemed *and mused* about how they could *trick Jesus*, sneak around and capture Him, and then kill Him.

Chief Priests: ⁵We shouldn't try to catch Him at the great public festival. The people would riot *if they knew what we were doing.*

⁶Meanwhile Jesus was at Bethany staying at the home of Simon the leper. ⁷*While He was at Simon's house*, a woman came to see Him. She had an alabaster flask of very valuable ointment with her, and as Jesus reclined at the table, she poured the ointment on His head. ⁸The disciples, seeing this scene, were furious.

Disciples: This is an absolute waste! ⁹The woman could have sold that ointment for lots of money, and then she could have given it to the poor.

[10]Jesus knew what the disciples were saying among themselves, *so He took them to task.*

Jesus: Why don't you leave this woman alone? She has done a good thing. [11]*It is good that you are concerned about the poor,* but the poor will always be with you—I will not be. [12]In pouring this ointment on My body, she has prepared Me for My burial. [13]I tell you this: the good news *of the kingdom of God* will be spread all over the world, *and wherever the good news travels,* people will tell the story of this woman and her good discipleship. And people will remember her.

[14]At that, one of the twelve, Judas Iscariot, went to the chief priests.

Judas Iscariot: [15]What will you give me to turn Him over to you?

They offered him 30 pieces of silver. [16]And from that moment, he began to watch for a chance to betray Jesus.

Here begins the account of Jesus' last night before His trial and crucifixion.

[17]On the first day of the Festival of Unleavened Bread, the disciples said to Jesus,

Disciples: Where would You like us to prepare the Passover meal for You?

Jesus: [18]Go into the city, find a certain man, and say to him, "The Teacher says, 'My time is near, and I am going to celebrate Passover at your house with My disciples.'"

They find the man's house and secure the owner's permission, and there they will praise God for redeeming His people from bondage in Egypt.

[19]So the disciples *went off,* followed Jesus' instructions, and got the Passover meal ready. [20]When evening came, Jesus sat down with the twelve. [21]And they ate their dinner.

Jesus: I tell you this: one of you here will betray Me.

[22]The disciples, *of course,* were horrified.

A Disciple: Not me!

Another Disciple: *It's not me, Master, is it?*

Jesus: [23]It's the one who shared this dish of food with Me. That is the one who will betray Me. [24]Just as our sacred Scripture has taught, the Son of Man is on His way. But there will be nothing but misery for he who hands Him over. That man will wish he had never been born.

[25]At that, Judas, who was indeed planning to betray Him, said,

Judas Iscariot: It's not me, Master, is it?

Jesus: I believe you've just answered your own question.

[26]As they were eating, Jesus took some bread. He offered a blessing *over the bread,* and then He broke it and gave it to His disciples.

Jesus: Take this and eat; it is My body.

[27]And then He took the cup *of wine,* He made a blessing over it, and He passed it around the table.

Jesus: Take this and drink, all of you: [28]this is My blood of the new covenant, which is poured out for many for the forgiveness of sins. [29]But I tell you: I will not drink of the fruit of the vine again until I am with you once more, drinking in the kingdom of My Father.

[30]*The meal concluded.* Together, all the men sang a hymn *of praise and thanksgiving,* and then they took a late evening walk to the Mount of Olives.

Jesus: [31]Scripture says,

> I shall strike the shepherd,
>   and the sheep of the flock will
>   scatter.*

Just so, each of you will stumble tonight, *stumble and fall,* on account of Me. [32]Afterward I will be raised up. And I will go before you to Galilee.

Peter: [33]*Lord,* maybe everyone else will *trip and* fall tonight, but I will not. *I'll be beside You. I won't falter.*

* 26:31 Zechariah 13:7

Jesus: [34]*If only that were true.* In fact, this very night, before the cock crows *in the morning*, you will deny Me three times.

Peter: [35]*No!* I won't deny You. Even if that means I have to die with You!

And each of the disciples echoed Peter.

It is indeed a dark, bitter night. The disciples are sad and confused, and maybe a little bit prideful. Peter can not believe that he could ever betray his Lord.

[36]At that, Jesus led His disciples to the place called Gethsemane.

Jesus: I am going over there to pray. You sit here *while I'm at prayer*.

[37]Then He took Peter and the two sons of Zebedee with Him, and He grew sorrowful and deeply distressed.

Jesus: [38]My soul is overwhelmed with grief, to the point of death. Stay here and keep watch with Me.

[39]He walked a little farther and finally fell prostrate and prayed.

Jesus: Father, *this is the last thing I want.* If there is any way, please take this *bitter cup* from Me. Not My will, but Yours be done.

[40]When He came back to the disciples, He saw that they were asleep. *Peter awoke a little less confident and slightly chagrined.*

Jesus (to Peter): So you couldn't keep watch with Me for just one short hour? [41]*Now maybe you're learning*: the spirit is willing, but the body is weak. Watch and pray and take care that you are not pulled down during a time of testing.

[42]With that, Jesus returned *to His secluded spot* to pray again.

Jesus: Father, if there is no other way for this cup to pass without My drinking it— *then not My will*, but Yours be done.

[43]Again Jesus returned to His disciples and found them asleep. Their eyes were heavy-lidded. [44]So Jesus left them again and returned to prayer, praying the same sentiments with the same words. [45]Again He returned to His disciples.

Jesus: Well, you are still sleeping; are you getting a good long rest? Now the time has come; the Son of Man is just about to be given over to *the betrayers and* the sinners. [46]Get up; we have to be going. Look, here comes the one who's going to betray Me.

[47]There he was, Judas, one of the twelve leading a crowd of people from the chief priests and elders with swords and clubs; the chief priests and the elders were right there, *ready to arrest* Jesus. [48]*And Judas,* the one who intended to betray Him, had said *to the elders and the chief priests* that he would give them a sign.

Judas Iscariot: *I'll greet Him with a kiss.* And you will know that the one I kiss is the one you should arrest.

[49]So at once, he went up to Jesus.

Judas Iscariot: Greetings, Teacher (he kisses Him).

Jesus: [50]My friend, do what you have come to do.

And at that, the company came and seized Him. [51]One of the men with Jesus grabbed his sword and swung toward the high priest's slave, slicing off his ear.

Jesus: [52]Put your sword back. People who live by the sword die by the sword. [53]Surely you realize that if I called on My Father, He would send 12 legions of messengers to rescue Me. [54]But if I were to do that, I would be thwarting the scriptural story, wouldn't I? And we must allow the story *of God's kingdom* to unfold. [55](to the crowds) Why did you bring these weapons, these clubs and bats? Did you think I would fight you? That I would try to dodge and escape like a common criminal? You could have arrested Me any day when I was teaching in the temple, but you didn't.

[56]This scene has come together just so, so that the prophecies in the sacred Scripture could be fulfilled.

And at that, all the disciples ran away and abandoned Him. [57]The crowd that had arrested Jesus took Him to Caiaphas, the high priest. The scribes and elders had gathered *at Caiaphas's house and were waiting for Jesus to be delivered.* [58]Peter followed Jesus (though at some distance *so as not to be seen*). He slipped into Caiaphas's house and attached himself to a group of servants. And he sat watching, waiting to see how things would unfold.

[59]The high priest and his council of advisors first produced *false evidence against Jesus*—false evidence meant to justify some charge and Jesus' execution. [60]But even though many men were willing to lie, the council couldn't come up with the evidence it wanted. Finally, two men stood up.

Two Men: [61]Look, He said, "I can destroy God's temple and rebuild it in three days." *What more evidence do you need?*

[62]Then Caiaphas the high priest stood up and addressed Jesus.

Caiaphas: Aren't You going to respond to these charges? What exactly are these two men accusing You of?

[63]Jesus remained silent.

Caiaphas *(to Jesus)*: Under a sacred oath before the living God, tell us plainly: are You the Anointed One, the Son of God?

Jesus: [64]So you *seem to be* saying. I will say this: beginning now, you will see the Son of Man sitting at the right hand of God's power and glory and coming on heavenly clouds.

[65]The high priest tore his robes *and screeched.*

Caiaphas: Blasphemy! We don't need any more witnesses—we've all just witnessed this most grievous blasphemy, *right here and now.* [66]So, gentlemen, what's your verdict?

Gentlemen: He deserves to die.

[67]Then they spat in His face and hit Him. Some of them smacked Him, slapped Him across the cheeks, [68]and jeered.

Some of the Men: Well, Anointed One, prophesy for us, *if You can*—who hit You? *And who is about to hit You next?*

[69]*As all this was going on in Caiaphas's chamber,* Peter was sitting in the courtyard with some servants. One of the servant girls came up to him.

Servant Girl: You were with Jesus the Galilean, *weren't you?*

[70]*And just as Jesus had predicted,* Peter denied it before everyone.

Peter: Not me! I don't know what you're talking about.

[71]He went out to stand by the gate. And as he walked past, another servant girl recognized him.

Another Servant Girl *(speaking to those standing around)*: That man over there—he was here with Jesus the Nazarene!

[72]Again, *just as Jesus had predicted,* Peter denied it, swearing an oath.

Peter: I don't know Him!

[73]Peter then went to chat with a few of the servants. A little while later, some other servants approached him:

Other Servants: Look, we know that you must be one of Jesus' followers. You speak like you are from the same area as His followers. You've got that tell-tale Galilean accent.

[74]Cursing and swearing, *Peter denied Him again.*

Peter: I do not know Him!

As the exclamation point left his mouth, a cock crowed. [75]And Peter remembered. He remembered that Jesus had *looked at him with something like pity and* said, "This very night, before the cock crows in the morning, you will deny Me three times." And Peter went outside, *sat down on the ground,* and wept.

27 Eventually the chief priests and the elders looked around and saw that it was morning. They convened a council meeting whose sole purpose was to hand down Jesus' death sentence. [2]They tied Jesus up, took Him away, and

handed Him over to the governor *of Judea*, a man called Pilate.

³Judas—the one who had betrayed Him *with a kiss for 30 pieces of silver*—saw that Jesus had been condemned, and suddenly Judas regretted what he had done. He took the silver back to the chief priests and elders *and tried to return it to them*.

Judas Iscariot: ⁴*I can't keep this money!* I've sinned! I've betrayed an innocent man! *His blood will be on my hands.*

The priests and elders want nothing to do with Judas, and they refuse to take his money.

Chief Priests and Elders: *We're through with you, friend.* The state of your soul is really none of our affair.

⁵Judas threw down the money in the temple, went off, and hanged himself. ⁶The chief priests looked at the silver coins and picked them up.

Chief Priests and Elders: You know, according to the law, we can't put blood money in the temple treasury.

⁷After some deliberation, they took the money and bought a plot of land called Potter's Field; they would use it to bury foreigners, *suicides, and others who were unfit for a full Jewish burial.* ⁸(To this day, the field is called Blood Field, *because it was bought with blood money.*) ⁹*And when the priests bought Potter's Field,* they *unwittingly* fulfilled a prophecy made long ago by the prophet Jeremiah: "They took 30 pieces of silver, the price set on the head of the man by the children of Israel, ¹⁰and they gave them for the Potter's Field as the Eternal One instructed."*

¹¹Jesus was standing before the governor, *Pilate*.

Pilate: Are You the King of the Jews?

Jesus: So you say.

¹²The chief priests and the elders *stood and poured out their accusations: that Jesus was a traitor, a seditious rebel, a crazy, a would-be Savior, and a would-be king.* Jesus stood in the stream of accusations, but He did not respond.

Pilate: ¹³Do You hear these accusations they are making against You?

¹⁴Still Jesus said nothing, which Pilate found rather astounding—*no protests, no defense, nothing.*

¹⁵Now the governor had a custom. During the *great Jewish* festival *of* Passover, he would allow the crowd to pick one of the condemned men, and he, *Pilate*, would set the man free. *Just like that. Gratuitous, gracious freedom.* ¹⁶At this time, they had a notorious prisoner named Barabbas. ¹⁷So when the crowd gathered, Pilate offered them a choice:

Pilate: Whom do you want me to free? Barabbas or Jesus, whom some call the Anointed One?

V

Pilate could call Him "Jesus of Nazareth" or "Jesus the Carpenter," but he says, "whom some call the Anointed One." It is significant that Pilate is in a position where he passes judgment. He determines who will live and who will die, and he is preparing to hold court.

---

¹⁸Pilate knew the chief priests and elders hated Jesus and had delivered Him up because they envied Him.

¹⁹Then Pilate sat down on his judgment seat, and he received a message from his wife: "Distance yourself utterly from *the proceedings against* this righteous man. I have had a dream about Him, a dream full of twisted sufferings—*He is innocent, I know it, and we should have nothing to do with Him.*"

²⁰But the chief priests and the elders convinced the crowd to demand that Barabbas, not Jesus, *whom-some-call-the-Anointed-One*, be freed and that Jesus be put to death.

Pilate (*standing before the crowd*): ²¹Which of these men would you have me free?

Crowd (*shouting*): Barabbas!

* 27:10 Zechariah 11:12-13; Jeremiah 32:6-9

Pilate: ²²What would you have me do with this Jesus, whom some call the Anointed One?

Crowd (shouting): Crucify Him!

Pilate: ²³Why? What crime has this man committed?

Crowd (responding with a shout): Crucify Him!

It is clear Pilate has laid his own trap. He realizes he has given the crowd a choice, but the crowd doesn't choose as he expects them to.

²⁴Pilate saw that unless he wanted a riot on his hands, he now had to bow to their wishes. So he took a pitcher of water, stood before the crowd, and washed his hands.

Pilate: You will see to this crucifixion, for this man's blood will be upon you and not upon me. I wash myself of it.

Crowd: ²⁵Indeed, let His blood be upon us—upon us and our children!

²⁶So Pilate released Barabbas, and he had Jesus flogged and handed over to be crucified.

²⁷The governor's soldiers took Jesus into a great hall, gathered a great crowd, ²⁸and stripped Jesus of His clothes, draping Him in a bold scarlet cloak, the kind that soldiers sometimes wore. ²⁹They gathered some thorny vines, wove them into a crown, and perched that crown upon His head. They stuck a reed in His right hand, and then they knelt before Him, this inside-out, upside-down King. They mocked Him with catcalls.

Soldiers: Hail, the King of the Jews!

³⁰They spat on Him and whipped Him on the head with His scepter of reeds, ³¹and when they had their fill, they pulled off the bold scarlet cloak, dressed Him in His own simple clothes, and led Him off to be crucified.

³²As they were walking, they found a man called Simon of Cyrene and forced him to carry the cross. ³³Eventually they came to a place called Golgotha, which means "Place of the Skull." ³⁴There they gave Him a drink—wine mixed with bitter herbs. He tasted it but refused to drink it.

³⁵And so they had Him crucified. They divided the clothes off His back by drawing lots,* ³⁶and they sat on the ground and watched Him hang. ³⁷They placed a sign over His head: "This is Jesus, King of the Jews." ³⁸And then they crucified two thieves next to Him, one at His right hand and one at His left hand.

³⁹Passersby shouted curses and blasphemies at Jesus. They wagged their heads at Him and hissed.

Passersby: ⁴⁰You're going to destroy the temple and then rebuild it in three days? Why don't You start with saving Yourself? Come down from the cross if You can, if You're God's Son.

Chief Priests, Scribes, and Elders (mocking Him): ⁴¹⁻⁴²He saved others, but He can't save Himself. If He's really the King of Israel, then let Him climb down from the cross—then we'll believe Him. ⁴³He claimed communion with God—well, let God save Him, if He's God's beloved Son.

⁴⁴Even the thieves hanging to His right and left poured insults upon Him. ⁴⁵And then, starting at noon, the entire land became dark. It was dark for three hours. ⁴⁶In the middle of the dark afternoon, Jesus cried out in a loud voice.

Jesus: Eli, Eli, lama sabachthani—My God, My God, why have You forsaken Me?*

Bystanders: ⁴⁷He's calling on Elijah.

⁴⁸One bystander grabbed a sponge, steeped it in vinegar, stuck it on a reed, and gave Jesus the vinegar to drink.

Others: ⁴⁹We'll see—we'll see if Elijah is going to come and rescue Him.

⁵⁰And then Jesus cried out once more, loudly, and then He breathed His last breath. ⁵¹At that instant, the temple curtain was torn in half, from top to bottom. The earth shook; rocks split in two; ⁵²tombs burst open, and bodies of many sleeping holy women and men were raised up. ⁵³After Jesus' resurrection, they came out of their tombs, went

* 27:35 Psalm 22:18   * 27:46 Psalm 22:1

into the holy city of Jerusalem, and showed themselves to people.

⁵⁴When the Centurion and soldiers who had been charged with guarding Jesus felt the earthquake *and saw the rocks splitting and the tombs opening*, they were, of course, terrified.

Soldiers: He really was God's Son.

⁵⁵A number of women, who had been devoted to Jesus and followed Him from Galilee, were present, too, watching from a distance. ⁵⁶Mary Magdalene was there, and Mary the mother of James and Joseph, and the mother of the sons of Zebedee.

⁵⁷At evening time, a rich man from Arimathea arrived. His name was Joseph, and he had become a disciple of Jesus. ⁵⁸He went to Pilate and asked to be given Jesus' body; Pilate assented and ordered his servants to turn Jesus' body over to Joseph. ⁵⁹So Joseph took the body, wrapped Jesus in a clean sheath of white linen, ⁶⁰and laid Jesus in his own new tomb, which he had carved from a rock. Then he rolled a great stone in front of the tomb's opening, and he went away. ⁶¹Mary Magdalene was there, and so was the other Mary. They sat across from the tomb, *watching, remembering.*

⁶²The next day, which is the day after the Preparation Day, the chief priests and the Pharisees went together to Pilate. ⁶³They reminded him that when Jesus was alive He had claimed that He would be raised from the dead after three days.

Chief Priests and Pharisees: ⁶⁴So please order someone to secure the tomb for at least three days. Otherwise His disciples might sneak in and steal His body away, and then claim that He has been raised from the dead. If that happens, then we would have been better off just leaving Him alive.

Pilate: ⁶⁵You have a guard. Go and secure the grave.

⁶⁶So they went to the tomb, sealed the stone in its mouth, and left the guard to keep watch.

28 After the Sabbath, as the light of the next day, the first day of the week, crept over Palestine, Mary Magdalene and the other Mary came to the tomb *to keep vigil.* ²Earlier there had been an earthquake. A messenger of the Lord had come down from heaven and had gone to the grave. He rolled away the stone and sat down on top of it. ³He *veritably* glowed. He was vibrating with light. *His clothes were light,* white *like transfiguration,* like fresh snow. ⁴The soldiers guarding the tomb were terrified. They froze like stone.

⁵The messenger spoke to the women, *to Mary Magdalene and the other Mary.*

Messenger of the Lord: Don't be afraid. I know you are here keeping watch for Jesus who was crucified. ⁶But Jesus is not here. He was raised, just as He said He would be. Come over to the grave, and see for yourself. ⁷And then go straight to His disciples, and tell them He's been raised from the dead and has gone on to Galilee. You'll find Him there. Listen carefully to what I am telling you.

⁸The women were both terrified and thrilled, and they quickly left the tomb and went to find the disciples and give them this *outstandingly good* news. ⁹But while they were on their way, they saw Jesus Himself.

Jesus *(greeting the women):* Rejoice.

The women fell down before Him, kissing His feet and worshiping Him.

Jesus: ¹⁰Don't be afraid. Go and tell My brothers to go to Galilee. Tell them I will meet them there.

¹¹As the women were making their way to the disciples, some of the soldiers who had been standing guard *by Jesus' tomb recovered themselves,* went to the city, and told the chief priests everything that had happened—*the earthquake just after dawn, the heavenly messenger, and his commission to the Marys.* ¹²The chief priests gathered together all the elders, *an emergency conference of sorts. They needed a plan. They decided the simplest course was bribery:* they would pay off the guards ¹³and order them to say that the disciples had come in the middle of the night and had stolen Jesus' corpse while they slept. ¹⁴The chief priests promised the soldiers they would run interference with the governor so that the soldiers wouldn't be punished *for falling asleep when they were supposed to be*

keeping watch. [15]The guards took the bribe and spread the story around town—and indeed, you can still find people today who will tell you *that Jesus did not really rise from the dead, that it was a trick, some sort of sleight of hand.*

[16]The eleven disciples, *having spoken to the Marys,* headed to Galilee, to the mountain where they were to meet Jesus. [17]When the disciples saw Jesus there, many of them fell down and worshiped, *as Mary and the other Mary had done.* But a few hung back. They were not sure *(and who can blame them?).* [18]Jesus came forward and addressed *His beloved disciples.*

The disciples don't know what to think or how to act. Nothing like this has ever happened before.

Jesus: I am here speaking with all the authority of God, *who has commanded Me to give you this commission:* [19]Go out and make disciples in all the nations. Ceremonially wash them through baptism in the name of the *triune God:* Father, Son, and Holy Spirit. [20]Then disciple them. *Form them in the practices and postures that* I have taught you, and show them how to follow the commands I have laid down for you. And I will be with you, day after day, to the end of the age.

MARK

Record of the servant of God

By Mark, a follower of Jesus

This Gospel is probably the first written account of the life of Jesus. It focuses on Jesus as the Servant of God who works miracles, makes disciples, and suffers on the way to bring salvation to the world. Tradition has it that Mark accompanied Paul on some of his missionary journeys and later became Peter's associate in his ministry, hearing and writing down his eyewitness accounts. Apparently Mark was a Jewish Christian who grew up in Jerusalem with his mother, Mary. His intended audience was likely Roman Christians who were not Jews; so his Gospel explains Jewish words, phrases, and customs. That may also be why it does not often appeal to the Hebrew Scriptures to explain Jesus' words and deeds.

For Mark, the life of Jesus—from His ritual cleansing by John in the Jordan River to His resurrection in Jerusalem—is the beginning of the good news. It is "the mustard seed stage" of the kingdom of God. Ultimately God's kingdom is destined to fill the world and become a place where the nations come to find shelter and salvation. So Mark invites his readers to understand that, in following Jesus, their lives make up the next part of the story. As the people of the Kingdom, they are the next step in preparing the way for God's salvation. So when Jesus invites His disciples to "follow Me," Mark takes that as an invitation to imitate His life and follow His teachings.

Mark's Gospel is the shortest of the New Testament Gospels. It is especially fast-paced and action-oriented. It moves quickly from episode to episode as Jesus demonstrates that He has authority over nature, disease, death, and evil. For Mark, Jesus' miracles are more than powerful acts done by a good man; they are manifestations of God's coming reign. They show us what the world will be like when God's kingdom comes finally and completely. But until then, Jesus and His followers are locked in conflict with powerful forces—spiritual, religious, and political. Ultimately these forces join together to oppose and crucify Him, but even this is God's plan; His torturous death is not the last word. Instead, the last word is God's, and it is a word of life and resurrection. Implicitly Mark's story of Jesus is a promise that those who suffer on their journey as His disciples will one day share in the resurrection. While the way of Jesus may well lead to suffering, it will ultimately lead to glory.

When Mark writes in the first chapter about a mysterious man entering the scene, instantly the reader recognizes there's something very different about Jesus. He comes into the picture not as a rock star but rather as someone humble, kind, and yet, still kingly. Mark describes the people who are drawn toward this man as regular people who have become affected by the character, passion, and light of this strange Galilean.

Maybe that's why Mark jumps right into the action of Jesus' story. He offers little by way of introduction. He writes nothing about Jesus' family tree. Unlike Matthew and Luke, he doesn't mention His birth. Mark's retelling begins with Scripture and the preaching of John the Baptist who calls people to repent. Like all the greats of history, Jesus doesn't just arrive—He is announced—and who better than John to do that? Right before Jesus makes His entrance into Mark's narrative, John says, "I've washed you here with water, *but when He gets here,* He will wash you in the Spirit of God."

---

1 This is the beginning of the good news of Jesus, the Anointed One, *the Liberating King,* the Son of God. ²Isaiah the prophet told us *what would happen before He came:*

Watch, I will send My messenger in front of You
    to prepare Your way and make it clear *and straight.**
³*You'll hear him,* a voice crying in the wilderness,
    "Prepare the way of the Eternal One,
    a straight way in the wandering desert,
    a highway for our God."*

⁴*That messenger was* John the Baptist,* who appeared in the desert *near the Jordan River* preaching that people should be ritually cleansed through baptism *with water as a sign of* both their changed hearts* and God's forgiveness of their sins. ⁵People from across the countryside of Judea and from the city of Jerusalem came to him and confessed that they were deeply flawed and needed help, so he cleansed* them with the waters of the Jordan. ⁶John dressed *as some of the Hebrew prophets had,* in clothes made of camel's hair with a leather belt around his waist. He made his meals *in the desert* from locusts and wild honey. ⁷He preached a message *in the wilderness.*

John the Baptist: Someone is coming who is a lot more powerful than I am—One whose sandals I'm not worthy to bend down and untie. ⁸I've washed you here through baptism* with water; *but when He gets here,* He will wash* you in the Spirit of God.

V

The Jordan River is the setting of some of the most memorable miracles in the Old Testament. On their journey through the wilderness to the promised land, the Israelites walked across the Jordan River on dry ground because God parted its waters. Elisha, one of the prophets of God, healed Naaman by telling him to bathe seven times in its waters. Partly because of miracles like these and partly because of a growing wilderness spirituality, many of the Jews in John's day are out to hear him and be ritually baptized in the Jordan's cool, cleansing waters. They are looking for God to intervene miraculously in their lives as He has done in the past. What they don't know is that God is about to intervene, for at that time Jesus leaves Nazareth and heads south.

---

⁹It was in those days that Jesus left Nazareth (*a village in the region* of Galilee) and came down to the Jordan, and John cleansed Him through baptism there *in the same way all the others were ritually cleansed.* ¹⁰But as Jesus was coming out of the waters, He looked up and saw the sky split open. The Spirit *of God* descended

* 1:2 Malachi 3:1   * 1:3 Isaiah 40:3   * 1:4 Literally, John who immersed, to show repentance   * 1:4 Literally, repentance   * 1:5 Literally, immersed, to show repentance   * 1:8 Literally, immersed, to show repentance   * 1:8 Literally, immerse, in a rite of initiation and purification

upon Him like a dove, [11]and a voice echoed in the heavens.

Voice: You are My Son,* My beloved One, and I am very pleased with You.

[12]After that the Spirit compelled Him to go into the wilderness, [13]and there in the desert He stayed for 40 days. He was tested by Satan himself and surrounded by wild animals; *but through these trials,* heavenly messengers *cared for Him and* ministered to Him.

[14]After John was arrested *by Herod, who ruled the Jewish lands on behalf of Roman interests,* Jesus went back into *the region of* Galilee and began to proclaim the good news of God.

Jesus: [15]It's time! The kingdom of God is near! Seek forgiveness, change your actions,* and believe this good news!

[16]As Jesus walked along the *shore of the* Sea of Galilee, He met *the first of His disciples,* two brothers, Simon and Andrew, both fishermen who were casting their fishing net into the shallow waters.

Jesus: [17]*Come and* follow Me, and I'll send you to catch people *instead of fish.*

[18]Simon and Andrew left their nets and followed Jesus at once.

[19]When He had walked a little farther, He saw the sons of Zebedee, James and John, in their boat repairing their nets. [20]Right away He called to them, and they dropped what they were doing and left their father Zebedee and the hired men aboard the boat to follow Him *as His disciples.*

[21]They came *at last* to the village of Capernaum *on the Sea of Galilee;* and on the Sabbath Day, Jesus went straight into a synagogue, *sat down,* and began to teach. [22]The people *looked at each other,* amazed, because this strange teacher acted as One authorized *by God, and what He taught affected them* in ways their own scribes' teachings could not. [23]Just then a man in the gathering who was overcome by an unclean spirit shouted.

Unclean Spirit: [24]What are You doing here, Jesus of Nazareth? Have You come to destroy us? I can see who You are! You're the Holy One of God.

Jesus *(rebuking him):* [25]Be quiet, and come out of him now!

[26]The man's body began to shake and shudder; and then, howling, the spirit flew out of the man. [27]The people couldn't stop talking about what they had seen.

People: *Who is this Jesus?* This is a new teaching—and it has such authority! Even the unclean spirits obey His commands!

[28]It wasn't long before news of Jesus spread over the countryside of Galilee.

[29]Right after they left the synagogue, Jesus went with James and John to the home of Simon and Andrew. [30]They told Him about Simon's mother-in-law who was there in bed, sick and feverish. [31]Jesus went to her side, took her hand, and lifted her up. As soon as He touched her, the fever left her *and she felt well again—strong enough to bustle around the house* taking care of her visitors.

[32]Just before night fell, others had gathered all the sick, *diseased,* and demon-infested people *they could find.* [33]*It seemed as if* the whole town had gathered at Simon and Andrew's door. [34]Jesus was kept busy healing people of every sort of ailment and casting out unclean spirits. He was very careful not to let the demons speak because they knew Him *and could reveal to the people who He really was.*

[35]Early in the morning, Jesus got up, left the house while it was still dark outside, and went to a deserted place to pray. [36]Simon and the others traveling with Jesus looked for Him. [37]They finally tracked Him down.

V

Whenever possible, Jesus seeks out solitude so He can pray and meditate. Jesus reveals His humanity. In these silent and reflective moments, He seems to refuel mentally, physically, and spiritually because Jesus hears His Father speak during His time alone. Throughout Jesus' ministry on earth, hearing from His Father seems to help Him focus on the mission at hand: redemption.

* 1:11 Psalm 2:7 * 1:15 Literally, repent

People: Everybody wants to know where You are!

Jesus: ³⁸It's time we went somewhere else—the next village, maybe—so I can tell more people *the good news about the kingdom of God.* After all, that's the reason I'm here.

³⁹So He traveled *to the next village and the one after that,* throughout the region of Galilee, teaching in the synagogues and casting out unclean spirits.

Jesus is confronted with a man who has leprosy—a skin disease that makes him ritually unclean according to Jewish law. This creates a problem with the authorities.

⁴⁰A leper walked right up to Jesus, dropped to his knees, and begged Him for help.

Leper: If You want to, You can make me clean.

⁴¹Jesus was powerfully moved. He reached out and actually touched the leper.

Jesus: I do want to. Be clean.

⁴²And at that very moment, the disease left him; the leper was cleansed *and made whole once again.* ⁴³Jesus sent him away, but first He warned him strongly.

Jesus: ⁴⁴Don't tell anybody how this happened. Just go and show yourself to the priest *so that he can certify you're clean.* Perform the ceremony prescribed by Moses as proof of your cleansing, *and then you may return home.*

⁴⁵The man talked everywhere about how Jesus had healed him, until Jesus could no longer come into a town openly *without the risk of being mobbed.* So He remained on the outskirts. Even so, people still sought Him out from far and wide.

2 ¹⁻²Some days later when Jesus came back to Capernaum, people heard that Jesus was back in town and many gathered at the house where He was staying. Soon the crowd overflowed from the house into the streets, *and still more people pressed forward* to hear Jesus teaching the message *of God's kingdom.* ³Four men tried to bring a crippled friend to Him; ⁴but since the crowd prevented their carrying him close enough to get Jesus' attention, they climbed up onto the roof, opened a hole in it, and lowered the paralyzed man on his mat down to Jesus.
⁵Jesus recognized the faith of these men.

Jesus *(to the paralyzed man):* Son, your sins are forgiven.

⁶⁻⁷Some scribes were sitting in the crowd, *and they didn't like what they were hearing.*

Scribes *(reasoning to themselves):* What does this Jesus think He is doing? This kind of talk is blasphemy, *an offense against the Most High!* Only God can forgive sins.

⁸At once Jesus realized what they were thinking. He turned to them.

Jesus: Why do My words trouble you so? ⁹*Think about this:* is it easier to tell this paralyzed man, "Your sins are forgiven," or to tell him, "Get up, pick up your mat, and walk"? ¹⁰Still, I want to show you that the Son of Man has been given the authority on earth to forgive sins. (to the paralytic) ¹¹Get up, pick up your mat, and go home.

¹²The man rose to his feet, immediately rolled up his mat, and walked out *into the streets.* Everyone in the crowd was amazed. All they could do was *shake their heads,* thank God for this miracle, and say to each other, "We've never seen anything like that!"

V

To some who believe wholeheartedly in God's laws, Jesus is a troublemaker, a mere man who has a bad habit of making statements that take away from the honor due to the one true God. The "scribes" who make these kinds of accusations against Jesus are usually connected to the Pharisees (a Jewish sect popular with the people, mostly middle class, and religiously strict when it comes to following God's laws) or the Sadducees (a smaller Jewish sect made up of priests and aristocrats from Jerusalem). While the two groups often clash with each other politically and theologically, they do find common ground—and sometimes even work together—in opposing Jesus.

13Another time Jesus was out walking alongside the Sea *of Galilee* teaching the gathering crowd as He went. 14He saw Levi, the son of Alphaeus, sitting at the booth where he collected taxes.

Jesus (*calling out to him*): Follow Me.

Levi left the booth and went along with Him.

Jesus' invitation to follow Him, like His invitations to all the disciples, involves a lot more than joining the caravan; Jesus' invitation is for sinners to change their ways of life. Jesus makes it clear, despite the criticisms of some observers, that this invitation is indeed open to all—especially to the sinners who need it most. Jesus grants to those who choose Him not just companionship and forgiveness but the ability to truly receive a new identity and live a new life.

15At Levi's house, many tax collectors and other sinners—*Jews who did not keep the strict purity laws of the Jewish holy texts*—were dining with Jesus and His disciples. Jesus had attracted such a large following that all kinds of people surrounded Him. 16When the Pharisees' scribes saw who shared the table with Jesus, they were quick to criticize:

Scribes (*to His disciples*): *If your master is such a righteous person,* then why does He eat and drink with tax collectors and sinners, *the worst among us*?

17Jesus heard them.

Jesus (*to the scribes*): People who have their health don't need to see a doctor. Only those who are sick do. I'm not here to call those already in good standing with God; I'm here to call sinners to turn back to Him.*

18The disciples of John *the Baptist* and the Pharisees made a practice of fasting.

Some Jews fast twice a week and pray three times daily, but Jesus has a different set of practices for His followers. Some of the pious are disturbed by this.

Some People (*to Jesus*): Why is it that John's followers and the Pharisees' followers fast, but Your disciples are eating and drinking *like it was any other day*?

Jesus: 19Guests at the wedding can't fast when the bridegroom is with them. It would be wrong to do anything but feast. 20When the bridegroom is snatched away from them, then the time will come to fast *and mourn.*
    21*These are new things I'm teaching, and they can't be reconciled with old habits.* Nobody would ever use a piece of new cloth to patch an old garment because when the patch shrinks, it pulls away and makes the tear even worse. 22And nobody puts new, *unfermented* wine into old wineskins because if he does, the wine will burst the skins; they would lose both the wineskins and the wine. No, the only appropriate thing is to put new wine into new wineskins.

23One Sabbath Jesus and His disciples were walking through a field of grain; as they walked, His disciples *grew hungry.* They began to pull from the stalks *and eat.*
    24The Pharisees confronted Him.

Pharisees: Did You see that? Why are Your disciples doing what our law forbids on the Sabbath?

Jesus (*turning toward the Pharisees*): 25Do you remember the story about what *King* David and his followers did when they were hungry and had nothing to eat?

They said nothing, so He continued.

Jesus: 26David went into the house of God, when Abiathar was the high priest, and ate the bread that was consecrated to God. Now our laws say no one but the priests can eat that holy bread; *but when David was*

* 2:17 Literally, repentance

hungry, he ate and also shared the bread with those who followed him.*

²⁷The Sabbath was made for *the needs of* human beings, and not the other way around. ²⁸So the Son of Man is Lord even over the Sabbath.

3 *On the Sabbath,* Jesus had come into a synagogue where He saw a man with a withered hand.

²The Pharisees held their breath: would Jesus cure this man on the Sabbath, *right there in front of everyone?* If so, they could charge Him *with breaking the Sabbath law.* ³*Jesus knew their hearts.* He called to the man with the withered hand.

Jesus: Come to Me.

⁴Then He turned to the Pharisees with a question.

Jesus: Do our laws tell us to do good or evil on the Sabbath? To save life, or to snuff it out?

They remained silent.

⁵Jesus was furious as He looked out over the crowd, and He was grieved by their hard hearts.

How can anyone care so much about the words of the law and so little about the spirit of it?

Jesus (*to the man with the withered hand*): So be it. Stretch out your hand.

The man stretched forth his hand; and as he did, it was completely healed. ⁶The Pharisees went directly from the synagogue to consult with the supporters of Herod, *the Romans' puppet ruler,* about how they could get rid of this dangerous dreamer.

⁷Meanwhile Jesus and His followers traveled to *the shore of* the Sea *of Galilee; as always,* a huge crowd from Galilee and Judea gathered. ⁸People had come *from miles* to see this man they were hearing so much about. They came from *the big cities, including* Jerusalem *of Judea,* Tyre and Sidon *of Phoenicia,* and from the region of Idumea, south of Judea. ⁹⁻¹⁰Since Jesus had healed so many, the sick and the infirm pushed forward constantly to touch Him, *to be healed, and to ask His blessing.* The crowd pressed so closely around Jesus that He asked His disciples

to get a boat He could board if the crush became too great.

¹¹*Most wanted to be near Him, except for those possessed by* unclean spirits. Those people fell down before Him.

Unclean Spirits: You are the Son of God.

¹²But He ordered them not to reveal His true identity.

¹³Jesus called together a select group *of His followers* and led them up onto a mountain. ¹⁴There He commissioned them the twelve. [*Later He calls them His emissaries.*]* He wanted them to be with Him. He sent them out to spread the good news ¹⁵and to cast out evil spirits [and heal diseases].*

¹⁶Here are the names of the original twelve: Simon (whom Jesus called Peter, *meaning "the rock"*), ¹⁷James and John the sons of Zebedee, whom Jesus called "the Sons of Thunder"), ¹⁸Andrew, Philip, Bartholomew, Matthew (*the tax collector, also called Levi*), Thomas, James (the son of Alphaeus), Thaddaeus, Simon of Canaan (who was also called "the Zealot"), ¹⁹and Judas Iscariot (who one day would betray Jesus *to the authorities in Jerusalem so God's purpose could be fulfilled*).

²⁰Jesus *and His disciples* went into a house to eat, but so many people pressed in to see Jesus that they could not be served. ²¹When Jesus' family heard *about this craziness,* they went to drag Him out of that place.

Jesus' Family (*to one another*): Jesus has lost His mind.

²²The scribes, *for their part,* came down from Jerusalem *and spread the slander that Jesus was in league with the devil.*

Scribes: That's how He casts out demons. He's casting them out by the power of Beelzebul—*the ancient Philistine god*—the prince of demons.

²³When Jesus heard this, He tried to reason with them using parables.

Jesus: *Listen.* How can Satan drive out Satan? ²⁴A kingdom that makes war against itself will collapse. ²⁵A household divided against itself cannot stand. ²⁶If Satan opposes himself, he cannot stand and is finished.

* 2:26 1 Samuel 21:3-6   * 3:14 Most manuscripts omit this portion.
* 3:15 Most manuscripts omit this portion.

[27]If you want to break into the house of a strong man and plunder it, you have to bind him first. Then you can do whatever you want with his possessions. [28]Listen, the truth is that people can be forgiven for almost anything. *God has been known to forgive many things,* even blasphemy. [29]But speaking evil of the Spirit of God is an unforgivable sin that will follow you into eternity.

[30]He said this because the scribes were telling people that Jesus got His power from dark forces instead of from God.

Popularity is often a dangerous thing, particularly in a land occupied by Roman soldiers. As Jesus' ministry grows, some of His friends and family start to get nervous: they wonder if He has "lost His mind" entirely. They just can't understand what is happening and why He is so important. It doesn't seem right—the boy next door from Nazareth receiving so much attention. In fact, they are so uncomfortable with it that they decide to intervene and take Him home.

But Jesus' family isn't the only group concerned about Him. The Pharisees are doing their best to spread doubt about His authority with the worst accusations possible: His power to heal comes from the devil himself. They are attacking Him publicly and questioning His identity as the Anointed One.

---

[31]When Jesus' mother and brothers arrived, *they couldn't break through the crowd,* so they sent word in to Jesus that He should come out to them. [32]The crowd was pressed in tight around Him when He received the message, "Your mother and brothers [and sisters]* are waiting outside for You."

[33]*Jesus looked around.*

Jesus *(answering them):* Who are My mother and brothers?

He called into the silence. No one spoke.

[34]At last His gaze swept across those gathered close, *and Jesus smiled.*

Jesus: You, here, are My mother and My brothers! [35]Whoever does the will of God is My true family.

4 [1-2]Jesus went out again to teach by the Sea *of Galilee.* When the crowd became unmanageable, He climbed aboard a boat and sat down to teach the people listening on the shore by telling them parables. One of His teachings went like this:

Jesus: [3]Listen! A farmer went out and sowed his seed. [4]As he scattered it, one seed fell along the *hardened* path, and a bird flapped down and snapped it up. [5]One seed fell onto rocky places where the soil was thin, so it sprang up quickly. [6]But when the hot sun scorched *the fragile stems and leaves,* the seedling withered because its roots didn't go deep in the soil. [7]One of the seeds fell among the *weeds and* thorns, which crowded the seedling out of producing a crop. [8]And the rest of the seeds fell in good, rich soil. When they sprouted, the plants grew and produced a crop 30, 60, even 100 times larger *than expected* for every seed that the farmer had sown.

[9]All who have ears to hear, let them listen.

[10]When they were alone, the twelve and others close to Him asked why He always taught in parables *instead of explaining His teachings clearly.*

Jesus: [11]God has let you in on the inside story regarding the workings of the Kingdom—the hidden meanings. But the crowds—I teach them in parables [12]*as the prophet Isaiah predicted,*

So that when they look, they see and yet do not understand.
When they hear, they listen and yet do not comprehend.
Otherwise, they might really turn and be forgiven.*

This makes the disciples scratch their heads. Why would He want to hide the truth from some people? His teachings are hard enough without putting them into parables.

* 3:32 Some manuscripts omit this portion.   * 4:12 Isaiah 6:9-10

¹³Do you mean to say that you didn't understand My parable of the sower? *That was the key parable. If you don't see what I was trying to teach there,* how will you be able to understand any of the others?

¹⁴The seed the farmer is sowing is *the good news,* God's word. ¹⁵Some people are the seed thrown onto the path, and the tempter snaps up the word *before it can even take root.* ¹⁶Others are the seed thrown among the rocks. Those people hear the word and receive it immediately with joy and enthusiasm; ¹⁷but without deep roots, *doubt,* trouble, or persecution instantly withers their faith. ¹⁸Still others are the seed tossed among *weeds and* brambles. The word has reached them, ¹⁹but the things of this life—the worries, the drive for more and more, the desire for other things—those things *cluster around close and* choke the life of God out of them until they cannot produce. ²⁰But those last seeds—those sown into good soil? Those people hear the word, accept it, *meditate on it, act on it,* and bear fruit—a crop 30, 60, or 100 times larger *than the farmer dropped to earth.*

Jesus' teaching often includes parables: stories that explain the truth about the Kingdom with examples from everyday life. Considering that most of His listeners know about farming, it's no wonder most of Jesus' parables are based on agricultural realities.

Parables like this force Jesus' listeners to think about the kingdom of God differently. He challenges their ideas, and He also knows they are unlikely to forget it. When they see farmers broadcasting their seeds, they will remember this parable and ponder the mysteries of the Kingdom. It never seems to bother Him that people are confused by His teaching. He doesn't expect them to understand everything; He wants them to wrestle with His teachings so His words will sit in their hearts and germinate—much like the seed sitting in good soil that eventually grows to bear fruit.

Jesus: ²¹When you bring a lamp *into the house,* do you put it under a box or *stuff it* under your bed? Or do you set it on top of a table *or chest*? ²²Those things that are hidden are meant to be revealed, and what is concealed is meant to be brought out where its light can shine.

²³All who have ears to hear, let them listen.

²⁴So consider carefully the things you're hearing. If you put it to use, you'll be given more to wrestle with—much more. ²⁵Those who have *listened* will receive more, but those who don't hear will forget even the little they've failed to understand.

²⁶Here is what the kingdom of God is like: a man who throws seeds onto the earth. ²⁷Day and night, as he works and as he sleeps, the seeds sprout and climb out into the light, even though he doesn't understand how it works. ²⁸*It's as though* the soil itself produced the grain *somehow*—from a sprouted stalk to ripened fruit. ²⁹But *however it happens,* when he sees that the grain has grown and ripened, he gets his sickle and begins to cut it because the harvest has come.

³⁰What else is the kingdom of God like? What earthly thing can we compare it to? ³¹The kingdom of God is like a mustard seed, the tiniest seed you can sow. ³²But after that seed is planted, it grows into the largest plant in the garden, a plant so big that birds can build their nests in the shade of its branches.

³³Jesus spoke many parables like these to the people who followed Him. ³⁴This was the only way He taught them, although when He was alone with His chosen few, He interpreted all the stories *so the disciples truly understood.*

³⁵The same evening, Jesus suggested they cross over to the other side *of the lake.* ³⁶With Jesus already in the boat, they left the crowd behind and set sail along with a few other boats that followed. ³⁷*As they sailed,* a storm formed. *The winds whipped up huge waves that broke over the bow, filling the boat with so much water that even the experienced sailors among them were sure they were going to sink.*

³⁸Jesus was back in the stern of the boat, sound asleep on a cushion, when the disciples shook Him awake.

Disciples (*shouting over the storm*): Jesus, Master, don't You care that we're going to die?

³⁹He got up, shouted words into the wind, and commanded the waves.

Jesus: That's enough! Be still!

And immediately the wind died down to nothing, the waves stopped.

Jesus: ⁴⁰How can you be so afraid? *After all you've seen,* where is your faith?

⁴¹The disciples were still afraid, *slowly coming to grips with what they had seen.*

Disciples (*to one another*): Who is this *Jesus*? How can it be that He has power over even the wind and the waves?

For most of Jesus' miracles, the disciples are observers: they watch Him healing the sick, raising dead bodies, and casting demons out of strangers. This time, however, it is the disciples—and even Jesus Himself—who are in danger. Maybe that's why they are having such a hard time trusting that His power is greater than their situation.

They have seen Him cast out demons. They know He has powers that are not of natural origin. But they have never seen—or even heard of—anything like this. It's one thing to heal human sickness or even to order demons around. But to order the waves and the wind? To command the sea and the storm? That's a miracle of an entirely different order.

---

5 They traveled across the sea to the land of Gerasa* *in Galilee.* ²⁻³When Jesus came ashore there, He was immediately met by a man who was tortured by an evil spirit. This man lived in the cemeteries, and no one could control him—not even those who tried to tie him up or chain him. ⁴He had often been bound in chains, but his strength was so great that he could break the chains and tear the irons loose *from his feet*

and hands. No one *and nothing* could subdue him. ⁵Day and night, he lurked among the tombs or *ran mad* in the hills, and *the darkness* made him scream or cut himself with *sharp-edged* stones. ⁶When this man saw Jesus coming in the distance, he ran to Him and fell to his knees in front of Him. ⁷⁻⁸Jesus started commanding the unclean spirit.

Jesus: Come out of that man, you wicked spirit!

Unclean Spirit (*shouting*): What's this all about, Jesus, Son of the Most High? In the name of God, I beg You—don't torture me!

Jesus: ⁹What is your name?

Unclean Spirit: They call me "Legion," for there are thousands of us *in this body.*

¹⁰And then Legion begged Jesus again *to leave them alone,* not to send them out of the country.

¹¹*Since the Gerasenes were not Jews (who considered pigs to be unclean),* there happened to be a large herd of swine, *some 2,000 of them,* feeding on the hill nearby.

Unclean Spirit (*begging*): ¹²Send us into those pigs *if You have to,* so that we may enter into them.

¹³Jesus granted the request. The darkness swept up out of the man and into the herd of pigs. And then they thundered down the hill into the water; and there they drowned, all 2,000 of them. ¹⁴The swineherds ran away, telling everybody they met what had happened. Eventually a crowd of people came to see for themselves. ¹⁵When they reached Jesus, they found the man Legion had afflicted sitting quietly, sane and fully clothed; when they saw this, they were overwhelmed with fear *and wonder.* ¹⁶Those who had witnessed everything told the others what had happened: how Jesus had healed the man, how the pigs had rushed into the sea, and how they had destroyed themselves. ¹⁷*When they had heard the whole story,* the Gerasenes turned to Jesus and begged Him to go away. ¹⁸When Jesus climbed back into the

* 5:1 The earliest manuscripts read "Gerasenes"; others read "Gadarenes."

boat, the cured demoniac asked if he could come and be with Him, but Jesus said no.

Jesus: [19]Stay here; I want you to go back home to your own people and let them see what the Lord has done—how He has had mercy on you.

[20]So the man went away and began telling this news in the Ten Cities* region; wherever he went, people were amazed by what he told them.

V

This is the only time in the Gospels when Jesus seems to listen to the pleading of a demon or a demon-possessed person. The demons immediately acknowledge Jesus as all-powerful; the possessed man's first reaction on seeing Jesus is to fall at His feet and call Him the "Son of the Most High." Although we can't know why Jesus listens to their pleading, the effect is clear: the people in that region see first-hand the power of evil and its ulti-mate destiny, namely, destruction.

Instead of being pleased that they are now free from the terror of the demon-possessed man, the people in the town ask Jesus to leave. After all, the local economy takes a pretty big hit when 2,000 of their choicest pigs rush into the sea.

---

[21]After Jesus returned across the sea, a large crowd quickly found Him, so He stayed by the sea. [22]One of the leaders of the synagogue—a man named Jairus—came and fell at Jesus' feet, [23]begging Him to heal his daughter.

Jairus: My daughter is dying, *and she's only 12 years old.* Please come to my house. Just place Your hands on her. I know that if You do, she will live.

[24]Jesus began traveling with Jairus toward his home.

In the crowd pressing around Jesus, [25]there was a woman who had suffered con-tinuous bleeding for 12 years, *bleeding that made her ritually unclean and an outcast according to the purity laws.* [26]She had suf-fered greatly; and although she spent all her money on her medical care, she had only got-ten worse. [27]She had heard of this *Miracle-Man,* Jesus, so she snuck up behind Him in the crowd and reached out her hand to touch His cloak.

Woman (*to herself*): [28]Even if all I touch are His clothes, I know I will be healed.

[29]*As soon as her fingers brushed His cloak,* the bleeding stopped. She could feel that she was whole again.

[30]Lots of people were pressed against Jesus at that moment, but He immediately felt her touch; He felt healing power flow out of Him.

He stopped. Everyone stopped. He looked around.

Jesus: Who just touched My robe?

[31]His disciples broke the uneasy silence.

Disciples: Jesus, the crowd is so thick that everyone is touching You. Why do You ask, "Who touched Me?"

[32]*But Jesus waited.* His gaze swept across the crowd to see who had done it. [33]At last, the woman—knowing He was talking about her—pushed forward and dropped to her knees. She was shaking with fear *and amazement.*

Woman: *I touched You.*

Then she told Him the reason why. [34]*Jesus listened to her story.*

Jesus: Daughter, you are well because you *dared to* believe. Go in peace, and stay well.

V

Jesus occasionally instigates His own miracles: He goes up to some-one, such as a paralyzed man, and offers to heal him. More often, as in the case of Jairus's daughter, peo-ple come to Jesus and ask for heal-ings. But the woman in this story is unique because she receives her healing without asking for it—simply by touching Jesus in faith. He is surrounded by crowds pressing in

---

* 5:20 Literally, the Decapolis

on every side, but Jesus feels that one person's touch is different, in a way that only He can perceive: one woman is touching Him deliberately, in hope and faith, knowing He has the power to heal her.

35While He was speaking, some members of Jairus's household pushed through the crowd.

Jairus's Servants *(to Jairus)*: Your daughter is dead. There's no need to drag the Teacher any farther.

36Jesus overheard their words. Then He turned to look at Jairus.

Jesus: *It's all right.* Don't be afraid; just believe.

37-38Jesus asked everyone but Peter, James, and John (James's brother) to remain outside when they reached Jairus's home. Inside the synagogue leader's house, the mourning had already begun; the weeping and wailing carried out into the street. 39Jesus *and His three disciples* went inside.

Jesus: Why are you making all this sorrowful noise? The child isn't dead. She's just sleeping.

40The mourners laughed *a horrible, bitter laugh and went back to their wailing*. Jesus cleared the house so that only His three disciples, Jairus, and Jairus's wife were left inside with Him. They all went to where the child lay. 41Then He took the child's hand.

Jesus: Little girl, it's time to wake up.

42Immediately the 12-year-old girl opened her eyes, arose, and began to walk. Her parents could not believe their eyes.

Jesus *(to the parents)*: 43Don't tell anybody what you've just seen. Why don't you give her something to eat? *I know she is hungry.*

Jesus at last arrives at the miracle He was asked to perform: the healing of Jairus's daughter. But

He is too late—the girl is already dead. Although Jesus later raises other dead people back to life, up to this point He has not yet performed such a powerful miracle. No one has an inkling of His power over the forces of life and death. He allows only His closest disciples to see this first miracle of resurrection, and He urges everyone who sees it to keep it quiet. Nevertheless, it is this miracle that first demonstrates to those who see it that He does indeed have power over death itself.

---

6 Jesus went back into His own hometown where He had grown up, and His disciples followed Him there. 2When the Sabbath came, He went into the synagogue *in Nazareth* and began to teach *as He had done elsewhere*, and many of those who heard Him were astonished.

Those in the Synagogue: Where did He gain this wisdom? And what are all these stories we've been hearing about the signs and healings He's performed? *Where did He get that kind of power?* 3Isn't this *Jesus, the little boy we used to see in Joseph's carpenter shop*? Didn't He grow up to be a carpenter *just like His father*? Isn't He the son of Mary *over there* and the brother of James, Joses, Judas, Simon, and their sisters? *Who does He think He is?*

And when they had thought about it that way, they became indignant and closed themselves to His message.

Jesus *(seeing this)*: 4A prophet can find honor anywhere except in his hometown, among his own people, and in his own household.

5He could not do any of His great works among them except with a few of the sick, whom He healed by laying His hands upon them. 6He was amazed by the stubbornness of their unbelief.

Jesus went out among the villages teaching, 7and He called the twelve to Him and began to send them out in pairs. He gave them authority over unclean spirits 8and instructed them to take nothing with them but a staff: no money, no bread, no bag, [9]nothing but the sandals on their feet and the coat* on their back.

Jesus: [10]When you go into a house, stay there until it is time for you to leave that town. [11]And if someone will not accept you and your message, when you leave, shake off the dust of that place from your feet as a judgment against it. [On the day of judgment, that city will wish for the punishment of Sodom and Gomorrah.]*

[12]And so His disciples went out *into the countryside,* preaching the changed life* *as Jesus had taught them,* [13]casting out unclean spirits and anointing the sick with oil to heal them.

[14]Jesus had become so well known that King Herod received reports of all that Jesus was doing. Some were saying* that John the Baptist* had been raised from the dead and that these mighty works were the fruits of his resurrection.

Others *(disagreeing):* [15]No, this Jesus is Elijah, *returned to work on the earth.*

And still others said He was another of the prophets.

Herod *(to himself):* [16]No, it is John, the prophet I beheaded, risen from the dead.

For the blood of John was on his hands. [17-18]Herod had imprisoned John *in the days before Jesus began His teaching.* John had preached to Herod that he should not have married his own brother's wife, Herodias, for *so it is written in the Hebrew Scriptures:* "It is not lawful for one to marry his brother's wife."*

[19]Herodias held a grudge against John and would have had him killed, but she couldn't. [20]Herod feared John as a holy and righteous man and did what he could to protect him. John taught hard truths,* and yet Herod found he usually liked hearing them.

So Herod had put John in prison instead of executing him; [21-22]*and there John sat until Herod's birthday,* when the governor held a great state dinner. That night, Herod's stepdaughter danced beautifully for the state officials; and the king proclaimed a solemn vow in the presence of *his honored guests,* military officers, and some of the leading men of Galilee.

Herod: Ask me whatever you wish, and I will grant it. [23]Whatever you want, I will give you—up to half my province.

[24]She went out and consulted with her mother, *Herodias, who had only one great desire* and told her daughter what she must say.

Herod's Stepdaughter *(immediately, in response to Herod):* [25]I want the head of John the Baptist*—right now—delivered to me on a platter.

[26]Herod was horrified, but he had sworn an oath and could not break his word in front of his invited guests. [27]So immediately he sent an executioner to the prison to behead John and bring them the head. [28]It was brought to the girl upon a platter, and she took it to her mother.

[29]When John's disciples were told of this, they came for his body and gave it a proper burial.

[30]Now the twelve returned from their travels and told Him what they had done, *whom they had seen,* and how they had spread the news of God's kingdom.

Jesus *(to the disciples):* [31]Let us go out into the wilderness for a while and rest ourselves.

The crowds gathered as always, and Jesus and the twelve couldn't eat because so many people came and went. [32]They could get no peace until they boarded a boat and sailed toward a deserted place.

[33]*But the people would not be put off so easily.* Those *along the shore* who recognized Jesus followed *along the coast.* People pushed out of all the cities and gathered ahead of Him [34]so that when Jesus came ashore and saw this crowd of people waiting for Him *in a place that should have been relatively deserted,* He was moved with compassion. They were like sheep without a shepherd.

He began to teach them many things [35]as the day passed; at last the disciples came to Jesus.

* 6:9 Literally, "not to wear two tunics"   * 6:11 Some of the earliest manuscripts omit this portion.   * 6:12 Literally, repentance
* 6:14 Some of the earliest manuscripts read "He was saying."
* 6:14 Literally, John who immersed, to show repentance
* 6:17-18 Leviticus 18:16; 20:21   * 6:20 Some early manuscripts read "he did many things."   * 6:25 Literally, John who immersed, to show repentance

Disciples: It is getting late, and there is nothing around for miles. 36Send these people to the surrounding villages so they can buy something to eat.

Jesus: 37Why don't you give them something to eat?

Disciples (looking at Him): What? It would cost a fortune* to buy bread for these people!

Jesus: 38Does anyone have any bread? Go and see.

Disciples (returning from the crowd): There are five pieces of flatbread and two fish, if that makes any difference.

Jesus: 39-40Listen, tell them to gather in smaller groups and sit on that green patch of grass.

And so the disciples gathered the people in groups of 100 or of 50, and they sat down. 41Jesus took the five pieces of flatbread and the two fish, looked up to heaven, thanked God for the food, and broke it. He gave the pieces to the disciples to distribute, 42and all of the people ate until no one was hungry. 43Then they gathered twelve baskets full of leftovers.

44That day, 5,000 men ate their fill of the bread when Jesus fed the hungry crowd.

how Jesus is making them a part of the miracle—despite their mundane concerns and their frustrations with Him.

45Not long after, He sent His disciples out onto their boat to sail to Bethsaida on the other shore, and He sent the crowd away. 46After everyone had gone, He slipped away to pray on a mountain overlooking the sea.

47When evening came, the boat was out on the sea and He was alone on the land. 48He saw that the disciples were making little progress because they were rowing against a stiff wind. Before daylight He came near them, walking on the water, and would have passed by them. 49Some of them saw Him walking on the surface of the water, thought He was a ghost, and cried out. 50When they all saw Him, they were terrified.

Jesus (immediately calling out): Don't be frightened. Do you see? It is I.

51He walked across the water to the boat; and as soon as He stepped aboard, the contrary wind ceased its blowing. They were greatly astonished; 52although they had just witnessed the miracle of Jesus feeding 5,000 with bread and fish, and other signs besides, they didn't understand what it all meant and their hearts remained hard.

The disciples pull Jesus aside to point out the obvious: everyone needs to go and eat something.

But Jesus, as usual, isn't about to be distracted by the obvious. His answer must irritate them even further: "Why don't you give them something to eat?" Jesus is seeing a much bigger reality. He is deliberately creating a turning point in His ministry: He wants to make them a part of His miracles. From recorders and observers, they will become participants. And so the disciples, not Jesus, tell the people to sit down, pass out the food, and collect the leftovers after everyone has eaten until they are stuffed. The disciples must feel pretty sheepish as they experience

How can the disciples still be in doubt about Jesus after having been part of so many miracles? Like the Israelites in the Old Testament, the disciples are discovering the truth that miracles don't produce faith. As Jesus so often points out, the process works the other way around: it's faith that produces miracles. Miracles are only signs—evidence of truth that you have to know before the miracle. As long as the disciples are still in doubt about who Jesus is, they find their faith constantly challenged and frequently wavering. It will not be until after the resurrection, the greatest miracle of

* 6:37 Literally, 200 denarii, Roman coins

all, that they will come to recognize and believe in Jesus for who He is; and then their hearts will at last open.

---

⁵³When they finished their journey, they landed the boat in Gennesaret. ⁵⁴People at once recognized Jesus *as the Healer.* ⁵⁵Immediately they hurried to collect the sick and infirm—bringing them to Him in beds if they had to—⁵⁶laying them out in the markets of any village, city, or field where He might pass.

Gennesarites: Just let us touch the fringe of Your robe.

Even the people who touched only it were made whole again.

7 Then the Pharisees returned to talk with Jesus, and with them came some of the scribes *and scholars* from Jerusalem.

Scribes and Scholars (*seeing the disciples eating*): ²Your disciples are eating bread with defiled, unwashed hands.

³Now *you need to know that* the Pharisees, and all Jews *for that matter,* held the tradition of their ancestors that hands must be washed before eating to avoid being ritually unclean. ⁴Likewise, they washed when they returned from the market and followed similar purity teachings as well, from the washing of their food to the washing of their bowls, cups, and kettles.

Scribes and Pharisees: ⁵Why don't Your disciples follow the traditions passed down to us? Why do they eat their bread with defiled hands?

Jesus: ⁶Isaiah prophesied wisely about your religious pretensions when he wrote,

These people honor Me *with words* off their lips;
meanwhile their hearts are far from Me.
⁷Their worship is empty, *void of true devotion.*
They teach a human commandment, *memorized and practiced by rote.**

⁸When you cling blindly to your own traditions [such as washing utensils and cups],* you completely miss God's command. ⁹Then, indeed, you have perfected setting aside God's commands for the sake of your tradition. ¹⁰Moses gave you God's commandment: "Honor your father and your mother."* And also, "If you curse your father or your mother, you will be put to death."* ¹¹But you say to your *aged* parents, "I've decided that the support you were expecting from me will now be the holy offering set aside for God." ¹²After that he is not allowed to do anything for his parents. ¹³Do you think God wants you to honor your traditions that you have passed down? This is only one of many places where you are blind. ¹⁴(to the crowd that had gathered) Listen, all of you, to this teaching. I want you to understand. ¹⁵There is nothing outside someone that can corrupt him. Only the things that come out of a person can corrupt him. [¹⁶All who have ears to hear, let them listen.]*

¹⁷When they had come in from the road, His disciples asked Him what He meant by this teaching.

Jesus: ¹⁸Do you mean you don't understand this one either? Whatever goes into people from outside can't defile them ¹⁹because it doesn't go into their hearts. Outside things go through their guts and back out, thus making all foods pure.* ²⁰No, it's what comes from within that corrupts. ²¹⁻²²It's what grows out of the hearts of people that leads to corruption: evil thoughts, immoral sex, theft, murder, adultery, greed, wicked acts, treachery, sensuality, jealousy, slander, pride, and foolishness. ²³All of these come from within, and these are the sins that truly corrupt a person.

V

Although Mark specifically states that Jesus is overriding the Old Testament dietary laws and declaring all foods pure, it will be a long time before the disciples are willing to act on that message. One of the biggest controversies in

* 7:6-7 Isaiah 29:13 * 7:8 Some of the earliest manuscripts omit this portion. * 7:10 Exodus 20:12; Deuteronomy 5:16 * 7:10 Exodus 21:17; Leviticus 20:9 * 7:16 Some manuscripts omit verse 16.
* 7:19 The earliest texts say "Jesus declared all foods pure."

the early church will be the question of dietary restrictions and how the Old Testament laws ought to be observed by Jewish and non-Jewish Christian believers. However, Jesus makes it clear in this passage that His main concern has nothing to do with what people eat. Instead, He is concerned about the hearts of His followers.

24From there Jesus and His followers traveled to the region of Tyre [and Sidon]* *on the Mediterranean coast.* He hoped to slip unnoticed into a house, but people discovered His presence. 25*Shortly after He arrived,* a woman whose daughter was filled with an unclean spirit heard that He was there, so she came directly to Him and prostrated herself at His feet.

26The woman was *not a Jew, but* a Syrophoenician (a Greek) by birth. *All the same,* she came to Jesus and begged Him to cast the unclean spirit out of her daughter.

Jesus *(shaking His head)*: 27I must feed the children first. It would do no good to take the children's bread and throw it to the dogs.

Syrophoenician Woman: 28Yes, Lord, but even the dogs under the table may eat of the children's crumbs.

Jesus *(smiling and nodding)*: 29This is a wise saying. Go back home. Your daughter is free of the spirit that troubled her.

30And when she returned to her house, *she discovered that it was as Jesus had told her.* Her daughter lay on her bed, in her right mind, *whole and healthy.*

 Although Jesus at first answers the Greek woman harshly, He ultimately responds to her request. By healing her daughter, He demonstrates that God's loving presence has come to all people and not just to Jews. It's one of the first glimpses in this Gospel of the truth that will become clearer later—the truth that, through Jesus, God is

making all people, and not just one chosen nation, clean and whole.

31Jesus traveled on His way through Tyre and Sidon, eventually returning to the region of the Sea of Galilee. From there He pressed on to the area of the Ten Cities.* 32*Among the sick* who were brought to Him was a man who was deaf and could barely speak at all, and those who brought him begged Jesus to lay His hands on the man. 33Jesus took him aside from the crowd, alone, and touched his ears with His fingers. Then after spitting on His fingers, Jesus touched the man's tongue. 34Looking heavenward to God, Jesus sighed and commanded,

Jesus: Open up* *and let this man speak.*

35[Immediately]* the man could hear, his tongue was loosed, and he spoke plainly. 36Jesus ordered those *who had witnessed this* to tell no one; but the more He insisted, the more zealously people spread the word.

People *(astonished)*: 37He does everything so well! He even returns sound to the deaf and mute.

8 Once again a huge crowd had followed them, and they had nothing to eat. So Jesus called His disciples together.

Jesus: 2These people have been with Me for three days without food. They're hungry, and I am concerned for them. 3If I try to send them home now, they'll faint along the way because many of them have come a long, long way *to hear and see Me.*

Disciples: 4Where can we find enough bread for these people in this desolate place?

Jesus: 5How much bread do we have left?

Disciples: Seven rounds of flatbread.

6*So, as before,* He commanded the people to sit down; and He took the rounds of flatbread, gave thanks for them, and broke them. His disciples took what He gave them and fed the people. 7They also had a few small

---

* 7:24 Some manuscripts omit this portion.   * 7:31 Literally, the Decapolis   * 7:34 Aramaic, *Ephphatha*   * 7:35 Some of the earliest manuscripts omit this word.

fish, which, after He had spoken a blessing, He likewise gave His followers to pass to the people. [8]When all had eaten their fill and they had gathered up the food that remained, seven baskets were full.

[9]*On this occasion,* there were about 4,000 people who had eaten the food *that Jesus provided.* Jesus sent the crowd home; [10] then, immediately, He got into a boat with His disciples and sailed away. Upon their arrival in Dalmanutha *in the district of Magdala,* [11]they were met by Pharisees—ready with their questions and tests—seeking some sign from heaven *that His teaching was from God.*

Jesus *(sighing with disappointment):* [12]Why does this generation ask for a sign *before they will believe?* Believe Me when I say that you will not see one.

[13]He left the Pharisees and sailed across to the other shore.

[14]The disciples had forgotten to buy provisions, so they had only one round of flatbread among them. [15]Jesus took this moment to warn them.

Jesus: Beware of the yeast of the Pharisees and the leaven of Herod.

The disciples *didn't understand what Jesus was talking about and* discussed it among themselves.

Some Disciples: [16]What?

Other Disciples: He's saying this because we have run out of bread.

Jesus *(overhearing them):* [17-19]Why are you focusing on bread? Don't you see yet? Don't you understand? You have eyes—why don't you see? You have ears—why don't you hear? Are you so hard-hearted?
Don't you remember when I broke the five rounds of flatbread among the 5,000? *Tell Me,* how many baskets of scraps were left over?

Disciples: Twelve.

Jesus: [20]And how many were left when I fed the 4,000 with seven rounds?

Disciples: Seven.

Jesus: [21]And still you don't understand?

[22]When they came into Bethsaida, a group brought a blind man to Jesus, and they begged Him to touch the man *and heal him.* [23]So Jesus guided the man out of the village, *away from the crowd;* and He spat on the man's eyes and touched them.

Jesus: What do you see?

Blind Man *(opening his eyes):* [24]I see people, but they look like trees—walking trees.

[25]Jesus touched his eyes again; and when the man looked up, he could see everything clearly.
[26]Jesus sent him away to his house.

Jesus *(to the healed man):* Don't go into town yet. [And don't tell anybody in town what happened here.]*

V

Bethsaida is the hometown of at least three of Jesus' emissaries—Peter, Andrew, and Philip—and possibly James and John as well. Jesus performs many miracles there, most notably the feeding of the 5,000. However, this miracle—the healing of the blind man—is the only miracle in all the Gospels that is done in stages instead of instantly.

Of course, there's no way to know for sure why Jesus chooses to heal this man partly before He heals him entirely. Jesus frequently links faith, or lack of faith, with the healings. Bethsaida is a town He criticizes for its lack of faith (Matthew 11:21-22). So it's likely He wants to demonstrate to His disciples that their inability to see His purpose can be healed, too, even if it takes time.

---

[27]As He traveled with His disciples into the villages of Caesarea Philippi, He posed an *important* question to them.

Jesus: Who do the people say that I am?

[28]They told Him *about the great speculation concerning His identity.*

* 8:26 Some manuscripts omit this portion.

Disciples: Some of them say *You are* John the Baptist,* others say Elijah, while others say one of the prophets *of old.*

Jesus (*pressing the question*): 29And who do you say that I am?

Peter: You are God's Anointed, *the Liberating King.*

Jesus: 30Don't tell anyone. *It is not yet time.*

31And He went on to teach them many things *about Himself:* how the Son of Man would suffer; how He would be rejected by the elders, chief priests, and scribes; how He would be killed; and how, after three days, *God would* raise Him from the dead. 32He said all these things in front of them all, but Peter took Jesus aside to rebuke Him.

Peter represents the best and worst in humanity. One day, Peter drops everything to become a follower of Jesus; the next, he's busy putting his foot in his mouth. Peter is always responding to Jesus, frequently making mistakes, but never drifting far from Jesus' side. In this passage, Peter verbalizes God's word and Satan's temptation—almost in the same breath. Peter thinks he understands who Jesus is, but he still has a lot to learn about what Jesus has come to do.

Jesus (*seeing His disciples surrounding them*): 33Get behind Me, you tempter! You're thinking only of human things, not of the things God has planned.

34He gathered the crowd and His disciples alike.

Jesus: If any one of you wants to follow Me, you will have to give yourself up to God's plan, take up your cross, and do as I do. 35For any one of you who wants to be rescued will lose your life, but any one of you who loses your life for My sake and for the sake of this good news will be liberated. 36Really, what profit is there for you to gain

the whole world and lose yourself *in the process?* 37What can you give in exchange for your life? 38If you are ashamed of Me and of what I came to teach to this adulterous and sinful generation, then the Son of Man will be ashamed of you when He comes in the glory of His Father along with the holy messengers *at the final judgment.*

9 Jesus: Truly, some of you who are here now will not experience death before you see the kingdom of God coming in *glory and* power.

2Six days after saying this, Jesus took Peter, James, and John and led them up onto a high mountaintop by themselves. There He was transformed 3so that His clothing became intensely white, brighter than any earthly cleaner could bleach them. 4Elijah and Moses appeared to them and talked with Jesus.

Peter (*to Jesus*): 5Teacher, it's a great thing that we're here. We should build three shelters here: one for You, one for Moses, and one for Elijah.

6He *was babbling and* did not know what he was saying because they were terrified *by what they were witnessing.*
7Then a cloud surrounded them, and they heard a voice within that cloud.

Voice: This is My beloved Son. Listen to Him.

8All of a sudden, they looked about and all they had seen was gone. They stood alone on the mountain with Jesus. 9On their way back down, He urged them not to tell anyone what they had witnessed until the Son of Man had risen from the dead, 10so they kept it all to themselves.

Mark doesn't usually record events with much attention to chronology; but in this case, he mentions that the transfiguration took place six days after Peter's confession of Jesus' identity. In a dramatic confirmation of the truth Peter has spoken, the three disciples see that Jesus is indeed the Anointed One

* 8:28 Literally, John who immersed, to show repentance

of God. The veil of Jesus' human nature is pulled away, and the glory of His divinity shines through.

The appearance of Moses and Elijah shows that Jesus is the fulfillment of the law and the answer to all the promises of the prophets. The disciples hear God's own voice commanding them to listen to Jesus as His beloved Son. What an incredible confirmation of the truth that Peter spoke in faith only six days before!

Disciples (*to one another*): What does He mean, "Until the Son of Man is risen"? [11](*to Jesus*) Master, why do the scribes say that Elijah must come first?

Jesus (*thinking of John the Baptist*): [12]Elijah does come first to restore all things. *They have it right.* But there is something else written in the Scriptures about the Son of Man: He will have to suffer and be rejected. [13]*Here's the truth:* Elijah has come; *his enemies treated him with contempt* and did what they wanted to him, just as it was written.

[14]When they reached the rest of the disciples, Jesus saw that a large crowd had gathered and that among them the scribes were asking questions. [15]Right when the crowd saw Jesus, they were overcome with awe and surged forward immediately, *nearly running over the disciples.*

Jesus (*to the scribes*): [16]What are you debating with My disciples? *What would you like to know?*

Father (*in the crowd*): [17]Teacher, I have brought my son to You. He is filled with an unclean spirit. He cannot speak, [18]and when the spirit takes control of him, he is thrown to the ground *to wail and moan,* to foam at the mouth, to grind his teeth, and to stiffen up. I brought him to Your followers, but they could do nothing with him. *Can You help us?*

Jesus: [19]O faithless generation, how long must I be among you? How long do I have to put up with you? Bring the boy to Me.

[20]They brought the boy toward Jesus; but as soon as He drew near, the spirit took control of the boy and threw him on the ground, where he rolled, foaming at the mouth.

Jesus (*to the father*): [21]How long has he been like this?

Father: Since he was a baby. [22]This spirit has thrown him often into the fire and sometimes into the water, trying to destroy him. *I have run out of options; I have tried everything.* But if there's anything You can do, please, have pity on us and help us.

Jesus: [23]*What do you mean,* "If there's anything?" All things are possible, if you only believe.

Father (*crying in desperation*): [24]I believe, Lord. Help me to believe!

[25]Jesus noticed that a crowd had gathered around them now. He issued a command to the unclean spirit.

Jesus: Listen up, you no-talking, no-hearing demon. I Myself am ordering you to come out of him now. Come out, and don't ever come back!

[26]The spirit shrieked and caused the boy to thrash about; then it came out of the boy and left him lying as still as death. Many of those in the crowd whispered that he was dead. [27]But Jesus took the boy by the hand and lifted him to his feet.

[28]Later He and His disciples gathered privately in a house.

Disciples (*to Jesus*): Why couldn't we cast out that unclean spirit?

Jesus: [29]That sort *of powerful spirit* can only be conquered with much prayer [and fasting].*

V

The father has enough faith to bring his son to Jesus for healing, but he asks hesitantly whether there is anything Jesus can do. In his desperation, the father recognizes the limits of his faith. Perhaps that very desperation is enough because Jesus immediately heals his son.

* 9:29 The earliest manuscripts omit this portion.

Having successfully healed many demon-possessed people when Jesus sent them out earlier, the disciples are at a loss to know why they are completely unable to heal this little boy. Jesus' reply is cryptic and surprising: "That sort *of powerful spirit* is only conquered with much prayer [and fasting]." It seems that although the disciples have faith that they can heal the boy, they are spiritually unprepared for the depth of evil residing in the world. They need to be saturated in the presence of God to face the challenge.

³⁰When they left that place, they passed secretly through Galilee.

Jesus *(to the disciples as they traveled)*: ³¹The Son of Man will be delivered into the hands of the people, and they will kill Him. And after He is killed, He will rise on the third day.

³²But again they did not understand His meaning, and they were afraid to ask Him *for an explanation.*

³³At last, they came to Capernaum where they gathered in a house.

Jesus: What was it I heard you arguing about along the way?

³⁴They *looked down at the floor and* wouldn't answer, for they had been arguing among themselves about who was the greatest *of Jesus' disciples.*

It is only natural for the disciples to wonder which of them will be His right-hand man. Even the three disciples who have just seen Jesus' glory revealed in the transfiguration cannot resist the attraction of honor. After all, who has a better claim than they do to being the greatest of Jesus' disciples?

Fortunately Jesus overhears what is said and is quick to respond in mercy to correct their mistake. Greatness in His eyes doesn't consist of seeing wonders or performing miracles or even fasting and praying. Instead, greatness is about humility and service. These are the heart of the kingdom of heaven.

³⁵He sat down with the twelve to teach them.

Jesus: Whoever wants to be first must be last, and *whoever wants to be the greatest* must be the servant of all.

³⁶He then called forward a child, set the child in the middle of them, and took the child in His arms.

Jesus: ³⁷Whoever welcomes a child like this in My name welcomes Me; and whoever welcomes Me is welcoming not Me, but the One who sent Me.

John *(to Jesus)*: ³⁸Master, we saw another man casting out unclean spirits in Your name, but he was not one of our group. So we told him to stop what he was doing.

Jesus: ³⁹You shouldn't have said that. Anyone using My name to do a miracle cannot turn quickly to speak evil of Me. ⁴⁰Anyone who isn't against us is for us. ⁴¹The truth of the matter is this: anyone who gives you a cup of *cool* water to drink because you carry the name of your Anointed One will be rewarded.

⁴²But if anyone turns even the smallest of My followers away from Me, it would be better for him if someone had hung a millstone around his neck and flung him into the deepest part of the sea.

⁴³If your hand turns you away from the things of God, then you should cut it off. It's better to come into *eternal* life maimed than to have two hands and be flung into hell—[⁴⁴where the worm will not die and the fire will not be smothered.]*

⁴⁵If your foot trips you on the path, you should cut it off. It's better to come into *eternal* life crawling than to have two feet and be flung into hell—[⁴⁶where the worm will not die and the fire will not be smothered.]*

* 9:44 The earliest manuscripts omit verse 44, a quote from Isaiah 66:24. * 9:46 The earliest manuscripts omit verse 46, a quote from Isaiah 66:24.

47And if your eye keeps you from seeing clearly, then you should pull it out. It's better to come into the kingdom of God with one eye than to have two eyes and be flung into hell, 48where the worm will not die and the fire will not be smothered.* 49Everyone will be salted with fire[, and every sacrifice will be seasoned with salt].* 50Salt is a good thing; but if it has lost its zest, how can it be seasoned again? You should have salt within yourselves and peace with one another.

10 From there Jesus traveled to Judea and beyond the Jordan River; He taught the crowds who gathered as was His custom.

2Some Pharisees came to Him to test Him on His adherence to the law of Moses.

Pharisees: Is it lawful for a husband to divorce his wife?

Jesus: 3What did Moses say to you?

Pharisees: 4Moses permitted us to write a certificate of dismissal and divorce her.*

Jesus: 5Moses gave you this law as a concession because of the hardness of your hearts. 6But truly, God created humans male and female in the beginning.* 7As it is written in the Hebrew Scriptures, "For this reason, a man will leave his father and mother [to marry his wife],* 8and the two of them will become one flesh and blood."* So they are no longer two people, but one. 9What God has joined together in this way, no one may sever.

10In the privacy of their dwelling that evening, the disciples asked Him about this teaching, 11and He went even further.

Jesus: If any husband divorces his wife and then marries another woman, he commits adultery against her. 12And if a wife should divorce her husband and marry another, then she commits adultery against him.

The Pharisees hope to trip Jesus. Instead of taking a side, Jesus goes to the purpose and meaning of marriage: not just from a social but a spiritual perspective.

13When the crowd gathered again, the people brought their children to see Jesus, hoping that He might grant them His blessing through His touch.

His disciples turned them all away; 14but when Jesus saw this, He was incensed.

Jesus (to the disciples): Let the children come to Me, and don't ever stand in their way, for this is what the kingdom of God is all about. 15Truly anyone who doesn't accept the kingdom of God as a little child does can never enter it.

16Jesus gathered the children in His arms, and He laid His hands on them to bless them.

17When He had traveled on, a young man came and knelt in the dust of the road in front of Jesus.

Young Man: Good Teacher! What must I do to gain life in the world to come?

Jesus: 18You are calling Me good? Don't you know that God and God alone is good? 19Anyway, why ask Me that question? You know the Commandments of Moses: "Do not murder, do not commit adultery, do not steal, do not slander, do not defraud, and honor your father and mother."*

Young Man: 20Yes, Teacher, I have done all these since I was a child.

21Then Jesus, looking at the young man, saw that he was sincere and responded out of His love for him.

Jesus: Son, there is still one thing you have not done. Go now. Sell everything you have and give the proceeds to the poor so that you will have treasure in heaven. After that, come, follow Me.

22The young man went away sick at heart at these words because he was very wealthy, 23and Jesus looked around to see if His disciples were understanding His teaching.

Jesus (to His disciples): Oh, it is hard for people with wealth to find their way into God's kingdom!

Disciples (amazed): 24What?

* 9:48 Isaiah 66:24   * 9:49 Some of the earliest manuscripts omit this portion.   * 10:4 Deuteronomy 24:1   * 10:6 Genesis 1:27; 5:2; the Hebrew name for the Book of Genesis is "In the beginning."   * 10:7 Some of the earliest manuscripts omit this portion.   * 10:7-8 Genesis 2:24   * 10:19 Exodus 20:12-16; Deuteronomy 5:16-20

Jesus: *You heard Me.* How hard it is to enter the kingdom of God [for those who trust in their wealth]!* ²⁵I think you'll see camels squeezing through the eye of a needle before you'll see the rich *celebrating and dancing as they* enter into *the joy of* God's kingdom!

²⁶The disciples looked around at each other, whispering.

Disciples *(aloud to Jesus)*: Then who can be liberated?

Jesus *(smiling and shaking His head)*: ²⁷For human beings it is impossible, but not for God: God makes everything possible.

Peter: ²⁸Master, we have left behind everything we had to follow You.

Jesus: ²⁹That is true. And those who have left their houses, their lands, their parents, or their families for My sake, and for the sake of this good news ³⁰will receive all of this 100 times greater than they have in this time—houses and farms and brothers, sisters, mothers, and children, along with persecutions—and in the world to come, they will receive eternal life. ³¹But many of those who are first *in this world* shall be last *in the world to come,* and the last, first.

This young man, like many wealthy people, is confident in his own abilities. He wants to make sure he will live well in the coming world, but he is not convinced he will not fall short of the mark. And without humbly recognizing his own sinfulness and need in the face of God's goodness and perfection, it is indeed very hard for him to find the Kingdom.

This is the only person in the Gospels outside of the twelve whom Jesus personally invites to follow Him. He is also the only person in the Gospels to walk away from that invitation.

---

³²At length, they made their way toward Jerusalem. Jesus was walking ahead of them. As they neared the city, wonder and amazement filled them. But soon those who were following began to tremble.

Jesus *(taking the twelve aside)*: ³³Look, we are going up to Jerusalem, and there the Son of Man is going to be delivered to the chief priests and the scribes. They shall seek His death and deliver Him to the outsiders *to carry out that sentence.* ³⁴Then people will mock Him, spit upon Him, whip Him, and kill Him. But on the third day, He will rise again.

³⁵Two of the twelve—the sons of Zebedee *as they were known*—approached Jesus and pulled Him aside.

James and John: Teacher, will You do something for us if we ask it of You?

Jesus: ³⁶What is it that you want?

James and John: ³⁷*Master,* grant that we might sit on either side of You, one at Your right hand and one at Your left, when You come into the glory *of Your kingdom.*

Jesus: ³⁸You don't know what it is you're asking. Can you drink from the cup I have to drink from or be ritually washed in baptism with the baptism* that awaits Me?

James and John: ³⁹We can.

Jesus: You will indeed drink from the cup I drink from and be baptized with the baptism* that awaits Me. ⁴⁰But to sit at My right or at My left is an honor I cannot grant. That will be given to those for whom it has been prepared.

⁴¹When the other ten heard about this request, they were angry with James and John; ⁴²but Jesus stopped them.

Jesus: You know that among the nations of the world the great ones lord it over the little people and act like tyrants. ⁴³But that is not the way it will be among you. Whoever would be great among you must serve and minister. ⁴⁴Whoever wants to be great among you must be slave of all. ⁴⁵Even the Son of Man came not to be served but to be a servant—to offer His life as a ransom for others.

---

* 10:24 Some manuscripts omit this portion.   * 10:38 Literally, immersion   * 10:39 Literally, be immersed with the immersion

V

None of the disciples understand what Jesus is telling them, and none of His predictions will become clear to them until after His resurrection. In the meantime, several of His disciples are not only failing to understand His warnings about the things to come but are missing His message on things right before their eyes. Jesus has already told them that to be great among His followers means to become humble like a child; but James and John still think that as two of His closest disciples, they can win worldly fame and power.

⁴⁶*By that time,* they had reached Jericho; as they passed through the town, a crowd of people followed along. They came to a blind beggar, Bartimaeus, the son of Timaeus, who sat beside the *main* road. ⁴⁷When he was told that Jesus of Nazareth was passing in that throng, he called out in a loud voice.

Bartimaeus: Jesus, Son of David, take pity on me and help me!

Disgusted by the blind man's public display, others in the crowd tried to silence him *until the Master passed.*

Some of the Crowd: ⁴⁸Be quiet. Shush.

Bartimaeus (*still louder*): Jesus, Son of David, have pity on me!

⁴⁹Jesus stopped where He stood. *The crowd stopped with Him.* He told those *near the front of the crowd* to call the blind man forward.

Some of the Crowd (*to Bartimaeus*): Good news! *Jesus has heard you. Listen*—He calls for you. Get up *and go to Him.*

⁵⁰Bartimaeus cast aside his *beggar's* robe and stepped forward, *feeling his way* toward Jesus.

Jesus: ⁵¹What do you want from Me?

Bartimaeus: Teacher, I want to see.

Jesus: ⁵²Your faith has made you whole. Go in peace.

In that moment, Bartimaeus could see again; and from that time on, he followed Jesus.

V

Few people in the Gospels show as much persistence and eagerness in their desire to be healed as blind Bartimaeus. He is not about to be swayed from his efforts to attract Jesus' attention. The discouragement from everyone around him only makes him shout louder, determined to get the attention of the healer he has heard about.

The blind man's actions demonstrate his faith. Beggars in first-century Palestine would spread a cloak on the ground in front of them to collect donations from compassionate passersby. It probably isn't much, but for Bartimaeus, his cloak is all he has. He throws it aside without a thought—probably along with the coins he collected that day—because he is certain that once he meets Jesus, he will not need to be a beggar anymore.

11 When they had gotten close to Jerusalem, near the two villages of Bethphage and Bethany and the Mount of Olives, Jesus sent two of His followers *ahead of them.*

Jesus: ²Go to that village over there. As soon as you get into the town, you'll see a young colt tied that nobody has ever ridden. Untie it and bring it back *to Me.* ³If anybody *stops you and* asks what you're doing, just say, "The Lord needs it, and He will send it back right after He's done."

⁴*Everything happened just as Jesus had told them.* They found the colt in the street tied near a door, and they untied it.

Bystanders: ⁵What are you doing?

⁶They answered as Jesus had instructed and were allowed to take it, ⁷so they brought the colt back to Jesus, piled garments on its back *to make a comfortable seat,* and Jesus rode

the animal *toward Jerusalem*. [8]*As they traveled*, people cast their cloaks onto the road and spread out leafy branches, which they had brought from the fields *along the way*. [9]People walked ahead of them, and others followed behind.

People (*shouting*): Hosanna! *Rescue us now, Lord!* Hosanna!

> Blessed be the One who comes in the
>   name of the Eternal One!*
> [10]And blessed is the kingdom of our father
>   David, which draws closer *to us
>   today*!
> Hosanna in the highest heavens!

V

Jesus enters Jerusalem, but this time He radically redefines the people's every expectation. His descriptions to His disciples of where they will find the colt He is to ride and how they shall get it has an air of prophecy and supernatural knowledge. He rides a donkey instead of being carried into town on the backs of servants (in a litter as a conquering king would do), fulfilling the prophecy that the King will come riding a donkey (Zechariah 9:9). After all, donkeys are a poor man's mount, and even in this triumphal entry, Jesus makes it clear He does not intend to conquer and rule in a worldly way. Now, for the first time, He allows the crowds to voice their excitement about who He is and all that He has been doing.

[11]*To the sound of this chanting*, Jesus rode through the gates of Jerusalem and up to the temple. He looked around and saw that evening was coming, so He and the twelve went back to Bethany *to spend the night*. [12]The next morning, when they departed Bethany *and were traveling back to the city*, Jesus was hungry. [13]Off in the distance, He saw a fig tree fully leafed out, so He headed toward it to see if it might have any ripe fruit. But when He reached it, He found only leaves because the fig season had not yet come. [14]As the disciples listened, *Jesus pronounced a curse on the tree*.

Jesus: No one will ever eat fruit from your branches again.

V

This is the only time recorded in the Gospels when Jesus uses His supernatural power to destroy. The tree is "fully leafed out"—a stage that usually comes after figs are ripe and not before. Because the tree looks as though it ought to have fruit but doesn't, it is a perfect illustration of people who believe they have the good fruit of righteousness even though their actions are void of true compassion and love, as empty and useless as leaves. And so Jesus curses the fig tree, not out of anger with the tree itself, but as a warning to hypocrites who think their appearance is more important than the fruit of their actions.

[15]They continued into Jerusalem *and made their way up to the temple*.

Upon reaching the temple *that morning*, Jesus dealt with those who were selling and buying *animals for sacrifices* and drove them out of the area. He turned over the tables of those who exchanged money *for the temple pilgrims* and the seats of those selling birds, [16]and He *physically* prevented anyone from carrying anything through the temple.

Jesus (*to those who were listening*): [17]Didn't the prophets write, "My house will be called a house of prayer, for all the people"*? But you have made it into a "haven for thieves."*

V

At the temple, Jesus responds in shock to the scene before Him. He acts decisively and with great emotion against those who have turned God's house into a place where pilgrims are exploited. He has a message and, like the prophets of old, this message is better seen than heard. Because the temple leadership has allowed

* 11:9 Psalm 118:26   * 11:17 Isaiah 56:7   * 11:17 Jeremiah 7:11

profiteers and merchants to set up shop in the court of the Gentiles, they are making ridiculous profits. For the people who come long distances to worship, it is a normal practice to have merchants selling animals for the pilgrims to sacrifice. What is not normal and what is immoral is where and how they transact business. Jesus takes issue with robbers profiteering in His Father's house.

---

[18]The chief priests and the scribes heard these words *and knew Jesus was referring to them,* so they plotted His destruction. They had grown afraid of Him because His teachings struck the crowds into astonishment.

[19]When evening came, [Jesus and His followers]* left the city again. [20]The next morning *on the way back to Jerusalem,* they passed a tree that had withered down to its very roots.

Peter (*remembering*): [21]That's the fig tree, Teacher, the one You cursed *just yesterday morning.* It's withered away *to nothing*!

Jesus: [22]Trust in God. [23]*If you do,* honestly, you can say to this mountain, "Mountain, uproot yourself and throw yourself into the sea." If you don't doubt, but trust that what you say will take place, then it will happen. [24]So listen to what I'm saying: Whatever you pray for or ask *from God,* believe that you'll receive it and you will. [25]When you pray, if you remember anyone who has wronged you, forgive him so that God above can also forgive you. [[26]If you don't forgive others, don't expect God's forgiveness.]*

[27]As they arrived in Jerusalem and were walking in the temple, the chief priests, scribes, and elders came to Jesus [28]and asked Him a question.

Leaders: Tell us, who has given You the authority to say and do the things You're saying and doing?

Jesus: [29]I will answer your question, if you will answer one for Me. Only then will I tell you who gives Me authority to do these things. [30]Tell Me, when John was ritually

cleansing through baptism *for the forgiveness of sins,* was his authority from heaven or was it merely human?

[31]The priests, scribes, and elders huddled together to think through an answer.

Leaders (*to themselves*): If we say, "It must have been from heaven," *then Jesus will have us.* He'll ask, "Then why didn't you listen to him and follow him?" [32]But if we say, "John's cleansing was only human," the people will be up in arms because they think John was a prophet *sent by God.* [33](responding to Jesus) We don't know what to tell You.

Jesus: *All right,* then don't expect Me to tell you where I get the authority to say and do these things.

V

The religious leaders ask Jesus where His authority comes from. What gives Him the right to heal people on the Sabbath, teach about God, do miracles, and cast out demons? Who exactly does He think He is—and where does His authority come from? This question is a trap: if He claims His authority is from God, then they can argue that God does not endorse someone who breaks His laws; but if He says His authority is His own, then He will be in trouble with the crowds and perhaps even with the Roman governor.

Jesus, however, issues a challenge: I'll tell you what you want to know if you'll answer My question first. But He asks them an impossible question—impossible not because they don't know the answer, but because they cannot say the answer.

---

12 Then He told a story.

Jesus: There was a man who established a vineyard. He put up a wall around it to fence it in; he dug a pit for a

---

* 11:19 Some of the earliest manuscripts read "He." * 11:26 Some of the earliest manuscripts omit verse 26.

winepress; he built a watchtower. *When he had finished this work,* he leased the vineyard to some tenant farmers and went away to a distant land.

²When the grapes were in season, he sent a slave to the vineyard to collect *his rent*—his share of the fruit. ³But the farmers grabbed the slave, beat him, and sent him back to his master empty-handed. ⁴The owner sent another slave, and this slave the farmers beat over the head and sent away dishonored. ⁵A third slave, the farmers killed. This went on for some time, with the farmers beating some of the messengers and killing others *until the owner had lost all patience.* ⁶He had a son whom he loved above all things, and he said to himself, *"When these thugs see my son, they'll know he carries my authority.* They'll have to respect him."

⁷*But when the tenant farmers saw the owner's son coming,* they said among themselves, "Look at this! It's the son, the heir to this vineyard. If we kill him, then the land will be ours!" ⁸So they seized him and killed him and threw him out of the vineyard.

⁹Now what do you suppose the owner will do *when he hears of this?* He'll come and destroy these farmers, and he'll give the land to others.

¹⁰Haven't you read the Scriptures? *As the psalmist says,*

The stone that the builders rejected
    has become the very stone that
        holds together the entire
            foundation.
¹¹This is the work of the Eternal One,
    and it is marvelous in our eyes.*

¹²The priests, scribes, temple leaders, and elders knew the story was directed against them. They couldn't figure out how to lay their hands on Jesus then because they were afraid the people *would rise up against them.* So they left Him alone, and they went away *furious.*

The leaders are stunned to learn they will face judgment themselves. It goes against everything they believe about themselves and about God.

¹³Then some Pharisees and some of Herod's supporters banded together to try to entrap Jesus. ¹⁴They came to Him and complimented Him.

Pharisees: Teacher, we know You are truthful *in what You say* and that You don't play favorites. You're not worried about what anyone thinks of You, so You teach with total honesty what God would have us do. *So tell us:* is it lawful that we Jews should pay taxes to the Roman emperor or not? ¹⁵Should we give or not?

Jesus *(seeing through their ruse):* Why do you test Me like this? Listen, bring Me a coin* so that I can take a look at it.

¹⁶When they had brought it to Him, He asked them another question.

Jesus: *Tell Me,* whose picture is on this coin? And of whom does this inscription speak?

Pharisees: Caesar, of course.

Jesus: ¹⁷Then give to the emperor what belongs to the emperor. And give to God what belongs to God.

They could not think of anything to say to His response.

Jesus turns the question back on them. It isn't about taxes. It is about knowing and being faithful to the one true God.

¹⁸Later a group of Sadducees, *Jewish religious leaders* who didn't believe the dead would be resurrected, came to test Jesus.

Sadducees: ¹⁹Teacher, the law of Moses tells us, "If a man's brother dies, leaving a widow without sons, then the man should marry his sister-in-law and *try to* have children with her in his brother's name."*

²⁰Now here's the situation: there were seven brothers. The oldest took a wife and left her a widow with no children. ²¹So the next oldest married her, left her a widow, and again there were no children. So the next brother married her and died, and the next, *and the next.* ²²Finally all seven brothers had married her, but none of them had conceived children with her, and at last she died also.

* 12:10-11 Psalm 118:22-23 * 12:15 Literally, denarius, a Roman coin * 12:19 Deuteronomy 25:5

[23]Tell us then, in the resurrection [when humans rise from the dead],* whose wife will she be? For all seven of them married her.

Jesus: [24]You can't see the truth because you don't know the Scriptures well and because you don't really believe that God is powerful. [25]The answer is this: when the dead rise, they won't be married or given in marriage. They'll be like the messengers in heaven, *who are not united with one another in marriage.* [26]But how can you fail to see the truth of resurrection? Don't you remember in the Book of Moses how God talked to Moses out of a burning bush and what God said to him then? "I am the God of Abraham, the God of Isaac, and the God of Jacob."* *"I am," God said. Not "I was."* [27]So God is not the God of the dead but of the living. You are sadly mistaken.

[28]One of the scribes *who studied and copied the Hebrew Scriptures* overheard this conversation and was impressed by the way Jesus had answered.

Scribe: Tell me, Teacher. What is the most important thing that God commands *in the law?*

Jesus: [29]The most important commandment is this: "Hear, O Israel, the Eternal One is our God, and the Eternal One is the only God. [30]You should love the Eternal, your God, with all your heart, with all your soul, with all your mind, and with all your strength."* [31]The second *great commandment* is this: "Love others in the same way you love yourself."* There are no commandments more important than these.

V

Although Jesus is asked for only the single most important commandment, He answers by naming two commands: love God and love others. He includes both because these two teachings can never be really separated from each other. Some people think they can love God and ignore the people around them, but Jesus frequently makes it clear that loving God apart from loving His people is impossible.

Scribe: [32]Teacher, You have spoken the truth. For there is one God and only one God, [33]and to love God with all our heart and soul and mind and strength and to love our neighbors as ourselves are more important than any burnt offering or sacrifice *we could ever give.*

[34]Jesus heard that the man had spoken with wisdom.

Jesus: *Well said; if you understand that,* then the kingdom of God is closer than you think.

Nobody asked Jesus any more questions after that.

[35]Later Jesus was teaching in the temple.

Jesus: Why do the scribes say that the Anointed One is the son of David? [36]*In the psalms,* David himself was led by the Holy Spirit to sing,

The Master said to my master,
"Sit at My right hand,
in the place of power and honor,
And I will gather Your enemies together,
lead them in on hands and knees,
and You will rest Your feet on their backs."*

[37]If David calls Him "Master," how can He be his son?

The crowd listened to Him with delight.

Jesus: [38]Watch out for the scribes *who act so religious*—who like to be seen in pious clothes and to be spoken to respectfully in the marketplace, [39]who take the best seats in the synagogues and the place of honor at every dinner, [40]who spend widows' inheritances and pray long prayers to impress others. These are the kind of people who will be condemned above all others.

[41]Jesus sat down opposite the treasury, where people came to bring their offerings, and He watched as they came and went. Many rich people threw in large sums of money, [42]but a poor widow came and put in only two small coins* worth only a fraction of a cent.*

---

* 12:23 Some manuscripts omit this portion. * 12:26 Exodus 3:6,15
* 12:30 Deuteronomy 6:4-5 * 12:31 Leviticus 19:18 * 12:36 Psalm 110:1 * 12:42 Literally lepta, a Roman coin worth an insignificant amount * 12:42 Literally, kodrantes, a Roman penny

Jesus *(calling His disciples together)*: ⁴³Truly this widow has given a greater gift than any other contribution. ⁴⁴All the others gave a little out of their great abundance, but this poor woman has given God everything she has.

13 As Jesus left the temple *later that day,* one of the disciples noticed *the grandeur of Herod's temple.*

Disciple: Teacher, I can't believe the size of these stones! Look at these magnificent buildings!

Jesus: ²Look closely at these magnificent buildings. *Someday* there won't be one of these great stones left on another. Everything will be thrown down.

³They took a seat on the Mount of Olives, across *the valley* from the temple; and Peter, James, John, and Andrew asked Jesus to explain His statement to them privately.

Peter, James, John, and Andrew: ⁴Don't keep us in the dark. When will the temple be destroyed? What sign will let us know that it's about to happen?

Jesus: ⁵Take care that no one deceives you. ⁶Many will come claiming to be Mine, saying, "I am the One," and they will fool lots of people. ⁷You will hear of wars, or that war is coming, but don't lose heart. These things will have to happen, although it won't mean the end yet. ⁸Tribe will rise up against tribe, nation against nation, and there will be earthquakes in place after place and famines. These are a prelude to "labor pains" *that precede the temple's fall.*

⁹Be careful, because you will be delivered to trial and beaten in the places of worship. Kings and governors will stand in judgment over you as you speak in My name. ¹⁰The good news *of the coming kingdom of God* must be delivered first in every land and every language. ¹¹When people bring you up on charges and it is your time to defend yourself, don't worry about what message you'll deliver. Whatever comes to your mind, speak it, because the Holy Spirit will inspire it.

¹²*But it will get worse.* Brothers will betray each other to death, and fathers will betray their children. Children will turn against their parents and cause them to be executed. ¹³Everyone will hate you because of your allegiance to Me. But if you're faithful until the end, you will be rescued.

¹⁴You will see that which desecrates our most holy place* [described by Daniel the prophet]* out of place.

Let the one who reads *and hears* understand.

Jesus: On the day you see it, whoever is in Judea should flee for the mountains. ¹⁵The person on the rooftop shouldn't reenter the house to get anything, ¹⁶and the person working in the field shouldn't turn back to grab his coat. ¹⁷It will be horrible for women who are pregnant or who are nursing their children when those days come. ¹⁸And pray that you don't have to run for your lives in the winter. ¹⁹When those days come, there will be suffering like nobody has seen from the beginning of the world that God created until now, and it never will be like this again. ²⁰And if the Lord didn't shorten those days for the sake of the ones He has chosen, then nobody would survive them.

²¹If anyone tells you in those days, "Look, there is the Anointed One!" or "Hey, that must be Him!" don't believe them. ²²False liberators and prophets will pop up *like weeds,* and they will work signs and perform miracles that would entice even God's chosen people, if that were possible. ²³So be alert, and remember how I have warned you.

²⁴⁻²⁵*As Isaiah said* in the days after that great suffering,

The sun will refuse to shine,
    and the moon will hold back its
        light.
The stars in heaven will fall,
    and the powers in the heavens will
        be shaken.*

²⁶Then you will see *(as Daniel predicted)* "the Son of Man coming in the clouds,"* *clothed* in power and majesty. ²⁷And He will send out His heavenly messengers and gather together to Himself those He has chosen from the four corners of the world, from every direction and every land.

* 13:14 Literally abomination of desolation, Daniel 9:27; 11:31; 12:11
* 13:14 The earliest manuscripts omit this portion.   * 13:24-25 Isaiah 13:10; 34:4   * 13:26 Daniel 7:13

The disciples can't help but notice that something is in the air during this week between His entry into Jerusalem and His crucifixion. Surely the moment when Jesus is to reveal Himself as the Anointed can't be far off. By repeatedly calling Himself the Son of Man, Jesus has told people His kingdom will be divinely instituted like the one described in Daniel 7. They are also thinking of promises about the coming Anointed One. But for Jesus, everything now is connected to His imminent death and resurrection. Even as He predicts the temple's fall—an event that will occur about 40 years later—and speaks of His second coming, He is still thinking about His death. After all, resurrection can't happen without death. And the old world must die before the world is made new.

Jesus: 28Learn this lesson from the fig tree: When its branch is new and tender and begins to put forth leaves, you know that summer must be near. 29In the same way, when you see *and hear* the things I've described to you taking place, you'll know the time is drawing near. 30It's true—this generation will not pass away before all these things have happened. 31Heaven and earth may pass away, but these words of Mine will never pass away.

32*Take heed:* no one knows the day or hour when the end is coming. The messengers in heaven don't know, nor does the Son. Only the Father knows.

33So be alert. Watch for it [and pray,]* for you never know when that time might approach.

34This situation is like a man who went on a journey; when he departed, he left his servants in charge of the house. Each of them had his own job to do; and the man left the porter to stand at the door, watching. 35So stay awake, because no one knows when the master of the house is coming back. It could be in the evening or at midnight or when the rooster crows or in the morning. 36*Stay awake;* be alert so that when he suddenly returns, the master won't find you sleeping.

37The teaching I am giving *the four of you* now is for everyone *who will follow Me:* stay awake, *and keep your eyes open.*

V

Later Christians will try to use this chapter to predict exactly when Jesus will come and how the world will end. But to do that is to do exactly the opposite of what Jesus intends as He speaks these words. He makes it very clear that He doesn't want anyone to use this description of signs to predict an exact time and date for His coming; even He Himself doesn't know that time and date, and no one else needs to know either. Instead, the purpose is to warn them to stay ready and alert.

14 The Passover and the Feast of Unleavened Bread were two days away. *The Jewish leaders*—the chief priests and the scribes—gathered to discuss how they might secretly arrest Jesus and kill Him.

Jewish Leaders: 2We can't do it during the festivals. It might create an uproar.

3While Jesus was eating dinner in Bethany at the house of Simon the leper, a woman came into the house carrying an alabaster flask filled with a precious, sweet-smelling ointment made from spikenard. She came to Jesus, broke the jar, and gently poured out the perfume onto His head. 4Some of those around the table were troubled by this and grumbled to each other.

Dinner Guests: Why did she waste this precious ointment? 5We could have sold this ointment for almost a year's wages,* and the money could have gone to the poor!

Their *private concerns* turned to public criticism against her.

Jesus: 6Leave her alone. Why are you attacking her? She has done a good thing. 7The poor will always be with you, and you

---

* 13:33 Some manuscripts omit this portion.   * 14:5 Literally, more than 300 denarii, Roman coins

can show kindness to them whenever you want. But I won't always be with you. [8]She has done what she could for Me—she has come to anoint My body and prepare it for burial. [9]Believe Me when I tell you that this act of hers will be told in her honor as long as there are people who tell the good news.

> The disciples can't see any value in pouring so much perfume on Jesus. It is obviously a waste. The woman is demonstrating her love for Him with an abandon and an emotional commitment that few people have ever shown, and He appreciates her love and her faith. To Him, it is more than a gesture; it is a practical preparation for His imminent death and burial. No one else there can see what use her action is; but to Jesus, it is incredibly precious—so much so that He promises to make sure her action is never forgotten.

[10]It was after this that Judas Iscariot, one of the twelve, went to meet the chief priests with the intention of betraying Jesus to them. [11]When they heard what he proposed, they were delighted and promised him money. So from that time on, Judas *thought and waited and* sought an opportunity to betray Jesus.

[12]On the first day of the Feast of Unleavened Bread, the customary day when the Passover lamb is sacrificed, His disciples wondered *where they would celebrate the feast.*

Disciples: Where do You want us to go and make preparations for You to eat the Passover meal?

[13]So *again* He sent two of His disciples ahead and told them to watch for a man carrying a jar of water.

Jesus: Follow that man; [14]and wherever he goes in, say to the owner of the house, "The Teacher asks, 'Where is the guest room where I can eat the Passover meal with My disciples?'" [15]He will take you upstairs and show you a large room furnished and ready. Make our preparations there.

[16]So the two left and went into the city. All was as Jesus had told them, and they prepared the meal in the upper room. [17]That evening Jesus and the twelve arrived *and went into the upper room;* [18]and each reclined around the table, *leaning upon an elbow* as he ate.

Jesus: I tell you in absolute sincerity, one of you eating with Me tonight is going to betray Me.

[19]The twelve were upset. *They looked around at each other.*

Disciples (one by one): Lord, it's not I, is it?

Jesus: [20]It is one of you, the twelve—one of you who is dipping your bread in the same dish that I am. [21]The Son of Man goes *to His fate.* That has already been predicted in the Scriptures. But still, it will be terrible for the one who betrays Him. It would have been better for him if he had never been born.

[22]As they ate, Jesus took bread, offered a blessing, and broke it. He handed the pieces to His disciples.

Jesus: Take this [and eat it].* This is My body.

[23]He took a cup *of wine;* and when He had given thanks *for it,* He passed it to them, and they all drank from it.

Jesus: [24]This is My blood, a covenant* poured out on behalf of many. [25]Truly I will never taste the fruit of the vine again until the day when I drink it new in the kingdom of God.

> This moment has been commemorated for two thousand years. Exactly what Jesus meant by calling the bread and wine His body and blood has been debated for centuries. By eating the bread and drinking the wine, believers participate not only in this supper but also in His death and resurrection because the bread is torn and the

* 14:22 Some manuscripts omit this portion. * 14:24 Some manuscripts read "the new covenant."

wine is poured, just as His body was torn and His blood poured out.

Just as Jesus' physical body housed the Spirit of God, the physicality of the bread and wine has a spiritual significance. Otherwise, we wouldn't need to eat the bread and drink the wine to celebrate this moment—it would be enough for us to read the story and remember what happened. But we, too, are physical as well as spiritual; and our physical actions can have spiritual importance.

---

²⁶*After the meal,* they sang a psalm and went out *of the city* to the Mount of Olives.

Jesus: ²⁷All of you will desert Me tonight. It was written *by Zechariah,*

I will strike the shepherd,
    and the sheep will scatter.*

²⁸But when I am raised up, I will go ahead of you to Galilee.

Peter (*protesting*): ²⁹It doesn't matter who else turns his back on You. I will never desert You.

Jesus: ³⁰Peter, mark My words. This very night before the cock crows twice, you will have denied Me three times.

Peter (*insisting*): ³¹*No, Teacher.* Even if it means that I have to die with You, I'll never deny You.

All the other disciples said similar things.
    ³²They came *at length* to a garden called Gethsemane.

Jesus: Stay here. I'm going *a little farther* to pray *and to think.*

³³He took Peter, James, and John with Him; *and as they left the larger group behind,* He became distressed and filled with sorrow.

Jesus: ³⁴My heart is so heavy; I feel as if I could die. Wait here for Me, and *stay awake to* keep watch.

³⁵He walked on a little farther. Then He threw Himself on the ground and prayed for deliverance from what was about to come.

Jesus: ³⁶Abba, Father, I know that anything is possible for You. Please take this cup away so I don't have to drink from it. But whatever happens, let Your will be done—not Mine.

³⁷He got up, went back *to the three,* and found them sleeping.

Jesus (*waking Peter*): Simon, are you sleeping? Couldn't you wait with Me for just an hour? ³⁸Stay awake, and pray that you aren't led into a trial of your own. *It's true*—even when the spirit is willing, the body can betray it.

³⁹He went away again, and prayed again the same prayer as before—*pleading with God but surrendering to His will.*
    ⁴⁰He came back and found the three asleep; *and when He woke them,* they didn't know what to say to Him.
    ⁴¹After He had gone away and prayed for a third time, *He returned to find them slumbering.*

Jesus: Again? Still sleeping and getting a good rest? Well, that's enough sleep. The time has come; the Son of Man is betrayed into the hands of sinners. ⁴²Get up now, and let's go. The one who is going to betray Me is close by.

V

In the moments before Jesus' death, He really knows what it feels like to be human and afraid. Jesus knows exactly what is about to happen to Him and exactly how bad it will be. Now that the time has come, He feels all the natural human emotions.

Most amazing of all is the prayer Jesus says in that moment: "Please take this cup away so I don't have to drink from it." Even though He divinely knows what is going to happen—what must happen—He still asks for a reprieve. At the same time, He submits His human desires and will to the plan of His Father: in order to experience fully what it means to be human, He has to go through even this—denying Himself and what

* 14:27 Zechariah 13:7

He wants—to face certain torture and death.

43Before He had finished talking, Judas (one of the twelve) approached with a large group of people—agents of the chief priests, scribes, and elders in Jerusalem armed with swords and clubs.

44The signal they had arranged *was a kiss.* "Watch to see whom I kiss; He's the One," Judas had told them. "Arrest Him, and take Him into secure custody."

45As soon as they arrived, Judas stepped forward.

Judas *(kissing Jesus)*: My Teacher.*

46*Immediately* the soldiers grabbed Jesus and took Him into custody.

47Now one *of the disciples* standing close by drew his sword and swung, cutting off the ear of a slave of *Caiaphas, the high priest.*

Jesus *(calling out)*: 48Am I a thief or a bandit that you have to come armed with swords and clubs to capture Me? 49I sat teaching in the temple every day with you. You could have taken Me at any time, but you never did. Let the Scriptures be fulfilled.

50*When they saw the armed crowd take Jesus into custody,* the disciples fled. 51One of those following Jesus was a young man who was wearing nothing but a linen cloth. When people from the mob grabbed for him, 52*he wriggled out of their grasp,* left them holding the cloth, and ran naked *into the night.*

53They led Jesus off to see the high priest, *who had gathered a council of religious and civic leaders,* scribes, chief priests, and elders *to hear the evidence and render some decision regarding Jesus.* 54Peter followed, at a safe distance, all the way into the courtyard of the high priest, and he sat down with the guards to warm himself at their fire. *He hoped no one would notice.*

55The chief priests and other religious leaders called for witnesses against Jesus so they could execute Him, but things didn't turn out the way they had planned. 56There were plenty of people willing to get up and accuse Jesus falsely, *distorting what Jesus had said or done*; but their testimonies disagreed with each other, *and the leaders were left with nothing.* 57Some gave the following distorted testimony:

Witnesses: 58We heard Him say, "I will destroy this temple that has been made by human hands, and in three days, I will build another that is not made by human hands."

59But even here the witnesses could not agree on exactly what He had said.

60The high priest stood up and turned to Jesus.

High Priest: Do You have anything to say *in Your own defense?* What do You think of what all these people have said about You?

61But Jesus *held His peace and* didn't say a word.

Jesus, God's Anointed, the Liberating King, has come not as a conquering king but as a sacrificial lamb who will die without defending Himself.

He is accused of setting Himself in the place of God, but He is innocent of that accusation because He is God. He does not defend Himself because His death protects from punishment the sinners who have made themselves like God ever since Adam ate the fruit in the garden.

High Priest: Are You God's Anointed, *the Liberating King,* the Son of the Blessed One?

Jesus: 62I am. *One day* you will see the Son of Man "sitting at His right hand, *in the place of honor and* power,"* and "coming in the clouds of heaven."*

63Then the high priest tore his clothes.

High Priest *(to the council)*: What else do we need to hear? 64You have heard the blasphemy from His own lips. What do you have to say about that?

The verdict was unanimous—Jesus was guilty of a capital crime.

65*So the people began to humiliate Him.*

* 14:45 Literally, Rabbi   * 14:62 Psalm 110:1   * 14:62 Daniel 7:13

Some even spat upon Him. Then He was blindfolded, and they slapped and punched Him.

People: *Come on, Prophet*, prophesy for us! *Tell us who just hit You.*

Then the guards took Him, beating Him as they did so.
⁶⁶⁻⁶⁷While Peter was waiting by the fire outside, one of the servant girls of the high priest saw him.

Servant Girl: You were one of those men with Jesus of Nazareth.

Peter: ⁶⁸Woman, I don't know what you're talking about.

He left the fire, and as he went out into the gateway, [a cock crowed.]*
⁶⁹The servant girl saw him again.

Servant Girl: Hey, this is one of them—*one of those who followed Jesus.*

Peter: ⁷⁰No, I'm not one of them.

A little later, some of the other bystanders turned to Peter.

Bystander: Surely you're one of them. You're a Galilean. [We can tell by your accent.]*

⁷¹And then he swore an oath that if he wasn't telling the truth that he would be cursed.

Peter: *Listen*, I don't even know the man you're talking about.

⁷²And as he said this, a cock crowed [a second time];* and Peter remembered what Jesus had told him: "Before the cock crows [twice],* you will have denied Me three times."
He began to weep.

15 When morning came, the chief priests met in council with all the Jewish leaders. They bound Jesus, led Him away, and turned Him over to *the Roman governor,* Pilate.

Pilate (*after hearing them*): ²Are You the King of the Jews?

Jesus: You have said so.

³The chief priests went on to accuse Jesus of many things, but Jesus simply stood quietly.

Pilate: ⁴Do You have anything to say? How do You respond to all these charges that have been made against You?

⁵But Jesus said nothing more, and Pilate was astonished.
⁶Now it was his custom at that feast that Pilate should release one prisoner from custody, whomever the people most desired. ⁷There was one rebel from those imprisoned for insurrection *against the Roman occupation.* He had committed murder during an uprising. His name was Barabbas. ⁸A crowd had gathered *in front of Pilate's judgment seat* to request that Pilate follow his usual custom.
⁹Pilate turned to them.

Pilate: Why don't I release to you the King of the Jews?

¹⁰He knew that the chief priests had delivered Jesus because they were threatened by Him, *not because Jesus was a criminal.*
¹¹But priests moved among the crowd and persuaded them to call for Barabbas instead.

Pilate: ¹²Then what do you want me to do with the King of the Jews?

Crowd: ¹³Crucify Him, *crucify Him!*

¹⁴But now he called to them.

Pilate: Why? What has He done to deserve such a sentence?

Crowd (*crying all the louder*): Crucify Him, *crucify Him!*

V

Barabbas is an active and a militant Jewish leader. In one sense, the choice that the crowd is offered—to have either Jesus or Barabbas released—can be seen as a choice between two types of revolutions. Do they want a revolution

* 14:68 Some early manuscripts omit this portion.   * 14:70 Some early manuscripts omit this portion.   * 14:72 Some early manuscripts omit this portion.   * 14:72 Some early manuscripts omit "twice."

of power, a revolution that is easily visible, a revolution that will conquer their enemies in a way they can understand? Or do they want a revolution of healing, a revolution of love, a revolution that will bring the kingdom of God to earth in a mystical, transcendental way? It's no wonder they make the choice they do. Who wants a gentle revolution in a time of war?

15When Pilate saw that he could not persuade the crowd to change its mind, he released Barabbas to them and had Jesus publicly whipped, *which was the normal prelude to crucifixion.* Then he had Jesus led away to be crucified. 16The soldiers took Him into the headquarters of the governor; and the rest of the soldiers in the detachment gathered there, *hundreds of them.* 17They put a purple robe on Him and made a crown of thorns that they forced onto His head, 18and they began to cry out in mock salute.

Soldiers: Hail to the King of the Jews!

19For a long while they beat Him on the head with a reed, spat upon Him, and knelt down *as if to honor Him.* 20When they had finished mocking Him, they stripped off His purple robe and put His own clothes back on Him. Then they took Him away to be executed.

21Along the way, they met a man from Cyrene, Simon (the father of Rufus and Alexander), who was coming in from the fields; and they ordered him to carry *the heavy crossbar of* the cross. 22And so they came at last to *the execution site,* a hill called Golgotha, which means the "Place of a Skull." 23The soldiers offered Jesus wine mixed with myrrh *to dull His pain,* but He refused it. 24And so they crucified Him, divided up His clothes, and cast lots (*an ancient equivalent of rolling dice*) to see who would keep the clothes *they had stripped from Him.*

25His crucifixion began about nine o'clock in the morning. 26Over His head hung a sign that indicated the charge for which He was being crucified. It read, "THE KING OF THE JEWS." 27On either side of Him were two insurgents *who also had received the death penalty.* [28And the Hebrew Scripture was completed that said, "He was considered *just another* criminal."]*

29Those passing by on their way into or out of Jerusalem insulted and ridiculed Him.

Some in the Crowd: So You're the One who was going to destroy the temple and rebuild it in three days? 30*Well, if You're so powerful,* then why don't You rescue Yourself? Come on down from the cross!

Chief Priests and Scribes (*mocking Jesus among themselves*): 31He rescued others, but He can't rescue Himself. 32Let the Anointed—the King of Israel—come down from the cross now, and we will see it and believe.

Even the insurgents who were being crucified next to Him taunted Him and reviled Him.

33At noon, the day suddenly darkened for three hours across the entire land. 34Sometime around three o'clock Jesus called out in a loud voice.

Jesus: Eloi, Eloi, lama sabachthani?

Jesus was speaking, as in the psalms, "My God, My God, why have You turned Your back on Me?"*

35Some of those standing nearby misunderstood Him.

Bystanders: Hey, He's calling for Elijah.

36One of them filled a sponge with wine that had turned to vinegar and lifted it to Jesus' lips on a stick so He could drink.

Bystander: Let's see if Elijah will come to take Him down.

37Then Jesus cried out with a loud voice, and He took His last breath.

38*At that moment,* the curtain in the temple was torn in two from top to bottom.

V

The tearing of the temple veil is a picture of what Jesus' death has accomplished. The temple sanctuary is divided into two sections: the holy place and the most holy place. The most holy place is a chamber so sanctified that only

* 15:28 Some manuscripts omit verse 28, a quote from Isaiah 53:12.   * 15:34 Psalm 22:1

the high priest can enter—and then only once a year. There God's presence is manifest on earth.

A long curtain divides the two areas, and at the moment of Jesus' death it is torn in two. The veil that serves as a means to protect everyone but the high priest from the power of God's presence is no longer needed because Jesus, on account of His sacrificial death, gives everyone access to God. Only God Himself can rip the curtain in two "from top to bottom," opening the way for people to come into His presence.

---

[39]The Roman Centurion, *the soldier in charge of the executions,* stood in front of Jesus, [heard His words,]* and saw the manner of His death.

Centurion: Surely this man was the Son of God!

[40]Off in the distance, *away from the crowds,* stood some women *who knew and had followed Jesus,* including Mary Magdalene and Mary the mother of the younger James, Joses, and Salome. [41]These were women who used to care for Him when He was in Galilee, and many other women who had followed Jesus to Jerusalem joined them.

[42]Evening came. The crucifixion had taken place on preparation day, Friday, before the Jewish Sabbath began *at sundown.* [43]Joseph of Arimathea, a member of the ruling council who was also *a believer anxiously* waiting for the kingdom of God, went to Pilate and boldly asked for the body of Jesus. [44]Pilate could not believe Jesus was already dead, so he sent for the Centurion, [45]who confirmed it. Then Pilate gave Joseph permission to take the body. [46]Joseph had the body wrapped in a linen burial cloth he had purchased and laid Him in a tomb that had been carved out of rock. Then he had a stone rolled over the opening *to seal it.* [47]Mary Magdalene and Mary the mother of Joses were watching as the body was interred.

16 [1-2]At the rising of the sun, after the Sabbath on the first day of the week, the two Marys and Salome brought sweet-smelling spices they had purchased to the tomb to anoint the body of Jesus. [3]Along the way, they wondered to themselves how they would roll the heavy stone away from the opening. [4]But when they arrived, the stone was already rolled away in spite of its weight and size.

[5]Stepping through the opening, they were startled to see a young man in a white robe seated inside and to the right.

Man in White: [6]Don't be afraid. You came seeking Jesus of Nazareth, the One who was crucified. He is gone. He has risen. See the place where His body was laid. [7]Go back, and tell Peter and His disciples that He goes before you into Galilee, just as He said. You will see Him there *when you arrive.*

[8]The women went out quickly; and when they were outside the tomb, they ran away trembling and astonished. Along their way, they didn't stop to say anything to anyone because they were too afraid.

Mark finishes his Gospel in the same way he begins it—quickly, without commentary or explanation. He also finishes it in a humble way: it is the lowly women who take center stage in this greatest miracle of Jesus. The heavenly messenger sends the women with a commission to tell the disciples what has happened, making them the first preachers of the resurrection.

[[9]After He rose from the dead early on Sunday,* Jesus appeared first to Mary Magdalene, a woman out of whom He had cast seven demons. [10]She brought this news back to all those who had followed Him and were still mourning and weeping, [11]but they refused to believe she had seen Jesus alive.

[12]After that, Jesus appeared in a different form to two of them as they walked through the countryside, [13]and again the others did not believe it.

[14]The eleven did not believe until Jesus appeared to them all as they sat at dinner.

---

* 15:39 Some early manuscripts omit this portion.　* 16:9 Literally, "the first day of the week." The new creation was underway.

He rebuked them for their hard hearts—for their lack of faith—because they had failed to believe those witnesses who had seen Him after He had risen.

Jesus: ¹⁵Go out into the world and share the good news with all of creation. ¹⁶Anyone who believes this good news and is ceremonially washed* will be rescued, but anyone who does not believe it will be condemned. ¹⁷And these signs will follow those who believe: they will be able to cast out demons in My name, speak with new tongues, ¹⁸take up serpents, drink poison without being harmed, and lay their hands on the sick to heal them.

¹⁹After the Lord Jesus had charged the disciples in this way, He was taken up into heaven and seated at the right hand of God. ²⁰The disciples went out proclaiming the good news; and the risen Lord continued working through them, confirming every word they spoke with the signs He performed through them.]*

[And the women did everything they had been told to do, speaking to Peter and the other disciples. Later Jesus Himself commissioned the disciples to take this sacred and eternal message of salvation far to the East and the West.]*

V

The remaining eleven disciples take this command as their life's mission. According to tradition, all but one of them (John) will be killed for their refusals to stop proclaiming the truth that Jesus is the Anointed One who has been crucified and who has arisen from the dead. They dedicate their lives—and their deaths—to the proclamation of this reality. If they are not absolutely certain of the truth of Jesus' resurrection, then why dedicate their lives to announcing it to the world?

---

* 16:16 Literally, immersed, to show repentance   * 16:9-20 are not contained in the earliest manuscripts. However, many manuscripts do contain these verses. It is likely the original Gospel ended in 16:8 or that the original ending was lost.   * 16:20 One manuscript concludes with these bracketed words.

LUKE

Carefully researched account of God's Anointed

By Luke, the physician

This Third Gospel account is the work of a physician named Luke. Unlike Matthew and John, Luke is not one of the twelve or an eyewitness to any of the life of Jesus. However, he is a close friend and traveling companion of the most influential missionary of the early church—Paul, the emissary.

Luke writes with a highly advanced literary style; his is the only Gospel that begins with a formal, literary introduction, a feature characteristic of many books written in his day. Luke clearly states the method and purpose for writing his Gospel. He has researched the life of Jesus thoroughly in order to correct the misinformation being spread about Him and to provide the most historically accurate report of Jesus' ministry possible. He wants to assure believers that the Christian faith is rooted in fact, not fiction.

Luke addresses his Gospel to Theophilus, a Roman official; but it's clear that he also writes with a broader audience in mind. In fact, the name "Theophilus" means "one who loves God," suggesting his account is for anyone who loves God. Luke himself may be an outsider to the Jewish faith. If so, he is the only Gentile author in the New Testament. Luke traces Jesus' genealogy all the way back to Adam (rather than starting with Abraham, as Matthew does) in order to emphasize that Jesus is the Savior of all humanity, not just the Jewish Messiah. Connecting Jesus with Adam also emphasizes the humanity of Jesus, which is repeatedly stressed in this Gospel. Luke, of course, does not deny Jesus' divinity; he just shows how Jesus exemplifies the perfect human being. Luke also focuses on the compassion of Jesus toward the disadvantaged members of society, including women, outcasts, and the poor. The Gospel according to Luke turns the world upside down and exalts the humble while humbling the exalted.

Luke's story of Jesus is the most comprehensive of the Gospels. It begins with the announcement of the birth of John the Baptist. It continues through Jesus' life, death, resurrection, and ascension into heaven. But Luke's story does not end there. After showing his readers how Jesus welcomes all people to follow Him, Luke gives the next chapter in his account of this movement Jesus began—the book known as the Acts of the Apostles. There he describes how the followers of Jesus moved beyond Jerusalem and the Jews and took the message of Jesus to the outsider nations across the known world.

In the time of Jesus, Jewish life is centered in the temple in Jerusalem. Priests are responsible for the temple's activities—which include receiving religious pilgrims and their sacrifices (cattle, sheep, goats, and doves). Animal sacrifices may sound strange to a modern society, but in the ancient world, they are quite common. The slaughter of animals is a daily experience; it is part of any meal that includes meat. So this meal brings together the Jewish family from near and far, seeking to affirm their connections to the one true and living God. Their gift of animals is their contribution to the meal. (The priests, by the way, are authorized to use the meat for the sustenance of their families.)

The presentation of the blood and meat of these sacrifices is accompanied by a number of prescribed rituals, performed by priests wearing prescribed ornamental clothing, according to a prescribed schedule. As the story continues, these solemn rituals are interrupted in an unprecedented way.

Luke travels widely with the Lord's emissary, Paul. Thus, he is a sort of cosmopolitan person, multicultural in his sensitivities, understanding both Jewish culture and the broader Greco-Roman culture of the Roman Empire. Moreover, as a physician he is more educated than the average person of his day and has an impressive ability to relate to common people. Luke is especially skilled as a storyteller, so he isn't presenting a theological treatise (as good and important as theological treatises may be); he's telling the story of Jesus, gathered from many eyewitnesses. Based on the name of the intended audience of his book (Theophilus—literally, "God-lover," translated here as "those who love God"), presumably he wants to help people who love God to love Him even more by knowing what He has done through Jesus.

1 ¹⁻³For those who love God, several other people have already written accounts of what God has been bringing to completion among us, using the reports of the original eyewitnesses, those who were there from the start to witness the fulfillment of prophecy. Like those other servants who have recorded the messages, I present to you my carefully researched, orderly account of these new teachings. ⁴I want you to know that you can fully rely on the things you have been taught about Jesus, God's Anointed One.

⁵*To understand the life of Jesus, I must first give you some background history, events that occurred when* Herod ruled Judea *for the Roman Empire.* Zacharias was serving as a priest *in the temple in Jerusalem* those days as his fathers had before him. He was a member of the priestly division of Abijah (*a grandson of Aaron who innovated temple practices*), and his wife, Elizabeth, was of the priestly lineage of Aaron, *Moses' brother.* ⁶They were good and just people in God's sight, walking with integrity in the Lord's ways and laws. ⁷Yet they had this sadness. Due to Elizabeth's infertility, they were childless, and at this time, they were both quite old—*well past normal childbearing years.*

⁸One day Zacharias was chosen to perform his priestly duties in God's presence, according to the temple's normal schedule and routine. ⁹He had been selected from all the priests by the customary procedure of casting lots *for a once-in-a-lifetime opportunity* to enter the sacred precincts of the temple. There he burned sweet incense, ¹⁰while outside a large crowd of people prayed. ¹¹*Suddenly Zacharias realized he was not alone:* a messenger of the Lord was there with him. The messenger stood just to the right of the altar of incense. ¹²Zacharias was shocked and afraid, ¹³but the messenger reassured him.

Messenger: Zacharias, calm down! Don't be afraid!

Zacharias is a priest working in the temple, but priests don't normally hear from God. Those who hear from God are called prophets, not priests. One becomes a priest by being born in a priestly family line. Prophets, on the other hand, arise unpredictably and have no special credentials except the message they carry. So Zacharias has no reason to believe his duties will be interrupted in this way. Often in the biblical story, when people receive a message from God—after getting over the initial shock—they start asking questions. They push back; they doubt.

Messenger: Zacharias, your prayers have been heard. Your wife is going to have a son, and you will name him John. [14]He will bring you great joy and happiness—and many will share your joy at John's birth.

[15]This son of yours will be a great man in God's sight. He will not drink alcohol in any form;* *instead of alcoholic spirits,* he will be filled with the Holy Spirit from the time he is in his mother's womb. [16]*Here is his mission:* he will turn many of the children of Israel around to follow the path to the Lord their God. [17]Do you remember the prophecy about someone to come in the spirit and power of the prophet Elijah; someone who will turn the hearts of the parents back to their children;* someone who will turn the hearts of the disobedient to the mind-set of the just and good? Your son is the one who will fulfill this prophecy: he will be the Lord's forerunner, the one who will prepare the people and make them ready for God.

Zacharias: [18]How can I be sure of what you're telling me? I am an old man, and my wife is far past the normal age for women to bear children. *This is hard to believe!*

Messenger (*sternly*): [19]I am Gabriel, the messenger who inhabits God's presence. I was sent here to talk with you and bring you this good news. [20]Because you didn't believe my message, you will not be able to talk—not another word—until you experience the fulfillment of my words.

[21]Meanwhile the crowd at the temple wondered why Zacharias hadn't come out of the sanctuary yet. It wasn't normal for the priest to be delayed so long. [22]When at last he came out, *he* was making signs with his hands to give the blessing, but he couldn't speak. They realized he had seen some sort of vision. [23]When his time on duty at the temple came to an end, he went back home to his wife. [24]Shortly after his return, Elizabeth became pregnant. She avoided public contact for the next five months.

Elizabeth: [25]I have lived with the disgrace of being barren for all these years. Now God has looked on me with favor. When I go out in public *with my baby,* I will not be disgraced any longer.

[26]Six months later in Nazareth, a city in *the rural province of* Galilee, the heavenly messenger Gabriel made another appearance. This time the messenger was sent by God [27]to meet with a virgin named Mary, who was engaged to a man named Joseph, a descendant of King David himself. [28]The messenger entered her home.

Messenger: Greetings! You are favored, and the Lord is with you! [Among all women on the earth, you have been blessed.]*

[29]The heavenly messenger's words baffled Mary, and she wondered what type of greeting this was.

Messenger: [30]Mary, don't be afraid. You have found favor with God. [31]Listen, you are going to become pregnant. You will have a son, and you must name Him "Savior," or Jesus.* [32]Jesus will become the greatest among men. He will be known as the Son of the Highest God. God will give Him the throne of His ancestor David, [33]and He will reign over the covenant family of Jacob forever.

Mary: [34]But I have never been with a man. How can this be possible?

Messenger: [35]The Holy Spirit will come upon you. The Most High will overshadow you. That's why this holy child will be known, *as not just your son, but also* as the Son of God. [36]*It sounds impossible,* but listen—you know your relative Elizabeth

* 1:15 Numbers 6:3; Leviticus 10:9   * 1:17 Malachi 4:5-6   * 1:28 The earliest manuscripts omit this portion.   * 1:31 Through the naming of Jesus, God is speaking prophetically about the role Jesus will play in our salvation.

has been unable to bear children and is now far too old to be a mother. Yet she has become pregnant, *as God willed it*. Yes, in three months, she will have a son. [37]So the impossible is possible with God.

Mary (*deciding in her heart*): [38]Here I am, the Lord's humble servant. As you have said, let it be done to me.

Luke is very interested in the ways that disadvantaged people of his day respond to God. Already there is a fascinating interplay between Zacharias's response to God and Mary's.

And the heavenly messenger was gone. [39]Mary immediately got up and hurried to the hill country, in the province of Judah, [40-41]where her cousins Zacharias and Elizabeth lived. When Mary entered their home and greeted Elizabeth, who felt her baby leap in her womb, Elizabeth was filled with the Holy Spirit.

Elizabeth (*shouting*): [42]You are blessed, *Mary*, blessed among all women, and the child you bear is blessed! [43]And blessed I am as well, that the mother of my Lord has come to me! [44]As soon as I heard your voice greet me, my baby leaped for joy within me. [45]How fortunate you are, Mary, for you believed that what the Lord told you would be fulfilled.

V

Mary is deeply moved by these amazing encounters—first with the messenger and then with her cousin, Elizabeth. Mary's response can't be contained in normal prose; her noble soul overflows in poetry. And this poetry isn't simply religious; it has powerful social and political overtones. It speaks of a great reversal—what might be called a social, economic, and political revolution. To people in Mary's day, there is little question as to what she is talking about. The Jewish people are oppressed by the Roman Empire, and to speak of a King who will demote the powerful and rich and elevate the poor and humble means one thing: God

is moving toward setting them free! Soon Zacharias will overflow in poetry of his own.

Mary: [46]My soul lifts up the Lord!
[47]My spirit celebrates God, my
    Liberator!
[48]For though I'm God's humble servant,
    God has noticed me.
Now and forever,
    I will be considered blessed by all
    generations.
[49]For the Mighty One has done great things
    for me;
    holy is God's name!
[50]From generation to generation,
    God's lovingkindness endures
    for those who revere Him.

[51]God's arm has accomplished mighty
    deeds.
    The proud in mind and heart,
    God has sent away in disarray.
[52]The rulers from their high positions of
    power,
    God has brought down low.
And those who were humble and
    lowly,
    God has elevated with dignity.
[53]The hungry—God has filled with fine
    food.
    The rich—God has dismissed with
    nothing in their hands.
[54]To Israel, God's servant,
    God has given help,
[55]As promised to our ancestors,
    remembering Abraham and his
    descendants in mercy forever.

[56]Mary stayed with Elizabeth *in Judea* for the next three months and then returned to her home *in Galilee*.

[57]When the time was right, Elizabeth gave birth to a son. [58]News about the Lord's special kindness to her had spread through her extended family and the community. Everyone shared her joy, *for after all these years of infertility, she had a son!* [59]As was customary, eight days after the baby's birth the time came for his circumcision *and naming*. Everyone assumed he would be named Zacharias, like his father.

Elizabeth (*disagreeing*): [60]No. We will name him John.

Her Relatives (protesting): ⁶¹That name is found nowhere in your family.

⁶²They turned to Zacharias and asked him what he wanted the baby's name to be. ⁶³He motioned for a tablet, and he wrote, "His name is John." Everyone was shocked by this breach of family custom. ⁶⁴They were even more surprised when, at that moment, Zacharias was able to talk again, and he shouted out praises to God. ⁶⁵A sense of reverence spread through the whole community. In fact, this story was spread throughout the hilly countryside of Judea. ⁶⁶People were certain that God's hand was on this child, and they wondered what sort of person John would turn out to be when he became a man.

⁶⁷When Zacharias's voice was restored to him, he sang from the fullness of the Spirit a prophetic blessing.

Zacharias: ⁶⁸May the Lord God of Israel be blessed indeed!
For God's intervention has begun, and He has moved to rescue us, the people of God.
⁶⁹And the Lord has raised up a powerful sign of liberation for us from among the descendants of God's servant, King David.
⁷⁰As was prophesied through the mouths of His holy prophets in ancient times:
⁷¹God will liberate us from our enemies and from the hand of our oppressors!*

⁷²⁻⁷⁴God will show mercy promised to our ancestors, upholding the abiding covenant He made with them,
Remembering the original vow He swore to Abraham, from whom we are all descended.
God will rescue us from the grasp of our enemies so that we may serve Him without fear all our days
⁷⁵In holiness and justice, in the presence of the Lord.

⁷⁶And you, my son, will be called the prophet of the Most High.
For you will be the one to prepare the way for the Lord*

⁷⁷So that the Lord's people will receive knowledge of their freedom through the forgiveness of their sins.

⁷⁸All this will flow from the kind and compassionate mercy of our God.
A new day is dawning:
the Sunrise from the heavens will break through in our darkness,
⁷⁹And those who huddle in night, those who sit in the shadow of death,
Will be able to rise and walk in the light,* guided in the pathway of peace.

⁸⁰And John grew up and became strong in spirit. He lived in the wilderness, outside the cities, until the day came for him to step into the public eye in Israel.

2 Around the time of Elizabeth's amazing pregnancy and John's birth, the emperor in Rome, Caesar Augustus, required everyone in the Roman Empire to participate in a massive census—²the first census since Quirinius had become governor of Syria. ³Each person had to go to his or her ancestral city to be counted.

V

This political background isn't incidental: it is crucial to the story. Conquering nations in the ancient world work in various ways. Some brutally destroy and plunder the nations they conquer. Some conquer people as slaves or servants. Other empires allow the people to remain in their land and work as before, but with one major change: the conquered people have to pay taxes to their rulers. The purpose of a census like the one Luke describes is to be sure that everyone is appropriately taxed and knows who is in charge.

---

⁴⁻⁵Mary's fiancé Joseph, from Nazareth in Galilee, had to participate in the census in the same way everyone else did. Because he was a descendant of King David, his ancestral city was Bethlehem, David's birthplace. Mary, who was now late in her pregnancy

* 1:71 Psalm 106:10 * 1:76 Isaiah 40:3 * 1:79 Isaiah 9:2

that the messenger Gabriel had predicted, [6]accompanied Joseph. While in Bethlehem, she went into labor [7]and gave birth to her firstborn son. She wrapped the baby in a blanket and laid Him in a feeding trough because the inn had no room for them.

[8]Nearby, in the fields outside of Bethlehem, a group of shepherds were guarding their flocks *from predators* in the darkness of night. [9]Suddenly a messenger of the Lord stood in front of them, and the darkness was replaced by a glorious light—the shining light of God's glory. They were terrified!

Messenger: [10]Don't be afraid! Listen! I bring good news, news of great joy, news that will affect all people everywhere. [11]Today, in the city of David, a Liberator has been born for you! He is the promised Anointed One, the Supreme Authority! [12]You will know you have found Him when you see a baby, wrapped in a blanket, lying in a feeding trough.

[13]At that moment, the first heavenly messenger was joined by thousands of other messengers—a vast heavenly choir. They praised God.

Heavenly Choir: [14]To the highest heights of
the universe, glory to God!
And on earth, peace among all people
who bring pleasure to God!

[15]As soon as the heavenly messengers disappeared into heaven, the shepherds were buzzing with conversation.

Shepherds: Let's rush down to Bethlehem right now! Let's see what's happening! Let's experience what the Lord has told us about!

[16]So they ran into town, and *eventually* they found Mary and Joseph and the baby lying in the feeding trough. After they saw the baby, [17]they spread the story of *what they had experienced and* what had been said to them about this child. [18]Everyone who heard their story couldn't stop thinking about its meaning. [19]Mary, too, pondered all of these events, treasuring each memory in her heart. [20]The shepherds returned *to their flocks,* praising God for all they had seen and heard, and they glorified God for the way the

experience had unfolded just as the heavenly messenger had predicted.

Here again is Luke's fascination with disadvantaged people. Jesus' first visitors are not ambassadors, dignitaries, or wealthy landowners. The first to pay Him homage are simple shepherds, minimum-wage workers in the ancient agrarian economy. They have little to no status in the world. They are the humble and the poor whom God is now raising up to receive heavenly messages and an audience with the great King. This theme recurs as the story continues.

---

[21]Eight days after His birth, the baby was circumcised *in keeping with Jewish religious requirements,* and He was named Jesus, the name the messenger had given Him before His conception in Mary's womb. [22]After Mary had observed the ceremonial days of *postpartum* purification required by Mosaic law, she and Joseph brought Jesus to the temple in Jerusalem to present Him to the Lord. [23]They were fulfilling the Lord's requirement that "every firstborn *Israelite* male will be dedicated to the Eternal One as holy."* [24]They also offered the sacrifice required by the law of the Lord, "two turtledoves or two young pigeons."*

[25]*While fulfilling these sacred obligations at the temple,* they encountered a man in Jerusalem named Simeon. He was a just and pious man, anticipating the liberation of Israel from her troubles. He was a man in touch with the Holy Spirit. [26]The Holy Spirit had revealed to Simeon that he would not die before he had seen the Lord's Anointed One. [27]The Spirit had led him to the temple that day, and there he saw the child Jesus in the arms of His parents, who were fulfilling their sacred obligations. [28]Simeon took Jesus into his arms and blessed God.

Simeon: [29]Now, Lord *and King,* You can let
me, Your humble servant, die in
peace.
[30]You promised me that I would see with
my own eyes
what I'm seeing now: Your freedom,

* 2:23 Exodus 13:2,12,15   * 2:24 Leviticus 5:11; 12:8

³¹Raised up in the presence of all peoples. ³²He is the light who reveals Your
    message to the other nations,
and He is the shining glory of Your
    covenant people, Israel.

³³His father and mother were stunned to hear Simeon say these things. ³⁴Simeon went on to bless them both, and to Mary in particular he gave predictions.

Simeon: Listen, this child will make many in Israel rise and fall. He will be a significant person whom many will oppose. ³⁵*In the end,* He will lay bare the secret thoughts of many hearts. And a sword will pierce even your own soul, Mary.

³⁶At that very moment, an elderly woman named Anna stepped forward. Anna was a prophetess, the daughter of Phanuel, of the tribe of Asher. She had been married for seven years *before her husband died* ³⁷and a widow to her current age of 84 years. She was *deeply devoted to the Lord,* constantly in the temple, fasting and praying. ³⁸When she approached *Mary, Joseph, and Jesus,* she began speaking out thanks to God, and she continued spreading the word about Jesus to all those who shared her hope for the rescue of Jerusalem.

³⁹After fulfilling their sacred duties according to the law of the Lord, Mary and Joseph returned *with Jesus* to their own city of Nazareth in the province of Galilee. ⁴⁰There Jesus grew up, maturing in physical strength and increasing in wisdom, and the grace of God rested on Him.

⁴¹Every year *during Jesus' childhood,* His parents traveled to Jerusalem for the Passover celebration. ⁴²When Jesus was 12, He made the journey with them. ⁴³They spent several days there, participating in the whole celebration. When His parents left for home, Jesus stayed in Jerusalem, but Joseph and Mary were not aware. ⁴⁴They assumed Jesus was elsewhere in the caravan *that was traveling together*. After they had already traveled a full day's journey *toward home,* they began searching for Him among their friends and relatives. ⁴⁵When no one had seen the boy, Mary and Joseph rushed back to Jerusalem and searched for Him.

⁴⁶After three days of separation, they finally found Him—sitting among a group of religious teachers in the temple—asking them questions, listening to their answers.

⁴⁷Everyone was surprised and impressed that a 12-year-old boy could have such deep understanding and could answer questions *with such wisdom.*

⁴⁸His parents, of course, had a different reaction.

Mary: Son, why have You treated us this way? Listen, Your father and I have been sick with worry *for the last three days, wondering where You were,* looking everywhere for You.

Jesus: ⁴⁹Why did you need to look for Me? Didn't you know that I must be working for My Father?

V

Little is recorded about Jesus' life between His birth and the age of 30. But this one episode tells so much. First, Jesus' family life is a lot like anyone's—full of mishaps and misunderstandings. Second, as Jesus enters young adulthood, He begins manifesting an extraordinary sense of identity. (Remember, a 12-year-old isn't "just a kid" in Israel—he is becoming a man.) He isn't just "Mary's boy" or "Joseph's stepson." He has a direct relationship with God as His Father, and He knows His life will follow a path of working for God.

---

⁵⁰Neither Mary nor Joseph really understood what He meant by this. ⁵¹Jesus went back to Nazareth with them and was obedient to them. His mother continued to store these memories like treasures in her heart. ⁵²And Jesus kept on growing—in wisdom, in physical stature, in favor with God, and in favor with others.

3 Our story continues 15 years after Tiberius Caesar had begun his reign over the empire. Pilate was governor of Judea, Herod ruled Galilee, his brother Philip ruled Ituraea and Trachonitis, and Lysanias ruled Abilene.

V

More than any other Gospel writer, Luke wants to situate the story of

John's father Zacharias is a priest who serves in Jerusalem at the temple. Among their other duties, priests perform ritual cleansings necessary for Jewish worshipers who become ceremonially unclean—perhaps through contact with outsiders (non-Jewish people), perhaps through contact with blood or a dead body, perhaps through a physical illness. But when John appears on the scene, he hasn't followed in his father's footsteps. He's not fulfilling the role of the priest, but rather of the prophet. He works far outside of Jerusalem, and he baptizes people in the Jordan River, not near the temple. It's as if John is performing a symbolic drama: If you want to be in tune with God, the temple and its normal routines can't help you anymore. Instead of being cleansed there, you should come out to this radical preacher and let him cleanse you in the river. And his message isn't a polite, tame message. It's fiery and intense! God isn't interested in just routine religion. He wants changed lives!

Jesus in secular history. In particular, he gives details of the emperor, governor, and other client rulers. With a toxic mixture of cruelty and might, these authorities lord their power over the common people. Yet these high and mighty are—as Mary's poem describes—destined to be brought down in the presence of a new kind of king and a new kind of kingdom. Jesus will exercise His authority in a radically different way—not through domination and violence, but through love, healing, compassion, and service.

[2]*In Jerusalem* Annas and Caiaphas were high priests in the temple. And in those days, out in the wilderness, John (son of Zacharias) received a message from God.

[3]John brought this divine message to all those who came to the Jordan River. He preached that people should be ritually cleansed through baptism as an expression of changed lives for the forgiveness of sins. [4]As Isaiah the prophet had said,

A solitary voice is calling:
"Go into the wilderness;
    prepare the road for the Eternal One's
        journey.
In the desert, repair and straighten
    every mile of our True God's highway.
[5]Every low place will be lifted
    and every high mountain,
    every hill will be humbled;
The crooked road will be straightened out
    and rough places ironed out smooth;

[6]Then the radiant glory of the Eternal One
    will be revealed.
All flesh together will take it in."*

[7]In fulfillment of those words, crowds streamed out *from the villages and towns* to be baptized* by John *at the Jordan*.

John the Baptist: You bunch of venomous snakes! Who told you that you could escape God's coming wrath? [8]Don't just talk of turning to God; you'd better bear the authentic fruit of a changed life. Don't take pride in your religious heritage, saying, "We have Abraham for our father!" Listen—God could turn these rocks into children of Abraham!

[9]*God wants you to bear fruit!* If you don't produce good fruit, then you'll be chopped down like a fruitless tree and made into firewood. God's ax is taking aim and ready to swing!

People: [10]What shall we do *to perform works from changed lives?*

John the Baptist: [11]The person who has two shirts must share with the person who has none. And the person with food must share with the one in need.

[12]Some tax collectors were among those in the crowd seeking baptism.*

Tax Collectors: Teacher, what kind of fruit is God looking for from us?

John the Baptist: [13]Stop overcharging people. Only collect what you must turn over to the Romans.

* 3:4-6 Isaiah 40:3-5   * 3:7 Literally, immersed, to show repentance
* 3:12 Literally, immersion, an act to show repentance

Soldiers: [14]What about us? What should we do *to show true change?*

John the Baptist: Don't extort money from people by throwing around your power or making false accusations, and be content with your pay.

[15]John's bold message seized public attention, and many began wondering if John might himself be the Anointed One *promised by God.*

John the Baptist: [16]I baptize* you with water, but One is coming—One far more powerful than I, One whose sandals I am not worthy to untie—who will baptize* you with the Holy Spirit and with fire. [17]He is coming *like a farmer at harvesttime,* tools in hand to separate the wheat from the chaff. He will burn the chaff with unquenchable fire, and He will gather the genuine wheat into His barn.

[18]He preached with many other provocative figures of speech and so conveyed God's message to the people—*the time had come to rethink everything.* [19]*But John's public preaching ended when* he confronted Herod, the ruler of Galilee, for his many corrupt deeds, including *taking* Herodias, the ruler's sister-in-law, *as his own wife.* [20]Herod responded by throwing John into prison.

[21]*But before John's imprisonment, when he was still preaching and* ritually cleansing through baptism* the people in the Jordan River, Jesus also came to him to be baptized. As Jesus prayed, the heavens opened, [22]and the Holy Spirit came upon Him in a physical manifestation that resembled a dove. A voice echoed out from heaven.

Voice from Heaven: You are My Son,* the Son I love, and in You I take great pleasure.

What does it mean for Jesus to be baptized by John? If John's baptism symbolizes a rejection of the religious establishment centered in the temple in Jerusalem, then Jesus' baptism by John symbolizes that He is aligned with this radical preacher. Jesus isn't simply coming to strengthen or even renew the centers of power. Instead, He is joining John at the margins to be part of something wild and new that God is doing. And the vivid manifestation of God's pleasure—the dovelike appearance and the voice from heaven—suggests that even though Jesus is in a sense aligning Himself with John, John is simply the opening act and Jesus is the main attraction. The choreography between John's work and Jesus' work continues, but from this point on, Jesus is in the center of the story.

---

[23]At this, the launch of Jesus' ministry, Jesus was about 30 years old.

He was assumed to be the son of Joseph, the son of Eli, [24]the son of Matthat, the son of Levi, the son of Melchi, the son of Jannai, the son of Joseph, [25]the son of Mattathias, the son of Amos, the son of Nahum, the son of Hesli, the son of Naggai, [26]the son of Maath, the son of Mattathias, the son of Semein, the son of Josech, the son of Joda, [27]the son of Joanan, the son of Rhesa, the son of Zerubbabel, the son of Shealtiel, the son of Neri, [28]the son of Melchi, the son of Addi, the son of Cosam, the son of Elmadam, the son of Er, [29]the son of Joshua, the son of Eliezer, the son of Jorim, the son of Matthat, the son of Levi, [30]the son of Simeon, the son of Judah, the son of Joseph, the son of Jonam, the son of Eliakim, [31]the son of Melea, the son of Menna, the son of Mattatha, the son of Nathan, the son of David, [32]the son of Jesse, the son of Obed, the son of Boaz, the son of Salmon, the son of Nahshon, [33]the son of Amminadab, the son of Admin, the son of Ram, the son of Hezron, the son of Perez, the son of Judah, [34]the son of Jacob, the son of Isaac, the son of Abraham, the son of Terah, the son of Nahor, [35]the son of Serug, the son of Reu, the son of Peleg, the son of Heber, the son of Shelah, [36]the son of Cainan, the son of Arphaxad, the son of Shem, the son of Noah, the son of Lamech, [37]the son of Methuselah, the son of Enoch, the son of Jared, the son of Mahalaleel, the son of Cainan, [38]the son of Enosh, the son of Seth, the son of Adam, the son of God.

---

* 3:16 Literally, immerse, to show repentance   * 3:21 Literally, immersing, to show repentance   * 3:22 Psalm 2:7

While genealogies may seem tedious, for people in many cultures (including Luke's), genealogies are important and meaningful because they give a sense of identity and history. Luke places Jesus in the mainstream of biblical history, connected to King David, Abraham, Noah, and Adam. By connecting Jesus with Adam, and ultimately with God, Luke shows how Jesus is connected to and relevant for all people, and he may also be suggesting that in Jesus God is launching a new humanity, with Jesus as the new Adam. Unlike the first Adam, though, Jesus will be completely faithful to God, as the next episode makes clear. Perhaps echoing Adam and Eve being tempted by the serpent in the garden (Genesis 3:1-7), Luke moves from the stories of Jesus' beginnings to His temptation.

4 When Jesus returned from the Jordan River, He was full of the Holy Spirit, and the Holy Spirit led Him away *from the cities and towns* and out into the desert.
2For 40 days, the Spirit led Him from place to place in the desert, and while there, the devil tempted Jesus. Jesus was fasting, eating nothing during this time, and at the end, He was terribly hungry. 3At that point, the devil came to Him.

Devil: Since You're the Son of God, You don't need to be hungry. Just tell this stone to transform itself into bread.

Jesus: 4It is written *in the Hebrew Scriptures,* "People need more than bread to live."*

5Then the devil gave Jesus a vision. It was as if He traveled around the world in an instant and saw all the kingdoms of the world at once.

Devil: 6All these kingdoms, all their glory, I'll give to You. They're mine to give because this whole world has been handed over to me. 7If You just worship me, then everything You see will all be Yours. All Yours!

Jesus: 8[Get out of My face, Satan!]* The Hebrew Scriptures say, "Worship and serve the Eternal One your God—only Him—and nobody else."*

9Then the devil led Jesus to Jerusalem, and he transported Jesus to stand upon the pinnacle of the temple.

Devil: Since You're the Son of God, just jump. Just throw Yourself into the air. 10*You keep quoting the Hebrew Scriptures.* They themselves say,

He will put His heavenly messengers in charge of You,
  to keep You safe in every way.

11And,

They will hold You up in their hands
  so that You do not smash Your foot against a stone.*

Jesus: 12*Yes, but* the *Hebrew* Scriptures also say, *"You will not presume on God;* you will not test the Lord, the one True God."*

13The devil had no more temptations to offer *that day,* so he left Jesus, preparing to return at some other opportune time.
14Jesus returned to Galilee in the power of the Holy Spirit, and soon people across the region had heard news of Him. 15He would regularly go into their synagogues and teach. His teaching earned Him the respect and admiration of everyone who heard Him.
16He eventually came to His hometown, Nazareth, and did there what He had done elsewhere *in Galilee*—entered the synagogue and stood up to read *from the Hebrew Scriptures.*
17The *synagogue attendant* gave Him the scroll of the prophet Isaiah, and Jesus unrolled it to the place where Isaiah had written these words:

18The Spirit of the Lord the Eternal One is on Me.
Why? Because the Eternal designated Me to be His representative to the poor, to preach good news to them.

* 4:4 Deuteronomy 8:3   * 4:8 Many early manuscripts omit this portion.   * 4:8 Deuteronomy 6:13; 10:20   * 4:10-11 Psalm 91:11-12
* 4:12 Deuteronomy 6:16

Luke's audience doesn't divide the world into sacred vs. secular or religious vs. political. For them, life is integrated. And for them, these "religious" words from Isaiah have a powerful and "political" meaning: because they see themselves as oppressed by the Roman occupation, Jesus' words suggest that His "good news" describes a powerful change about to come—a change that will rescue the people from their oppression. His fellow Jews have long been waiting for a savior to free them from Roman oppression. Jesus tells them their hopes are about to be fulfilled. But then, just as people speak well of Jesus, He lets them know their expectations aren't in line with God's plans. He tells them not to expect God to fit into their boxes and suggests the unthinkable: that God cares for the Gentiles, the very people who are oppressing them! They aren't too pleased by this.

He sent Me to tell those who are held
    captive that they can now be set
    free,
and to tell the blind that they can now
    see.
He sent Me to liberate those held down by
    oppression.
19*In short, the Spirit is upon Me* to
    proclaim that now is the time;
    this is the jubilee season of the Eternal
    One's grace.*

20Jesus rolled up the scroll and returned it to the synagogue attendant. Then He sat down, *as a teacher would do,* and all in the synagogue focused their attention on Jesus, *waiting for Him to speak.* 21He told them that these words from the Hebrew Scriptures were being fulfilled then and there, in their hearing.

22At first everyone was deeply impressed with the gracious words that poured from Jesus' lips. Everyone spoke well of Him and was amazed that He could say these things.

Everyone: Wait. This is only the son of Joseph, right?

Jesus: 23You're about to quote the old proverb to Me, "Doctor, heal yourself!" Then you're going to ask Me to prove Myself to you by doing the same miracles I did in Capernaum. 24But face the truth: hometowns always reject their homegrown prophets. 25Think back to the prophet Elijah. There were many needy Jewish widows in *his homeland,* Israel, when a terrible famine persisted there for three and a half years. 26Yet the only widow God sent Elijah to help was *an outsider* from Zarephath in Sidon.*

27It was the same with the prophet Elisha. There were many Jewish lepers in his homeland, but the only one he healed—Naaman—*was an outsider* from Syria.*

28The people in the synagogue became furious when He said these things. 29They seized Jesus, took Him to the edge of town, and pushed Him right to the edge of the cliff on which the city was built. They would have pushed Him off and killed Him, 30but He passed through the crowd and went on His way.

31-33Next He went to Capernaum, another Galilean city. Again He was *in the synagogue* teaching on the Sabbath, and as before, the people were enthralled by His words. He had a way of saying things—a special authority, *a unique power.*

In attendance that day was a man with a demonic spirit.

Demon-Possessed Man (*screaming at Jesus*): 34*Get out of here!* Leave us alone! What's Your agenda, Jesus of Nazareth? Have You come to destroy us? I know who You are: You're the Holy One, the One sent by God!

Jesus (*firmly rebuking the demon*): 35Be quiet. Get out of that man!

Then the demonic spirit immediately threw the man into a fit, and he collapsed right there in the middle of the synagogue. It was clear the demon had come out, and the man was completely fine after that. 36Everyone was shocked to see this, and they couldn't help but talk about it.

Synagogue Members: What's this about? What's the meaning of this message? Jesus

* 4:18-19 Isaiah 61:1-2   * 4:26 1 Kings 17:8-16   * 4:27 2 Kings 5:1-14

The essential message of Jesus can be summed up this way: the kingdom of God is available to everyone, starting now. When Jesus refers to the kingdom of God, He doesn't mean something that happens after death, far off in heaven; He equates the kingdom of God with God's will being done on earth as it is in heaven. So the kingdom of God is life as God intends it to be—life to the full, life in peace and justice, life in abundance and love. Individuals enter the Kingdom when they enter into a relationship with Jesus, when they trust Him enough to follow His ways. But make no mistake, the Kingdom is about more than individual lives; it is about the transformation and renewal of all God has created. It may start with individual responses, but it doesn't stop there.

Jesus describes His purpose as proclaiming this message. But Jesus not only expresses His message of the kingdom of God in words, He also dramatizes it in deeds. Luke calls these amazing deeds "signs and wonders," suggesting that these actions have symbolic meaning, which is *sign*ificant, and are *wonder*ful, which means they fill people with awe and *wonder*. In the coming chapters, the wonder that the original eyewitnesses feel is palpable, and Jesus' actions are significant signs of the kingdom of God.

---

speaks with authority, and He has power to command demonic spirits to go away.

³⁷The excitement about Jesus spread into every corner of the surrounding region.

³⁸ *Picture this:*

Jesus then leaves that synagogue and goes over to Simon's place. Simon's mother-in-law is there. She is sick with a high fever. Simon's family asks Jesus to help her. ³⁹Jesus stands over her, *and just as He had rebuked the demon,* He rebukes the fever, and the woman's temperature returns to normal. She feels so much better that she gets right up and cooks them all a big meal.

⁴⁰By this time, it's just before nightfall, and as the sun sets, *groups of families, friends, and bystanders come* until a huge crowd has gathered. Each group has brought along family members or friends who are sick with any number of diseases. One by one, Jesus lays His hands on them and heals them. ⁴¹On several occasions, demonic spirits are expelled from these people, after shouting at Jesus, "You are the Son of God!"

Jesus always rebukes them and tells them to be quiet. They know He is the Anointed One, *but He doesn't want to be acclaimed in this way.*

⁴²The next morning, Jesus sneaks away. He finds a place away from the crowds, but soon they find Him. The crowd tries their best to keep Him from leaving.

Jesus: ⁴³No, I cannot stay. I need to preach the kingdom of God to other cities too. This is the purpose I was sent to fulfill.

⁴⁴So He proceeds from synagogue to synagogue across Judea,* preaching His message *of the kingdom of God.*

5 *Picture these events:*
On the banks of Gennesaret Lake, a huge crowd, Jesus in the center of it, presses in to hear His message from God. ²Off to the side, fishermen are washing their nets, leaving their boats unattended on the shore.

³Jesus gets into one of the boats and asks its owner, Simon, to push off *and anchor* a short distance from the beach. Jesus sits down and teaches the people standing on the beach.

⁴After speaking for a while, Jesus speaks to Simon.

Jesus: Move out into deeper water, and drop your nets to see what you'll catch.

Simon (*perplexed*) : ⁵Master, we've been fishing all night, and we haven't caught even a minnow. But . . . all right, I'll do it if You say so.

⁶Simon then gets his fellow fishermen to help him let down their nets, *and to their surprise,* the water is bubbling with thrashing fish—*a huge school.* The strands of their

* 4:44 Other early manuscripts read "Galilee."

The miracles Jesus performs come in all types: He heals the sick. He frees the oppressed. He shows His power over nature. He will even raise the dead. But as the story in verses 21-26 shows, one of the greatest miracles of all is forgiveness. To have sins forgiven—to start over again, to have God separate believers from their mistakes and moral failures, to lift the weight of shame and guilt—this may well be the weightiest evidence that God's Son is on the move. The kingdom of God doesn't throw all guilty people in jail; it doesn't execute everyone who has made mistakes or tell them they're just getting what they deserve. Instead, it brings forgiveness, reconciliation, a new start, a second chance. In this way, it mobilizes believers to have a new future.

Certainly Jesus has communicated the message of the Kingdom through words and through signs and wonders. Now Jesus embodies the message in the way He treats people, including outcasts like Levi. As a tax collector, Levi is a Jew who works for the Romans, the oppressors, the enemies. No wonder tax collectors are despised! But how does Jesus treat this compromiser? He doesn't leave him paralyzed in his compromised position; He invites him—like the paralyzed man—to get up and walk, and to walk in a new direction toward a new King and Kingdom.

---

nets start snapping under the weight of the catch, [7]so the crew shouts to the other boat to come out and give them a hand. They start scooping fish out of the nets and into their boats, and before long, their boats are so full of fish they almost sink!

[8-10]Simon's fishing partners, James and John (two of Zebedee's sons), along with the rest of the fishermen, see this incredible haul of fish. They're all stunned, especially Simon. He comes close to Jesus and kneels in front of His knees.

Simon: I can't take this, Lord. I'm a sinful man. You shouldn't be around the likes of me.

Jesus: Don't be afraid, Simon. From now on, I'll ask you to bring Me people instead of fish.

[11]The fishermen haul their fish-heavy boats to land, and they leave everything to follow Jesus.

[12]Another time in a city nearby, a man covered with skin lesions comes along. As soon as he sees Jesus, he prostrates himself.

Leper: Lord, if You wish to, You can heal me of my disease.

[13]Jesus reaches out His hand and touches the man, *something no one would normally do for fear of being infected or of becoming ritually unclean.*

Jesus: I want to heal you. Be cleansed!

Immediately the man is cured. [14]Jesus tells him firmly not to tell anyone about this.

Jesus: Go, show yourself to the priest, and do what Moses commanded by making an appropriate offering to celebrate your cleansing. This will prove to everyone what has happened.

[15]Even though Jesus said not to talk about what happened, soon every conversation was consumed by these events. The crowds swelled even larger as people went to hear Jesus preach and to be healed of their many afflictions. [16]Jesus repeatedly left the crowds, though, stealing away into the wilderness to pray.

[17]One day Jesus was teaching *in a house*, and the healing power of the Lord was with Him. Pharisees and religious scholars were sitting and listening, having come from villages all across the regions of Galilee and Judea and from *the holy city of* Jerusalem.

[18]Some men came *to the house*, carrying a paralyzed man on his bed pallet. They wanted to bring him in and present him to Jesus, [19]but the house was so packed with people that they couldn't get in. So they climbed up on the roof and pulled off some roof tiles. Then they lowered the man *by ropes* so he came to rest right in front of Jesus.

[20]In this way, their faith was visible to Jesus.

Jesus (to the man on the pallet): My friend, all your sins are forgiven.

[21]The Pharisees and religious scholars were offended at this. They turned to one another and asked questions.

Pharisees and Religious Scholars: Who does He think He is? Wasn't that blasphemous? Who can pronounce that a person's sins are forgiven? Who but God alone?

Jesus (*responding with His own question*): [22]Why are your hearts full of questions? [23]Which is easier to say, "Your sins are forgiven" or "Get up and walk"? [24]Just so you'll know that the Son of Man is fully authorized to forgive sins on earth (He turned to the paralyzed fellow *lying on the pallet*), I say, get up, take your mat, and go home.

[25]Then, right in front of their eyes, the man stood up, picked up his bed, and left to go home—full of praises for God! [26]Everyone was stunned. They couldn't help but feel awestruck, and they praised God too.

People: We've seen extraordinary things today.

[27]Some time later, Jesus walked along the street and saw a tax collector named Levi sitting in his tax office.

Jesus: Follow Me.

[28]And Levi did. He got up from his desk, left everything (*just as the fishermen had*), and followed Jesus.

[29]Shortly after this, Levi invited his many friends and associates, including many tax collectors, to his home for a *large* feast in Jesus' honor. Everyone sat at a table together.

The Pharisees are back again, and they stay through the rest of the story. Pharisaism is a religious movement, consisting of lay people (not clergy) who share a deep commitment to the Hebrew Scriptures and traditions. They believe the Jewish people have not yet been freed from the Romans because of the Jews' tolerance of sin. There are too many drunks, prostitutes, and gluttons. "If we could just get these sinners to change their ways," they feel, "then God would send the One who will free us." How angry they are at

Jesus not just for forgiving sins but also for eating with sinners! After all, to eat with people means to accept them. The kind of Rescuer they expect will judge and destroy sinners, not forgive them and enjoy their company!

---

[30]The Pharisees and their associates, the religious scholars, got the attention of some of Jesus' disciples.

Pharisees (*in low voices*): What's wrong with you? Why are you eating and drinking with tax collectors and other immoral people?

Jesus (*answering for the disciples*): [31]Healthy people don't need a doctor, but sick people do. [32]I haven't come for the pure and upstanding; I've come to call *notorious* sinners to rethink their lives and turn to God.

Pharisees: [33]Explain to us why You and Your disciples are so commonly found partying like this, when our disciples—and even the disciples of John—are known for fasting rather than feasting, and for saying prayers rather than drinking *wine*.

Jesus: [34]Imagine there's a wedding going on. Is that the time to tell the guests to ignore the bridegroom and fast? [35]Sure, there's a time for fasting—when the bridegroom has been taken away. [36]Look, nobody tears up a new garment to make a patch for an old garment. If he did, the new patch would shrink and rip the old, and the old garment would be worse off than before. [37]And nobody takes freshly squeezed juice and puts it into old, stiff wineskins. If he did, the fresh wine would make the old skins burst open, and both the wine and the wineskins would be ruined. [38]New demands new—new wine for new wineskins. [39]Anyway, those who've never tasted the new wine won't know what they're missing; they'll always say, "The old wine is good enough for me!"

6 [1-2]One Sabbath Day,* some Pharisees confronted Jesus again. This time, they saw the disciples picking some grain as they walked through the fields. The disciples

* 6:1 Other manuscripts read "On the second Sabbath after the first."

Jesus certainly has His detractors. They watch Him closely and voice their opposition to His words and actions. Sometimes they even try to stump Him with questions or publicly humiliate Him. But Jesus refuses to be intimidated. For every charge they level, He has an answer. To the charge of blasphemy, He responds, "I have the authority to forgive sins." To the charge that He befriends sinners and parties too much, He answers, "These are My people; I've come for them." To the accusation that He breaks Sabbath law, He quips, "The Sabbath is a great servant, but it's not your master. I am Lord of the Sabbath." The crowds are amazed at the tense give-and-take between Jesus and His opponents. They seem to respect the Pharisees for their strict observance of God's law, or perhaps they fear them because they don't want to become targets of Pharisaic criticism. Yet the people are attracted to Jesus because of the peculiar moral authority He exhibits. As time goes on, Jesus crosses more and more lines drawn in the sand. The tension between Jesus and the Pharisees now becomes a major plotline of Luke's story.

would dehusk the grain by rubbing the kernels in their hands, and then they would eat it raw.

Pharisees: *Don't You know the sacred law says You can't harvest and mill grain* on the Sabbath Day—the day on which all work is forbidden? Why do You think You can ignore the sacred law?

V

The Pharisees think they have God all figured out. They claim to be experts in the sacred writings—the Hebrew Scriptures. But Jesus doesn't fit in with their assumptions and expectations, and He doesn't submit to their presumed expertise. So they are constantly criticizing Him and trying to trap Him in some obvious wrongdoing or unorthodoxy. But Jesus responds with questions instead of answers. He seems to decide that the best way to help them is by challenging them to think, to question their assumptions, to see things from a higher or deeper perspective. For example, they argue about what is permissible on the Sabbath Day (the seventh day, the day of rest); this is how Jesus gets them thinking about the deeper purpose of the Sabbath Day.

Jesus: ³*Speaking of the sacred law,* haven't you ever read about the time when David

and his companions were hungry? ⁴Don't you remember how he went into the house of God and took the sacred bread of the presence—which, you may recall, only the priests were lawfully permitted to eat? Remember that he not only ate it, but he also gave it to his companions?* ⁵Likewise, the Son of Man has authority over the Sabbath.

⁶On another Sabbath, Jesus entered the synagogue and taught there. In the congregation was a man who had a deformed right hand. ⁷The religious scholars and Pharisees watched Jesus; they suspected that He might try to perform a healing on that day, which they would use as evidence to convict Him of Sabbath-breaking.

⁸Jesus knew about their plan, and He told the man with the deformed hand to come and stand in front of everyone. The man did so. ⁹Then Jesus spoke directly to the religious scholars and Pharisees.

Jesus: Here's a question for you: On the Sabbath Day, is it lawful to do good or to do harm? Is it lawful to save life or to destroy it?

¹⁰He turned His gaze to each of them, *one at a time.* Then He spoke to the man.

Jesus: Stretch your hand out.

As the man did, his deformed hand was made normal again. ¹¹This made the Pharisees and religious scholars furious. They

* 6:4 1 Samuel 21:2-6

began discussing together what they would do to Jesus.

¹²Around this time, Jesus went outside the city to a nearby mountain, *along with a large crowd of His disciples*. He prayed through the night to God. ¹³The next morning, He chose 12 of them and gave each a new title of "emissary. "

They are no longer simply disciples, which means "learners"; now they are also apostles, which means "emissaries."

¹⁴They included Simon (Jesus called him Peter) and Andrew (Simon's brother); James and John; Philip and Bartholomew; ¹⁵Matthew and Thomas; James (son of Alphaeus) and Simon (known as the Zealot); ¹⁶Judas (son of James) and the other Judas (Judas Iscariot, who later betrayed *Jesus*).

¹⁷The whole crowd of disciples *(including the 12 now designated as His emissaries)* came down together, and they stood on a level area nearby. They were joined by an even greater crowd of people who had come from across the whole region—from all of Judea, from Jerusalem, from the coastal areas of Tyre and Sidon. ¹⁸These people came to hear Jesus teach and to be healed by Jesus of their diseases. Those who were troubled by demonic spirits were liberated.

¹⁹Everyone wanted to touch Jesus because when they did, power emanated from Him and they were healed. ²⁰He looked across the faces of His disciples.

Jesus: All you who are poor, you are blessed
for the kingdom of God belongs to you.
²¹All you who are hungry now, you are blessed
for your hunger will be satisfied.
All you who weep now, you are blessed
for you shall laugh!
²²When people hate you,
when they exclude you
and insult you
and write you off as evil
on account of the Son of Man, you are blessed.
²³When these things happen, rejoice! Jump for joy!
Then you have a great reward in heaven
For at that moment, you are experiencing what the ancient prophets did when they were similarly treated by the ancestors of your detractors.

²⁴All you who are rich now, you are in danger
for you have received your comfort in full.
²⁵All you who are full now, you are in danger
for you shall be hungry.
All you who laugh now, you are in danger
for you shall grieve and cry.
²⁶And when everyone speaks well of you, you are in danger
for their ancestors spoke well of the false prophets too.

Here is Luke's most concentrated summary of Jesus' teachings for His followers. Here He describes what life in the kingdom of God looks like.

²⁷If you're listening, here's My message: Keep loving your enemies no matter what they do. Keep doing good to those who hate you. ²⁸Keep speaking blessings on those who curse you. Keep praying for those who mistreat you. ²⁹If someone strikes you on one cheek, offer the other cheek too. If someone steals your coat, offer him your shirt too. ³⁰If someone begs from you, give to him. If someone robs you of your valuables, don't demand them back. ³¹Think of the kindness you wish others would show you; do the same for them.

³²Listen, what's the big deal if you love people who already love you? Even scoundrels do that much! ³³So what if you do good to those who do good to you? Even scoundrels do that much! ³⁴So what if you lend to people who are likely to repay you? Even scoundrels lend to scoundrels if they think they'll be fully repaid.

³⁵If you want to be extraordinary—love your enemies! Do good *without restraint*! Lend *with abandon*! Don't expect anything in return! Then you'll receive the truly great reward—you will be children of the Most High—for God is kind to the ungrateful and those who are wicked. ³⁶So imitate God and be truly compassionate, the way your Father is.

³⁷If you don't want to be judged, don't judge. If you don't want to be condemned, don't condemn. If you want to be forgiven, forgive. ³⁸Don't hold back—give freely, and you'll have plenty poured back into your lap—a good measure, pressed down, shaken together, brimming over. You'll receive in the same measure you give.

39 Jesus told them this parable:

Jesus: What happens if a blind man leads a blind man? Won't both of them fall into a pit? 40 You can't turn out better than your teacher; when you're fully taught, you will resemble your teacher.

41 Speaking of blindness: Why do you focus on the speck in your brother's eye? Why don't you see the log in your own? 42 How can you say to your brother, "Oh, brother, let me help you take that little speck out of your eye," when you don't even see the big log in your own eye? What a hypocrite! First, take the log out of your own eye. Then you'll be able to see clearly enough to help your brother with the speck in his eye.

43 *Count on this:* no good tree bears bad fruit, and no bad tree bears good fruit. 44 You can know a tree by the fruit it bears. You don't find figs on a thorn bush, and you can't pick grapes from a briar bush. 45 *It's the same with people.* A person full of goodness in his heart produces good things; a person with an evil reservoir in his heart pours out evil things. The heart overflows in the words a person speaks; your words reveal what's within your heart.

46 What good is it to mouth the words, "Lord! Lord!" if you don't live by My teachings? 47 What matters is that you come to Me, hear My words, and actually live by them. 48 If you do that, you'll be like the man who wanted to build a sturdy house. He dug down deep and anchored his foundation to solid rock. During a violent storm, the floodwaters slammed against the house, but they couldn't shake it because of solid craftsmanship. [It was built upon rock.]*

49 On the other hand, if you hear *My teachings* but don't put them into practice, you'll be like the careless builder who didn't bother to build a foundation under his house. The floodwaters barely touched that pathetic house, and it crashed in ruins in the mud.

In addition to teaching and healing, Jesus also gathers disciples, who are simply students or apprentices. Their classroom is the world—hillsides and beaches, homes and country roads, fields and city streets. Their subject is life—life in the kingdom of God. Jesus has many students, both men and women, but He forms a special inner circle known as "the twelve." The number "twelve" is highly symbolic because the Jewish people were originally composed of twelve tribes. However, over the centuries, some of the tribes were decimated. By calling together a new twelve, Jesus seems to be dramatizing a new beginning for the people of God. The original twelve tribes found their identity in the law of Moses, but now Jesus is giving a new way of life for His twelve to learn and follow.

7 Jesus shared all these sayings with the crowd that day on the plain. When He was finished, He went into the town of Capernaum. 2 There, a Centurion had a slave he loved dearly. The slave was sick—about to die—3 so when the Centurion heard about Jesus, he contacted some Jewish elders. He sent them to ask Jesus to come and heal his dear slave. 4 With great emotion and respect, the elders presented their request to Jesus.

Jewish Elders: This man is worthy of Your help. *It's true that he's a Centurion,* 5 but he loves our nation. In fact, he paid for our synagogue to be built.

6 So Jesus accompanied them. When they approached the Centurion's home, the Centurion sent out some friends to bring a message to Jesus.

Message of the Centurion: Lord, don't go to the trouble of coming inside. I am not worthy to have You come under my roof. 7 That's why I sent others with my request. Just say the word, and that will be enough to heal my servant. 8 I understand how authority works, being under authority myself and having soldiers under my authority. I command to one, "Go," and he goes. I say to another, "Come," and he comes. I say to my slave, "Do this," and he obeys me.

9 Jesus was deeply impressed when He heard this. He turned to the crowd that followed Him.

* 6:48 The earliest manuscripts omit this portion.

John, it seems, is having second thoughts. Is Jesus really the One we have expected? Is He the Anointed One? But who can blame John for these doubts? After all, John is in prison, unjustly held by a corrupt, immoral ruler. Ultimately the desert prophet will have his head severed from his body when the drunken, lusty king makes a silly promise in front of dinner guests. So who can blame John for seeking assurance from the Lord? Jesus, realizing fully the kinds of expectations others have, gently reminds John and his disciples of the Scriptures: "the blind see, the lame walk, the lepers are cleansed, the deaf hear, the dead live, and the poor receive the good news." Luke doesn't say how John responds to the report as he nears his own end. What is clear is that Jesus has the utmost respect for His colleague and cousin. He doesn't reject him for his doubts but tries to send him reassurance.

Jesus: Listen, everyone. *This outsider, this Roman,* has more faith than I have found even among our own Jewish people.

¹⁰The friends of the Centurion returned home, and they found the slave was completely healed.

¹¹It wasn't long after this when Jesus entered a city called Nain. Again all of His disciples accompanied Him, along with a huge crowd. ¹²He was coming near the gate of the city as a corpse was being carried out. This man was the only child *and support* of his widowed mother, and she was accompanied by a large funeral crowd. ¹³As soon as the Lord saw her, He felt compassion for her.

Jesus: Don't weep.

¹⁴Then He came to the stretcher, and those carrying it stood still.

Jesus: Young man, listen! Get up!

¹⁵The dead man immediately sat up and began talking. Jesus presented him to his mother, ¹⁶and everyone was both shocked and jubilant. They praised God.

Funeral Crowd: A tremendous prophet has arisen in our midst! God has visited His people!

¹⁷News of Jesus spread across the whole province of Judea and beyond to the surrounding regions. ¹⁸When these reports reached John's disciples, they brought news to John himself, *who was known for his preaching and ritual cleansing.** ¹⁹John sent two of his disciples to ask the Lord, "Are You the Promised One, or shall we keep looking for someone else?"

²⁰They came to Jesus and asked their question exactly as directed by John the Baptist. ²¹Before He answered John's messengers, Jesus cured many from various diseases, health conditions, and evil spirits. He even caused many blind people to regain their sight.

Jesus (to John's disciples): ²²Go and tell John what you've witnessed with your own eyes and ears: the blind are seeing again, the lame are walking again, the lepers are clean again, the deaf hear again, the dead live again, and good news is preached to the poor.* ²³Whoever is not offended by Me is blessed indeed.

²⁴When John's messengers left, Jesus talked to the crowds about John.

Jesus: When you went out into the wilderness to see John, what were you expecting? A reed shaking in the wind? ²⁵What were you looking for? A man in expensive clothing? Look, if you were looking for fancy clothes and luxurious living, you went to the wrong place—you should have gone to the kings' courts, *not to the wilderness!* ²⁶What were you seeking? A prophet? Ah yes, that's what John is, and even more than a prophet. ²⁷*The prophet Malachi* was talking about John when he wrote,

I will send My messenger *before You,*
    to clear Your path in front of You.*

²⁸Listen, there is no human being greater than this man, John the Baptist. Yet even

* 7:18 Literally, immersing, to show repentance   * 7:22 Isaiah 29:18; 35:5-6   * 7:27 Malachi 3:1

the least significant person in the coming kingdom of God is greater than John.

²⁹The common people and tax collectors heard God's own wisdom in Jesus' assessment of John because they had been ritually cleansed through baptism by John. ³⁰But the Pharisees and religious scholars hardened their hearts and turned their backs on God's purposes for them because they had refused John's baptism.*

Jesus: ³¹The people of this generation—what are they like? To what can they be compared? ³²I'll tell you: they're like spoiled kids sitting in the marketplace *playing games,* calling out,

> We played the pipes for you,
>   but you didn't dance to our tune!
> We cried like mourners,
>   but you didn't cry with us!

³³*You can't win with this generation.* John the Baptist comes along, fasting and abstaining from wine, and you say, "This guy is demon-possessed!" ³⁴The Son of Man comes along, feasting and drinking *wine,* and you say, "This guy is a glutton and a drunk, a friend of scoundrels and tax collectors!" ³⁵Well, wisdom's true children know wisdom when they hear it.

³⁶⁻⁴⁰Once a Pharisee named Simon invited Jesus to be a guest for a meal.

Picture this:

Just as Jesus enters the man's home and takes His place at the table, a woman from the city—notorious as a woman of ill repute—follows Him in. She has heard that Jesus will be at the Pharisee's home, so she comes in and approaches Him, carrying an alabaster flask of perfumed oil. Then she begins to cry, she kneels down so her tears fall on Jesus' feet, and she starts wiping His feet with her own hair. Then she actually kisses His feet, and she pours the perfumed oil on them.

Simon *(thinking): Now I know this guy is a fraud.* If He were a real prophet, He would have known this woman is a sinner and He would never let her get near Him, much less touch Him . . . *or kiss Him!*

Jesus *(knowing what the Pharisee is thinking):* Simon, I want to tell you a story.

Simon: Tell me, Teacher.

Jesus: ⁴¹Two men owed a certain lender a lot of money. One owed 100 weeks' wages, and the other owed 10 weeks' wages. ⁴²Both men defaulted on their loans, but the lender forgave them both. Here's a question for you: which man will love the lender more?

Simon: ⁴³Well, I guess it would be the one who was forgiven more.

Jesus: Good answer.

⁴⁴⁻⁴⁶Now Jesus turns around so He's facing the woman, although He's still speaking to Simon.

Jesus: Do you see this woman here? *It's kind of funny.* I entered your home, and you didn't provide a basin of water so I could wash the road dust from My feet. You didn't give Me a customary kiss of greeting and welcome. You didn't offer Me the common courtesy of providing oil to brighten My face. But this woman has wet My feet with her own tears and washed them with her own hair. She hasn't stopped kissing My feet since I came in. And she has applied perfumed oil to My feet. ⁴⁷This woman has been forgiven much, and she is showing much love. But the person who has shown little love shows how little forgiveness he has received. ⁴⁸(to the woman) Your sins are forgiven.

Simon and Friends *(muttering among themselves):* ⁴⁹Who does this guy think He is? He has the audacity to claim the authority to forgive sins?

Jesus *(to the woman):* ⁵⁰Your faith has liberated you. Go in peace.

8 Soon after this incident, Jesus preached from city to city, village to village, carrying the good news of the kingdom of God. He was accompanied by a group called "the twelve," ²and also by a larger group including some women who had been rescued from evil spirits and healed of diseases. There was Mary, called Magdalene, who had been released from seven demons. ³There were others like Susanna and Joanna, who

* 7:30 Literally, immersed, to show repentance

was married to Chuza, a steward of King Herod. And there were many others too. *These women played an important role in Jesus' ministry,* using their wealth to provide for Him and His other companions.

⁴While a huge crowd gathered with people from many surrounding towns streaming to hear Jesus, He told them a parable.

Jesus: ⁵Once a farmer went out to scatter seed *in his fields.* Some seeds fell along a trail where they were crushed underfoot by people walking by. Birds flew in and ate those seeds. ⁶Other seeds fell on gravel. Those seeds sprouted but soon withered, depleted of moisture *under the scorching sun.* ⁷Still other seeds landed among thorns where they grew for a while, but eventually the thorns stunted them so they couldn't thrive or bear fruit. ⁸But some seeds fell into good soil—*soft, moist, free from thorns.* These seeds not only grew, but they also produced *more seeds,* a hundred times what the farmer originally planted. If you have ears, hear My meaning!

⁹His disciples heard the words, but the deeper meaning eluded them.

Disciples: What were You trying to say?

Jesus: ¹⁰The kingdom of God contains many
    secrets.
They keep listening, but do not
    comprehend;
    keep observing, but do not
    understand.*

I want you to understand, so ¹¹here's the interpretation: The voice of God falls on

human hearts like seeds scattered across a field. ¹²Some people hear that message, but the devil opposes the liberation that would come to them by believing. So he swoops in and steals the message from their hard hearts like birds stealing the seeds from the footpath. ¹³Others receive the message enthusiastically, but their vitality is short-lived because the message cannot be deeply rooted in their shallow hearts. In the heat of temptation, their faith withers, like the seeds that sprouted in gravelly soil. ¹⁴A third group hears the message, but as time passes, the daily anxieties, the pursuit of wealth, and life's addicting delights outpace the growth of the message in their hearts. Even if the message blossoms and fruit begins to form, the fruit never fully matures because the thorns choke out the plants' vitality.

¹⁵But some people hear the message and let it take root deeply in receptive hearts made fertile by honesty and goodness. With patient dependability, they bear good fruit.

¹⁶If you light a lamp, you're not going to cover it with a clay pot. You're not going to hide it under your bed. If you light a lamp, you're going to put it out in the open so your guests *can feel welcome and* see where they're going.

¹⁷Hidden things will always come out into the open. Secret things will come to light and be exposed. ¹⁸*I hope you're still listening.* And I hope you're listening carefully. If you get what I'm saying, you'll get more. If you miss My meaning, even the understanding you think you have will be taken from you.

¹⁹Around this time, Jesus was speaking to a crowd of people gathered in a house. His mother and brothers arrived to see Him, but the crowd around Him was so huge that they couldn't even get through the door. ²⁰Word spread through the crowd.

Someone from the Crowd: Jesus, Your mother and brothers are outside the house hoping to see You.

Jesus: ²¹Do you want to know who My mother and brothers are? They're the ones who truly understand God's message and obey it.

* 8:10 Isaiah 6:9

²²*Picture this:*

One day Jesus and His disciples get into a boat.

Jesus: Let's cross the lake.

So they push off from shore and begin sailing to the far side. ²³As they progress across the lake, Jesus falls sound asleep. Soon a raging storm blows in. The waves wash over the sides of the boat, and the boat starts filling up with water. Every second the situation becomes more dangerous.

²⁴The disciples *shake Jesus and* wake Him.

Disciples (*shouting*): Master! Master! We're all going to die!

Jesus wakes up and tells the wind to stop whipping them around, and He tells the furious waves to calm down. They do just that. ²⁵Then Jesus turns to the disciples.

Jesus: What happened to your faith?

The disciples had been terrified during the storm, but now they're afraid in another way. They turn to each other and start whispering, chattering, and wondering.

Disciples: Who is this man? How can He command wind and water so they do what He says?

²⁶When they get to the other side of the lake, in the Gerasene country opposite Galilee, ²⁷a man from the city is waiting for Jesus when He steps out of the boat. The man is full of demonic spirits. He's been running around for a long time stark naked, and he's homeless, sleeping among the dead in a cemetery. ²⁸⁻²⁹This man has on many occasions been tied up and chained and kept under guard, but each time he has broken free and the demonic power has driven him back into remote places *away from human contact.* Jesus commands the demonic force to leave him. The man looks at Jesus and starts screaming. He falls down in front of Jesus.

Possessed Man (*shouting*): Don't torment me, Jesus, Son of the Most High God! Why are You here?

Jesus (*calmly and simply*): ³⁰What's your name?

Possessed Man: Battalion.

He says this because an army of demons is inside of him. ³¹The demons start begging Jesus not to send them into the bottomless pit. ³²They plead instead to enter into a herd of pigs feeding on a steep hillside near the shore. Jesus gives them permission to do so. ³³Suddenly the man is liberated from the demons, but the pigs—they stampede, squealing down the hill and into the lake where they drown themselves.

³⁴The pig owners see all this. They run back to their town and tell everyone in the region about it. ³⁵Soon a crowd rushes from the town to see what's going on out by the lake. There they find Jesus seated *to teach* with the newly liberated man sitting at His feet *learning in the posture of a disciple.* This former madman is now properly dressed and completely sane. This frightens the people. ³⁶The pig owners tell them the whole story—the healing, *the pigs' mass suicide, everything.*

³⁷The people are scared to death, and they don't want this scary abnormality happening in their territory. They ask Jesus to leave immediately. *Jesus doesn't argue.* He prepares to leave, ³⁸but before they embark, the newly liberated man begs to come along and join the band of disciples.

Jesus: ³⁹No. Go home. Tell your people this amazing story about how much God has done for you.

The man does so. In fact, he tells everyone in the whole city how much Jesus did for him that day *on the shore.*

⁴⁰When Jesus and His disciples crossed the lake, another crowd was waiting to welcome Him. ⁴¹A man made his way through the crowd. His name was Jairus, and he was a synagogue official. *Like the man on the other side of the lake,* this dignified man also fell at Jesus' feet, begging Jesus to visit his home ⁴²where his only daughter, a girl of 12, lay dying. Jesus set out with Jairus. The crowd came along, too, pressing hard against Him.

⁴³In the crowd was a woman. She had suffered from an incurable menstrual disorder for 12 years [and had spent her livelihood on doctors with no effect].* *It had kept her miserable and ritually unclean, unable to participate fully in Jewish life.* ⁴⁴She followed

* 8:43 This portion is omitted in some early manuscripts.

Jesus, until she could reach Him. She touched the fringe of the robe Jesus wore, and at that moment the bleeding stopped.

Jesus (stopping and looking about): ⁴⁵Who touched Me?

Some in the Crowd (everyone speaking at once): Not me.

Another in the Crowd: It wasn't me either.

Peter [and those with him]* (intervening): Master, what kind of question is that, with this huge crowd all around You and many people touching You on all sides?

Jesus: ⁴⁶I felt something. I felt power going out from Me. I know that somebody touched Me.

⁴⁷The woman now realized her secret was going to come out sooner or later, so she stepped out of the crowd, shaking with fear, and she fell down in front of Jesus. Then she told her story in front of everyone—why she touched Him, what happened as a result.

Jesus: ⁴⁸Your faith has made you well again, daughter. Go in peace.

⁴⁹Right at that instant, one of Jairus's household servants arrived.

Servant: Sir, your daughter is dead. It's no use bothering the Teacher with this anymore.

Jesus (interrupting Jairus before he could speak): ⁵⁰Don't be afraid. Just believe. She'll be well again.

⁵¹⁻⁵²As they approached the house, the whole neighborhood was full of the sound of mourning—weeping, wailing, loud crying. Jesus told everyone to stay outside—everyone except Peter, John, James, and, of course, the girl's father and mother.

Jesus (to the mourners): Please stop weeping. The girl isn't dead. She's only asleep.

⁵³They knew for certain that she was dead, so their bitter tears now mixed with mocking laughter. ⁵⁴Meanwhile, inside, Jesus took the girl's hand.

Jesus: Child, get up!

⁵⁵She started breathing again, and she sat right up.

Jesus: Get her something to eat.

⁵⁶Her parents were amazed, but Jesus sternly told them to keep what had happened a secret.

So concludes an almost breathtaking succession of encounters between Jesus and people in need. Each story is unique; Jesus responds to each person as an individual, and there is no detectable formula to His way of treating people—except that in every case, His interactions are characterized by love and compassion.

Now Jesus takes His ministry of teaching the kingdom of God in word and deed to a new level: He sends out His disciples to do what they have seen Him do. Jesus commissions the twelve to multiply His ministry. They will go out from and then return to Jesus with reports of what they've experienced and learned. But it's hard for them to get any time alone to talk. There are so many people who want time with Jesus!

---

9 Jesus convened a gathering of the twelve. He gave them power and authority to free people from all demonic spirits and to heal them of diseases. ²He sent them out to preach the kingdom of God and to heal the sick. ³⁻⁵These were His instructions:

1. Travel light on your journey: don't take a staff, backpack, bread, money, or even an extra change of clothes.
2. When you enter a house, stay there until you leave that city.
3. If a town rejects you, shake the dust from your feet as you leave as a witness against them.

* 8:45 The earliest manuscripts omit this portion.

[6]The disciples left on their journeys from village to village. They preached the good news, and they healed the sick everywhere they went.

[7-8]*Their mission didn't go unnoticed.* The local official installed by Rome, Herod, was especially anxious about the news because rumors were flying. Some people said that Elijah or one of the other ancient prophets had been resurrected, while others said that John, *famous for his ritual cleansing,* was alive *and preaching again.*

Herod: [9]I am the one who beheaded John. So who is this man who is causing such a stir?

Herod *was curious about Jesus and* wanted to see Him.

[10]The emissaries* whom Jesus had sent out returned, and Jesus took them away from the crowds for a time of retreat in a city called Bethsaida. They gave Jesus a full report of their accomplishments and experiences. [11]But soon the crowds discovered where they were and pursued Him. Jesus didn't turn them away; He welcomed them, spoke of the kingdom of God to them, and brought health to those who needed healing.

[12]*Picture what happened* while in Bethsaida, where Jesus and His disciples were spending time with the crowds:

The sun is low in the sky, and soon it will be dusk. The twelve come to Jesus with advice.

Disciples: Send the crowd away so they can find lodging and food in the nearby villages and countryside. We're out here in the middle of nowhere.

Jesus: [13-14]No. You give them something to eat.

Disciples: *Are You kidding?* There are at least 5,000 men here, *not to mention women and children.* All we have are five loaves and two fish. The only way we could provide for them would be to go to a nearby city and buy cartloads of food. *That would cost a small fortune.*

Jesus: Just do this: organize them in little communities of about 50 people each and have them sit down.

[15]They do what Jesus says, and soon groups of 50 are scattered across the landscape.

[16]Then Jesus takes the five loaves and two fish, and He looks up to heaven. He praises God for the food, takes each item, and breaks it into fragments. Then He gives fragments to the twelve disciples and tells them to distribute the food to the crowd.

[17]Everyone eats. Everyone is satisfied. Nobody goes away hungry. In fact, when the disciples recover the leftovers, they have 12 baskets full of broken pieces.

[18]Once Jesus was praying in solitude. The disciples were nearby, and He came to them with a question.

Jesus: What are the people saying about Me?

Disciples: [19]Some people think You're John the Baptist. Others say You're the prophet Elijah, or else one of the other ancient prophets who has come back from the dead.

Jesus: [20]Ah, but what about you? Who do you say that I am?

Peter: God's Anointed, *the Liberating King.*

Jesus (sternly): [21]Don't tell anyone this. [22]The Son of Man must suffer intensely. He must be rejected by the religious establishment—the elders, the chief priests, the religious scholars. Then He will be killed. And then, on the third day He will be raised.

[23]If any of you want to walk My path, you're going to have to deny yourself. You'll have to take up your cross every day and follow Me. [24]If you try to avoid danger and risk, then you'll lose everything. If you let go of your life and risk all for My sake, then your life will be rescued, *healed, made whole and full.* [25]Listen, what good does it do you if you gain everything—if the whole world is in your pocket—but then your own life slips through your fingers and is lost to you?

[26]If you're ashamed of who I am and what I teach, then the Son of Man will be ashamed of you when He comes in all His glory, the glory of the Father, and the glory of the holy messengers. [27]*Are you ready for this?* I'm telling you the truth: some of you

* 9:10 Literally, apostles

will not taste death until your eyes see the kingdom of God.

In this section of Luke, Jesus is working hard with the disciples. They have a lot to learn and not much time left to learn it. But their "not-getting-it factor" is quite amazing. Luke's tone betrays him shaking his head and chuckling as he writes, thinking about how foolish the disciples can be at times. And, of course, he's probably thinking of himself too . . . just as he hopes his readers will when they read about the stupid things the disciples say and do—one moment seeing and hearing glorious things, the next moment missing the point entirely.

28Those words had about eight days *to settle in with the disciples.* Then, once again, Jesus went away to pray. This time He took along only Peter, John, and James. They climbed a mountainside *and came to a place of solitude.*

29-32Jesus began to pray and the disciples tried to stay awake, but their eyes grew heavier and heavier and finally they all fell asleep. When they awakened, they looked over at Jesus and saw something inexplicable happening. Jesus was changing before their eyes, beginning with His face. It seemed to glow. The glow spread, and even His clothing took on a blinding whiteness. Then, two figures appeared in the glorious radiance emanating from Jesus. The three disciples somehow knew that these figures were Moses and Elijah. Peter, James, and John overheard the conversation that took place among Jesus, Moses, and Elijah—a conversation that centered on Jesus' "departure"* and how He would accomplish this departure from the capital city, Jerusalem.

33*The glow began to fade, and* it was clear that Moses and Elijah were about to disappear.

Peter *(to Jesus)*: Please, Master, it is good for us to be here *and see this.* Can we make three structures—one to honor You, one to honor Moses, and one to honor Elijah, *to try to capture what's happening here?*

Peter had no idea what he was saying. 34While he spoke a cloud descended, and they were enveloped in it, and fear fell on them. 35Then a voice came out of everywhere and nowhere at once.

Voice from Heaven: This is My Son!* This is the One I have chosen! Listen to Him!*

36Then the voice was silent, *the cloud disappeared,* and Moses and Elijah were gone. Peter, James, and John were left speechless, *stunned, staring at* Jesus who now stood before them alone. For a long time, they did not say a word about this whole experience.

37They came down the mountain, and the next day yet another huge crowd gathered around Jesus. There was a man in the crowd who shouted out.

Man in Crowd: 38Teacher! Please come and look at my son here, my only child. 39From time to time, a demonic spirit seizes him. It makes him scream and go into convulsions. He foams at the mouth. It nearly destroys him and only leaves after causing him great distress. 40*While You were up on the mountain,* I begged Your disciples to liberate him from this spirit, but they were incapable of helping us.

Jesus: 41O generation faithless, twisted, and crooked, how long can I be with you? How much can I bear? Bring your boy here.

42The boy had taken a few steps toward Jesus when suddenly the demon seemed to rip into the boy, throwing him into convulsions. Jesus spoke sternly to the demonic spirit, and the boy was healed. Jesus presented the boy to his father.

43*The crowd began cheering and* discussing this amazing healing and the power of God, but Jesus turned to His disciples.

Jesus: 44Listen. Listen hard. Let these words get down deep: the Son of Man is going to be turned over to the authorities and arrested.

45They had no idea what He meant by this; they heard the words but missed the meaning, and they felt too afraid to ask Him to explain further.

* 9:32 Literally, His exodus   * 9:35 Psalm 2:7; Luke 3:22
* 9:35 Deuteronomy 18:15; Isaiah 42:1

46Later the close followers of Jesus began to argue over the *stupid and vain* question, "Which one of us is the greatest disciple?"

47Jesus saw what was going on—*not just the argument, but* the deeper heart issues—so He found a child and had the child stand beside Him.

Jesus: 48*See this little one?* Whoever welcomes a little child in My name welcomes Me. And whoever welcomes Me welcomes the One who sent Me. The smallest one among you is therefore the greatest.

John: 49Master, we found this fellow casting out demons. He said he was doing it in Your name, but he's not one of our group. So we told him to stop.

Jesus: 50*What?* No! Don't think like that! Whoever is not working against you is working with you.

51The time approached for Him to be taken back up *to the Father;* so strong with resolve, Jesus made Jerusalem His destination.

52He sent some people ahead of Him into the territory of the Samaritans, *a minority group at odds with the Jewish majority.* He wanted His messengers to find a place for them to stay in a village *along the road to Jerusalem.* 53But because the Samaritans realized Jesus was going to Jerusalem, they refused to welcome them.

James and John (outraged): 54Lord, do You want us to call down fire from heaven to destroy these people who have rejected You?* [Just as Elijah did.]*

Jesus (turning toward them and shaking His head): 55You just don't get it. [56The Son of Man didn't come to ruin the lives of people, but He came to liberate them.]*

He led them on toward another village. 57Farther along on the road, a man volunteered to become a disciple.

Volunteer: I'll follow You to any destination.

Jesus: 58Foxes are at home in their burrows. Birds are at home in their nests. But the Son of Man has no home. 59You (to another person)—I want you to follow Me!

Another Volunteer: *I'd be glad to,* Teacher, but let me first attend to my father's funeral.

Jesus: 60Let the dead bury their dead. I'm giving you a different calling—to go and proclaim the kingdom of God.

A Third Volunteer: 61I'll come, Jesus. I'll follow You. But just let me first run home to say good-bye to my family.

Jesus: 62Listen, if your hand is on the plow but your eyes are looking backward, then you're not fit for the kingdom of God.

10 The Lord then recruited and deployed 70* more disciples. He sent them ahead, in teams of two, to visit all the towns and settlements between them and Jerusalem. 2This is what He ordered.

Jesus: There's a great harvest waiting in the fields, but there aren't many good workers to harvest it. Pray that the Harvest Master will send out good workers to the fields.

3It's time for you 70 to go. I'm sending you out *armed with vulnerability,* like lambs walking into a pack of wolves. 4Don't bring a wallet. Don't carry a backpack. I don't even want you to wear sandals. Walk along *barefoot, quietly,* without stopping for small talk. 5When you enter a house seeking lodging, say, "Peace on this house!" 6If a child of peace—one who welcomes God's message of peace—is there, your peace will rest on him. If not, don't worry; nothing is wasted. 7Stay where you're welcomed. *Become part of the family,* eating and drinking whatever they give you. You're My workers, and you deserve to be cared for. Again, don't go from house to house, 8but settle down in a town and eat whatever they serve you. 9Heal the sick and say to the townspeople, "The kingdom of God has come near to you."

10Of course, not every town will welcome you. If you're rejected, walk through the streets and say, 11*"We're leaving this town.* We'll wipe off the dust that clings to our feet in protest against you. But even so, know this: the kingdom of God has come near." 12I tell you the truth, on

* 9:54 2 Kings 1:10,12   * 9:54 Most early manuscripts omit this portion.   * 9:56 The earliest manuscripts omit this portion.
* 10:1 Other early manuscripts read "72."

judgment day, Sodom will have an easier time of it than the town *that rejects My messengers.*

[13]It's going to be bad for you, Chorazin! It's going to be bad for you, Bethsaida! If the mighty works done in your streets had been done in the cities of Tyre and Sidon, they would have been moved to turn to God and cry out in sackcloth and ashes. [14]On judgment day, Tyre and Sidon will have an easier time of it than you. [15]It's going to be bad for you, too, Capernaum! Will you be celebrated to heaven? No, you will go down to the place of the dead.

[16]*Listen, disciples:* if people give you a hearing, they're giving Me a hearing. If they reject you, they're rejecting Me. And if they reject Me, they're rejecting the One who sent Me. *So—go now!*

[17]When the 70* *completed their mission and* returned *to report on their experiences,* they were elated.

Seventy: It's amazing, Lord! When we use Your name, the demons do what we say!

Jesus: [18]*I know.* I saw Satan falling from above like a lightning bolt. [19]I've given you true authority. You can smash vipers and scorpions under your feet.* You can walk all over the power of the enemy. You can't be harmed. [20]But listen—that's not the point. Don't be elated that evil spirits leave when you say to leave. Rejoice that your names are written in heaven.

[21]Then Jesus Himself became elated. The Holy Spirit was on Him, and He began to pray with joy.

Jesus: Thank You, Father, Lord of heaven and earth. Thank You for hiding Your mysteries from the wise and intellectual, instead revealing them to little children. Your ways are truly gracious. [22]My Father has given Me everything. No one knows the full identity of the Son except the Father, and nobody knows the full identity of the Father except the Son, and the Son fully reveals the Father to whomever He wishes. [23](then almost in a whisper to the disciples) How blessed are your eyes to see what you see! [24]Many prophets and kings dreamed of seeing what you see, but they never got a glimpse. They dreamed of hearing what you hear, but they never heard it.

[25]Just then a scholar *of the Hebrew Scriptures* tried to trap Jesus.

Scholar: Teacher, what must I do to experience the eternal life?

Jesus *(answering with a question):* [26]What is written in the *Hebrew* Scriptures? How do you interpret their answer to your question?

Scholar: [27]You shall love—"love the Eternal One your God with everything you have: all your heart, all your soul, all your strength, and all your mind"* —and "love your neighbor as yourself."*

Jesus: [28]*Perfect.* Your answer is correct. Follow these commands and you will live.

[29]The scholar *was frustrated by this response because he* was hoping to make himself appear smarter than Jesus.

Scholar: Ah, but who is my neighbor?

Jesus: [30]This fellow was traveling down from Jerusalem to Jericho when some robbers mugged him. They took his clothes, beat him to a pulp, and left him naked and bleeding and in critical condition. [31]By chance, a priest was going down that same road, and when he saw the wounded man, he crossed over to the other side and passed by. [32]Then a Levite *who was on his way to assist in the temple* also came and saw the victim lying there, and he too kept his distance. [33]Then a *despised* Samaritan journeyed by. When he saw the fellow, he felt compassion for him. [34]The Samaritan went over to him, stopped the bleeding, applied some first aid, and put the poor fellow on his donkey. He brought the man to an inn and cared for him through the night.

[35]The next day, the Samaritan took out *some money*—two days' wages* to be exact—and paid the innkeeper, saying, "Please take care of this fellow, and if this isn't enough, I'll repay you next time I pass through."

[36]Which of these three proved himself a neighbor to the man who had been mugged by the robbers?

---

* 10:17 Other early manuscripts read "72."   * 10:19 Psalm 91:13
* 10:27 Deuteronomy 6:5   * 10:27 Leviticus 19:18   * 10:35 Literally, denarii, Roman coins

Scholar: 37The one who showed mercy to him.

Jesus: Well then, go and behave like that Samaritan.

V

This story brings together many themes from Jesus' teaching of the Kingdom. Samaritans are seen as "half-breeds" by Jesus' fellow Jews—racially mixed and also religiously compromised. By making a Samaritan the hero of the story, Jesus is once again tweaking assumptions and breaking out of conventional boxes: "In the kingdom of God," Jesus is saying, "the outcasts and last can move to the front of the line." The focus for Jesus is not on the kinds of sophisticated arguments preferred by the religious scholar; for Jesus the kingdom of God is about living life, and in particular, living a life of love for God and for neighbor—whoever that neighbor may be.

38Jesus continued from there *toward Jerusalem* and came to another village. Martha, a resident of that village, welcomed Jesus into her home. 39Her sister, Mary, went and sat at Jesus' feet, listening to Him teach. 40Meanwhile Martha was anxious about all the hospitality arrangements.

Martha *(interrupting Jesus):* Lord, why don't You care that my sister is leaving me to do all the work by myself? Tell her to get over here and help me.

Jesus: 41Oh Martha, Martha, you are so anxious and concerned about a million details, 42but really, only one thing matters. Mary has chosen that one thing, and I won't take it away from her.

11 Another time Jesus was praying, and when He finished, one of His disciples approached Him.

Disciple: Teacher, would You teach us Your way of prayer? John taught his disciples his way of prayer, *and we're hoping You'll do the same.*

Jesus: 2Here's how to pray:

Father [in heaven], may Your name be revered.
    May Your kingdom come.
[May Your will be accomplished on earth as it is in heaven.]
3Give us the food we need for tomorrow,
4And forgive us for our wrongs,
    for we forgive those who wrong us.
And lead us away from temptation.
[And save us from the evil one.]*

5Imagine that one of your friends comes over at midnight. He bangs on the door and shouts, "Friend, will you lend me three loaves of bread? 6A friend of mine just showed up unexpectedly from a journey, and I don't have anything to feed him." 7Would you shout out from your bed, "I'm already in bed, and so are the kids. I already locked the door. I can't be bothered"? 8You know this as well as I do: even if you didn't care that this fellow was your friend, if he keeps knocking long enough, you'll get up and give him whatever he needs simply because of his brash persistence!

9So listen: Keep on asking, and you will receive. Keep on seeking, and you will find. Keep on knocking, and the door will be opened for you. 10All who keep asking will receive, all who keep seeking will find, and doors will open to those who keep knocking.

11Some of you are fathers, so ask yourselves this: if your son comes up to you and asks for a fish for dinner, will you give him a snake instead? 12If your boy wants an egg to eat, will you give him a scorpion? 13Look, all of you are flawed in so many ways, yet in spite of all your faults, you know how to give good gifts to your children. How much more will your Father in heaven give the Holy Spirit to all who ask!

14*Picture this:*
    Jesus is exorcising a demon that has long kept a man from speaking. When the demon is expelled, the man starts talking and the people are amazed. 15*But then controversy erupts.*

Some People: Do you know why He can cast out demons? It's because He's in league with the demon prince, Beelzebul.

* 11:2-4 The earliest manuscripts omit the bracketed text.

16Other people want to see more, so they challenge Jesus to give them another miraculous sign. 17Jesus knows what they're thinking.

Jesus: *People, be logical.* If a kingdom is divided against itself, it will collapse. If a ruling family is divided against itself, it will fall apart.
    18So if Satan's kingdom is divided against itself, won't his whole enterprise collapse? Does it make any sense to say I'm casting out demons by Beelzebul? 19Besides, if you're saying it takes satanic power to cast out Satan, by whose power do your own exorcists work? If you condemn Me for an exorcism, you'll have to condemn them. 20But if I by the power of God cast out demonic spirits, then *face this fact*: the kingdom of God is here, *just as I've been saying.*
    21When a man of power with his full array of weapons guards his own palace, everything inside is secure. 22But when a new man who is stronger *and better armed* attacks the palace, the old ruler will be overcome, his weapons and trusted defenses will be removed, and his treasures will be plundered. 23Can you see that I'm asking you to choose whose side you're on—working with Me or fighting against Me?

These people think they are experts on demonic spirits, but Jesus instructs them in how these things actually work.

    24When a demonic spirit is expelled from someone, he wanders through waterless wastelands seeking rest. But there is no rest for him anywhere, so he says, "I'm going back to my old house." 25He returns and finds the old house has been swept clean and fixed up again. 26So he goes and finds seven other spirits even worse than he is, and they make themselves at home in the man's life so that he's worse off now than he was before.

27As He is speaking, a woman shouts out from the crowd and interrupts Him.

Woman: How blessed is Your mother's womb for bearing You! How blessed are her 28breasts for nursing You!

Jesus: No, how blessed are those who hear God's voice and make God's message their way of life.

29*Jesus was becoming more and more popular, and the crowds swelled wherever He went. He wasn't impressed.*

Jesus: This generation is evil. These people are seeking signs *and spectacles, but I'm not going to play their game.* The only sign they will be given is the sign of Jonah. 30Just as Jonah became a sign to the people of Nineveh, so will the Son of Man be to this generation.
    31The queen of Ethiopia will stand to condemn the people of this generation on the day of judgment. She, *an outsider,* came from so far away to hear the wisdom given to Solomon, but now, something greater than Solomon is here: *how are the people of this generation responding?*
    32Similarly, the people of Nineveh will stand to condemn the people of this generation on the day of judgment. They, *outsiders,* responded and changed because of the preaching of Jonah, but now, something greater than Jonah is here: *how are the people of this generation responding?*
    33*You need a light to see.* Only an idiot would light a lamp and then put it beneath the floor or under a bucket. No, any intelligent person would put the lamp on a table so everyone who comes in the house can see. 34Listen, your eye, *your outlook, the way you see* is your lamp. If your way of seeing is functioning well, then your whole life will be enlightened. But if your way of seeing is darkened, then your life will be a dark, dark place. 35So be careful, people, because your light may be malfunctioning. 36If your outlook is good, then your whole life will be bright, with no shadowy corners, as when a radiant lamp brightens your home.

Jesus is fearless with Pharisees and scholars. To get through to them He agrees to eat in the home of a Pharisee where a religious scholar has also been invited.

37A Pharisee interrupted His speech with an invitation to dinner. Jesus accepted the invitation and took His place at his table. 38The Pharisee was offended that Jesus didn't perform the ceremonial handwashing before eating—*something Pharisees were fastidious about doing.*

Jesus: ³⁹You Pharisees *are a walking contradiction.* You are so concerned about external things—like someone who washes the outside of a cup and bowl but never cleans the inside, *which is what counts!* Beneath your fastidious exterior is a mess of extortion and filth.

⁴⁰You guys don't get it. Did the potter make the outside but not the inside too? ⁴¹*If you were full of goodness within,* you could overflow with generosity from within, and if you did that, everything would be clean for you.

⁴²Woe to you, Pharisees! *Judgment will come on you!* You are fastidious about tithing—keeping account of every little leaf of mint and herb—but you neglect what really matters: justice and the love of God! If you'd get straight on what really matters, then your fastidiousness about little things would be worth something.

⁴³Woe to you, Pharisees! *Judgment will come on you!* What you really love is having people fawn over you when you take the seat of honor in the synagogue or when you are greeted in the public market.

⁴⁴*Wake up! See what you've become!* Woe to you; you're like a field full of unmarked graves. People walk on the field and have no idea of the corruption that's a few inches beneath their feet.

Scholar (*sitting at Jesus' table*): ⁴⁵Rabbi, if You insult the Pharisees, then You insult us too.

Jesus: ⁴⁶Well, *now that you mention it,* watch out, all you religious scholars! *Judgment will come on you too!* You load other people down with unbearable burdens *of rules and regulations,* but you don't lift a finger to help others. ⁴⁷⁻⁴⁸Woe to you; *you don't fool anybody! You seem very religious*—honoring the prophets by building them elaborate memorial tombs. Come to think of it, that's very fitting, since you're so much like the people who killed the prophets! They killed the prophets; you build their tombs—*you're all in the same family business!*

⁴⁹This is why the Wisdom of God said, "I will send these people My prophets and emissaries,* and these people will kill and persecute many of them." ⁵⁰As a result, this generation will be held accountable for the blood of all the prophets shed from the very beginning of time, ⁵¹from Abel's blood to Zechariah's blood, who was killed in the temple itself between the altar and the holy place. I'm serious: this generation will be held accountable.

⁵²So, religious scholars, judgment will come on you! *You're supposed to be teachers, unlocking the door of knowledge and guiding people through it.* But the fact is, you've never even passed through the doorway yourselves. You've taken the key, left the door locked tight, and stood in the way of everyone who sought entry.

⁵³After that dinner, things were never the same. The religious scholars and Pharisees put constant pressure on Jesus, ⁵⁴trying to trap Him and trick Him into saying things they could use to bring Him down.

12

The crowds at this time were packed in so tightly that thousands of people were stepping on each other. Jesus spoke to His disciples, *knowing that the crowds could overhear.*

Jesus: Guard yourselves from the yeast that puffs up the Pharisees—hypocrisy, *false appearance, trying to look better than you really are.*

²Nothing is covered up that won't be discovered; nothing is hidden that won't be exposed. ³Whatever a person says in the dark will be published in the light of day, and whatever a person whispers in private rooms will be broadcast from the housetops.

⁴Listen, My friends, if people are trying to kill you, why be afraid? After you're dead, what more can they do? ⁵⁻⁶Here's whose opinion you should be concerned about: the One who can take your life and then throw you into hell! He's the only One you should fear! *But don't misunderstand: you don't really need to be afraid of God,* because God cares for every little sparrow. How much is a sparrow worth—don't five of them sell for a few cents?* ⁷Since you are so much more precious to God than a thousand flocks of sparrows, *and since God knows you in every detail*—down to the number of hairs on your head *at this moment—you can be secure and unafraid of*

* 11:49 Literally, apostles   * 12:5-6 Literally, two assaria

any person, and you have nothing to fear from God either.

⁸That's why I keep telling you not to be intimidated. If you identify unashamedly with Me before others, I, the Son of Man, will affirm you before God and all the heavenly messengers. ⁹But if you deny Me before others, you will be denied before God and all the heavenly messengers. ¹⁰People can speak a word against Me, the Son of Man, and the sin is forgivable. But they can go too far, slandering the testimony of the Holy Spirit by rejecting His message about Me, and they won't be forgiven for that.

¹¹So you can anticipate that you will be put on trial before the synagogues and religious officials. Don't worry how you'll respond, and don't worry what you should say. ¹²The Holy Spirit will give you the words to say at the moment when you need them.

In the kingdom of God, money is valued in a very different way. In fact, concern for money can easily turn the spiritual life into a lukewarm, halfhearted affair.

¹³A person in the crowd got Jesus' attention.

Person in the Crowd: Teacher, intervene and tell my brother to share the family inheritance with me.

Jesus: ¹⁴Since when am I your judge or arbitrator?

¹⁵Then He used that opportunity to speak to the crowd.

Jesus: You'd better be on your guard against any type of greed, for a person's life is not about having a lot of possessions.

¹⁶(then, beginning another parable) A wealthy man owned some land that produced a huge harvest. ¹⁷He often thought to himself, "I have a problem here. I don't have anywhere to store all my crops. What should I do? ¹⁸I know! I'll tear down my small barns and build even bigger ones, and then I'll have plenty of storage space for my grain and all my other goods. ¹⁹Then I'll be able to say to myself, 'I have it made! I can relax and take it easy for years! So I'll just sit back, eat, drink, and have a good time!'"

²⁰Then God interrupted the man's conversation with himself. "Excuse Me, Mr. Brilliant, but your time has come. Tonight you will die. Now who will enjoy everything you've earned and saved?"

²¹This is how it will be for people who accumulate huge assets for themselves but have no assets in relation to God.

²²(then, to His disciples) This is why I keep telling you not to worry about anything in life—about what you'll eat, about how you'll clothe your body. ²³Life is more than food, and the body is more than fancy clothes. ²⁴Think about those crows flying over there: do they plant and harvest crops? Do they own silos or barns? Look at them fly. It looks like God is taking pretty good care of them, doesn't it? Remember that you are more precious to God than birds! ²⁵Which one of you can add a single hour to your life or 18 inches* to your height by worrying really hard? ²⁶If worry can't change anything, why do you do it so much?

²⁷Think about those beautiful wild lilies growing over there. They don't work up a sweat toiling for needs or wants—they don't worry about clothing. Yet the great King Solomon never had an outfit that was half as glorious as theirs!

²⁸Look at the grass growing over there. One day it's thriving in the fields. The next day it's being used as fuel. If God takes such good care of such transient things, how much more you can depend on God to care for you, weak in faith as you are. ²⁹Don't reduce your life to the pursuit of food and drink; don't let your mind be filled with anxiety. ³⁰People of the world who don't know God pursue these things, but you have a Father caring for you, a Father who knows all your needs.

³¹Since you don't need to worry—about security and safety, about food and clothing—then pursue God's kingdom first and foremost, and these other things will come to you as well.

³²My little flock, don't be afraid. God is your Father, and your Father's great joy is to give you His kingdom.

³³That means you can sell your possessions and give generously to the poor. You can have a different kind of savings plan: one that never depreciates, one that never defaults, one that can't be plundered by crooks or destroyed by natural calamities.

* 12:25 Literally, one cubit

³⁴*Your treasure will be stored in the heavens,* and since your treasure is there, your heart will be lodged there as well.

³⁵⁻³⁶*I'm not just talking theory. There is urgency in all this.* If you're apathetic and complacent, then you'll miss the moment of opportunity. You should be wide awake and on your toes like servants who are waiting for their master to return from a big wedding reception. They'll have their shoes on and their lamps lit so they can open the door for him as soon as he arrives home. ³⁷How fortunate those servants will be when the master knocks and they open the door immediately! You know what the master will do? He'll put on an apron, sit them down at the kitchen table, and he'll serve them a midnight snack. ³⁸The later he comes home—whether it's at midnight or even later, just before dawn—the more fortunate the alert servants will be.

³⁹*In contrast, imagine a complacent, apathetic household manager whose house gets robbed.* If he had been aware that thieves *were waiting in the bushes* and what hour they were coming, [he would have watched and]* he never would have left the house! ⁴⁰I'm trying to tell you that these are times for alertness, times requiring a sense of urgency and intensity, because *like the master in the first story or the thief in the second,* the Son of Man shows up by surprise.

Peter: ⁴¹Lord, I'm not sure if this parable is intended only for us disciples or if this is for everyone else too.

Jesus: ⁴²Imagine the stories of two household managers, and decide for yourself which one is faithful and smart. Each household manager is told by his master *to take good care of all his possessions and* to oversee the other employees—*the butlers, cooks, gardeners, and so on.* ⁴³One servant immediately busies himself in doing just what he was told. His master eventually comes to check on him ⁴⁴and rewards him with a major promotion and with more responsibility and trust. ⁴⁵The other household manager thinks, "Look, my boss is going to be gone for a long time. *I can be complacent; there's no urgency here.*" So he beats the other employees—the women as well as the men. He sits around *like a slob,* eating and getting drunk. ⁴⁶Then the boss comes home unexpectedly and catches him by surprise. One household manager will

be fortunate indeed, and the other will be cut into pieces and thrown out.

⁴⁷Now if a servant who is given clear instructions by his master doesn't follow those instructions but instead is complacent and apathetic, then he will be punished severely. ⁴⁸But if a servant doesn't know what his master expects and behaves badly, then he will receive a lighter punishment. If you are given much, much will be required of you. If much is entrusted to you, much will be expected of you.

⁴⁹*This is serious business we're involved in.* My mission is to send a purging fire on the earth! In fact, I can hardly wait to see the smoke rising. ⁵⁰I have a kind of baptism to go through, and I can't relax until My mission is accomplished! ⁵¹Do you think I've come with a nice little message of peace? No way. Believe Me, My message will divide. ⁵²It will divide a household of five into three against two or two against three. ⁵³It will divide father against son and son against father; mother against daughter and daughter against mother; mother-in-law against daughter-in-law and daughter-in-law against mother-in-law.*

⁵⁴(speaking to the crowd) You see a cloud arise *from the sea* in the west, and you can say, "Here comes a shower!" And you're right. ⁵⁵Or you feel the hot wind blowing in from *the desert in* the south and you say, "It's going to be really hot!" And you're right. ⁵⁶Listen, hypocrites! You can predict the weather by paying attention to the sky and the earth, but why can't you interpret the urgency of this present moment? ⁵⁷Why don't you see it for yourselves?

⁵⁸Imagine you're being sued. You and your accuser are on your way to court. Wouldn't you do everything in your power to settle out of court before you stand before the magistrate? After all, he might drag you to stand before the judge, and the judge might hand you over to the police, and they might throw you in jail. ⁵⁹Once you're in jail, it's too late: you're not going anywhere until you've paid in full.

13 As He said this, some people told Him the latest news about a group of Galilean pilgrims *in Jerusalem—a group not unlike Jesus' own entourage.* Pilate butchered them *while they were at worship,*

* 12:39 The earliest manuscripts omit the bracketed portion.
* 12:53 Micah 7:6

their own blood mingling with the blood of their sacrifices.

Jesus: [2]Do you think these Galileans *were somehow being singled out for their sins,* that they were worse than any other Galileans, because they suffered this terrible death? [3]Of course not. But listen, if you do not consider God's ways and truly change, then friends, you should prepare to face His judgment and eternal death.

[4]*Speaking of current events,* you've all heard about the 18 people killed *in that building accident* when the tower in Siloam fell. Were they extraordinarily bad people, worse than anyone else in Jerusalem, *so that they would deserve such an untimely death?* [5]Of course not. *But all the buildings of Jerusalem will come crashing down on you* if you don't wake up and change direction now.

[6](following up with this parable) A man has a fig tree planted in his vineyard. One day he comes out looking for fruit on it, but there are no figs. [7]He says to the vineyard keeper, "Look at this tree. For three years, I've come hoping to find some fresh figs, but what do I find? Nothing. So just go ahead and cut it down. Why waste the space with a fruitless tree?"

[8]The vineyard keeper replies, "Give it another chance, sir. Give me one more year working with it. I'll cultivate the soil and heap on some manure to fertilize it. [9]If it surprises us and bears fruit next year, that will be great, but if not, then we'll cut it down."

[10]Around this time, He was teaching in a synagogue on the Sabbath, *the Jewish day of rest.* [11]A woman there had been sick for 18 years; she was weak, hunched over, and unable to stand up straight. [12-13]Jesus placed His hands on her and suddenly she could stand straight again. She started praising God, [14]but the synagogue official was indignant because Jesus had not kept their Sabbath regulations by performing this healing.

Synagogue Official: Look, there are six other days when it's appropriate to get work done. Come on those days to be healed, not on the Sabbath!

Jesus: [15]You *religious leaders* are such hypocrites! Every single one of you unties his ox or donkey from its manger every single Sabbath Day, and then you lead it out to get a drink of water, right? [16]Do you care more about your farm animals than you care about this woman, one of Abraham's daughters, oppressed by Satan for 18 years? Can't we untie her from her oppression on the Sabbath?

[17]As the impact of His words settled in, His critics were humiliated, but everyone else loved what Jesus said and celebrated everything He was doing.

Jesus (explaining): [18]Do you want to understand the kingdom of God? Do you want Me to tell you what it's like? [19]It's like a single mustard seed that someone took and planted in his garden. That tiny seed grew and became a tree so large that the birds could fly in and make their nests in its branches.

[20]Do you want Me to tell you what the kingdom of God is like? [21]It's like some yeast which a woman hid within a huge quantity of flour; soon the whole batch of dough was rising.

[22]He was pressing toward Jerusalem, His journey taking Him through various towns and villages. In each one, He taught the people. [23]Once a person asked this question:

Inquiring Individual: Lord, will only a few people be rescued?

Jesus: [24]Strive to enter through the narrow door now, because many people—hear Me on this—will try to enter *later on* and will not be able to. [25]Imagine you want to enter someone's home, but you wait until after the homeowner has shut the door. Then you stand outside and bang on the door, and you say, "Sir, please open the door for us!" But he will answer, "I don't know where you're from."

[26]Then you'll say, "Just a minute. We ate and drank with you, and you taught in our streets." [27]But he'll say, "Sorry, I have no idea where you're from. Leave me, all of you evildoers." [28]Then you'll see something that will make you cry and grind your teeth together—you'll see Abraham and Isaac and Jacob and all the prophets in the kingdom of God, but you yourselves will be on the outside looking in.

[29]And then you'll see people streaming in from east and west, from north and

south, gathering around the table in the kingdom of God, *but you'll be on the outside looking in.* ³⁰That's how it will be; some are last now who will be first then, and some are first now who will be last then.

V

Jesus' response shows that the Jewish people will be surprised by who enters the kingdom of God. It will not be just the Jews but people from all around the world—east and west, north and south. And they will also be surprised by who does not enter the kingdom, since some Jews will be on the outside looking in.

---

³¹Right then some Pharisees came and warned Him.

Pharisees: You'd better get out of here because Herod is plotting Your murder.

Jesus: ³²You can give that sly fox this message: "Watch as I cast out demons and perform healings today and tomorrow, and on the third day I'll reach My destination. ³³But for today and tomorrow and the next day, I have to continue My journey, for no prophet should perish outside of Jerusalem."

³⁴O Jerusalem! O Jerusalem! You kill the prophets and you stone the messengers who are sent to you. How often I wanted to gather in your children as a hen gathers in her chicks under her wings, but you were not willing to come to Me. ³⁵Look now, your house is abandoned and empty. You won't see Me until you welcome Me with the words *of the psalms,* "Anyone who comes in the name of the Eternal One will be blessed!"*

14 Another Sabbath Day came and Jesus was invited to an official's home for a meal. This fellow was a leader of the Pharisees, and Jesus was still under close surveillance by them. ²Jesus noticed a man suffering from a swelling disorder. ³He questioned the religious scholars and Pharisees.

Jesus: Is it permitted by traditions and the Hebrew Scriptures to heal people on the Sabbath, or is it forbidden?

⁴They didn't reply. Then Jesus healed the man and sent him on his way.

Jesus: ⁵Would any single one of you leave his son* or even his ox in a well on the Sabbath if he had fallen into it, or would you pull him out immediately?

⁶They still didn't reply.
⁷Then He noticed how the guests were jockeying for places of honor at the dinner, so He gave them advice.

Jesus: ⁸Whenever someone invites you to a wedding dinner, don't sit at the head table. Someone more important than you might also have been invited, ⁹and your host will have to humiliate you publicly by telling you to give your seat to the other guest and to go find an open seat in the back of the room. ¹⁰Instead, go and sit in the back of the room. Then your host may find you and say, "My friend! Why are you sitting back here? Come up to this table near the front!" Then you will be publicly honored in front of everyone. ¹¹Listen, if you lift yourself up, you'll be put down, but if you humble yourself, you'll be honored.

¹²Jesus still wasn't finished. Now He turned to the host who had invited Him to this gathering.

Jesus: When you host a dinner or banquet, don't invite your friends, your brothers, your relatives, or your rich neighbors. If you do, they might invite you to a party of their own, and you'll be repaid for your kindness. ¹³Instead, invite the poor, the amputees, the cripples, the blind. ¹⁴Then you'll be blessed because they can never repay you. Your reward will come from God at the resurrection of the just and good.

Guest: ¹⁵Blessed is everyone who will eat bread in the kingdom of God!

Jesus: ¹⁶A man once hosted a huge banquet and invited many guests. ¹⁷When the time came, he sent his servant to tell the guests who had agreed to come, "We're ready! Come now!" ¹⁸But then every single guest began to make excuses. One said, "*Oh, I'm sorry.* I just bought some land, and I need

* 13:35 Psalm 118:26   * 14:5 Some manuscripts read "donkey."

to go see it. Please excuse me." [19]Another said, "*So sorry.* I just bought five pairs of oxen. I need to go check them out. Please excuse me." [20]Another said, "I just got married, so I can't come."

[21]The servant returned and reported their responses to his master. His master was angry and told the servant, "Go out quickly to the streets and alleys around town and bring the poor, the amputees, the blind, and the cripples."

[22]The servant came back again: "Sir, I've done as you said, but there is still more room." [23]And the host said, "Well then, go out to the highways and hedges and bring in the complete strangers you find there, until my house is completely full. [24]One thing is for sure, not one single person on the original guest list shall enjoy this banquet."

V

Jesus continues to challenge Jewish ideas about who will be in the kingdom of God and how the Kingdom will work. Those who have been dishonored on earth will be honored in the Kingdom, and those in positions of economic and religious honor here will be dishonored there. He also challenges individuals to reconsider their personal value systems. They should not honor their own lives and family above Christ, but rather give them up for Him.

---

[25]Great crowds joined Him on His journey, and He turned to them.

Jesus: [26]If any of you come to Me without hating your own father, mother, wife, children, brothers, sisters, and yes, even your own life, you can't be My disciple. [27]If you don't carry your own cross *as if to your own execution* as you follow Me, you can't be part of My movement. [28]Just imagine that you want to build a tower. Wouldn't you first sit down and estimate the cost to be sure you have enough to finish what you start? [29]If you lay the foundation but then can't afford to finish the tower, everyone will mock you: [30]"Look at that guy who started something that he couldn't finish!"

[31]Or imagine a king gearing up to go to war. Wouldn't he begin by sitting down *with his advisors* to determine whether his 10,000 troops could defeat the opponent's 20,000 troops? [32]If not, he'll send a peace delegation quickly and negotiate a peace treaty. [33]In the same way, if you want to be My disciple, it will cost you everything. *Don't underestimate that cost!*

[34]Don't be like salt that has lost its taste. How can its saltiness be restored? *Flavorless salt is absolutely worthless.* [35]You can't even use it as fertilizer, so it's worth less than manure! Don't just listen to My words here. Get the deeper meaning.

15 Jesus became increasingly popular among *notorious* sinners—tax collectors and other social outcasts. [2]The Pharisees and religious scholars noticed this.

Pharisees and Religious Scholars: This man welcomes immoral people and enjoys their company over a meal!

Jesus (*with another parable*): [3-4]Wouldn't every single one of you, if you have 100 sheep and lose one, leave the 99 in their grazing lands and go out searching for the lost sheep until you find it? [5]When you find the lost sheep, wouldn't you hoist it up on your shoulders, feeling wonderful? [6]And when you go home, wouldn't you call together your friends and neighbors? Wouldn't you say, "Come over and celebrate with me, because I've found my lost sheep"? [7]This is how it is in heaven. They're happier over one sinner who changes his way of life than they are over 99 good and just people who don't need to change their ways of life.

[8]Or imagine a woman who has 10 silver coins. She loses one. Doesn't she light a lamp, sweep the whole house, and search diligently until that coin is found? [9]And when she finds it, doesn't she invite her friends and neighbors and say, "Celebrate with me! I've found that silver coin that I lost"? [10]Can't you understand? There is joy in the presence of all God's messengers over even one sinner who changes his way of life.

[11]Once there was this man who had two sons. [12]One day the younger son came to his father and said, "Father, eventually I'm going to inherit my share of your estate. Rather than waiting until you die, I want you to give me my share now." And so the

father *liquidated assets and* divided them. [13]A few days passed and this younger son gathered all his wealth and set off on a journey to a distant land. Once there he wasted everything he owned on wild living. [14]He was broke, a terrible famine struck that land, and he felt desperately hungry and in need. [15]He got a job with one of the locals, who sent him into the fields to feed the pigs. [16]The young man felt so miserably hungry that he wished he could eat the slop the pigs were eating. Nobody gave him anything.

[17]So he had this moment of self-reflection: *"What am I doing here?* Back home, my father's hired servants have plenty of food. Why am I here starving to death? [18]I'll get up and return to my father, and I'll say, 'Father, I have done wrong—wrong against God and against you. [19]I have forfeited any right to be treated like your son, but I'm wondering if you'd treat me as one of your hired servants?'" [20]So he got up and returned to his father. The father looked off in the distance and saw the young man returning. He felt compassion for his son and ran out to him, enfolded him in an embrace, and kissed him.

[21]The son said, "Father, I have done a terrible wrong in God's sight and in your sight too. I have forfeited any right to be treated as your son."

[22]But the father turned to his servants and said, "Quick! Bring the best robe we have and put it on him. Put a ring on his finger and shoes on his feet. [23]Go get the fattest calf and butcher it. Let's have a feast and celebrate [24]because my son was dead and is alive again. He was lost and has been found." So they had this huge party.

[25]Now the man's older son was still out in the fields working. He came home at the end of the day and heard music and dancing. [26]He called one of the servants and asked what was going on. [27]The servant said, "Your brother has returned, and your father has butchered the fattest calf to celebrate his safe return."

[28]The older brother got really angry and refused to come inside, so his father came out and pleaded with him to join the celebration. [29]But he argued back, "Listen, all these years I've worked hard for you. I've never disobeyed one of your orders. But how many times have you even given me a little goat to roast for a party with my friends? Not once! *This is not fair!* [30]So this son of yours comes, this wasteful delinquent who has spent your hard-earned wealth on loose women, and what do you do? You butcher the fattest calf from our herd!"

[31]The father replied, "My son, you are always with me, and all I have is yours. [32]Isn't it right to join in the celebration and be happy? This is your brother we're talking about. He was dead and is alive again; he was lost and is found again!"

V

The parable ends. Jesus never reveals how it came out. Did the older brother join the party and reconcile with his younger, wayward brother? Or did he stay outside, fuming over the seeming injustice of his father's extravagant love? The story remains unresolved because it is, in fact, an invitation—an invitation to the Pharisees and other opponents of Jesus to join Him in welcoming sinners and other outsiders into the joyful party of the Kingdom.

---

16 Here's a parable He told the disciples:

Jesus: Once there was a rich *and powerful* man who had an asset manager. One day, the man received word that his asset manager was squandering his assets.

[2]The rich man brought in the asset manager and said, "You've been accused of wrongdoing. I want a full and accurate accounting of all your financial transactions because you are really close to being fired."

[3]The manager said to himself, *"Oh, no!* Now what am I going to do? I'm going to lose my job here, and I'm too weak to dig ditches and too proud to beg. [4]I have an idea. This plan will mean that I have a lot of hospitable friends when I get fired."

[5]So the asset manager set up appointments with each person who owed his master money. He said to the first debtor, "How much do you owe my boss?" [6]The debtor replied, "A hundred barrels* of oil." The manager said, "I'm discounting your

*16:6 About 600-800 gallons

bill by half. Just write 50 on this contract."
⁷Then he said to the second debtor, "How much do you owe?" This fellow said, "A hundred bales* of wheat." The manager said, "I'm discounting your debt by 20 percent. Just write down 80 bales on this contract."

⁸When the manager's boss realized what he had done, he congratulated him for at least being clever. That's how it is: those attuned to this evil age are more clever in dealing with their affairs than the enlightened are in dealing with their affairs!

⁹*Learn some lessons from this crooked but clever asset manager.* Realize that the purpose of money is to strengthen friendships, to provide opportunities for being generous and kind. Eventually money will be useless to you—but if you use it generously to serve others, you will be welcomed joyfully into your eternal destination.

¹⁰If you're faithful in small-scale matters, you'll be faithful with far bigger responsibilities. If you're crooked in small responsibilities, you'll be no different in bigger things. ¹¹If you can't even handle a small thing like money, who's going to entrust you with spiritual riches that really matter? ¹²If you don't manage well someone else's assets that are entrusted to you, who's going to give over to you important spiritual and personal relationships to manage?

¹³Imagine you're a servant and you have two masters giving you orders. *What are you going to do when they have conflicting demands?* You can't serve both, so you'll either hate the first and love the second, or you'll faithfully serve the first and despise the second. One master is God and the other is money. You can't serve them both.

¹⁴The Pharisees overheard all this, and they started mocking Jesus because they really loved money.

Jesus (to the Pharisees): ¹⁵*You've made your choice.* Your ambition is to look good in front of other people, not God. But God sees through to your hearts. He values things differently from you. The goals you and your peers are reaching for God detests.

¹⁶The law and the prophets had their role until the coming of John *the Baptist.* Since John's arrival, the good news of the kingdom of God has been taught while

people are clamoring to enter it. ¹⁷*That's not to say that God's rules for living are useless.* The stars in the sky and the earth beneath your feet will pass away before one letter of God's rules for living become worthless.

¹⁸*Take God's rules regarding marriage for example.* If a man divorces his wife and marries somebody else, then it's still adultery *because that man has broken his vow to God.* And if a man marries a woman divorced from her husband, he's committing adultery *for the same reason.*

¹⁹There was this rich man who had everything—purple clothing of fine quality and high fashion, gourmet meals every day, and a large house. ²⁰Just outside his front gate lay this poor *homeless* fellow named Lazarus. Lazarus was covered in ugly skin lesions. ²¹He was so hungry he wished he could scavenge scraps from the rich man's trash. Dogs would come and lick the sores on his skin. ²²The poor fellow died and was carried on the arms of the heavenly messengers to the embrace of Abraham. Then the rich fellow died and was buried ²³and found himself in the place of the dead. In his torment, he looked up, and off in the distance he saw Abraham, with Lazarus in his embrace.

²⁴He shouted out, "Father Abraham! Please show me mercy! Would you send *that beggar* Lazarus to dip his fingertip in water and cool my tongue? These flames are hot, and I'm in agony!"

²⁵But Abraham said, "Son, you seem to be forgetting something: your life was full to overflowing with comforts and pleasures, and the life of Lazarus was just as full with suffering and pain. So now is his time of comfort, and now is your time of agony. ²⁶Besides, a great canyon separates you and us. Nobody can cross over from our side to yours, or from your side to ours."

²⁷"Please, Father *Abraham,* I beg you," the formerly rich man continued, "send Lazarus to my father's house. ²⁸I have five brothers there, *and they're on the same path I was on.* If Lazarus warns them, they'll choose another path and won't end up here in torment."

²⁹But Abraham said, "*Why send Lazarus?* They already have the law of Moses and the writings of the prophets to instruct them. Let your brothers hear them."

* 16:7 About 700 bushels

30"No, Father Abraham," he said, *"they're already ignoring the law and the prophets.* But if someone came back from the dead, then they'd listen for sure; then they'd change their way of life."

31Abraham answered, "If they're not listening to Moses and the prophets, they won't be convinced even if someone comes back from the dead."

V

The theme of money and wealth has come up again and again. It's what really motivates the Pharisees, it turns out. Money might be God's top competitor. In the previous parable, Jesus turns the tables. The rich man, who represents what most people wish they could become, turns out to be the one who is hopeless in God's judgment; he is rich in possessions but poor in compassion, and compassion is what God measures, not wealth. The kingdom of God, Jesus is making clear, calls rich people to stop working to increase their personal wealth portfolio; instead, it challenges them to join God by using their wealth and power on behalf of the poor.

---

17 **Jesus** (*to His disciples*): You can't stop temptations to do wrong from coming. But how tragic it will be for the person who becomes the source of the temptation! 2It would be better if a millstone were hung around his neck and he were thrown into the sea, than that he should offend one of these little ones.

3So each of you needs to be careful. If your brother sins [against you],* confront him about it, and if he has a change of mind and heart, then forgive him. 4Even if he wrongs you seven times in a single day, if he turns back to you each time and says he's sorry and will change, you must forgive him.

The Lord's Emissaries: 5*We don't have enough faith for this!* Help our faith to grow!

Jesus (*pointing to a nearby mulberry tree*): 6*It's not like you need a huge amount of*

faith. If you just had faith the size of a single, tiny mustard seed, you could say to this huge tree, "Pull up your roots and replant yourself in the sea," and it would *fly through the sky and* do what you said. *So even a little faith can accomplish the seemingly impossible.*

7*Imagine this scenario.* You have a servant—say he's been out plowing a field or taking care of the sheep—and he comes in hot and sweaty from his work. Are you going to say, "*You poor thing!* Come in and sit down right away"? Of course not! 8Wouldn't you be more likely to say, "First, cook my supper and set the table, and then after I've eaten, you can get something to eat and drink for yourself"? 9And after your servant has done everything you told him to do, are you going to make a big deal about it and thank him? [I don't think so!]* 10Now apply this situation to yourselves. When you've done everything I'm telling you to do, just say, "We're servants, unworthy of extra consideration or thanks; we're just doing our duty."

11Jesus was still pressing toward Jerusalem, taking a road that went along the border between Samaria (*considered undesirable territory*) and Galilee. 12On the outskirts of a border town along this road, He was greeted from a distance by a group of 10 people who were under quarantine because of an ugly and disgusting skin disease known as leprosy.

Lepers (*shouting across the distance*): 13Jesus, Master, show mercy to us!

Jesus: 14Go now and present yourselves to the priests *for inspection of your disease.*

They went, and before they reached the priests, their skin disease was healed, *leaving no trace of the disease that scarred them and separated them from the community.*

15One of them, the instant he realized he had been healed, turned and ran back to Jesus, shouting praises to God. 16He prostrated himself facedown at Jesus' feet.

Leper: Thank You! Thank You!

Now this fellow happened to be, *not a Jew,* but a Samaritan.

* 17:3 The earliest manuscripts omit this portion.   * 17:9 The earliest manuscripts omit this portion.

Jesus: [17]Didn't all ten receive the same healing this fellow did? Where are the other nine? [18]Was the only one who came back to give God praise an outsider? [19](to the Samaritan man) Get up, and go your way. Your faith has made you healthy again.

[20]Some Pharisees asked Jesus when the kingdom of God would come.

Jesus: The kingdom of God comes—but not with signs that you can observe. [21]People are not going to say, "Look! Here it is!" They're not going to say, "Look! It's over there!" You want to see the kingdom of God? The kingdom of God is already here among you.

[22](to His disciples) Days are coming when you will wish you could see just one of the days of the Son of Man, but you won't see it. [23]People will say, "Look, it's there!" or "Look! It's here!" Don't even bother looking. Don't follow their lead. [24]You know how lightning flashes across the sky, bringing light from one horizon to the other. That's how the Son of Man will be when His time comes.

[25]But first, He must face many sufferings. He must be rejected by this generation. [26]The days of the Son of Man will be like the days of Noah. [27]People were eating, drinking, marrying, and being given in marriage. *Everything seemed completely normal* until the day Noah entered the ark. Then it started raining, and soon they were all destroyed by the flood.

[28]It was just the same in the days of Lot. People were eating, drinking, buying, selling, planting, building, *and carrying on business as usual.* [29]But then came the day when Lot left Sodom—a different kind of rain began to fall, and they were all destroyed by fire and sulfur falling from the sky.* [30]That's how it will be on the day when the Son of Man is revealed.

Since people are easily distracted, Jesus says that they shouldn't get so caught up in the routines of daily life that they forget to remain faithful to Him.

[31]When that day comes, if you're on the housetop, don't run inside to try to save any of your belongings. If you're in the field, don't bother running back *to the house.* [32]Remember Lot's wife. *Turning back is*

fatal for those who do so. [33]If you try to hold on to your life, it will slip through your fingers; if you let go of your life, you'll keep it. [34]Listen, on the day of the Son of Man, two people will be asleep in bed; destruction will take one and the other will be left to survive. [35]Two women will be grinding grain together; destruction will take one and the other will survive. [[36]Two men will be working out in the field; destruction will overtake one and the other will survive.]*

Disciples: [37]Where, Lord?

Jesus: Where vultures circle over rotting corpses.

18

He told them a parable, urging them to keep praying and never grow discouraged. The parable went like this:

Jesus: [2]There was a judge living in a certain city. He showed no respect for God or humanity. [3]In that same city there was a widow. Again and again she kept coming to him seeking justice: "Clear my name from my adversary's false accusations!" [4]He paid no attention to her request for a while, but then he said to himself, "I don't care about what God thinks of me, much less what any mere human thinks. [5]But this widow is driving me crazy. She's never going to quit coming to see me unless I hear her case and provide her legal protection."

[6]Did you catch what this self-assured judge said? [7]*If he can be moved to act justly,* won't God bring justice for His chosen people when they cry to Him day and night? Will He be slow to bring them justice? [8]Mark My words: God will intervene fast with vindication. But here's the question: when the Son of Man comes, will He find anyone who still has faith?

Jesus emphasizes that the kingdom of God will not come through valiant efforts but as people pray, "may Your kingdom come," with persistence and with humility.

[9]He told another parable—this one addressed to people who were confident in their self-righteousness and looked down on other people with disgust.

* 17:29 Genesis 19:24   * 17:36 Most manuscripts omit verse 36.

Jesus: [10]Imagine two men *walking up a road*, going to the temple to pray. One of them is a Pharisee and the other is a *despised* tax collector. [11]Once inside the temple, the Pharisee stands up and prays this prayer in honor of himself: "God, how I thank You that I am not on the same level as other people—crooks, cheaters, the sexually immoral—like this tax collector over here. [12]*Just look at me!* I fast *not once but* twice a week, and I faithfully pay my tithes on every penny of income." [13]Over in the corner, the tax collector begins to pray, but he won't even lift his eyes to heaven. He pounds on his chest *in sorrow* and says, "God, be merciful to me, a sinner!"

[14]*Now imagine these two men walking back down the road to their homes.* Listen, it's the tax collector who walks home clean before God, and not the Pharisee, because whoever lifts himself up will be put down and whoever takes a humble place will be lifted up.

[15]Some people brought infants to Jesus, hoping He would touch them *in blessing.* The disciples rebuked them for doing so, [16]but Jesus called to the people.

Jesus: Let the little children come to Me. Never hinder them! Don't you realize—the kingdom of God belongs to those who are like children? [17]You can depend on this: if you don't receive the Kingdom as a child would, you won't enter it at all.

Public Official: [18]Good Teacher, what do I need to do to inherit the life of the age to come?

Jesus: [19]Why did you just call Me good? No one is good but God—only God. [20]You know what the *Hebrew* Scriptures command: "Do not commit adultery; do not murder; do not steal; do not bear false witness; honor your father and mother."*

Public Official: [21]I've already been doing these things—since I came of age.

Jesus: [22]One thing you still lack—one thing; sell all your possessions and distribute the proceeds to the poor. Then you will have treasure in heaven. Then you can come and follow Me.

[23]The man heard these words and sadness came over his face, for his wealth was considerable.

Jesus: [24]What a hard thing it is for those with much wealth to enter the kingdom of God! [25]In fact, it would be easier for a camel to squeeze through the eye of a needle than it would be for a rich person to enter the kingdom of God!

Listeners: [26]Then who can be liberated?

Jesus: [27]Remember, what is humanly impossible is possible with God.

Peter: [28]We have left our homes and followed You.

Jesus: [29]I'm telling you the truth: there is nobody who leaves his house or wife or siblings or parents or children for the sake of the kingdom of God [30]who will not receive more than he has given up—much more—in this age and in the age to come. He will receive eternal life.

[31]He took the twelve aside and spoke privately to them.

Jesus: Look, *my friends,* we are going up to Jerusalem. Everything the prophets have written about the Son of Man will be fulfilled. [32]He will be handed over to the outsiders. They will mock Him, disgrace Him, and spit on Him; [33]they will scourge Him, and they will kill Him. And on the third day, He will rise from death.

[34]But they had no comprehension of what He was talking about. The meaning was hidden from them, and they couldn't grasp it.

[35]*Picture this:*

Jesus is nearing the city of Jericho. A blind man is sitting there, begging by the roadside. [36]He can hear the sounds of the crowd *accompanying Jesus,* and he asks what's going on.

Crowd: [37]Jesus of Nazareth is passing this way.

[38]Then the man starts shouting.

* 18:20 Exodus 20:12-16; Deuteronomy 5:16-20

Blind Man: Jesus, Son of *King* David, show mercy to me!

[39]The people in the front of the crowd reprimand him and tell him to be quiet, but he just shouts louder.

Blind Man: Son of *King* David, show mercy to me!

[40]Jesus stops and tells the people to bring the man over to Him. The man stands in front of Jesus.

Jesus: [41]What do you want Me to do for you?

Blind Man: Lord, let me receive my sight.

Jesus: [42]Receive your sight; your faith has made you well.

[43]At that very instant, the man is able to see. He begins following Jesus, shouting praises to God; and everyone in the crowd, when they see what has happened, starts praising God too.

19 Jesus enters Jericho and seems only to be passing through. [2]Living in Jericho is a man named Zaccheus. He's the head tax collector and is very rich. [3]He is also very short. He wants to see Jesus as He passes through the center of town, but he can't get a glimpse because the crowd blocks his view. [4]So he runs ahead of the crowd and climbs up into a sycamore tree so he can see Jesus when He passes beneath him.

[5]Jesus comes along and looks up into the tree[, and there He sees Zaccheus].*

Jesus: Zaccheus, hurry down from that tree because I need to stay at your house *tonight*.

[6]Zaccheus scrambles down and joyfully brings Jesus back to his house. [7]Now the crowd sees this, and they're upset.

Crowd (*grumbling*): Jesus has become the houseguest of this fellow who is a notorious sinner.

Zaccheus: [8]Lord, I am giving half of my goods to the poor, and whomever I have cheated I will pay back four times what I took.

Jesus: [9]Today liberation has come to this house, since even Zaccheus is living as a son of Abraham. [10]For the Son of Man came to seek and to liberate the lost.

[11]The crowd has been listening to all this, and everyone assumes that the kingdom of God is going to appear at any moment, since He's nearing Jerusalem. So He tells them this parable:

Jesus: [12]A ruler once planned a journey to a distant country to take the throne of that country and then return home. [13]Before his departure, he called 10 of his servants and gave them each about three months of wages.* "Use this money to buy and sell until I return." [14]After he departed, the people under his rule despised him and sent messengers with a clear message: "We do not want this man to rule over us."

[15]He successfully assumed kingship *of the distant country* and returned home. He called his 10 servants together and told them to give an account of their success in doing business with the money he had entrusted to them.

[16]The first came before him and said, "Lord, I have made 10 times the amount you entrusted to me." [17]The ruler replied, "Well done! You're a good servant indeed! Since you have been faithful in handling a small amount of money, I'll entrust you with authority over 10 cities *in my new kingdom*."

[18]The second came and said, "Lord, I've made five times the original amount." [19]The ruler replied, "I'll entrust you with authority over five cities."

[20]A third came and said, "Lord, I have successfully preserved the money you gave me. I wrapped it up in a napkin and hid it away [21]because I was afraid of you. After all, you're a tough man. You have a way of taking a profit without making an investment and harvesting when you didn't plant any seed."

[22]The ruler replied, "I will condemn you using your very own words, you worthless servant! So I'm a severe man, am I? So I take a profit without making an investment and harvest without planting seed? [23]Then why didn't you invest my money in the bank so I could have at least gained some interest on it?" [24]The ruler told the

* 19:5 The earliest manuscripts omit this portion.   * 19:13 Literally, mina, Roman coins

It is common to speculate about when the kingdom of God will fully arrive. But Jesus, through the previous parable, makes it clear that such speculation is a waste of time. Instead, people should be busy investing their lives in the kingdom of God. Earlier, in His encounter with the rich young ruler, Jesus invited the man to stop collaborating with the Roman Empire for his own benefit and to switch sides—so he could start working with the kingdom of God for the sake of the poor. The man refused; but soon after, a man named Zaccheus volunteered to do that very thing: to stop working for his own wealth by collaborating with Caesar's kingdom and to start working for justice for the poor by collaborating with God's kingdom. Speculation about the dates and times of the coming of the Kingdom can obscure the point—believers should live, starting now, in the way of the Kingdom.

---

onlookers, "Take the money I gave him, and give it to the one who multiplied my investment by 10."

25Then the onlookers replied, "Lord, he already has 10 times the original amount!"

26The ruler responded, "Listen, whoever has some will be given more, and whoever doesn't have anything will lose what he thinks he has. 27And these enemies of mine who didn't want me to rule over them—bring them here and execute them in my presence."

28When He finished the parable, He pushed onward, climbing the steep hills toward Jerusalem.

29He approached the towns of Bethphage and Bethany, which are near Mount Olivet. He sent two of the disciples ahead.

Jesus: 30Go to the next village. When you enter, you will find a colt tied—a colt that has never been ridden before. Untie it and bring it here. 31If anyone asks you why you're untying it, just say, "The Lord needs it."

32So the two disciples found things just as He had told them. 33When its owners did indeed ask why they were untying the colt, 34the disciples answered *as they had been instructed.*

Disciples: The Lord needs it.

35They brought the colt to Jesus, threw their coats on the colt's back, and then sat Jesus on it. 36As Jesus rode along, some people began to spread their garments on the road *as a carpet.* 37When they passed the crest of Mount Olivet and began descending toward Jerusalem, a huge crowd of disciples began

to celebrate and praise God with loud shouts, glorifying God for the mighty works they had witnessed.

Crowd of Disciples: 38The King who comes in the name of the Eternal One is blessed!*
    Peace in heaven! Glory in the highest!

Pharisees (*who were in the crowd*):
    39Teacher, tell these people to stop making these wild claims and acting this way!

Jesus: 40Listen—if they were silent, the very rocks would start to shout!

41When Jerusalem came into view, He looked intently at the city and began to weep.

Jesus: 42How I wish you knew today what would bring peace! But you can't see. 43Days will come when your enemies will build up a siege ramp, and you will be surrounded and contained on every side.* 44Your enemies will smash you into rubble and not leave one stone standing on another, and they will cut your children down too, because you did not recognize the day when God's Anointed One visited you.

In this powerful scene as Jesus comes into the city, echoing the words of Zechariah 9:9, Jesus shows how His kingdom is upside down compared to the kingdoms of this world. Caesar enters a town riding a white stallion, accompanied by dignitaries and soldiers with weapons. Jesus comes on

* 19:38 Psalm 118:26   * 19:43 Ezekiel 4:2; 26:8

a little donkey, cheered by common people tossing their coats in the donkey's path. The contrast between the two ways, He suggests through tears, is the difference between violent destruction and peace.

---

⁴⁵He entered *Jerusalem* and went into the temple. He began driving out the temple merchants.

Jesus: ⁴⁶The *Hebrew* Scriptures say, "My house shall be a house of prayer,"* but you have turned it into a shelter for thieves.*

⁴⁷He came back day after day to teach in the temple. The chief priests, the religious scholars, and the leading men of the city wanted to kill Him, ⁴⁸but because He was so popular among the people—who hung upon each word He spoke—they were unable to do anything.

20 One day when He was teaching the people in the temple and proclaiming the good news, the chief priests, religious scholars, and elders came up and questioned Him.

Elders: ²Tell us by what authority You march into the temple and disrupt our worship. Who gave You this authority?

Jesus: ³Let Me ask you a question first. Tell Me this: ⁴was the ritual cleansing of baptism John did from God, or was it merely a human thing?

Chief Priests, Religious Scholars, and Elders (*conferring together*): ⁵If we say it was from God, then He'll ask us why we didn't believe John. ⁶If we say it was merely human, all the people will stone us because they are convinced that John was a true prophet.

⁷So they said they didn't know where John's ritual washing came from.

Jesus: ⁸Well then, if you won't answer My question, I won't tell you by what authority I have acted.

⁹He told the people another parable:

Jesus: A man planted a vineyard. He rented it to tenants and went for a long trip to another country. ¹⁰At the harvest time, he sent a servant to the tenants so he could be paid his share of the vineyard's fruit, but the tenants beat the servant and sent him away empty-handed. ¹¹The man sent another servant, and they beat him and treated him disgracefully and sent him away empty-handed too. ¹²He sent a third servant who was injured and thrown out. ¹³Then the vineyard owner said, "Now what am I going to do? I'll send my much-loved son. They should treat him with respect."

¹⁴But when the tenants recognized the owner's son, they said, "*Here's our chance to actually own this vineyard! Let's kill the owner's heir so we can claim this place as our own!*" ¹⁵So they threw him out of the vineyard and murdered him. What do you think the owner will do to these scoundrels?

¹⁶*I'll tell you what he'll do;* he'll come and wipe those tenants out, and he'll give the vineyard to others.

Crowd: No! God forbid that this should happen!

Jesus: ¹⁷Why then do the *Hebrew* Scriptures contain these words:

The stone that the builders rejected
has become the very stone
that holds together the entire
foundation?*

¹⁸Everyone who falls on that stone will be broken to fragments, and if that stone falls on anyone, he will be ground to dust.

¹⁹*That was the last straw for* the religious scholars and the chief priests; they were ready to attack Him right then and there. But they couldn't for fear of public opinion, and they realized that Jesus, through this parable, had exposed their violent intentions.

Since they can't use overt violence against Him, they develop a covert plan.

²⁰They would keep Him under constant surveillance. They would send spies, pretending to ask sincere questions, listening for

* 19:46 Isaiah 56:7　* 19:46 Jeremiah 7:11　* 20:17 Psalm 118:22

In addition to the Pharisees, there is a religious sect in Roman-occupied Israel called the Sadducees. They are religious conservatives holding to an ancient tradition in Judaism that doesn't believe in an afterlife. Their disbelief in an afterlife seems to make them conclude, "There's only one life, and this is it, so you'd better play it safe." That means they are very happy to collaborate with the Romans—and make a healthy profit—rather than risk any kind of rebellion or revolt. For this reason, they are closely allied with another group called the Herodians, allies of Caesar's puppet king Herod. Their contemporaries, the Pharisees, who believe in an afterlife, are more prone to risk their lives in a rebellion since they hope martyrs will be rewarded with resurrection. For this reason, the Pharisees are closely allied with the Zealots, who are more overtly revolutionary. Each group tries to trap Jesus, but He turns the tables on them, using each encounter to shed more light on the message of the kingdom of God. In case after case, Jesus brings His hearers to the heart of the matter; and again and again, the bottom-line issue is money.

something they could seize upon that would justify His arrest and condemnation under the governor's authority.

Chief Priests, Religious Scholars, and Elders: [21]Teacher, we respect You because You speak and teach only what is right, You show no partiality to anyone, and You truly teach the way of God. [22]So—is it lawful for us to pay taxes to Caesar's *occupying regime*, or should we refuse?

[23]He saw through their transparent trick.

Jesus: [Why are you trying to trick Me?]* [24]Show Me a coin. Whose image and name are on this coin?

Chief Priests, Religious Scholars, and Elders: Caesar's.

Jesus: [25]Well then, you should give to Caesar whatever is Caesar's, and you should give to God whatever is God's.

[26]Once again they failed to humiliate Him in public or catch Him in a punishable offense. They were confounded by His reply and couldn't say anything in response.

[27]Another group came to test Him—this time from the Sadducees, a *rival party of the Pharisees*, who believe that there is no resurrection.

Sadducees: [28]Teacher, Moses wrote *in the Hebrew Scriptures* that a man must marry his brother's wife and the new couple should bear children for his brother if his brother dies without heirs.* [29]Well, once

there were seven brothers, and the first took a wife and then died without fathering children. [30]The second [took her as his wife and then he died childless,]* [31]and then the third, and so on through the seven. They all died leaving no children. [32]Finally the woman died too. [33]*Here's our question:* in the resurrection, whose wife will she be, since all seven had her for a while? *Will she be the wife of seven men at once?*

Jesus: [34]The children of this era marry and are given in marriage, [35]but those who are considered worthy to attain the resurrection of the dead in the coming era do not marry and are not given in marriage. [36]They are beyond mortality; they are on the level of heavenly messengers; they are children of God and children of the resurrection. [37]*Since you brought up the issue of resurrection,* even Moses made clear in the passage about the burning bush that the dead are, in fact, raised. After all, he calls the Lord the God of Abraham, Isaac, and Jacob.* [38]*By Moses' time, they were all dead,* but God isn't God of the dead, but of the living. So all live to God.

Religious Scholars: [39]Teacher, that was a good answer.

[40]After this no one had the courage to ask Him any more questions. [41]But He asked them a question.

Jesus: How is it that people say the Anointed One is David's descendant?

* 20:23 The earliest manuscripts omit this portion.   * 20:28 Deuteronomy 25:5   * 20:30 The earliest manuscripts omit this portion.
* 20:37 Exodus 3:6,15

42Don't you remember how David himself wrote in the psalms,

The Master said to my master:
"Sit here at My right hand,
in the place of honor and power.
43And I will gather Your enemies together,
lead them in on hands and knees,
and You will rest Your feet on their backs."*

44Did you hear that? David calls his son "Lord." *Elders don't defer to those who are younger in that way.* How is David's son also "Lord"?

45Jesus turned to His disciples, speaking loudly enough for the others to hear.

Jesus: 46Beware of the religious scholars. They like to parade around in long robes. They love being greeted in the marketplaces. They love taking the best seats in the synagogues. They adore being seated around the head table at banquets. 47But *in their greed* they rob widows of their houses and *cover up their greed* with long pretentious prayers. Their condemnation will be all the worse *because of their hypocrisy.*

21 And then He turned His attention from the religious scholars to some wealthy people who were depositing their donations in the offering boxes. 2A widow, obviously poor, came up and dropped two copper coins in one of the boxes.

Jesus: 3I'm telling you the truth, this poor widow has made a bigger contribution than all of those rich fellows. 4They're just giving from their surplus, but she is giving from her poverty—she's giving all she has to give.

5Some people were impressed with the temple's opulence—the precious stones and expensive decorations—but Jesus countered their observations.

Jesus: 6Go ahead, look around, and be impressed; but days are coming when one stone will not be left standing on another. Everything here will be demolished.

Crowd: 7When will this happen, Teacher? What signs will tell us this is about to occur?

Jesus: 8Be careful. It's easy to be deceived. Many people will come claiming to have My authority. They'll shout, "I'm the One!" or "The time is now!" Don't take a step in their direction. 9You'll hear about wars and conflicts, but don't be frightened at all because these things must surely come, although they don't signify the immediate coming of the end. 10*You can count on this:* nation will attack nation, and kingdom will make war on kingdom. 11There will be disturbances around the world—from great earthquakes to famines to epidemics. Terrifying things will happen, and there will be shocking signs from heaven. 12But before any of this happens, they will capture you and persecute you. They'll send you to synagogues *for trial* and to prisons *for punishment;* you'll stand before kings and government officials for the sake of My name. 13This will be your opportunity— your opportunity to tell your story. 14Make up your mind in advance not to plan your strategy for answering their questions, 15for when the time comes, I will give you the words to say—wise words—which none of your adversaries will be able to answer or argue against. 16Your own parents, brothers, relatives, and friends will turn on you and turn you in. Some of you will be killed, 17and all of you will be hated by everyone for the sake of My name.

18But whatever happens, not a single hair of your heads will be harmed. 19By enduring all of these things, you will find *not loss but gain*—not death but authentic life.

20Here's how you will know that the destruction of Jerusalem *and her temple* is imminent: Jerusalem will be surrounded by armies. 21When that happens, *there's only one thing to do:* if you're in Judea, flee to the mountains; and if you're inside the city, escape; and if you're outside the city, stay there—don't enter—22because the time has come for the promised judgment to fall. 23How sad it will be for all the pregnant women, for all the nursing mothers in those days! All the land of Israel and all her people will feel the distress, the anger, falling on them *like rain.* 24The sword will cut some down, the outsider nations will take others captive, and this holy city, this Jerusalem, will be trampled upon by the outsiders until their times are fulfilled.

* 20:42-43 Psalm 110:1

²⁵*There will be earth-shattering events—* the heavens themselves will seem to be shaken with signs in the sun, in the moon, and in the stars. And across the earth the *outsider* nations will feel powerless and terrified in the face of a roaring flood *of fear and foreboding,* crashing like tidal waves upon them. ²⁶"What's happening to the world?" people will wonder. The cosmic order will be destabilized. ²⁷And then, at that point, they will see the Son of Man coming in a cloud with power and blazing glory. ²⁸So when the troubles begin, *don't be afraid.* Look up—raise your head high, because the truth is that your liberation is fast approaching.

²⁹(continuing with a parable) Look over there at that fig tree—and all the trees surrounding it. ³⁰When the leaves break out of their buds, nobody has to tell you that summer is approaching; it's obvious to you. ³¹*It's the same in the larger scheme of things.* When you see all these things happening, you can be confident that the kingdom of God is approaching. ³²I'm telling you the truth: this generation will not pass from the scene before everything I'm telling you has occurred. ³³Heaven and earth will cease to exist before My words ever fail.

³⁴So be careful. Guard your hearts. They can be made heavy with moral laxity, with drunkenness, with the hassles of daily life. Then the day I've been telling you about might catch you unaware and trap you. ³⁵Because it's coming—nobody on earth will escape it. ³⁶So you have to stay alert, praying that you'll be able to escape the coming trials so you can stand tall in the presence of the Son of Man.

³⁷⁻³⁸Through this whole period of time, He taught in the temple each day. People would arrive at the temple early in the morning to listen. Then, at day's end, He would leave the city and sleep on Mount Olivet.

22 *This daily pattern continued as they came closer to the holiday of Unleavened Bread, also known as the Passover.*

²The chief priests and religious scholars continued looking for a way to kill Jesus; they hadn't been able to act yet due to their fear of the people's reaction. ³At this point, Satan entered into one of the twelve, Judas (also called Iscariot). ⁴Judas set up a private meeting with the chief priests and the captains of the temple police to discuss a plan for betraying Jesus and putting Him in their hands. ⁵*This was just the kind of break they had been waiting for,* so they were thrilled and agreed to a handsome payment. ⁶Everything was settled, and Judas simply waited for the right moment, when the crowds weren't around, to betray Jesus into their custody.

⁷They came to the Day of Unleavened Bread, a holy day when a special lamb (called the Passover lamb) had to be sacrificed. ⁸Jesus chose Peter and John and gave them instructions.

Jesus: Go and make all the necessary preparations for the Passover meal so we can eat together.

Peter and John: ⁹Where do You want us to make preparations?

Jesus: ¹⁰When you enter the city, you'll encounter a man carrying a jar of water. Just follow him *wherever he goes,* and when he enters a house, ¹¹tell the homeowner, "The Teacher has this question for you: 'Where is the guest room where I can share the Passover meal with My disciples?'" ¹²He'll show you a spacious second-story room that has all the necessary furniture. That's where you should prepare our meal.

¹³They did as He said and found everything just as He said it would be, and they prepared the Passover meal. ¹⁴When the meal was prepared, Jesus sat at the table, joined by His emissaries.*

* 22:14 Literally, apostles

them yet another lesson about life in the kingdom of God. Jesus even spoke of His own suffering and their betrayal and denial. Yet through it all, Jesus' focus remained on the central theme of His life and mission: the coming of the kingdom of God.

Jesus: [15]It has been My deep desire to eat this Passover meal with you before My suffering begins. [16]Know this: I will not eat another Passover meal until its meaning is fulfilled in the kingdom of God.

[17]He took a cup *of wine* and gave thanks for it.

Jesus: Take this; share it among yourselves. [18]Know this: I will not drink another sip of wine until the kingdom of God has arrived in fullness.

[19]Then He took bread, gave thanks, broke it, and shared it with them.

Jesus: This is My body, My body given for you. Do this to remember Me.

[20]And similarly, after the meal had been eaten, He took the cup.

Jesus: This cup, which is poured out for you, is the new covenant, made in My blood. [21]But even now, the hand of My betrayer is with Me on this table. [22]As it has been determined, the Son of Man, *that firstfruit of a new generation of humanity*, must be betrayed, but how pitiful it will be for the person who betrays Him.

[23]They immediately began questioning each other.

Disciples: Which one of us could do such a horrible thing?

[24]Soon they found themselves arguing about the opposite question.

Disciples: Which one of us is the most faithful, the most important?

Jesus *(interrupting)*: [25]The authority figures of the outsiders play this game, flexing their muscles in competition for power over one another, masking their quest for domination behind words like "benefactor" or "public servant." [26]But you must not indulge in this charade. Instead, among you, the greatest must become like the youngest and the leader must become a true servant. [27]Who is greater right here as we eat this meal—those of us who sit at the table, or those who serve us? Doesn't everyone normally assume those who are served are greater than those who serve? But consider My role among you. I have been with you as a servant.

[28]You have stood beside Me faithfully through My trials. [29]I give you a kingdom, just as the Father has given Me a kingdom. [30]You will eat and drink at My table in My kingdom, and you will have authority over the twelve tribes of Israel.

[31]Simon, Simon, how Satan has pursued you, that he might make you part of his harvest. [32]But I have prayed for you. I have prayed that your faith will hold firm and that you will recover from your failure and become a source of strength for your brothers here.

Peter: [33]*Lord, what are You talking about? I'm going all the way to the end with You—to prison, to execution—I'm prepared to do anything for You.*

Jesus: [34]No, Peter, the truth is that before the rooster crows at dawn, you will have denied that you even know Me, not just once, but three times. [35]Remember when I sent you out with no money, no pack, not even sandals? Did you lack anything?

Disciples: Not a thing.

Jesus: [36]It's different now. If you have some savings, take them with you. If you have a pack, *fill it and* bring it. If you don't have a sword, sell your coat and buy one. [37]Here's the truth: what the Hebrew Scriptures said, "And He was taken as one of the criminals,"* must come to fruition in Me. These words must come true.

Disciples: [38]Look, Lord, we have two swords here.

Jesus: That's enough.

* 22:37 Isaiah 53:12

There is powerful consistency in Jesus' life. Again and again, He withdraws from the crowds to pray in solitude. Now, at this dramatic moment, Jesus again withdraws to pray—in a solitude made more intense by the fact that He has asked His disciples to pray, too, but they have fallen asleep. And in this moment of anguished emotion, Jesus mouths a prayer that resonates with His consistent message of the Kingdom. He has taught His disciples to pray, "May Your kingdom come," which is a request for God's will to be done on earth as it is in heaven. Now, drenched in sweat, Jesus Himself prays simply for God's will to be done, even if it means He must drink the cup of suffering that awaits Him in the hours ahead.

We often speak of having faith *in* Jesus; but we seldom speak of the faith *of* Jesus, a faith He demonstrated consistently throughout His life and especially at its end. In a moment of agony, Jesus still trusted God, still yielded His will to God, and still approached God as "Father," placing Himself in the position of a child, in trust—profound, tested, sincere.

---

³⁹Once again He left the city as He had been doing during recent days, returning to Mount Olivet along with His disciples. ⁴⁰And He came to a certain place.

Jesus: Pray for yourselves, that you will not sink into temptation.

⁴¹He distanced Himself from them about a stone's throw and knelt there, ⁴²praying.

Jesus: Father, if You are willing, take this cup away from Me. Yet not My will, but Your will, be done.

[⁴³Then a messenger from heaven appeared to strengthen Him. ⁴⁴And in His anguish, He prayed even more intensely, and His sweat was like drops of blood falling to the ground.]* ⁴⁵When He rose from prayer and returned to the disciples, He found them asleep, weighed down with sorrow. ⁴⁶He roused them.

Jesus: Why are you sleeping? Wake up and pray that you will not sink into temptation.

⁴⁷Even as He said these words, *the sound of a crowd could be heard in the distance,* and as the crowd came into view, it was clear that Judas was leading them. He came close to Jesus and gave Jesus *the traditional greeting of* a kiss.

Jesus: ⁴⁸Ah, Judas, is this how you betray the Son of Man—with a kiss?

Disciples (*realizing what was going on*): ⁴⁹Lord, is this why You told us to bring the swords? Should we attack?

⁵⁰Before Jesus could answer, one of them had swung his sword at the high priest's slave, cutting off his right ear.

Jesus: ⁵¹Stop! No more of this!

Then He reached out to touch—and heal—the man's ear. ⁵²Jesus turned to the chief priests, the captains of the temple, and the elders and spoke.

Jesus: Do you think I'm some sort of violent criminal? Is that why you came with swords and clubs? ⁵³*I haven't been hard to find*—each day I've been in the temple in broad daylight, and you never tried to seize Me there. But this is your time—*night*—and this is your power—the power of darkness.

⁵⁴They grabbed Him at this point and took Him away to the high priest's home. Peter followed—at a distance. ⁵⁵*He watched from the shadows as* those who had seized Jesus made a fire in the center of the courtyard and sat down around it. Then Peter *slipped in quietly and* sat with them. ⁵⁶But a young servant girl saw his face in the firelight. She stared for a while and then spoke.

Servant Girl: This fellow here was with Jesus. *I recognize him.*

Peter (*denying it*): ⁵⁷Woman, I don't even know the man.

⁵⁸A little later, a man also recognized him.

Man: *I recognize you.* You're one of Jesus' followers.

* 22:43-44 Some early manuscripts omit these verses.

Peter: Man, you're wrong. I'm not.

59An hour or so passed, and then another person pointed to Peter.

Another Person: This fellow is obviously Galilean. He must be a member of Jesus' group.

Peter: 60Look, I have no idea what you're talking about.

And he hadn't even finished the sentence when a nearby rooster crowed. 61The Lord turned toward Peter, and their eyes met. Peter remembered Jesus' words about his triple denial before the rooster would crow, 62so he left the courtyard and wept bitter tears.

63At this point, the men who were holding Jesus began to mock Him and beat Him. 64They put a blindfold on Him.

Men Holding Jesus: *Hey, Prophet!* Use Your prophetic powers to tell us who just whacked You!

65They kept on with this sort of insulting, degrading treatment for quite some time. 66When dawn had given way to full day, the Sanhedrin council assembled, consisting of religious leaders *of the Sadducean party,* along with the chief priests and religious scholars. They took Him to their headquarters *for interrogation.*

Sanhedrin: 67If you are the Anointed One whom God promised us, tell us plainly.

Jesus: If I give you an answer, you won't believe it. 68And if I ask you a question, you won't answer it. 69But *this I will say to you:* from now on, the Son of Man will take His seat at the right hand of the power of God.

Sanhedrin: 70So You are the Son of God, then?

Jesus: It's as you say.

Sanhedrin: 71What more evidence do we need? We've heard it with our own ears from His own lips.

23 So the whole council got up and took Jesus to Pilate. 2They brought accusations against Him.

Sanhedrin: We have observed this man leading our nation astray. He even forbade us to pay our taxes to Caesar. He claims to be the Anointed One and a King Himself.

Pilate: 3Are You the King of the Jews?

Jesus: It's as you say.

Pilate (*to the chief priest and crowd*): 4I find this man guilty of no crime.

Sanhedrin (*growing more intense*): 5He has been stirring up discontent among the people all over Judea. He started up in Galilee, and now He's brought His brand of trouble all the way to Jerusalem!

Pilate: 6*Just a minute.* Is this man a Galilean?

7When Pilate learned *that Jesus was indeed Galilean*—which meant He was officially under Herod's jurisdiction—Pilate sent Him over to Herod, who was currently in Jerusalem. 8Herod was fascinated to meet Jesus for he had heard about Him for a long time. He was hoping he might be treated to a miracle or two. 9He interrogated Jesus for quite a while, but Jesus remained silent, refusing to answer his questions. 10Meanwhile the chief priests and religious scholars had plenty to say—angrily hurling accusations at Jesus. 11Eventually Herod and his soldiers began to insult Jesus, mocking and degrading Him. They put expensive clothing on Him and sent Him back to Pilate. 12This ended a long-standing rift between Herod and Pilate; they became friends from that day forward.

13Pilate assembled the chief priests and other Jewish authorities.

Pilate: 14You presented this man to me as a rabble-rouser, but I examined Him in your presence and found Him not guilty of the charges you have leveled against Him. 15Herod also examined Him and released Him to my custody. So He hasn't done anything deserving the death penalty. 16I'll see to it that He is properly whipped and then let Him go.

[17It was the custom for Pilate to set one prisoner free during the holiday festivities.]*

Crowd (*all shouting at once*): 18Away with this man! Free Barabbas instead!

* 23:17 The earliest manuscripts omit verse 17.

Crucifixion is a favorite Roman punishment for insurrectionists, slaves, and prisoners of war. Anyone daring to defy the power and authority of Caesar is executed in this public and humiliating way. Jesus indeed is a revolutionary. He doesn't come to proclaim a new religion, but a new kingdom—a new way of life. He is indeed a threat to Caesar's way of doing things, a way that co-opts the religious leaders.

Jesus' revolution is a peaceful revolution. He doesn't advocate the use of violence—in fact, when one of His disciples uses the sword to try to protect Jesus from arrest, Jesus heals the "enemy" and rebukes His disciple. So Jesus doesn't support the regime of Caesar or follow the usual violent path of revolution: He leads a revolutionary revolution—in a path of love, healing, justice, and reconciliation.

Jesus appropriates and transforms the symbol of their power into a symbol of His greater power. He makes the cross not the icon of violent domination, but the reverse. By hanging on the cross and speaking of forgiveness, Jesus shows that there is a greater power at work in the world than the power of domination: it's the power of God's saving and reconciling love.

---

[19]Barabbas had been imprisoned after being convicted of an insurrection he had led in Jerusalem. He had also committed murder. [20]Pilate argued with them, wishing he could release Jesus, [21]but they wouldn't be silenced.

Crowd (*shouting*): Crucify Him! Crucify Him!

Pilate (*countering a third time*): [22]Why? What has He done that is so evil? I have found in Him no offense worthy of capital punishment. As I said, I will punish Him and then release Him.

[23]But they would not relent. They shouted louder and louder that He should be crucified, and eventually Pilate capitulated. [24]So he pronounced the punishment they demanded.

[25]He released the rebel and murderer *Barabbas*—the insurrectionist they had pleaded for in His place—and he handed Jesus over to them to do with as they desired.

[26]On the way to the place of crucifixion, they pulled a man from the crowd—his name was Simon of Cyrene, a person from the countryside who happened to be entering the city at that moment. They put Jesus' cross on Simon's shoulders, and he followed behind Jesus. [27]Along with Him was a huge crowd of common people, including many women shrieking and wailing in grief.

Jesus (*to the people in the crowd*): [28]Daughters of Jerusalem, do not weep for Me. Weep instead for yourselves and weep for your children. [29]Days are coming when people will say, "Blessed are the infertile; blessed are the wombs that never bore *a child*; blessed are the breasts that never nursed *an infant*." [30]People will beg the mountains, "Surround us!" They'll plead with the hills, "Cover us!"* [31]For if they treat Me like this when I'm like green unseasoned wood, what will they do to a nation that's ready to burn like seasoned firewood?

[32]*Jesus wasn't the only one being crucified that day.* There were two others, criminals, who were also being led to their execution. [33]When they came to the place known as "The Skull," they crucified Jesus there, in the company of criminals, one to the right of Jesus and the other to His left.

Jesus: [34][Father, forgive them, for they don't know what they're doing.]*

Meanwhile they were drawing lots to see who would win Jesus' clothing. [35]The crowd of people stood, watching.

Authorities (*mocking Jesus*): So He was supposed to rescue others, was He? He was supposed to be God's Anointed, *the Liberating King*? Let's see Him start by liberating Himself!

[36]The soldiers joined in the mockery. First, they *pretended to offer Him a soothing drink*—but it was sour wine.

* 23:30 Hosea 10:8   * 23:34 The earliest manuscripts omit this portion.

Soldiers: ³⁷Hey, if You're the King of the Jews, why don't You free Yourself!

³⁸Even the inscription they placed over Him was intended to mock Him—"This is the King of the Jews!" [This was written in Greek, Latin, and Hebrew.]*
    ³⁹One of the criminals joined in the cruel talk.

Cynical Criminal: You're supposed to be the Anointed One, right? *Well—do it!* Rescue Yourself and us!

⁴⁰But the other criminal told him to be quiet.

Believing Criminal: Don't you have any fear of God at all? You're getting the same death sentence He is! ⁴¹We're getting what we deserve since we've committed crimes, but this man hasn't done anything wrong at all! ⁴²(turning to Jesus) Jesus, when You come into Your kingdom, please remember me.

Jesus: ⁴³I promise you that this very day you will be with Me in paradise.

⁴⁴At this point, it was about noon, and a darkness fell over the whole region. The darkness persisted until about three in the afternoon, ⁴⁵and at some point during this darkness, the curtain in the temple was torn in two.

Jesus *(shouting out loudly)*: ⁴⁶Father, I entrust My spirit into Your hands!*

And with those words, He exhaled—and breathed no more.
    ⁴⁷The Centurion*—*one of the soldiers who performed the execution*—saw all this, and he praised God.

Centurion: No doubt, this man must have been innocent.

⁴⁸The crowds of common people who had gathered and watched the whole ordeal through to its conclusion left for their homes, pounding on their own chests *in profound grief.* ⁴⁹And all who knew Jesus personally, including the group of women who had been with Him *from the beginning* in Galilee, stood at a distance, watching all of these things unfold.
    ⁵⁰Meanwhile a man named Joseph *had been at work.* He was a member of the council, a good and fair man, ⁵¹from a Judean town called Arimathea. He had objected to the plans and actions of the council; he was seeking the kingdom of God. ⁵²He had gone to Pilate and asked for the body of Jesus. ⁵³He removed the body from the cross and wrapped it in a shroud made of *fine* linen. He then laid the body in a cavelike tomb cut from solid rock, a tomb that never had been used before. ⁵⁴It was Preparation Day—*the day before the holy* Sabbath—and it was about to begin *at sundown.* ⁵⁵The women who had accompanied Jesus *from the beginning* in Galilee now came, took note of where the tomb was and how His body had been prepared, ⁵⁶then left to prepare spices and ointments *for His proper burial.* They ceased their work on the Sabbath so they could rest as the *Hebrew* Scriptures required.

24 Early on Sunday morning, even before the sun had fully risen, these women made their way back to the tomb with the spices *and ointments* they had prepared. ²When they arrived, they found the stone was rolled away from the tomb entrance, ³and when they looked inside, the body of the Lord Jesus was nowhere to be seen. ⁴They didn't know what to think. As they stood there in confusion, two men suddenly appeared standing beside them. These men seemed to

---

* 23:38 Some early manuscripts omit this portion.   * 23:46 Psalm 31:5   * 23:47 A Roman military officer in charge of 100 soldiers

This phrase, "Son of Man," is very important in Luke's story and may have many layers of meaning. It may mean "epitome of humanity" or "prime example of what a human can be." But it also evokes a specific passage of Scripture that is very important to Jewish people, Daniel 7:13-27. There the phrase "Son of Man" refers to a king who receives an eternal and universal kingdom, and it also represents "the saints of the Most High"—the people of God. In light of Jesus' central message about the kingdom of God, it is likely that the phrase suggests Jesus is the long-awaited Anointed One who launches a new era in human history and who creates a community of people who represent the eternal and universal kingdom of God. In this way, "Son of" suggests "new generation of," and "Man" suggests "humanity." Jesus is Himself the new generation of humanity (a second Adam, a new beginning), and the community He creates shares this identity (a new creation, a new humanity in Jesus). The two messengers here use this pregnant phrase in a way that shocks everyone: The way this long-awaited Anointed One receives His kingdom is not through conventional military victory where enemies are defeated and killed. No, this King receives His kingdom by suffering, dying, and rising again Himself. Amazing news—good news!

glow with light. [5]The women were so terrified that they fell to the ground facedown.

Two Men: Why are you seeking the living One in the place of the dead? [6]He is not here. He has risen *from the dead*. Don't you remember what He told you way back in Galilee? [7]He told you that the Son of Man must be handed over to wicked men, He must be crucified, and then on the third day He must rise.

[8]The women did remember Jesus' words about this, [9]so they returned from the tomb and found the eleven and recounted for them—and others with them—everything they had experienced. [10-11]The Lord's emissaries* heard their stories as fiction, a lie; they didn't believe a word of it. (By the way, this group of women included Mary Magdalene, Joanna, and Mary the mother of James, along with a number of others.) [12]Peter, however, got up and ran to the tomb. *When he reached the opening,* he bent down, looked inside, and saw the linen burial cloths lying there. But the body was gone. He walked away, full of wonder about what had happened.

[13]*Picture this:*
That same day, two other disciples (*not of the eleven*) are traveling the seven miles from Jerusalem to Emmaus. [14]As they walk along, they talk back and forth about all that has transpired during recent days. [15]While they're talking, discussing, and conversing, Jesus catches up to them and begins walking with them, [16]but for some reason they don't recognize Him.

Jesus: [17]*You two seem deeply engrossed in conversation.* What are you talking about as you walk along this road?

They stop walking and just stand there, looking sad. [18]One of them—Cleopas is his name—speaks up.

Cleopas: You must be the only visitor in Jerusalem who hasn't heard about what's been going on over the last few days.

Jesus: [19]What are you talking about?

Two Disciples: It's all about the man named Jesus of Nazareth. He was a mighty prophet who did amazing miracles and preached powerful messages in the sight of God and everyone around. [20]Our chief priests and authorities handed Him over to be executed—crucified, in fact.
[21]We had been hoping that He was the One—you know, the One who would liberate all Israel *and bring God's promises.* Anyway, on top of all this, just this morning—the third day after the execution—[22]some women in our group really shocked us. They went to the tomb early this morning, [23]but they didn't see His body anywhere. Then they came back and told us they did see something— a vision of heavenly messengers—and

* 24:10-11 Literally, apostles

Luke has told his story. It ends with joy and praise. The crucified Jesus has been resurrected and has ascended to heaven to take His place at God's right hand just as the ancient prophets predicted. For the band of disciples, Easter joy has eclipsed Good Friday sorrow.

This ending point becomes the starting point for Luke's sequel, known as the Acts of the Apostles. The story isn't really over; it's just begun. The life and ministry of Jesus that Luke has just recounted is the mustard-seed stage of the kingdom of God that continues to grow and grow and grow. Now it's time for this Kingdom to fill the world. If Luke's Gospel is about what Jesus began to do and teach, then Luke's sequel is about what the risen Jesus continues to do and teach through His followers for millennia. Luke writes in hope that future believers will be taken up into this beautiful story that will never, ever end.

---

these messengers said that Jesus was alive. 24Some people in our group went to the tomb to check it out, and just as the women had said, it was empty. But they didn't see Jesus.

Jesus: 25Come on, men! Why are you being so foolish? Why are your hearts so sluggish when it comes to believing what the prophets have been saying all along? 26Didn't it have to be this way? Didn't the Anointed One have to experience these sufferings in order to come into His glory?

27Then He begins with Moses and continues, prophet by prophet, explaining the meaning of the Hebrew Scriptures, showing how they were talking about the very things that had happened to Jesus.

28About this time, they are nearing their destination. Jesus keeps walking ahead as if He has no plans to stop there, 29but they convince Him to join them.

Two Disciples: Please, be our guest. It's getting late, and soon it will be too dark to walk.

So He accompanies them to their home. 30When they sit down at the table for dinner, He takes the bread in His hands, He gives thanks for it, and then He breaks it and hands it to them. 31At that instant, *two things happen simultaneously:* their eyes are suddenly opened so they recognize Him, and He instantly vanishes—just disappears before their eyes.

Two Disciples (to each other): 32Amazing! Weren't our hearts on fire within us while He was talking to us on the road? *Didn't*

you feel it all coming clear as He explained the meaning of the Hebrew Scriptures?

33So they get up immediately and rush back to Jerusalem—*all seven miles*—where they find the eleven gathered together—the eleven plus a number of others. 34*Before Cleopas and his companion can tell their story,* the others have their own story to tell.

Other Disciples: The Lord has risen indeed! It's true! He appeared to Simon!

35Then the two men report their own experience—their conversation along the road, their moment of realization and recognition as He broke the bread. 36At that very instant, as they're still telling the story, Jesus is there, standing among them!

Jesus: May you have peace!

You might expect them to be overjoyed, but they aren't.

37They're startled and terrified; they think they're seeing a ghost.

Jesus: 38Why are you upset? Why are your hearts churning with questions? 39Look— look at My hands and My feet! See that it's Me! Come on; touch Me; see for yourselves. A ghost doesn't have flesh and bones, as you can see that I have!

[40Then He shows them His hands and His feet.]*

41Now their fear gives way to joy; but it seems too good to be true, and they're still unsure.

* 24:40 Some manuscripts omit verse 40.

Jesus: Do you have anything here to eat?

[42]They hand Him a piece of broiled fish, [43]and He takes it and eats it in front of them.

Jesus: [44]I've been telling you this all along, that everything written about Me in the Hebrew Scriptures must be fulfilled— everything from the law of Moses to the prophets to the psalms.

[45]Then He opens their minds so they can comprehend the meaning of the Hebrew Scriptures.

Jesus: [46]This is what the Scriptures said: that the promised Anointed One should suffer and rise from the dead on the third day, [47]that in His name a radical change of thought and life should be preached, and that in His name the forgiveness of sins should be preached, beginning in Jerusalem and extending to all nations. [48]You have witnessed the fulfillment of these things. [49]So I am sending My Father's promise to you. Stay in the city until you receive it— until power from heaven comes upon you.

[50]Then He leads them out to Bethany. He lifts up His hands and blesses them, [51]and at that moment, with His hands raised in blessing, He leaves them and is carried up into heaven. [52]They worship Him, then they return to Jerusalem, filled with intense joy, [53]and they return again and again to the temple to celebrate God.

JOHN

Visitation of God's Son

By John, the apostle

According to tradition, this Gospel was written by John the apostle toward the end of his life from Ephesus in Asia Minor. Along with Peter and James, John was part of an inner circle of disciples closest to Jesus. Many interpreters think that "the beloved disciple"—a unique description in this book for one of Jesus' followers—refers to John. If so, John enjoyed a special relationship with Jesus that allowed him to offer a unique account of Jesus' life.

This Gospel is distinct from the other New Testament Gospels. Matthew, Mark, and Luke present the life of Jesus from a similar perspective. They share a number of parallel accounts, arrange them in a similar order, and use many of the same words and expressions. Because of their similarities, Matthew, Mark, and Luke are often called the Synoptic Gospels. "Synoptic" means "with the same eye" or "seeing together." The Gospel of John, on the other hand, contains only a little of the material found in the other Gospels. John takes us behind the scenes into Jesus' conversations with people and into long, often private talks He has with His disciples. Jesus is clearly a miracle worker in this Fourth Gospel, but His miracles are regarded as "signs" because they point to a greater reality, the reality of life—abundant and eternal—that has entered our world. Further, John makes many bold claims to Jesus' deity. For example, John includes a number of "I am" sayings spoken by Jesus (for example, "I am the bread that gives life," "I am the light of the world," and "I am the resurrection and the source of all life"). These statements associate Jesus with God's holy, unspeakable name and are implicit claims to His divinity. Plus, in John's theological prologue (John 1:1-18), the author calls Jesus the *Logos* ("the Voice") that preexists with God, is the agent of creation, and is made flesh for the world's salvation.

Another unique feature of this Gospel is its simplicity. Its language and grammar are easily grasped. Its ideas—while deeply symbolic and evocative—can be understood by people of all ages and experiences. It is filled with dualisms that emphasize the difference eternal life makes when it enters into the world: life and death, belief and unbelief, light and darkness, to name a few. For many people, the simplicity of this Gospel, with its intimate look at Jesus' life, makes it their favorite story of the Anointed One sent from God.

This Gospel begins not with Jesus' birth or John's baptism but with a deliberate echo of the creation story in Genesis. It takes us back before time began to the moment when God interrupts the silence and speaks the cosmos into existence. Only John's Gospel names Jesus as the *Logos* and declares that He existed long before time was measured. This Greek word carries a variety of meanings, all relating to the act of speaking. It could be translated "word," a thought that comes to expression, message, declaration, reason, or the content of preaching; most are found in various translations. It is clear that John means that *logos* is declared to all creation.

John's use of *logos* is unique and has often been rendered as "Word." While this is a useful translation, even a casual understanding demonstrates that "Word" reflects only part of its meaning. Most readers will interpret "word" as a unit of language—a combination of sounds generally spoken but also written—that carries meaning. To understand what John means, readers need something more than their cultural understanding of "word"; they need a new way of thinking about it. This is why we have chosen to offer another rendering, an interpretive, poetic translation, of what may be one of the most theologically loaded words in Scripture. Since *logos* essentially refers to the act of speaking or bringing thoughts to expression, we have decided to use the word "voice" to capture that reality. John declares that truth has culminated in the person of Jesus. No single word captures the complete meaning of *logos*, but "voice" has a number of advantages.

First, "voice" manifests the act of speaking. Voice is that which is spoken and that which is heard; it comes on both sides of any communication event, bridging the gap between sender and receiver. John intends that in Jesus God is speaking and revealing Himself to the world.

Second, a voice is distinct and personal. We can distinguish people from one another simply by their voices. In John 10 Jesus describes the fact that the sheep hear the voice of the shepherd when he calls and they follow, but they refuse to follow a stranger because they do not know his voice (John 10:1-5). John desires that we know Jesus as the Son of God and believe in Him personally as the Good Shepherd.

Third, "voice" is dynamic in that it reflects the robust and powerful activity of a living God. It is historical in that any act of speaking comes to expression and takes place in the real world as a "voice" calling, demanding a response. It challenges any notion that the Christian faith can be reduced to rules, propositions, or doctrines that can be merely believed or dismissed and not lived out in our lives. Since in Jesus God is speaking and revealing Himself to the world, and since in Jesus we hear the Voice of God, then this new reality changes everything so we, too, must change.

In the beginning

1 Before time itself was measured, the Voice was speaking.

The Voice was and is God.
[2] This *celestial* Word remained ever present
    with the Creator;
    [3] His speech shaped the entire cosmos.
Immersed in the practice of creating,
    all things that exist were birthed in
      Him.
[4] His breath filled all things
    with a living, breathing light—
[5] A light that thrives in the depths of
      darkness,
    blazes through murky bottoms.
It cannot and will not be quenched.

[6] A man named John, who was sent by God, *was the first to clearly articulate the source of this Light.* [7] This *baptizer* put in plain words the *elusive mystery of the Divine* Light so all might believe through him. *Some wondered whether he might be the Light,* [8] but John was not the Light. He merely pointed to the Light. [9] The true Light, who shines upon *the heart of* everyone, was coming into the cosmos.

Jesus as the Light does not call out from a distant place but draws near by coming into the world.

[10] He entered our world, a world He made; yet the world did not recognize Him. [11] Even though He came to His own people, they

refused to *listen and* receive Him. [12]But for all who did receive and trust in Him, He gave them the right to be *reborn as* children of God; [13]He bestowed this birthright not by human power or initiative but by God's will.

[14]The Voice took on flesh *and became human* and chose to live alongside us. We have seen Him, enveloped in undeniable splendor—the one *true* Son of the Father— *evidenced in* the perfect balance of grace and truth. [15]John *the Baptist* testified about Him and shouted, "This is the one I've been telling you is coming. He is much greater than I am because He existed *long* before me." [16]Through this man we all receive *gifts of* grace beyond our imagination. [17]You see, Moses gave *us* rules to live by, but Jesus the Anointed offered *us* gifts of grace and truth. [18]God, unseen until now, is revealed in the Voice, God's only Son, *straight from* the Father's heart.

Before Jesus comes along, many wonder whether John the Baptist might be the Anointed One sent by God. But when Jesus appears in the wilderness, John points others to Him. John knows his place in God's redemptive plan: he speaks God's message, but Jesus is the Word of God. John rejects any messianic claim outright. Jesus, though, accepts it with a smile, but only from a few devoted followers—at least at first. Of course John is crucial to the unfolding drama, but he isn't the long awaited One sent to free His people. He preaches repentance and tells everybody to get ready for One greater to come along. The One who comes will cleanse humanity in fire and power, he says. John even urges some of his followers to leave him and go follow Jesus.

---

[19]The reputation of John was *growing*; and many had questions, including Jewish religious leaders from Jerusalem. [28]So some *priests and Levites* approached John in Bethany just beyond the Jordan River while he was baptizing *and bombarded him with questions:**

Religious Leaders: Who are you?

John the Baptist: [20]I'm not the Anointed One, *if that is what you are asking.*

Religious Leaders: [21]*Your words sound familiar, like a prophet's.* Is that how we should address you? Are you the Prophet Elijah?

John the Baptist: No, I am not Elijah.

Religious Leaders: Are you the Prophet *Moses told us would come?*

John the Baptist: No.

Religious Leaders: [22]Then tell us who you are and what you are about because everyone is asking us, *especially the Pharisees,* and we must prepare an answer.

[23]John replied with the words of Isaiah the prophet:

John the Baptist: *Listen!* I am a voice calling out in the wilderness.
    Straighten out the road for the Lord.
    He's on His way.*

[24-25]Then some of those sent by the Pharisees questioned him again.

Religious Leaders: How can you *travel the countryside* baptizing* people if you are not the Anointed One or Elijah or the Prophet?

John the Baptist: [26]Baptizing with water is what I do; but the One *whom I speak of, whom we all await,* is standing among you; and you have no idea who He is. [27]Though He comes after me, I am not even worthy to unlace His sandals.*

The mystery of Jesus' identity occupies His contemporaries and will continue to occupy generations of believers for centuries to come. As the twelve journey with Him, it gradually becomes clearer who this man is, where He

---

* 1:28 Verse 28 has been inserted here to help retain the continuity of events.   * 1:23 Isaiah 40:3   * 1:24-25 Literally, immersing, to show repentance   * 1:27 Verse 28 has been moved before verse 20 to retain the continuity of events.

comes from, and how His existence will profoundly affect the rest of human history. The question of "Who is this man?" cannot be answered overnight.

---

²⁹The morning after *this conversation,* John sees Jesus coming toward him. *In eager astonishment,* he shouts out:

John the Baptist: Look! *This man is more than He seems!* He is the Lamb sent from God, *the sacrifice* to erase the sins of the world! ³⁰He is the One I have been saying will come after me, who existed long before me and is much greater than I am. ³¹*No one* recognized Him—myself included. But I came baptizing* with water so that He might be revealed to Israel. ³²As I watched, the Spirit came down like a dove from heaven and rested on Him. ³³I didn't recognize Him *at first,* but the One who sent me to baptize told me, "The One who will baptize with the Holy Spirit will be the person you see the Spirit come down and rest upon." ³⁴I have seen this *with my own eyes* and can attest that this One is the Son of God!

³⁵⁻³⁶The day after, John *saw Him again as he* was visiting with two of his disciples. As Jesus walked by, he announced again:

John the Baptist: Do you see Him? This man is the Lamb of God, *God's sacrifice to cleanse our sins.*

³⁷At that moment, the two disciples began to follow Jesus, ³⁸⁻³⁹who turned back to them, saying:

Jesus: What is it that you want?

Two Disciples: We'd like to know where You are staying. Teacher, *may we remain at Your side today?*

Jesus: Come and see. *Follow Me, and we will camp together.*

It was about four o'clock in the afternoon *when they met Jesus.* They came and saw where He was staying, *but they got more than they imagined.* They remained with Him the rest of the day *and followed Him for the rest of their lives.* ⁴⁰⁻⁴¹One of these new disciples,

Andrew, rushed to find his brother Simon and tell him they had found the One who is promised, God's Anointed *who will heal the world.* ⁴²As Andrew approached with Simon, Jesus looked into him.

Jesus: Your name is Simon, and your father is called John. But from this day forward you will be known as Peter,* the rock.

⁴³⁻⁴⁴The next day Jesus set out to go into Galilee; and when He came upon Philip, He invited him to join them.

Jesus: Follow Me.

Philip, like Andrew and Peter, came from a town called Bethsaida; *and he decided to make the journey with Him.* ⁴⁵Philip found Nathanael, *a friend, and burst in with excitement:*

Philip: We have found the One. Moses wrote about Him in the Law, all the prophets spoke of the day when He would come, and now He is here—His name is Jesus, son of Joseph *the carpenter;* and He comes from Nazareth.

Nathanael: ⁴⁶How can anything good come from *a place like* Nazareth?

Philip: Come with me, and see for yourself.

⁴⁷As Philip and Nathanael approached, Jesus saw Nathanael and spoke to those standing around Him.

Jesus: Look closely, and you will see an Israelite who is a truth-teller.

Nathanael *(overhearing Jesus)*: ⁴⁸How would You know this about me? *We have never met.*

Jesus: *I have been watching you* before Philip invited you here. *Earlier in the day,* you were enjoying *the shade and fruit of* the fig tree. I saw you then.

Nathanael: ⁴⁹Teacher, You are the One—God's own Son and Israel's King.

Jesus: ⁵⁰Nathanael, if all it takes for you to believe is My telling you I saw you under the fig tree, then what you will see later

* 1:31 Literally, immersing, to show repentance * 1:42 Literally, Cephas

will astound you. ⁵¹I tell you the truth: *before our journey is complete*, you will see the heavens standing open while heavenly messengers ascend and descend, *swirling around the Son of Man.*

2 Three days later, they all went to celebrate a wedding feast in Cana of Galilee. Mary, the mother of Jesus, was invited ²together with Him and His disciples. ³While they were celebrating, the wine ran out; and Jesus' mother hurried over to her son.

Mary: *The host stands on the brink of embarrassment; there are many guests, and* there is no more wine.

Jesus: ⁴Dear woman, is it our problem *they miscalculated when buying wine and inviting guests*? My time has not arrived.

⁵*But* she turned to the servants.

Mary: Do whatever my son tells you.

⁶In that area were six *massive* stone water pots that could each hold 20 to 30 gallons.* They were typically used for Jewish purification rites. ⁷Jesus' instructions *were clear:*

Jesus: Fill each water pot with water until it's ready to spill over the top; ⁸then fill a cup, and deliver it to the headwaiter.

They did exactly as they were instructed. ⁹After tasting the water that had become wine, the headwaiter couldn't figure out where such wine came from (even though the servants knew), and he called over the bridegroom *in amazement.*

Headwaiter: ¹⁰*This wine is delectable.* Why would you save the most exquisite fruit of the vine? A host would generally serve the good wine first and, when his inebriated guests don't notice or care, he would serve the inferior wine. You have held back the best for last.

¹¹Jesus performed this miracle, the first of His signs, in Cana of Galilee. *They did not know how this happened;* but when the disciples *and the servants* witnessed this miracle, their faith blossomed.

With a wedding as the setting of Jesus' first sign, John shows how

Jesus' ministry isn't limited to just "spiritual" things, but is His blessing for all of life.

¹²Jesus then gathered His clan—His family members and disciples—for a journey to Capernaum where they lingered several days. ¹³The time was near to celebrate the Passover, *the festival commemorating when God rescued His children from slavery in Egypt,* so Jesus went to Jerusalem *for the celebration.* ¹⁴*Upon arriving,* He entered the temple *to worship. But the porches and colonnades* were filled with merchants selling *sacrificial animals (such as* doves, oxen, and sheep) and exchanging money. ¹⁵Jesus fashioned a whip of cords and used it *with skill* driving out animals; He scattered the money and overturned the tables, emptying profiteers from the house of God. ¹⁶There were dove merchants *still standing around,* and Jesus reprimanded them.

Jesus: *What are you still doing here?* Get all your stuff, and haul it out of here! Stop making My Father's house a place for your own profit!

¹⁷*The disciples were astounded,* but they remembered that the Hebrew Scriptures said, "Jealous devotion for God's house consumes me."* ¹⁸Some of the Jews cried out to Him *in unison.*

Jews: Who gave You the right to shut us down? *If it is God, then* show us a sign.

Jesus: ¹⁹*You want a sign? Here it is.* Destroy this temple, and I will rebuild it in 3 days.

Jews: ²⁰*Three days?* This temple took more than 46 years to complete. You think You can replicate that feat in 3 days?

²¹The true temple was His body. ²²His disciples remembered this bold prediction after He was resurrected. *Because of this knowledge,* their faith in the Hebrew Scriptures and in Jesus' teachings grew. ²³During the Passover feast in Jerusalem, *the crowds were watching Jesus closely*; and many began to believe in Him because of the signs He was doing. ²⁴⁻²⁵But Jesus saw through to the heart of humankind, and He chose not to give them what they requested. He didn't need anyone to prove to Him the

* 2:6 Literally, two to three measures   * 2:17 Psalm 69:9

character of humanity. He knew what man was made of.

3 Nicodemus was one of the Pharisees, a man with some clout among his people. [2]He came to Jesus under the cloak of darkness to question Him.

Nicodemus: Teacher, some of us have been talking. You are obviously a teacher who has come from God. The signs You are doing are proof that God is with You.

V

At this time, Israel's Roman occupiers have given a small group of Sadducees and Pharisees limited powers to rule, and Nicodemus is one of the Pharisees. He holds a seat on the ruling council known as the Sanhedrin, and surprisingly Nicodemus is among those who seek Jesus for His teaching. It appears that he believes more about Jesus than he wants others to know, so he comes at night.

Jesus: [3]I tell you the truth: only someone who experiences birth for a second time* can *hope to* see the kingdom of God.

Nicodemus: [4]*I am a grown man.* How can someone be born again when he is old *like me*? Am I to crawl back into my mother's womb for a second birth? *That's impossible!*

Jesus: [5]I tell you the truth, if someone does not experience water and Spirit birth, there's no chance he will make it into God's kingdom. [6]*Like from like.* Whatever is born from flesh is flesh; whatever is born from Spirit is spirit. [7]Don't be shocked by My words, *but I tell you the truth.* Even you, *an educated and respected man among your people,* must be reborn *by the Spirit to enter the kingdom of God.* [8]The wind* blows all around us as if it has a will of its own; we *feel and* hear it, but we do not understand where it has come from or where it will end up. Life in the Spirit is as if it were the wind of God.

Nicodemus: [9]I still do not understand how this can be.

Jesus: [10]Your responsibility is to instruct Israel *in matters of faith,* but you do not comprehend *the necessity of life in the Spirit?* [11]I tell you the truth: we speak about the things we know, and we give evidence about the things we have seen, and you choose to reject *the truth of* our witness. [12]If you do not believe when I talk to you about ordinary, earthly realities, then heavenly realities will certainly elude you. [13]No one has ever journeyed to heaven above except the One who has come down from heaven—the Son of Man, who is of heaven. [14]Moses lifted up the serpent in the wilderness. In the same way, the Son of Man must be lifted up; [15]then all those who believe in Him will experience everlasting life.

[16]For God expressed His love for the world in this way: He gave His only Son so that whoever believes in Him will not face everlasting destruction, but will have everlasting life. [17]Here's the point. God didn't send His Son into the world to judge it; instead, He is here to rescue a world *headed toward certain destruction.*

[18]No one who believes in Him has to fear condemnation, yet condemnation is already the reality for everyone who refuses to believe because they reject the name of the only Son of God. [19]Why does God allow for judgment *and condemnation*? Because the Light, *sent from God,* pierced through the world's darkness *to expose ill motives, hatred, gossip, greed, violence, and the like.* Still some people preferred the darkness over the light because their actions were dark. [20]Some of humankind hated the light. They *scampered hurriedly* back into the darkness where vices thrive and wickedness flourishes. [21]Those who *abandon deceit and* embrace what is true, they will enter into the light where it will be clear that all their deeds come from God.

V

Jesus makes the point clear: stay connected to Him, and have no reason to fear. Jesus doesn't mean that at the instant someone has faith, fear simply vanishes or only good things happen in that person's life. In fact, the blessings that come with eternal life often

* 3:3 Or "from above" * 3:8 "Wind" and "spirit" are the same word in Greek.

have nothing to do with present or future circumstances, but they have everything to do with the individual's connections to God and others. That is John's message to his listeners. God came to earth embodied in flesh, and then He reached His greatest acclaim through a torturous death. If this is all true, then believers will find strength and beauty in places never imagined. Abiding in Jesus the Anointed is the good life, regardless of the external circumstances.

---

²²Not long after, Jesus and His disciples traveled to the Judean countryside where they could enjoy one another's company and ritually cleanse *new followers* through baptism.* ²³-²⁴About the same time, *Jesus' cousin* John—*the wandering prophet* who had not yet been imprisoned—was *upriver* at Aenon near Salim baptizing *scores of* people in the abundant waters there. ²⁵John's activities raised questions about the nature of purification among his followers and a religious leader, ²⁶so they approached him with their questions.

John's Followers: Teacher, the One who was with you *earlier* on the other side of the Jordan, the One whom you have been pointing to, is baptizing* the multitudes who are coming to Him.

John the Baptist: ²⁷Apart from the gifts that come from heaven, no one can receive anything at all. ²⁸I have said it many times, and you have heard me—I am not the Anointed One; I am the one who comes before Him. ²⁹If you are confused, consider this: the groom is the one with the bride. The best man takes his place close by and listens for him. When he hears the voice of the groom, he is swept up in the joy *of the moment*. So hear me. My joy could not be more complete. ³⁰He, *the groom*, must take center stage; and I, *the best man*, must step to His side.

³¹If someone comes from heaven above, he ranks above it all *and speaks of heavenly things*. If someone comes from earth, he speaks of earthly things. The One from the heavens is superior; He is over all. ³²He reveals the mysteries seen and *realities* heard *of the heavens above*, but no one below is listening. ³³Those who are listening and accept His witness *to these truths* have gone on record. They acknowledge the fact that God is true! ³⁴The One sent from God speaks with the very words of God and abounds with the very Spirit and essence of God. ³⁵The Father loves the Son and withholds nothing from Him. ³⁶Those who believe in the Son will bask in eternal life, but those who disobey the Son will never experience life. They will know only God's lingering wrath.

4 The picture was becoming clear to the Pharisees that Jesus had gained a following much larger than that of John the Baptist, *the wandering prophet*. Now He could see *that the Pharisees were beginning to plot against Him*. ²This was because His disciples were busy ritually cleansing many new disciples through baptism,* ³He chose to leave Judea *where most Pharisees lived* and return to *a safer location in* Galilee. ⁴This was a trip that would take them through Samaria.

For Jews in Israel, Samaria is a place to be avoided. Before Solomon's death 1,000 years earlier, the regions of Samaria and Judea were part of a united Israel. After the rebellion that divided the kingdom, Samaria became a hotbed of idol worship. The northern kings made alliances that corrupted the people by introducing foreign customs and strange gods. They even had the nerve to build a temple to the True God on Mt. Gerizim to rival the one in Jerusalem. By the time the twelve are traveling with Jesus, it has long been evident that the Samaritans have lost their way. By marrying outsiders, they have polluted the land. Israel's Jews consider them to be half-breeds—mongrels—and the Jews know to watch out for them or else be bitten by temptation.

---

* 3:22 Literally, immerse, to show repentance   * 3:26 Literally, immersing, to show repentance   * 4:2 Literally, immersing, to show repentance

5-8In a *small* Samaritan town known as Sychar, Jesus *and His entourage* stopped to rest at the historic well that Jacob gave his son Joseph. It was about noon when Jesus found a spot to sit close to the well while the disciples ventured off to find provisions. *From His vantage, He watched as* a Samaritan woman approached to draw some water. *Unexpectedly* He spoke to her.

Jesus: Would you *draw water, and* give Me a drink?

Woman: 9I cannot believe that You, a Jew, would associate with me, a Samaritan woman; much less ask me to give You a drink.

Jews, you see, have no dealings with Samaritans.

Also, a man never approaches a woman like this in public. Jesus is breaking accepted social barriers with this confrontation.

Jesus: 10You don't know the gift of God or who is asking you for a drink *of this water from Jacob's well.* Because if you did, you would have asked Him *for something greater;* and He would have given you the living water.

Woman: 11Sir, You sit by this deep well *a thirsty man* without a bucket in sight. Where does this living water come from? 12Are You claiming superiority to our father Jacob who labored long and hard to dig *and maintain* this well so that he could share clean water with his sons, *grandchildren,* and cattle?

Jesus: 13Drink this water, and your thirst is quenched only for a moment. *You must return to this well again and again.* 14I offer water that will become a wellspring within you that gives life throughout eternity. You will never be thirsty again.

Woman: 15*Please,* Sir, give me some of this water, so I'll never be thirsty and never again have to make the trip to this well.

Jesus: 16Then bring your husband to Me.

Woman: 17-18I do not have a husband.

Jesus: Technically you are telling the truth. But you have had five husbands and are currently living with a man you are not married to.

Woman: 19Sir, it is obvious to me that You are a prophet. 20Our fathers worshiped here on this mountain, but Your people say that Jerusalem is the only place for all to worship. *Which is it?*

Jesus: 21-24Woman, I tell you that neither *is so.* Believe this: a new day is coming—in fact, it's already here—when the importance will not be placed on the time and place of worship but on the truthful hearts of worshipers. You worship what you don't know while we worship what we do know, for God's salvation is coming through the Jews. The Father is spirit, and He is seeking followers whose worship is sourced in truth and deeply spiritual as well. Regardless of whether you are in Jerusalem or on this mountain, if you do not seek the Father, then you do not worship.

Woman: 25These mysteries will be made clear by He who is promised, the Anointed One.

Jesus: 26The Anointed is speaking to you. I am the One you have been looking for.

27The disciples returned to Him *and gathered around Him* in amazement that He would *openly break their customs by* speaking to this woman, but none of them would ask Him what He was looking for or why He was speaking with her. 28The woman went back to the town, leaving her water pot behind. She stopped men and women on the streets and told them about what had happened.

Woman: 29*I met* a stranger who knew everything about me. Come and see for yourselves; can He be the Anointed One?

30A crowd came out of the city and approached Jesus. 31During all of this, the disciples were urging Jesus to eat the food they gathered.

Jesus: 32I have food to eat that you know nothing about.

Disciples *(to one another)*: 33Is it possible someone else has brought Him food while we were away?

Jesus: ³⁴I receive My nourishment by serving the will of the Father who sent Me and completing His work. ³⁵You have heard others say, *"Be patient; we have four more months to wait until the crops are ready for the harvest."* I say, take a closer look and you will see that the fields are ripe and ready for the harvest. ³⁶The harvester is collecting his pay, harvesting fruit ripe for eternal life. So even now, he and the sower are celebrating *their fortune.* ³⁷The saying *may be old, but it* is true: "One person sows, and another reaps." ³⁸I sent you to harvest where you have not labored; someone else took the time to plant and cultivate, and you feast on the fruit of their labor.

³⁹Meanwhile, because one woman shared with her neighbors how Jesus exposed her past and present, the village *of Sychar* was transformed—many Samaritans heard and believed. ⁴⁰The Samaritans approached Jesus and repeatedly invited Him to stay with them, so He lingered there for two days *on their account.* ⁴¹With the words that came from His mouth, there were many more believing Samaritans. ⁴²They began their faith journey because of the testimony of the woman *beside the well*; but when they heard for themselves, they were convinced the One they were hearing was and is God's Anointed, *the Liberating King,* sent to rescue the entire world.

⁴³⁻⁴⁵After two days *of teaching and conversation,* Jesus proceeded to Galilee where His countrymen received Him *with familiar smiles.* After all, they witnessed His miracle at the feast in Jerusalem; but Jesus understood and often quoted *the maxim:* "No one honors a hometown prophet."

These old friends should be the first to believe, but it takes outsiders like the Samaritans to recognize Him.

⁴⁶⁻⁴⁷As Jesus traveled to Cana (the village in Galilee where He transformed the water into *fine* wine), He was met by a government official. This man had heard *a rumor that* Jesus had left Judea and was heading to Galilee, and he came *in desperation* begging for Jesus' help because his young son was near death. *He was fearful that unless* Jesus would go with him to Capernaum, his son would have no hope.

Jesus *(to the official)*: ⁴⁸*My word is not enough*; you only believe when you see miraculous signs.

Official: ⁴⁹Sir, this is my son; please come with me before he dies.

Jesus *(interrupting him)*: ⁵⁰Go home. Your son will live.

When he heard the voice of Jesus, faith took hold of him and he turned to go home. ⁵¹Before he reached his village, his servants met him on the road celebrating his son's miraculous recovery.

Official: ⁵²What time did this happen?

Servants: Yesterday about one o'clock in the afternoon.

⁵³At that moment, it dawned on the father the exact time that Jesus spoke the words, "He will live." After that, he believed; and *when he told* his family *about his amazing encounter with this Jesus,* they believed too. ⁵⁴This was the second sign Jesus performed when He came back to Galilee from Judea.

5 When these events were completed, Jesus led His followers to Jerusalem where they would celebrate a Jewish feast* together.

Jesus takes His disciples into one of the most miserable places they have ever seen. The suffering and impurity is frightening, but He comes to serve these precious people.

²⁻³In Jerusalem they came upon a pool by the sheep gate surrounded by five covered porches. In Hebrew this place is called Bethesda.

Crowds of people lined the area, lying around the porches. All of these people were *disabled in some way;* some were blind, lame, paralyzed, or plagued by diseases[; and they were waiting for the waters to move. ⁴From time to time, a heavenly messenger would come to stir the water in the pool. Whoever reached the water first and got in after it was agitated would be healed of his or her disease].* ⁵⁻⁶In the crowd, Jesus noticed one particular man who had been living with his

* 5:1 Perhaps Passover   * 5:4 Some early manuscripts omit the end of verse 3 and all of verse 4.

disability for 38 years. He knew this man had been waiting here a long time.

Jesus *(to the disabled man):* Are you *here in this place* hoping to be healed?

Disabled Man: [7]Kind Sir, I wait, *like all of these people,* for the waters to stir; *but I cannot walk. If I am to be healed in the waters,* someone must carry me into the pool. Without a helping hand, someone else beats me to the water's edge each time it is stirred.

Jesus: [8]Stand up, carry your mat, and walk.

[9]At the moment Jesus uttered these words, a healing energy coursed through the man and returned life to his limbs—he stood and walked *for the first time in 38 years.* But this was the Sabbath Day; *and any work, including carrying a mat, was prohibited on this day.*

It is impossible to imagine this man's excitement. His entire life has been defined by his illness. Now he is free from it. Free from the pain and weakness. Free from the depression that gripped his soul. Free, too, from the shame he always knew. Now he does not just walk—he runs and celebrates with friends and family. Everyone is rejoicing with him, except for some of the Jewish leaders. Instead, they drill him with questions as if they can disregard this miracle.

Jewish Leaders *(to the man who had been healed):* [10]Must you be reminded that it is the Sabbath? You are not allowed to carry your mat today!

Formerly Disabled Man: [11]The man who healed me gave me specific instructions to carry my mat and go.

Jewish Leaders: [12]Who is the man who gave you these instructions? *How can we identify Him?*

[13]The man genuinely did not know who it was that healed him. In the midst of the crowd *and the excitement of his renewed*

health, Jesus had slipped away. [14]Some time later, Jesus found him in the temple and again spoke to him.

Jesus: Take a look at your body; it has been made whole and strong. So avoid a life of sin, or else a calamity greater than any disability may befall you.

[15]The man went immediately to tell the Jewish leaders that Jesus was the mysterious healer. [16]So they began pursuing and attacking Jesus because He performed these miracles on the Sabbath.

Jesus *(to His attackers):* [17]My Father is at work. So I, too, am working.

This issue keeps arising from the Jewish leaders. They do not appreciate the good things Jesus does on the Sabbath. Most Jews cower at the rebuke from these men, but Jesus does not. He is very clear about this. He cares for the poor, the sick, and the marginalized more than He cares for how some people may interpret and apply God's law. It is easy to follow a set of rules; it is much harder to care for the things of the heart. He also makes it clear that those who follow His path are put on earth to serve. His followers' service comes out of love for Him. All who follow Him are to love and to serve, especially on the Sabbath.

[18]He was justifying the importance of His work on the Sabbath, claiming God as His Father in ways that suggested He was equal to God. These pious religious leaders sought an opportunity to kill Jesus, and these words fueled their hatred.

Jesus: [19]The truth is that the Son does nothing on His own; *all these actions are led by the Father.* The Son watches the Father closely and then mimics the work of the Father. [20]The Father loves the Son, so He does not hide His actions. Instead, He shows Him everything, and the things not yet revealed by the Father will dumbfound you. [21]The Father can give life to those who are dead; in the same way, the Son can give the gift of life to those He chooses.

²²The Father does not *exert His power to* judge anyone. Instead, He has given the authority as Judge to the Son. ²³So all of creation will honor *and worship* the Son as they do the Father. If you do not honor the Son, then you dishonor the Father who sent Him.

²⁴I tell you the truth: eternal life belongs to those who hear My voice and believe in the One who sent Me. These people have no reason to fear judgment because they have already left death and entered life.

²⁵I tell you the truth: a new day is imminent—in fact, it has arrived—when the voice of the Son of God will penetrate death's domain, and everyone who hears will live. ²⁶⁻²⁷You see, the Father radiates with life; and He also animates the Son *of God* with the same life-giving *beauty and* power to exercise judgment *over all of creation.* Indeed, the Son of God is also the Son of Man. ²⁸If this sounds amazing to you, what is even more amazing is that when the time comes, those buried long ago will hear His voice *through all the rocks, sod, and soil* ²⁹and step out *of decay into resurrection. When this hour arrives,* those who did good will be resurrected to life, and those who did evil will be resurrected to judgment.

³⁰I have not ever acted, and will not in the future act, on My own. I listen *to the directions of the One who sent Me* and act *on these divine instructions. For this reason,* My judgment is always fair and never self-serving. I'm committed to pursuing God's agenda and not My own.

³¹If I stand as the lone witness to My true identity, then I can be dismissed as a liar. ³²But *if you listen,* you will hear another testify about Me, and I know what He says about Me is genuine and true. ³³You sent *messengers* to John, and he told the truth *to everyone who would listen.* ³⁴Still his message about Me *originated in heaven,* not in mortal man. I am telling you these things *for one reason*—so that you might be rescued. ³⁵*The voice of* John the Baptist, *the wandering prophet,* is like a light in the darkness; and for a time, you took great joy and pleasure in the light he offered.

³⁶There's another witness standing in My corner who is greater than John *or any other man.* The mission that brings

Me here, and the things I am called to do, demonstrate the authenticity of My calling which comes directly from the Father. ³⁷In the act of sending Me, the Father has endorsed Me. *None of you really knows the Father.* You have never heard His voice or seen His profile. ³⁸His word does not abide in you because you do not believe in the One sent by the Father.

³⁹Here you are scouring through the Scriptures, hoping that you will find eternal life among a pile of scrolls. *What you don't seem to understand is that* the Scriptures point to Me. ⁴⁰*Here I am with you,* and still you reject the truth *contained in the law and prophets* by refusing to come to Me so that you can have life.

Jesus is the source of life, the animating energy of creation that humanity desperately lacks.

⁴¹This kind of glory does not come from mortal men. ⁴²And I see that you do not possess the love of God. ⁴³I have *pursued you,* coming here in My Father's name, and you have turned Me away. If someone else were to approach you with a different set of credentials, you would welcome him. ⁴⁴*That's why it is hard to see* how true faith is even possible for you: you are consumed by the approval of other men, *longing to look good in their eyes;* and yet you disregard the approval of the one true God. ⁴⁵Don't worry that I might bring you up on charges before My Father. Moses is your accuser even though you've put your hope in him ⁴⁶because if you believed *what* Moses had to *say,* then you would believe in Me because he wrote about Me. ⁴⁷But if you ignore Moses and the deeper meaning of his writings, then how will you ever believe what I have to say?

6 Once this had transpired, Jesus made His way to the other side of the Sea of Galilee (which some these days call the Sea of Tiberias). ²As Jesus walked, a large crowd pursued Him hoping to see new signs *and miracles;* His healings of the sick and lame were garnering great attention. ³Jesus went up a mountain and found a place to sit down *and teach.* His disciples gathered around. ⁴The celebration of the Passover, one of the principal Jewish feasts, would take place soon. ⁵But when Jesus looked up, He

could see an immense crowd coming toward Him. Jesus approached Philip.

Jesus *(to Philip)*: Where is a place to buy bread so these people may eat?

[6]Jesus knew what He was planning to do, but He asked Philip nonetheless. He had something to teach, and it started with a test.

Philip: [7]I could work for more than half of a year* and still not have the money to buy enough bread to give each person a very small piece.

[8]Andrew, the disciple who was Simon Peter's brother, spoke up.

Andrew: [9]I met a young boy in the crowd carrying five barley loaves and two fish, but that is practically useless in feeding a crowd this large.

Jesus: [10]Tell the people to sit down.

They all sat together on a large grassy area. *Those counting the people reported* approximately 5,000 men—*not including the women and children*—sitting in the crowd. [11]Jesus picked up the bread, gave thanks to God, and passed it to everyone. He repeated this ritual with the fish. *Men, women, and children* all ate until their hearts were content. [12]When the people had all they could eat, He told the disciples *to gather the leftovers.*

Jesus: Go and collect the leftovers, so we are not wasteful.

[13]They filled 12 baskets with fragments of the five barley loaves. [14]After witnessing this sign that Jesus did, the people stirred in conversation.

Crowd: This man must be the Prophet *God said was* coming into the world.

[15]Jesus sensed the people were planning to mount a revolution *against Israel's Roman occupiers* and make Him king, so He withdrew farther up the mountain by Himself.

another in their land. As conquerors go, the Romans aren't all that bad. They allow the Jews to worship God in His temple, and they appoint some of them to government positions. Of course, the Judeans still long to rule themselves and throw the Roman rulers out. Some think Jesus is just the man to lead that revolution. But political upheaval isn't what He is teaching, and it isn't why He has come to earth.

---

[16]Later that evening the disciples walked down to the sea, [17]boarded a boat, and set sail toward Capernaum. Twilight gave way to darkness. Jesus had not yet joined them. [18]*Suddenly,* the waves rose and a fierce wind began *to rock the boat.* [19]After rowing three or four miles* *through the stormy seas,* they spotted Jesus approaching the boat walking mysteriously upon the deep waters that surrounded them. They panicked.

Jesus *(to the disciples)*: [20]I am the One. Don't be afraid.

[21]They welcomed Jesus aboard their small vessel; and when He stepped into the boat, the next thing they knew, they were ashore at their destination.

[22]The following day some people gathered on the other side of the sea and saw that only one boat had been there; *they were perplexed.* They remembered seeing the disciples getting into the boat without Jesus.

[23]Other boats were arriving from Tiberias near the grassy area where the Lord offered thanks and passed out bread. [24]When this crowd could not find Him or His disciples, they boarded their small boats and crossed the sea to Capernaum looking for Him. [25]When they found Jesus across the sea, they questioned Him.

Crowd: Teacher, when did You arrive at Capernaum?

Jesus: [26]I tell you the truth—you are tracking Me down because I fed you, not because you saw signs from God. [27]Don't spend your life chasing food that spoils and rots.

Since the Babylonians seized Judah in 586 B.C., the Jews have endured one foreign occupier after

* 6:7 Literally, 200 denarii   * 6:19 Literally, 25 or 30 stadia

Instead, seek the food that lasts into all the ages and comes from the Son of Man, the One on whom God the Father has placed His seal.

Crowd: [28]What do we have to do to accomplish the Father's works?

Jesus: [29]If you want to do God's work, then believe in the One He sent.

Crowd: [30]Can You show us a miraculous sign? *Something spectacular?* If we see something like that, it will help us to believe. [31]Our fathers ate manna when they wandered in the desert. The Hebrew Scriptures say, "He gave them bread from heaven to eat."*

Jesus: [32]I tell you the truth: Moses did not give you bread from heaven; it is My Father who offers you true bread from heaven. [33]The bread of God comes down out of heaven and breathes life into the cosmos.

Crowd: [34]Master, we want a boundless supply of this bread.

Jesus: [35]I am the bread that gives life. If you come to My table and eat, you will never go hungry. Believe in Me, and you will never go thirsty. [36]Here I am standing in front of you, and still you don't believe. [37]All that My Father gives to Me comes to Me. I will receive everyone; I will not send away anyone who comes to Me. [38]And here's the reason: I have come down from heaven not to pursue My own agenda but to do what He desires. I am here on behalf of the Father who sent Me. [39]He sent Me to care for all He has given Me so that nothing *and no one* will perish. *In the end,* on the last day, He wants everything to be resurrected *into new life.* [40]So if you want to know the will of the Father, know this: everyone who sees the Son and believes in Him will live eternally; and on the last day, I am the One who will resurrect him.

[41]Some of the Jews began to grumble *quietly* against Him because He said, "I am the bread that came down from heaven."

Crowd: [42]Isn't Jesus the son of Joseph? We know His parents! *We know where He came from,* so how can He claim to have "come down from heaven"?

Jesus: [43]Stop grumbling *under your breaths.* [44]If the Father who sent Me does not draw you, then there's no way you can come to Me. But I will resurrect everyone who does come on the last day. [45]Among the prophets, it's written, "Everyone will be taught of God."* So everyone who has heard and learned from the Father finds Me. [46]No one has seen the Father, except the One sent from God. He has seen the Father. [47]I am telling you the truth: the one who accepts these things has eternal life. [48]I am the bread that gives life. [49]Your fathers ate manna in the wilderness, and they died *as you know.* [50]But there is another bread that comes from heaven; if you eat this bread, you will not die. [51]I am the living bread that has come down from heaven *to rescue those who eat it.* Anyone who eats this bread will live forever. The bread that I will give breathes life into the cosmos. This bread is My flesh.

[52]*The low whispers of* some of Jesus' detractors turned into an out-and-out debate.

Crowd: *What is He talking about?* How is He able to give us His flesh to eat?

Jesus: [53]I tell you the truth; unless you eat the flesh of the Son of Man and drink His blood, you will not know life. [54]If you eat My flesh and drink My blood, then you will have eternal life and I will raise you up at the end of time. [55]My flesh and blood provide true nourishment. [56]If you eat My flesh and drink My blood, you will abide in Me and I will abide in you. [57]The Father of life who sent Me has given life to Me; and as you eat My flesh, I will give life to you. [58]This is bread that came down from heaven; I am not like the manna that your fathers ate and then died! If you eat this bread, your life will never end.

[59]He spoke these words in the synagogue as part of His teaching mission in Capernaum. [60]Many disciples heard what He said, and they had questions *of their own.*

Disciples: How are we supposed to understand all of this? It is a hard teaching.

[61]Jesus was aware that even His disciples were murmuring about this.

* 6:31 Exodus 16:4   * 6:45 Isaiah 54:13

How is it possible to follow this path and believe these truths? To be honest, it is not easy. In fact, some find this so hard that they leave Jesus for good. The rest readily admit they are still working on what it means to follow Him. So Jesus leaves behind a number of practices to help believers. One of these is known as the Lord's Supper. Jesus instructs His disciples to break bread and share wine to remember how He will allow His body to be broken for all humankind. In some beautiful, mysterious way, Jesus is present in the simple elements of bread and wine, so the worshiper may touch Him, taste His richness, and remember His most glorious hours on the cross. In that moment, He embraces all darkness and shame and transforms them into light. As believers come to the table together and feast on His light, life seems more hopeful and complete. Taking the bread and the wine means affirming the reality that the One who has come to liberate souls is among and within His people.

Jesus: Has My teaching offended you? [62]What if you were to see the Son of Man ascend *to return* to where He came from? [63]The Spirit brings life. The flesh has nothing to offer. The words I have been teaching you are spirit and life, [64]but some of you do not believe.

From the first day *Jesus began to call disciples*, He knew those who did not have genuine faith. He knew, too, who would betray Him.

Jesus: [65]This is why I have been telling you that no one comes to Me without the Father's blessing and guidance.

[66]After hearing these teachings, many of His disciples walked away and no longer followed Jesus.

Jesus (to the twelve): [67]Do you want to walk away too?

Simon Peter: [68]Lord, if we were to go, whom would we follow? You speak the words that give everlasting life. [69]We believe and recognize that You are the Holy One sent by God.*

Jesus: [70]I chose each one of you, the twelve, Myself. But one of you is a devil.

[71]This cryptic comment referred to Judas, the son of Simon Iscariot, for he was the one of the twelve who was going to betray Him.

7 After these events, *it was time for Jesus to move on.* He began a long walk through the Galilean countryside. He was purposefully avoiding Judea because

of *the violent threats made against Him by* the Jews there who wanted to kill Him. [2]*It was fall,* the time of year when the Jews celebrated the Festival of Booths.

On this holiday, everyone camps in temporary quarters, called booths, to remember that God was with their ancestors when they wandered for 40 years without a home.

Brothers of Jesus (to Jesus): [3]Let's get out of here and go *south* to Judea so You can show Your disciples there what You are capable of doing. [4]No one who seeks the public eye is content to work in secret. If You want to perform these signs, then step forward on the world's stage; *don't hide up here in the hills, Jesus.*

[5]Jesus' own brothers *were speaking contemptuously*; they did not yet believe in Him, *just as the people in His hometown did not see Him as anything more than Joseph's son.*

Jesus: [6]My time has not yet arrived; but for you My brothers, *by all means,* it is always the right time. [7]*You have nothing to worry about because* the world doesn't hate you, but it despises Me because I am always exposing the dark evil in its works. [8]Go on to the feast without Me; I am not going *right now* because My time is not yet at hand.

[9]This conversation came to an *abrupt* end, and Jesus stayed in Galilee [10]until His brothers were gone. Then He, too, went up to Jerusalem. But He traveled in secret to avoid

* 6:69 Other ancient manuscripts read, "You are God's Anointed, *the Liberating King,* the Son of the Living God."

drawing any public attention. [11]Some Jewish leaders were searching for Him at the feast and asking the crowds where they could find Him. [12]The crowds would talk in groups: some favored Jesus and thought He was a good man; others disliked Him and thought He was leading people astray. [13]*All of these conversations took place in whispers.* No one was willing to speak openly about Jesus for fear of the religious leaders.

[14]In the middle of the festival, Jesus marched directly into the temple and started to teach. [15]Some of the Jews *who heard Him* were amazed at Jesus' ability, and people questioned repeatedly:

Jews: How can this man be so wise *about the Hebrew Scriptures*? He has never had a formal education.

Jesus: [16]I do not claim ownership of My words; they are *a gift* from the One who sent Me. [17]If anyone is willing to act according to His purposes *and is open to hearing truth*, he will know the source of My teaching. Does it come from God or from Me? [18]If a man speaks his own words, *constantly quoting himself,* he is after adulation. But I chase only after glory for the One who sent Me. My intention is *authentic and* true. You'll find no wrong *motives* in Me.

[19]Moses gave you the law, didn't he? Then how can you *blatantly* ignore the law and look for an opportunity to murder Me?

Notice how Jesus changes in tone and subject. This shift seems abrupt because the Pharisees' plotting is yet to be exposed.

Crowd: [20]You must be possessed with a demon! Who is trying to kill You?

Jesus: [21]*Listen,* all it took was for Me to do one thing, *heal a crippled man,* and you all were astonished. [22]Don't you remember how Moses passed down circumcision as a tradition of our ancestors? When you pick up a knife to circumcise on the Sabbath, *isn't that work?* [23]If a male is circumcised on the Sabbath to keep the law of Moses intact, how can making one man whole on the Sabbath be a cause for your violent rage? [24]You should not judge by outward appearance. When you judge, search for what is right and just.

Some People of Jerusalem: [25]There is the man they are seeking to kill; surely He must be the one. [26]But here He is, speaking out in the open to the crowd, while they have not spoken a word to *stop or challenge* Him. Do these leaders now believe He is the Anointed One? [27]But He can't be; we know where this man comes from, but the true origin of the Anointed will be a mystery to all of us.

Jesus *(speaking aloud as He teaches on the temple's porch)*: [28]*You think* you know Me and where I have come from, but I have not come here on My own. I have been sent by the One who embodies truth. You do not know Him. [29]I know Him because I came from Him. He has sent Me.

[30]Some were trying to seize Him because of His words, but no one laid as much as a finger on Him—His time had not yet arrived. [31]In the crowd, there were many in whom faith was taking hold.

Believers in the Crowd: When the Anointed arrives, will He perform any more signs than this man has done?

[32]Some Pharisees *were hanging back in the crowd,* overhearing the gossip about Him. The temple authorities and the Pharisees *took action and* sent officers to arrest Jesus.

Jesus: [33]I am going to be with you for a little while longer; then I will return to the One who sent Me. [34]You will look for Me, but you will not be able to find Me. Where I am, you are unable to come.

Some Jews in the Crowd *(to each other)*: [35]Where could He possibly go that we could not find Him? You don't think He's about to go into the Dispersion* and teach our people scattered among the Greeks, do you? [36]What do you think He means, "You will look for Me, but you will not be able to find Me," and, "Where I am, you are unable to come"?

[37]On the last day, the biggest day of the festival, Jesus stood again and spoke aloud.

Jesus: If any of you is thirsty, come to Me and drink. [38]If you believe in Me, the

* 7:35 Literally, the Diaspora (Greek for "scattering"). The Diaspora refers to those Jews who were exiled or settled outside the traditional lands of Israel.

Hebrew Scriptures say that rivers of living water will flow from within you.*

[39]Jesus was referring to *the realities of life in the Spirit made available to everyone who believes in Him.* But the Spirit had not yet arrived because Jesus had not been glorified.

The Holy Spirit connects believers to the Father and His Son. So any fear about being disconnected from God may be abandoned; the Creator of the Universe dwells within His people, sustains them, and will accomplish the impossible through them.

Some of the Crowd: [40]This man is definitely the Prophet.

Others: [41]This is God's Anointed, *the Liberating King!*

Still Others: Is it possible for the Anointed to come from Galilee? [42]Don't the Hebrew Scriptures say that He will come from Bethlehem,* King David's village, and be a descendant of King David?

[43]*Rumors and* opinions about the true identity of Jesus divided the crowd. [44]Some wanted to arrest Him, but no one dared to touch Him.

[45]The officers *who had been sent by the* chief priests and Pharisees *to take Jesus into custody* returned *empty-handed,* and they faced some hard questions.

Chief Priest and Pharisees: *Where is Jesus?* Why didn't you capture Him?

Officers: [46]*We listened to Him.* Never has a man spoken like this man.

Pharisees: [47]So you have also been led astray? [48]Can you find one leader or educated Pharisee who believes this man? *Of course not.* [49]This crowd is plagued by ignorance about the teachings of the law; *that is why they will listen to Him.* That is also why they are under God's curse.

[50]Nicodemus, *the Pharisee who approached Jesus under the cloak of darkness,* was present when the officers returned empty-handed. He addressed the leaders.

Nicodemus: [51]Does our law condemn someone without first giving him a fair hearing and learning something about him?

Pharisees *(ignoring Nicodemus's legal point):* [52]Are you from Galilee too? Look it up for yourself; no real prophet is supposed to come from Galilee.

[[53]The time came for everyone to go home.

8 Jesus went to the Mount of Olives. [2]He awoke early in the morning to return to the temple. *When He arrived,* the people surrounded Him, so He sat down and began to teach them. [3]*While He was teaching,* the scribes and Pharisees brought in a woman who was caught in the act of adultery; and they stood her before Jesus.

Pharisees: [4]Teacher, this woman was caught in the act of adultery. [5]Moses says in the law that we are to kill such women by stoning. What do You say about it?

[6]This was all set up as a test for Jesus; His answers would give them grounds to accuse Him *of crimes against Moses' law.* Jesus bent over and wrote something in the dirt with His finger. [7]They persisted in badgering Jesus, so He stood up straight.

Jesus: Let the first stone be thrown by the one among you who has not sinned.

[8]Once again Jesus bent down to the ground and resumed writing with His finger. [9]The Pharisees who heard Him *stood still for a few moments and then* began to leave slowly, one by one, beginning with the older men. Eventually only Jesus and the woman remained, [10]and Jesus looked up.

Jesus: *Dear* woman, where is everyone? *Are we alone?* Did no one step forward to condemn you?

Woman Caught in Adultery: [11]Lord, no one *has condemned me.*

* 7:38 Isaiah 44:3; 55:1; 58:11 * 7:42 Micah 5:1-2

Jesus: Well, I do not condemn you either; *all I ask is that you* go and from now on avoid the sins that plague you.]*

12*On another occasion,* Jesus spoke to the crowds again.

Jesus: I am the light that shines through the cosmos; if you walk with Me, you will thrive in the *nourishing* light that gives life and will not know darkness.

Pharisees: 13Jesus, what You are claiming about Yourself cannot possibly be true. The only person bearing witness is You.

Jesus: 14Even if I am making *bold* claims about Myself—*who I am, what I have come to do*—I am speaking the truth. You see, I know where I came from and where I will go *when I am done here.* You know neither where I come from nor where I will go. 15You spend your time judging *by the wrong criteria,* by human standards; but I am not here to judge anyone. 16If I were to judge, then My judgment would be based on truth; but I would not judge anyone alone. I act in harmony with the One who sent Me. 17Your law states that if the testimonies of two witnesses agree, their testimony is true. 18Well, I testify about Myself, and so does the Father who sent Me here.

Pharisees: 19Where is the Father *who testifies on Your behalf?*

Jesus: You don't know the Father or Me. If you knew Me, then you would also know the Father.

20Jesus said all of these things in the treasury while He was teaching in the temple; *followers and opponents alike gathered to hear Him,* but none of His enemies tried to seize Him because His time had not yet come.

Jesus *(to the crowds)*: 21I am leaving this place, and you will look for Me and die in your sin. For where I am going, you are unable to come.

Jews: 22Is He suicidal? He keeps saying, "Where I am going, you are unable to come."

Jesus: 23You originate from *the earth* below, and I have come from *the heavens* above. You are from this world, and I am not.

24That's why I told you that you will die here as a result of your sins. Unless you believe I am who I have said I am, your sins will lead to your death.

Jews: 25Who exactly are You?

Jesus: From the beginning of My mission, I have been telling you who I am. 26I have so much to say about you, so many judgments to render; *but if you hear one thing,* hear that the One who sent Me is true, and all the things I have heard from Him I speak into the world.

27The people had not understood that Jesus was teaching about the Father.

Jesus: 28Whenever *the day comes and* you lift up the Son of Man, then you will know that I am He. *It will be clear then* that I am not acting alone, but that I am speaking the things I have learned directly from the Father. 29The One who sent Me is with Me; He has not abandoned Me because I always do what pleases Him.

30As Jesus was speaking, many in the crowd believed in Him.

Even though many believe, they cannot imagine what He means about the lifting up of the Son of Man.

Jesus *(to the new Jewish believers)*: 31If you *hear My voice and* abide in My word, you are truly My disciples; 32you will know the truth, and that truth will give you freedom.

Jewish Believers: 33We are Abraham's children, and we have never been enslaved to anyone. How can You say to us, "You will be set free"?

Jesus: 34I tell you the truth: everyone who commits sin surrenders his freedom to sin. He is a *slave to sin's power.* 35Even a household slave does not live in the home like a member of the family, but a son belongs there forever. 36So *think of it this way:* if the Son comes to make you free, you will really be free.

Jesus notices that some of His opponents are listening, so He speaks louder and turns His remarks to them.

* 7:53-8:11 Many early manuscripts omit these verses.

[37]I know you are descendants of Abraham, but here you are plotting to murder Me because you do not welcome My voice into your lives. [38]As I speak, I am painting you a picture of what I have seen with My Father; here you are repeating the things you have seen from your father.

Jews: [39]Abraham is our father.

Jesus: If you are truly Abraham's children, then act like Abraham! [40]From what I see you are trying to kill Me, a man who has told you the truth that comes from the Father. This is not something Abraham would do, [41]but you are doing what you have learned from your father.

Jews: We were not born from adulterous parents; we have one Father: God.

Jesus: [42]I come from the one True God, and I'm not here on My own. He sent Me *on a mission*. If God were your Father, you would *know that and would* love Me. [43]You don't even understand what I'm saying. *Do you?* Why not? It is because You cannot stand to hear My voice. [44]You are just like your true father, the devil; and you spend your time pursuing the things your father loves. He started out as a killer, and he cannot tolerate truth because he is void of anything true. At the core of his character, he is a liar; everything he speaks originates in these lies because he is the father of lies. [45]So when I speak truth, you don't believe Me. [46-47]If I speak the truth, why don't you believe Me? If you belong to God's family, then why can't you hear God speak? The answer is clear; you are not in God's family. *I speak truth, and you don't believe Me.* Can any of you convict Me of sin?

Jews: [48]We were right when we called You a demon-possessed Samaritan.

Jesus: [49-50]I'm not taken by demons. You dishonor Me, but I give *all glory and* honor to the Father. But I am not pursuing My own fame. There is only One who pursues and renders justice. [51]I tell you the truth, anyone who *hears My voice and* keeps My word will never experience death.

Jews: [52]We are even more confident now that You are demon-possessed. *Just go down the list:* Abraham died, the prophets all died. Yet You say, "If you keep My word, you will never taste death." [53]Are you greater than our father Abraham? He died; *remember?* Prophets—are any of them still alive? No. Who do You think You are?

Jesus: [54]If I were trying to make Myself somebody important, *it would be a waste of time.* That kind of fame is worth nothing. It is the Father who *is behind Me, urging Me on,* giving Me praise. You say, "He is our God," [55]but you are not in relationship with Him. I know Him *intimately;* even if I said anything other than the truth, I would be a liar, like you. I know Him, and I do as He says. [56]Your father Abraham anticipated the time when I would come, and he celebrated My coming.

Jews: [57]You aren't even 50 years old, yet You have seen *and talked with* Abraham?

Jesus: [58]I tell you the truth; I AM before Abraham was born.

[59]The people picked up stones to hurl at Him, but Jesus slipped out of the temple. *Their murderous rage would have to wait.*

V

John and many people in his community are Jews. As a son of Abraham, his criticism of certain Jewish leaders is not a criticism of a whole people. He's not stereotyping or making generalizations. "The Jews" he remembers in this passage are a corrupt group of power brokers who conspire against Jesus with the Romans to have Him crucified and who later have John's own followers expelled from the synagogue. Their behavior may be compared to the behavior of those Israelites condemned by Old Testament prophets. Prophets have the duty—Jeremiah said he had "a fire in his bones" (20:9)—to speak for God and condemn hypocrisy and unbelief wherever it is found, especially when it's found close to home. That's what John's doing when recalling this event.

9 While walking along the road, Jesus saw a man who was blind since his birth.

Disciples: ²Teacher, who sinned? *Who is responsible for this man's blindness?* Did he commit sins that merited this punishment? If not his sins, is it the sins of his parents?

Jesus: ³Neither. His blindness cannot be *explained or* traced to any particular person's sins. He is blind so the deeds of God may be put on display. ⁴While it is daytime, we must do the works of the One who sent Me. But when the *sun sets and* night falls, this work is impossible. ⁵Whenever I am in the world, I am the Light of the world.

⁶After He said these things, He spat on the ground and mixed saliva and dirt to form mud, which He smeared across the blind man's eyes.

Jesus *(to the blind man):* ⁷Go, wash yourself in the pool of Siloam.

Siloam means "sent," *and its name reminded us that his healing was sent by God.* The man went, washed, and returned to Jesus, his eyes now alive with sight. ⁸Then neighbors and others who knew him were confused to see a man so closely resembling the blind beggar running about.

Townspeople: Isn't this the man we see *every day* sitting and begging *in the streets*?

Others: ⁹This is the same man.

Still Others: This cannot be him. But this fellow bears an uncanny resemblance to the blind man.

Formerly Blind Man: I am the same man. *It's me!*

Townspeople: ¹⁰How have your *lifeless* eyes been opened?

Formerly Blind Man: ¹¹A man named Jesus *approached me and* made mud from the ground and applied it to my eyes. He then said to me, "Go, wash yourself in the pool of Siloam." I went and washed, and suddenly I could see.

Townspeople: ¹²Where is this man *who healed you*?

Formerly Blind Man: I don't know.

¹³⁻¹⁴The townspeople brought the formerly blind beggar to appear before the Pharisees *the same day Jesus healed him*, which happened to be on the Sabbath Day. ¹⁵The Pharisees began questioning him, looking for some explanation for how he could now see.

Formerly Blind Man: He smeared mud on my eyes, and I washed; now I see.

Some Pharisees: ¹⁶God can't possibly be behind this man because He is breaking the rules of the Sabbath.

Other Pharisees: How can such a lawbreaking scoundrel do something like this?

The Pharisees were at odds with one another about Jesus and could not agree *whether His power came from God or the devil.*

Pharisees *(to the formerly blind man):* ¹⁷What do you say about this man, about the fact He opened your eyes so you could see?

Formerly Blind Man: *I have no doubt*—this man is a prophet.

¹⁸Some of the Jews suspected the whole situation was a charade, that this man was never blind. So they summoned the man's parents to testify about his condition.

Pharisees: ¹⁹Is this man your son? Do you testify that he has been blind from birth? How therefore does he now see?

Parents: ²⁰We can tell you this much: he is our son, and he was born blind. ²¹But his new sight is a complete mystery to us! We do not know the man who opened his eyes. Why don't you ask our son? He is old enough to speak for himself.

²²The man's parents were a bit evasive because they were afraid of the Jewish leaders. It had been rumored that anyone who spoke of Jesus as the Anointed One would be expelled from the synagogue. ²³So they deferred the thorny question to their son, ²⁴and the Pharisees called on him a second time.

Pharisees: Give God the credit. *He's the One who healed you.* All glory belongs to God.

We are persuaded this man you speak of is a sinner *who defies God.*

Formerly Blind Man: 25If this man is a sinner, I don't know. *I am not qualified to say.* I only know one thing: I was blind, and now I see.

Pharisees: 26What did He do to you? How did He give you sight?

Formerly Blind Man: 27*Listen,* I've already answered all these questions, and you don't like my answers. Do you really need me to say it all over again? Are you thinking about joining up with Him and becoming His followers?

Pharisees (berating him): 28You're one of His followers, but we follow Moses. 29We have confidence that God spoke to Moses, but this man *you speak of is a mystery;* we don't even know where He comes from.

Formerly Blind Man: 30Isn't it ironic that you, *our religious leaders,* don't even know where He comes from; yet He gave me sight! 31We know that God does not listen to sinners, but He does respond and work through those who worship Him and do His will. 32No one has ever heard of someone opening the eyes of any person blind from birth. 33This man must come from God; otherwise, this miracle would not be possible. *Only God can do such things.*

Pharisees: 34You were born under a cloud of sin. How can you, *of all people,* lecture us?

The religious leaders banished him from their presence. 35Jesus heard what had happened and sought out the man.

Jesus: Do you believe in the Son of Man?

Formerly Blind Man: 36I want to believe, Lord. Who is He?

Jesus: 37You have seen His face *with your new eyes,* and you are talking to Him now.

Formerly Blind Man: 38Lord, I do believe.

The man bowed low to worship Jesus.

Jesus: 39I have entered this world to announce a verdict *that changes everything.*

Now those without sight may begin to see, and those who see may become blind.

Some Pharisees (who overheard Jesus): 40Surely we are not blind, are we?

Jesus: 41If you were blind, you would be without sin. But because you claim you can see, your sin is ever present.

V

The Pharisees are frequently around to challenge whatever Jesus says and does, but He always gets the better of them. Once again, Jesus turns what the Pharisees say inside out. They think blindness is a curse that evidences sin, and they think vision ensures knowledge and understanding—even concerning spiritual matters. Instead, the Pharisees' confidence in their vision and discernment make them unable to see the truth about Jesus. Ironically, they have blind trust in their sighted leaders. By refusing to believe in Him, they are the sinners—not the blind man.

10

Jesus: I tell you the truth: the man who crawls through the fence of the sheep pen, rather than walking through the gate, is a thief or a vandal. 2The shepherd walks openly through the entrance. 3The guard who is posted to protect the sheep opens the gate for the shepherd, and the sheep hear his voice. He calls his own sheep by name and leads them out. 4When all the sheep have been gathered, he walks on ahead of them; and they follow him because they know his voice. 5The sheep would not be willing to follow a stranger; they run because they do not know the voice of a stranger.

6Jesus explained a profound truth through this metaphor, but they did not understand His teaching. 7So He explained further.

Jesus: I tell you the truth: I am the gate of the sheep. 8All who approached the sheep before Me came as thieves and robbers, and the sheep did not listen to their voices. 9I am the gate; whoever enters through Me will be liberated, will go in and go out, and will find pastures. ¹⁰The thief approaches *with malicious intent*, looking to steal, slaughter, and destroy; I came to give life with joy and abundance.

¹¹I am the good shepherd. The good shepherd lays down His life for the sheep *in His care.* ¹²The hired hand is not like the shepherd caring for His own sheep. When a wolf attacks, snatching and scattering the sheep, he runs for his life, leaving them *defenseless.* ¹³The hired hand runs because he works only for wages and does not care for the sheep. ¹⁴I am the good shepherd; I know My sheep, and My sheep know Me. ¹⁵As the Father knows Me, I know the Father; I will give My life for the sheep. ¹⁶There are many more sheep than you can see here, and I will bring them as well. They will hear My voice, and the flock will be united. One flock. One shepherd. ¹⁷The Father loves Me because I *am willing to* lay down My life—but I will take it up again. ¹⁸My life cannot be taken away by anybody else; I am giving it of My own free will. My authority allows Me to give My life and to take it again. All this has been commanded by My Father.

V

Jesus loves to explain truth through everyday things like vines, fruit, fishing, building, and shepherding, as He does here. He is a master communicator. In this metaphor, Jesus is the shepherd. Eventually He becomes the sheep as well. On the cross, He is destined to become the innocent sacrifice that makes all future sin sacrifices and burnt offerings unnecessary.

---

¹⁹When He spoke these words, some of the Jews began to argue.

Many Jews: ²⁰He has a demon and is a raving maniac. Why are you people listening to Him?

Other Jews: ²¹No demon-possessed man ever spoke like this. Do demons give sight to the blind?

²²⁻²³It was winter and time for the Festival of Dedication.* While in Jerusalem, Jesus was walking through the temple in an area known as Solomon's porch, ²⁴and Jews gathered around Him.

Jews: How long are You going to keep us guessing? If You are God's Anointed, *the Liberating King,* announce it clearly.

Jesus: ²⁵I have told you, and you do not believe. The works I am doing in My Father's name tell the truth about Me. *You do not listen;* ²⁶you lack faith because you are not My sheep. ²⁷My sheep *respond as they* hear My voice; I know them *intimately,* and they follow Me. ²⁸I give them a life that is unceasing, and death will not have the last word. *Nothing or* no one can steal them from My hand. ²⁹My Father has given the flock to Me, and He is superior to all *beings and things.* No one is powerful enough to snatch the flock from My Father's hand. ³⁰The Father and I are one.

³¹The Jews gathered stones to execute Jesus right then and there.

Jesus: ³²I have performed many beautiful works before you in the name of the Father. Which of these can be judged as an offense that merits My execution?

Jews: ³³You are not condemned for performing miracles. We demand Your life because You are a man, yet you claim to be God. This is blasphemy!

Jesus: ³⁴*You know* what is written in the Scriptures. Doesn't it read, "I said, you are gods"?* ³⁵If the Scriptures called your ancestors (*mere mortals*) gods to whom the word of God came—and the Scriptures cannot be set aside—³⁶what should you call One *who is unique,* sanctified by and sent from the Father into the world? I have said, "I am God's Son." How can you call that blasphemy? ³⁷*By all means,* do not believe in Me, if I am not doing the things of the Father. ³⁸But examine My actions, *and you will see that My work is the work of the Father.* Regardless of whether you believe in Me—believe the miracles. Then you will know that the Father is in Me, and I am in the Father.

³⁹Once again, *some of* the Jews tried to capture Him, but He slipped away, eluding their

* 10:22-23 The Festival of Lights or Hanukkah   * 10:34 Psalm 82:6

grasp. [40]Jesus crossed the Jordan River and returned to the place where John was ritually cleansing the people through baptism* in the early days. He lingered in the area, [41]and scores of people gathered around Him.

Crowds: John never performed any miracles, but every word he spoke about this man has come to pass. It is all true!

[42]In that place, many believed in Him.

V

John points to stories where Jesus returns to the issue of faith again and again. The crowds are fickle, believing sometimes and not others. The religious leaders refuse to believe because Jesus doesn't fit their paradigms. The disciples and close friends constantly face situations that challenge their faith, and this especially happens when Lazarus dies. John is implicitly urging his readers to have faith in Christ, even in difficult times, because He is the source of life and well being.

---

11 There was a certain man who was very ill. He was known as Lazarus from Bethany, which is the hometown of Mary and her sister Martha. [2]Mary *did a beautiful thing for Jesus. She* anointed the Lord with a pleasant-smelling oil and wiped His feet with her hair. Her brother Lazarus became deathly ill, [3]so the sisters immediately sent a message to Jesus which said, "Lord, the one You love is very ill." [4]Jesus heard the message.

Jesus: His sickness will not end in his death but will bring great glory to God. As these events unfold, the Son of God will be exalted.

[5]Jesus *dearly* loved Mary, Martha, and Lazarus. [6]However, after receiving this news, He waited two more days where He was.

Jesus (*speaking to the disciples*): [7]It is time to return to Judea.

Disciples: [8]Teacher, the last time You were there, some Jews attempted to execute You

by crushing You with stones. Why would You go back?

Jesus: [9]There are 12 hours of daylight, correct? If anyone walks in the day, that person does not stumble because he or she sees the light of the world. [10]If anyone walks at night, he will trip and fall because he does not have the light within. [11](Jesus briefly pauses.) Our friend Lazarus has gone to sleep, so I will go to awaken him.

Disciples: [12]Lord, if he is sleeping, then he will be all right.

[13]Jesus used "sleep" *as a metaphor* for death, but the disciples took Him literally *and did not understand.* [14]Then Jesus spoke plainly.

Jesus: Lazarus is dead, [15]and I am grateful for your sakes that I was not there when he died. Now you will *see and* believe. Gather yourselves, and let's go to him.

Thomas, the Twin (*to the disciples*): [16]Let's go so we can die with Him.

[17-18]As Jesus was approaching Bethany (which is about two miles east of Jerusalem), He heard that Lazarus had been in the tomb four days. [19]Now many people had come to comfort Mary and Martha as they mourned the loss of their brother. [20]Martha went to meet Jesus when word arrived that He was approaching Bethany, but Mary stayed behind at the house.

Martha: [21]Lord, if You had been with us, my brother would not have died. [22]Even so I still believe that anything You ask of God will be done.

Jesus: [23]Your brother will rise to life.

Martha: [24]I know. He will rise again when everyone is resurrected on the last day.

Jesus: [25]I am the resurrection and the source of all life; those who believe in Me will live even in death. [26]Everyone who lives and believes in Me will never truly die. Do you believe this?

Martha: [27]Yes, Lord, I believe that You are the Anointed, *the Liberating King,* God's own Son who *we have heard* is coming into the world.

* 10:40 Literally, immersing, to show repentance

28After this Martha ran home to Mary.

Martha (*whispering to Mary*): Come with me. The Teacher is here, and He has asked for you.

29Mary did not waste a minute. She got up and went 30to the same spot where Martha had found Jesus outside the village. 31The people gathered in her home offering support and comfort assumed she was going back to the tomb to cry and mourn, so they followed her. 32Mary approached Jesus, saw Him, and fell at His feet.

Mary: Lord, if only You had been here, my brother would still be alive.

33When Jesus saw Mary's *profound grief and the moaning and* weeping of her companions, He was deeply moved *by their pain* in His spirit and was intensely troubled.

Jesus: 34Where have you laid his body?

Jews: Come and see, Lord.

35*As they walked,* Jesus wept; 36and everyone noticed how much Jesus must have loved Lazarus. 37But others were skeptical.

Others: If this man can give sight to the blind, He could have kept him from dying.

They are asking, if Jesus loves Lazarus so much, why didn't He get here much sooner?

38Then Jesus, who was intensely troubled by all of this, approached the tomb—a *small* cave covered by a *massive* stone.

Jesus: 39Remove the stone.

Martha: Lord, he has been dead four days; the stench will be unbearable.

Jesus: 40Remember, I told you that if you believe, you will see the glory of God.

41They removed the stone, and Jesus lifted His eyes toward heaven.

Jesus: Father, I am grateful that You have heard Me. 42I know that You are always listening, but I proclaim it loudly so that everyone here will believe You have sent Me.

43After these words, He called out in a thunderous voice.

Jesus: Lazarus, come out!

44Then, the man who was dead walked out of his tomb bound from head to toe in a burial shroud.

Jesus: Untie him, and let him go.

Once again Jesus amazes everyone around Him. How does He raise Lazarus? What kind of man can speak life into death's darkness? Throughout His time on earth, those around Him are continually surprised by Jesus. He is unique. How does He have power over death? It takes a while, but more and more His followers become convinced this is no ordinary man.

45As a result, many of the Jews who had come with Mary saw what happened and believed in Him. 46But some went to the Pharisees to report what they witnessed Jesus doing. 47As a result of these reports—*and on short notice*—the chief priests and Pharisees called a meeting of the high council.

Pharisees: What are we going to do about this man? He is performing many miracles. 48If we don't stop this now, every man, woman, and child will believe in Him. *You know what will happen next?* The Romans *will think He's mounting a revolution and* will destroy our temple. It will be the end of our nation.

Caiaphas, the High Priest That Year: 49You have no idea what you are talking about; 50what you don't understand is that it's better for you that one man should die for the people so the whole nation won't perish.

51*His speech was more than it seemed.* As high priest that year, Caiaphas prophesied (without knowing it) that Jesus would die on behalf of the entire nation, 52and not just for the *children of* Israel—He would die so all God's children could be gathered from the four corners of the world into one people. ⁵³In that moment, they cemented their intentions to have Jesus executed.

⁵⁴From that day forward, Jesus refrained from walking publicly among the people in Judea. He withdrew to a small town known as Ephraim, a rural area near the wilderness, where He set up camp with His disciples.

⁵⁵The Passover was approaching, and Jews everywhere traveled to Jerusalem early so they could purify themselves and prepare for Passover. ⁵⁶People were looking for Jesus, hoping to catch a glimpse of Him in the city. All the while, some Jews were discussing Him in the temple.

Some Jews: Do you think He will decide not to come *to Jerusalem this year* for the feast?

⁵⁷*In the midst of this confusion,* the Pharisees and the chief priests ordered that if anyone knew the whereabouts of Jesus *of Nazareth,* it must be reported immediately so they could arrest Him.

12 Six days before the Passover feast, Jesus journeyed to the village of Bethany, to the home of Lazarus who had recently been raised from the dead, ²where they hosted Him for dinner. Martha was busy serving *as the hostess,* Lazarus reclined at the table with Him, ³and Mary took a pound of fine ointment, pure nard (which is *both rare and* expensive), and anointed Jesus' feet with it; and then she wiped them with her hair. As the pleasant fragrance of this extravagant ointment filled the entire house, ⁴Judas Iscariot, one of His disciples (who was plotting to betray Jesus), began to speak.

Judas Iscariot: ⁵*How could she pour out* this vast amount of fine oil? Why didn't she sell it? It is worth nearly a year's wages;* the money could have been given to the poor.

⁶This had nothing to do with Judas's desire to help the poor. The truth is he served as the treasurer, and he helped himself to the money from the common pot at every opportunity.

Jesus: ⁷Leave her alone. She has observed this custom in anticipation of the day of My burial. ⁸The poor are ever present, but I will be leaving.

⁹Word spread of Jesus' presence, and a large crowd was gathering to see Jesus and the formerly deceased Lazarus, whom He had brought back from the dead. ¹⁰The chief priests were secretly plotting Lazarus's murder since, ¹¹because of him, many Jews were leaving their teachings and believing in Jesus.

¹²The next day, a great crowd of people who had come to the festival heard that Jesus was coming to Jerusalem; ¹³so they gathered branches of palm trees to wave as they celebrated His arrival.

Crowds (*shouting*): Hosanna!
>   He who comes in the name of the Lord is
>   truly blessed*
>   and is King of all Israel.

¹⁴Jesus found a young donkey, sat on it, *and rode through the crowds mounted on this small beast.* The Scriptures foretold of this day:

> ¹⁵Daughter of Zion, do not be afraid.
>   Watch! Your King is coming.
>   *You will find Him* seated on the colt of
>   a donkey.*

¹⁶The disciples did not understand any of this at the time; these truths did not sink in until Jesus had been glorified. As they reflected on their memories of Jesus, they realized these things happened just as they were written. ¹⁷Those who witnessed the resurrection of Lazarus enthusiastically spoke of Jesus to all who would listen, ¹⁸and that is why the crowd went out to meet Him. They had heard of the miraculous sign He had done.

V

His followers may suspect during their time with Jesus that He is more than a man, but it takes the power and glory of the resurrection to convince them completely that Jesus is divine. When they see Him, touch Him, and hear the sound of His voice thunder in their souls, the disciples know they are face-to-face with God's immense glory, the unique Son of God. Reading

* 12:5 Literally, 300 denarii, Roman coins   * 12:13 Psalm 118:26
* 12:15 Zechariah 9:9

and rereading the Scriptures in light of their experiences of Him, it becomes clear that Jesus' life and story are the climax of God's covenants with His people.

Pharisees *(to one another):* ¹⁹Our efforts to squelch Him have not worked, *but now is not the time for action.* Look, the world is following after Him.

²⁰Among the crowds traveling to Jerusalem were Greeks seeking to *follow God and* worship at the great feast. ²¹⁻²²Some of them came to Philip with an important request.

Greek Pilgrims *(to Philip):* Sir, we are hoping to meet Jesus.

Philip, a disciple from the Galilean village of Bethsaida, told Andrew *that these Greeks wanted to see Jesus.* Together Andrew and Philip approached Jesus to inform Him about the request.

Jesus *(to Philip and Andrew):* ²³The time has come for the Son of Man to be glorified. ²⁴I tell you the truth: unless a grain of wheat is planted in the ground and dies, it remains a solitary seed. But when it is planted, it produces in death a great harvest. ²⁵The one who loves this life will lose it, and the one who despises it in this world will have life forevermore. ²⁶Anyone who serves Me must follow My path; anyone who serves Me will want to be where I am, and he will be honored by the Father. ²⁷My spirit is low and unsettled. How can I ask the Father to save Me from this hour? This hour is the purpose for which I have come *into the world. But what I can say is this:* ²⁸"Father, glorify Your name!"

Suddenly a voice echoed from the heavens.

The Father: I have glorified My name. And again I will bring glory *in this hour that will resound throughout time.*

²⁹The crowd of people surrounding Jesus were confused.

Some in the Crowd: It sounded like thunder.

Others: A heavenly messenger spoke to Him.

Jesus: ³⁰The voice you hear has not spoken for My benefit, but for yours. ³¹Now judgment comes upon this world, *and everything will change.* The tyrant of this world, *Satan,* will be thrown out. ³²When I am lifted up from the earth, then all of humanity will be drawn to Me.

³³These words foreshadowed the nature of His death.

Crowd: ³⁴The law teaches that the Anointed is the One who will remain without end. How can You say it is essential that the Son of Man be lifted up? Who is this Son of Man *You are talking about*?

Jesus: ³⁵Light is among you, but very soon it will flicker out. Walk as you have the light, and then the darkness will not surround you. Those who walk in darkness don't know where they are going. ³⁶While the light is with you, believe in the light; and you will be reborn as sons *and daughters* of the light.

After speaking these words, Jesus left the people to go to a place of seclusion. ³⁷Despite all the signs He performed, they still did not believe in Him. ³⁸Isaiah spoke of this reality, saying,

> Lord, who could accept what we've been told?
>   And who has seen the awesome power of the Lord revealed?*

³⁹This is the reason they are unable to believe. ⁴⁰Isaiah also said,

> God has blinded their eyes
>   and hardened their hearts
> So that their eyes cannot see *properly*
>   and their hearts cannot understand
>   *and be persuaded*
>   *by the truth* to turn to Me
>   and be reconciled by My healing hand.*

⁴¹Isaiah could say this because he had seen the glory of the Lord *with his own eyes* and declared His beauty aloud. ⁴²Yet many leaders secretly believed in Him but would not declare their faith because the Pharisees continued their threats to expel all His

* 12:38 Isaiah 53:1   * 12:40 Isaiah 6:10

followers from the synagogue; [43]here's why: they loved to please men more than they desired to glorify God.

Jesus (crying out before the people): [44]Anyone who believes in Me is not placing his faith in Me, but in the One who sent Me here. [45]If one sees Me, he sees the One who sent Me. [46]I am here to bring light in this world, freeing everyone who believes in Me from the darkness that blinds him. [47]If anyone listening to My teachings chooses to ignore them, so be it: I have come to liberate the world, not to judge it. [48]However, those who reject Me and My teachings will be judged: in the last day, My words will be their judge [49]because I am not speaking of My own volition and from My own authority. The Father who sent Me has commanded Me what to say and speak. [50]I know His command is eternal life, so every word I utter originates in Him.

13 Before the Passover festival began, Jesus was keenly aware that His hour had come to depart from this world and to return to the Father. From beginning to end, Jesus' days were marked by His love for His people. [2]Before Jesus and His disciples gathered for dinner, the adversary filled Judas Iscariot's heart with plans of deceit and betrayal. [3]Jesus, knowing that He had come from God and was going away to God, [4]stood up from dinner and removed His outer garments. He then wrapped Himself in a towel, [5]poured water in a basin, and began to wash the feet of the disciples, drying them with His towel.

Simon Peter (as Jesus approaches): [6]Lord, are You going to wash my feet?

Jesus: [7]Peter, you don't realize what I am doing, but you will understand later.

Peter: [8]You will not wash my feet, now or ever!

Jesus: If I don't wash you, you will have nothing to do with Me.

Peter: [9]Then wash me but don't stop with my feet. Cleanse my hands and head as well.

Jesus: [10]Listen, anyone who has bathed is clean all over except for the feet. But I tell you this, not all of you are clean.

Within pain and filth, there is an opportunity to extend God's kingdom through an expression of love, humility, and service. This simple act of washing feet is a metaphor for how the world looks through the lens of Jesus' grace. He sees the people—the world He created—which He loves. He also sees the filthy corruption in the world that torments everyone. His mission is to cleanse those whom He loves from those horrors. This is His redemptive work with feet, families, disease, famine, and hearts.

When Jesus sees disease, He sees the opportunity to heal. When He sees sin, He sees a chance to forgive and redeem. When He sees dirty feet, He sees a chance to wash them.

[11]He knew the one with plans of betraying Him, which is why He said, "not all of you are clean." [12]After washing their feet and picking up His garments, He reclined at the table again.

Jesus: Do you understand what I have done to you? [13]You call Me Teacher and Lord, and truly, that is who I am. [14]So if your Lord and Teacher washes your feet, then you should wash one another's feet. [15]I am your example; keep doing what I do. [16]I tell you the truth: a servant is not greater than the master. Those who are sent are not greater than the one who sends them.* [17]If you know these things, and if you put them into practice, you will find happiness. [18]I am not speaking about all of you. I know whom I have chosen, but let the Hebrew Scripture be fulfilled that says, "The very same man who eats My bread with Me will stab Me in the back." [19]Assuredly, I tell you these truths before they happen so that when it all transpires, you will believe that I am. [20]I tell you the truth: anyone who accepts the ones I send accepts Me. In turn, the ones who accept Me also accept the One who sent Me.

[21]Jesus was becoming visibly distressed.

* 13:16 Literally, apostle

Jesus: I tell you the truth: one of you will betray Me.

[22]The disciples began to stare at one another, wondering who was the unfaithful disciple. [23]One disciple in particular, who was loved by Jesus, reclined next to Him at the table. [24]Peter motioned to the disciple at Jesus' side.

Peter *(to the beloved disciple)*: Find out who the betrayer is.

Beloved Disciple *(leaning in to Jesus)*: [25]Lord, who is it?

Jesus: [26]I will dip a piece of bread in My cup and give it to the one who will betray Me.

He dipped one piece in the cup and gave it to Judas, the son of Simon Iscariot. [27]After this occurred, Satan entered into Judas.

Jesus *(to Judas)*: Make haste, and do what you are going to do.

[28]No one understood Jesus' instructions to Judas. [29]Because Judas carried the money, some thought he was being instructed to buy the necessary items for the feast or give some money to the poor. [30]So Judas took his piece of bread and departed into the night.
[31]Upon Judas's departure, Jesus spoke:

Jesus: Now the Son of Man will be glorified as God is glorified in Him. [32]If God's glory is in Him, His glory is also in God. The moment of this astounding glory is imminent. [33]My children, My time here is brief. You will be searching for Me; and as I told the Jews, "You cannot go where I am going." [34]So I give you a new command: Love each other *deeply and fully*. Remember the ways that I have loved you, and demonstrate your love for others in those same ways. [35]Everyone will know you as My followers if you demonstrate your love to others.

Simon Peter: [36]Lord, where are You going?

Jesus: Peter, you cannot come with Me now, but later you will join Me.

Peter: [37]Why can't I go now? I'll give my life for You!

Jesus: [38]Will you really give your life for Me? I tell you the truth: you will deny Me three times before the rooster crows.

Ultimately Peter is telling the truth. He is more than willing to lay down his life. But none of His disciples understand the magnitude of the persecution and hatred that is about to be unleashed.

Even Peter, Jesus' dear Peter, is afraid. He protests any inference to Jesus' impending departure. Each of the twelve would do the same. Jesus calms their fears over and over again with stories, metaphors, and outright promises, saying, "I will never abandon you like orphans; I will return to be with you" (14:18).

---

14 **Jesus:** Don't get lost in despair; believe in God, and keep on believing in Me. [2]My Father's home is designed to accommodate all of you. If there were not room for everyone, I would have told you that. I am going to make arrangements for your arrival. [3]I will be there to greet you personally and welcome you home, where we will be together. [4]You know where I am going and how to get there.

Thomas: [5]Lord, we don't know where You are going, so how can we know the path?

Jesus: [6]I am the path, the truth, and the *energy of* life. No one comes to the Father except through Me. [7]If you know Me, you know the Father. Rest assured now; you know Him and have seen Him.

Philip: [8]Lord, all I am asking is that You show us the Father.

Jesus *(to Philip)*: [9]I have lived with you all this time, and you still don't know who I am? If you have seen Me, you have seen the Father. How can you keep asking to see the Father? [10]Don't you believe Me when I say I abide in the Father and the Father dwells in Me? I'm not making this up as I go along. The Father has given Me these truths that I have been speaking to you, and

He empowers all My actions. [11]Accept these truths: I am in the Father, and the Father is in Me. If you have trouble believing based on My words, believe because of the things I have done. [12]I tell you the truth: whoever believes in Me will be able to do what I have done, but they will do even greater things, because I will return to be with the Father. [13]Whatever you ask for in My name, I will do it so that the Father will get glory from the Son. [14]*Let Me say it again:* if you ask for anything in My name, I will do it. [15]If you love Me, obey the commandments I have given you. [16]I will ask the Father to send you another Helper, *the Spirit of truth,* who will remain constantly with you. [17]The world does not recognize the Spirit of truth, because it does not know the Spirit and is unable to receive Him. But you do know the Spirit because He lives with you, and He will dwell in you. [18]I will never abandon you like orphans; I will return to be with you. [19]In a little while, the world will not see Me; but I will not vanish completely from your sight. Because I live, you will also live. [20]At that time, you will know that I am in the Father, you are in Me, and I am in you. [21]The one who loves Me will do the things I have commanded. My Father loves everyone who loves Me; and I will love you and reveal My heart, will, and nature to you.

The Other Judas: [22]Lord, why will You reveal Yourself to us, but not to the world?

Jesus: [23]Anyone who loves Me will listen to My voice and obey. The Father will love him, and We will draw close to him and make a dwelling place within him. [24]The one who does not love Me ignores My message, which is not from Me, but from the Father who sent Me.

[25]I have spoken these words while I am here with you. [26]The Father is sending a great Helper, the Holy Spirit, in My name to teach you everything and to remind you of all I have said to you. [27]My peace is the legacy I leave to you. I don't give gifts like those of this world. Do not let your heart be troubled or fearful. [28]You were listening when I said, "I will go away, but I will also return to be with you." If you love Me, celebrate the fact that I am going to be with the Father because He is far greater than I am. [29]I have told you all these things in advance so that your faith will grow as these things come to pass. [30]I am almost finished speaking to you. The one who rules the world is stepping forward, and he has no part in Me; [31]but to demonstrate to the cosmos My love for the Father, I will do just as He commands. Stand up. It is time for us to leave this place.

15 **Jesus:** I am the true vine, and My Father is the keeper of the vineyard. [2]My Father examines every branch in Me and cuts away those who do not bear fruit. He leaves those bearing fruit and carefully prunes them so that they will bear more fruit; [3]already you are clean because you have heard My voice. [4]Abide in Me, and I will abide in you. A branch cannot bear fruit if it is disconnected from the vine, and neither will you if you are not connected to Me.

[5]I am the vine, and you are the branches. If you abide in Me and I in you, you will bear great fruit. Without Me, you will accomplish nothing. [6]If anyone does not abide in Me, he is like a branch that is tossed out and shrivels up and is later gathered to be tossed into the fire to burn. [7]If you abide in Me and My voice abides in you, anything you ask will come to pass for you. [8]Your abundant growth and your faithfulness as My followers will bring glory to the Father.

God becomes flesh and lives among humanity, not just to have a transaction with people and ultimately die, but to continue to be with them and to send His Spirit to be present with believers. So God calls His Spirit-indwelled people to something greater, something more significant: they are here as redeeming forces on this earth; their time here is about reclaiming the things He has created. Believing God has created the entire cosmos and that it is restored in Jesus, the believer's work here through the Spirit is to say, "This belongs to God," and to help point out the beauty of creation to everyone. And most of all, to live in it themselves by the power of the Holy Spirit who plants the teachings of the Lord in their hearts.

At a time when all of His disciples are feeling as if they are about to be uprooted, Jesus sketches a picture of this new life as a flourishing vineyard—a labyrinth of vines and strong branches steeped in rich soil, abundant grapes hanging from their vines ripening in the sun. Jesus sculpts a new garden of Eden in their imaginations—one that is bustling with fruit, sustenance, and satisfying aromas. This is the Kingdom life. It is all about connection, sustenance, and beauty. But within this promise of life is the warning that people must be in Christ or they will not experience these blessings.

Jesus: [9]I have loved you as the Father has loved Me. Abide in My love. [10]Follow My example in obeying the Father's commandments and receiving His love. If you obey My commandments, you will stay in My love. [11]I want you to know the delight I experience, to find ultimate satisfaction, which is why I am telling you all of this.

[12]My commandment to you is this: love others as I have loved you. [13]There is no greater way to love than to give your life for your friends. [14]You celebrate our friendship if you obey this command. [15]I don't call you servants any longer; servants don't know what the master is doing, but I have told you everything the Father has said to Me. I call you friends. [16]You did not choose Me. I chose you, and I orchestrated all of this so that you would be sent out and bear great and perpetual fruit. As you do this, anything you ask the Father in My name will be done. [17]This is My command to you: love one another.

[18]If you find that the world despises you, remember that before it despised you, it first despised Me. [19]If you were a product of the world order, then it would love you. But you are not a product of the world because I have taken you out of it, and it despises you for that very reason. [20]Don't forget what I have spoken to you: "a servant is not greater than the master." If I was mistreated, you should expect nothing less. If they accepted what I have spoken, they will also hear you. [21]Everything

they do to you they will do on My account because they do not know the One who has sent Me. [22]If I had not spoken within their hearing, they would not be guilty of sin; but now they have no excuse for ignoring My voice.

[23]If someone despises Me, he also despises My Father. [24]If I had not demonstrated things for them that have never been done, they would not be guilty of sin. But the reality is they have stared Me in the face, and they have despised Me and the Father nonetheless. [25]Yet their law, which says, "They despised Me without any cause,"* has again been proven true.

[26]I will send a great Helper to you from the Father, one known as the Spirit of truth. He comes from the Father and will point to the truth as it concerns Me. [27]But you will also point others to the truth about My identity, because you have journeyed with Me since this all began.

As Jesus warns of the mistreatment His followers can expect, He disarms fears by noting the most important things. If the Spirit is within, there is no reason to fear. In fact, the church will thrive under persecution. Yet humans are obsessed with power and political prominence as a means to influence the culture. Christian citizens have an obligation to strive for justice and freedom through the transforming power of the Spirit in people's lives. Rather than exerting temporal power, the real work of the Kingdom often thrives under fierce attack and opposition. Jesus announces this coming persecution to His followers, believing this will lead to their finest hour.

16

Jesus: I am telling you all of this so that you may avoid the offenses that are coming. [2]The time will come when they will kick you out of the synagogue because some believe God desires them to execute you as an act of faithful service. [3]They will do this because they don't know the Father, or else they

* 15:25 Psalm 35:19

would know Me. ⁴I'm telling you all this so that when it comes to pass you will remember what you have heard. It was not important for Me to give you this information in the beginning when I was with you. ⁵But now, I am going to the One who has sent Me, and none of you ask Me, "Where are You going?"

⁶I know that hearing news like this is overwhelming and sad. ⁷But the truth is that My departure will be a gift that will serve you well, because if I don't leave, the great Helper will not come to your aid. When I leave, I will send Him to you. ⁸⁻⁹When He arrives, He will uncover the sins of the world, expose unbelief as sin, and allow all to see their sins in the light of righteousness for the first time. ¹⁰This new awareness of righteousness is important because I am going to the Father and will no longer be present with you. ¹¹The Spirit will also carry My judgment because the one who rules in this world has already been defeated.

¹²I have so much more to say, but you cannot absorb it right now. ¹³⁻¹⁵The Spirit of truth will come and guide you in all truth. He will not speak His own words to you; He will speak what He hears, revealing to you the things to come and bringing glory to Me. The Spirit has unlimited access to Me, to all that I possess and know, just as everything the Father has is Mine. That is the reason I am confident He will care for My own and reveal the path to you. ¹⁶For a little while you will not see Me; but after that, a time will come when you will see Me again.

Some of His Disciples: ¹⁷What does He mean? "I'll be here, and then I won't be here, because I'll be with the Father"?

Other Disciples: ¹⁸What is He saying? "A little while"? We don't understand.

be encouraged that in eternity all needs will be fulfilled in the presence of God.

---

¹⁹Jesus knew they had questions to ask of Him, so He approached them.

Jesus: Are you trying to figure out what I mean when I say you will see Me in a little while? ²⁰I tell you the truth, a time is approaching when you will weep and mourn while the world is celebrating. You will grieve, but that grief will give birth to great joy. ²¹⁻²²In the same way that a woman labors in great pain during childbirth only to forget the intensity of the pain when she holds her child, when I return, your labored grief will also change into a joy that cannot be stolen.

²³When all this transpires, you will finally have the answers you have been seeking. I tell you the truth, anything you ask of the Father in My name, He will give to you. ²⁴Until this moment, you have not sought after anything in My name. Ask and you will receive so that you will be filled with joy.

²⁵I have been teaching you all of these truths through stories and metaphors, but the time is coming for Me to speak openly and directly of the Father. ²⁶The day is coming when you will make a request in My name, but I will not represent you before the Father. ²⁷*You will be heard directly by the Father*. The Father loves you because you love Me and know that I come from the Father. ²⁸I came from the Father into the cosmos, but soon I will leave it and return to the Father.

V

The promise of eternity is a reminder that God's children are made for a renewed world. There is great comfort amid fear, knowing believers will be reunited with Jesus and joined with the Father. As believers labor together in this world—enduring pain, loss, and unfulfilled desires—they should

V

All His disciples mourn Jesus' refusal to take His rightful place as a king and lead a revolution. Jesus knows political might, brute force, and earthly governments are not helpful tools in a battle for hearts. Spiritual revolutions are subversive. They are led by defiant acts of love (for example, healing, foot washing, and martyrdom). Laws do not change hearts, and violence induces hatred and fear. But a sincere community of faith in which love and hope are demonstrated even in the darkest hours will lead a spiritual revolution. It is time to go forward with open eyes and continue to labor as Christian citizens, placing hope only in the redemptive work of the gospel.

Disciples: 29We hear You speaking clearly and not in metaphors. *How could we misunderstand?* 30We see now that You are aware of everything and You reveal things at the proper time. So we do not need to question You, because we believe You have come from God.

Jesus: 31So you believe now? 32Be aware that a time is coming when you will be scattered *like seeds*. You will return to your own way, and I will be left alone. But I will not be alone, because the Father will be with Me. 33I have told you these things so that you will be *whole and* at peace. In this world, you will be plagued with times of trouble, but you need not fear; I have triumphed over this corrupt world order.

17 Jesus (*lifting His face to the heavens*): Father, My time has come. Glorify Your Son, and I will bring You great glory 2-3because You have given Me total authority over humanity. *I have come bearing the plentiful gifts of God*; and all who receive Me will experience everlasting life, a new intimate relationship with You (the one True God) and Jesus the Anointed (the One You have sent). 4I have glorified You on earth and fulfilled the mission You set before Me.

5In this moment, Father, fuse Our collective glory and bring Us together as We were before creation existed. 6You have entrusted Me with these men who have come out of this corrupt world order. I have told them about Your nature and declared Your name to them, and they have held on to Your words and understood that these words, 7like everything else You have given Me, come from You. 8It is true that these men You gave Me have received the words that come from You and not only understood them but also believed that You sent Me. 9I am now making an appeal to You on their behalf. This request is not for the entire world; it is for those whom You have given to Me because they are Yours.

10Yours and Mine, Mine and Yours, for all that are Mine are Yours. Through them I have been glorified.

11I will no longer be physically present in this world, but they will remain in this world. As I return to be with You, holy Father, remain with them through Your name, *the name You have given Me*. May they be one even as We are one. 12While I was physically present with them, I protected them through Your name. I watched over them closely; and only one was lost, the one the Scriptures said was the son of destruction. 13Now I am returning to You. I am speaking this prayer here in the created cosmos *alongside friends and foes* so that in hearing it they might be consumed with joy. 14I have given them Your word; and the world has despised them because they are not products of the world, in the same way that I am not a product of the corrupt world order. 15Do not take them out of this world; protect them from the evil one.

16Like Me, they are not products of the corrupt world order. 17Immerse them in the truth, the truth Your voice speaks. 18In the same way You sent Me into this world, I am sending them. 19It is entirely for their benefit that I have set Myself apart so that they may be set apart by truth. 20I am not asking solely for their benefit; this prayer is also for all the believers who will follow them and hear them speak. 21Father, may they all be one as You are in Me and I am in You; may they be in Us, for by this unity the world will believe that You sent Me.

22All the glory You have given to Me, I pass on to them. May that glory unify them and make them one as We are one, 23I in them and You in Me, that they may be refined so that all will know that You sent Me, and You love them in the same way You love Me.

In this great prayer that Jesus prays for His disciples, He returns repeatedly to the gathering of believers unified with the Father and the Son.

24Father, I long for the time when those You have given Me can join Me in My place so they may witness My glory, which comes from You. You have loved Me before the foundations of the cosmos were laid. 25Father, You are just; though this corrupt world order does not know You, I do.

These followers know that You have sent Me. ²⁶I have told them about Your nature; and I will continue to speak of Your name in order that Your love, which was poured out on Me, will be in them. And I will also be in them.

18 When Jesus finished praying, He began a brief journey with His disciples to the other side of the Kidron Valley, a deep ravine that floods in the winter rains, then farther on to a garden where He gathered His disciples.

²⁻³Judas Iscariot (who had already set his betrayal in motion and knew that Jesus often met with the disciples in this olive grove) entered the garden with an entourage of Roman soldiers and officials sent by the chief priests and Pharisees. They brandished their weapons under the light of torches and lamps. ⁴Jesus stepped forward. It was clear He was not surprised because He knew all things.

Jesus: Whom are you looking for?

Judas's Entourage: ⁵Jesus the Nazarene.

Jesus: I am the One.

Judas, the betrayer, stood with the military force. ⁶As Jesus spoke "I am the One," the forces fell back on the ground. ⁷Jesus asked them a second time:

Jesus: Whom are you searching for?

Judas's Entourage: Jesus the Nazarene.

Jesus: ⁸I have already said that I am the One. If you are looking for Me, then let these men go free.

⁹This happened to fulfill the promise He made that none of those entrusted to Him will be lost.* ¹⁰Suddenly Peter lunged toward Malchus, one of the high priest's servants; and with his sword, Peter severed the man's right ear.

Jesus (to Peter): ¹¹Put down your sword, and return it to the sheath. Am I to turn away from the cup the Father has given Me to drink?

¹²So the Roman commander, soldiers, and Jewish officials arrested Jesus, cuffed His hands and feet, ¹³and brought Him to Annas (the father-in-law of Caiaphas the high priest). ¹⁴You may remember that Caiaphas counseled the Jews that one should die for all people. ¹⁵⁻¹⁶Simon Peter and another disciple followed behind Jesus. When they arrived, Peter waited in the doorway while the other disciple was granted access because of his relationship with the high priest. That disciple spoke to the woman at the door, and Peter was allowed inside.

Servant Girl (to Peter): ¹⁷You are one of this man's disciples, aren't you?

Peter: I am not.

¹⁸All the servants and officers gathered around a charcoal fire to keep warm. It was a cold day, and Peter made his way into the circle to warm himself.

Annas (to Jesus): ¹⁹Who are Your disciples, and what do You teach?

Jesus: ²⁰I have spoken in public where the world can hear, always teaching in the synagogue and in the temple where the Jewish people gather. I have never spoken in secret. ²¹So why would you need to interrogate Me? Many have heard Me teach. Why don't you question them? They know what I have taught.

²²While Jesus offered His response, an officer standing nearby struck Jesus with his hand.

Officer: Is that how You speak to the high priest?

Jesus: ²³If I have spoken incorrectly, why don't you point out the untruths that I speak? Why do you hit Me if what I have said is correct?

²⁴Annas sent Jesus to Caiaphas bound as a prisoner. ²⁵As this was happening, Peter was still warming himself by the fire.

Servants and Officers: You, too, are one of His disciples, aren't you?

Peter: No, I am not.

²⁶One of the high priest's servants who was related to *Malchus*—the person Peter *attacked and* cut off his ear—*recognized Peter.*

* 18:9 John 6:39

Initially, Pilate tells the Jewish leaders to take Jesus and try Him according to Jewish law, but when they hint at capital charges, Pilate agrees to interrogate Jesus as a traitor to the empire. Rome reserves the right to decide who lives and dies in the provinces. They don't delegate that to the Jewish high council. The charge of blasphemy carries no weight in Roman jurisprudence, for it is a matter of Jewish religious law. Rome has no opinion on such matters. So a new charge must be concocted, a charge that Rome does care about. Rome does care about taxes, of course, and takes a dim view of anyone making royal claims under their noses.

Pilate agrees to hear the charge, not wasting a Roman minute. He takes Jesus inside and begins asking Him about these charges. Pilate can't handle the truth when he asks, "Are You the King of the Jews?" Jesus is the King of the Jews, and that is the truth. But as Jesus knows, the world doesn't recognize His kingdom. That's because it is sourced in heaven above, not in Rome. His authority comes from God the Father, Creator, Sustainer—not from the Roman senate.

High Priest's Servant: Didn't I see you in the garden with Him?

[27]Peter denied it again, and instantly a rooster crowed.

[28]Before the sun had risen, Jesus was taken from Caiaphas to the governor's palace. The Jewish leaders would not enter the palace because their presence in a Roman office would defile them and cause them to miss the Passover feast. Pilate, the governor, met them outside.

Now Caiaphas is high priest at this time. The sacred office he occupies has been corrupted for more than a century by Jewish collaboration with Greeks and Romans. Reformers are few, and they have been unable to cleanse the high office from its pollutants. Because of this, many Jews have stopped coming to the temple. How can God's holy habitation on earth be pure if its primary representative is coddling the enemies of Israel? Caiaphas knows he needs friends in high places to put an end to Jesus, so he turns to Pilate, the Roman governor. It is Pilate's job to look out for Roman interests in Judea. He is an irritable man, unnecessarily cruel and intentionally provocative. Many Jews will die on his watch. For Pilate, Jesus is just one more.

Pilate: [29]What charges do you bring against this man?

Priests and Officials: [30]If He weren't a law-breaker, we wouldn't have brought Him to you.

Pilate: [31]Then judge Him yourselves, by your own law.

Jews: Our authority does not allow us to give Him the death penalty.

[32]All these things were a fulfillment of the words Jesus had spoken indicating the way that He would die. [33]So Pilate reentered the governor's palace and called for Jesus to follow him.

Pilate: Are You the King of the Jews?

Jesus: [34]Are you asking Me because you believe this is true, or have others said this about Me?

Pilate: [35]I'm not a Jew, am I? Your people, including the chief priests, have arrested You and placed You in my custody. What have You done?

Jesus: [36]My kingdom is not recognized in this world. If this were My kingdom, My servants would be fighting for My freedom. But My kingdom is not in this physical realm.

Pilate: [37]So You are a king?

Jesus: You say that I am king. For this I have been born, and for this I have come into the cosmos: to demonstrate the power of truth. Everyone who seeks truth hears My voice.

Pilate (to Jesus): ³⁸What is truth?

Pilate left Jesus to go and speak to the Jewish people.

Pilate (to the Jews): I have not found any cause for charges to be brought against this man. ³⁹Your custom is that I should release a prisoner to you each year in honor of the Passover celebration; shall I release the King of the Jews to you?

Jews: ⁴⁰No, not this man! Give us Barabbas!

You should know that Barabbas was a terrorist.

19 Pilate took Jesus and had Him flogged. ²The soldiers twisted thorny branches together as a crown and placed it onto His brow and wrapped Him in a purple cloth. ³They drew near to Him, shouting:

Soldiers (striking at Jesus): Bow down, everyone! This is the King of the Jews!

Pilate (going out to the crowd): ⁴Listen, I stand in front of you with this man to make myself clear: I find this man innocent of any crimes.

⁵Then Jesus was paraded out before the people, wearing the crown of thorns and the purple robe.

Pilate: Here is the man!

Chief Priests and Officers (shouting): ⁶Crucify, crucify!

Pilate: You take Him and crucify Him; I have declared Him not guilty of any punishable crime!

Jews: ⁷Our law says that He should die because He claims to be the Son of God.

⁸Pilate was terrified to hear the Jews making their claims for His execution; ⁹so he retired to his court, the Praetorium.

Pilate (to Jesus): Where are You from?

Jesus did not speak.

Pilate: ¹⁰How can You ignore me? Are You not aware that I have the authority either to free You or to crucify You?

Jesus: ¹¹Any authority you have over Me comes from above, not from your political position. Because of this, the one who handed Me to you is guilty of the greater sin.

¹²Pilate listened to Jesus' words. Taking them to heart, he attempted to release Jesus; but the Jews opposed him, shouting:

Jews: If you release this man, you have betrayed Caesar. Anyone who claims to be a king threatens Caesar's throne.

¹³After Pilate heard these accusations, he sent Jesus out and took his seat in the place where he rendered judgment. This place was called the Pavement, or Gabbatha in Hebrew. ¹⁴All this occurred at the sixth hour on the day everyone prepares for the Passover.

Pilate (to the Jews): Look, here is your King!

Jews: ¹⁵Put Him away; crucify Him!

Pilate: You want me to crucify your King?

Chief Priests: We have no king but Caesar!

¹⁶Pilate handed Him over to his soldiers, knowing that He would be crucified. ¹⁷They sent Jesus out carrying His own instrument of execution, the cross, to a hill known as the Place of the Skull, or Golgotha in Hebrew. ¹⁸In that place, they crucified Him along with two others. One was on His right and the other on His left. ¹⁹Pilate ordered that a plaque be placed above Jesus' head. It read, "Jesus of Nazareth, the King of the Jews." ²⁰Because the site was near an urban region, it was written in three languages (Greek, Latin, and Hebrew) so that all could understand.

Chief Priests (to Pilate): ²¹Don't write, "The King of the Jews." Write, "He said, 'I am King of the Jews'!"

Pilate: ²²I have written what I have written.

²³As Jesus was being crucified, the soldiers tore His outer garments into four pieces,

one for each of them. They wanted to do the same with His tunic, but it was seamless—one piece of fabric woven from the top down. [24]So they said,

Soldier (*to other soldiers*): Don't tear it. Let's cast lots, and the winner will take the whole thing.

This happened in keeping with the Hebrew Scriptures, which said, "They divided My outer garments and cast lots for My clothes."* These soldiers did exactly what was foretold in the Hebrew Scriptures. [25]Jesus' mother was standing next to His cross along with her sister, Mary the wife of Clopas, and Mary Magdalene. [26]Jesus looked to see His mother and the disciple He loved standing nearby.

Jesus (*to Mary, His mother*): Dear woman, this is your son (*motioning to the beloved disciple*)! [27](*to John, His disciple*) This is now your mother.

V

Now you know who "the beloved disciple" is: the last eyewitness to the life, death, and resurrection of Jesus. Mary has become family to John, fulfilling the dying wish of Jesus, his Savior. For those who are gathered at the foot of the cross, family is less about blood kinship than it is about covenant obedience.

The mother of the Lord will serve the redemptive purposes of her son and the Savior of the world until her last day on earth. Anyone feeling sorry for himself should think about Jesus. He spent all this time before His death, and through His death, demonstrating how to love and how to serve. He is asking John to do no more in serving Mary than He did in serving us.

From that moment, the disciple treated her like his own mother and welcomed her into his house. [28]Jesus knew now that His work had been accomplished, and the Hebrew Scriptures were being fulfilled.

Jesus: I am thirsty.

[29]A jar of sour wine had been left there, so they took a hyssop branch with a sponge soaked in the vinegar and put it to His mouth. [30]When Jesus drank, He spoke:

Jesus: It is finished!

In that moment, His head fell; and He gave up the spirit. [31]The Jews asked Pilate to have their legs broken so the bodies would not remain on the crosses on the Sabbath. It was the day of preparation for the Passover, and that year the Passover fell on the Sabbath. [32]The soldiers came and broke the legs of both the men crucified next to Jesus. [33]When they came up to Jesus' cross, they could see that He was dead; so they did not break His legs. [34]Instead, one soldier took his spear and pierced His abdomen, which brought a gush of blood and water.

[35]This testimony is true. In fact, it is an eyewitness account; and he has reported what he saw so that you also may believe. [36]It happened this way to fulfill the Hebrew Scriptures that "not one of His bones shall be broken";* [37]and the Hebrew Scriptures also say, "They will look upon Him whom they pierced."*

[38]After all this, Joseph of Arimathea, a disciple who kept his faith a secret for fear of the Jewish officials, made a request to Pilate for the body of Jesus. Pilate granted his request, and Joseph retrieved the body. [39]Nicodemus, who first came to Jesus under the cloak of darkness, brought over 100 pounds of myrrh and ointments for His burial. [40]Together, they took Jesus' body and wrapped Him in linens soaked in essential oils and spices, according to Jewish burial customs.

[41]Near the place He was crucified, there was a garden with a newly prepared tomb. [42]Because it was the day of preparation, they arranged to lay Jesus in this tomb so they could rest on the Sabbath.

V

As the lifeless body of Jesus is laid into the virgin tomb, those who witnessed the spectacle retreat into the city that has claimed the lives of so many prophets. All are crushed that their teacher and friend has died such a horrible

---

* 19:24 Psalm 22:18   * 19:36 Exodus 12:46; Numbers 9:12; Psalm 34:20   * 19:37 Zechariah 12:10

death. Their hopes are dashed against the rocks of Golgotha. In the first hours of grief, Jesus' followers huddle together in secret in the city, hoping to avoid arrests and executions. They mourn. They grieve. They remember. Three days later, some venture outside the city and return to the place where He was buried. Miraculously, the stone has been rolled back, and the rock-hewn tomb is empty. Has someone taken His body? Are His enemies laying a trap for His followers? Or perhaps—could it be—that the last days have arrived?

---

20 Before the sun had risen on Sunday morning, Mary Magdalene made a trip to the tomb where His body was laid to rest. In the darkness, she discovered the covering had been rolled away. ²She darted out of the garden to find Simon Peter and the dearly loved disciple to deliver this startling news.

Mary Magdalene: They have taken the body of our Lord, and we cannot find Him!

³Together, they all departed for the tomb to see for themselves. ⁴They began to run, and Peter could not keep up. The beloved disciple arrived first ⁵but did not go in. There was no corpse in the tomb, only the linens and cloths He was wrapped in. ⁶When Simon Peter finally arrived, he went into the tomb and observed the same: ⁷the cloth that covered His face appeared to have been folded carefully and placed, not with the linen cloths, but to the side. ⁸After Peter pointed this out, the other disciple (who had arrived long before Peter) also entered the tomb; and based on what he saw, faith began to well up inside him! ⁹Before this moment, none of them understood the Scriptures and why He must be raised from the dead. ¹⁰Then they all went to their homes.

¹¹Mary, however, stood outside the tomb sobbing, crying, and kneeling at its entrance. ¹²As she cried, two heavenly messengers appeared before her sitting where Jesus' head and feet had been laid.

Heavenly Messengers: ¹³Dear woman, why are you weeping?

Mary Magdalene: They have taken away my Lord, and I cannot find Him.

¹⁴After uttering these words, she turned around to see Jesus standing before her, but she did not recognize Him.

Jesus: ¹⁵Dear woman, why are you sobbing? Who is it you are looking for?

She still had no idea who it was before her. Thinking He was the gardener, she muttered:

Mary Magdalene: Sir, if you are the one who carried Him away, then tell me where He is and I will retrieve Him.

Jesus: ¹⁶Mary!

Mary Magdalene (*turning to Jesus and speaking in Hebrew*): Rabboni, my Teacher!

Jesus: ¹⁷Mary, you cannot hold Me. I must rise above this world to be with My Father, who is also your Father; My God, who is also your God. Go tell this to all My brothers.

¹⁸Mary Magdalene obeyed and went directly to His disciples.

The hope of resurrection has often been a topic on the lips of Jesus. Now it is taking shape. Confusion gives way to conviction as Jesus appears alive over the next few Sundays. One by one He convinces His followers that God has raised Him from the dead.

Mary Magdalene (*announcing to the disciples*): I have seen the Lord, and this is what He said to me . . .

¹⁹On that same evening (Resurrection Sunday), the followers gathered together behind locked doors in fear that some of the Jewish leaders in Jerusalem were still searching for them. Out of nowhere, Jesus appeared in the center of the room.

Jesus: May each one of you be at peace.

²⁰As He was speaking, He revealed the wounds in His hands and side. The disciples

began to celebrate as it sank in that they were really seeing the Lord.

Jesus: ²¹I give you the gift of peace. In the same way the Father sent Me, I am now sending you.

²²Now He drew close enough to each of them that *they could feel His breath.* He breathed on them:

Jesus: Welcome the Holy Spirit of the living God. ²³You now have the mantle of God's forgiveness. As you go, you are able to share the life-giving power to forgive sins, or to withhold forgiveness.

²⁴All of the eleven were present with the exception of Thomas. ²⁵He heard the accounts of each brother's interaction with the Lord.

The Other Disciples: We have seen the Lord!

Thomas: Until I see His hands, feel the wounds of the nails, and put my hand to His side, I won't believe what you are saying.

²⁶Eight days later, they gathered again behind locked doors; and Jesus reappeared. This time Thomas was with them.

Jesus: May each one of you be at peace.

²⁷He drew close to Thomas.

Jesus: Reach out and touch Me. See the punctures in My hands; reach out your hand, and put it to My side; leave behind your faithlessness, and believe.

Thomas *(filled with emotion)*: ²⁸You are the one True God and Lord of my life.

Jesus: ²⁹Thomas, you have faith because you have seen Me. Blessed are all those who never see Me and yet they still believe.

³⁰Jesus performed many other wondrous signs that are not written in this book. ³¹These accounts are recorded so that you, too, might believe that Jesus is the Anointed, *the Liberating King,* the Son of God, because believing grants you the life He came to share.

21 There was one other time when Jesus appeared to the disciples—this time by the Sea of Tiberias. This is how it happened: ²Simon Peter, Thomas (the Twin), Nathanael (the Galilean from Cana), the sons of Zebedee, and two other disciples were together.

Simon Peter *(to disciples)*: ³I am going fishing.

Disciples: Then we will come with you.

After Jesus' death, the disciples don't know what to do with themselves, other than return to their old livelihood of fishing. This band of fishermen is lost and lonely, but just when they think things can't be stranger, Jesus shows up. He tells them to fish on the other side of the boat. They do, and they are suddenly overwhelmed with fish. The nets are bulging.

What He shows here is that not only will their old ways of living leave His followers as empty as the nets, but their old habits will not work either. He has impacted their lives in a way that changed them forever. They can't go back. And He knows they don't know how to go forward.

They went out in the boat and caught nothing through the night. ⁴As day was breaking, Jesus was standing on the beach; but they did not know it was Jesus.

Jesus: ⁵My sons, you haven't caught any fish, have you?

Disciples: No.

Jesus: ⁶Throw your net on the starboard side of the boat, and your net will find the fish.

They did what He said, and suddenly they could not lift their net because of the massive weight of the fish that filled it. ⁷The disciple loved by Jesus turned to Peter and said:

Beloved Disciple: It is the Lord.

Immediately, when Simon Peter heard these words, he threw on his shirt (which he would take off while he was working) and dove into the sea. [8]The rest of the disciples followed him, bringing in the boat and dragging in their net full of fish. They were close to the shore, fishing only about 100 yards out. [9]When they arrived on shore, they saw a charcoal fire laid with fish on the grill. *He had* bread too.

Jesus *(to disciples)*: [10]Bring some of the fish you just caught.

[11]Simon Peter went back to the boat to unload the fish from the net. He pulled 153 large fish from the net. Despite the number of the fish, the net held without a tear.

Jesus: [12]Come, and join Me for breakfast.

V

Jesus reveals to His disciples a world where God is intimately involved, the main actor in the drama of history. These fish, all 153, are a sign from God representing the community of men and women transformed by faith. Some of them sit down and don't say a word as they ponder all of this. Others busy themselves in work. Each in his own way thinks, wonders, and prays.

That's how John always begins and ends his stories of Jesus: reminding believers to become the sons of God. The resurrection of Jesus shows the world He is the resurrection and the life. That isn't life after death; it is the reality that through Jesus believers can have abundant life, a full and meaningful life, here and now through faith.

Not one of the disciples dared to ask, "Who are You?" They knew it was the Lord. [13]Jesus took the bread and gave it to each of them, and then He did the same with the fish. [14]This was the third time the disciples had seen Jesus since His death and resurrection. [15]They finished eating breakfast.

Jesus: Simon, son of John, do you love Me more than these other things?

Simon Peter: Yes, Lord. You know that I love You.

Jesus: Take care of My lambs.

[16]Jesus asked him a second time . . .

Jesus: Simon, son of John, do you love Me?

Simon Peter: Yes, Lord. You must surely know that I love You.

Jesus: Shepherd My sheep.
[17](for the third time) Simon, son of John, do you love Me?

Peter was hurt because He asked him the same question a third time, "Do you love Me?"

Simon Peter: Lord, You know everything! You know that I love You.

Jesus: Look after My sheep. [18]I tell you the truth: when you were younger, you would pick up and go wherever you pleased; but when you grow old, someone else will help you and take you places you do not want to go.

V

Ever since the night Judas betrayed Jesus and Peter denied knowing Christ three times, Peter has felt small. He has felt he betrayed Jesus too. Matching the three denials, Jesus has Peter reaffirm his love for Him three times. At the same time, Jesus reaffirms Peter's call to ministry each time by challenging him to serve as a leader. The conversation on the beach that day affects him profoundly. From then on, Simon Peter is one of the most humble followers of Jesus, but he is also one of the great leaders of the early church, as Acts explains.

The disciples all learn a lesson that day. No matter what someone may have done, the Master wants the miracle of forgiveness to restore that person to be whom He made and called him or her to be.

[19]Jesus said all this as an indicator of the nature of Peter's death, which would glorify God. After this conversation, Jesus said,

Jesus: Follow Me!

[20]Peter turned around to see the disciple loved by Jesus following the two of them, the same disciple who leaned back on Jesus' side during their supper and asked, "Lord, who is going to betray You?"

Peter: [21]Lord, and what will happen to this man?

Jesus: [22]If I choose for him to remain till I return, what difference will this make to you? You follow Me!

[23]It is from this exchange with Jesus that some thought this disciple would not die. But Jesus never said that. He said, "If I choose for him to remain till I return, what difference will this make to you?" [24]That very same disciple is the one offering this truthful account written just for you. [25]There are so many other things that Jesus said and did; and if these accounts were also written down, the books could not be contained in the entire cosmos.

V

John has reached the end of his story. Future believers will go on without him, but not without his words. John's voice is added to the voices of the prophets and the witnesses declaring God has become flesh as Jesus, who manifested true life in the midst of humanity. Now that's a pretty big idea for a fisherman, but John goes to his grave bearing witness that it is true.

This account, in particular, shows how to enter into God's kingdom through faith in Jesus so they can experience eternal life. This is his invitation to join him in this marvelous journey.

ACTS

History of the early church

By Luke, the physician

The Acts of the Apostles, written by Luke as a sequel to his Gospel, presents a selective history of the early church from Jesus' resurrection and ascension to the dispersion of the good news from Jerusalem to Rome, the center of the known world. Luke writes in the manner of an apologist, describing how the amazing growth of this Kingdom movement could have come only through the power of God. He presents it as an outgrowth of the Jewish faith and not a new religion in the Roman Empire. It begins in Jerusalem, the center of Jewish life, and fulfills the promises spoken centuries earlier by Israel's poets and prophets. Acts shows how the gospel message moves culturally from the Jews to the Samaritans to the non-Jews, and geographically from Jerusalem to Asia Minor to Greece and, finally, to Rome.

As with his Gospel, Luke dedicates Acts to Theophilus, likely a high-ranking Roman official. He describes this account as the continuing story of what Jesus began to do and teach. Now the risen Jesus is working through people He chooses to carry the message of redemption to the ends of the earth. Despite the name of this book, not all of His apostles or emissaries are discussed in this history. Luke focuses his account on the contributions of two men: Simon Peter, one of "the twelve," and Paul (also called Saul), a Pharisee who persecuted the movement until he encountered the risen Jesus on his way to Damascus. Luke also traces the history of two churches: the church in Jerusalem, the mother church consisting mainly of Jewish Christians, and the church in Antioch, consisting of both Jewish and non-Jewish believers. It is the church in Antioch that helps to launch Paul's missionary efforts to Asia and Greece, and it is there that believers are first called Christians. At the heart of Luke's story are the conflicts and changes that take place as Jesus' kingdom message goes from place to place and people to people. Jesus was a polarizing figure in His day, so it's no wonder that Jesus' followers also create controversy as they carry on His message.

In spite of persecution by the Romans and disagreements within the church, the early church grows rapidly. When believers are forced out of Jerusalem and into other cities, they take the good news with them. Believers use their suffering as a catalyst to spread the message of Jesus, which is a lesson that will continue to inspire the church into the future.

Luke, in this his second volume concerning the genesis of the Christian movement, doesn't preserve Jesus' teachings during those mysterious meetings with His emissaries after His death. Surely they are filled with joy, curiosity, and amazement as His followers hang on His every word and gaze on the reality of His bodily resurrection as He describes the kingdom of God. His words are undoubtedly intended to prepare each of them for this journey, a journey with a clear destination in sight—the kingdom of God.

An integral part of this kingdom is the activity of the Holy Spirit to empower the people of God as they expand the kingdom beyond the region of Palestine. Luke records surprisingly little about the day-to-day life of these early Christians, about how they integrated their faith into their culture; but he does emphasize the work of the Spirit who empowers miracles and gives believers the means to testify of their faith before Jews and the outsiders.

---

1 To *a lover of God,* Theophilus: In my first book, I recounted the events of Jesus' life—His actions, His teachings—2-3*from the beginning of His life* until He was taken up into heaven. After His great suffering *and vindication,* He showed His apostles that He was alive—appearing to them repeatedly over a period of 40 days, giving them many convincing proofs of His resurrection. *As before,* He spoke constantly of the kingdom of God. During these appearances, He had instructed His chosen messengers through the Holy Spirit, 4prohibiting them from leaving Jerusalem, but rather requiring them to wait there until they received what He called "the promise of the Father."

Jesus: This is what you heard Me teach— 5that just as John ritually cleansed people with water through baptism,* so you will be washed with the Holy Spirit very soon.

6When they had gathered *just outside Jerusalem at the Mount of Olives,* they asked Jesus,

Disciples: Is now the time, Lord—the time when You will reestablish Your kingdom in *our land of* Israel?

Jesus: 7The Father, on His own authority, has determined the ages and epochs *of history,* but you have not been given this knowledge. 8*Here's the knowledge you need:* you will receive power when the Holy Spirit comes on you. And you will be My witnesses, first here in Jerusalem, then beyond to Judea and Samaria, and finally to the farthest places on earth.

9As He finished this commission, He began to rise from the ground before their eyes

until the clouds obscured Him from their vision. 10As they strained to get one last glimpse of Him going into heaven, the Lord's emissaries* realized two men in white robes were standing among them.

Two Men: 11You Galileans, why are you standing here staring up into the sky? This Jesus who is leaving you and ascending to heaven will return in the same way you see Him departing.

12Then the disciples returned to Jerusalem— their short journey from the Mount of Olives was an acceptable Sabbath Day's walk.

13-14Back in the city, they went to the room where they were staying—a second-floor room. This whole group devoted themselves to constant prayer with one accord: Peter, John, James, Andrew, Philip, Thomas, Bartholomew, Matthew, James (son of Alphaeus), Simon (the Zealot), Judas (son of James), a number of women including Mary (Jesus' mother), and some of Jesus' brothers.

15As the disciples prayed, Peter stood among the group of about 120 people and made this proposal:

Peter: 16-17My friends, everything in the Hebrew Scriptures had to be fulfilled, including what the Holy Spirit foretold through David about Judas. *As you know,* Judas was one of us and participated in our ministry until he guided the authorities to arrest Jesus. 18(He was paid handsomely for his betrayal, and he bought a field with the blood money. But he died *on that land*—falling so that his abdomen burst and his internal organs gushed out. 19News of this death

---

* 1:5 Literally, immersed, to show repentance   * 1:10 Literally, apostles

The Creator of heaven and earth is orchestrating a redemptive story that will radically change the course of history. The most significant supernatural event in the history of this newly formed church will be the filling of the Holy Spirit. Through the Holy Spirit, God will direct the church's growth. But how does the early church make important decisions before the Holy Spirit descends on them?

The company of disciples turns to the practice of "drawing lots," a practice used by saints for centuries to discover God's providential leading. After much prayer, Joseph and Matthias most likely write their names on scraps; then someone draws the replacement's name out of a bag. What seems like a 50/50 chance is, in fact, God's way of imparting His will. The disciples aren't putting their faith in "chance"; they are putting their faith in a God who lives. This living God isn't distant; He is a player in their lives, active when His people seek Him and His will. They know God directs the process, start to finish, and determines whose name is drawn to join the eleven.

---

spread to everyone in Jerusalem, so Judas's property is known as Hakeldama, which means "field of blood.") [20]In this way, one of *David's* psalms was fulfilled: "May their camps be bleak, with not one left in any tent."* But the psalms also include these words: "Let his position of oversight be given to another."* [21]So we need *to determine his replacement* from among the men who have been with us during all of the Lord Jesus' travels among us—[22]from His baptism* by John until His ascension. We need someone to join us as a witness of Jesus' resurrection.

[23]The group put forward two men: Joseph (who was also known as Barsabbas or Justus) and Matthias.

Disciples: [24]Lord, You know everyone's heart. Make it clear to us which of these two is Your choice [25]to take on this ministry as Your apostle, replacing Judas who went his own way to his own destination.

[26]Then they drew lots, and the lot fell to Matthias, so he was added to the eleven apostles *to reconstitute the twelve.*

2 When the holy day of Pentecost came *50 days after Passover,* they were gathered together in one place.

[2]*Picture yourself among the disciples:*
A sound roars from the sky without warning, the roar of a violent wind, and the whole house where you are gathered reverberates with the sound. [3]Then a flame appears, dividing into smaller flames and spreading from one person to the next.

[4]All the people present are filled with the Holy Spirit and begin speaking in languages they've never spoken, as the Spirit empowers them.

[5]*Because of the holy festival,* there are devout Jews staying as pilgrims in Jerusalem from every nation under the sun. [6]They hear the sound, and a crowd gathers. They are amazed because each of them can hear the group speaking in their native languages. [7]They are shocked and amazed by this.

Pilgrims: Just a minute. Aren't all of these people Galileans? [8]How in the world do we all hear our native languages being spoken? [9]*Look*—there are Parthians here, and Medes, Elamites, Mesopotamians, and Judeans, residents of Cappadocia, Pontus, and Asia, [10]Phrygians and Pamphylians, Egyptians and Libyans from Cyrene, Romans including both Jews *by birth* and converts, [11]Cretans, and Arabs. We're each, in our own languages, hearing these people talk about God's powerful deeds.

[12]Their amazement becomes confusion as they wonder,

Pilgrims: What does this mean?

Skeptics: [13]It doesn't mean anything. They're all drunk on some fresh wine!

This miraculous sign of God's kingdom is astounding. The followers of Jesus are not known as people

* 1:20 Psalm 69:25-26   * 1:20 Psalm 109:8   * 1:22 Literally, immersion, an act to show repentance

who drink too much wine with breakfast, so this fantastic episode requires some other kind of explanation. Unfortunately it is impossible to comprehend or explain what transpires on Pentecost. But this is not a novelty performance; rather, it is the foundation of the kingdom of God in that it establishes the church as the place where God moves on the earth through His Spirit. They expect a political kingdom, but God moves in people's hearts to transform individuals and communities.

---

[14]As the twelve stood together, Peter shouted to the crowd,

Peter: Men of Judea and all who are staying here in Jerusalem, listen. I want you to understand: [15]these people aren't drunk as you may think. Look, it's only nine o'clock in the morning! [16]*No, this isn't drunkenness;* this is the fulfillment of the prophecy of Joel. [17]Hear what God says!

In the last days,
I will offer My Spirit to humanity as a
    libation.
Your children will boldly speak *the word
    of the Lord.*
Young warriors will see visions,
    and your elders will dream dreams.
[18]Yes, in those days I shall offer My Spirit to
    all servants,
    both male and female, and they will
    boldly speak My word.
[19]And in the heaven above and on the earth
    below,
I shall give signs *of impending judgment*:
    blood, fire, and clouds of smoke.
[20]The sun will become a void of darkness,
    and the moon will become blood.
Then the great and dreadful day of the
    Lord will arrive,
[21]And everyone who calls on the name of
    the Lord
    will be liberated *into God's freedom
    and peace.**

[22]All of you Israelites, listen to my message: it's about Jesus of Nazareth, a man whom God authenticated for you by performing in your presence powerful deeds, wonders, and signs through Him, just as

you yourselves know. [23]This man, *Jesus,* who came into your hands by God's sure plan and advanced knowledge, you nailed to a cross and killed in collaboration with lawless outsiders. [24]But God raised Jesus and unleashed Him from the agonizing birth pangs of death, for death could not possibly keep Jesus in its power. [25]David spoke of Jesus' *resurrection,* saying:

I see the Lord is ever present with me.
I will not live in fear *or abandon my
    calling* because He guides my right
    hand.
[26]My heart is glad; my soul rejoices;
    my body is safe.
[27]You will not abandon me to experience
    the suffering of a miserable
    afterlife,
    nor leave Your Holy One to rot *alone.*
[28]*Instead,* You direct me on a path that leads
    to a beautiful life.
As I walk with You, the pleasures are
    never-ending, and I know true joy
    and contentment.*

[29]My fellow Israelites, I can say without question that David our ancestor died and was buried, and his tomb is with us today. [30]*David wasn't speaking of himself;* he was speaking as a prophet. He saw *with prophetic insight* that God had made a solemn promise to him: God would put one of his descendants on His throne. [31]Here's what David was seeing in advance; here's what David was talking about—the Anointed One would be resurrected. Think *of David's words* about Him not being abandoned to the place of the dead nor being left to decay in the grave. [32]*He was talking about* Jesus, the One God has raised, whom all of us have seen with our own eyes *and announce to you today.* [33]Since Jesus has been lifted to the right hand of God—*the highest place of authority and power*—and since Jesus has received the promise of the Holy Spirit from the Father, He has now poured out what you have seen and heard here today. [34]*Remember:* David couldn't have been speaking of himself rising to the heavens when he said,

The Master said to my master,
"Sit here at My right hand,
    in the place of honor and power,

* 2:17-21 Joel 2:28-32   * 2:25-28 Psalm 16:8-11

V

³⁵And I will gather Your enemies together,
  lead them in on hands and knees,
  and You will rest Your feet on their
    backs."*

³⁶Everyone in Israel should now realize with certainty *what God has done*: God has made Jesus both Lord and Anointed King—this same Jesus whom you crucified.

³⁷When the people heard this, their hearts were pierced; and they said to Peter and his fellow apostles,

Pilgrims: Our brothers, what should we do?

Peter: ³⁸Reconsider your lives; change your direction. Participate in the ceremonial washing of baptism* in the name of Jesus God's Anointed, *the Liberating King.* Then your sins will be forgiven, and the gift of the Holy Spirit will be yours. ³⁹For the promise *of the Spirit* is for you, for your children, for all people—even those considered outsiders and outcasts—the Lord our God invites everyone to come to Him.

Just as God raised Jesus from a decaying body, Peter holds out hope for God to liberate those who follow Him from their decaying culture.

⁴⁰Peter was pleading and offering many logical reasons to believe. ⁴¹Whoever made a place for his message in their hearts received the baptism;* in fact, that day alone, about 3,000 people joined the disciples.

⁴²The community continually committed themselves to learning what the apostles taught them, gathering for fellowship, breaking bread, and praying. ⁴³Everyone felt a sense of awe because the apostles were doing many signs and wonders among them. ⁴⁴There was an intense sense of togetherness among all who believed; they shared all their material possessions in trust. ⁴⁵They sold any possessions and goods *that did not benefit the community* and used the money to help everyone in need. ⁴⁶They were unified as they worshiped at the temple day after day. In homes, they broke bread and shared meals with glad and generous hearts. ⁴⁷The new disciples praised God, and they enjoyed the goodwill of all the people *of the city.* Day after day the Lord added to their number everyone who was experiencing liberation.

Although this young and thriving church has no political influence, property, fame, or wealth, it is powerful. Its power is centered in living the gospel. The people value one another more than any possessions. They come together as a large, passionate, healthy family where it is natural to pray and share all of life together. The kingdom of God is blossoming on earth as these lovers of God embrace the teachings of Jesus. In the days ahead, the church will lose much of this initial beauty and appeal; it will become consumed with a desire for material possessions, cultural influence, and power.

3 One day at three o'clock in the afternoon, a customary time for daily prayer, Peter and John walked to the temple. ²Some people were carrying in a man who had been paralyzed since birth. Every day they brought him to a place near the beautiful gate *(one of the temple entrances)* so he could beg for money from people entering *to worship.* ³He saw Peter and John coming and asked them for a contribution. ⁴Peter gazed intensely at him—so did John.

Peter: Look at us.

⁵The man looked up at them, assuming they were about to give him some money.

Peter: ⁶I want to give you something, but I don't have any silver or gold. Here's what I can offer you: stand up and walk in the name of Jesus of Nazareth, the Anointed One.

⁷Then Peter took the man's right hand and lifted him to his feet. Instantly the man's feet and ankles grew strong. ⁸He jumped and walked, accompanying Peter and John into the temple where he walked, jumped for joy, and shouted praises to God. ⁹⁻¹¹A crowd ran to the commotion, and they gathered around this man in an open area called Solomon's Porch. There he was, standing on his

* 2:34-35 Psalm 110:1   * 2:38 Literally, immersion, a rite of initiation and purification   * 2:41 Literally, immersion, a rite of initiation and purification

own two feet, holding on to Peter and John. They knew exactly who he was—the beggar they passed at the beautiful gate every day. Everyone was absolutely amazed at this wonderful miracle; they were speechless, stunned.

Just as Jesus promised, the Spirit comes on believers in power, enabling them to do miracles like this. Now they can participate in the truth of the good news.

Peter *(to the crowd):* [12]Why are you so amazed, my fellow Israelites? Why are you staring at my friend and me as though we did this miracle through our own power or made this fellow walk by our own holiness? [13]*We didn't do this—God did!* The God of Abraham, the God of Isaac, the God of Jacob—the God of our ancestors has glorified Jesus, God's servant—the same Jesus whom you betrayed and rejected in front of Pilate, even though Pilate was going to release Him. [14]He is the Holy and Righteous One, but you rejected Him and asked for a murderer to be released to you instead. [15]*You not only rejected Him,* but you killed Him—the very Author of life! But God raised Jesus from the dead, whom my friend John and I have seen with our own eyes. [16]So that's how this miracle happened: we have faith in the name of Jesus, and He is the power that made this man strong—this man who is known to all of you. It is faith in Jesus that has given this man his complete health here today, in front of all of you.

[17]Listen, friends, I know you didn't fully realize what you were doing *when you rejected and betrayed Jesus.* I know that you, and your rulers as well, were acting in ignorance. [18]God was at work in all this, fulfilling what He had predicted through all the prophets—that the Anointed One would suffer. [19]So now you need to rethink everything and turn to God so your sins will be forgiven and a new day can dawn, days of refreshing times flowing from the Lord. [20]Then God may send Jesus the Anointed, whom God has chosen for you. [21]He is in heaven now and must remain there until the day of universal restoration comes—the restoration which in ancient times God announced through the holy prophets. [22]Moses, *for example,* said, "The Eternal One your God will raise up from among your people a prophet who will be like me. You must listen to Him. [23]And whoever does not listen to His words will be completely uprooted from among the people."*

[24]Every prophet, from Samuel through all of his successors, agreed. [25]You are the descendants of these prophets, and you are the people of God's covenant to your ancestors. God's word to Abraham includes you: "Because of your descendants, all the *families* of the earth will be blessed."* [26]So when God raised up His Servant, God sent Him first to you, to begin blessing you by calling you to change your path from evil ways *to God's ways.*

4 The conversation continued *for a few hours there in Solomon's porch.* Suddenly, the head of the temple police and some members of the Sadducean party interrupted Peter and John. [2]They were annoyed because Peter and John were *enthusiastically* teaching that in Jesus, resurrection of the dead is possible—*an idea the Sadducees completely rejected.* [3]So they arrested Peter, John, *and the man who was healed* and kept them in jail overnight. [4]*But during these few afternoon hours between the man's miraculous healing and their arrest,* Peter and John already had convinced about 5,000 more people to believe their message about Jesus!

[5]*The next morning, the Jewish leaders*—their officials, elders, and scholars—called a meeting in Jerusalem [6]presided over by Annas (the patriarch of the ruling priestly clan), along with Caiaphas *(his son-in-law),* John, Alexander, and other members of their clan. [7]They made their prisoners stand in the middle of the assembly and questioned them.

Jewish Leaders: Who gave you the authority to create that spectacle in the temple yesterday?

Peter *(filled with the Spirit):* [8]Rulers and elders of the people, [9]yesterday a good deed was done. Someone who was sick was healed. If you're asking us how this happened, [10]I want all of you and all of the people of Israel to know this man standing in front of you—obviously in good health—was healed by the authority of Jesus of Nazareth, the Anointed One. This is the

* 3:23 Deuteronomy 18:15,18-19   * 3:25 Genesis 22:18; 26:4

same Jesus whom you crucified and whom God raised from the dead. [11]He is "the stone that you builders rejected who has become the very stone that holds together the entire foundation"* *on which a new temple is being built.* [12]There is no one else who can rescue us, and there is no other name under heaven given to any human by whom we may be rescued.

[13]Now the leaders were surprised and confused. They looked at Peter and John and realized they were *typical peasants—*uneducated, utterly ordinary fellows—with extraordinary confidence. The leaders recognized them as companions of Jesus, [14]then they turned their attention to the third man standing beside them—recently lame, now standing tall and healthy. What could they say in response to all this?

[15]*Because they were at a loss about what to do,* they excused the prisoners so the council could deliberate in private.

Jewish Leaders: [16]What do we do with these fellows? Anyone who lives in Jerusalem will know an unexplainable sign has been performed through these two preachers. We can't deny their story. [17]The best we can do is try to keep it from spreading. So let's warn them to stop speaking to anybody in this name.

[18]The leaders brought the prisoners back in and prohibited them from doing any more speaking or teaching in the name of Jesus. [19]Peter and John *listened quietly and then* replied,

Peter and John: You are the judges here, so we'll leave it up to you to judge whether it is right in the sight of God to obey your commands or God's. [20]*But one thing we can tell you:* we cannot possibly restrain ourselves from speaking about what we have seen and heard *with our own eyes and ears.*

[21-22]The council threatened them again, but finally let them go because public opinion strongly supported Peter and John and this man who had received this miraculous sign. He was over 40 years old, *so his situation was known to many people,* and they couldn't help but glorify God for his healing.

[23]Peter and John, upon their release, went right to their friends and told the story—including the warning from the council. [24]The whole community responded with this prayer to God:

Community of Believers: God, our King, You made the heaven and the earth and the sea and everything they contain.* [25]You are the One who, by the Holy Spirit, spoke through our ancestor David, Your servant, with these words:

Why did the nations rage?
    Why did they imagine useless things?
[26]The kings of the earth took their stand;
    their rulers assembled in opposition
    against the Eternal One and His
        Anointed King.*

[27]This is exactly what has happened among us, here in this city. *The foreign ruler* Pontius Pilate and *the Jewish ruler* Herod, along with their respective peoples, have assembled in opposition to Your holy servant Jesus, the One You chose. [28]They have done whatever Your hand and plan predetermined should happen. [29]And now, Lord, take note of their intimidations *intended to silence us.* Grant us, Your servants, the courageous confidence we need to go ahead and proclaim Your message [30]while You reach out Your hand to heal people, enabling us to perform signs and wonders through the name of Your holy servant Jesus.

[31]They finished their prayer, and immediately the whole place where they had gathered began to shake. All the disciples were filled with the Holy Spirit, and they began speaking God's message with courageous confidence.

V

The Holy Spirit changes everyone and everything. If there is any doubt about the power of the Spirit, just take a look at Peter. When Jesus was captured, Peter cowered in fear that he might be identified as a man who loved Jesus. Now this same man is preaching, healing, and pointing his finger in the face of Jewish officials who have captured him and

* 4:11 Psalm 118:22 * 4:24 A prayer inspired by other biblical prayers: 2 Kings 19:15; Nehemiah 9:6; Psalm 146:6; Isaiah 37:16
* 4:25-26 Psalm 2:1-2

John. With a boldness that is not his own, he blames them for the death of Jesus and does not cower at their show of violence.

---

³²*During those days,* the entire community of believers was deeply united in heart and soul to such an extent that they stopped claiming private ownership of their possessions. Instead, they held everything in common. ³³The apostles with great power gave their eyewitness reports of the resurrection of the Lord Jesus. Everyone was surrounded by an extraordinary grace. ³⁴Not a single person in the community was in need because those who had been affluent sold their houses or lands and brought the proceeds ³⁵to the emissaries* of the Lord. They then distributed the funds to individuals according to their needs. ³⁶⁻³⁷One fellow, a Cyprian Levite named Joseph, earned a nickname *because of his generosity* in selling a field and bringing the money to the apostles *in this way*. From that time on, they called him Barnabas, which means "son of encouragement."

This portrait of the early church as an unselfish community is captivating and inspiring. It presents a challenge for many followers of the Anointed One who want to show sacrificially their love to Him and His church. Many today wonder how to translate this into a modern culture so shaped by consumerism and self-interest, but no translation is necessary. These problems weren't foreign to the early community. In contrast to the generosity and sincerity of some like Barnabas, Luke now explains that others gave not out of love, but out of a desire to be honored by the community.

---

5 Once a man named Ananias, with his wife Sapphira fully cooperating, *committed fraud*. He sold some property ²and kept some of the proceeds, but he pretended to make a full donation to the Lord's emissaries.*

Peter: ³Ananias, have you allowed Satan to influence your lies to the Holy Spirit and hold back some of the money? ⁴Look, it was your property before you sold it, and the money was all yours after you sold it. Why have you concocted this scheme in your heart? You weren't just lying to us; you were lying to God.

⁵Ananias heard these words and immediately dropped to the ground, dead; fear overcame all those who heard of the incident. ⁶Some young men came, wrapped the body, and buried it immediately. ⁷About three hours had passed when Sapphira arrived. She had no idea what had happened.

Peter: ⁸Did you sell the land for such-and-such a price?

Sapphira: Yes, that was the price.

Peter: ⁹Why did the two of you conspire to test the Spirit of the Lord? Do you hear those footsteps outside? Those are the young men who just buried your husband, and now they will carry you out as well.

¹⁰She—*like her husband*—immediately fell dead at Peter's feet. The young men came in and carried her corpse outside and buried it beside her husband. ¹¹The whole church was terrified by this story, as were others who heard it.

In these formative days, God sends some strong messages about His work in the church: the power to heal, the beauty of life in the Spirit, and His hatred for arrogant religion. If God does not rebuke the married couple who chooses to make a show of their supposed generosity, then Christianity might drift in the wrong direction. While the Jewish leaders are using religion as a means to gain power and increase their reputations, the teachings of Jesus lead down a path toward the kingdom of God rather than toward human advancement. God chooses to expose these bad motives quickly, so that the church can give out of

---

* 4:35 Literally, apostles * 5:2 Literally, apostles

pure motives rather than out of a desire to appear righteous.

12*Those were amazing days*—with many signs and wonders being performed through the apostles among the people. The church would gather as a unified group in Solomon's Porch, 13enjoying great respect by the people of the city—though most people wouldn't risk publicly affiliating with them. 14Even so, record numbers of believers—both men and women—were added to the Lord. 15*The church's renown was so great that* when Peter walked down the street, people would carry out their sick relatives hoping his shadow would fall on some of them as he passed. 16Even people from towns surrounding Jerusalem would come, bringing others who were sick or tormented by unclean spirits, all of whom were cured.

17*Of course, this popularity elicited a response:* the high priest and his affiliates in the Sadducean party were jealous, 18so they arrested the apostles and put them in the public prison. 19But that night, a messenger of the Lord opened the doors of the prison and led them to freedom.

Messenger of the Lord: 20Go to the temple, and stand up to tell the people the whole message about this way of life *from Jesus.*

21At dawn they did as they were told; they returned to their teaching in the temple.

Meanwhile the council of Jewish elders was gathering—convened by the high priest and his colleagues. They sent the temple police to the prison to have the Lord's emissaries* brought *for further examination;* 22but of course, the temple police soon realized they weren't there. They returned and reported,

Temple Police: 23The prison was secure and locked, and the guards were standing in front of the doors; but when we unlocked the doors, the cell was empty.

24The captain of the temple police and the senior priests were completely mystified when they heard this. They had no idea what had happened. 25Just then, someone arrived with this news:

Temple Messenger: You know those men you put in prison last night? *Well, they're*

free. At this moment, they're *at it again,* teaching our people in the temple!

26The temple police—this time, accompanied by their captain—rushed over *to the temple* and brought the emissaries* of the Lord to the council. They were careful not to use violence, because the people were so supportive of them that the police feared being stoned by the crowd *if they were too rough.* 27Once again the men stood before the council. The high priest began the questioning.

High Priest: 28Didn't we give you strict orders to stop teaching in this name? But here you are, spreading your teaching throughout Jerusalem. And you are determined to blame us for this man's death.

Peter and the Apostles: 29If we have to choose between obedience to God and obedience to any human authority, then we must obey God. 30The God of our ancestors raised Jesus from death. You killed Jesus by hanging Him on a tree, 31but God has lifted Him high, to God's own right hand, as the Prince, as the Liberator. God intends to bring Israel to a radical rethinking of our lives and to a complete forgiveness of our sins. 32We are witnesses to these things. There is another witness, too—the Holy Spirit—whom God has given to all who choose to obey Him.

33The council was furious and would have killed them; 34but Gamaliel, a Pharisee in the council respected as a teacher of the Hebrew Scriptures, stood up and ordered the men to be sent out *so the council could confer privately.*

Gamaliel: 35Fellow Jews, you need to act with great care in your treatment of these fellows. 36Remember when a man named Theudas rose to notoriety? He claimed to be somebody important, and he attracted about 400 followers. But when he was killed, his entire movement disintegrated and nothing came of it. 37After him came Judas, that Galilean fellow, at the time of the census. He also attracted a following; but when he died, his entire movement fell apart. 38So here's my advice: in this case, just let these men go. Ignore them. If this is just another movement arising from human

* 5:21 Literally, apostles   * 5:26 Literally, apostles

enthusiasm, it will die out soon enough.
³⁹But then again, if God is in this, you won't
be able to stop it—unless, of course, you're
ready to fight against God!

⁴⁰The council was convinced, so they
brought the apostles back in. They were
flogged, again told not to speak in the name
of Jesus, and then released. ⁴¹As they left the
council, they *weren't discouraged at all. In
fact, they* were filled with joy over being considered worthy to suffer disgrace for the sake
of His name. ⁴²And constantly, *whether in
public,* in the temple, or in their homes, they
kept teaching and proclaiming Jesus as the
Anointed One, *the Liberating King.*

| V |

These emissaries of Jesus inspire
us with their passion to serve Jesus
and advance the gospel in the face
of torture and abuse. After a night
in prison and a public flogging,
they moved forward with smiles on
their faces. Believers in the Western church often enjoy the benefits of social and political power
and are unwilling to suffer persecution for their faith as these men
did. At the same time, many believers throughout the world face daily
pressure to renounce their faith but
choose boldly to remain faithful
despite social, economic, and even
physical persecution. These believers follow closely the path trodden
by the Anointed One and His early
followers.

---

6 *Things were going well,* and the number of disciples was growing. But a
problem arose. The Greek-speaking
believers became frustrated with the
Hebrew-speaking believers. The Greeks
complained that the Greek-speaking widows
were being discriminated against in the daily
distribution of food. ²The twelve convened
the entire community of disciples.

The Twelve: We could solve this problem
ourselves, but that wouldn't be right. We
need to focus on proclaiming God's message, not on distributing food. ³So, friends,
find seven respected men from the community of faith. These men should be full of

the Holy Spirit and full of wisdom. Whomever you select we will commission to
resolve this matter ⁴so we can maintain our
focus on praying and serving—*not meals*—
but the message.

| V |

Life in the new community isn't
perfect. However, the believers
don't allow their linguistic and
social barriers to divide the church;
instead, the emissaries seize this
opportunity to create greater unity
between disparate groups. They
appoint seven leaders, mostly
Greek-speaking (based on their
names), to oversee the distribution
of food. This movement toward
unity will be a challenge to the
future church that will so easily be
divided by any problem, real or
perceived.

---

⁵The whole community—*Greek-speaking and
Hebrew-speaking*—was very pleased with this
plan, so they chose *seven men:* Stephen (a
man full of faith and full of the Holy Spirit),
Philip, Prochorus, Nicanor, Timon, Parme-
nas, and Nicolas (a Greek-speaking convert
from Antioch). ⁶These men were presented
to the apostles, who then prayed for them
and commissioned them by laying their
hands on them. ⁷The message of God continued to spread, and the number of disciples
continued to increase significantly there in
Jerusalem. Even priests in large numbers
became obedient to the faith.

⁸Stephen continually overflowed with
extraordinary grace and power, and he was
able to perform a number of miraculous
signs and wonders in public view. ⁹But eventually a group arose to oppose Stephen *and
the message to which his signs and wonders
pointed.* (These men were from a group
called the Free Synagogue and included
Cyrenians, Alexandrians, Cilicians, and
Asians.) ¹⁰The Holy Spirit gave Stephen such
wisdom in responding to their arguments
that they were humiliated; ¹¹*in retaliation,*
they spread a vicious rumor: "We heard Stephen speak blasphemies against Moses and
God."

¹²Their rumor prompted an uprising
that included common people, religious officials, and scholars. They surprised Stephen,

grabbed him, and hauled him before the council. [13]They convinced some witnesses to give false testimony.

False Witnesses: This fellow constantly degrades the holy temple and mocks our holy law. [14]*With our own ears,* we've heard him say this Jesus fellow, this Nazarene *he's always talking about,* will actually destroy the holy temple and will try to change the sacred customs we received from Moses.

[15]The entire council turned its gaze on Stephen *to see how he would respond.* They *were shocked to* see his face radiant *with peace*—as if he were a heavenly messenger.

7 **High Priest:** *What do you have to say for yourself?* Are these accusations accurate?

Stephen: [2]Brothers, fathers, please listen to me. Our glorious God revealed Himself to our common ancestor Abraham, when he lived far away in Mesopotamia before he immigrated to Haran. [3]God gave him this command: "Leave your country. Leave your family *and your inheritance.* Move into unknown territory, where I will show you a new homeland."* [4]First, he left Chaldea *in southern Mesopotamia* and settled in Haran until his father died. Then God led him still farther from his original home—until he settled here, in our land. [5]*But at that point,* God still hadn't given him any of this land as his permanent possession—not even the footprint under his sandal actually belonged to him yet. But God did give Abraham a promise—a promise that yes, someday, the entire land would indeed belong to him and his descendants. *Of course, this promise was all the more amazing because* at that moment, Abraham had no descendants at all.

[6]God said that Abraham's descendants would first live in a foreign country as resident aliens, *as refugees,* for 400 years. During this time, they would be enslaved and treated horribly. *But that would not be the end of the story.* [7]God promised, "I will judge the nation that enslaves them,"* and "I will bring them to this mountain to serve Me."* [8]God gave him the covenant ritual of circumcision *as a sign of His sacred promise.* When Abraham fathered his son, Isaac, he performed this ritual of circumcision on the eighth day. Then Isaac

fathered Jacob, and Jacob fathered the twelve patriarchs.

[9]The patriarchs were jealous of *their brother* Joseph, so they sold him as a slave into Egypt. Even so, God was with him; [10]and *time after time,* God rescued Joseph from whatever trials befell him. God gave Joseph the favor and wisdom *to overcome each adversity* and eventually to win the confidence and respect of *his captors, including* Pharaoh, the king of Egypt himself. So Pharaoh entrusted his whole nation and his whole household to Joseph's stewardship. [11]*Some time later,* a terrible famine spread through the entire region—from Canaan down to Egypt—and everyone suffered greatly. Our ancestors, *living here in the region of Canaan,* could find nothing to eat. [12]Jacob heard that Egypt had stores of grain; so he sent our forefathers, *his sons, to procure food* there. [13]Later, when they returned to Egypt a second time, Joseph revealed his true identity to them. He also told Pharaoh his family story.

[14-16]Joseph then invited his father Jacob and all his clan to come and live with him in Egypt. So Jacob came, along with 75 extended family members. After their deaths, their remains were brought back to this land so they could be buried in the same tomb where Abraham *had buried Sarah* (he had purchased the tomb for a certain amount of silver from the family of Hamor in *the town of* Shechem).

[17]Still God's promise to Abraham had not yet been fulfilled, but the time for that fulfillment was drawing very near. In the meantime, our ancestors living in Egypt rapidly multiplied. [18]Eventually a new king came to power—one who had not known Joseph *when he was the most powerful man in Egypt.* [19]This new leader *feared the growing population of our ancestors and* manipulated them for his own benefit, eventually seeking to control their population by forcing them to abandon their infants so they would die. [20]Into this horrible situation *our ancestor* Moses was born, and he was a beautiful child in God's eyes. He was raised for three months in his father's home, [21]and then he was abandoned *as the brutal regime required.* However, Pharaoh's daughter found, adopted, and raised him as her own son. [22]So Moses learned the culture and wisdom of the Egyptians and

* 7:3 Genesis 12:1   * 7:7 Genesis 15:14   * 7:7 Exodus 3:12

became a powerful man—both as an intellectual and as a leader. ²³When he reached the age of 40, his heart drew him to visit his kinfolk, our ancestors, the Israelites. ²⁴During his visit, he saw one of our people being wronged, and he took sides with our people by killing an Egyptian. ²⁵He thought his kinfolk would recognize him as their God-given liberator, but they didn't realize *who he was and what he represented.*

²⁶The next day Moses was walking among the Israelites again when he observed a fight—but this time, it was between two Israelites. He intervened and tried to reconcile the men. "You two are brothers," he said. "Why do you attack each other?" ²⁷But the aggressor pushed Moses away and responded *with contempt:* "Who made you our prince and judge? ²⁸Are you going to slay me *and hide my body* as you did with the Egyptian yesterday?"* ²⁹Realizing this murder had not gone unnoticed, he quickly escaped Egypt and lived as a refugee in the land of Midian. He *married there and* had two sons.

³⁰Forty more years passed. One day while Moses was in the desert near Mount Sinai, a heavenly messenger appeared to him in the flames of a burning bush. ³¹The phenomenon intrigued Moses; and as he approached for a closer look, he heard a voice—the voice of the Lord: ³²"I am the God of your own fathers, the God of Abraham, Isaac, and Jacob."* This terrified Moses—he began to tremble and looked away in fear. ³³The voice continued: "Take off your sandals *and stand barefoot on the ground in My presence,* for this ground is holy ground. ³⁴I have avidly watched how My people are being mistreated by the Egyptians. I have heard their groaning *at the treatment of their oppressors.* I am descending *personally* to rescue them. So get up. I'm sending you to Egypt."*

³⁵*Now remember:* this was the same Moses who had been rejected by his kinfolk when they said, "Who made you our prince and judge?" This man, *rejected by his own people,* was the one God had truly sent and commissioned by the heavenly messenger who appeared in the bush, to be their leader and deliverer.

³⁶Moses indeed led our ancestors to freedom, and he performed miraculous signs and wonders in Egypt, at the Red Sea, and in the wilderness over a period of 40 years. ³⁷This Moses promised our ancestors, "The Eternal One your God will raise up from among your people a Prophet who will be like me."* ³⁸This is the same one who led the people to Mount Sinai, where a heavenly messenger spoke to him and our ancestors, and who received the living message of God to give to us.

³⁹But our ancestors still resisted. They again pushed Moses away and refused to follow him. In their hearts, they were ready to return to *their former slavery in* Egypt. ⁴⁰*While Moses was on the mountain communing with God,* they begged Aaron to make idols to lead them. "We have no idea what happened to this fellow, Moses, who brought us from Egypt,"* they said. ⁴¹So they made a calf as their new god, and they even sacrificed to it and celebrated an object they had fabricated *as if it were their God.*

⁴²*And you remember what God did next:* He let them go. He turned from them and let them follow their idolatrous path—worshiping sun, moon, and stars *just as their unenlightened neighbors did.* The prophet *Amos* spoke for God *about this horrible betrayal:*

Did you offer Me sacrifices or give Me
        offerings
    during your 40-year wilderness
        journey, you Israelites?
⁴³*No, but* you have taken along your sacred
        tent for the worship of Moloch,
    and you honored the star of Rompha,
        your false god.
So, if you want to worship your man-made
        images,
    you may do so—beyond Babylon.*

⁴⁴Now recall that our ancestors had a sacred tent in the wilderness, the tent God directed Moses to build according to the pattern revealed to him. ⁴⁵When Joshua led our ancestors to dispossess the nations God drove out before them, our ancestors carried this sacred tent. It remained here in the land until the time of David. ⁴⁶David found favor with God and asked Him for permission to build a permanent structure (*rather than a portable tent*) to honor Him. ⁴⁷It was, of course, Solomon who actually built God's house. ⁴⁸Yet we all know the Most High God doesn't actually dwell in

* 7:28 Exodus 2:13-14   * 7:32 Exodus 3:6   * 7:34 Exodus 3:5,7-8,10
* 7:37 Deuteronomy 18:15   * 7:40 Exodus 32:1   * 7:42-43 Amos
5:26-27

structures made by human hands, as the prophet *Isaiah* said,

49"Since My throne is heaven
    and since My footstool is earth—
What kind of structure can you build to
    contain Me?
What *man-made* space could provide Me
    a resting place?" asks the Eternal
    One.
50"Didn't I make all things with My own
    hand?"*

As Stephen recounts how God has worked with the Jews in spite of their faltering fidelity, his speech up to this point sounds like any good synagogue sermon. In the stories of Abraham, Joseph, and Moses, he narrates the history of God's work of salvation among the Jewish people in the midst of their repeated struggle with unfaithfulness and idolatry. However, it is one thing for his audience to agree that idolatry was a problem in the past and another when they are charged with the accusation of the same idolatry in the present. According to Stephen, those who reject Jesus are following the same path as the people who rejected Moses to follow idols. Such a strong message strikes a nerve, and Stephen becomes the first martyr of the church because of it.

Stephen: 51You stubborn, stiff-necked people! Sure, you are physically Jews, but you are no different from outsiders in your hearts and ears! You are just like your ancestors, constantly fighting against the Holy Spirit. 52Didn't your ancestors persecute the prophets? First, they killed those prophets who predicted the coming of the Just One; and now, you have betrayed and murdered the Just One Himself! 53Yes, you received the law as given by heavenly messengers, but you haven't kept the law which you received.

54Upon hearing this, *his audience could contain themselves no longer.* They boiled in fury at Stephen; they clenched their jaws and

ground their teeth. 55But Stephen was filled with the Holy Spirit. Gazing upward into heaven, he saw *something they couldn't see:* the glory of God, and Jesus standing at His right hand.

Stephen: 56Look, I see the heavens opening! I see the Son of Man standing at the right hand of God!

57At this, they covered their ears and started shouting. The whole crowd rushed at Stephen, converged on him, 58dragged him out of the city, and stoned him.

    They laid their coats at the feet of a young man named Saul, 59while they were pelting Stephen with rocks.

Stephen (*as rocks fell upon him*): Lord Jesus, receive my spirit.

60Then he knelt *in prayer*, shouting at the top of his lungs,

Stephen: Lord, do not hold this evil against them!

Those were his final words; then he fell asleep *in death.*

Stephen's sermon weaves together the story of the Jews and the life of Jesus. The point of the message is that God pursues His children despite their constant failure. The crucifixion of Jesus is the greatest of all of these failures.
    Stephen affirms that through circumcision they have made themselves look like Jews, but their hearts and ears need circumcising as well. Of course, telling the Jewish leaders to get their hearts and ears circumcised elicits a rather violent response. Stephen speaks the truth so that all might hear, including a man named Saul.

8 1-2Some devout men buried Stephen and mourned his passing with loud cries of grief. But Saul, *this young man who seemed to be supervising the whole*

* 7:49-50 Isaiah 66:1-2

violent event, was pleased by Stephen's death. That very day, the *whole* church in Jerusalem began experiencing severe persecution. All *of the followers of Jesus*—except for the emissaries* themselves—fled to the countryside of Judea and Samaria. ³*Young* Saul went on a rampage—hunting the church, house after house, dragging both men and women to prison.

>
> They flee to the very places where Jesus said His disciples would be His witnesses at the beginning of this book. As a result, the persecution spreads the message of Christ rather than hinders it. Commenting about similar events a century later, church father Tertullian will write, "The blood of martyrs is the seed of the Church."

⁴All those who had been scattered *by the persecution* moved from place to place; *and wherever they went, they weren't afraid or silent. Instead,* they spread the message of Jesus.

⁵Philip, *for example,* headed north to the city of Samaria, and he told them the news of the Anointed One. ⁶The crowds were united in their desire to understand Philip's message. They not only listened with their ears, but they witnessed miraculous signs with their eyes. ⁷Unclean spirits cried out with loud screams as they were exorcised from people. Paralyzed people and lame people moved and walked in plain view. ⁸So the city was swept with joy.

⁹⁻¹¹There was a fellow named Simon who had a widespread and long-standing reputation as a sorcerer in Samaria. Everyone—not just poor or uneducated people, but also the city's elite—paid him great respect. Because he had amazed them with his magic, they thought, "This is a truly great man, full of the power of the God of Greatness." ¹²But they were even more impressed with Philip as he proclaimed the good news of the kingdom of God and the name of Jesus the Anointed. Both men and women received ceremonial washing through baptism*—¹³and even Simon himself became a believer. After his baptism, he shadowed Philip constantly, and he was as amazed as everyone else when he saw great and miraculous signs taking place.

¹⁴Meanwhile word had reached the Lord's emissaries* in Jerusalem that the message of God was welcomed in Samaria—*a land of half-breeds and heretics in the minds of many Judeans.* They sent Peter and John ¹⁵to pray for the Samaritans. They were especially eager to see if the new believers would receive the Holy Spirit ¹⁶because until this point they had been baptized* in the name of the Lord Jesus but had not experienced the Holy Spirit. ¹⁷When Peter and John laid hands on the people, the Holy Spirit did indeed come upon them *all.*

¹⁸Simon *watched all this closely.* He saw the Holy Spirit coming to the people when the apostles laid hands on them. So he *came to Peter and John and* offered them money.

Simon: ¹⁹I want to purchase this ability to confer the Holy Spirit on people through the laying on of my hands.

Peter: ²⁰May your silver rot right along with you, Simon! To think the Holy Spirit is some kind of magic that can be procured with money! ²¹You aren't even close to being ready for this kind of ministry; your heart is not right with God. ²²You need to turn from your past, and you need to pray that the Lord will forgive the evil intent of your heart. ²³I can see deep bitterness has poisoned you, and wickedness has locked you in chains.

Simon: ²⁴*Please*—you must pray to the Lord for me. I don't want these terrible things to be true of me.

²⁵Peter and John preached to and talked *with the Samaritans* about the message of the Lord; and then they returned to Jerusalem, stopping in many other Samaritan villages along the way to proclaim the good news.

²⁶A heavenly messenger brought this *short* message from the Lord to Philip *during his time preaching in Samaria:*

Messenger of the Lord: Leave Samaria. Go south to the Jerusalem-Gaza road.

The message was especially unusual because this road runs through the middle of uninhabited desert. ²⁷But Philip got up, *left the*

---

* 8:1-2 Literally, apostles   * 8:12 Literally, immersion, a rite of initiation and purification   * 8:14 Literally, apostles   * 8:16 Literally, immersed, in a rite of initiation and purification

excitement of Samaria, and did as he was told to do. *Along this road, Philip saw a chariot in the distance. In the chariot was* a dignitary from Ethiopia (the treasurer for Queen Candace), *an African man* who had been castrated. He had gone north to Jerusalem to worship *at the Jewish temple,* 28and he was now *heading southwest* on his way home. He was seated in the chariot and was reading aloud from a scroll of the prophet Isaiah.

29Philip received another prompting from the Holy Spirit:

Holy Spirit: Go over to the chariot and climb on board.

30So he started running until he was even with the chariot. Philip heard the Ethiopian reading aloud and recognized the words from the prophet Isaiah.

Philip: Do you understand the meaning of what you're reading?

The Ethiopian: 31How can I understand it unless I have a mentor?

Then he invited Philip to sit in the chariot. 32Here's the passage he was reading from the Hebrew Scriptures:

Like a sheep, He was led to be slaughtered.
Like a lamb about to be shorn of its wool,
He was completely silent.
33He was humiliated, and He received no justice.
Who can describe His peers? *Who would treat Him this way?*
For they snuffed out His life.*

The Ethiopian: 34*Here's my first question.* Is the prophet describing his own situation, or is he describing someone else's *calamity?*

35That began a conversation in which Philip used the passage to explain the good news of Jesus. 36Eventually the chariot passed a body of water beside the road.

The Ethiopian: Since there is water here, is there anything that might prevent me from being ceremonially washed through baptism* *and identified as a disciple of Jesus?*

Philip: [37If you believe in your heart that Jesus the Anointed is God's Son, then nothing can stop you.

The Ethiopian said that he believed.]*

Possibly a reference to the Jewish prohibition of full participation in temple worship by men who have been castrated—a prohibition he likely encounters in this very visit to Jerusalem.

38He commanded the charioteer to stop the horses. Then Philip and the Ethiopian official walked together into the water. There Philip baptized* him, *initiating him as a fellow disciple.* 39When they came out of the water, Philip was immediately caught up by the Holy Spirit and taken from the sight of the Ethiopian, who climbed back into his chariot and continued on his journey, overflowing with joy. 40Philip found himself at a town called Azotus (*formerly the Philistine capital city of Ashdod, on the Mediterranean*); and from there he traveled north again, proclaiming the good news in town after town until he came to Caesarea.

9 Back to Saul—this fuming, raging, hateful man who wanted to kill every last one of the Lord's disciples: he went to the high priest *in Jerusalem* 2for authorization to purge all the synagogues in Damascus of followers of the way of Jesus.* His plan was to arrest and chain any of Jesus' followers—women as well as men—and transport them back to Jerusalem. 3He traveled north toward Damascus *with a group of companions.*

Imagine this: Suddenly a light flashes from the sky around Saul, 4and he falls to the ground at the sound of a voice.

The Lord: Saul, Saul, why are you attacking Me?

Saul: 5Lord, who are You?

Then he hears these words:

The Lord: I am Jesus. I am the One you are attacking. 6Get up. Enter the city. You will learn there what you are to do.

These are shocking, unexpected words that will change his life forever.

* 8:32-33 Isaiah 53:7-8   * 8:36 Literally, immersed, in a rite of initiation and purification   * 8:37 The earliest manuscripts omit verse 37.   * 8:38 Literally, immersed, in a rite of initiation and purification   * 9:2 The Christian movement

[7]His other traveling companions just stand there, *paralyzed,* speechless because they, too, heard the voice; but there is nobody in sight. [8]Saul rises to his feet, his eyes wide open, but he can't see a thing. So his companions lead their blind friend by the hand and take him into Damascus. [9]He waits for three days—completely blind—and does not eat a bite or drink a drop of anything.

[10]Meanwhile, in Damascus a disciple named Ananias had a vision in which the Lord Jesus spoke to him.

The Lord: Ananias.

Ananias: Here I am, Lord.

The Lord: [11]Get up and go to Straight Boulevard. Go to the house of Judas, and inquire about a man from Tarsus, Saul by name. He is praying *to Me at this very instant.* [12]He has had a vision—a vision of a man by your name who will come, lay hands on him, and heal his eyesight.

Ananias: [13]Lord, *I know whom You're talking about.* I've heard rumors about this fellow. He's *an evil man and* has caused great harm for Your special people in Jerusalem. [14]I've heard that he has been authorized by the religious authorities to come here and chain everyone who associates with Your name.

The Lord: [15]*Yes, but* you must go! I have chosen him to be My instrument to bring My name far and wide—to outsiders, to kings, and to the people of Israel as well. [16]I have much to show him, including how much he must suffer for My name.

[17]So Ananias went and entered the house *where Saul was staying.* He laid his hands on Saul and called to him.

Ananias: Brother Saul, the Lord Jesus, who appeared to you on your way here, sent me so you can regain your sight and be filled with the Holy Spirit.

[18]At that instant, something like scales fell from Saul's eyes, and he could see. So he got up, received the ceremonial washing of baptism* *identifying him as a disciple,* [19]ate some food (*remember, he had not eaten for three days*), and regained his strength. He spent a lot of time with the disciples in Damascus

over the next several days. [20]Then he went into the very synagogues he had intended to purge, proclaiming,

Saul: Jesus is God's Son!

[21]Obviously this amazed everybody, and the buzz spread.

The People: Isn't he the man who caused so much trouble in Jerusalem for everyone identified with Jesus? Didn't he come here to arrest followers of Jesus and bring them in chains to the religious authorities? *Now he's switched sides and is preaching Jesus?*

[22]As time passed, Saul's confidence grew stronger and stronger, so much so that he debated with the Jews of Damascus and made an irrefutable case that Jesus is, in fact, God's Anointed, *the Liberating King.*

[23]*They didn't like being confounded like this;* so after several days, the Jews plotted to assassinate Saul. [24]But he learned of the plot. He knew they were keeping the city gates under constant surveillance, so they could follow and kill him when he left. [25]*To save Saul, the disciples came up with a plan of their own.* During the night, they put Saul in a basket and lowered him by ropes from an opening in the wall of the city *rather than passing through the gates. Their plan worked,* [26]and he returned to Jerusalem.

He tried to join the disciples there, but they didn't think he was sincere.

[27]*Only one person accepted Saul as a genuine disciple,* Barnabas, who became Saul's advocate to the apostles. He told the whole story of what happened in Damascus, from Saul's vision and message from the Lord to his transformation into a confident proclaimer of the name of Jesus. [28]Finally they accepted Saul and gave him access to their community, and he continued to speak confidently in the name of the Lord. [29]He dialogued—and argued—with a group of Greek-speaking Jews. *That didn't go well either, because soon* they were plotting to kill him also. [30]His fellow believers helped him escape by bringing him to Caesarea and sending him to *his hometown,* Tarsus.

[31]And so the church enjoyed a period of peace and growth throughout the regions of Judea, Galilee, and Samaria. The disciples lived in deep reverence for the Lord, they

---

* 9:18 Literally, immersion, a rite of initiation and purification

experienced the strong comfort of the Holy Spirit, and their numbers increased.

³²*Peter hadn't been idle during all this time.* He was having a number of amazing experiences of his own, traveling from group to group and visiting the various communities of believers. Once he came to a town called Lydda, *a border town between Samaria and Judea,* and met with God's special people there. ³³He visited a man named Aeneas. This poor fellow had been paralyzed for eight years, unable to leave his bed.

Peter: ³⁴Aeneas, Jesus the Anointed heals you. Get up! Now you can make your own bed!

And immediately—he got up! ³⁵All the local residents—both of Lydda and nearby Sharon—saw Aeneas *healthy and strong again,* so they turned to the Lord.

³⁶In *a nearby coastal city,* Joppa, there lived a disciple whose *Aramaic* name was Tabitha, or Dorcas in Greek. She was a good woman—devotedly doing good and giving to the poor. ³⁷While Peter was in Lydda, she fell sick and died. Her fellow disciples washed her body and laid her in an upstairs room. ³⁸They had heard Peter was nearby, so two of them went with an urgent message, "Please come to Joppa as soon as possible."

³⁹Peter went with them and immediately entered the room where the corpse had been placed. *It was quite a scene*—the widows *of the community* were crowded in the room, weeping, showing the various items of clothing that Dorcas had made for them.

⁴⁰Peter asked them to leave the room; then he got on his knees. He prayed *for a while* and then turned to her body.

Peter: Tabitha, get up!

She opened her eyes, saw Peter, and sat up. ⁴¹Giving her his hand, Peter lifted her up. Then he called in the other disciples—including the widows—and reintroduced them to their beloved friend. ⁴²The news of this miracle spread throughout the city, and many believed in the Lord. ⁴³Peter stayed in Joppa for some time as the guest of Simon, a tanner by profession.

While Peter is in Joppa, another story is developing a day's journey to the north along the Mediterranean coast.

10 Cornelius, a Roman Centurion and a member of *a unit called* the Italian Cohort, lived in Caesarea. ²Cornelius was *an outsider, but he was* a devout man—a God-fearing fellow with a God-fearing family. He consistently and generously gave to the poor, and he practiced constant prayer to God. ³About three o'clock one afternoon, he had a vision of a messenger of God.

Messenger of God: Cornelius!

Cornelius *(terrified):* ⁴What is it, sir?

Messenger of God: God has heard your prayers, and He has seen your kindness to the poor. *God has taken notice of you.* ⁵⁻⁶Send men *south* to Joppa, to the house of a tanner named Simon. Ask to speak to a guest of his named Simon, but also called Peter. You'll find this house near the waterfront.

⁷After the messenger departed, Cornelius immediately called two of his slaves and a soldier under his command—an especially devout soldier. ⁸He told them the whole story and sent them to Joppa.

⁹Just as these men were nearing Joppa about noon the next day, Peter went up on the flat rooftop *of Simon the tanner's house.* He planned to pray, ¹⁰but he soon grew hungry. While his lunch was being prepared, Peter had a vision of his own—*a vision that linked his present hunger with what was about to happen:* ¹¹A rift opened in the sky, and a wide container—something like a huge sheet suspended by its four corners—descended through the torn opening toward the ground. ¹²This container teemed with four-footed animals, creatures that crawl, and birds—*pigs, bats, lizards, snakes, frogs, toads, and vultures.*

A Voice: ¹³Get up, Peter! Kill! Eat!

Peter: ¹⁴No way, Lord! *These animals are forbidden in the dietary laws of the Hebrew Scriptures!* I've never eaten nonkosher foods like these before—*not once in my life!*

A Voice: ¹⁵If God calls something permissible and clean, you must not call it forbidden and dirty!

¹⁶Peter saw this vision three times; but the third time, the container of animals flew up

through the rift in the sky, *the rift healed,*
¹⁷and Peter was confused and unsettled as he
tried to make sense of this strange vision.

At that very moment, *Peter heard the
voices of* Cornelius's delegation, who had
asked for directions to Simon's house, coming from the front gate.

Delegation: ¹⁸Is there a man named Simon,
also called Peter, staying at this house?

¹⁹⁻²⁰Peter's mind was still racing about the
vision when the voice of the Holy Spirit
broke through his churning thoughts.

Holy Spirit: The three men who are searching for you have been sent by Me. So get
up! Go with them. Don't hesitate *or argue.*

²¹Peter rushed downstairs to the men.

Peter: I'm the one you're seeking. Can you
tell me why you've come?

Delegation: ²²We've been sent by *our commander and master,* Cornelius. He is a Centurion, and he is a good, honest man who
worships your God. All the Jewish people
speak well of him. A holy messenger told
him to send for you, so you would come to
his home and he could hear your message.

²³Peter extended hospitality to them and
gave them lodging overnight. When they
departed together the next morning, Peter
brought some believers from Joppa.
²⁴They arrived in Caesarea the next
afternoon *just before three o'clock.* Cornelius had anticipated their arrival and had
assembled his relatives and close friends *to
welcome them.* ²⁵When Peter and Cornelius
met, Cornelius fell at Peter's feet in worship,
²⁶but Peter helped him up.

Peter: Stand up, man! I am just a human
being!

²⁷They talked and entered the house to meet
the whole crowd inside.

Peter: ²⁸You know *I am a Jew.* We Jews consider it a breach of divine law to associate,
much less share hospitality, with outsiders. But God has shown me something in
recent days: I should no longer consider
any human beneath me or unclean. ²⁹That's
why I made no objection when you invited

me; rather, I came willingly. Now let me
hear the story of why you invited me here.

Cornelius: ³⁰It was about this time of day
four days ago when I was here, in my
house, praying the customary midafternoon
prayer. Suddenly a man appeared out of
nowhere. His clothes were dazzling white,
and he stood directly in front of me ³¹and
addressed me: "Cornelius, your prayer has
been heard, and your kindness to the poor
has been noticed by God. ³²God wants you
to find a man in Joppa, Simon who is also
called Peter, who is staying at the home of
a tanner named Simon, near the seaside."
³³I wasted no time, *did just as I was told,*
and you have generously accepted my invitation. So here we are, in the presence of
God, ready to take in all that the Lord has
told you to tell us.

Peter: ³⁴It is clear to me now that God plays
no favorites, ³⁵that God accepts every person whatever his or her culture or ethnic
background, that God welcomes all who
revere Him and do right. ³⁶*You already
know that* God sent a message to the people
of Israel; it was a message of peace, peace
through Jesus the Anointed—who is King
of all people. ³⁷You know this message
spread through Judea, beginning in Galilee
where John called people to be ritually
cleansed through baptism.* ³⁸You know
God identified Jesus as the uniquely chosen One by pouring out the Holy Spirit on
Him, by empowering Him. You know Jesus
went through the land doing good *for all*
and healing all who were suffering under
the oppression of the evil one, for God was
with Him. ³⁹My friends and I stand as witnesses to all Jesus did in *the region of* Judea
and *the city of* Jerusalem. The people of
our capital city killed Him by hanging Him
on a tree, ⁴⁰but God raised Him up on the
third day and made it possible for us to see
Him. ⁴¹Not everyone was granted this privilege, only those of us whom God chose as
witnesses. We actually ate and drank with
Him after His resurrection. ⁴²He told us
to spread His message to everyone and to
tell them that He is the One whom God has
chosen to be Judge, *to make a just assessment of all people*—both living and dead.
⁴³All the prophets tell us about Him and
assert that every person who believes in

* 10:37 Literally, immersed, to show repentance

Jesus receives forgiveness of sins through His name.

V

The true gospel is becoming increasingly clear as the church spreads and develops. What happens that day in Caesarea changes the face of Christianity forever. It builds a bridge from Jews to Gentiles, from insiders to outsiders, and sends the community of Jesus on a journey beyond the kind of religious and cultural barriers that all people erect. Through Peter's short trip, the church makes an important journey toward reaching the ends of the earth because the message of Jesus is not for the Jews alone but for all people of all time. This is a hard lesson, and not everyone is eager to learn it.

⁴⁴*Peter wasn't planning to stop at this point, but* the Holy Spirit suddenly interrupted and came upon all the people who were listening. ⁴⁵⁻⁴⁶They began speaking in foreign languages (*just as the Jewish disciples did on the Day of Pentecost*), and their hearts overflowed in joyful praises to God. Peter's friends *from Joppa—all of them Jewish,* all circumcised—were stunned to see that the gift of the Holy Spirit was poured out even on outsiders.

Peter: ⁴⁷Can anyone give any good reason not to ceremonially wash these people through baptism* *as fellow disciples? After all, it's obvious* they have received the Holy Spirit just as we did *on the Day of Pentecost.*

⁴⁸So he had them baptized in the name of the Lord Jesus. The new disciples asked him to stay for several more days.

11 ¹⁻²*By the time Peter and his friends from Joppa returned to Jerusalem,* news about outsiders accepting God's message had already spread to the Lord's emissaries* and believers there. *Some of* the circumcised believers didn't welcome Peter with joy, but with criticism.

Circumcised Believers: ³*Why did you violate divine law by* associating with outsiders and

sitting at the table with them for a meal? *This is an outrage!*

⁴Peter patiently told them what had happened, laying out in detail the whole story.

Peter: ⁵I was in Joppa, I was praying, and I fell into a trance. In my vision, something like a huge sheet descended from the sky as if it were being lowered by its four corners. It landed right in front of me. ⁶It was full of all kinds of four-footed creatures *that we would call unclean*—I could identify mammals, snakes, lizards, and birds. ⁷Then I heard a voice say, "Get up, Peter! Kill these creatures and eat them!" ⁸Of course, I replied, "No way, Lord! Not a single bite of forbidden, nonkosher food has ever touched my lips." ⁹But then the voice spoke from heaven a second time: "If God makes something clean, you must not call it dirty or forbidden." ¹⁰This whole drama was repeated three times, and then it was all pulled back up into the sky.

¹¹At that very second, three men arrived at the house where I was staying. They had come to me from Caesarea. ¹²The Holy Spirit told me I should go with them, that I shouldn't make any distinction *between them as Gentiles and us as Jews.* These six brothers *from Joppa* came with me; and yes, we entered the man's home *even though he was an outsider.*

¹³The outsider told us the story of how he had seen a heavenly messenger standing in his house who said, "Send to Joppa and bring back Simon, also called Peter, ¹⁴and he will give you a message that will rescue both you and your household." ¹⁵Then I began to speak; and as I did, the Holy Spirit fell upon them—it was exactly as it had been with us at the beginning. ¹⁶Then I remembered what Jesus had said to us: "John ritually cleansed people with water through baptism,* but you will be washed with the Holy Spirit."* ¹⁷So, if God gave them the same gift we were given when we believed in the Lord Jesus, the Anointed One, who was I to stand in God's way?

¹⁸There was no argument, only silence.

Circumcised Believers: Well then, we must conclude that God has given to the

---

* 10:47 Literally, immerse, in a rite of initiation and purification * 11:1-2 Literally, apostles * 11:16 Literally, immersed, to show repentance * 11:16 Acts 1:5

outsiders the opportunity to rethink their lives, turn to God,* and gain a new life.

> Just as the experience of the Holy Spirit transforms that small community of believers into the church at the beginning of this book, the presence of the Spirit's work among these outsiders, the ones who were not a part of God's covenant with Moses, demonstrates that they, too, are part of the church. This isn't what many expected, and questions about inclusion of outsiders consume the early life of the church.

¹⁹The believers who were scattered *from Judea* because of the persecution following Stephen's stoning kept moving out, reaching Phoenicia, Cyprus, and Antioch. Until this time, they had only shared their message with Jews. ²⁰Then some men from Cyprus and Cyrene who had become believers came to Antioch, and they began sharing the message of the Lord Jesus with some Greek *converts to Judaism.* ²¹The Lord was at work through them, and a large number *of these Greeks* became believers and turned to the Lord Jesus.

²²Word of this new development came to the church in Jerusalem, and they sent Barnabas to Antioch *to investigate.* ²³He arrived and saw God's grace in action there, so he rejoiced and urged them to remain faithful to the Lord, to maintain an enduring, unshakable devotion. ²⁴This Barnabas truly was a good man, full of the Holy Spirit, full of faith. A very large number of people were brought to the Lord.

²⁵Barnabas soon was off again—now to Tarsus to look for Saul. ²⁶He found Saul and brought him back to Antioch. The two of them spent an entire year there, meeting with the church and teaching huge numbers of people. It was there, in Antioch, where the term "Christian" was first used to identify disciples of Jesus.

²⁷During that year, some prophets came north from Jerusalem to Antioch. ²⁸A prophet named Agabus stood in a meeting and made a prediction by the Holy Spirit: there would be an expansive, terrible famine in the whole region during the reign of Claudius. ²⁹*In anticipation of the famine,* the disciples determined to give an amount proportionate to their financial ability and create a relief fund for all the believers in Judea. ³⁰They sent Barnabas and Saul to carry this fund to the elders *in Jerusalem.*

12 *Back in Jerusalem, hard times came to the disciples.* King Herod violently seized some who belonged to the church with the intention of mistreating them. ²He ordered James (brother of John) to be executed by the sword, *the first of those appointed as emissaries to be martyred.* ³This move pleased Jewish public opinion, so he decided to arrest Peter also. During the holy festival of Unleavened Bread, ⁴he caught Peter and imprisoned him, assigning four squads of soldiers to guard him. He planned to bring him to trial publicly after the Passover holiday.

⁵During Peter's imprisonment, the church prayed constantly and intensely to God for his safety. ⁶*Their prayers were not answered,* until the night before Peter's execution.

Picture this event: Peter is sound asleep between two soldiers, double-chained, with still more guards outside the prison door watching for external intruders. ⁷Suddenly the cell fills with light: it is a messenger of the Lord manifesting himself. He taps Peter on the side, awakening him.

Messenger of the Lord: Get up, quickly.

The chains fall off Peter's wrists.

Messenger of the Lord: ⁸Come on! Put on your belt. Put on your sandals.

Peter puts them on *and just stands there.*

Messenger of the Lord: Pull your cloak over your shoulders. *Come on!* Follow me!

⁹Peter does so, but he is completely dazed. He doesn't think this is really happening—he assumes he is dreaming or having a vision. ¹⁰They pass the first guard. They pass the second guard. They come to the iron gate that opens to the city. The gate swings open for them on its own, and they walk into a lane. Suddenly the messenger disappears.

* 11:18 Literally, repent

[11]Peter finally realized all that had really happened.

Peter: *Amazing!* The Lord has sent His messenger to rescue me from Herod and the public spectacle *of my execution* which the Jews fully expected.

[12]Peter immediately rushed over to the home of a woman named Mary. (Mary's son, John Mark, *would eventually become an important associate of the apostles.*) A large group had gathered there to pray *for Peter and his safety.* [13]He knocked at the outer gate; and a maid, Rhoda, answered. [14]She recognized Peter's voice, but she was so overcome with excitement that she left him standing on the street and ran inside to tell everyone.

Rhoda: *Our prayers were answered!* Peter is at the front gate!

Praying Believers: [15]*Rhoda, you're crazy!*

Rhoda: *No! Peter's out there! I'm sure of it!*

Praying Believers: Well, maybe it's his *guardian* angel *or something.*

[16]All this time, Peter was still out in the street, knocking on the gate. *Finally* they came and let him in. *Of course,* the disciples were stunned, *and everyone was talking at once.* [17]Peter motioned for them to quiet down and then told them the amazing story of how the Lord engineered his escape.

On the night before his execution, Peter sleeps like a baby. Here he is, chained in a room full of soldiers while James's blood is still moist on the ground. Although he can only assume this is his one last night before his own torturous death, he is not afraid. So peacefully does he rest, in fact, that the heavenly messenger has to prod him to wake up; and while he is walking, he questions if he is dreaming. Does the thought that believers are on their knees all day appealing to God for him give him peace? Maybe. But certainly Peter trusts that God is in control. A church that started with a few

people is now over 8,000, and God is redeeming the rest of the world through these people.

Peter: Could you please get word to James, *our Lord's brother,* and the other believers *that I'm all right?*

Then he left to find a safer place to stay. [18]But when morning came and Peter was gone, there was a huge uproar among the soldiers. [19]Herod *sent troops* to find Peter, but he was missing. Herod interrogated the guards and ordered their executions. Peter headed down toward the coast to Caesarea, and he remained there.

[20]*At this time there was major political upheaval.* Herod was at odds with the populace of neighboring Tyre and Sidon, so the two cities sent a large group of representatives to meet with him. They won over one of Herod's closest associates, Blastus, the director of the treasury; then they pressured Herod to drop his grudge. Cooperation was important to the two cities because they *were all major trading partners and* depended on Herod's territory for food. [21]*They struck a deal, and* Herod came over *to ratify it.* Dressed in all his royal finery and seated high above them on a platform, he made a speech; [22]and the people of Tyre and Sidon interrupted with cheers to flatter him.

The People: This is the voice of a god! This is no mere mortal!

[23]Herod should have given glory to the true God; *but since he vainly accepted their flattery,* that very day a messenger of the Lord struck him with an illness. *It was an ugly disease,* involving putrefaction and worms eating his flesh. Eventually he died.

[24]*Through all this upheaval,* God's message spread to new frontiers and attracted more and more people. [25]Meanwhile, the time Barnabas and Saul spent *in Jerusalem* came to an end, and they reported back *to Antioch,* bringing along John, who was also called Mark.

After Barnabas and Saul help deliver the relief fund to Jerusalem (11:29-30), the three men return to Antioch. With this trip by Saul (who will shortly be renamed Paul) back to Antioch, Luke's emphasis for the rest of the book shifts away from Peter and the church in Jerusalem to focus on Paul and his mission to spread the good news to Jews and outsiders throughout the northern Mediterranean area.

---

13 The church in Antioch *had grown strong*, with many prophets and teachers: Barnabas, Simeon (a dark man *from Central Africa*), Lucius (from Cyrene *in North Africa*), Manaen (a member of Herod's governing council), and Saul. ²Once they were engaged in a time of worship and fasting when the Holy Spirit spoke to them, "Commission Barnabas and Saul to a project I have called them to accomplish." ³They fasted and prayed some more, laid their hands on the two selected men, and sent them off on their new mission. ⁴Having received special commissioning by the Holy Spirit, Barnabas and Saul went to nearby Seleucia *on the coast*. Then they caught a ship to the island of Cyprus.

⁵At the city of Salamis *on the east side of Cyprus*, they proclaimed the message of God in Jewish synagogues, assisted by John Mark. ⁶⁻⁷They went *westward from town to town*, finally reaching Paphos on the western shore. There the proconsul named Sergius Paulus, an intelligent man, summoned Barnabas and Saul because he wanted to hear their message. At his side was an occult spiritualist and Jewish false prophet named Bar-Jesus ⁸or Elymas (which means "magician"). Elymas argued with Barnabas and Saul, trying to keep Sergius Paulus from coming to faith.

⁹Saul, who is also known as Paul, was suddenly full of the Holy Spirit. He stared directly into Elymas's face.

Paul: ¹⁰You're a son of the devil. You're an enemy of justice, you're full of lies, and you steal opportunities from others. Why do you insist on confusing and twisting the clear, straight paths of the Lord? ¹¹Hear this, *Elymas*: the Lord's hand is against you, and you will be *as blind as a bat* for a period of time, *beginning right now*!

At that instant, *it was as if* a mist came over Elymas and then total darkness. He stumbled around, groping for a hand so he could be led *back home*. ¹²When Sergius Paulus saw this happen, he came to faith and was attracted to and amazed by the teaching about the Lord.

¹³Paul and his entourage *boarded a ship and* set sail from Paphos. They traveled *north* to Perga in Pamphylia. John Mark, however, abandoned the mission and returned to Jerusalem.

¹⁴Paul and Barnabas continued from Perga to Pisidian Antioch; and on the Sabbath, they entered the synagogue and sat down. ¹⁵After the regular reading *of the Hebrew Scriptures—including* passages from the Law and the Prophets—the synagogue leaders sent a message to them: "Brothers, if you would like to give us some exhortation, please do so." ¹⁶Paul rose to his feet, offered a gesture of greeting, and began his message.

Paul: Israelites and other God-fearing people, please hear me. ¹⁷The God of the Israelites chose our ancestors and helped them become a large population while they were living in Egypt many years ago. He displayed His great power by leading them out *of that powerful nation*. ¹⁸For about 40 years, He endured their constant complaining in the wilderness. ¹⁹He opened up some land for them in Canaan by destroying the seven nations living there, and that land became their inheritance for about 450 years. ²⁰They had tribal leaders* through the time of the prophet Samuel. ²¹Then they asked for a king, and God gave them one—Saul, son of Kish, of the tribe of Benjamin—who reigned for 40 years. ²²After God moved Saul aside, He made David king in his place. God had this to say about David: "I have found David, son of Jesse, to be a man after My own heart. He's the kind of king who will rule in ways that please Me."* ²³God has selected one of David's descendants as the long-promised Liberator of Israel. I am speaking of Jesus.

²⁴*Before Jesus arrived on the scene, His cousin John* was hard at work, proclaiming to all the people of Israel a ceremonial washing through baptism* and pointing to a new direction in thought and life. ²⁵John's ministry climaxed when he said, "Who do you assume me to be? I am not the One *you're looking for*. No, but One is

---

* 13:20 In the Hebrew Scriptures, these leaders were called "judges." * 13:22 1 Samuel 13:14 * 13:24 Literally, immersion, an act to show repentance

coming after me, One whose sandal thong I am unworthy to untie."* ²⁶My brothers, fellow descendants of our common father Abraham, and others here who fear God, we are the ones to whom God has sent this message of salvation.

²⁷But you know the people of Jerusalem and their leaders did not recognize Jesus. They didn't understand the words of the prophets that are read *in the synagogues* on Sabbath after Sabbath. As a result, they fulfilled the ancient prophecies by condemning Jesus. ²⁸Even though they could find no offense punishable by death, still they asked Pilate to execute Jesus. ²⁹When they carried out everything that had been foretold by the prophets, they took His body down from the tree and laid Him in a tomb. ³⁰But *that was not the end:* God raised Him from the dead, ³¹and over a period of many days, He appeared to those who had been His companions from *the beginning of their journey in* Galilee until *its end in* Jerusalem. They are now witnesses to everyone. ³²We are here to bring you the good news of God's promise to our ancestors, ³³which He has now fulfilled for our children by raising Jesus. *Consider the promises fulfilled in Jesus.* The psalmist says, "You are My Son; today I have become Your Father."*

³⁴Elsewhere God promises that Jesus will rise and never return to death and corruption again: "I will make You the holy and faithful promises I made to David."* ³⁵Similarly, another psalm says, "You will not abandon Me to experience death and the grave or leave Me to rot alone."* ³⁶*We all know* David died and was reduced to dust after he served God's purpose in his generation; ³⁷these words *obviously* apply *not to David but to* the One God raised from death before suffering decay. ³⁸So you must realize, my brothers, that through this *resurrected* man forgiveness of sins is assured to you. ³⁹Through Jesus, everyone who believes is set free from all sins—sins which the law of Moses could not release you from. ⁴⁰In light of all this, be careful that you do not fulfill these words of the prophet *Habakkuk:*

⁴¹Look, you scoffers!
  Be shocked to death.
For in your days I am doing a work,
  a work you will never believe, even if
    someone tells you plainly!*

⁴²Paul and Barnabas prepared to leave *the synagogue,* but the people wanted to hear more and urged them to return the following Sabbath. ⁴³As the people dispersed after the meeting, many Jews and converts to Judaism followed Paul and Barnabas. *Privately* Paul and Barnabas continued teaching them and urged them to remain steadfast in the grace of God. ⁴⁴The next Sabbath, it seemed the whole city had gathered to hear the message of the Lord. ⁴⁵But some of the Jewish leaders were jealous when they saw these huge crowds. They began to *argue with and* contradict Paul's message, as well as slander him. ⁴⁶Paul and Barnabas together responded with great confidence.

Paul and Barnabas: *OK, then.* It was only right that we should bring God's message to you *Jewish people* first. But now, since you are rejecting our message and identifying yourselves as unworthy of eternal life, we are turning to the outsiders. ⁴⁷The Lord has commanded us to do this. *Remember His words:*

I have appointed you a light to the nations
    beyond Israel,
  so you can bring redemption to every
    corner of the earth.*

⁴⁸*These words created two strong reactions.* The outsiders were thrilled and praised God's message, and all those who had been appointed for eternal life became believers. ⁴⁹*Through them* the Lord's message spread through the whole region. ⁵⁰But the Jewish leaders united the aristocratic religious women and the city's leading men in opposition to Paul and Barnabas, and soon they were persecuted and driven out of the region. ⁵¹They simply shook the dust off their feet in protest and moved on to Iconium. ⁵²The disciples *weren't intimidated at all;* rather, they were full of joy and the Holy Spirit.

V

Paul never forsakes the Jews, the ones to whom the covenants were given. He shares with them first the good news about how God has fulfilled His promises through Jesus. Only when he faces opposition

* 13:25 Luke 3:16   * 13:33 Psalm 2:7   * 13:34 Isaiah 55:3   * 13:35 Psalm 16:10   * 13:41 Habakkuk 1:5   * 13:47 Isaiah 49:6

does he turn to the outsiders, because this hope is for them too.

---

14 *The results* in Iconium *were similar*. Paul and Barnabas began in the Jewish synagogue, bringing a great number of ethnic Jews and Greek converts to faith in Jesus. [2]But the other Jews who wouldn't believe agitated the outsiders and poisoned their minds against the brothers. [3]Paul and Barnabas stayed in Iconium for a long time, speaking with great confidence for the Lord. He confirmed the message of His grace by granting them the power to do signs and wonders. [4]But *over time* the people were divided, some siding with the *unbelieving* Jews and some siding with the apostles. [5]Finally the Jews and outsiders who opposed them joined forces and enlisted the political leaders in their plan to beat and stone Paul and Barnabas. [6]They learned of the plan and escaped to Lystra and Derbe in Lycaonia, and the surrounding countryside, [7]where they continued proclaiming the good news.

[8]In Lystra they met a man who had been crippled since birth; his feet were completely useless. [9]He listened to Paul speak, and Paul could see in this man's face that he had faith to be healed.

Paul (*shouting*): [10]Stand up on your own two feet, man!

The man jumped up and walked! [11]When the crowds saw this, they started shouting in Lycaonian.

Crowd: The gods have come down to us! They've come in human form!

[12]They decided that Barnabas was Zeus and Paul was Hermes (since he was the main speaker). [13]*Before they knew it,* the priest of Zeus, whose temple was prominent in that city, came to the city gates with oxen and garlands of flowers so the Lycaonians could offer sacrifices in worship *to Paul and Barnabas!* [14]When they heard of this, Paul and Barnabas were beside themselves with frustration—they ripped their tunics *as an expression of disapproval* and rushed out into the crowd.

Paul and Barnabas (*shouting*): [15]Friends! No! No! Don't do this! We're just humans like all of you! *We're not here to be worshiped!* We're here to bring you good news—good news that you should turn from these worthless forms of worship and instead serve the living God, the God who made the heaven and the earth and the sea and all that they contain. [16]Through all previous generations, God has allowed all the nations to follow their own customs and religions, [17]but even then God revealed Himself by doing good to you—giving you rain for your crops and fruitful harvests season after season, filling your stomachs with food and your hearts with joy.

[18]In spite of these words, they were barely able to keep the crowds from making sacrifices to them.

V

When God uses men to bless the world, many mistakenly exalt those men to the place of God. This inevitably leads to pain and disappointment. Paul and Barnabas did the right thing by shouting as loudly as possible, "We are only men!" It is time for many leaders and celebrities to follow their example, root out the religious hero worship, claim our humanity, and start sharing our own struggles—sin, depression, despair— to remind people we are all alike. Then we can focus on the one true God instead of His messengers.

---

[19]Then *unbelieving* Jews came from Antioch and Iconium and *incited the crowds against the Lord's emissaries.* The crowds turned on Paul, stoned him, dragged him out of the city, and left him there, thinking he was dead. [20]As the disciples gathered around him, he suddenly rose to his feet and returned to the city. The next day he and Barnabas left for Derbe. [21]After they proclaimed the good news there and taught many disciples, they returned to *some of the cities they had recently visited*—Lystra, Iconium, and Antioch *in Pisidia.* [22]In each place, they brought strength to the disciples, encouraging them to remain true to the faith.

Paul and Barnabas: We must go through many persecutions as we enter the kingdom of God.

23In each church, they would appoint leaders, pray and fast together, and entrust them to the Lord in whom they had come to believe.

24They then passed through Pisidia and came to Pamphylia. 25They preached their message in Perga and then went to the port of Attalia. 26There they set sail for Antioch, where they were first entrusted to the grace of God for the mission they had now completed. 27They called the church together when they arrived and reported all God had done with *and through* them, how God had welcomed outsiders through the doorway of faith. 28They stayed with the disciples *in Antioch* for quite a while.

15 *Their peace was disturbed, however,* when certain Judeans came with this teaching: "Unless you are circumcised according to Mosaic custom, you cannot be saved." 2Paul and Barnabas argued against this teaching and debated with the Judeans vehemently, so the church selected several people—including Paul and Barnabas—to travel to Jerusalem to dialogue about this issue with the apostles and elders there. 3The church sent them on their way. They passed through Phoenicia and Samaria, stopping to report to the groups of believers there that outsiders were now being converted. This brought great joy to them all. 4Upon arrival in Jerusalem, the church, the apostles, and the elders welcomed them warmly; and they reported all they had seen God do. 5But there were some believers present who belonged to the sect of the Pharisees. They stood up and asserted,

Pharisees: *No, this is not acceptable.* These people must be circumcised, and we must require them to keep the whole Mosaic law.

6The apostles and elders met privately to discuss how this issue should be resolved. 7There was a lot of debate, and finally Peter stood up.

These debates give a glimpse of the cultural tensions present between Jewish and Gentile believers throughout the New Testament writings. The early Jewish believers still follow the traditional Jewish practices of Sabbath rest and kosher food. This is fine, until Jewish and Gentile Christians must share a table. How can they be truly unified as one church without being able to sit down together for a meal? This council affirms—under the influence of the Spirit's work—that the outsiders may become Christians without becoming Jews first; but the outsiders should respect their Jewish brothers' beliefs so they can fellowship together. The decision is a model for church unity: artificial hurdles should not be imposed for inclusion, but groups should willingly sacrifice their freedoms to promote unity in the church.

Peter: My brothers, you all know that in the early days *of our movement,* God decided that I should be the one through whom the first outsiders would hear the good news and become believers. 8God knows the human heart, and He showed approval of their hearts by giving them the Holy Spirit just as He did for us. 9In cleansing their hearts by faith, God has made no distinction between them and us. 10So it makes no sense to me that some of you are testing God by burdening His disciples with a load that neither our forefathers nor we have been able to carry. 11No, we all believe that we will be liberated through the grace of the Lord Jesus—they also will be rescued in the same way.

12There was silence among them while Barnabas and Paul reported all the miraculous signs and wonders God had done through them among outsiders. 13When they finished, James spoke.

James: My brothers, hear me. 14Simon *Peter* reminded us how God first included outsiders in His favor, taking people from among them for His name. 15This resonates with the words of the prophets:

16"After this, I will return
    and rebuild the house of David, which
        has fallen into ruins.
    From its wreckage I will rebuild it;

17So all the nations may seek the Eternal
One—
including every person among the
outsiders who has been called by
My name."*
This is the word of the Lord, 18who has
been revealing these things since
ancient times.*

19So here is my counsel: we should not
burden these outsiders who are turning
to God. 20We should instead write a letter, instructing them to abstain from four
things: first, things associated with idol
worship; second, sexual immorality; third,
food killed by strangling; and fourth, blood.
21My reason for these four exceptions is
that in every city there are Jewish communities where, for generations, the laws
of Moses have been proclaimed; and on
every Sabbath, Moses is read in synagogues
everywhere.

22This seemed like a good idea to the apostles, the elders, and the entire church. They
commissioned men from among them and
sent them to Antioch with Paul and Barnabas. They sent two prominent men among
the believers, Judas (also known as Barsabbas) and Silas, 23to deliver this letter:

The brotherhood, including the apostles
and elders in Jerusalem, send greetings
to the outsider believers in Antioch,
Syria, and Cilicia. 24We have heard
that certain people from among us—
without authorization from us—have
said things that, in turn, upset you and
unsettle your minds. 25We have decided
unanimously to choose and send two
representatives, along with our beloved
Barnabas and Paul 26who, as you know,
have risked their lives for our Lord
Jesus the Anointed. 27These representatives, Judas and Silas, will confirm
verbally what you will read in this letter.
28It has seemed good to the Holy Spirit
and to us to keep you free from all burdens except these four: 29abstain from
anything sacrificed to idols, from blood,
from food killed by strangling, and from
sexual immorality. Avoid these things,
and you will be just fine. Farewell.

30So the men were sent to Antioch.
When they arrived, they gathered the community together and read the letter. 31The

community rejoiced at the resolution to the
controversy. 32Judas and Silas, being prophets themselves, offered lengthy encourage-
ments to strengthen the believers. 33After
some time there, their mission was complete;
so the leaders in Antioch released Judas and
Silas to return to Jerusalem with a blessing
of peace. [34But after some thought, Silas
decided to remain behind.]* 35Paul and Barnabas stayed in Antioch, where they teamed
with many others to teach and preach the
message of the Lord.

36Some days later, Paul proposed
another journey to Barnabas.

Paul: Let's return and visit the believers in
each city where we preached the Lord's
message last time to see how they're doing.

37Barnabas agreed and wanted to bring
John Mark along, 38but Paul felt that was a
mistake since John Mark had abandoned
them in Pamphylia and hadn't finished the
previous mission. 39Their difference of opinion was so heated that they decided not to
work together anymore. Barnabas took John
Mark and sailed to Cyprus, 40while Paul
chose Silas as his companion. The believers
in Antioch commissioned him for this work,
entrusting him to the grace of the Lord.
41They traveled through Syria and Cilicia to
strengthen the churches there.

16 1-3When Paul reached Derbe and
Lystra, he invited a disciple named
Timothy to join him and Silas.
Timothy had a good reputation among the
believers in Lystra and Iconium, but there
was a problem: although Timothy's mother
was a believing Jew, his father was Greek,
which meant Timothy was uncircumcised.
Because the Jewish people of those cities
knew he was the son of a Greek man, Paul
felt it would be best for Timothy to be circumcised before proceeding.
4Leaving there, now accompanied by
Timothy, they delivered to the churches in
each town the decisions and instructions
given by the apostles and elders in Jerusalem. 5The churches were strengthened in the
faith by their visit and kept growing in numbers on a daily basis.
6They sensed the Holy Spirit telling
them not to preach their message in Asia at
this time, so they traveled through Phrygia

* 15:16-17 Amos 9:11-12   * 15:17-18 Isaiah 45:21   * 15:34 The earliest
manuscripts omit verse 34.

and Galatia. [7]They came near Mysia and planned to go into Bithynia, but again they felt restrained from doing so by the Spirit of Jesus. [8]So they bypassed Mysia and went down to Troas. [9]That night Paul had a vision in which a Macedonian man was pleading with him.

Macedonian Man: Come over to Macedonia! Come help us!

Luke now shifts his narration from impersonal observation to a first-person account of events because he has joined Paul, Silas, and Timothy.

[10]This vision convinced us all that God was calling us to bring the good news to that region. [11]We set sail from the port city of Troas, first stopping in Samothrace, then the next day in Neapolis, [12]finally arriving in Philippi, a Roman colony and one of Macedonia's leading cities. We stayed in Philippi for several days. [13]On the Sabbath day, we went outside the city walls to the nearby river, assuming that *some Jewish* people might be gathering for prayer. We found a group of women there, so we sat down and spoke to them. [14]One of them, Lydia, was *a business woman* originally from Thyatira. She made a living *buying and* selling fine purple fabric. She was a true worshiper of God and listened to Paul *with special interest.* The Lord opened her heart to take in the message with enthusiasm. [15]She and her whole household were ceremonially washed through baptism.*

Lydia: If you believe I'm truly faithful to the Lord, please, you must come and stay at my home.

We couldn't turn down her invitation. [16]One day, as we were going to the place set aside for prayer, we encountered a slave girl. She made a lot of money for her owners as a fortune-teller, assisted by some sort of occult spirit. [17]She began following us.

Slave Girl *(shouting):* These men are slaves like me, but slaves of the Most High God! They will proclaim to you the way of liberation!

[18]The next day as we passed by, she did the same thing—and again on the following days. One day Paul was really annoyed, so he turned and spoke to the spirit that was enslaving her.

Paul: I order you in the name of Jesus, God's Anointed: Come out of her!

It came right out. [19]But when her owners realized she would be worthless now as a fortune-teller, they grabbed Paul and Silas, dragged them into the open market area, and presented them to the authorities.

Slave Owners: [20]These men are troublemakers, disturbing the peace of our great city. They are from some Jewish sect, [21]and they promote foreign customs that violate our Roman standards of conduct.

[22]The crowd joined in with insults and insinuations, prompting the city officials to strip them naked *in the public square* so they could be beaten with rods. [23]They were flogged mercilessly and then were thrown into a prison cell. The jailer was ordered to keep them under the strictest supervision. [24]The jailer complied, first restraining them in ankle chains, then locking them in the most secure cell in the center of the jail.

[25]*Picture this:* It's midnight. *In the darkness of their cell,* Paul and Silas—*after surviving the severe beating—aren't moaning and groaning;* they're praying and singing hymns to God. The prisoners *in adjoining cells are wide awake,* listening to them pray and sing. [26]Suddenly the ground begins to shake, and the prison foundations begin to crack. You can hear the sound of jangling chains and the squeak of cell doors opening. Every prisoner realizes that his chains have come unfastened. [27]The jailer wakes up and runs into the jail. His heart sinks as he sees the doors have all swung open. He is sure his prisoners have escaped, *and he knows this will mean death for him,* so he pulls out his sword to commit suicide. [28]At that moment, Paul *sees what is happening and* shouts out at the top of his lungs,

Paul: *Wait, man!* Don't harm yourself! We're all here! *None of us has escaped.*

[29]The jailer sends his assistants to get some torches and rushes into the cell of Paul and

* 16:15 Literally, immersed, in a rite of initiation and purification

Silas. He falls on his knees before them, trembling. [30]Then he brings them outside.

Jailer: Gentlemen, please tell me, what must I do to be liberated?

Paul and Silas: [31]Just believe—believe in the ultimate King, Jesus, and not only will you be rescued, but your whole household will as well.

[32-34]The jailer brings them to his home, and they have a long conversation with the man and his family. Paul and Silas explain the message of Jesus to them all. The man washes their wounds and *feeds them*, then they baptize* the man and his family. The night ends with Paul and Silas in the jailer's home, sharing a meal together, the whole family rejoicing that they have come to faith in God.

[35]At dawn the city officials send the police *to the jailer's home* with a command: "Let those men go free."

Jailer: [36]The city officials have ordered me to release you, so you may go now in peace.

Paul (*loud enough that the police can hear*): [37]Just a minute. This is unjust. We've been *stripped naked*, beaten in public, and thrown into jail, all without a trial of any kind. Now they want to release us secretly as if nothing happened? No way: we're Roman citizens—*we shouldn't be treated like this*! If the city officials want to release us, then they can come and tell us to our faces.

[38]The police report back to the city officials; and when they come to the part about Paul and Silas being Roman citizens, the officials turn pale with fear. [39]They rush to the jail in person and apologize. They personally escort Paul and Silas from their cell and politely ask them to leave the city. [40]Paul and Silas oblige—after stopping at Lydia's home to gather with the brothers and sisters there and give them parting words of encouragement.

Paul and Silas are keeping a low profile in order to advance the cause of Jesus. Paul's first miracle in the area is to cast out an evil spirit from a girl. This sets off an unexpected chain of events bringing the men into the city court to be beaten before the crowds. This sounds like the start of a very bad day. Silas must wonder, "Paul, what were you doing? Is your aggravation with this wandering girl worth all this trouble?" But they neither fight nor despair; instead, they sing, pray to God, and love their captors. Paul and Silas demonstrate that believers are not easily distracted or depressed as long as serving God is their priority.

---

17 After *leaving Philippi and* passing through Amphipolis and Apollonia, Paul and Silas came to Thessalonica. There was a Jewish synagogue there. [2-3]As he had done in other cities, Paul attended the synagogue and presented arguments, based on the Hebrew Scriptures, that the Anointed had to suffer and rise from the dead.

Paul: Who is this suffering and rising Anointed One I am proclaiming to you? He is Jesus.

He came back the next two Sabbaths—repeating the same pattern. [4]Some of the *ethnically Jewish* people *from the synagogue* were persuaded and joined Paul and Silas. Even more devout Greeks *who had affiliated with Judaism* came to believe—along with quite a few of the city's leading women. [5-6]*Seeing this movement growing,* the unconvinced Jewish people became protective and angry. They found some ruffians hanging out in the marketplaces and convinced them to help start a riot. Soon a mob formed, *and the whole city was seething with tension.* The mob was *going street by street,* looking for Paul and Silas—who were nowhere to be found. Frustrated, when the mob came to the house of a man named Jason, *now known as a believer*, they grabbed him and some other believers they found there and dragged them to the city officials.

Mob: These people—they're *political agitators* turning the world upside down! They've come here to our fine city, [7]and this man, Jason, has given them sanctuary *and made his house a base for their*

* 16:32-34 Literally, immerse, in a rite of initiation and purification

operations. We want to expose their real intent: they are trying to overturn Caesar's sensible decrees. They're saying that Jesus is king, *not Caesar!*

[8]Of course, this disturbed the crowd at large and the city officials especially, [9]so they demanded bail from Jason and the others before releasing them.

[10]The believers waited until dark and then sent Paul and Silas off to Berea. When they arrived, they went to the synagogue.

Though Paul is known as the Emissary to the Gentiles, wherever he goes he proclaims Jesus to the Jews in the synagogue from the Hebrew Scriptures first.

[11]The Jewish people here were more receptive than they had been in Thessalonica. They warmly and enthusiastically welcomed the message and then, day by day, would check for themselves to see if what they heard *from Paul and Silas* was truly in harmony with the Hebrew Scriptures. [12]Many of them were convinced, and the new believers included—*as in Thessalonica*—quite a few of the city's leading Greek women and important men also. [13]Reports got back to Thessalonica that Paul and Silas were now spreading God's message in Berea; the Jewish people who had incited the riot in Thessalonica quickly came to Berea to do the same once again. [14-15]The believers sent Paul away. A small group escorted him, first to the coast, and then all the way to Athens. Silas and Timothy, however, remained in Berea. Later they received instructions from Paul to join him in Athens as soon as possible.

[16]So Paul found himself alone for some time in Athens. He would walk through the city, feeling deeply frustrated about the abundance of idols there. [17]*As in the previous cities,* he went to the synagogue. Once again, he engaged in debate *about Jesus* with both ethnic Jews and devout *Greek-born* converts *to Judaism.* He would even wander around in the marketplace, speaking with anyone he happened to meet. [18]Eventually he got into a debate with some Epicurean and Stoic philosophers. Some were dismissive from the start.

Philosophers: What's this fast-talker trying to pitch?

Others: He seems to be advocating the gods of distant lands.

They said this because of what Paul had been preaching about Jesus and the resurrection.

The philosophers misunderstand Paul's message. They think he is talking about two deities: Jesus and Anastasis (the Greek word for "resurrection").

[19-21]This stirred their curiosity, because the favorite pastime of Athenians (including foreigners who had settled there) was conversation about new and unusual ideas. So they brought him to the *rock outcropping known as the* Areopagus, *where Athens' intellectuals regularly gathered for debate,* and they invited him to speak.

Athenians: May we understand this new teaching of yours? It is intriguingly unusual. We would love to know its meaning.

Paul: [22]Athenians, *as I have walked your streets,* I have observed your strong and diverse religious ethos. You truly are a religious people. [23]I have stopped again and again to examine carefully the religious statues and inscriptions that fill your city. On one such altar, I read this inscription: "TO AN UNKNOWN GOD." I am not here to tell you about a strange foreign deity, but about this One whom you already worship, though without full knowledge. [24]This is the God who made the universe and all it contains, the God who is the King of all heaven and all earth. It would be illogical to assume that a God of this magnitude could possibly be contained in any manmade structure, no matter how majestic. [25]Nor would it be logical to think that this God would need human beings to provide Him with food and shelter—after all, He Himself would have given to humans everything they need—life, breath, *food, shelter, and so on.*

This is the only universal God, the One who makes all people whatever their nationality or culture or religion.

[26]This God made us in all our diversity from one original person, allowing each culture to have its own time to develop,

giving each its own place to live and thrive in its distinct ways. ²⁷*His purpose in all this was* that people *of every culture and religion* would search for this ultimate God, grope for Him *in the darkness, as it were,* hoping to find Him. Yet, in truth, God is not far from any of us. ²⁸For *you know the saying,* "We live in God; we move in God; we exist in God." And still another said, "We are indeed God's children." ²⁹*Since this is true,* since we are indeed offspring of God's creative act, we shouldn't think of the Deity as our own artifact, something made by our own hands—as if this great, universal, ultimate Creator were simply a combination of elements like gold, silver, and stone. ³⁰No, God has patiently tolerated this kind of ignorance in the past, but now God says it is time to rethink our lives *and reject these unenlightened assumptions.* ³¹He has fixed a day of accountability, when the whole world will be justly evaluated by a new, higher standard: *not by a statue,* but by a living man. God selected this man and made Him credible to all by raising Him from the dead.

³²When they heard that last phrase about resurrection from the dead, some shook their heads and scoffed, but others were even more curious.

Others: We would like you to come and speak to us again.

³³Paul left at that point, ³⁴but some people followed him and came to faith, including one from Areopagus named Dionysius, a *prominent* woman named Damaris, and others.

This exchange is the most potent example of cross-cultural evangelism in the Bible. Paul provokes his audience to think and invites them to pursue God, but he does not attempt to summarize the gospel in simple propositions or acronyms. He connects their culture with the truth of the gospel and the beauty of the person who is Jesus. After that, it's the job of the Holy Spirit.

---

18 From Athens, Paul traveled to Corinth *alone.* ²He found a Jewish man there named Aquila, originally from Pontus. Aquila and his wife Priscilla had recently come to Corinth from Italy because Claudius had banished all Jews from Rome. Paul visited them *in their home* ³and discovered they shared the same trade of tent making. He then became their long-term guest and joined them in their tentmaking business. ⁴Each Sabbath he would engage both Jews and Greeks in debate in the synagogue in an attempt to persuade them of his message. ⁵Eventually Silas and Timothy left Macedonia and joined him in Corinth. They found him fully occupied by proclaiming the message, testifying to the Jewish people that Jesus was God's Anointed, *the Liberating King.* ⁶Eventually, though, some of them stopped listening and began insulting him. He shook the dust off his garments in protest.

Paul: OK. I've done all I can for you. You are responsible for your own destiny before God. From now on, I will bring the good news to the outsiders!

⁷He walked out of the synagogue and went next door to the home of *an outsider,* Titius Justus, who worshiped God. ⁸*Paul formed a gathering of believers there that included* Crispus (the synagogue leader) and his whole household and many other Corinthians who heard Paul, believed, and were ceremonially washed through baptism. ⁹One night Paul had a vision in which he heard the Lord's voice.

The Lord: Do not be afraid, Paul. Speak! Don't be silent! ¹⁰I am with you, and no one will lay a finger on you to harm you. I have many in this city who are already My people.

¹¹*After such turmoil in previous cities,* these words encouraged Paul to extend his stay in Corinth, teaching the message of God among them for a year and six months.

Paul is no machine. He needs encouragement to faithfully pursue his calling in the face of persecution. While God allows Paul to experience serious persecution in many other cities, He spares him that trouble in Corinth even though the Jewish leaders still try to stir up the government officials against him. Paul knows that the greatest joys in life are found in passionately pursuing the dangerous mission of Jesus, and that God sustains His followers in good times and bad.

---

¹²During this time, some Jews organized an attack on Paul and made formal charges against him to Gallio, the proconsul of Achaia.

Jews: ¹³This man is convincing people to worship God in ways that contradict our Hebrew Scriptures.

Paul was about to speak, but Gallio spoke first.

Gallio: ¹⁴Look, if this were some serious crime, I would accept your complaint as a legitimate legal case, ¹⁵but this is just more of your typical Jewish squabbling about trivialities in your sacred literature. I have no interest in getting dragged into this kind of thing.

¹⁶So he threw out their case and drove them away from his bench. ¹⁷They were furious and seized Sosthenes, the synagogue official; then they beat him in front of the tribunal. Gallio just ignored them.

¹⁸At the end of 18 months, Paul said good-bye to the believers in Corinth. He wanted to travel to the east and south to Syria by ship; so, accompanied by Priscilla and Aquila, he went to the nearby port city of Cenchrea, where he fulfilled a vow he had made by cutting his hair. ¹⁹The three of them sailed east to Ephesus where Paul would leave Priscilla and Aquila. Paul again went to the synagogue where he dialogued with the Jews. ²⁰They were receptive and invited him to stay longer. But he politely declined.

Paul: ²¹⁻²²If God wills, I'll return at some point.

He caught a ship bound south and east for Caesarea by the sea. There he went up for a brief visit with the believers in the church at Jerusalem; then he headed north to Antioch. ²³He spent considerable time there and then left again, visiting city after city throughout Galatia and Phrygia, strengthening the disciples in each place.

²⁴Meanwhile, back in Ephesus, a Jew named Apollos made contact with the community of believers. He had been raised in Alexandria.

In Alexandria, Egyptian Jews such as Philo are known for seeking to integrate Greek philosophy with their faith.

Apollos was eloquent and well educated in the Hebrew Scriptures. ²⁵He was partially instructed in the way of the Lord, and he added to his native eloquence a burning enthusiasm to teach about Jesus. He taught accurately what he knew; but he had only understood part of the good news, specifically the ritual cleansing through baptism* preached by John, the forerunner of Jesus. ²⁶So, when Priscilla and Aquila heard him speak boldly in the synagogue, they discerned both his gift and his lack of full understanding. They took him aside and in private explained the way of God to him more accurately and fully. ²⁷He wanted to head west into Achaia, where Paul had recently been, to preach there. The believers encouraged him to do so and sent a letter instructing the Greek disciples to welcome him. Upon his arrival, he was of great help to all in Achaia who had, by the grace of God, become believers. ²⁸This gifted speaker publicly demonstrated, based on the Hebrew Scriptures, that the promised Anointed One is Jesus. Then, when the Jews there raised counterarguments, he refuted them with great power.

19 ¹,⁷While Apollos was in Corinth, Paul's overland journey brought him back to Ephesus. He encountered a group of about a dozen disciples there.*

Paul: ²Did you receive the Holy Spirit when you became believers?

John's Disciples: We've never heard about the Holy Spirit.

* 18:25 Literally, immersion, an act to show repentance
* 19:1,7 Verses 1 and 7 have been combined to help the reader understand the continuity of the passage.

Paul: [3]Well then, what kind of ceremonial washing through baptism* did you receive?

John's Disciples: We received the ritual cleansing of baptism* that John taught.

Paul: [4]John taught the truth—that people should be baptized with renewed thinking and turn toward God. But he also taught that the people should believe in the One whose way he was preparing, that is, Jesus the Anointed.

[5]As soon as they heard this, they were baptized, this time in the name of our Lord Jesus. [6]When Paul laid his hands on them, the Holy Spirit came upon them *in the same way the original disciples experienced at Pentecost*: they spoke in tongues and prophesied.

V

Both Apollos and this small band of John's disciples hear an incomplete gospel. The church is called not only to bring the gospel to those who have never heard, but also to expand the truth to those who understand only partial truth. All people are on a journey to know God—no one has "arrived." Everyone has something more to learn because the truth constantly reveals itself.

---

[8]For three months, Paul continued his standard practice: he went *week by week* to the synagogue, speaking with great confidence, arguing with great persuasiveness, proclaiming the kingdom of God. [9-10]*Once again*, some members of the synagogue refused to believe and insulted the Way* publicly before the whole synagogue community. Paul withdrew and took those with him who had become disciples. For the next two years, he used the public lecture hall of Tyrannus, presenting the Word of the Lord every day, debating with all who would come. As a result, everyone in the region, whether Jews or Greeks, heard the message. [11]Meanwhile, God did amazing miracles through Paul. [12]People would take a handkerchief or article of clothing that had touched Paul's skin and bring it to their sick *friends or relatives*, and the patients would be cured of their diseases or released from the evil spirits that oppressed them.

[13-14]Some itinerant Jewish exorcists *noticed Paul's success in this regard, so they* tried to use the name of Jesus, the King, in an exorcism they were performing.

Imagine this: There are seven of them, all sons of a Jewish chief priest named Sceva, *gathered around a demonized man in a house.*

One of the Jewish Exorcists: I command you to depart, by the Jesus proclaimed by Paul!

Evil Spirit: [15]Jesus I know. Paul I know. But who are you?

[16]Then the man leaps up, attacks them all, rips off their clothing, and beats them so badly that they run out of the house stark naked and covered in bruises.
[17]Word of this strange event spread throughout Ephesus among both Jews and Greeks. Everyone was shocked and realized that the name of Jesus was indeed powerful and praiseworthy. [18]As a result, a number of people involved *in various occult practices* came to faith. They confessed their secret practices and rituals. [19]Some of them had considerable libraries about their magic arts; they piled up their books and burned them publicly. Someone estimated the value of the books to be 50,000 silver coins. [20]Again, word spread, and the message of the Lord overcame resistance and spread powerfully.
[21]Eventually Paul felt he should move on again. The Holy Spirit confirmed that he should first travel through Macedonia and Achaia and then return to Jerusalem.

Paul: I must eventually see Rome.

[22]So he sent Timothy and Erastus, two of his helpers, ahead to Macedonia while he stayed a while longer in Asia. [23]It was during this time that a major incident occurred involving the Way.

In most cities, the Jews stand in opposition to the Way; but in this instance, the outsiders cause the disturbance.

---

* 19:3 Literally, immersion, a rite of initiation and purification
* 19:3 Literally, immersion, an act to show repentance   * 19:9-10 The Christian movement (9:2)

²⁴An idol maker named Demetrius had a profitable business, for himself and for others, making silver shrines for Artemis (*also known as Diana by the Romans*), *one of the deities worshiped in Ephesus.*

²⁵*Picture this:* Demetrius calls a meeting of all the artisans who are similarly employed in idol making. *Everyone in the idol industry comes together.*

Demetrius: Men, we are all colleagues in this fine line of work. We're making a good living doing what we're doing. But we'd better wake up, or we're all going to go broke. ²⁶You've heard about this fellow Paul. Here in Ephesus, he's already convinced a large number of people to give up using idols. He tells them that our products are worthless. He's been doing this same kind of thing almost everywhere in Asia. ²⁷It's bad enough that he is slandering our fine and honorable profession, *but do you see where this will lead?* If his lies catch on, the temple of Artemis itself will be called a fraud. The great goddess of our region, the majestic deity who is revered here in Asia and around the world, will be disgraced.

²⁸The crowd goes wild with rage. They start chanting.

Crowd: Great is Artemis of the Ephesians! *Great is Artemis of the Ephesians!*

²⁹Soon the whole city is filled with confusion, and a mob forms. They find Paul's Macedonian travel companions, Gaius and Aristarchus, and drag them to the theater. ³⁰Paul wants to go confront the crowd *and protect his friends,* but the disciples hold him back. ³¹Even some provincial officials of Asia who are friendly to Paul send him an urgent message, warning him to stay away from the theater.

³²Enraged voices are shouting *on top of each other,* some saying one thing, some saying something else. The crowd is completely out of control. Most of the people don't even know what caused the commotion in the first place. ³³Some of the Jewish people push a man named Alexander to the front of the crowd, hoping he can calm the disturbance. He raises his hands to silence the crowd and gets a few sentences out; ³⁴but then the crowd realizes he's a Jew, and once again they start chanting.

Crowd: Great is Artemis of the Ephesians!

For two solid hours they keep the chant going. ³⁵Finally the town clerk manages to calm the crowd.

Town Clerk: My fellow citizens of Ephesus, everyone in the world knows that our great city is the caretaker of the temple of Artemis! Everyone knows that we are the home of the great statue that fell from heaven! ³⁶Our status as the economic center of the idolmaking industry is not in danger, so please, calm down. Don't do anything rash. ³⁷The men whom you have seized aren't temple robbers, nor have they blasphemed our great goddess. ³⁸If Demetrius and the artisans who share his important trade have a legal complaint, don't bring it here to the theater; take it to the courts—they're open today. ³⁹If you need to charge someone with a crime or launch an inquiry, take the matter to the regional judges. ⁴⁰We need to do this according to regulations, or we'll all be charged with rioting. This kind of behavior can't be justified.

⁴¹So he succeeds in dispersing the crowd.

V

The message of Jesus not only has the power to annihilate economic supremacy, but also turns the world upside down in the process. In the kingdom of God, a worker is always paid a wage worthy of his work: anyone who works has enough to eat, and no one is left out of the profitable bounty of God. No longer do businesses profit from dishonesty, manipulation, or selfishness.

---

20 As soon as the uproar ended, Paul gathered the disciples together, encouraged them once more, said farewell, and left *on foot.* He decided to pass through Macedonia, ²encouraging believers wherever he found them, and came to Greece. ³He spent three months there, and then he planned to set sail once again for Syria. But he learned that a group of Jewish opponents was plotting to kill him, so he decided to travel through Macedonia.

4-5*There was a large group of us traveling with him at this time, and we decided it was best, in light of the plot, to split up and then reunite in the city of Troas.* This group included Paul, a Berean named Sopater (son of Pyrrhus), two Thessalonians named Aristarchus and Secundus, a Derbean named Gaius, two Asians named Tychicus and Trophimus, and Timothy. 6Some of us waited until the Days of Unleavened Bread were over; then we went to Philippi where we boarded a ship for Troas. The other group left immediately *on foot, passing through Macedonia.* When my group landed in Troas five days later, Paul's group had already arrived. We stayed in Troas another week.

7-8The Sunday night before our Monday departure, we gathered to celebrate the breaking of bread.

Many wondrous events happen as Paul travels, ministering among the churches. One evening a most unusual event occurs.

Imagine you are celebrating with them:
    We are in an upstairs room, with *the gentle light and shadows cast by* several lamps. Paul is carrying on an extended dialogue with the believers, taking advantage of every moment since we plan to leave at first light. The conversation stretches on until midnight. 9A young fellow named Eutychus, *seeking some fresh air,* moves to an open window. Paul keeps on talking. Eutychus perches in the open window itself. *Paul keeps talking.* Eutychus drifts off to sleep. *Paul continues talking* until Eutychus, now overcome by deep sleep, drops out of the window and falls three stories to the ground, where he is found dead. 10Paul joins us downstairs, bends over, and takes Eutychus in his arms.

Paul: It's OK. He's alive again.

11Then Paul goes back upstairs, celebrates the breaking of bread, and—*just as you might guess*—keeps on conversing until first light. Then he leaves. 12(I should add that Eutychus had been taken home *long before,* his friends more than a little relieved that the boy was alive!)

This may be one of the strangest stories ever told. Paul was talking

about faith while one young man dozed off and fell out the window. Many a pastor has secretly prayed that slumbering congregants would fall out of their chairs. It might have been funny had he not died; instead, it was a scene of great horror. That is, until God used Paul to turn horror into celebration with a death-defying miracle. But the people were so enamored with Paul's teaching about Jesus that they returned to their conversations, which continued until sunrise.

13Again Paul wanted us to split up. He wanted to go by land by himself while we went by ship to Assos. 14There he came on board with us, and we sailed on to Mitylene. 15From there we sailed near Chios, passing by it the next day, docking briefly at Samos the day after that, then arriving at Miletus the following day. 16This route kept us safely out of Ephesus and didn't require Paul to spend any time at all in Asia, since he wanted to arrive in Jerusalem quickly—before Pentecost, he hoped.
    17In Miletus he sent word to the church in Ephesus, asking the elders to come down to meet with him. 18When they arrived, he talked with them.

Paul: We will have many memories of our time together in Ephesus; *but of all the memories, most of all I want you to remember my way of life.* From the first day I arrived in Asia, 19I served the Lord with humility and tears, patiently enduring the many trials that came my way through the plots of my Jewish opponents. 20I did everything I could to help you; I held nothing back. I taught you publicly, and I taught you in your homes. 21I told everyone the same message—Jews and Greeks alike—that we must turn toward God and have faith in our Lord Jesus the Anointed. 22Now I feel that the Holy Spirit has taken me captive. I am being led to Jerusalem. My future is uncertain, 23but I know—the Holy Spirit has told me—that everywhere I go from now on, I will find imprisonment and persecution waiting for me. 24*But that's OK. That's no tragedy for me because* I don't cling to my life for my own sake. The only value I place on my life is that I may finish my race, that I may fulfill the ministry that Jesus our King has given me, that I may gladly tell the good news of God's grace. [25]I now realize that this is our last good-bye. *You have been like family* in all my travels to proclaim the kingdom of God, but after today none of you will see my face again. [26]So I want to make this clear: I am not responsible for your destiny from this point on [27]because I have not held back from telling you the purpose of God in all its dimensions.

[28]*Here are my instructions:* diligently guard yourselves, and diligently guard the whole flock over which the Holy Spirit has given you oversight. Shepherd the church of God, this precious church which He made His own through the blood of His own Son. [29]I know that after I've gone, dangerous wolves will sneak in among you, savaging the flock. [30]Some of you here today will begin twisting the truth, enticing disciples to go your way, to follow you. [31]You must be on guard, and you must remember *my way of life among you.* For three years, I have kept on, persistently warning everyone, day and night, with tears.

[32]So now I put you in God's hands. I entrust you to the message of God's grace, a message that has the power to build you up and to give you rich heritage among all who are set apart for God's holy purposes. [33]*Remember my example:* I never once coveted a single coin of silver or gold. I never looked twice at someone's fine clothing. [34]No, you know this: I worked with my own two hands *making tents*, and I paid my own expenses and my companions' expenses as well. [35]This is my last gift to you, this example of a way of life: a life of hard work, a life of helping the weak, a life that echoes every day those words of Jesus our King, who said, "It is more blessed to give than to receive."

[36]*Once again, imagine this scene:*

As Paul finishes speaking, he kneels down; and we all join him, kneeling. He prays, and we all join him, praying. [37]There's the sound of weeping, and then more weeping, and then more still. One by one, we embrace Paul and kiss him, [38]our sadness multiplied because of his words about this being our last good-bye. We walk with him to the ship, *and he sets sail.*

The last words of Paul to his Ephesian disciples are emotional, inspiring, but unbelievably arrogant. Who would place himself on a pedestal and encourage everyone to be more like him? It sounds like a cult of personality, but it is not. Paul understands that the gospel must be incarnate; it is more than a set of ideas, so someone must demonstrate how to walk the path of faith. He calls them to watch him carefully and emulate his behavior: watch how I treat people, how I eat, what I say, the way I give; and do likewise. If all believers could possess the same boldness to say, "do as I do," then the world would be a better place. Believers would not just speak the good news; they would live the good news.

21 Cos was our next stop, and the next day, Rhodes, and the next, Patara. [2]We found another ship in Patara that would take us *south and east* toward Phoenicia. [3]We saw Cyprus to our left and sailed on to Syria, landing at Tyre where the ship had cargo to unload. [4]We found the disciples there and stayed with them for seven days. The Spirit moved them to tell Paul not to go on to Jerusalem; [5]but the day came for our departure, and the whole community of disciples, including wives and children, escorted us outside the city. We knelt down together on the beach, prayed together, said farewell, and then parted company—[6]the disciples returning to their homes, we sailing on. [7]From Tyre we docked at Ptolemais where we met with the believers and spent a day with them. [8]Then we moved on to Caesarea. In Caesarea we stayed with Philip the evangelist, one of the seven.* [9]His four virgin daughters lived with him, each having the gift of prophecy. [10]While we were with them, another gifted prophet named Agabus came *north* from Judea. [11]He took Paul's belt and used it to bind his own feet and hands.

Agabus: This is a message from the Holy Spirit: *unbelieving* Jews in Jerusalem will in this way bind the owner of this belt and will hand him over to the outsiders.

* 21:8 Acts 6:1-6; 8:4-40

Paul is a man of great mystery. This persecutor-turned-preacher seems more like a character from pages of fiction than the instigator of the spread of Christianity. He becomes what he once despised and willingly suffers on behalf of his new Savior. Paul is accused of many things, but he is no fool. He fully understands what is waiting for him in Jerusalem: persecution, suffering, and ultimately death. His friends beg him not to return to this holy city, but Paul is called to live in the footsteps of the One who was crucified—He who was destined to suffer yet called for no drugs. His suffering served a greater purpose, and Paul never loses sight of this spiritual reality because he is living in the kingdom of God.

The masses hope for a gospel that makes them happy, healthy, and wealthy. Jesus said the way of life is a hard road, with only a few on it. Ironically this hard road ends in life. The easy, broad street—which may be paved with good intentions—always leads to death and destruction.

---

¹²Now we all joined in imploring Paul—we, *his companions, and Philip and his daughters,* everyone present—begging him not to go one step closer to the city.

Paul: ¹³Please, you're breaking my heart with your tears! *I know exactly what I'm doing.* I'm fully prepared to be bound, and more— to die for the name of Jesus, the King.

¹⁴We realized our persuasion was fruitless, so we stopped pleading with him and simply said, "The Lord's will be done."

¹⁵So we knew what we were getting into as we prepared to ascend the foothills toward Jerusalem. ¹⁶Some of the disciples from Caesarea accompanied us and led us to the home of Mnason, a Cypriot and one of the first disciples, with whom we stayed. ¹⁷We continued on to Jerusalem and were welcomed warmly by the brothers there. ¹⁸The next day, we went together to visit James, and all the elders were there with him. ¹⁹Paul greeted them and then reported account after account of what God had done through him among the outsiders. ²⁰When they heard his story, they praised God.

James and the Elders: Brother, *we have a problem.* You can see that we have thousands of Jewish believers here, and all of them are zealous law keepers. ²¹They've heard all kinds of rumors about you—that you teach all the Jews living among the outside nations to forget about Moses entirely, that you tell believers not to circumcise their sons, that you teach them to abandon all our customs. ²²We need to deal with this situation, since word will spread that you're here in the city. ²³So here's what

we would like you to do. We have four men here who are fulfilling a vow. ²⁴Join them. Go through the rituals of purification with them. Pay for their heads to be shaved *according to our ritual.* That will show that the rumors are false and that you are still observing and upholding the law. ²⁵For the outside believers, we've already written in a letter our judgment on their situation: they should not eat food that has been sacrificed to idols, they should not eat meat with blood in it or meat from animals killed by strangulation, and they should abstain from all sexual misconduct.

²⁶Paul complied with their request. The very next day, he publicly joined the four men, completed the initial purification rites, entered the temple with them, and began the *seven-day* ritual purification process, after which a sacrifice would be made for each of them.

²⁷The seven days of purification were almost completed when some Jews from Asia recognized Paul in the temple. They grabbed him.

Asian Jews (*shouting*): ²⁸Help! Fellow Israelites! This man is an enemy of our people, *our religion,* our law, and this temple! He travels around the world subverting our holiest customs! He is at this moment desecrating this holy temple by bringing outsiders into this sacred place.

²⁹*In this accusation, they were confused*—they had seen Paul elsewhere in the city with Trophimus the Ephesian, and they assumed that one of his current companions was Trophimus. ³⁰*It was too late to clarify, though, because*

word spread and soon a huge crowd rushed to the temple. They held Paul and dragged him from the temple and shut the doors behind them. [31]*They beat Paul,* and it was clear they intended to kill him. By this time, word of the uproar reached the commandant of the Roman guard assigned to Jerusalem.

[32]He led a group of soldiers and officers to the scene. When the mob looked up and saw the soldiers running toward them, they stopped beating Paul. [33]The commandant took him into custody and ordered him to be bound with two chains. He conducted a preliminary interrogation—asking Paul's name, what he had done. [34]Members of the crowd were shouting over each other, and the tribune couldn't hear a thing, so he ordered Paul to be taken back to the barracks. [35]When they came to the steps leading down from the temple, the crowd was seething with such violence *toward Paul* that the soldiers had to pick him up and carry him. [36]Then the crowd followed.

Crowd: Away with him! *Away with him!*

[37]They were just leaving the temple area when Paul asked the commandant,

Paul: May I say something to you?

Commandant: Do you speak Greek? [38]We thought you were that Egyptian who recently stirred a rebellion and led 4,000 assassins out into the desert. *But if you speak Greek, then obviously you're not the person we supposed.*

Paul: [39]No, I'm a Jew, originally from Tarsus in Cilicia. I'm a citizen from an important city. Please, I beg you, let me speak to the people.

[40]The commandant agreed, and Paul stood there on the steps, motioning for the people to be silent. The crowd settled down, and Paul spoke in their native tongue, Aramaic.

22 Paul: Brothers and fathers, please let me defend myself against these charges.

[2]When they heard him speaking Aramaic, a hush came over the crowd.

Paul: [3]I am a Jew, born in Tarsus in Cilicia. I was raised here in Jerusalem and was tutored in the great school of Gamaliel. My education trained me in the strict interpretation of the law of our ancestors, and I grew zealous for God, just as all of you are today. [4]I encountered a movement known as the Way, *and I considered it a threat to our religion,* so I persecuted it violently. I put both men and women in chains, had them imprisoned, and would have killed them—[5]as the high priest and the entire council of elders will tell you. I received documentation from them to go to Damascus and work with the brothers there to arrest followers of the Way and bring them back to Jerusalem in chains so they could be properly punished. [6]I was on my way to Damascus. It was about noon. Suddenly a powerful light shone around me, [7]and I fell to the ground. A voice spoke: "Saul, Saul, why do you persecute Me?" [8]I answered, "Who are You, Lord?" The voice replied, "I am Jesus of Nazareth, the One you persecute."

[9]My companions saw the light, but they didn't hear the voice. [10]I asked, "What do You want me to do, Lord?" The Lord replied, "Get up and go to Damascus; you will be given your instructions there." [11]Since the intense light had blinded me, my companions led me by the hand into Damascus. [12]I was visited there by a devout man named Ananias, a law-keeping Jew who was well spoken of by all the Jews living in Damascus. [13]He said, "Brother Saul, regain your sight!" I could immediately see again, beginning with Ananias standing before me. [14]Then he said, "You have been chosen by the God of our ancestors to know His will, to see the Righteous One, and to hear the voice of God. [15]You will tell the story of what you have seen and heard to the whole world. [16]So now, don't delay. Get up, be ceremonially cleansed through baptism,* and have your sins washed away, as you call on His name *in prayer.*"

[17]I returned to Jerusalem, and I was praying here in the temple one day. I slipped into a trance [18]and had a vision in which Jesus said to me, "Hurry! Get out of Jerusalem fast! The people here will not receive your testimony about Me." [19]I replied, "But Lord, they all know that I went from synagogue to synagogue imprisoning and beating everyone who believed

* 22:16 Literally, immersed, in a rite of initiation and purification

These Jewish leaders are prepared to squabble with Paul about the law. But in his wisdom, Paul disarms them with his story. He is one of them; and on his journey to defend Judaism against these Christian heretics, he encountered the living God. How can anyone dispute his experience? He was trained by trustworthy Jews and lived his life according to their strict interpretation of the law. When Paul invites his audience into his experience with the supernatural, it makes debating the finer points of the law seem ridiculous. It would be like antagonizing Moses while he reiterated God's message heard through the burning bush. But prejudice is apparently stronger than any divine message. Paul has them hanging on to every word from his mouth, until he speaks of the outsiders. The crowd immediately rises from their silence into a furious rage. The message is clear—if your revelation extends beyond our people, we will hear nothing of it. How could all of these students of the Hebrew Scriptures have been so ignorant about God's intentions to rescue all people? The prophets declared God's plan to offer grace to Jews and non-Jews, but no one in this crowd considered that good news.

---

in You. ²⁰They know *what I was like and how I stood in approval of the execution of Stephen, Your witness, when he was stoned. I even held the coats of those who actually stoned him.*" ²¹Jesus replied, "Go, for I am going to send you to distant lands to teach the outsiders."

²²They were listening quietly up until he mentioned *the outsiders*.

Crowd (*shouting*): Away with him! Such a man can't be allowed to remain here. Kill him! He must die!

²³*Chaos broke out again.* People were shouting, slamming their coats down on the ground, and throwing fistfuls of dust up in the air. ²⁴The commandant ordered the soldiers to bring Paul to the barracks and flog him until he confessed to whatever he had done to stir up this outrage.

²⁵Back at the barracks, as they tied him up with leather thongs, Paul spoke to a nearby officer.

Paul: Is this legal—for you to flog a Roman citizen without a trial?

²⁶The officer went and spoke to the commandant.

Officer: What can you do about this? Did you know this fellow is a Roman citizen?

Commandant (*rushing to Paul's side*): ²⁷What's this? Are you really a Roman citizen?

Paul: Yes.

Commandant: ²⁸I paid a small fortune for my citizenship.

Paul: I was born a citizen.

²⁹Hearing this, those who were about to start the flogging pulled back, and the commandant was concerned because he had arrested and bound a citizen *without cause.* ³⁰He still needed to conduct an investigation to uncover the Jews' accusations against Paul. So the next day, he removed the ties on Paul and called a meeting with the chief priests and council of elders. He brought Paul in and had him stand before the group.

23 Paul stared at the council and spoke.

Paul: Brothers, I have always lived my life to this very day with a clear conscience before God.

²Ananias the high priest signaled those standing near Paul to hit him on the mouth.

Paul: ³You hypocrite! God will slap you! How dare you sit in judgment and claim to represent the law, while you violate the law by ordering me to be struck *for no reason*?

Bystanders: ⁴The nerve of you insulting the high priest of God!

Paul is brilliant. Accused by a group of religious intellectuals, he gets them fighting with one another. Paul understands the axiom, "The enemy of my enemy is my friend," so he picks a fight with the Sadducees knowing the rest of the room will defend him. The thing society opposes often defines it, so manipulation is easy. (Consider some of the conservative political pundits who have never espoused any inclination toward Christianity. They gain millions of Christian followers by opposing the political enemies of conservative Christians.) Paul embraces a similar strategy here—if he can get these guys to fight, they will forget why they are actually convening. In many ways, the culture war is equally distracting to the early church. In the middle of the Jews vs. Gentiles battle, the church is realizing believers are not here to fight about morality and culture, but to bring the kingdom of God to earth. His kingdom will not come by debate, but by the working of the Holy Spirit within the church.

Paul: [5]I'm sorry, my brothers. I didn't realize this was the high priest. The law warns us to not curse the ruler of the people.*

[6]Paul noticed that some members of the council were Sadducees and some were Pharisees, so he quickly spoke to the council.

Paul: Brothers, I am a Pharisee, born to a Pharisee. I am on trial because I have hope that the dead are raised!

[7]That got the two parties arguing with one another [8]because the Sadducees say there is no such thing as resurrection, heavenly messengers, or spirits, and the Pharisees believe in all three. [9]Soon these leaders were shouting, and some of the scholars from the party of the Pharisees rose to their feet.

Pharisees: There is nothing wrong with this man. Maybe he really has encountered a spirit or a heavenly messenger.

[10]The two parties were about to start throwing punches, and the commandant was afraid Paul would be torn to pieces, so he sent in his soldiers to intervene. They took Paul back into custody and returned him to their barracks. [11]That night the Lord came near and spoke to him.

The Lord: Keep up your courage, Paul! You have successfully told your story about Me in Jerusalem, and soon you will do the same in Rome.

[12-13]That morning a group of more than 40 Jewish opponents conspired to kill Paul. They bound themselves by an oath that they wouldn't eat or drink until he was dead.

[14]They told the chief priests and elders about their plan.

Jewish Opponents: We've made an oath not to eat or drink until this man is dead. [15]So you and the council must ask the commandant to bring Paul to meet with you. Tell him that you want to further investigate Paul's case. We'll get rid of the troublemaker on his way here.

[16]Now Paul had a nephew who heard about the planned ambush; he managed to gain entry into the barracks and alerted Paul. [17]Paul called one of the officers.

Paul: Take this young man to the commandant. He has news the commandant needs to hear.

[18]The officer took him to the commandant.

Officer: The prisoner named Paul asked me to bring this man to you. He has some kind of information.

[19]The commandant led him away so they could speak in private.

Commandant: What do you want to tell me?

Young Man: [20]The Jewish council is going to ask you to bring Paul down to the council tomorrow under the pretext that there will be a thorough examination. [21]But don't agree to do it, because 40 assassins have bound themselves to an oath not to eat or drink until they've killed Paul. Their plan is in motion, and they're simply waiting for you to play your part.

* 23:5 Exodus 22:28

[22]The commandant sent the young man home with these instructions: "Don't tell a soul that you've spoken with me." [23]Then he called for two officers.

Commandant: At nine o'clock tonight, you will leave for Caesarea with 200 soldiers, 70 horsemen, and 200 spearmen. [24]Have a mount for Paul to ride, and conduct him safely to Felix the governor.

[25]He wrote the following letter:

[26]*Commandant* Claudius Lysias greets his excellency, Felix, Governor. [27]The accompanying prisoner was seized by Jews who were about to kill him. I learned he was a Roman citizen and intervened with the guard here to protect him. [28]I arranged for a hearing before their council [29]and learned that he was accused for reasons relating to their religious law, but that he has done nothing deserving imprisonment or execution. [30]I was informed that a group was planning to assassinate him, so I sent him to you immediately. I will require his accusers to present their complaint before you.

[31]So the soldiers followed their orders and safely conducted Paul as far as Antipatris that night. [32-33]The next day, the horsemen conducted him on to Caesarea as the foot soldiers returned to the barracks. The horsemen delivered the letter and the prisoner to Felix who read the letter. [34]The only question Felix asked concerned the province of Paul's birth. When he learned Paul was from Cilicia, [35]he said,

Felix: As soon as your accusers arrive I will hear your case.

He placed Paul under guard within Herod's headquarters.

24 The high priest Ananias came north *to Caesarea* five days later, accompanied by some elders and an attorney named Tertullus. They explained their case to Felix *without Paul present*. [2]When Paul was brought in, Tertullus launched into an accusation.

Tertullus: Most Excellent Felix, through your esteemed leadership we have enjoyed a long and happy peace. Your foresight in governance has brought many reforms for the people I represent. [3]We always and everywhere welcome every thought of you with high and deep gratitude. [4]But knowing how busy you are and how limited your time must be, I beg you to hear us briefly present our case to you with the legendary graciousness for which you are known everywhere.

[5]Here are the facts: this man is a disease to the body politic. He agitates trouble in Jewish communities throughout our empire as a ringleader of the *heretical* sect known as the Nazarenes. [6]He even tried to desecrate the temple, so we seized him. [Our aim was to try him by the Jewish law, [7]but Commandant Lysias interfered and removed this man from our control. [8]Because of his meddling, you are now forced to hear those making the accusation.]* You will find, through your own examination, that everything we say of Paul is true.

[9]The Jewish opponents present added their vigorous testimony in support of the lawyer's opening statement. [10]The governor *didn't say anything, but he* motioned for Paul to speak.

Paul: I am happy now to make my defense to you, sir, knowing that you have been a judge over this nation for many years. [11]Just 12 days ago, I went up to Jerusalem to worship, as you can easily verify. [12]I wasn't arguing with anyone in the temple. I wasn't stirring up a crowd in any of the synagogues. I wasn't disturbing the peace of the city in any way. They did not find me doing these things in Jerusalem, [13]nor can they prove that I have done any of the things of which they have accused me. [14]But I can make this confession: I believe everything established by the Law and written in the Prophets, and I worship the God of our ancestors according to the Way, which they call a *heretical* sect.

[15]*Here is my crime:* I have a hope in God that there will be a resurrection of both the just and unjust, which my opponents also share. [16]Because of this hope, I always do my best to live with a clear conscience toward God and all people. [17]I have been away for several years, so recently I brought gifts for the poor of my nation and offered sacrifices. [18]When they found me, I was not disturbing anyone, nor was I

* 24:6-8 Some early manuscripts omit this portion.

gathering a crowd. No, I was quietly completing the rite of purification. Some Jews from Asia *are the ones who started the disturbance*—[19]and if they have an accusation, they should be here to make it. [20]If these men here have some crime they have found me guilty of when I stood before their council, they should present it. [21]Perhaps my crime is that I spoke this one sentence in my testimony before them: "I am on trial here today because I have hope that the dead are raised."

[22]Felix was quite knowledgeable about the Way. He adjourned the preliminary hearing.

Felix: When Lysias the commandant comes *to Caesarea,* I will decide your case.

[23]He then ordered the officer to keep Paul in custody, but to permit him some freedom and to allow any of his friends to take care of his needs.

[24]A few days later, Felix sent for Paul and gave him an opportunity to speak about faith in the Anointed One. Felix was accompanied by his wife Drusilla, who was Jewish. [25]As Paul spoke of justice, self-control, and the coming judgment, Felix became fearful.

Felix: That's enough for now. When I have time, I will send for you again.

[26]They had a number of conversations of this sort; *but Felix* actually was hoping that, by having frequent contact with him, Paul might offer him a bribe. [27]As a favor to the Jews, he did nothing to resolve the case and left Paul in prison for two years. Then Felix completed his assignment as governor, and Porcius Festus succeeded him.

V

There are rumors that a large sum of money is at Paul's disposal— that is, the relief offering for the church in Jerusalem. But Paul does not choose to buy his freedom. Despite the corruption of the government, Paul understands that ultimately his justice is in the hands of God. In the near future, he will appear before the government of Rome, and that encounter will likely lead to his death.

---

25 Three days after arriving in the province, Festus traveled south from Caesarea to Jerusalem. [2-3]The chief priests and Jewish leaders still had a plan to kill Paul and gave a report to Festus about their unresolved grievances against Paul. They suggested that as a favor to them, Festus should move Paul to Jerusalem. Of course, this was part of the plan to set an ambush for Paul and kill him en route. [4]Festus *instead offered to reopen the case.* He would be going back to Caesarea soon.

Festus: [5]So let your leaders accompany me, and bring your accusations against the man.

[6]Eight or ten days later, Festus returned to Caesarea, and the next day he took his seat in court. He ordered Paul to be brought before him. [7]The Jewish opponents from Jerusalem immediately surrounded Paul and from all directions bombarded him with all sorts of serious charges, none of which could be proven.

Paul (*quietly and simply*): [8]In no way have I committed any offense against Jewish law, against the Jewish temple and all it represents, or against the emperor.

[9]Here Festus saw an opportunity to do just the favor Paul's Jewish opponents had requested.

Festus: Would you like to have your trial in Jerusalem? I'd be willing to try your case there.

Paul: [10-11]If I had committed a capital offense, I would accept my punishment. But I'm sure it's clear to you that I have done no wrong to the Jews. Since their charges against me are completely empty, it would be wrong to turn me over to them. *No, I do not wish to go to Jerusalem.* I am appealing to the court of the emperor in Rome.

[12]Festus conferred privately with his council and returned with this decision:

Festus: You have appealed to the emperor, so to the emperor you will go.

[13]Several days later, the provincial king Agrippa arrived in Caesarea with *his wife* Bernice to welcome the new governor.

[14]Their visit lasted several days, which gave Festus the chance to describe Paul's case to the king.

Festus: Felix left me some unfinished business involving a prisoner *named Paul.* [15]When I was in Jerusalem, I got an earful about him from the chief priests and Jewish elders. They wanted me simply to decide against him, [16]but I informed them that we Romans don't work that way. We don't condemn a person accused of a crime unless the accusers present their case in person so the accused has ample opportunity to defend himself against the charge. [17]I arranged for them to come here for a proper hearing. In fact, the first day after I returned *to Caesarea,* I took my seat in court and heard his case without delay. [18]Contrary to my expectations, the accusers brought no substantial charges against him at all. [19]Instead, they were bickering about their own religious beliefs related to a fellow named Jesus, who had died, but whom Paul claimed was raised to life again. [20]I had no idea how to handle a religious squabble pretending to be a legal case, so I suggested Paul be taken to Jerusalem so he could be tried on Jewish turf, so to speak. [21]But Paul refused, and instead he appealed to be kept in custody so the case could be referred to his Imperial Majesty. So I have held him until we can arrange to send him to the emperor.

Agrippa: [22]This sounds interesting. I'd like to hear this fellow in person.

Festus: You will, then. We'll bring him in tomorrow.

[23]The next day, King Agrippa and Bernice arrived at the great hall with great formality, accompanied by the military commanders and the city's leading men. Festus ordered Paul to be brought before them.

Festus: [24]King Agrippa and all our honored guests, here is the man who has been charged with wrongdoing by the Jewish community—both in Jerusalem and here. They yelled for his execution, [25]but I found him guilty of no capital offense. Then he appealed to our Imperial Majesty, so I have agreed that he will be sent *to Rome.* [26-27]*Here is where I need your help.* I can't send a man to our emperor without a letter logically detailing the charges against him, but I have no idea what to write. So, King Agrippa, and all of you honored guests, I'm requesting your help in determining what to write in my letter to the emperor.

26

Agrippa *(to Paul):* Go ahead. You may speak for yourself.

Paul *(extending his hand):* [2]I am indeed fortunate to be standing before you, King Agrippa, to humbly defend myself against accusations from my Jewish opponents. [3]You are extraordinarily familiar with Jewish customs and controversies, so I beg your patience as I begin. [4]My way of life is well known to the whole Jewish community, how I have lived in the Jewish community abroad and in Jerusalem. [5]If they are willing to speak, they themselves will tell you something they have long known—that I was a member of the strictest sect of our religion and lived *for many years* as a Pharisee. [6]But now I am on trial here *for this simple reason:* I have hope. I have hope rooted in a promise God made to our ancestors. [7]All our twelve tribes have hope in this promise—they express their hope as they worship day and night. How strange it is, then, Your Excellency, that I am accused by the Jews of having hope! [8]Why would any of you think it is absurd to have hope that God raises the dead? [9]As you know, *we're talking specifically* about Jesus of Nazareth. For a long time, I was convinced that I should work against that name. [10]I opposed it in Jerusalem. I received authorization from the chief priests to lock many of His followers in prison. When they were threatened with execution, I voted against them. [11]I would find them in synagogues across Jerusalem and try to force them to blaspheme. My fury drove me to pursue them to foreign cities as well.

The importance of Paul's conversion experience on the way to Damascus is highlighted as he recounts it in his defense.

[12]On one occasion, I was traveling to Damascus, authorized and commissioned by the chief priests *to find and imprison more of His followers.* [13]It was about midday, Your Excellency, when I saw a light from heaven—brighter than the noonday

sun—shining around my companions and me. [14]We all fell to the ground *in fear*, and I then heard a voice. The words were in Aramaic: "Saul, Saul, why are you persecuting Me? When you kick against the cattle prods, you're only hurting yourself." [15]I asked, "Lord, who are You?" and the Lord answered, "I am Jesus, the One you are persecuting. [16]Get up now, and stand upright on your feet. I have appeared to you for a reason. I am appointing you to serve Me. You are to tell My story and how you have now seen Me, and you are to continue to tell the story in the future. [17]I will rescue you from your Jewish opponents and from the outsiders—for it is to the outsiders I am sending you. [18]It will be your mission to open their eyes so that they may turn from darkness to light and from the kingdom of Satan to the kingdom of God. This is so that they may receive forgiveness of all their sins and have a place among those who are set apart for a holy purpose through having faith in Me."

[19]King Agrippa, I did not disobey this vision from heaven. [20]I began in Damascus, then continued in Jerusalem, then throughout the Judean countryside, then among the outsiders—telling everyone they must turn from their past and toward God and align their deeds and way of life with this new direction. [21]So then, this is my crime. This is why my Jewish opponents seized me that day in the temple and tried to kill me. [22]God has helped me right up to this very moment, so I can stand here telling my story to both the humble and the powerful alike. I only say what the prophets and Moses said would happen—[23]that the Anointed One must suffer, and then, by being the first to rise from the dead, He would proclaim light to both Jews and outsiders.

Festus (*interrupting*): [24]You've gone crazy, Paul! You've read one book too many and have gone insane!

Paul: [25]No, most excellent Festus, I am not insane. I am telling the sane and sober truth. [26]The king understands what I'm talking about, which is why I could speak so freely to him. None of these things have been covered up and hidden away in a corner, so I'm sure none of these things have escaped his notice. [27]King Agrippa, do you believe the prophets? I know you must believe.

Agrippa: [28]Paul, have you so quickly moved on from defending yourself to trying to persuade me to become a Christian?

Paul: [29]Whether I have done so quickly or not, I pray to God that not only you but also everyone who is listening to me today might become what I am—minus these chains.

[30]The king stood to leave at this point, along with Festus, Bernice, and all those who had been seated; [31]and as they left, everyone was saying the same thing: "This man isn't doing anything deserving death—he shouldn't even be in prison."

Agrippa (*to Festus*): [32]This man could have been released completely if he had not appealed to the emperor.

V

At different points in Acts, Luke shows how the good news of Jesus challenges Greco-Roman culture and religion, but he also shows that Christianity is not subversive to the Roman government. These direct statements by Roman officials about Paul's innocence support this message. However, a challenge to culture and religion always ends up becoming a challenge to the government, as later Christians will learn.

---

27 The date was set for us to depart for Rome, and Paul and some other prisoners were transferred to the custody of a Roman officer named Julius, a member of the Augustan Division. [2]*I, Luke, was permitted to join Paul for his journey to Rome,* along with Aristarchus, a Macedonian brother from Thessalonica. We boarded a ship from Adramyttium that was stopping in ports along the coast of Asia. [3]We stopped the next day at Sidon, and Julius kindly allowed Paul to visit friends and be taken care of by them. [4]We sailed from there north of Cyprus because the winds were unfavorable. [5]We passed Cilicia and Pamphylia *on our right* and then came to Myra in Lycia. [6]There Julius found a ship from Alexandria heading directly to Italy, to which we transferred. [7]The winds were still contrary, so we made slow progress for a number of days and with difficulty passed Cnidus and sailed south toward Crete and past Cape Salmone *on its eastern end.* [8]Sailing conditions were adverse to say the least. Finally we came to a place called Fair Havens, near the city of Lasea *on the south coast of Crete.* [9]We had lost a lot of time already—it was *late in the year for sailing*—following the Day of Atonement, and conditions had deteriorated from adverse to dangerous. Paul tried to warn those in charge.

Paul: [10]Sirs, if we proceed, I can see that our voyage will be dangerous and will involve heavy loss, not only of cargo, but of the ship itself; not only of the ship, but also of our lives.

[11]But the officer ignored Paul and instead trusted the ship's pilot and owner who felt they could proceed.

[12]*We had two choices.* We could anchor in the harbor at Fair Havens and spend the winter, or we could proceed *west along the coastline,* hoping to reach Phoenix and wait there for calmer spring weather. *Fair Havens* was not a good option, though, being vulnerable to winter storms; so most of us agreed we should try to reach Phoenix, whose harbor was more protected. [13]One day a moderate south wind began to blow, which made an attempt possible. We weighed anchor and sailed *west,* staying near shore. [14]*Then things got scary.* A violent northeaster, the Euraquilo, blew down across Crete. [15]We were caught. We couldn't turn and sail into this fierce wind, so we had no choice but to let it drive us. [16]We briefly found a bit of shelter from the wind near the island of Clauda. We had been having trouble securing the ship's lifeboat; [17]but we were able there to hoist it up and send down cables to brace the hull, *which was in danger of breaking apart under the strain of the storm. The wind was relentless, and* soon we were again being driven *southwest at the mercy of the storm.* We feared it would drive us all the way to the Syrtis Banks, *down near the North African coast,* so we threw out the sea anchor to slow us down. [18]All through the night, the storm pounded us violently. The next day, the crew threw the ship's cargo overboard; [19]and the day after that, they discarded any of the ship's equipment they could do without. [20]Days passed without relief from the furious winds, without a single break in the clouds to see sun or stars, even for a moment. Despair set in, as if all hope of rescue had been cast overboard as well. [21]On top of all of this, the crew had been unable to eat anything *because of the turmoil. Paul saw the crew had reached a critical moment.* He gathered them.

Paul: Men, if you had listened to my warning, we would still be safe in Crete and would have avoided this damage and loss. [22]*I was correct in my warning,* so I urge you to believe me now: none of you will die. We will lose the ship, but we will not lose one life. So keep up your courage, men! [23]The God I belong to, the God I worship, sent a heavenly messenger to me this night. [24]He said, "Do not be afraid, Paul. *I'm not finished with you yet.* You are going to stand before the emperor! You can be certain that God has granted safety to you and all your companions." [25]So listen, men: *you must not give up hope!* Keep up your courage! I have faith in God that things will turn out exactly as I was told last night. [26]*Here's what I foresee:* we will run aground on some island.

[27-28]*Imagine what happened:* It's the 14th night *of our nightmare voyage;* we're being driven by the storm somewhere in the Adriatic Sea. It's about midnight, and the sailors are taking soundings, fearing we might run aground. "Twenty fathoms," somebody calls out in the darkness, then a little later, "Fifteen fathoms." We're nearing land! [29]But hope quickly gives way to a new fear. At any moment in this darkness, they realize, we could be smashed onto unseen rocks. So they drop four anchors from the stern and pray for first light.

[30]Then some of the crew decide to make a run for it on their own. They say they need to let out more anchors from the bow, and this will require lowering the ship's lifeboat. *They actually plan to abandon us; we realize what's going on.* [31]Paul quickly speaks to the officer and soldiers.

Paul: Unless these men stay on board, you won't survive.

[32]So the soldiers intervene, cut away the lifeboat, and let it drift away. [33,37]*We wait.* Just before dawn, Paul again gathers everyone on

the ship—all 276 of us. He urges everyone to eat *and encourages us not to lose hope.**

Paul: Listen, men, we've all been under incredible stress for 14 days. You haven't eaten anything during this whole time. [34]I urge you to take some food now because it will help you survive what we're about to face. And I want to assure you—not one of you will lose a single hair from your head. *We're all going to make it—all 276 of us!*

[35]Then Paul takes a loaf of bread and gives thanks to God in front of all of them. He breaks it, takes a piece, and begins to eat. [36]A fresh surge of courage seems to fill their hearts as they also begin to eat. [38]After satisfying their hunger, the crew lightens the ship by throwing the remaining wheat overboard. [39]Day finally breaks. They survey the coastline and don't recognize it, but they do notice a bay with a beach—the best place to try to run ashore.

[40]So they cut the anchor ropes, untie the steering oars, hoist the foresail to the wind, and make for the beach. [41]But *then there's a horrible sound, and* we realize we've struck a reef; the bow is jammed solid, and the waves are smashing the stern to pieces. [42]The soldiers start talking about killing the prisoners so they won't swim away and escape; [43]but the officer wants to save Paul, so he stops them. He tells those who can swim to jump overboard and swim to the shore, [44]and those who can't, he tells to hold on to planks and other pieces of the ship when it breaks apart. *Some hours later,* we reassemble on the beach, each one safe and sound.

28 We quickly learned that we were on the island of Malta. [2]The Maltese people found us and were extraordinarily kind to us. They kindled a bonfire and welcomed us around it, *which we greatly appreciated* because it was raining and cold. [3]Paul was gathering firewood and helping build the fire. A viper had been hiding in some of the wood, and as it tried to escape the heat, it bit Paul on the hand. It sank its fangs in and wouldn't let go. [4]The natives saw it dangling from his hand.

Natives: This man must be a murderer. He escaped the sea, but now justice has caught up with him.

[5]Paul simply shook the snake off into the fire and suffered no harm. [6]The natives knew what to expect—rapid swelling followed by death—but when they waited a long time and saw that Paul suffered no ill effects of the bite, they changed their minds and concluded that he was a god.

[7]The leading man of the island, Publius, owned large amounts of land near this beach. Publius received us and hosted us for three days. [8]Publius's father was sick, bedridden with fever and dysentery. Paul visited the invalid and prayed for him, placing his hands on Publius's father. The man was cured. [9]Soon people from all over the island who had diseases came, and they were cured as well.

[10-11]We stayed on Malta for the next three months and were treated with great honor. *When spring arrived,* we prepared to continue our journey on a ship that had wintered there—an Alexandrian vessel with the Twin Brothers as its figurehead. The Maltese people showed us a final kindness as we departed: they came with all the provisions we needed for our journey and put them on board.

[12]We *set sail from Malta and* stopped first at Syracuse. After three days, [13]we weighed anchor and came to Rhegium. We waited there a day, and then a south wind sprang up and sped us to Puteoli. [14]We found some believers there, and they invited us to stay with them for seven days. Then we reached Rome. [15]The believers from Rome heard we were coming, so they traveled out to meet us at the Forum of Appius and Three Taverns. Paul thanked God and felt encouraged to see them. [16]Once inside the city, Paul lived under house arrest by himself, with only one soldier to guard him.

[17]Three days after his arrival, he called together the local Jewish leaders.

Paul: Brothers, although I committed no wrong against our Jewish people or our ancestral customs, I was arrested in Jerusalem and handed over to the Romans. [18]The Romans examined me and wanted to set me free because I had committed no capital offense. [19]But my Jewish opponents objected, so I had to appeal to the emperor—even though I had no charges against me and had filed no charges

---

* 27:33,37 Verses 33 and 37 have been combined to help the reader understand the continuity of the passage.

Luke's account of the early church ends abruptly: one of the story's heroes, Paul, is under house arrest in Rome awaiting trial. Other sources will recount how Paul is later martyred in Rome, a victim of Nero's paranoia and cruelty. But Luke's story isn't a biography of Paul; it is a narration about "the Way" as it moved geographically and culturally from Jerusalem (at the edge of the empire) to Rome (the celebrated center of the world). Therefore, Luke's story finishes once the message of Jesus is spreading without hindrance.

As it moves geographically, "the Way," as Jesus' followers preferred to call it, crosses cultural, linguistic, and religious boundaries. At each and every point, Luke assures, the Spirit is there demonstrating God's blessing on and approval of the emissaries who walk in the footsteps of Jesus and in fulfillment of prophecies. Clearly what happened in those early decades was driven by the Spirit-wind of heaven; and God's purposes are realized through the faithful obedience of disciples such as Peter, Stephen, Philip, and Paul.

Luke's account has ended, but the story about the acts of God through the church continues into our day. We are the characters in the current volume of salvation history. Through our faithful obedience, also empowered by the Spirit-wind of heaven, our stories are part of the anthology of God's new creation.

---

against my nation. 20I wanted to gather you together and explain all this to you. I want you to understand that it is because of Israel's hope that I am bound with this chain.

Jewish Leaders: 21We haven't received letters from Judea about you, and no visiting brother has reported anything or said anything negative about you. 22So we are interested in hearing your viewpoint on the sect *you represent*. The only thing we know about it is that people everywhere speak against it.

23They scheduled a day to meet again, and a large number came to his lodging. From morning until evening, he explained his message to them—giving his account of the kingdom of God, trying to convince them about Jesus from the Law of Moses and the Prophets' writings. 24Some were convinced, but others refused to believe.

Paul (*adding as they left in disagreement*):
25The Holy Spirit rightly spoke to your ancestors through the prophet Isaiah,

26Go to this people and say,
  "You certainly do hear, but you will
      never understand;
  you certainly do see, but you will
      never have insight.
27Make their hearts hard,
  their ears deaf, and their eyes
      blind.
Otherwise, they would look and see,
  listen and hear,
  understand and repent,
  and be healed."*

28So let it be known to you that God's liberation, *God's healing,* has been sent to the outsiders, and they will listen.

[29Then the local Jewish leaders left Paul to discuss all he had told them.]*

30For two full years, he lived there in Rome, paying all his own expenses, receiving all who came to him. 31With great confidence and with no hindrance, he proclaimed the kingdom of God and taught about *the ultimate authority*—the Lord Jesus, God's Anointed, *the Liberating King.*

* 28:26-27 Isaiah 6:9-10   * 28:29 Some early manuscripts omit verse 29.

ROMANS

Letter to the church in Rome

From Paul, the apostle to the Gentiles

Rome was the center of the known world; it was the cradle of civilization, commerce, culture—and home to a military machine under the command of Caesar, the most powerful man in the world. The most influential city on the planet was on the frontier of the Jesus movement, a place where God was bringing together Jews and non-Jews into one community to follow Jesus' teachings. A group of believers was gathering, and a church of great importance was forming from ragamuffin believers who had been touched by the power of the gospel. But they do not appear to have had the leadership of the Lord's emissaries—those who had walked with and had been handpicked by Jesus. This church would become the seedbed for the spread of the gospel across the known world, so Paul recognized the importance of articulating the whole gospel to this body of believers and preparing them for their missional calling in the world.

This letter from Paul, the emissary of Jesus, breaks all the previous molds. He is writing to many people he does not know, is instructing a church he did not plant, and is challenging them to embrace their role in bringing the gospel to the people of Italy and Spain, despite the fact that he has not been able to model the work of missions and church planting in Rome as he had in other places. What would Paul have to say to believers he had never met? How would he proclaim the gospel in a letter? In planting other churches, Paul surely told how the risen Jesus appeared to him. Paul must have preached to them for untold hours (he was known for being quite verbose) about sin, redemption, justification, the cross, adoption, grace, love, life in the Spirit, and the power of the Anointed One to redeem all things.

This letter set the church in Rome on a firm foundation and ultimately became one of the most important pieces of literature ever written. It has influenced some of the greatest minds and agents of change the world has known: Augustine, Martin Luther, John Wesley, Martin Luther King Jr., and Desmond Tutu, just to name a few. It was one of the primary inspirations for the Protestant Reformation in the 16th century. But most importantly, this letter written to Christians in an ancient city penetrates our hearts and minds today with a beautiful and persuasive view of the power of the gospel!

According to Paul, in and by itself, the gospel is power—God's power. The simple message of Jesus brings healing and rescue to all people. It starts with God's people, the Jews, but does not end until all people hear and respond to its call.

The gospel reveals how right and faithful God has been all along. It begins with God's faithfulness to His creation and His covenant people. Then God acts, finally and decisively, in the cross of Jesus. For Paul the cross, more than any other event, displays Jesus' faithfulness to God the Father. As the Gospels tell us, in the garden of Gethsemane, Jesus entrusts Himself completely to God's will. As a result, this good news brings faith and hope to those who hear and respond to its elegant message. Because God is faithful, He acts in a most extraordinary way. Somehow in the scandal of the cross, He offers His own Son in order to redeem the fallen world.

---

1 Paul, a servant of Jesus the Anointed called by God to be His emissary* and appointed to tell the good news [2]of the things promised long ago by God, spoken by prophets, and recorded in the Holy Scriptures. [3]All of this good news is about His Son: who was (from a human perspective) born of David's royal line [4]and ultimately designated to be the true Son of God with power upon His resurrection from the dead by the Spirit of holiness. I am speaking of Jesus, the Anointed One, our Lord.

The prophets express God's mind and will in the world. Sometimes their messages are a word-on-target to the people and powers of their day; at other times, they see and speak about the future. Their words not only predict the future—they speak the word of the Lord, which creates reality and shapes the future.

Paul describes the gospel of Jesus by bringing in the good news on two levels: On a human level, the good news is about God's Son, David's descendant, entering the world to begin the task of restoring it from the damage sin and death have left behind. But the resurrection of Jesus from the dead takes Jesus' sonship to a new level. Now He is the Son-of-God-in-Power, the One called Lord and Master.

mission is to spread the one true and obedient faith to all people in the name of Jesus. [6]This includes you: you have been called by Jesus, God's Anointed.

[7]To all those who are God's beloved saints in Rome:

May grace and peace from God our Father and the Lord Jesus, the Anointed One, surround you.

[8]First, I thank my God through Jesus the Anointed for all of you because we are joined by faith as family, and your faith is spreading across the world. [9-10]For I call God as my witness—whom I worship in my spirit and serve in making known the gospel—He alone knows how often I mention you in my prayers. I find myself constantly praying for you and hoping it's in God's will for me to be with you soon. [11]I desperately want to see you so that I can share some gift of the Spirit to strengthen you. [12]Plus I know that when we come together something beautiful will happen as we are encouraged by each other's faith.

[13]If, my brothers and sisters, you did not already know, my plans were set to meet you in Rome, but time and circumstances have forced every trip to be canceled until now. I have deeply desired to see some good fruit among you just as I have seen with so many non-Jewish believers. [14]You see, I am in tremendous debt to those of various nationalities, from non-Jews to barbarians, from the wisest of the wise to the idle wanderer. [15]So you can imagine how eager I am to join you and to teach the good news in the mighty and diverse city of Rome.

[16]For I am not the least bit embarrassed about the gospel. I won't shy away from it, because it is God's power to save every person who believes: first the Jew, and then the

[5]And here's what He's done: He has graced us and sanctioned us as His emissaries* whose

* 1:1 Literally, apostle * 1:5 Literally, apostles

non-Jew. [17]You see, in the good news, God's restorative justice is revealed. *And as we will see*, it begins with and ends in faith. As the Scripture declares, "By faith the just will obtain life."*

[18]For the wrath of God is breaking through from heaven, opposing all *manifestations of* ungodliness and wickedness by the people who do wrong to keep God's truth in check. [19]These people are not ignorant about what can be known of God, because He has shown it to them *with great clarity*. [20]From the beginning, creation in its magnificence enlightens us to His nature. Creation itself makes His undying power and divine identity clear, even though they are invisible; and it voids the excuses *and ignorant claims* of these people [21]because, despite the fact that they knew the one true God, they have failed to show the *love*, honor, and appreciation due to the One who created them! Instead, their lives are consumed by vain thoughts that poison their foolish hearts. [22]They claim to be wise; but they have been exposed as fools, *frauds, and con artists*—[23]only a fool would trade the splendor and beauty of the immortal God to worship images of the common man or woman, bird or reptile, or *the next beast that tromps along.*

[24]So God gave them just what their lustful hearts desired. *As a result,* they violated their bodies and invited shame into their lives. [25]*How?* By choosing a foolish lie over God's truth. They gave their lives and devotion to the creature rather than to the Creator Himself, who is blessed forever and ever. Amen. [26-27]This is why God released them to their own vile pursuits, *and this is what happened*: they chose sexual counterfeits—women had sexual relations with other women and men committed unnatural, shameful acts because they burned with lust for other men. This sin was rife, and they suffered painful consequences.

[28]Since they had no mind to recognize God, He turned them loose to follow the unseemly designs of their depraved minds and to do things that should not be done. [29]Their days are filled with all sorts of godless living, wicked schemes, greed, hatred, endless desire for more, murder, violence, deceit, and spitefulness. And, *as if that were not enough,* they are gossiping, [30]slanderous, God-hating, rude, egotistical, smug people who are always coming up with even more dreadful ways to treat one another. They don't listen to their parents; [31]they lack understanding *and character*. They are simple-minded, covenant-breaking, heartless, and unmerciful; *they are not to be trusted.* [32]Despite the fact that they are fully aware that God's law says this way of life deserves death, they fail to stop. And *worse*—they applaud others on this destructive path.

Paul sounds a sober warning. God's wrath is here; it is not some far-off future event. Paul says that God's wrath is already at work in the world in what is effectively God's "hands-off" policy. God, he says, steps aside and gives us over to idolatry, sexual sins, and depraved minds. Human sin and depravity are both its cause and effect. You see, we are not only punished for our sins, but we are punished by our sins. If God's salvation consists essentially of His presence with us, then His wrath consists of His absence or separation from us. The bad news is this: God's wrath is real. Without the good news of Jesus, no hope exists.

---

2 So you can see there are no excuses for any of us. If your eyes shift their focus from yourselves to others—to judge *how they are doing*—you have already condemned yourselves! *You don't realize that* you are pointing your fingers at others for the exact things you do as well. [2]There's no doubt that the judgment of God will justly fall upon hypocrites who practice such things. [3]*Here's what is happening*: you attack and criticize others and then turn around to commit the same offenses yourselves! Do you think you will somehow dodge God's judgment? [4]Do you take the kindness of God for granted? Do you see His patience and tolerance as signs that He is a pushover *when it comes to sin*? How could you not know that His kindness is guiding our hearts to turn away from *distractions and habitual* sin to walk a new path?*

[5]But because your heart is obstinate and shameless, you're storing up wrath that will count against you. On the day of His choosing, God's wrath and judgment will be

* 1:17 Habakkuk 2:4   * 2:4 Literally, repentance

unleashed to make things right. [6]As it goes, everyone will receive what his actions in life have cultivated. [7]Whoever has labored diligently and patiently to do what is right—seeking glory, honor, and immortality—God will grant him *endless joy in* life eternal. [8]But selfish individuals who *make trouble,* resist the truth, or sell out to wickedness *will meet a very different fate—they* will find fury and indignation *as the fruit of living in the wrong.* [9]Suffering and pain await everyone whose life is marked by evil living (first for the Jew, and next for the non-Jew). [10]But if you do what is right, you will receive glory, admiration, and peace (again, first for the Jew, then for the non-Jew). [11]God has no favorites.

[12]If one lives life without knowledge of the law—*the teachings of the Torah*—he will sin and die apart from the law. If someone else lives life under the law, his sin will be judged by what the law teaches. [13]*Here's my point:* just because a person hears the law *read or recited* does not mean he is right before the one True God; it is following the law that makes one right, *not just hearing it.* [14-15]*For instance, some* outsiders who are not required to follow the law often live quite naturally by its teachings. Even though the law wasn't given to them, in themselves they have the law. *Here's the thing:* their lives demonstrate that God has inscribed the law's teachings on their hearts. *On judgment day,* their consciences will testify for them, and their thoughts will both accuse and defend them. [16]This good news given to me declares that this *affirmation and accusation* will take place on that day when God, through Jesus, the Anointed One, judges every person's life secrets.

[17]Listen, if you claim to be a Jew, count on the law, and boast in *your relationship with* God; [18]if you know His will and can determine what is essential (because you have been instructed in the law); and [19]if you stand convinced that you are *chosen to be* a guide to the blind, a light to those who live in darkness, [20]a teacher of foolish wanderers and children, and have in the law what is essentially the form of knowledge and truth—[21]then tell me, why don't you practice what you preach? If you are going to sermonize against stealing, then stop stealing. [22]If you are going to teach others not to commit adultery, then be completely faithful to your spouse. If you hate idolatry, then stop robbing the temples! [23]If you pride yourself in having God's law, then stop dishonoring God by failing to keep its teaching. [24]Here's what it says: "Because of you, God's reputation is slandered by those outside the covenant."*

[25]You see, circumcision is of value only if you keep the law's teachings. But if you keep breaking God's rules, you are no different than those without the mark. [26]So if an uncircumcised man abides by God's just precepts, doesn't that make his standing before God the same as one who is circumcised? [27]The man who is physically uncircumcised but still keeps the law, he will stand in judgment over the person who is circumcised and yet continually breaks God's law. [28]A mark that is evident doesn't necessarily make one a Jew, and circumcision that is evident only in the flesh is not true. [29]But the true Jew is Jewish on the inside—*in secret places no one but God can see*—and true circumcision involves the heart; it comes from the Spirit, not from some written code. The praise *and reputation* of that kind of Jew come from God, not from man.

When God's people—or people who claim to be God's people—are hypocrites, then God is the one who gets the bad name. How often do we say one thing and do another? How often have we set a standard for others only to break it ourselves? The saying is true: we practice every day what we believe; all the rest is religious talk. There is a lot of religious talk out there, a lot of smugness and self-satisfaction. But every day people readily violate their consciences and the Lord's reasonable teachings. For faith to matter, it has to get under your skin.

---

3 So then, do the Jews have an advantage *over the other nations*? Does circumcision do anything for you? [2]The answer is yes, in every way. To begin with, God spoke to and through the Jewish people. [3]But what if some *Jews* have been unfaithful? Does the fact that they abandoned their faith zero out God's faithfulness? [4]Absolutely not! If every person *on the planet* were a liar

* 2:24 Isaiah 52:5; Ezekiel 36:22

and thief, God would still be true. It stands written:

> Whenever You speak, You are in the right.
> When You come to judge, You will prevail.*

[5]If our perpetual injustice and corruption merely accentuate the purity of God's justice, what can we say? Is God unjust for unleashing His fury against us? (I am speaking from our limited human perspective.) [6]Again, absolutely not! If this were so, how could God stand as Judge over the world? [7]But if my lie serves only to point out God's truth and bring Him glory, then why am I being judged for my sin? [8]There are slanderous charges out there that we are saying things like, "Let's be as wicked as possible so that something good will come from it." Those malicious gossips will get what they deserve.

[9]So what then? Are we Jews better off? Not at all. We have made it clear that people everywhere, Jews and non-Jews, are living under the power of sin. [10]Here's what Scripture says:

> No one is righteous—not even one.
> [11]There is no one who understands *the truth*;
>   no one is seeking after the *one True God.*
> [12]All have turned away; together they've become worthless.
>   No one does good, not even one.*
> [13]What comes out of their mouths is as foul as a rotting corpse;
>   their words stink of flattery.*
> Viper venom hides beneath their lips;*
>   [14]their mouths are full of curses, lies, and oppression.*
> [15]Their feet race to *violence and* bloodshed;
>   [16]destruction and trouble line the roads of their lives,
> [17]And they've never taken the road to peace.*
>   [18]You will never see the fear of God in their eyes.*

V

Sin is more than just wrong choices, bad decisions, and willful acts of disobedience that violate God's Word and are contrary to His will. It is that and much more. Paul knows sin is missing the mark or deliberately stepping over the line, but he also knows that sin is a power at work in him and every child of Adam. As strange as it may sound, sin seems to have a will of its own. Like an addiction, sin takes hold of us and causes us to act in ways we never wanted. For Paul the cross of Jesus deals finally and definitively with the dual reality of sin. Not only are we forgiven of our sins—our willful acts of disobedience—but we are also liberated from the power of sin.

---

[19]We want to be clear that whatever the law says, it says to everyone who is under its authority. Its purpose is to muzzle every mouth, *to silence idle talk,* and to bring the whole world under the standard of God's justice. [20]Therefore, doing what the law prescribes will not make anyone right in the eyes of God—*that's not its purpose*—but the law is capable of exposing the true nature of sin.

[21]But now *for the good news*: God's restorative justice has entered the world, independent of the law. Both the law and the prophets told us this day would come. [22]This redeeming justice comes through the faithfulness of Jesus,* the Anointed One, *the Liberating King,* who makes salvation a reality for all who believe—without the slightest partiality. [23]You see, all have sinned, and all their futile attempts to reach God in His glory fail. [24]Yet they are now saved and set right by His free gift of grace through the redemption available only in Jesus the Anointed. [25]When God set Him up to be the sacrifice—the seat of mercy where sins are atoned through faith—His blood became the demonstration of God's own restorative justice. All of this confirms His faithfulness *to the promise,* for over the course of human history God patiently held back as He dealt with the sins being committed. [26]This expression of God's restorative justice displays in the present that He is just and righteous and that He makes right those who trust and commit themselves to Jesus.

V

In the incarnation and sacrificial death of Jesus, God is at work to

* 3:4 Psalm 51:4   * 3:10-12 Psalms 14:1-3; 53:1-3   * 3:13 Psalm 5:9
* 3:13 Psalm 140:3   * 3:14 Psalm 10:7   * 3:15-17 Isaiah 59:7-8
* 3:18 Psalm 36:1   * 3:22 Often translated "faith in Jesus"

extend salvation to those who fall under sin's addiction. They are liberated from its power, cleansed of its stain. By "God's restorative justice," Paul means first the justice that belongs to God and reflects His character. God is just, fair, or in a word, righteous. But character is dynamic, not static. This means that God's justice must express itself in some way. So it is in the nature of God's justice that He acts to restore and repair a world that is not the way it should be. Above all, it is God's saving actions through Jesus that constitute the gift of God's restorative justice.

---

²⁷So is there any place left for boasting? No. It's been shut out completely. *And how?* By what sort of law? The law of works perhaps? No! By the law of faith. ²⁸We hold that people are justified, *that is, made right with God* through faith, which has nothing to do with the deeds the law prescribes.

²⁹Is God the God of the Jews only? *If He created all things, then doesn't that make Him* the God of all people? Jews and non-Jews, *insiders and outsiders alike*? Yes, He is also the God of all the outsiders. ³⁰So since God is one, *there is one way for Jews and outsiders,* circumcised and uncircumcised, to be right with Him. That is the way of faith. ³¹So are we trying to use faith to abolish the law? Absolutely not! In fact, we *now are free to* uphold the law *as God intended.*

4 In light of all of this, what should we say about our ancestor Abraham? ²If Abraham was made right by performing certain works, then he would surely have something to brag about. Right? Not before *the Creator* God, ³because as the Scriptures say, "Abraham believed God *and trusted in His promises,* so God counted it to his favor as righteousness."* ⁴Now, when you work a job, do your wages come as a gift *or as compensation for your work*? It is *most certainly* not a gift—you are only paid what you have earned. ⁵So for the person who does not work, but instead trusts in the One who makes the ungodly right, his faith is counted for him as righteousness.

⁶*Remember the psalm where* David speaks about the benefits that come to the person whom God credits with righteousness apart from works? He said,

⁷Blessed are those whose wrongs have been forgiven
and whose sins have been covered.
⁸Blessed is the person whose sin the Lord will not take into account.*

⁹So is this blessing spoken only for the circumcised or for all uncircumcised people too? We remind *you what the Scripture has to say*: faith was credited to Abraham as righteousness.*

¹⁰So when was the credit awarded *to Abraham*? Was it before or after his circumcision? Well, it certainly wasn't after—it was before he was circumcised. ¹¹*Eventually* he was given circumcision as a sign of his right standing, indicating that he was credited on the basis of the faith he possessed before he was circumcised. It happened this way so that Abraham might become the spiritual father of all those who are not circumcised but are made right through their faith. ¹²In the same way, *God destined him to be* the spiritual father of all those who are circumcised as more than an outward sign, but who walk in our father Abraham's faithful footsteps—a faith he possessed while he was still uncircumcised.

¹³The promise given to Abraham and his children, that one day they would inherit the world, did not come because he followed the rules of the law. It came as a result of his right standing *before God, a standing he* obtained through faith. ¹⁴If this inheritance is available only to those who keep the law, then faith is a useless commodity and the promise is canceled. ¹⁵For the law brings God's wrath *against sin.* But where the law doesn't draw the line, there can be no crime.

¹⁶This is the reason that faith is the single source of the promise—so that grace would be offered to all Abraham's children, those whose lives are defined by the law and those who follow the path of faith charted by Abraham, our common father. ¹⁷As it is recorded *in the Scriptures,* "I have appointed you the father of many nations."* In the presence of the God who creates out of nothing and holds the power to bring to life what is dead, Abraham believed *and so became our father.*

* 4:3 Genesis 15:6   * 4:7-8 Psalm 32:1-2   * 4:9 Genesis 15:6
* 4:17 Genesis 17:5

¹⁸Against the odds, Abraham's hope grew into full-fledged faith that he would turn out to be the father of many nations, just as God had promised when He said, "That's how *many* your descendants will be."* ¹⁹His faith did not fail, although he was well aware that his impotent body, after nearly 100 years, was as good as dead and that Sarah's womb, too, was dead. ²⁰In spite of all this, his faith in God's promise did not falter. In fact, his faith grew as he gave glory to God ²¹because he was supremely confident that God could deliver on His promise. ²²This is why, *you see, God saw* his faith *and* counted him as righteous; *this is how he became* right with God.

²³The story of how faith was credited to Abraham was not recorded for him and him alone, ²⁴but was written for all of us who would one day be credited for having faith in God, the One who raised Jesus our Lord from the realm of the dead. ²⁵He was delivered over to death for our trespasses and raised so that we might be made right *with God.*

In God's plan to restore a fallen and disfigured world, Abraham became the father of all of us, the agent of blessing to everyone. Jesus completes what God started centuries before when He established Abraham's covenant family. Those who put faith in Jesus and call Him "Lord" become part of Abraham's faith family. Because God is gracious, loving, and merciful, men and women from every corner of the earth are not only declared right, but ultimately are made right as well. It happens through God's actions—not our efforts—in the death, burial, and resurrection of Jesus who was crucified for our misdeeds and raised to repair what has been wrong all along. So the promises of God made long years ago are being realized in men and women who hear the call of faith and answer "yes" to it.

---

5 Since we have been *acquitted and* made right through faith, we are able to experience *true and lasting* peace with

God through our Lord Jesus, the Anointed One, *the Liberating King.* ²Jesus leads us into a place of *radical* grace where we are able to celebrate the hope of experiencing God's glory. ³And that's not all. We also celebrate in seasons of suffering because we know that when we suffer we develop endurance, ⁴which shapes our characters. When our characters are refined, we learn what it means to hope *and anticipate God's goodness.* ⁵And hope will never fail to satisfy our deepest need because the Holy Spirit that was given to us has flooded our hearts with God's love.

⁶When the time was right, the Anointed One died for all of us who were far from God, powerless, and weak. ⁷Now it is rare to find someone willing to die for an upright person, although it's possible that someone may give up his life for one who is truly good. ⁸But *think about this:* while we were wasting our lives in sin, God revealed His powerful love to us *in a tangible display*—the Anointed One died for us. ⁹As a result, the blood of Jesus has made us right with God now, and certainly we will be rescued by Him from God's wrath *in the future.* ¹⁰If we were in the heat of combat with God when His Son reconciled us by laying down His life, then how much more will we be saved by Jesus' *resurrection* life? ¹¹In fact, we stand now reconciled *and at peace* with God. That's why we celebrate in God through our Lord Jesus, the Anointed.

¹²Consider this: sin entered our world through one man, *Adam;* and through sin, death followed *in hot pursuit.* Death spread rapidly to infect all people on the earth as they engaged in sin.

God's gift of grace and salvation is amazing. Paul struggles to find the words to describe it. He looks everywhere around him to find a metaphor, an image, a word to put into language one aspect of this awesome gift. One of those is "reconciliation." There is hardly anything more beautiful than to see two people who have been enemies or estranged or separated coming back together. When Paul reflects on what God has done through Jesus, he thinks about

* 4:18 Genesis 15:5

reconciliation. Before we receive God's blessing through His Son, we are enemies of God, sinners of the worst sort. But God makes the first move to restore us to a right relationship with Him.

---

[13]Before God gave the law, sin existed, *but there was no way to account for it.* Outside the law, how could anyone be charged and found guilty of sin? [14]Still, death plagued all humanity from Adam to Moses, even those whose sin was of a different sort than Adam's. *You see, in God's plan,* Adam was a prototype of the One who comes *to usher in a new day.* [15]But the free gift of grace bears no resemblance to Adam's crime *that brings a death sentence to all of humanity; in fact, it is quite the opposite.* For if the one man's sin brings death to so many, how much more does the gift of God's *radical* grace extend to humanity since Jesus the Anointed offered His generous gift. [16]His free gift is nothing like the scourge of the first man's sin. The judgment that fell because of one false step brought condemnation, but the free gift following countless offenses results in a favorable verdict—not guilty. [17]If one man's sin brought a reign of death—*that's Adam's legacy*—how much more will those who receive grace in abundance and the free gift of redeeming justice reign in life by means of one other man—Jesus the Anointed.

[18]So here is the result: as one man's sin brought about condemnation *and punishment* for all people, so one man's act of faithfulness makes all of us right with God and brings us to new life. [19]Just as through one man's *defiant* disobedience every one of us were made sinners, so through the *willing* obedience of the one man many of us will be made right.

[20]When the law came into the picture, sin grew and grew; but wherever sin grew and spread, God's grace was there in fuller, greater measure. *No matter how much sin crept in, there was always more grace.* [21]In the same way that sin reigned in the sphere of death, now grace reigns through God's restorative justice, *eclipsing death and* leading to eternal life through the Anointed One, Jesus our Lord, *the Liberating King.*

We arrive here, children of a common ancestor, Adam. As such, we have inherited his traits, physically and spiritually. Although our sin may be of a different sort than his, we sin no less than Adam. The proof of that is death. Adam opens the way for sin and death to pursue us and run rampant across the earth. But from the beginning, God has a plan to reverse the curse. At just the right moment in human history, Jesus arrives, a son of Adam and the Son of God. Through His faithful obedience to His Father, He challenges the twin powers of sin and death and defeats them. Sin no longer reigns unchecked. Death no longer has the last word.

---

6 How should we respond to all of this? Is it good to persist in a life of sin so that grace may multiply even more? [2]Absolutely not! How can we die to a life where sin ruled over us and then invite sin back into our lives? [3]Did someone forget to tell you that when we were initiated into Jesus the Anointed through baptism's ceremonial washing,* we entered into His death? [4]Therefore, we were buried with Him through this baptism into death so that just as God the Father, in all His glory, resurrected the Anointed One, we, too, might walk *confidently out of the grave* into a new life. [5]*To put it another way:* if we have been united with Him to share in a death like His, don't you understand that we will also share in His resurrection? [6]We know this: whatever we used to be with our old sinful ways has been nailed to His cross. So our entire record of sin has been canceled, and we no longer have to bow down to sin's power. [7]A dead man, you see, cannot be bound by sin. [8]But if we have died with the Anointed One, we believe that we shall also live together with Him. [9]So we stand firm in the conviction that death holds no power over God's Anointed, because He was resurrected from the dead never to face death again. [10]When He died, He died to whatever power sin had, once and for all, and now He lives completely to God. [11]So here is how to picture yourself now that you have been initiated into Jesus the Anointed: you are dead to sin's

---

* 6:3 Literally, immersion, in a rite of initiation and purification

power and influence, but you are alive to God's rule.

[12]Don't invite *that insufferable tyrant of* sin back into your mortal body so you won't become obedient to its *destructive* desires. [13]Don't offer your bodily members to sin's service as tools of wickedness; instead, offer your body to God as those who are alive from the dead, and devote the parts of your body to God as tools for justice *and goodness in this world.* [14]For sin is no longer a tyrant over you; indeed you are under grace and not the law.

> Now sin and death no longer define us, but grace does: God's favor has been given freely to us through His Son, Jesus, who liberates us from sin's power.

[15]So what do we do now? Throw ourselves into lives of sin because we are cloaked in grace and don't have to answer to the law? Absolutely not! [16]Doesn't it make sense that if you sign yourself over as a slave, you will have to obey your master? The question *before you is, What will be your master?* Will it be sin—which will lead to certain death— or obedience—which will lead to a right *and reconciled* life? [17]Thank God that your slavery to sin has ended and that *in your new freedom* you pledged your heartfelt obedience to that teaching which was passed on to you. [18]*The beauty of your new situation is this*: now that you are free from sin, you are free to serve *a different master, God's redeeming* justice.

[19]Forgive me for using casual language to compensate for your natural weakness of human understanding. *I want to be perfectly clear*. In the same way you gave your bodily members away as slaves to corrupt and lawless living and found yourselves deeper in your unruly lives, now devote your members as slaves to right *and reconciled* lives so you will find yourselves deeper in holy living. [20]In the days when you lived as slaves to sin, you had no obligation to do the right thing. *In that regard, you were free.* [21]But what do you have to show from your former lives besides shame? The outcome of that life is death*, guaranteed*. [22]But now that you have been emancipated from the death grip of sin and are God's slave, you have a *different sort of life*, a growing holiness. The outcome of that life is eternal life. [23]The payoff for a life of sin is death, but God is offering us a free

gift—eternal life through our Lord Jesus, the Anointed One, *the Liberating King.*

V

Grace is no license to sin. As creatures, we are made to serve our Creator. In the absence of truth, we will serve somebody or something. It's an essential part of our nature. Our only choice is this: whom will we serve? At one time, we all served sin and grew weak under its deadly power over us. Now, through God's grace, we have become servants of obedience that sets us right with God, each other, and ourselves. We must daily decide whose servant we are and offer Him our hands, our feet, our hearts, our eyes.

---

7 My brothers and sisters who are well versed in the law, don't you realize that a person is subject to the law only as long as he is alive? [2]So, for example, a wife is obligated by the law to her husband until his death; if the husband dies, she is freed from the parts of the law that relate to her marriage. [3]If she is sleeping with another man while her husband is alive, she is rightly labeled an adulteress. But if her husband dies, she is free from the law and can marry another man. In such a case, she is not an adulteress.

[4]My brothers and sisters, in the same way, you have died when it comes to the law because of *your connection with* the body of the Anointed One. His death—*and your death with Him*—frees you to belong to the One who was raised from the dead so we can bear fruit for God. [5]As we were living in the flesh, the law *could not solve the problem of sin; it* only awakened our lust for more and cultivated the fruit of death in our bodily members. [6]But now that we have died to those chains that imprisoned us, we have been released from the law to serve in a new Spirit-empowered life, not the old written code.

[7]So what is the story? Is the law itself sin? Absolutely not! *It is the exact opposite.* I would never have known what sin is if it were not for the law. *For example,* I would not have known that desiring something that belongs to my neighbor is sin if the law had

not said, "You are not to covet."* ⁸Sin took advantage of the commandment to create a constant stream of greed and desire within me; *I began to want everything.* You see, apart from the law, sin lies dormant. ⁹There was a time when I was living without the law, but the commandment came *and changed everything:* sin came to life, and I died. ¹⁰This commandment was supposed to bring life; but in my experience, it brought death. ¹¹Sin took advantage of the commandment, tricked me, and exploited it in order to kill me. ¹²So *hear me out:* the law is holy; and its commandments are holy, right, and good.

¹³So did the good *law* bring about my death? Absolutely not! It was sin that killed me, *not the law.* It's the nature of sin to produce death through what is good and exploit the commandments to multiply sin's vile effects. ¹⁴This is what we know: the law comes from the spiritual realm. *My problem is that* I am of the fallen human realm, owned by sin, *which tries to keep me in its service.*

God gives Israel the law as part of His covenant promises. The law does a great deal for His people; mainly it sets them apart from all other nations of the world and gives them a blueprint for God's will. But, according to Paul, the law cannot fix everything that is wrong with this broken world. Although the law is perfectly suited for bringing sin to the surface and exposing it, the law cannot free people from the power of sin and its evil twin, death.

---

¹⁵*Listen,* I can't explain my actions. Here's why: I am not able to do the things I want; and at the same time, I do the things I despise. ¹⁶If I am doing the things I have already decided not to do, I am agreeing with the law regarding what is good. ¹⁷But now I am no longer the one acting—*I've lost control*—sin has taken up residence in me *and is wreaking havoc.* ¹⁸I know that in me, that is, in my fallen human nature, there is nothing good. I can will myself to do something good, but that does not help me carry it out. ¹⁹I can determine that I am going to do good, but I don't do it; instead, I end up living out

the evil that I decided not to do. ²⁰If I end up doing the exact thing I pledged not to do, I am no longer doing it because sin has taken up residence in me.

²¹Here's an *important* principle I've discovered: regardless of my desire to do the right thing, *it is clear that* evil is never far away. ²²For deep down I am in happy agreement with God's law; ²³but the rest of me does not concur. I see a very different principle at work in my bodily members, and it is at war with my mind; I have become a prisoner in this war to the rule of sin in my body. ²⁴I am absolutely miserable! Is there anyone who can free me from this body where *sin and* death reign *so supremely?* ²⁵I am thankful to God *for the freedom that comes* through our Lord Jesus, the Anointed One! So on the one hand, I devotedly serve God's law with my mind; but on the other hand, with my flesh, I serve the principle of sin.

8 Therefore, now no condemnation awaits those who are living in Jesus the Anointed, *the Liberating King,* ²because when you live in the Anointed One, Jesus, *a new law takes effect.* The law of the Spirit of life *breathes into you and* liberates you from the law of sin and death. ³God did something the law could never do. *You see, human flesh took its toll on God's law. In and of itself, the law is not weak; but* the flesh weakens it. So to condemn the sin that was *ruling* in the flesh, God sent His own Son, bearing the likeness of sinful flesh, as a sin offering. ⁴Now we are able to live up to the justice demanded by the law. But that ability has not come from living by our fallen human nature; it has come because we walk according to the movement of the Spirit in our lives.

⁵If you live your life animated by the flesh—*namely, your fallen, corrupt nature*—then your mind is focused on the matters of the flesh. But if you live your life animated by the Spirit—*namely, God's indwelling presence*—then your focus is on the work of the Spirit. ⁶A mind focused on the flesh is doomed to death, but a mind focused on the Spirit will find full life and complete peace. ⁷You see, a mind focused on the flesh is declaring war against God; it defies the authority of God's law and is incapable of following His path. ⁸*So it is clear that* God

* 7:7 Exodus 20:17; Deuteronomy 5:21

takes no pleasure in those who live oriented to the flesh.

The power of sin and death has been eclipsed by the power of the Spirit. The Spirit breathes life into our mortal, sin-infested bodies—thanks to what Jesus has done for us. By sending His Son in "the likeness of sinful flesh," God judges sin finally and completely. The sins of the world are concentrated and condemned in the flesh of Jesus as He hangs on the cross. So now there is no condemnation remaining for those who've entered into the life, death, and resurrection of Jesus.

---

[9]But you do not live in the flesh. You live in the Spirit, assuming, of course, that the Spirit of God lives inside of you. *The truth is that* anyone who does not have the Spirit of the Anointed living within does not belong to God. [10]If the Anointed One lives within you, even though the body is *as good as* dead because of *the effects of* sin, the Spirit is infusing you with life now that you are right with God. [11]If the Spirit of the One who resurrected Jesus from the dead lives inside of you, then *you can be sure that* He who raised Him will cast *the light of* life into your mortal bodies through the life-giving power of the Spirit residing in you.

As Paul ponders the story of redemption, he finds in the family unit a beautiful image of what salvation means. Those who enter into God's salvation are adopted into God's family. Before we receive the gift of God's grace, we are homeless orphans searching for some place to belong. But now all that has changed. The Father reaches out through His Son to all those orphaned by sin and death, and He brings them into His family. We are adopted into His forever family and fully enfranchised as His heirs.

---

[12]So, my brothers and sisters, you owe the flesh nothing! You do not need to live according to its ways, *so abandon its oppressive regime.* [13]For if your life is just about satisfying the impulses of your sinful nature, then prepare to die. But if you have invited the Spirit to destroy these selfish desires, you will experience life. [14]If the Spirit of God is leading you, then *take comfort in knowing* you are His children. [15]You see, you have not received a spirit that returns you to slavery, so you have nothing to fear. The Spirit you have received adopts you *and welcomes you* into God's own family. That's why we call out to Him, "Abba! Father!" *as we would address a loving daddy.* [16]*Through that prayer,* God's Spirit confirms in our spirits that we are His children. [17]If we are God's children, that means we are His heirs along with the Anointed, set to inherit everything that is His. If we share His sufferings, *we know that* we will ultimately share in His glory.

[18]Now I'm sure of this: the sufferings we endure now are not even worth comparing to the glory that is coming and will be revealed in us. [19]For all of creation is waiting, yearning for the time when the children of God will be revealed. [20]You see, all of creation has collapsed into emptiness, not by its own choosing, but by God's. Still He placed within it a *deep and abiding* hope [21]that creation would one day be liberated from its slavery to corruption and experience the glorious freedom of the children of God. [22]For we know that all creation groans *in unison* with birthing pains up until now. [23]*And there is more;* it's not just creation—all of us are groaning together too. Though we have already tasted the firstfruits of the Spirit, we are longing for the total redemption of our bodies that comes when our adoption as children *of God* is complete—[24]for we have been saved in this hope *and for this future.* But hope does not involve what we already *have or* see. For who goes around hoping for what he already has? [25]But if we wait expectantly for things we have never seen, then we hope with true perseverance and eager anticipation.

[26]A similar thing happens *when we pray.* We are weak and do not know how to pray, so the Spirit steps in and articulates prayers for us with groaning too profound for words. [27]*Don't you know that* He who pursues and explores the human heart *intimately* knows the Spirit's mind because He pleads to God for His saints to align their lives with the

will of God? [28]We are confident that God is able to orchestrate everything to work toward something good *and beautiful* when we love Him and accept His invitation to live according to His plan. [29-30]*From the distant past, His eternal love reached into the future. You see, He knew those who would be His one day, and He chose them beforehand to be conformed to the image of His Son so that Jesus would be the firstborn of a new family of believers, all brothers and sisters.* As for those He chose beforehand, He called them to a different destiny so that they would experience what it means to be made right with God and share in His glory.

[31]So what should we say about all of this? If God is on our side, *then tell me: whom should we fear?* [32]If He did not spare His own Son, but handed Him over on our account, then *don't you think that* He will graciously give us all things with Him? [33]Can anyone be so bold as to level a charge against God's chosen? *Especially since* God's *"not guilty"* verdict is already declared. [34]Who has the authority to condemn? Jesus the Anointed who died, but *more importantly, conquered death when He* was raised to sit at the right hand of God where He pleads on our behalf. [35]So who can separate us? What can come between us and the love of God's Anointed? Can troubles, hardships, persecution, hunger, poverty, danger, or even death? *The answer is, absolutely nothing.* [36]As the psalm says,

> On Your behalf, our lives are endangered constantly;
> we are like sheep awaiting slaughter.*

[37]But no matter what comes, we will always taste victory through Him who loved us. [38]For I have every confidence that nothing— not death, life, heavenly messengers, *dark* spirits, the present, the future, spiritual powers, [39]height, depth, nor any created thing— can come between us and the love of God revealed in the Anointed, Jesus our Lord.

In all of Paul's letters, there is no more triumphant note than in this declaration. He has reached the climax of what it means to live empowered by God's Spirit. We are champions, one and all. We will taste victory and sweet success

made possible by His love and gifts to us. We may fear the harsh judgment of the majority. We may bristle under the scowls of others. We may even be unsettled by thoughts of death, persecution, and dark spiritual powers. But Paul celebrates the absolute assurance that no one and nothing can come between us and the love of God.

---

9 Now let me speak the truth *as plainly as I know it* in the Anointed One. I am not lying when I say that my conscience and the Holy Spirit are witnesses [2]to my state of constant grief. [3]*It may sound extreme;* but I wish that I were lost, cursed, and totally separated from the Anointed—if that would change *the eternal destination of* my brothers and sisters, my flesh *and countrymen.* [4]They are, *after all,* Israelites who have been adopted into God's family; the glory, the covenants, the *gift of the* law, the temple service, and God's promises are their rightful heritage. [5]The patriarchs are theirs, too; and from their bloodline comes the Anointed One, *the Liberating King,* who reigns supreme over all things, God blessed forever. Amen.

The tone changes abruptly. One minute Paul is celebrating the power of Jesus' love; the next he is grieving because they are not pressing their way into the Kingdom.

[6]Clearly it is not that God's word has failed. The truth is that not everyone descended from Israel is truly Israel. [7]Just because people can claim Abraham as their father does not make them his true children. But *in the Scriptures, it says,* "Through Isaac your *covenant* children will be named."* [8]The proper interpretation is this: Abraham's children by natural descent are not *necessarily* God's covenant people; what matters is that His children receive and live the promise. [9]For this is the word God promised: "In due time, I will come, and Sarah will give birth to a son."* [10]But the story didn't stop there. Remember when Rebekah conceived her twin boys by our father Isaac? [11-12]The twins were in Rebekah's womb when God said to her, "The older will serve the younger."* *This*

* 8:36 Psalm 44:22   * 9:7 Genesis 21:12   * 9:9 Genesis 18:10,14
* 9:11-12 Genesis 25:23

was not based on merit or actions; the twins had not done anything to please or displease God. This was God's call on each son and His desired purposes. [13]Just as the Scriptures say, "I loved Jacob, but I hated Esau."*

[14]So how do we talk about that? Are God's dealings unjust? Absolutely not! [15]Because He said to Moses, "I will show mercy to whomever I choose to show mercy, and I will demonstrate compassion on whomever I choose to have compassion."* [16]The point is that God's mercy has nothing to do with our will or the things we pursue. It is completely up to God. [17]The Scriptures even speak to the Pharaoh himself: "I have given you a position of power so that I might show My *greater* power through you and so that My name might be declared throughout every land upon the earth."* [18]So when and where God decides to show mercy is completely up to Him. Likewise, when He chooses to harden one's heart, how can we argue?

[19]I can hear one of you asking, "Then how can He blame us *if He is the one in complete control?* How can we do anything He has not chosen for us?" [20]*Here's my answer:* Who are you, a mere human, to argue with God? If God takes the time to shape us from the dust, is it right to point a finger at Him and ask, "Why have You made me this way?" [21]Doesn't the potter have the right to shape the clay in any way he chooses? Can't he make one lump into an elegant vase, and another into a common jug? *Absolutely.* [22]Even though God desires to demonstrate His anger and to reveal His power, He has shown tremendous restraint toward those vessels of wrath that are doomed to be cracked and shattered. [23]And why is that? To make the wealth of His glory known to vessels of mercy that are prepared for great beauty. [24]*These vessels of mercy* include all of us. God has invited Jews and non-Jews, *insiders and outsiders;* it makes no difference. [25]The prophet Hosea says:

I will give a new name to those who are not My people; I'll call them "My people,"
and to the one who has not been loved, I'll rename her "beloved."*

[26]And it shall turn out that in the very place where it was said to them, "You are not My people,"
they will be called "children of the living God."*

[27]And *this is what* Isaiah cries out when he speaks of Israel, "Even though the number of the children of Israel had once been like the sand of the sea, only a remnant of My people will be rescued and remain. [28]For the Lord will waste no time in carrying out every detail of His sentence upon the earth."* [29]It is as Isaiah predicts:

Except for the fraction of us who hang on by *the grace of* the Lord, Commander of *heavenly* armies,
we'd be *destroyed and deserted* like Sodom
and Gomorrah, *utterly done in.**

V

For Paul, the astonishing truth of the gospel has to do with what God is now doing with the non-Jews. Apparently God's plan all along is to make those who are not His people into His people. All those who never experienced God's love are now experiencing it as they enter into the life of the Spirit through faith. But what does this mean for Israel? Israel, too, is included in the people of God; but again, this does not mean all of Israel. Pedigree is not what counts; faith is. As it was in the days of the prophets, so it is again. Divine judgment is falling on disobedience, but a remnant of faithful Jews—a fraction of the whole—is being saved.

---

[30]So what does all of this mean? Did the non-Jews stumble into a right standing with God without chasing after it? Yes, they found it through faith. [31]And has Israel, who pursued the law to secure a right standing *with God,* failed to keep the law? Yes again. [32]And why is that? Because Israel did not follow the path of faith. They thought that whatever they needed *to be right with God* could be accomplished by doing the works of the law; they tripped over the stumbling stone. [33]As the Scriptures say,

* 9:13 Malachi 1:2-3   * 9:15 Exodus 33:19   * 9:17 Exodus 9:16
* 9:25 Hosea 2:23   * 9:26 Hosea 1:10   * 9:27-28 Isaiah 10:22-23
* 9:29 Isaiah 1:9

Look *what I am going to do* in Zion.
I'll put in place a stone that makes them
      stumble, a rock that trips them up,
and those who trust in it will not be
      disgraced.*

10 My brothers and sisters, I pray
constantly to God for the salvation
of my people; it is the deep desire
of my heart. ²What I can say about them is
that they are enthusiastic about God, but
that won't lead them to Him because their
zeal is not based on true knowledge. ³In
their ignorance about how God is working to
make things right, they have been trying to
establish their own right standing with God
through the law. But they are not operating
under God's saving, restorative justice. ⁴You
see, God's purpose for the law reaches its climax when the Anointed One arrives; now all
who trust *in Him* can have their lives made
right with God.

God's plan to restore the world disfigured by sin and death reaches
its climax with the resurrection of
Jesus. When the King enters, all
the prophecies, all the hopes, all
the longings find in Him their true
fulfillment. There may have been
earlier fulfillments; but these are
only partial fulfillments, signposts
along the way to God's true goal.
The goal has been the restoration of people to a holy God. With
Jesus, we find the only perfect
man with right standing before
God. He comes to blaze a path
defined by God's justice, not by
our own sense of right and wrong.
All men, women, and children who
commit their lives to Him will be
made right with God and will begin
new lives defined by faith and
God's new covenant.

---

⁵Moses *made this clear long ago when he*
wrote about *what it takes to have* a right
relationship with God based on the law:
"The person devoted to the law's commands will live by them."* ⁶But a right
relationship based on faith sounds like this:
"Do not say to yourselves, 'Who will go up
into heaven?'"* (that is, to bring down the

Anointed One), ⁷"or, 'Who will go down into
the abyss?'"* (that is, to bring the Anointed
One up from the dead). ⁸But what does it
actually say? "The word is near you, in your
mouth and in your heart"* (that is, the good
news we *have been called to* preach to you).
⁹So if you believe deep in your heart that
God raised Jesus from the *pit of* death and if
you voice your allegiance by confessing *the
truth* that "Jesus is Lord," then you will be
saved! ¹⁰Belief begins in the heart and leads
to *a life that's* right with God; confession
departs from our lips and brings *eternal* salvation. ¹¹Because what Isaiah said *was true*:
"The one who trusts in Him will not be disgraced."* ¹²Remember that the Lord draws
no distinction between Jew and non-Jew—
He is Lord over all things, and He pours out
His treasures on all who invoke His name
¹³because *as Scripture says*, "Everyone who
calls on the name of the Lord will be saved."*

**Faith is not something we do. It is
a response to what God has done
already on our behalf, the response of
a spirit restless in a fragmented world.**

¹⁴How can people invoke His name when
they do not believe? How can they believe
in Him when they have not heard? How
can they hear if there is no one proclaiming
Him? ¹⁵How can some give voice to the truth
if they are not sent *by God*? As *Isaiah* said,
"Ah, how beautiful the feet of those who
declare the good news *of victory, of peace and
liberation*."* ¹⁶But some will hear the good
news and refuse to submit to the truth they
hear. Isaiah *the prophet also* says, "Lord, who
would ever believe it? Who would possibly
accept what we've been told?"* ¹⁷So faith
proceeds from hearing, as we listen to the
message about God's Anointed.

¹⁸But let me ask this: have my people
ever heard? Indeed, they have:

Yet from here to the ends of the earth,
    their voice has gone out;
    the whole world has heard what they
      have to say.*

¹⁹But again let me ask: did Israel *perhaps
hear and* not understand all of this? *Well,*
Moses was the first to say,

---

* 9:33 Isaiah 8:14; 28:16   * 10:5 Leviticus 18:5   * 10:6 Deuteronomy
30:12   * 10:7 Deuteronomy 30:13   * 10:8 Deuteronomy 30:14
* 10:11 Isaiah 28:16   * 10:13 Joel 2:32   * 10:15 Isaiah 52:7
* 10:16 Isaiah 53:1   * 10:18 Psalm 19:4

I will make you jealous with a people who
    are not a nation.
  With a senseless people I will anger
    you.*

²⁰Then Isaiah the fearless *prophet* says it this
way:

I was found by people who did not seek Me;
  I showed My face to those who never
    asked for Me.*

²¹And as to *the fate of* Israel, God says,

All day long I opened My hands
  to a rebellious people, who constantly
    work against Me.*

11 Now I ask you, has God rejected
His people? Absolutely not! *I'm living
proof that God is faithful.* I am an Israelite, Abraham's my father, and Benjamin's
my tribe. ²God has not, *and will not,* abandon
His covenant people; He always knew they
would belong to Him. Don't you remember
the story of what happens when Elijah pleads
with God to deal with Israel? The Scripture
tells us *his protest*: ³"Lord, they have murdered
Your prophets, they have demolished Your
altars, and I alone am left *faithful to You*; now
they are seeking to kill me."* ⁴How does God
answer his pleas for help? He says, "I have
held back 7,000 men who are faithful to Me;
none have bowed a knee to worship Baal."*
⁵The same thing is happening now. God has
preserved a remnant, elected by grace. ⁶Grace
is central in God's action here, and it has nothing to do with deeds prescribed by the law. If
it did, grace would not be grace.

---

⁷Now what does all this mean? Israel has
chased an end it has never reached. Yet those
chosen by God *through grace* have reached
it while all others were made hard *as stones.*
⁸The Scriptures continue to say *it best:*

God has confounded them so they are not
    able to think,
  given them eyes that do not see, and
    ears that do not hear,
Down to this very day.*

⁹David says *it this way*:

Let their table be turned into a snare and
    a trap,
  an obstacle *to peace* and payback *for
    their hostility.*
¹⁰Let their *bright* eyes become cloudy,
    darkened so they cannot see,
  and bend their *proud* backs through
    it all.*

¹¹So I ask: did God's people stumble and fall
off the deep end? Absolutely not! *They are not
lost forever;* but through their misconduct,
the door has been opened for salvation to
extend even to the outsiders. *This has been
part of God's plan all along, and* so is the
jealousy that comes when they realize *the
outsiders have been welcomed into God's new
covenant.* ¹²So if their misconduct leads ultimately to God's riches coming to the world
and if their failure turns into the blessing
of salvation to all people, then how much
greater will be the riches and blessing when
they are included fully?
    ¹³But I have this to say to all of you who
are not ethnic Jews: I am God's emissary*
to you, and I honor this call by focusing on
what God is doing *with and through you.*
¹⁴I do this so that somehow my own blood
brothers and sisters will be made jealous;
and that, *I trust,* will bring some to salvation.
¹⁵If the fact that they are currently set aside
resolves the hostility between God and the
rest of the world, what will their acceptance
bring if not life from the dead? ¹⁶If the first
and best of the dough you offer is sacred, the
entire loaf will be as well. If the root *of the
tree* is sacred, the branches will be also.
    ¹⁷Imagine some branches are cut off *of
the cultivated olive tree* and other branches

---

* 10:19 Deuteronomy 32:21   * 10:20 Isaiah 65:1   * 10:21 Isaiah
65:2   * 11:3 1 Kings 19:10,14   * 11:4 1 Kings 19:18. Baal is the name for
a Canaanite god.   * 11:8 Deuteronomy 29:4; Isaiah 29:10
* 11:9-10 Psalm 69:22-23   * 11:13 Literally, apostle

of a wild olive (which represents all of you *outsiders*) are grafted in their place. You are nourished by the root of the *cultivated* olive tree. [18]It doesn't give you license to become proud and self-righteous about the fact that you've been grafted in. If you do boast, remember that the branches do not sustain the root—it is the system of roots that *nourishes and* supports you.

[19]I can almost hear some of you saying, "Branches had to be pruned to make room for me." [20]Yes, they were. They were removed because they did not believe; and you will stay attached, be strong, *and be productive* only through faith. So don't think too highly of yourselves; instead, stand in awe *of God's mercy.* [21]Besides *we know that* God did not spare the natural branches, so there is no reason to think He will spare you. [22]Witness the simultaneous balance of the kindness and severity of our God. Severity is directed at the fallen *branches withering without faith.* Yet kindness is directed at you. So live in the kindness of God or else prepare to be cut off yourselves. [23]If those *branches that have been cut from the tree* do not stay in unbelief, then God will carefully graft them back *onto the tree* because He has the power to do that. [24]So if it is possible for you to be taken from a wild olive tree and become part of a cultivated olive tree, imagine how much easier it would be to reconnect branches that originally grew on that olive tree.

[25]My brothers and sisters, I do not want you to be in the dark about this mystery—*I am going to let you in on the plan* so that you will not think too highly of yourselves. A part of Israel has been hardened *to the good news* until the full number of those outside the Jewish family have entered in. [26]This is the way that all of Israel will be saved. As it was written, *so it also stands*:

> The Deliverer will come from Zion;
>   He will drive away wickedness from
>   Jacob.
> [27]And this is My covenant promise to them,
>   *on the day* when I take away their
>   sins.*

[28]*It may seem strange.* When it comes to *the work of* the gospel, the fact that they oppose it is actually for your benefit. But when you factor in God's election, they are truly loved because they descended from faithful forefathers. [29]You see, when God gives a *grace* gift and issues a call *to a people*, He does not change His mind and take it back. [30]There was a time when you *outsiders* were disobedient to God *and at odds with His purpose*, but now you have experienced mercy as a result of their disobedience. [31]In the same way, their disobedience now will make a way for them to receive mercy as a result of the mercy shown to you. [32]For God has assigned all of us together—*Jews and non-Jews, insiders and outsiders*—to disobedience so He can show His mercy to all.

V

The cultivated olive tree provides Paul with a beautiful image of how believing Jews and non-Jews were organically connected in the plan of God. Life flows from the earth to the branches—some natural, some grafted in—through the root-stock. Paul wants to make sure the grafted branches know they have not arrived on their own; their spiritual life and vitality flow from the root, Israel. God is the Farmer who has tenderly grafted them into the sturdy stock on the basis of faith. So pride and arrogance are completely out of place for those grafted branches. They will bear fruit only as they remain connected by faith to the stock.

V

Paul says that God's mysterious plan for the ages is being revealed as the number of outsiders swells in the churches and as a part of Israel is hardened, at least for a time. But let's not forget that hardening is not God's unilateral action. Whatever hardening takes place happens first on our side before God reluctantly agrees. That part of Israel now hardened has already rejected God's Anointed. Yet when the full complement of non-Jewish outsiders enters God's kingdom, "all Israel will be saved." But clearly "all Israel" can't mean every last Jew, because Paul has already shown that not every son

---

* 11:26-27 Isaiah 27:9; 59:20-21; Jeremiah 31:33-34

or daughter of Abraham is an heir to the promise.

33*We cannot wrap our minds around* God's wisdom and knowledge! Its depths can never be measured! We cannot understand His judgments or explain the mysterious ways that He works! For,

34Who can fathom the mind of the Lord?
   Or who can claim to be His
      advisor?*

35Or,

Who can give to God in advance
   so that God must pay him back?*

36For all that exists originates in Him, comes through Him, and is moving toward Him; so give Him the glory forever. Amen.

12 Brothers and sisters, in light of *all I have shared with you about* God's mercies, I urge you to offer your bodies as a living and holy sacrifice *to God*, a sacred offering that brings Him pleasure; this is your reasonable, essential worship. 2Do not allow this world to mold you in its own image. Instead, be transformed *from the inside out* by renewing your mind. As a result, you will be able to discern what God wills and whatever God finds good, pleasing, and complete.

V

Paul urges those who read and hear his letter to respond to the good news by offering their bodies—eyes, ears, mouths, hands, feet—to God as a "living sacrifice." Paul knows well enough that sacrifices end in death, not life. But the sacrifice of Jesus changes everything. His resurrection steals life from death and makes it possible for those who trust in Him to become a sacrifice and yet live. But how do we live? We do not live as before, wrapping ourselves in the world and its bankrupt values. We live in constant renewal and transformation of our minds.

3Because of the grace allotted to me, I can *respectfully* tell you not to think of yourselves as being more important than you are; devote your minds to sound judgment since God has assigned to each of us a measure of faith. 4For in the same way that one body has so many different parts, each with different functions; 5we, too—the many—are different parts that form one body in the Anointed One. Each one of us is joined with one another, *and we become together what we could not be alone.* 6Since our gifts vary depending on the grace poured out on each of us, *it is important that* we exercise the gifts *we have been given.* If prophecy is your gift, then speak as a prophet according to your proportion of faith. 7If service is your gift, then serve well. If teaching is your gift, then teach well. 8If you have been given a voice of encouragement, then use it *often.* If giving is your gift, then be generous. If leading, then be eager to get started. If sharing God's mercy, then be cheerful in sharing it.

9Love others *well, and* don't hide behind a mask; love authentically. Despise evil; pursue what is good *as if your life depends on it.* 10Live in true devotion to one another, loving each other as sisters and brothers. Be first to honor others *by putting them first.* 11Do not slack in your faithfulness and hard work. Let your spirit be on fire, bubbling up and boiling over, as you serve the Lord. 12*Do not forget to* rejoice, for hope is always just around the corner. Hold up through the hard times that are coming, and devote yourselves to prayer. 13Share what you have with the saints, so they lack nothing; take every opportunity to open your *life and* home to others.

14If people mistreat or malign you, bless them. Always speak blessings, not curses. 15If some have cause to celebrate, join in the celebration. And if others are weeping, join in that as well. 16Work toward unity, and live in harmony with one another. Avoid thinking you are better than others or wiser than the rest; instead, embrace common people *and ordinary tasks.* 17Do not retaliate with evil, regardless of the evil brought against you. Try to do what is good *and right and honorable* as agreed upon by all people. 18If it is within your power, make peace with all people. 19*Again,* my loved ones, do not seek revenge; instead, allow God's wrath *to make sure justice is served.* Turn it over to Him. For the Scriptures say, "Revenge is Mine. I will

* 11:34 Isaiah 40:13   * 11:35 Job 41:11

settle all scores."* [20]But *consider this bit of wisdom:* "If your enemy is hungry, give him something to eat. If he is thirsty, give him something to drink; because if you treat him kindly, it will be like heaping hot coals on top of his head."* [21]Never let evil get the best of you; instead, overpower evil with the good.

13 It is important that all of us submit to the authorities who have charge over us because God establishes all authority *in heaven and on the earth.* [2]Therefore, a person who rebels against authority rebels against the order He established, and people like that can expect to face certain judgment. [3]You see, if you do the right thing, you have nothing to be worried about from the rulers; but if you do what you know is wrong, the rulers will make sure you pay a price. Would you not rather live with a clear conscience than always have to be looking over your shoulder? Then keep doing what you know to be good and right, and they will publicly honor you.

[4]*Look at it this way:* The ruler is a servant of God called to serve and benefit you. But he is also a servant of God executing wrath upon those who practice evil. If you do what is wrong, then you'd better be afraid because he wields the power of the sword and doesn't make empty threats.

At the time, Christians are a tiny minority within Judaism, a minor religion in the largest empire the world has ever seen. Minorities are often the subjects of rumors, suspicions, and innuendos. Christians don't need to add to the problem by developing a reputation as lawbreakers and rebels. So Kingdom citizens are not to dodge taxes or cheat on fees imposed by legitimate governing authorities. They are to show the proper respect for officials in power. Ultimately those who follow the truth of the gospel under the banner of the Anointed One may find themselves at odds with the powers that be. But Paul's counsel here is not a blanket approval of any and every government that may arise in a broken world.

[5]So submission is not optional; it's required. But don't just submit for the sake of avoiding punishment; submit *and abide by the laws* because your conscience leads you to do the right thing. [6]Pay your taxes for the same reason because the authorities are servants of God, giving their full attention to take care of these things. [7]Pay all of them what you owe. If you owe taxes, then pay. If you owe fees, then pay. In the same way, give honor and respect to those who deserve it.

[8]Don't owe anyone anything, with the exception of love to one another—*that is a debt which never ends*—because the person who loves others has fulfilled the law. [9]The commands *given to you in the Scriptures*—do not commit adultery, do not murder, do not take what is not yours, do not covet*—and any other command *you have heard* are summarized in God's instruction: "Love your neighbor as yourself."* [10]Does love hurt anyone? Absolutely not. In fact, love achieves everything the law requires.

Believers are not to have any obligation of any kind. Borrowed money and granted favors always come with strings attached. How many lives and families have been ruined by debts and deals made in haste! There is only one obligation Paul allows, and that is love. When we share God's care and compassion with others, we fulfill His law whether we realize it or not. Fundamentally, God's law has always been about love.

[11]And *now consider* this. You know well the times *you are living in.* It is time for you to wake up *and see what is right before your eyes:* for salvation is nearer to us now than when we first believed. [12]The darkness of night is dissolving as dawn's light draws near, so walk out on your old dark life and put on the armor of light. [13]May we all act as good and respectable people, living today the same way as we will in the day *of His coming.* Do not fall into patterns of dark living: wild partying, drunkenness, sexual depravity, decadent gratification, quarreling, and jealousy. [14]Instead, wrap yourselves in the Lord Jesus,

* 12:19 Deuteronomy 32:35   * 12:20 Proverbs 25:21-22
* 13:9 Leviticus 19:18

God's Anointed, and do not fuel your sinful imagination by indulging *your self-seeking desire* for the pleasures of the flesh.

14 *It's high time that you* welcome all people weak in the faith without debating and disputing their opinions.

²*Here's the issue:* One person believes that nothing's off the menu; *he'll eat any food put before him.* But there's another believer—*we'll call him* the weaker—who eats only vegetables *because the meat is tainted through contact with an idol.* ³If you are an eater of all things, do not be condescending to your vegetarian brother or sister. In turn, those who abstain *from certain foods on religious principles* should not judge your brothers and sisters who eat meat—if God has accepted them, *you have no reason to reject them.* ⁴How could *you think for a moment that* you have the right to judge another person's servant? Each *servant* answers to his own Master, and he will either stand or fall in His presence. *The good news is that* he will stand because the Master is able to make it so.

⁵There may be a believer who regards one day as more sacred than any other, while another views every day as sacred as the next. *In these matters,* all must reach their own conclusions *and satisfy their own minds.* ⁶If someone observes a day *as holy,* he observes it in honor of the Lord. If another eats *a particular diet,* he eats in honor of the Lord since he begins by giving thanks! If yet another abstains *from that same food,* he abstains out of respect for the Lord and begins his meal by thanking God too. ⁷*The truth is that* none of us live for ourselves, and none die for ourselves. ⁸For if we live, we live for the Lord. If we die, we die for the Lord. So in both life and death, we belong to the Lord. ⁹The Anointed One, *the Liberating King,* died and returned to life to make this a reality: through His death and resurrection, He became Lord of the living and the dead.

¹⁰So how is it that you continue to judge your brother? How is it possible for you to look down on a sister? We will all stand before the judgment seat of God. ¹¹For it is written,

"As I live, *so I promise*," says the Lord,
"every knee will bow down to Me.
Every tongue will confess to God."*

¹²So every one of us, *regardless of our eating habits,* should expect to give an account for our own lives to God.

¹³In light of this, we must resolve never to judge others and never to place an obstacle or impediment in their paths that could cause them to trip and fall. ¹⁴Personally I have been completely convinced that in Jesus, our Lord, no object in and of itself is unclean; but if my fellow believers are convinced that something is unclean, then it is unclean to them. ¹⁵If the food you eat harms your brother, then you have failed to love him. Do not let what you eat tear down your brother; after all, the Anointed laid down His life for him. ¹⁶Do not allow people to slander something you find to be good ¹⁷because the kingdom of God is not about eating and drinking. *When God reigns, the order of the day is* redeeming justice, true peace, and joy made possible by the Holy Spirit. ¹⁸You see, those who serve the Anointed in this way will be welcomed into the whole acceptance of God and valued by all men. ¹⁹Join us, and pursue a life that creates peace and builds up our brothers and sisters.

²⁰Do not sacrifice God's work for the sake of certain foods. *It is true that* all things are clean, but it's wrong to eat if you know that eating something will cause offense. ²¹It is right for you to abstain from certain meats and wine (or anything else for that matter) if it prevents your brother from falling *in his faith.* ²²Hold on to what you believe *about these issues,* but keep them between you and God. A happy man does not judge himself by the lifestyle he endorses. ²³But a man who decides for himself what to eat is condemned because he is not living by his faith. Any action not consistent with faith is sin.

V

Paul says he is free to eat, but he is not free to injure another in what he eats. Personal freedom must always give way to corporate responsibility. To put it another way, the gospel of love demands that we surrender individual liberties for the sake of our brothers and sisters. We see this demonstrated powerfully in the example of Jesus who gave up His life and freedom for the sake of the world. When we live by this ethic, we

* 14:11 Isaiah 45:23

create a community marked by warmth and hospitality. Food, drink, and holidays may well be personal options within the Kingdom. But justice, peace, and joy are communal essentials for life in the Kingdom.

15

So now what? We who are strong are not just to satisfy our own desires. We are called to carry the weaknesses of those who are not strong. [2]Each of us must strive to please our neighbors, pursuing their welfare so they will become strong. [3]The Anointed One Himself *is our model for this kind of living,* for He did not live to please Himself. And as the Scriptures declared, "When they insult You, they insult me."* [4]You see, everything written in the days of old was recorded to give us instructions *for living.* We find encouragement through the Scriptures and a call to perseverance that will produce hopeful living. [5]I pray that our God, who calls you and gives you perseverance and encouragement, will join all of you together to share one mind according to Jesus the Anointed. [6]In this unity, you will share one voice as you glorify *the one True* God, the Father of our Lord Jesus, the Anointed One, *our Liberating King.*

[7]So accept one another in the same way the Anointed has accepted you so that God will get the praise He is due. [8]For, as I am *fond of* saying, the Anointed One has become a servant of the Jews* in order to demonstrate God's truth. Effectively this confirms the promises He made to our ancestors [9]and causes the non-Jewish nations to glorify God for His mercy. As the Scriptures say,

For this I will praise You among the
  nations
and sing praises to Your name.*

[10]Again the Scriptures say,

Nations, celebrate with His *covenant*
  people.*

[11]And again,

Praise the Lord, all nations.
  Raise your voices, all people; let your
  praises flow to God.*

[12]Again Isaiah says,

Then, the root of Jesse will
  emerge—
He rises to rule all the peoples of the
  world
  *who come to Him for guidance and
  direction.*
In Him they place their hope.*

[13]I pray that God, the source of all hope, will infuse your lives with an abundance of joy and peace in the midst of your faith so that your hope will overflow through the power of the Holy Spirit.

[14]My brothers and sisters, I am ultimately confident that you are full of goodness, knowledge, and the ability to *help and* instruct one another. [15]I have written to you with unflinching honesty on many topics because I do not want you to ever lose sight of the *tremendous* grace God has given me. [16]*His grace makes me who* I am, a minister of the Anointed One, Jesus, called to serve the nations.

Though Paul's churches are made up of Jews and non-Jews, Paul's special calling is to be God's emissary to the nations beyond Israel, known as the Gentiles.

The good news of God is the focus of my priestly work. In effect, these nations have become an offering to God, totally acceptable, indeed made holy by the work of the Holy Spirit. [17]So in Jesus, the Anointed One, I have reason to celebrate the things I do for God. [18]I don't want to be presumptuous, so I will restrict myself to what the Anointed has accomplished through my words and actions, which has culminated in the obedience of the nations. [19]*My words and actions have been rooted* in Spirit-empowered signs and miracles. *The upshot is this:* I have been able to preach the good news of the Anointed One *in city after city* from Jerusalem all the way *around the Mediterranean* to Illyricum. [20]I have dreamed of preaching the gospel in places where no one has ever heard of the Anointed so that I do not build on a foundation laid by anyone else. [21]But as the Scriptures say,

* 15:3 Psalm 69:9   * 15:8 Literally, "the circumcision"
* 15:9 Psalm 18:49   * 15:10 Deuteronomy 32:43   * 15:11 Psalm 117:1
* 15:12 Isaiah 11:10

They will see Him even though they've
never been told about Him;
they will understand even though they
never heard of Him.*

22Because of many issues, I have not been
able to visit you *in the city of Rome.* 23But *my
time to serve those here is coming to an end,*
there's no room left for me in this region,
and I have longed to come to you for many
years. So I plan to visit you 24on my journey
to Spain. I am hoping that I will not only
see you face-to-face, but that you will assist
me in the journey *west* after I have enjoyed
our time together. 25But right now I must
make the journey to Jerusalem to serve
the saints there. 26Those in Macedonia and
Achaia decided it was a good idea to share
their funds to help the poor among the saints
in Jerusalem. 27*I must tell you that* they
were thrilled to be able to help. *They realize that* they are indebted to the believers in
Jerusalem. If the nations share in the Jews'
spiritual goods, then it's only right that they
minister back to them in material goods.
28When this work is complete and the funds
we've collected are delivered, I will make
my way to Spain through your *grand* city
of Rome and enjoy some of your hospitality.
29I'm sure that when I come to you I will
come as a blessing and as one fully blessed
by the Anointed One.

30My brothers and sisters, I urgently
plead with you by the name of our Lord
Jesus, the Anointed, and by the love of
the Spirit to join together with me in your
prayers to God for my success *in these next
endeavors.* 31Pray that I will be rescued from
those who deny *and persecute* the faith in
Judea and that my service in Jerusalem will
meet the approval of all the saints there. 32If
that happens, then my journey to you will
be filled with joy; and, if God wills, I can *rest
and* be refreshed in your presence. 33*I pray*
the God of all peace will be with you all.
Amen.

Before Paul treks west to Rome, he
must complete an important mission he started years earlier. He
must carry to Jerusalem an offering for the poor collected from the
outsider churches. Paul, the emissary, hopes not only that the offering will alleviate the human need
and suffering brought on by years
of famine, but that it will also build
a bridge between his mainly non-
Jewish churches and the Jewish
mother church in Jerusalem. But
when he arrives in Jerusalem, Paul's
enemies trump up charges against
him that ultimately land him in jail.
So Paul makes it to Rome, but not
as he planned. Several years later,
after a lengthy confinement in
Caesarea and a perilous journey at
sea, he is led into Rome as a prisoner of the empire.

---

16 I commend to you our *beloved* sister
Phoebe; she serves the church in
Cenchrea as a *faithful* deacon. 2*It is
important* that you welcome her in the Lord
in a manner befitting your saintly status.
Join in her work, and assist her in any way
she needs you. She has spent her energy and
resources helping others, and *I am blessed to
have her* as my benefactor as well.

3Give my best to Prisca and Aquila; *they
are not only my colleagues in my profession of
tent making, but more importantly* they are
my fellow servants of Jesus the Anointed.
4They put their lives on the line to keep me
safe. Not only do I owe them my thanks, so
do all the churches of the non-Jews. 5Send
my regards to the church that meets in their
house.

Send greetings to Epaenetus. I love
him dearly *and celebrate his journey to faith
because* he was the first to believe in the
Anointed One in all of Asia.

6Salute Mary for me; she has worked
hard for all of you.

7Give my regards to Andronicus and
Junias, who are part of my own family and
served time in prison with me. They are well
known among the emissaries* and have been
in the Anointed longer than I.

8Give my best to Ampliatus whom I love
in the Lord, 9and greet Urbanus (our fellow
worker in service to the Anointed One) and
my beloved Stachys.

10Send greetings to Apelles, a tried and
true *believer* in the Anointed, and to the
entire family of Aristobulus.

11*Do not forget to* greet Herodion,
another of my relatives, and everyone in the
family of Narcissus who belong to the Lord.

* 15:21 Isaiah 52:15   * 16:7 Literally, apostles

[12]Greet Tryphaena and Tryphosa, *faithful* laborers in the Lord, and our beloved Persis, who also has accomplished a great deal in the Lord.

[13]Give my best to Rufus, clearly one of the Lord's chosen, and also his mother. She's like a mother to me.

[14]My regards also go to Asyncritus, Phlegon, Hermes, Patrobas, Hermas, and all the brothers and sisters who are along with them.

[15]Greet Philologus and Julia, Nereus and his sister, and *let me not forget* Olympas and all the saints who journey with them.

[16]Greet each other with a holy kiss. All of the churches of the Anointed *under my care* send their greetings to all of you.

[17]I am pleading with all of you, brothers and sisters, to keep up your guard against anyone who is causing conflicts and enticing others with teachings contrary to what you have already learned. *If there are people like that in your churches,* stay away from them. [18]These kinds of people are not truly serving our Lord Jesus the Anointed; they have devoted their lives to satisfying their own appetites. With smooth talking and a *well-rehearsed* blessing, they lead a lot of unsuspecting people down the wrong path. [19]The stories about the way you are living in obedience to God have traveled to all *the churches.* So celebrate *your faithfulness to God* that is being displayed in your lives—seek wisdom about the good life, and remain innocent when it comes to evil. [20]*If you do this,* the God of peace will crush Satan under your feet soon. May the grace of our Lord Jesus, the Anointed One, *the Liberating King,* be ever present with you.

[21]Timothy, my coworker *in the spreading of the gospel,* also sends his greeting to all of you, as do my kinsmen, Lucius, Jason, and Sosipater.

[22]I, Tertius, the one who wrote this letter *for Paul,* greet you in *the name of* the Lord. [23]Gaius, my host here as well as patron for the whole church, sends his* best to all of you. Erastus, the city administrator, sends his greetings along with brother Quartus. [[24]May the grace of our Lord Jesus, the Anointed One, touch you all. Amen.]*

[25]So to the One who is able to strengthen you to live consistently with my good news and the preaching of Jesus, the Anointed, with the revelation of the ancient mystery that has been kept secret since the earliest days, [26]this mystery is revealed through the prophetic voices passed down in the Scriptures, as they have been commanded by the Eternal God. *In this time,* this mystery is being made known to the nations so that all may be led to faith-filled obedience.

[27]To the one *true and* wise God, we offer glory for all times through Jesus, the Anointed One. Amen.

* 16:23 Some early manuscripts read "their." * 16:24 Some early manuscripts omit this verse.

1 CORINTHIANS

Letter to the church in Corinth

From Paul, the apostle to the Gentiles

Jesus invested His life in twelve unlikely characters, a ragtag group of common Jews, and used them as the foundation of His church. Then He miraculously revealed Himself to Saul (also known as Paul), who had previously devoted his life to the destruction of Jewish Christians. Not only was Paul an unlikely emissary, but he also planted churches in unlikely places. Corinth was the last place one would imagine starting one of the first churches. This small strip of land in Achaia (southern Greece) served as a seaport on two seas and was home to sailors and merchants. It was known primarily as a place of sin, decadence, and corruption. If someone was looking for prostitutes, orgies, pagan festivals, or abundant alcohol, then Corinth was the place. However, if a person was looking for a faithful church, then this would seem an impossible location—but not with God.

Paul stayed in Corinth for almost two years. In that time, he led many people to faith in Jesus. Some of these people were transients who boarded ships and carried the good news to distant shores, but others stayed in Corinth as members of this early Christian community. Once Paul left to plant churches elsewhere, the situation in Corinth began to deteriorate. This first generation of believers struggled with what it meant to live the gospel faithfully in this challenging and immoral city. When Paul heard reports that the church was deeply divided and immorality was rampant, he had no trouble believing it. He addresses those issues in the first part of this letter (chapters 1–6). But Paul also received a letter from the church posing to him a number of questions about celibacy, food offered to idols, spiritual gifts, and the resurrection. He deals with their questions in the last part of his letter (chapters 7–15).

Although this letter is known today as 1 Corinthians, it is clear Paul wrote this church an earlier letter which apparently some misunderstood (see 1 Corinthians 5:9). So 1 Corinthians is at least Paul's second letter to them. But the situation becomes more complex, as we see in 2 Corinthians, when Paul speaks of another tearful letter written between 1 and 2 Corinthians. In all, we know of four letters Paul writes to this community, but there may have been more. Of all the churches Paul established, the Corinthian church was the most troubled; so it received more visits, more letters, and more instruction than any other. Paul's letters to the Corinthians exhibit his deep, pastoral concern for these urban believers who live in a truly secular city. His teachings continue to speak today to our own troubled times.

1 Paul, called out by God's will to be an emissary* for Jesus the Anointed, along with brother Sosthenes, ²to God's church gathering in the city of Corinth. As people who are united with Jesus, the Anointed One, you have been set apart for service. You are all called into community to live as saints with all who invoke the name of our Lord Jesus, the Anointed

³I pray that God our Father and the Lord Jesus, the Anointed One, will shower you with grace and peace.

⁴I am continuously thanking my God for you when I think about the grace God has offered you in Jesus the Anointed. ⁵*In this grace,* God is enriching every aspect of your lives by gifting you with the right words to say and everything you need to know. ⁶In this way, your life story confirms the life story of the Anointed One, ⁷so you are not ill-equipped or slighted on any necessary gifts as you patiently anticipate the day when our Lord Jesus, the Anointed One, is revealed. ⁸Until that final day, He will preserve you; and on that day, He will consider you faultless. ⁹*Count on this:* God is faithful and in His faithfulness called you out into an intimate relationship with His Son, our Lord Jesus the Anointed.

¹⁰My brothers and sisters, I urge you by the name of our Lord Jesus, the Anointed, to come together in agreement. Do not allow anything *or anyone* to create division among you. Instead, be restored, completely fastened together with one mind and shared judgment. ¹¹I have heard *troubling* reports from Chloe's people that you, my siblings, are consumed by fighting *and petty disagreements.* ¹²What I have heard is that each of you is taking sides, saying, "I am with Paul," or "I am with Apollos," or "I am with Cephas," or "I am with the Anointed One." ¹³Has the Anointed One been split up *into many small pieces?* Do you think Paul was crucified for you? Were you ceremonially washed through baptism* into the name of Paul? *Absolutely not!*

and central message of Jesus. Any cult of personality is intoxicating, and it is often easier to claim to follow a person who can be seen and touched. But Christianity is founded upon the belief that Jesus is the head of the church and that all of His followers serve His will as a part of the royal priesthood.

---

¹⁴Now I am thankful that I baptized* only Crispus and Gaius, ¹⁵so none of you can *falsely* declare you were baptized in my name. ¹⁶*Now wait, as I think about it,* I also baptized the household of Stephanas; if there are others in your community whom I baptized, I cannot recall at this moment. ¹⁷The mission given to me by the Anointed One is not about baptism, but about preaching good news. The point is not *to impress others by* spinning an eloquent, intellectual argument; that *type of rhetorical showboating* would only nullify the cross of the Anointed.

¹⁸For people who are stumbling toward ruin, the message of the cross is nothing but a tall tale for fools by a fool. But for those of us who are already experiencing the reality of being rescued *and made right*, it is nothing short of God's power. ¹⁹This is why the Scripture says:

I will put an end to the wisdom of the
    so-called wise,
and I will invalidate the insight of your
    so-called experts.*

²⁰*So now,* where is the philosopher? Where is the scholar? Where is the skilled debater, the best of your time? *Step up, if you dare.* Hasn't God made fools out of *those who count on* the wisdom of this *rebellious, broken* world? ²¹For in God's *deep* wisdom, *He made it so that* the world could not even begin to comprehend Him through its own style of wisdom; in fact, God took immense pleasure in rescuing people of faith through the foolishness of the message we preach. ²²It seems the Jews are always asking for signs and the Greeks are always on the prowl for wisdom. ²³*But we tell a different story.* We proclaim a crucified Jesus, God's Anointed. For Jews

---

Paul knows that if the work of Jesus' gospel degenerates into a cult of personality, it will hardly resemble true Christianity. If the focus is on Paul, Cephas, Apollos, or any famous religious leader, then that distracts from the person this is scandalous, for outsiders* this is moronic, [24]but for those of us living out God's call—regardless of our Jewish or Greek heritage—we know the Anointed embodies God's *dynamic* power and God's *deep* wisdom. [25]*You can count on this:* God's foolishness will always be wiser than mere human wisdom, and God's weakness will always be stronger than mere human strength.

The cross challenges human values because no one expects to find freedom through capital punishment. Unlike most of the thousands who faced crucifixion before and after Jesus, He was clearly not a criminal. God uses this contradiction to reveal His power and wisdom: Jesus has offered Himself to death and has been raised to life to bring liberation to others. Those who truly follow this crucified king do not seek power and authority through the normal patterns of the world; they offer themselves in loving sacrifice for others. That is where God's transforming power is truly revealed in the church.

---

[26]Look carefully at your call, brothers and sisters. By human standards, not many of you are deemed to be wise. Not many are considered powerful. Not many of you come from royalty, right? [27]But *celebrate this:* God selected the world's foolish to bring shame upon *those who think they are* wise; likewise, He selected the world's weak to bring disgrace upon *those who think they are* strong. [28]God selected the common and the castoff, whatever lacks status, so He could invalidate the claims of those who think those things are significant. [29]So it makes no sense for any person to boast in God's presence. [30]Instead, credit God with your new situation: you are united with Jesus the Anointed. He is God's wisdom for us and more. He is our righteousness and holiness and redemption. [31]As the Scripture says: "If someone wants to boast, he should boast in the Lord."*

2 My brothers and sisters, I did not pose *as an expert with all the answers.* I did not pretend to explain the mystery of God with eloquent speech and *human*

wisdom. [2]I claimed to know nothing *with certainty* other than *the reality that* Jesus is the Anointed One, *the Liberating King,* who was crucified on our behalf. [3]I was moved to utter despair during my time with you. I would find myself trembling in *dread and fear.* [4]The sermons I preached were not delivered with *the kind of* persuasive elegance *some have come to expect,* but they were effective because I relied on God's Spirit to demonstrate God's power. [5]If this were not so, your faith would be based on human wisdom and not the power of God.

Christianity is not merely a set of ideas and propositions. One can agree with all the truths in the Bible and still miss the power of God. Paul knows the brothers and sisters in Corinth might attempt to reduce Christianity to a new philosophy based on human understanding, but the power of God cannot be fully grasped by our eight-pound brains. We must approach God humbly as creations, not as those aspiring to fully explain the Creator of the universe.

---

[6]However, in the presence of mature believers, we do impart *true* wisdom—not the *phony* wisdom typical of this *rebellious* age or of the *hostile* powers who rule this age. *Despite what you may think,* these ruling spirits are losing their grip on this world. [7]But we do impart God's mysterious and hidden wisdom. Before the ages began, God graciously decided to use His wisdom for our glory. [8]This wisdom has not been grasped by the ruling powers of this age; if they had understood, they would not have crucified the Lord of Glory. [9]But as the Scriptures say,

> No eye has ever seen and no ear has ever heard
>> and it has never occurred to the human heart
> All the things God prepared for those who love Him.*

[10]God has shown us these *profound and startling* realities through His Spirit. The

* 1:23 Literally, Gentiles   * 1:31 Jeremiah 9:23-24   * 2:9 Isaiah 64:4

Spirit searches all things, even the deep mysteries of God. [11]Who can see into a man's heart and know his thoughts? Only the spirit that dwells within the man. In the same way, the thoughts of God are known only by His Spirit. [12]*You must know that* we have not received the spirit of this *rebellious and broken* world but the Spirit that comes from God, so that we may experience and comprehend the gifts that come from God. [13]We do not speak of these *gifts of God* in words shaped by human wisdom; we speak in words crafted by the Spirit because our collective judgment on spiritual matters is accessible to those who have the Spirit. [14]But a person who denies spiritual realities will not accept the things that come through the Spirit of God; they all sound like foolishness to him. He is incapable of grasping them because they are *disseminated,* discerned, *and valued* by the Spirit. [15]A person who walks by the Spirit examines everything, *sizing it up and seeking out truth.* But no one is able to examine or size up that *kind of* spiritual person, [16]for *the Scripture asks,* "Does anyone know the mind of the Lord well enough to become His advisor?"* But we do possess the mind of the Anointed One.

3 My brothers and sisters, I cannot address you as people who walk by the Spirit; I have to speak to you as people who tend to think in merely human terms, as spiritual infants in the Anointed One. [2]I nursed you with milk, *as a mother would feed her baby,* because you were not, and still are not, developed enough to digest complex spiritual food. [3]*And here's why:* you are still living in the flesh, not in the Spirit. How do I know? Are you fighting one another? Are you *comparing yourselves to others and* becoming consumed with jealousy? Then it sounds like you are living in the flesh, no different from the rest *who live by the standards of this rebellious and broken world.* [4]If one of you is saying, "I am with Paul," and the other says, "I am with Apollos," aren't you like everybody else? [5]So who is Apollos really? Or Paul for that matter? *We are only* servants, agents who led you to faith, and the Lord commissioned each of us to do a particular job.

Paul's test for spiritually immaturity: Do you argue? Do you compare yourself to others? Are you jealous?

Answer "yes" to any of these, then you are spiritually immature.

[6]My job was to plant *the seed,* and Apollos was called to water it. Any growth comes from God, [7]so the ones who water and plant have nothing *to brag about.* God, who causes the growth, is the only One who matters. [8]The one who plants is no greater than the one who waters; both will be rewarded based on their work. [9]We are *gardeners and field* workers laboring with God. You are *the vineyard,* the garden, the house where God dwells. [10]Like a *skilled architect and* master builder, I laid a foundation based upon God's grace given to me. Now others will come along to build on the foundation. Each *serves in a different way and* is to build upon it with great care. [11]There is, in fact, only one foundation, and no one can lay any foundation other than Jesus the Anointed. [12]As others build on the foundation (whether with gold, silver, gemstones, wood, hay, or straw), [13]the quality of each person's work will be revealed in time as it is tested by fire. [14]If a man's work stands *the test of fire,* he will be rewarded. [15]If a man's work is consumed by the fire, his reward will be lost but he will be spared, rescued from the fire. [16]Don't you understand that together you form a temple to *the living* God and His Spirit lives among you? [17]If someone comes along to *corrupt, vandalize, and* destroy the temple of God, *you can be sure that* God will see to it that he meets destruction because the temple of God is sacred. You, *together,* are His temple.

[18]Don't let anyone deceive himself. If any one of you thinks he is wise in matters pertaining to this world, *he is going to be really disappointed.* In fact, one must be deemed a fool *by worldly standards* in order to become truly wise [19]because the wisdom of this *rebellious and broken* world looks like foolishness when put next to God. So it stands in Scripture, "He catches the wise in their deceitful plotting."* [20]And the Scriptures add, "The Lord knows the *highest* thoughts of the wise, and they are worthless."* [21]So there is no reason for anyone to boast in human leaders. You already have it all. [22]So whether it is Paul, Apollos, Cephas, the world, life or death, the present or the future—it all belongs to you. [23]You belong to the Anointed One, and the Anointed One belongs to God.

* 2:16 Isaiah 40:13   * 3:19 Job 5:13   * 3:20 Psalm 94:11

4 *Rather than power brokers*, think of us as servants of the Anointed One, *the Liberating King*, caretakers of the mysteries of God. [2]Because we are in this particular role, it is especially important that we are people of fidelity and integrity. [3]It makes little difference to me how you or any human court passes judgment on me. I even resist the temptation to compare myself *to the ever-changing human standard.* [4]Although I am not aware of any flaw that might exclude me *from this divine service,* that's not the reason I stand acquitted—*the only supreme judge,* our Lord, will examine me in the proper time. [5]So resist the temptation to act as judges before all the evidence is in. When the Lord comes, He will draw our buried motives, thoughts, and deeds *(even things we don't know or admit to ourselves)* out of the dark shadows of our hearts into His light. When this happens, the voice of God will speak to each of us the *only* praise *that will ever matter.*

[6]Right now, brothers and sisters, the best thing I can do for you is to apply these principles to the situation with Apollos and me. Maybe we can show you the meaning of the saying, "not beyond the things written." If you learn that, perhaps none of you will swell with pride because you fall into the seductive trap of pitting one against the other. [7]Is there any reason to consider yourselves better than others? What do you have that you didn't receive? If you received it as a gift, why do you boast like it is something you achieved on your own?

[8]*Now let's see if I have it straight.* You *suppose that you* already have all you need. You already are rich *and prosperous.* And without us you've already begun to reign like kings. To be honest, I wish you did reign so that we could reign with you [9]because it seems to me that God has put His emissaries* at the end of the line, like convicts in their final walk to certain death. We have become a spectacle to the rest of the world—to all people and heaven's messengers. [10]We are nothing but fools for the cause of the Anointed One while you are wise in Him. *Am I right?* We are feeble *and tired* while you are mighty *and full of life.* You are well respected by others while we're treated as contemptuous creatures *by pretty much everyone everywhere.* [11]Up to this very minute, we are famished, we are thirsty, and our clothes are shabby, *practically rotted to pieces.* We are homeless, *hapless wanderers.*

[12]But still we labor, working with our hands *to meet our needs because, despite all of this,* when a fist is raised against us, we respond with a blessing; when we face *violence and* persecution, we stay on mission; and [13]when others choose *taunts and* slander against us, we speak words of encouragement and reconciliation. We're treated as the scum of the earth—*and I am not talking in the past tense; I mean today!* We're the scraps of society, *nothing more than the foulest human rubbish.*

Paul explains and exemplifies the goals of a mature believer in a way that may be easily contrasted with the desires of an immature believer. He is seeking love and truth more than popularity, embracing suffering rather than comfort. In fact, he disregards popularity and comfort completely so that he isn't distracted from the love and truth of Jesus. This could be a powerful force in the world if believers embraced this kind of maturity.

---

[14]I am not telling you all this so that you'll *feel guilty or* be ashamed of how you have acted. I am only trying to warn you, just as a father would warn his children. [15]You may have 10,000 instructors in the *faith of the* Anointed One, but you have only one father. In Jesus the Anointed I have become your father through *my efforts in spreading* the good news. [16]So as your father in the faith, *I want to encourage you to live as I have lived.* Imitate my life. [17]This is one of the reasons I sent Timothy to be with you. He is my dearly loved and faithful child in the Lord. His mission is to remind you of the way I experience life in the Anointed. In all the churches everywhere I go, I teach the same lessons the same way, *and I live out those lessons.* [18]But the reality is, some of you *have put yourselves on pedestals and* live like you are high above the rest—it's as if you assumed I would not return *to confront your misguided pride.* [19]But I am coming. Lord willing, I will be with you soon. Then I will know what power is backing those arrogant folks and their words. [20]The kingdom of God is not a realm of

* 4:9 Literally, apostles

grandiose talk; it is a realm of power. ²¹So tell me what you want. Should I visit you, rod in hand *ready to discipline a crew of self-important people*; or should I *embrace you*, love you, and gently teach you *as we celebrate the blessings of God together*?

5 *Because of my deep love for you, I must express my concern about* the report brought to me regarding the *lewd and immoral behavior* exhibited in your community. This scandal has come to my attention because this kind of thing is unheard of even among the outsiders around us: I understand a man is having sexual relations with his father's wife. ²You have turned into an arrogant lot who refuse to *see the tragedy right in front of your eyes and* mourn for it. If you would face these hard realities, the one living in this sin would be removed from the community.

³Despite the fact that I am not physically present with you, I am there in spirit and already have spoken judgment against the man who has engaged in this conduct. ⁴When you gather in the name of the Lord Jesus and I am present with you in spirit, and the infinite power of our Lord Jesus is present also, ⁵I direct you to release this man over to Satan so his rebellious nature will be destroyed and his spirit might be rescued in the day the Lord Jesus returns.

⁶Your proud boasting *in this matter* is terrible. *Don't you understand that the tiniest infraction can bring about an unwelcome chain of events?* That just a little yeast causes all the dough to rise? ⁷Get rid of all the old yeast; then you'll become new dough, just as you are already a people without *sin's* leavening influence. You see, the Anointed One is our Passover lamb; He has been sacrificed for us. ⁸So let the real feast begin. Get rid of all the old yeast, the yeast of hatred and evil. *Throw it out* so we can feast on the unleavened bread of sincerity and truth.

Sexual sin is always painful, but incest decimates families and communities, and it leaves people isolated and angry. The danger for believers who understand the reality of sin is that they may lose sight of redemption and become complacent in their brokenness. In Corinth the believers have become so complacent that they are ignoring the incest in their community. The church's reputation is beginning to suffer among outsiders.

Church discipline if properly done accomplishes two things: first, it protects the community from harm caused by the sin; second, it can lead to a restoration of the sinner to God and the community. Ignoring the sin actually makes the lives of the sinners worse. Real love confronts the sin and leads the sinners toward redemption and wholeness.

---

⁹In the letter I wrote to you *previously, I made it clear* that you are not to band together with those who have embraced immoral lives. ¹⁰Don't misunderstand; *I'm not telling you to hole up and hunker down from the rest of the world. That's impossible.* The world is filled with immoral people consumed by their desire for more; they steal *from one another without hesitation* and will worship man-made idols *with no shame at all.* If you attempted to avoid these people, you would have to leave the world itself. ¹¹What I was saying is that you should not associate with someone who calls himself a brother or sister but lives *contrary to all we stand for:* committing immoral sexual acts, consumed with desire for more, worshiping tangible lifeless things, using profanity, drinking into oblivion, swindling and cheating others. Do not even sit at the table with a person like this. ¹²Why would I ever attempt to judge those outside *the church?* Aren't we *called* to judge those within *the church?* ¹³God judges the outsiders. *Your job is this:* "Expel the wicked from your own community."*

6 *Here's another troubling issue.* If you have a grievance against another *follower of Jesus,* do you have the audacity to bring that brother or sister into the civil courts rather than submitting yourselves to the authority of God's people? ²Don't you know that His people are destined to judge the world? If you have the authority to judge the world, can't you handle these small matters *and render a better judgment than the civil courts?* ³Further, don't you know that

* 5:13 Deuteronomy 17:7

we are destined to judge the heavenly messengers? *So if we are to exercise authority in the heavenly realms,* can't we take care of the conflicts that arise in this life? [4]To put it another way, if you are asking the courts to adjudicate your mundane conflicts, aren't you placing your problems under the authority of judges who have no standing within the church? [5]My words should embarrass you. Is it possible that you have no one among you with the wisdom to mediate between two siblings? [6]So one brother sues another brother *in public and drags the dispute* before outsiders who have no allegiance to Jesus?

[7]The truth is that these *public* lawsuits cause all of you to lose and lose big. Wouldn't it be better to be ripped off or defrauded? [8]In fact, you are guilty of ripping off and defrauding your own brothers and sisters, *not the other way around.*

[9-10]Do you need reminding that the unjust have no share in the blessings of the kingdom of God? Do not be misled. A lot of people stand to inherit nothing of God's coming kingdom, including those whose lives are defined by sexual immorality, idolatry, adultery, sexual deviancy, theft, greed, drunkenness, slander, and swindling. [11]Some of you used to live in these ways, but *you are different* now; you have been washed clean, set apart, restored, *and set on the right path* in the name of the Lord Jesus, the Anointed, by the Spirit of our living God.

V

In the same way that some seek to reduce Christianity to a philosophy or a set of ideas, others seek to reduce it to a set of rules for living. If true faith is only about eating certain foods, abstaining from others, and avoiding certain practices, then willpower must be more important than the Spirit of God. But following stringent rules is not that easy. Actually, living by willpower is hard—some might say impossible. Paul is preaching about an alternative to a life governed by rules and restrictions, and that's a life of faith that embraces grace. What Paul is about to describe is a life of freedom that surpasses a life of rule keeping.

[12]*I can hear some of you saying,* "For me, all things are permitted." But *face the facts:* all things are not beneficial. *So you say,* "For me, all things are permitted." *Here's my response:* I will not allow anything to control me. [13]*Another chimes in:* "Food is for the stomach, and the stomach is for food." *I suppose so, but a day will come when* God will dispense with both food and the stomach. The body is not meant for sexual immorality but for the Lord; the Lord *is over all, and* He cares about your body. [14]God has raised the Lord *Jesus from death,* but He won't stop there. His dynamic power will raise us up *from the grips of death* as well. [15]Don't you realize that your bodies are members of the Anointed One? So should I take the members of the Anointed One and unite them to a prostitute? This *illicit union* should never take place! [16]Don't you understand that when your body is joined with a prostitute, the two of you have become one body? For as it says, "The two come together as one flesh."* [17]But when you are joined with the Lord, you become one spirit with Him. [18]Run from immoral behavior. All other sins are disconnected from the body, but sexual immorality is a sin against your own body. [19]Don't you know that your body is the temple of the Holy Spirit who comes from God and dwells inside of you? You do not own yourself. [20]You have been purchased at a great price, so use your body to bring glory to God!

Salvation is a costly proposition. You and your body belong to God, so use your body for the work of God, not for selfish pursuits.

7 Now to the topics you raised *in your last letter. Some have said,* "It is better for a man to abstain from having sex with his wife." [2]Well, *I disagree.* Because of our tendency to embrace immoralities, each man should feel free to join together in sexual intimacy with his own wife, and each woman should join with her own husband. [3]*Husbands and wives have reciprocal duties.* Each husband has the responsibility to meet his wife's *sexual* desires, and each wife should do the same for her husband. [4]In marriage neither the husband nor the wife should act as if his or her body is private property—your bodies now belong to one another, *and together they are whole.*

* 6:16 Genesis 2:24

Paul's teaching to the Corinthians about marriage stands in contrast to the message in Genesis 2, where God declares that it is not good to be alone. There He sculpts woman from the rib of the man: she was molded so that man and woman fit perfectly together. And God blesses marriage as a good and beautiful thing.

So is Paul contradicting the declaration of the Creator God when he suggests that it might be better for some people to choose an unmarried life? Absolutely not! Marriage is a sacred union, but it is possible that many will be able to serve God more fully if they do not have the limitations that come with marriage and family. Paul shares his advice humbly based on his own experience. The tension between the beauty of marriage and the freedom from marital obligations is one we should all explore. As we come to our own conclusions, we must also carry them humbly, remembering that one is not better than the other.

---

⁵So do not withhold *sex* from one another, unless both of you have agreed to devote a certain period of time to prayer. When the agreed time is over, come together again so that Satan will not tempt you when you are short on self-control. ⁶I am trying to encourage you and give you some wise counsel, so don't take this advice as a command. ⁷I wish that all of you could live as I do, *unmarried.* But the truth is all people are different, each gifted by God in various and dissimilar ways.

⁸To those who are unmarried or widowed, here's my advice: it is a good thing to stay *single* as I do. ⁹If they do not have self-control, they should go ahead and get married. It is much better to marry than to be obsessed by sexual urges.

¹⁰To those who are married, here's my command (*to be clear,* this isn't merely my opinion; it comes from the teaching of the Lord Jesus): it is not right for a wife to leave her husband. ¹¹If she does, she must either remain single or reconcile with her husband, *but she should not marry someone else.* Likewise, the husband should not divorce his wife.

¹²⁻¹³To everyone else, here's my counsel (this is not a direct command from the Lord; *it is my opinion*): if a brother has a wife who does not believe Jesus' teachings and the truth of His resurrection, he is to stay with her as long as she is willing to live with him. The same is true for any sister; you should not leave your husband even if he has no allegiance to Jesus. ¹⁴Here's the reason: An unbelieving husband is consecrated *by that union—touched by the grace of God* through his believing wife—and *the same is true* when the husband is a man of faith and he's wed to an unbelieving wife. His wife is consecrated through their union. If this weren't

so, your children wouldn't be pure; *but as it is when faith enters in,* God sets apart these children *to be used uniquely for His purposes.* ¹⁵If the unbelieving spouse decides the marriage is over, then let him or her go; the believing partner is freed *from the marital vows* because God has called you to peace. ¹⁶Remember that *anything is possible, so* the life you lead *and the love you show under this strain* may be what finally liberates your partner.

¹⁷So here is my instruction to all the churches: each must live with the gifts the Lord *Jesus* grants you and with the call God offers you. ¹⁸When you heard the voice of Jesus, *what were your circumstances?* Were you living as a circumcised *Jew*? If so, don't try to undo your circumcision. Were you living as an uncircumcised *outsider*? If so, you don't need to become a Jew. ¹⁹You see, whether you are circumcised or not—these outward signs aren't the issue—the way you live out the commands of God is what really matters. ²⁰It is important for all people to live *out faith* in the circumstances they know.

V

The call to faith is not a call to abandon your life, family, neighborhood, and culture. We must play with the hand God deals us, not look for a new deck. He works through faith to redeem broken lives and wasted years, not to provide a change of scenery. Even in the worst circumstances, faith can change the believer from the inside.

21Did you hear God's voice while you were a slave? Don't be concerned. (But if the opportunity comes to gain your freedom, then take it.) 22For the slave who hears the Lord's call is set free to belong to the Lord. In the same way, the so-called free person is called to become a slave of the Anointed One. 23A high price has been paid for your freedom, so don't *devalue God's investment by* becoming a slave to people. 24My brothers and sisters, each of you should remain in whatever external circumstances you were in when God called you.

25Now when it comes to unmarried young women, I do not have a command from our Lord. The best I can do is to give you my advice as a trustworthy brother who knows the Lord's mercy well. 26Because of the challenging times we live in, I think the best plan is to stay as you are. 27If you are married, don't divorce. If you are single, there is no need to get married. 28But if you decide to get married, this is not a sin; there is nothing wrong with a young woman taking a husband, *but know that marriage is not easy* and those who marry will face hard times. I am only trying to protect you. 29But *hear what* I say, brothers and sisters: the time is short *and growing shorter.* So for the time remaining, even if you have wives, live *with the undivided focus* of those who do not have them. 30Those who cry should live as those who have no tears. Those who rejoice should live as those who have no pleasure. Those who buy things should live as those who do not possess anything. 31If you make use of this *rebellious and broken* world, live as if you have no use for it—because the form of this world is fading away.

32My primary desire is for you to be free from the worries *that plague humanity.* A single man can focus on the things of the Lord and how to please the Lord, 33but a married man has to worry about the details of the here and now and how to please his wife. 34A married man will always have divided loyalties. *The same idea is true for* a young unmarried woman. She concerns herself only with the work of the Lord and how to dedicate herself entirely, body and spirit, *to her Lord.* On the other hand, a married woman has vast responsibilities for her family and a desire to please her husband. 35I am not trying to give you more rules and regulations. I only want to give you advice that is fitting and helpful. I want to help you live lives of faithful devotion to the Lord without any distraction.

36*But I have this advice for every single man:* If anyone thinks he is behaving badly toward his fiancée, if his desires prove to be too much for him, and if he feels they ought to marry, then he should do what he wants; it is not wrong *to marry her.* It is better that we let men *and women in this situation do as they wish and* get married. 37If a man has no compulsion and chooses not to marry his fiancée, but commits himself to live *a celibate life for the sake of following God* and has the strength to live out his conviction, then he is doing a good thing. 38So those who marry do a good thing, *and they will share in a holy blessing;* those who do not marry do an even better thing *because they are part of an even greater blessing in the service of God.*

39A wife should stay by her husband's side all of his life. But if he dies, she is free to marry any man she wishes as long as it is in the Lord. 40*You can likely guess that* in my opinion this woman would be better off to remain single, and I think that I have *this insight from* God's Spirit.

8 As to the concern of eating food dedicated to idols: we know that all of us have knowledge, *but knowledge can be risky.* Knowledge promotes *overconfidence and worse* arrogance, but *charity of the heart* (love, that is) looks to build up *others.* 2Just because a person presumes to have some bit of knowledge, that person doesn't necessarily have the right kind of knowledge. 3But if someone loves God, *it is certain that* God has already known that one.

4So to address your concerns about eating food offered to idols, let me start with what we know. An idol is essentially nothing, as there is no other God but the One. 5And even if *the majority believes* there are many so-called gods in heaven and on earth (certainly many *worship* such "gods" and "lords"), *this is not our view.* 6For us, there is one God, the Father who is the ultimate source of all things and the goal of our lives. And there is one Lord—Jesus the Anointed, *the Liberating King;* through Him all things *were created,* and by Him we are *redeemed.*

7But this knowledge is not in everyone. Up until now, some have been so familiar with idols *and what goes on in the temples* that when they eat meat that has been offered first to some idol, their weak consciences are polluted. *This is the issue.* [8]*Again, here's what we know:* what we eat will not bring us closer to God—we gain nothing in feasting and lose nothing by fasting. [9]Now let me warn you: don't let your newfound liberty cause those who don't know this to fall face-first. [10]Let's say a person (*someone who knows of Jesus*) sees you eating in the temple of an idol; and because the person with a weaker conscience is still unsure of things, he becomes confident, follows your lead, and eats idol food. [11]Now, because of your knowledge *on display in your conduct,* the weaker brother or sister—for whom the Anointed One died—is destroyed! Ruined! [12]What's more, *by living according to your knowledge,* you have sinned against these brothers and sisters and wounded their weak consciences—and because you sinned against them, you have sinned against the Anointed One, *the Liberating King.*

[13]So if any type of food is an issue that causes my brothers and sisters to fall away *from God,* then God forbid I should ever eat it again so that I would never be *the crack, the rise, or the rock on the road* that causes them to stumble.

V

Meat left over from pagan temple sacrifices was sold daily in the market. It was about the only option available for those who didn't raise their own livestock. Paul knows that idols are nothing really because there is only one God, but another brother thinks he is engaging in a heinous act and supporting a pagan temple by eating food that comes from a pagan sacrifice. So what is a believer to do? Well, it is not a matter of knowledge: Who's right? Who's wrong? It's a matter of love. Paul says that he has the right to eat the meat, but that he gladly gives up that right for the sake of the other brother. Paul limits his freedom out of love for the Corinthians.

---

9 Am I not truly free? Am I not an emissary* *of the Liberating King?* Have I not personally encountered Jesus our Lord? Are you not my work, *my mission in* the Lord? [2]Even if others don't recognize

that I am His emissary,* at least you do because you are the seal, *the living proof* that the Lord commissioned me to be His representative.

[3]Let me speak in my own defense against those *keeping themselves* busy picking me apart. [4]Have we lost the right to eat and drink? [5]Have we lost the right to bring along our wives, our sisters in Jesus? Other emissaries travel with their wives, and so do the brothers of our Lord, not to mention Cephas. [6]Is it just Barnabas and I who have lost the right to earn a living? [7]Is a soldier in combat required to pay his own salary? Who would plant a vineyard and not enjoy one grape from it? Who would care for *and nurture* a flock but never taste the fresh milk?

[8]These ideas aren't based on merely human notions; the law says these same things. [9]In Moses' law, it is written: "Do not muzzle the ox while it is treading out your grain."* Is God's concern here limited to oxen, [10]or does He speak here ultimately for our benefit? These things were written for us, so as the plowman plows and the worker gathers, they can labor with the hopeful expectation that they, too, will share in the good harvest. [11]*The same principle applies here:* Is it too much to ask that we would be compensated materially for planting *life- and world-changing* spiritual realities? [12]If you have rightfully supported others, shouldn't we deserve your support even more?

But we have never insisted on this right; instead, we would rather put up with anything than to put some obstacle in the way that prevents *even one person from experiencing* the good news of the Anointed One. [13]Perhaps it has escaped your notice that leaders and priests of the temple make their livings off the temple and that those who tend the altar eat their dinners from part of the sacrifices. [14]So *it shouldn't be a stretch that* the Lord has arranged for preachers of the gospel to make a living by *those who have embraced and been liberated by* the gospel.

V

Paul works hard. He travels the known world starting new churches and writes letters instructing other churches. Simultaneously, he makes and sells tents to fund his basic needs and missionary

---

* 9:1 Literally, apostle   * 9:2 Literally, apostle   * 9:9 Deuteronomy 25:4

travels. Would Paul's time be better spent training young pastors or preaching to a group of church leaders rather than making tents? By giving his churches his service for free, is he doing a disservice to those who will serve these churches in the future and have families to care for?

---

[15]*Despite what I've said here,* I have never staked a claim for such things, and I have no intention to start now; that's not why I'm writing. I would rather die than have anyone *(including me)* invalidate my right to boast. [16]You see, if I preach the good news, it's nothing to brag about. *This urgency,* this necessity has been laid on me. In fact, if I were to stop sharing this good news, I'd be in big trouble. [17]*You see, my story is different. I didn't volunteer for this.* Had I volunteered to preach the good news, then I would deserve a wage, a reward, *or something.* But I didn't choose this. God chose me and entrusted me with this mission. [18]*You're looking for the catch. I know you're wondering,* "What reward is he talking about?" My reward, *besides being with you and knowing you,* is sharing the good news of the Anointed One with you free and clear. That means I don't insist on all my rights for support in the good news; [19]that also means that I am free of obligations to all people. And, even though no one *(except Jesus)* owns me, I have become a slave *by my own free will* to everyone *in hopes* that I would gather more *believers.* [20]When around Jews, I emphasize my Jewishness in order to win them over. When around those who live *strictly* under the law, I live by its regulations—even though I have a different perspective on the law now—in order to win them over. [21]*In the same way,* I've made a life outside the law to gather those who live outside the law (although I personally abide by and live under the Anointed One's law). [22]I've been *broken, lost, depressed, oppressed, and* weak that I might *find favor and* gain the weak. I'm *flexible, adaptable, and* able to do and be whatever is needed for all kinds of people so that *in the end* I can use every means at my disposal to offer them salvation. [23]I do it all for the gospel *and for the hope* that I may participate with everyone who is blessed by the proclamation of the good news.

[24]We all know that when there's a race, all the runners bolt for the finish line, but only one will take the prize. When you run, run for the prize! [25]Athletes in training *are very strict with themselves,* exercising self-control *over desires, and for what?* For a wreath that soon withers *or is crushed or simply forgotten.* That is not our race. We run for the crown that we will wear for eternity. [26]So I don't run aimlessly. *I don't let my eyes drift off the finish line.* When I box, I don't throw punches in the air. [27]I discipline my body and make it my slave so that after *all this,* after I have brought the gospel to others, I will still be qualified *to win the prize.*

10 I wouldn't want you to be ignorant *of our history,* brothers and sisters. Our ancestors were once *safeguarded* under a *miraculous* cloud *in the wilderness* and brought *safely* through the sea. [2]*Enveloped in water* by cloud and by sea, they were, *you might say,* ritually cleansed into Moses through baptism.* [3]*Together they were sustained supernaturally:* they all ate the same spiritual food, *manna;* [4]and they all drank the same spiritual water, flowing from a spiritual rock that was always with them, for the rock was the Anointed One, *our Liberating King.* [5]Despite all of this, they were punished in the wilderness because God was unhappy with most of them.

[6]Look at what happened to them as an example; *it's right there in the Scriptures* so that we won't make the same mistakes and hunger after evil as they did. *So here's my advice:* [7]don't *degrade yourselves by* worshiping anything less than the living God as some of them did. *Remember* it is written, "The people sat down to eat and drink and then rose up in *dance and play.*"* [8]We must be careful not to engage in sexual sins as some of them did. In one day, 23,000 died *because of sin.** [9]None of us must test *the limits of* the Lord's patience. Some of the Israelites did, and serpents *bit them and* killed them. [10]You need to stop your groaning and whining. *Remember the story.* Some of them complained, and the messenger of death came for them and destroyed them. [11]All these happened for a reason: to sound a warning. They were written down and passed down to us to teach us. *They were meant especially for us* because *the beginning of* the end is happening in our time. [12]So let

---

* 10:2 Literally, immersed   * 10:7 Exodus 32:6   * 10:8 Numbers 25:9

One of the strengths of the Jewish people is their corporate identity that comes from belonging to a unique, suffering people deeply loved by God. The tendency for the new, non-Jewish believers may be to create a new identity among themselves because they lack the sense of belonging shared by Israel's descendants. A new day is dawning, a day when all may come to God regardless of ethnicity, locale, or social class. Believers in Corinth are not part of a new movement; they are a fresh expression of the historic movement of God.

The twenty-first century church needs to hear this truth today as much as the church in Corinth did two millennia ago. The world has changed drastically since the times of Abraham, David, John the Baptist, and even Martin Luther. In the midst of radical economic and technological advances, some within the church are embracing new or contemporary practices and regarding them as somehow superior to ancient and historic practices. Paul is challenging this idea and calling all believers to see themselves as a part of the local, global, and historic church.

even the most confident believers *remember their examples and* be very careful not to fall *as some of them did.*

¹³Any temptation you face will be nothing new. But God is faithful, and He will not let you be tempted beyond what you can handle. But He always provides a way of escape so that you will be able to endure *and keep moving forward.* ¹⁴So then, my beloved friends, run from idolatry *in any form.* ¹⁵As wise as I know you are, understand clearly what I am saying and determine the right course of action. ¹⁶When we give thanks *and share* the cup of blessing, are we not sharing in the blood of the Anointed One? When we *give thanks and* break bread, are we not sharing in His body? ¹⁷Because there is one bread, we, though many, are also one body since we all share one bread. ¹⁸Look no further than Israel *and the temple practices, and you'll see what I mean.* Isn't it true that those who eat sacrificial foods are communing at the altar, sharing its benefits? ¹⁹So what does all this mean? I'm not suggesting that idol food itself has any special qualities or that an idol itself possesses any special powers, ²⁰but I am saying that the outsiders' sacrifices are actually offered to demons, not to God. *So if you feast upon this food, you are feasting with demons*—I don't want you involved with demons! ²¹You can't hold the *holy* cup of the Lord *in one hand* and the cup of demons *in the other.* You can't share in the Lord's table while picking off the altar of demons. ²²Are we trying to provoke the Lord Jesus? *Do we think it's a good idea* to stir up His jealousy? Do we have *ridiculous delusions about matching or even* surpassing His power?

²³*There's a slogan often quoted on matters like this:* "All things are permitted." *Yes,* but not all things are beneficial. "All things are permitted," *they say. Yes,* but not all things build up *and strengthen others in the body.* ²⁴We should stop looking out for our own interests and instead focus on the people living and breathing around us. ²⁵Feel free to eat any meat sold in the market without your conscience raising questions about scruples ²⁶because "the earth and all that's upon it belong to the Lord."*

Paul's instruction on this matter is clear: believers should give up their rights and freedoms for the sake of others. This is the essence of sacrifice. This is what Jesus did. This is what Paul does. Otherwise, community becomes impossible. But no state or church authority should force compliance; it must arise from a heart of love and a disposition that puts the needs of others first.

²⁷So if some unbelievers invite you to dinner and you want to go, feel free to eat whatever they offer you without raising questions about conscience. ²⁸⁻²⁹But if someone says, "This is meat from the temple altar, *a sacrifice to god so-and-so,*" then do not eat it. Not so much because of your own conscience [because the earth and everything on it belongs to the Lord],* but out

* 10:26 Psalm 24:1   * 10:28-29 Some manuscripts omit this portion.

of consideration for the conscience of the other fellow who told you about it. So *you ask,* "Why should I give up my freedom to accommodate the scruples of another?" [30]or, "If I am eating with gratitude to God, why am I insulted for eating food that I have properly given thanks for?" *These are good questions.*

[31]Whatever you do—whether you eat or drink *or not*—do it all to the glory of God! [32]Do not offend Jews or Greeks or any part of the church of God *for that matter.* [33]*Consider my example:* I strive to please all people in all my actions and words—but don't think I am in this for myself—their rescued souls are the only profit.

11 So imitate me, *watch my ways, follow my example,* just as I, too, *always seek to* imitate the Anointed One.

[2]I must say how pleased I am *to hear that* you remember me in everything and continue to hold on to the traditions I have passed on to you. [3]But *it is important* that you understand this *about headship:* the Anointed One is the head of every man, the husband is the head of his wife, and God is the head of the Anointed. [4]*Knowing this,* any man wearing a covering over his head while praying or prophesying *in your gathering* disgraces his head, *Jesus.* [5-6]On the other hand, any woman—*I mean, of course, a married woman*—not wearing a veil over her head while praying or prophesying disgraces her head, *her husband.* It wouldn't be much different than if she walked into worship with her head shaved. For if a woman isn't going to be veiled properly, she ought to *go ahead and* cut off her hair; but if it brings shame to the woman *and her husband* to have all her hair cut off or her head shaved clean, then by all means let her wear a veil.

[7]*Here's the distinction:* man is created in God's image and for His glory, so he should not cover his head. But a wife is the glory of her husband. *She ought to be covered.* [8]Man, *you remember,* was not fashioned from the body of a woman. But woman, *though she was sculpted by the hands of God,* was fashioned from *the bones and flesh of* man.* [9]Furthermore, *don't forget that* man was not created for woman; woman was created for man *to be his helper in everything.* [10]This means that a wife should wear *a veil* on her head as a sign she is under authority, especially when gathering in the company of heavenly messengers. [11]Regardless *of how it all began,* husbands and wives should recognize they are not independent; [12]for just as woman was pulled from *the side of* man, man is pulled from *the womb of* woman. *In a similar way,* all things *and all people* share the same ultimate source, God.

[13]Judge for yourselves: *when you gather to worship,* is it appropriate for a woman to pray to God without covering her head? [14]*Consider the ways of nature:* doesn't nature itself teach you that a man who wears his hair long invites *shame and* dishonor to cover him? [15]But *doesn't nature also teach* that when a woman has long hair, it is her glory? It *radiates her beauty and* acts as a natural veil. [16]If you feel like debating more on this, *just know that* we, along with all other churches of God, have adopted the same custom.

[17]On this next matter, I wish I could applaud you; but I can't because your gatherings have *become counterproductive,* making things worse *for the community* rather than better. [18]Let me start *with this:* I hear that your gatherings are polarizing the community; and to be honest, this doesn't surprise me. [19]I've accepted the fact that factions are *sometimes useful and even* necessary so that those who are authentic *and those who are counterfeit* may be recognized. [20]*This distinction is obvious* when you come together *because* it is not the Lord's Supper you are eating *at all.* [21]When it's time to eat, some hastily dig right in; *but look—some have more than others:* over there someone is hungry, and over here someone is drunk! [22]What is going on? *If a self-centered meal is what you want,* can't you eat and drink at home? Do you have so little respect for God's people *and this community* that you shame the poor *at the Lord's table*? I don't even know what to say to you! Are you looking for my approval? You won't find it.

[23]I passed on to you the tradition the Lord gave to me: On the same night the Lord Jesus was betrayed, He took the bread *in His hands*; [24]and after giving thanks *to God,* He broke it and said, "This is My body, *broken* for you. Keep doing this so that you *and all who come after* will have a vivid reminder of Me." [25]After they had finished dinner, He took the cup and in the same way said, "This cup is the new covenant, *executed* in My blood. Keep doing this; and whenever you drink it, you *and all who come after* will

* 11:8 Genesis 2:21-25

have a vivid reminder of Me." ²⁶Every time you taste this bread and every time you place the cup *to your mouths* and drink, you are declaring the Lord's death, *which is the ultimate expression of His faithfulness and love,* until He comes again.

> **God doesn't demand perfection to partake at the Lord's table, rather brokenness. Their pride is causing division during the meal; instead they need to fellowship in a shared, broken spirit.**

²⁷So if someone takes of this bread and drinks from the Lord's cup improperly—*as you are doing*—he is guilty of *violating* the body and blood of our Lord. ²⁸Examine yourselves first. Then you can properly approach *the table* to eat the bread and drink from the cup; ²⁹because otherwise, if you eat and drink without properly discerning the significance of the Lord's body, then you eat and drink *a mouthful of* judgment upon yourself. ³⁰Because of this violation, many in your community are now sick and weak; some have even died. ³¹But if we took care to judge ourselves, then we wouldn't have to worry about being judged *by another*. ³²*In fact,* the Lord's hand of judgment is correcting us so that we don't suffer the same fate as the rest of the *rebellious* world: condemnation.

³³From now on, brothers and sisters, *this is what I want you to do:* when you come together to eat *at the Lord's table*, wait for each other. If someone is hungry *and can't wait*, he should go home and eat. In that way, your gatherings won't result in *God's* judgment. The rest of the instructions I have *for you* will have to wait until I come.

12 Now let me turn to *some issues about* spiritual gifts, brothers and sisters. There's much you need to learn. ²Remember *the way you used to live* when you were pagans *apart from God*? You were engrossed—enchanted with voiceless idols, led astray *by mere images carved by human hands*. ³With that in mind, I want you to understand that no one saying "Jesus is cursed" is operating under God's Spirit, and no one confessing "Jesus is Lord" can do so without the Holy Spirit's inspiration.

⁴Now there are many kinds of *grace* gifts, but they are all from the same Spirit. ⁵There are many different ways to serve, but *they're all directed by* the same Lord. ⁶There are many amazing working gifts in the church, but it is the same God who energizes them all in all *who have the gifts.*

> Paul's description of the works of the Spirit, the Lord (Jesus), and God (the Father) links the three persons together in remarkable ways. Although Paul never articulates the doctrine of the Trinity, what he writes here about the Godhead relationship—their community of persons—becomes the raw materials used by later believers to construct the church's teaching on the Trinity. In this chapter the apostle emphasizes the agency of the Spirit. For him the Spirit is not just an impersonal force or feeling; He is just as much a person within the Trinity as the Father and the Son. Accordingly, the Spirit chooses where to impart gifts as He works together with the Father and the Son to build up the church.

---

⁷Each believer has received a gift that manifests the Spirit's *power and presence*. That gift is given for the good of the whole community. ⁸The Spirit gives one person a word of wisdom, but to the next person the same Spirit gives a word of knowledge. ⁹Another will receive *the gift of* faith by the same Spirit, and still another gifts of healing—all from the one Spirit. ¹⁰One person is enabled *by the Spirit* to perform miracles, another to prophesy, while another is enabled to distinguish *those prophetic* spirits. The next one speaks in various kinds of unknown languages, while another is able to interpret those languages. ¹¹One Spirit works all these things in each of them individually as He sees fit.

¹²Just as a body is one whole made up of many different parts, and all the different parts comprise the one body, so it is with the Anointed One. ¹³We were all ceremonially washed through baptism* together into one body by one Spirit. *No matter our heritage—* Jew or Greek, insider or outsider—*no matter our status*—oppressed or free—we were all given the one Spirit to drink. ¹⁴*Here's what I*

* 12:13 Literally, immersed, in a rite of initiation and purification mean: the body is not made of one large part but of many *different parts*. ¹⁵Would it seem right for the foot to cry, "I am not a hand, so I couldn't be part of this body"? Even if it did, it wouldn't be any less joined to the body. ¹⁶And what about an ear? If an ear started to whine, "I am not an eye; I shouldn't be attached to this body," in all its pouting, it is still part of the body. ¹⁷Imagine the entire body as an eye. How would a giant eye be able to hear? And if the entire body were an ear, how would an ear be able to smell? ¹⁸*This is where God comes in*. God has meticulously put this body together; He placed each part in the exact place to perform the exact function He wanted. ¹⁹If all members were a single part, where would the body be? ²⁰So now, many members *function* within the one body. ²¹The eye cannot wail at the hand, "I have no need for you," nor could the head bellow at the feet, "I won't go one more step with you." ²²It's actually the opposite. The members who seem to have the weaker functions are necessary to keep the body moving; ²³the body parts that seem less important we treat as some of the most valuable; and those unfit, untamed, unpresentable members we treat with an even greater modesty. ²⁴That's something the more presentable members don't need. But God designed the body in such a way that greater significance is given to the *seemingly* insignificant part. ²⁵That way there should be no division in the body; instead, all the parts mutually depend on and care for one another. ²⁶If one part is suffering, then all the members suffer alongside it. If one member is honored, then all the members celebrate alongside it. ²⁷You are the body of the Anointed, *the Liberating King*; each and every one of you is a *vital* member. ²⁸God has appointed *gifts* in the assembly: first emissaries,* second prophets, third teachers, then miracle workers, healers, helpers, administrators, and then those who speak with various unknown languages. ²⁹Are all members gifted as emissaries? Are all gifted with prophetic utterance? Are all teachers? Do all work miracles? ³⁰Or are all gifted in healing arts? Do all speak or interpret unknown languages? *Of course not.* ³¹Pursue the greater gifts, and let me tell you of a more excellent way—*love*.

because members of the church elevate those who possess the more visible gifts over those whose gifts function in the background. In fact, this is the very problem facing the Corinthians. So while talking about the importance and function of these gifts in chapters 12 and 14, Paul shifts his focus to the central role love plays in a believer's life in chapter 13. Love is essential for the body to be unified and for members to work together. Members of the body that are very different, with little in common, are able to appreciate and even enjoy others because of the love that comes when a life is submitted to God.

---

13 What if I speak in the *most elegant* languages of people or in the *exotic* languages of the heavenly messengers, but I live without love? Well then, anything I say is like the clanging of brass or a crashing cymbal. ²What if I have the gift of prophecy, am blessed with knowledge and insight to all the mysteries, or what if my faith is strong enough to scoop a mountain *from its bedrock*, yet I live without love? If so, I am nothing. ³I could give all that I have to feed the poor, I could surrender my body to be burned *as a martyr*, but if I do not live in love, I gain nothing *by my selfless acts*.

V

Paul boils it all down for the believers in Corinth. Religious people often spend their time practicing rituals, projecting dogma, and going through routines that might look like Christianity on the outside but that lack the essential ingredient that brings all of it together—love! It is a loving God who birthed creation and now pursues a broken people in the most spectacular way. That same love must guide believers, so faith doesn't appear to be meaningless noise.

V

Gifts of the Spirit, which are intended to strengthen the church body, often divide the body

⁴Love is patient; love is kind. Love isn't envious, doesn't boast, *brag, or strut about.*

* 12:28 Literally, apostles

There's no arrogance in love; [5]it's never rude, crude, or indecent—it's not self-absorbed. Love isn't easily upset. Love doesn't tally wrongs [6]or celebrate injustice; but truth—*yes, truth*—is love's delight! [7]Love puts up with anything and everything that comes along; it trusts, hopes, and endures no matter what. [8]Love will never become obsolete. Now as for the prophetic gifts, they will not last; unknown languages will become silent, and the gift of knowledge will no longer be needed. [9]Gifts of knowledge and prophecy are partial at best, *at least for now,* [10]but when the perfection *and fullness of God's kingdom* arrive, all the parts will end. [11]When I was a child, I spoke, thought, and reasoned in childlike ways *as we all do.* But when I became a man, I left my childish ways behind. [12]For now, we can only see a dim and blurry picture of things, as when we stare into polished metal. I realize that everything I know is only part of the big picture. But one day, *when Jesus arrives,* we will see clearly, face-to-face. In that day, I will fully know just as I have been wholly known *by God.* [13]But now faith, hope, and love remain; these three *virtues must characterize our lives.* The greatest of these is love.

14 So *in everything* strive to love. Passionately seek the gifts of the Spirit, especially the gift of prophecy. [2]*You see,* a person speaking in an *unknown* language is not addressing the church because he is really addressing God—those who overhear don't understand because he is speaking in the Spirit the depths of the mysteries *of the Lord.* [3]But a person who has the gift of prophecy teaches in a way that builds up the community, draws them near, and comforts them. [4]Those who speak in an unknown language only strengthen themselves, but those who prophesy strengthen the community. [5]While I'd like for you all to be able to speak *by the Spirit* in unknown languages, my preference would be for you all to prophesy *by the Spirit.* Those who speak prophetically *are God's mouthpiece and* are far more useful to the church than those who speak in exotic languages—unless there is another who interprets so that the community may be strengthened.

[6]If I come to you, brothers and sisters, talking in unknown languages, what good would that be for any of you? You receive no benefit unless I speak to you some word of revelation, knowledge, prophecy, or instruction *in your own language.* [7]Look, if inanimate objects, *musical instruments* like a pipe or harp, don't make a clear, distinct sound, how would you know what tune is being played? [8]If the bugle blares more like a clank, who would know to prepare for battle? [9]It's the same with you. Unless you speak a message in a language everyone understands, they won't know what you're talking about. You'll be talking into the wind. [10]This world is full of languages, each and every one of them having meaning; [11]but if I don't understand the meaning of some sound, then I become like a foreigner to the person speaking, and the person speaking will be like a foreigner to me. [12]It's the same with you; in your passion for spiritual gifts, seek to strengthen the community of believers, *and you will all be better off.*

[13]So anyone who speaks in an unknown language should pray for the ability to interpret [14]because if I pray in such a language, although my spirit prays, my mind isn't productive. [15]What do I do then? I pray. I pray with my spirit but also with my mind engaged; I sing with my spirit but also with my mind engaged. [16]If you speak a word of blessing in the spirit only, then how will an uninformed person who can't understand your prayer say "Amen" when you are done giving thanks? [17]Even though you give thanks *to God* well, the unknowing person doesn't benefit. [18]I thank God that I speak in unknown languages more than the rest of you; [19]but when the church gathers, I would rather speak five words with my mind so I can be understood and train others than utter 10,000 exotic words.

[20]Brothers and sisters, don't think like children. Be innocent of malice but mature in understanding. [21]In the law, it states:

> "I will send My message to this people
>> with strange languages and foreign
>> lips.
> And even when that happens,
>> they will not listen to Me," says the
>> Lord.*

[22]So speaking in unknown languages is not a sign to the believing but *a miracle* to the unbelieving; prophecy, though, is not a sign to the unbelieving but for the believing. [23]*Imagine what would happen* if the entire church gathered together speaking in

* 14:21 Isaiah 28:11-12

different languages, *one foreign to the next.* Then people who have never heard of such a thing or unbelieving people walk up on all that's going on. Would they not think each and every one of you were raving lunatics? [24]But let's say an outsider or unbeliever walks in on a different scene: all are speaking for God with great power and insight *in a language they know. What then? Well,* the outsider would come under the conviction *of his own sins* and be called to accountability by the words of all *the prophets.* [25]The very secrets of his heart would be revealed, *and right there—mystified—*he would fall on his face in worship to God, proclaiming *all the while* that God most certainly dwells among you.

[26]What should you do then, brothers and sisters? When you come together, *each person has a vital role because each has gifts.* One person might have a song, another a lesson to teach, still another a revelation *from God.* One person might speak in an unknown language, another will offer the interpretation, but all of this should be done to strengthen *the life and faith of the community.* [27]But if any do speak in an exotic language, limit it to two or three people at the most, and have them speak one at a time, while another interprets for the rest. [28]If there is not an interpreter present, then the one should stay silent during the gathering, speaking only to himself and God. [29]Have two to three prophets speak, and let others *with discerning gifts* evaluate the messages they hear. [30]Now if *in the course of things* a message comes to another who is seated, then the first one speaking should be silent *until this new message can be spoken.* [31]To *avoid confusion and* create a space where all can learn and be encouraged, let only one prophet speak at a time *without interruption.* [32]*You see,* the prophetic spirits are under the control of the prophets [33]because God is the author of order, not confusion. This is how it is in all gatherings of the saints. [34]Wives should be respectfully silent at the gatherings, as they are not allowed to speak; and they should yield *themselves to those in authority* just as it is written in the law. [35]When they want to learn anything *in particular,* they should ask their husbands when they get home. It creates a shameful situation for them to speak at church. [36]Do you think the word of God came to the world by you? Or that it came only to you?

Paul clearly wants to correct the excessive use of speeches given in these exotic, unknown languages, but he doesn't want them banned either.

[37]Let any person who thinks he is a prophet or a spiritual person affirm that these things I write to you are the commands of the Lord. [38]Whoever chooses to be ignorant of this will be treated as ignorant. [39]So, my dear brothers and sisters, passionately desire to prophesy; but don't ban the gift of speaking in unknown languages. [40]Just maintain the proper order in all things.

15 Let me remind you, brothers and sisters, of the good news that I preached to you *when we first met. It's the essential message* that you have taken to heart, the central story you now base your life on; [2]and through this gospel, you are liberated—unless, of course, your faith has come to nothing. [3-4]For I passed down to you the crux of it all which I had also received *from others,* that the Anointed One, *the Liberating King,* died for our sins and was buried and raised from the dead on the third day. All this happened to fulfill the Scriptures; *it was the perfect climax to God's covenant story.* [5]Afterward He appeared alive to Cephas* *(you may know him as Simon Peter),* then to the rest of the twelve. [6]*If that were not amazing enough,* on one occasion, He appeared to more than 500 believers at one time. Many of those brothers and sisters are still around *to tell the story,* though some have fallen asleep* in Jesus. [7]Soon He appeared to James, *His brother and the leader of the Jerusalem church,* and then to all the rest of the emissaries* *He Himself commissioned.** [8]Last of all, He appeared to me;* I was like a child snatched from his mother's womb. [9]You see, I am the least of all His emissaries, not fit to be called His emissary because I hunted down and persecuted God's church. [10]Today I am who I am because of God's grace, and *I have made sure that* the grace He offered me has not been wasted. I have worked harder, *longer, and smarter* than all the rest; but *I realize* it is not me—it is God's grace with me *that has made the difference.* [11]In the end, *it doesn't matter* whether it was I or the other witnesses *who brought you the message.* What matters is that we keep

* 15:5 Luke 24:34   * 15:6 Literally, died   * 15:7 Literally, apostles
* 15:7 Acts 1:3-4   * 15:8 Acts 9:3-6

preaching and that you have faith in this message.

¹²Now if we have told you about the Anointed One (how He has risen from the dead *and appeared to us fully alive*), then how can you *stand there and* say there is no such thing as resurrection from death? ¹³*Friends*, if there is no resurrection of the dead, then even the Anointed hasn't been raised; ¹⁴if that is so, then all our preaching has been for nothing and your faith *in the message* is worthless. ¹⁵And what's worse, all of us *who have been preaching the gospel* are now guilty of misrepresenting God because we have been spreading the news that He raised the Anointed One from the dead (which must be a lie if what you are saying about the dead not being raised is the truth). ¹⁶*Please listen*. If *you* say, "the dead are not raised," then *what you are telling me is that* the Anointed One has not been raised. *Friends*, ¹⁷if the Anointed has not been raised *from the dead*, then your faith is worth less *than yesterday's garbage*, you are all doomed in your sins, ¹⁸and all the *dearly* departed who trusted in His liberation are left decaying *in the ground*. ¹⁹If what we have hoped for in the Anointed doesn't take us beyond this life, then we are world-class fools, deserving everyone's pity.

²⁰But the Anointed One was raised from death's slumber and is the firstfruits of those who have fallen asleep *in death*. ²¹For since death entered *this world* by a man, it took another man to make the resurrection of the dead *our new* reality. ²²*Look at it this way:* through Adam all of us die, but through the Anointed One all of us can live again. ²³But this is how it will happen: the Anointed's *awakening* is the firstfruits. It will be followed by the resurrection of all those who belong to Him at His coming, ²⁴and then the end will come. After He has *conquered His enemies and* shut down every rule and authority vying for power, He will hand over the Kingdom to God, the Father *of all that is*. ²⁵And He must reign as King until He has put all His enemies under His feet. ²⁶The last hostile power to be destroyed is death itself. ²⁷*All this will happen to fulfill the Scripture that says,* "You placed everything on earth beneath His feet."* (Although it says "everything," it is clear that this does not also pertain to God, *who created everything* and made it all subject to Him.) ²⁸Then, when all creation has taken its rightful place beneath God's sovereign reign, the Son will follow, subject to the Father who exalted Him over all created things; then God will be God over all.

Resurrection is central to the gospel. In fact, without the bodily resurrection of Jesus there is no good news at all. For in Jesus, God personifies His redeeming work and demonstrates the scope of that redemption. He is a God who brings life from death, peace from war, prosperity from adversity, and bounty from famine. The resurrection of Jesus marks a new era of God's dealing with the world. He intends nothing less than the total reclamation of His good creation damaged by human folly, sin, and death.

---

²⁹*You have probably heard that* some people are undergoing ritual cleansings of baptism* for the dead. Why are they doing that? If the dead are not going to be raised, then why are people being baptized for them? ³⁰Why are we putting our lives on the line all the time *if there's no resurrection*? ³¹I die every day! I swear that it's true! That's something you take pride in, brothers and sisters, as I do in Jesus the Anointed, our Lord. ³²But if I have fought against the wild beasts in Ephesus for some human cause, then what good has that done me? If the dead are not raised, then there's nothing more to do than—*as the saying goes*—eat and drink, for tomorrow we die.*

³³But don't be so naïve—*there's another saying you know well*—Bad company corrupts good habits. ³⁴Come to your senses, live justly, and stop sinning. *It's true that* some have no knowledge of God. I am saying this to shame you *into better habits*.

³⁵Now I know what some of you are thinking: "Just how are the dead going to be raised? What kind of bodies will they have when they come *back to life*?" ³⁶*Don't be a fool!* The seed you plant doesn't produce life unless it dies. *Right?* ³⁷The seed doesn't have *the same look,* the same body, *if you will,*

---

* 15:27 Psalm 8:6   * 15:29 Literally, immersions, to show repentance   * 15:32 Isaiah 22:13

of what it will have once it starts to grow. It starts out a single, naked seed—whether wheat or some other grain, *it doesn't matter*—38and God gives to that seed a body just as He has desired. For each of the different kinds of seeds God prepares a unique body. 39*Or look at it this way:* not all flesh is the same. *Right?* There is *skin* flesh on humans, *furry* flesh on animals, *feathery* flesh on birds, and *scaly* flesh on fish. 40*Likewise* there are bodies made for the heavens and bodies made for the earth. The heavenly bodies have a different kind of glory *or luminescence* compared to bodies below. 41*Even among the heavenly bodies, there is a different level of brilliance:* the sun shines differently than the moon, the moon differently than the stars, and the stars themselves differ in their brightness.

42It's like this with the resurrection of those who have died. The body planted in the earth decays. But the body raised from the earth cannot decay. 43The body is planted in disgrace and weakness. But the body is raised in splendor and power. 44The body planted *in the earth* was animated by the physical, material realm. But the body raised *from the earth* will be animated by the spiritual. Since there is a physical, material body, there will also be a spiritual body. 45That's why it was written, "The first man Adam became a living soul"; the last Adam has become a life-giving spirit. 46*Everything has an order.* The body is not animated first by the spiritual but the physical; then the spiritual *becomes its life-giving source.* 47The first man, *Adam,* came from the earth and was made from dust; the second man, *Jesus,* has come from heaven. 48The earth man shares his earth nature with all those made of earth; likewise the heavenly man shares His heavenly nature with all those made of heaven. 49Just as we have carried the image of the earth man in our bodies, we will* also carry the image of the heavenly man *in our new bodies at the resurrection.*

V

Redemption is not merely forgiveness of sin's guilt so our souls can go to heaven someday. Our true hope is to be free from physical death just as Jesus was raised from the dead. Accordingly, this hope of bodily resurrection stands against the expectation that souls escape from their mortal bodies (as if your soul is the real "you" and your body is a disposable external space suit) and merely float up to heaven. Rather, Paul presents resurrection as a new creation; and this restored bodily existence affirms and fulfills the original intent of creation. Believers don't have to wait until the future to experience this Spirit-enabled life because living in obedience to God through the Spirit is a foretaste of the total experience that will come when all is restored later.

50Now listen to this: brothers and sisters, this present body is not able to inherit the kingdom of God any more than decay can inherit that which lasts forever. 51Stay close because I am going to tell you a mystery—something you may have trouble understanding: we will not all fall asleep in death, but we will all be transformed. 52*It will all happen so fast,* in a blink, a mere flutter of the eye. The last trumpet will call, and the dead will be raised from their graves with a body that does not, cannot decay. All of us will be changed! 53We'll step out of our mortal clothes and slide into immortal bodies, *replacing everything that is subject to death with eternal life.* 54And, when we are all redressed with bodies that do not, cannot decay, when we put immortality over our mortal frames, then it will be as *Scripture* says:

> *Life everlasting* has victoriously
>   swallowed death.*
> 55Hey, Death! What happened to your big
>   win?
>   Hey, Death! What happened to your
>   sting?*

56Sin came *into this world,* and death's sting *followed.* Then sin took aim at the law and gained power *over those who follow the law.* 57Thank God, then, for our Lord Jesus, the Anointed, *the Liberating King,* who brought us victory *over the grave.*

58My dear brothers and sisters, stay firmly planted—be unshakable—do many good works in the name of God, and know

* 15:49 Other manuscripts read "so let us."   * 15:54 Isaiah 25:8
* 15:55 Hosea 13:14

that all your labor is not for nothing when it is for God.

16 Now I call you, just as I did the churches gathering in Galatia, to collect funds to support God's people *in Jerusalem.* [2]On *Sunday,* the first day of the week, *I want* each of you to set aside an amount, as God has blessed you, so the funds will be collected by the time I come. [3]When I get there, I will send those you recommend by your own letters to carry your *generous and gracious* donation to Jerusalem. [4]If you think it seems appropriate for me to travel with them, then we'll go together.

[5]*Get ready.* I will come your way after traveling through Macedonia. For I'm just passing through Macedonia [6]and will probably stay with you through the winter so that you may provide for my next journey (wherever that may be). [7]I want to reconnect with you, not just pass through; if the Lord is willing, I hope to stay awhile. [8]But until Pentecost, I plan to stay in Ephesus [9]because, not only has *God* opened a significant door here for me to serve, but also there is a lot of opposition against me.

V

Churches are often characterized by words such as "independent" and "autonomous." But one would be hard-pressed to find any of these ideas in the Scriptures. Instead, Paul seems to be modeling submission and interdependence. We must always consider others and shape our actions to bless them. But he does not stop there—it is clear that we are responsible to care for one another in physical and monetary ways. What might Paul say to the church today, given the drastic disparity between the wealthy churches of the West and the brothers and sisters in the rest

of the world who lack food, water, or shelter?

---

[10]If Timothy comes, see that he is comfortable and untroubled; his work is the Lord's, as is mine. [11]No one should treat him badly. Send him on to meet me in peace because the brothers and sisters here and I are looking for him. [12]You shouldn't expect to see our brother Apollos, although I tried to persuade him to come to you with the rest of the brothers and sisters, because now is not the best time for him to come. When it's his time, he will come.

[13]*Listen,* stay alert, stand tall in the faith, be courageous, and be strong. [14]Let love prevail in your life, words, and actions.

[15]*Finally,* brothers and sisters, I call on you *to follow your leaders.* People like those in the house of Stephanas—you know they were among the first believers in Achaia, and they have devoted their lives to serving God's people—[16]*I urge you* to submit to the authority of such leaders, to every coworker, and to those who *offer their backs and shoulders for the* work. [17]I celebrate the arrival of Stephanas, Fortunatus, and Achaicus, as they have supplied me with what you could not. [18]They have been a breath of fresh air for me as I know they are for you, so respect and honor those like them.

[19]The churches in Asia salute you. Aquila and Prisca send a heartfelt greeting in the Lord along with those who gather at their house. [20]The entire family in faith here sends their greetings. *Be sure you* greet one another by a holy kiss.

[21]This *closing* greeting is written by my own hand—Paul's: [22]May those who have no love for the Lord be cursed. Maranatha, *"Our Lord, come!"* [23]May the grace of the Lord Jesus be with you. [24]My love to you all in *the name of* the Anointed One, Jesus. [Amen.]*

* 16:24 Some manuscripts omit this word.

2 CORINTHIANS

Letter to the church in Corinth

From Paul, the apostle to the Gentiles

After Paul wrote 1 Corinthians, he heard from Timothy that the situation between him and the church he loved was deteriorating. Apparently in Paul's absence, a number of false teachers had instructed the church and claimed that Paul was not a true emissary of Jesus. They criticized his message and his methods; they charged that he was inferior to the real emissaries. So Paul made a hasty trip across the Aegean from Ephesus—where he was working—in hopes of repairing the rift between them. But the visit backfired. Instead of making things better, it made things worse. He returned to Ephesus from the "agonizing visit," as he later characterized it, and wrote a letter "covered with tears." This time Paul dispatched Titus with the letter. Perhaps he could intervene before a permanent break resulted.

When Titus caught up with Paul in Macedonia, he had good news and bad news. The good news was that a majority of believers in Corinth were back with Paul. The tearful letter—now lost—and Titus's vigilant efforts apparently worked. The bad news was that there was a minority of believers and influential leaders who were still unconvinced. So Paul wrote the letter we now call 2 Corinthians to congratulate the majority and to confront the minority, urging both to stay with the true gospel, and to pave the way for a peaceful, positive visit.

More than any letter Paul wrote, 2 Corinthians offers insight into his work as Jesus' emissary. As he responds to the accusations of his opponents, he articulates clearly his understanding of the good news and his call as one divinely commissioned to carry the good news to both Jews and outsiders. In response to their negative appraisals of Paul's ministry, he challenges them to recognize that faithful ministry entails suffering for others as an embodiment of Jesus' death. It's clear he is embarrassed by the way he has to defend himself at times; still he refuses to sit idly by as his work and the church are in jeopardy. At the heart of the letter is an appeal for the Corinthians to join in the collection for the Jerusalem church. The initiative has a dual purpose. First, Paul hopes to provide substantial relief to the poor in Judea after a lengthy period of famine and hard times. Second, he wants to build a bridge from the churches he is establishing in Asia and Greece to the "mother church" in Jerusalem. Paul understands well the heart of his Lord, and he does everything he possibly can to promote peace and unity among all the churches.

1 Paul, an emissary* of Jesus the Anointed *pressed into service* by the will of God, and our brother Timothy to God's church that gathers in Corinth and all the saints in the region of Achaia.

²May grace and peace from God our Father and the Lord Jesus, the Anointed One, surround you.

³All praise goes to God, Father of our Lord Jesus, the Anointed One. He is the Father of compassion, the God of all comfort. ⁴He consoles us as we endure the pain and hardship of life so that we may draw from His comfort and share it with others in their own struggles. ⁵For even as His suffering continues to flood over us, through the Anointed we experience the wealth of His comfort just the same. ⁶If we are afflicted *with such trouble and pain*, then know it is so that you might ultimately experience comfort and salvation. If we experience comfort, it is to encourage you so that you can hold up while you endure the same sufferings we all share. ⁷Remember that our hope for you stands firm, *unshaken and unshakable*. That's because we know that as you share in our sufferings, so you will also share in our comfort.

⁸My brothers and sisters, we have to tell you that when we were in Asia the troubles we faced were nearly more than we could handle. The burdens we bore nearly crushed us. Our strength dwindled to nothing. For a while, we weren't sure we would make it through the whole ordeal. ⁹We thought we would have to serve out our death sentences right then and there. As a result, we realized that we could no longer rely on ourselves and that we must trust solely in God, who possesses the power to raise the dead. ¹⁰*Miraculously* God Himself delivered us from the cold hands of death. We again place our hope in Him alone, and we know He will deliver us. ¹¹Join us in this work. Lend us a hand through prayer so that many will give thanks for the gift that comes to us when God answers the prayers of so many.

as your comforter. In these letters, and often in our own lives, it is when we seem to have come to the end of ourselves that we see and experience the fullness of God in entirely new ways. This is not to say that any of us should or would seek out the kind of suffering Paul experienced; we do not long to be imprisoned, beaten, shipwrecked, or hunted by authorities. But when our dark days come, we should be ready to learn, grow, and experience the fullness of God in the midst of our troubles.

¹²We are proud of the fact that we have lived before the world and especially before you with clear consciences, living holy lives mixed with genuine sincerity before God. We have not relied on any human wisdom but on the grace *and favor* of God. ¹³We are not writing to you in anything *resembling codes or riddles*; we only write those lessons you are ready to read and understand. I hope you will *study them, value them, and* truly understand them until the end. ¹⁴You have already begun to grasp what we mean in part; but on the day when our Lord Jesus returns, we will be as proud of you as you are of us.

¹⁵⁻¹⁶In *this spirit of* trust and confidence, I was intending to come your way first *on my current journey*. So that you might have a double dose of this grace and assurance, my plan was to visit you on my way to Macedonia and return to you again on the journey back so that you could assist me on the trip to Judea. ¹⁷*But since this didn't happen,* was I just being indecisive? Were my plans made in the flesh *rather than by God's Spirit*? How can I say "yes" and "no" in the same breath? ¹⁸Because our God is always faithful *to His promises*, our word to you was not both "yes" and "no"—*Yes, I'll come,"* and then, *"No, I've changed my mind."* ¹⁹For the Son of God—Jesus the Anointed whom we (Silvanus,* Timothy, and I) have preached to you—was not both "yes" and then "no." With Him the answer is always "yes." ²⁰In Jesus we hear a resounding "yes" to all of God's many promises. This is the reason we say "Amen" to and through Jesus when giving glory to God. ²¹*Remember that* God has established our

* 1:1 Literally, apostle   * 1:19 Silvanus is better known in Acts as Silas.

relationship with you in the Anointed One, and He has anointed *and commissioned* us *for this special mission.* [22]He has marked us with His seal and placed His Spirit in our hearts as a guarantee, a down payment *of the things to come.*

[23]*If I were in court today,* I'd call God as a witness to my soul. *Here's the truth:* I decided not to come back to Corinth in order to spare you *further pain and sorrow.* [24]It's not that we want to coerce you in any matter of faith; we are coworkers called to increase your joy because you have stood firm in faith.

The believers in Corinth are exhausting Paul and one another with their negativity and criticism. Nothing destroys the beauty of Christian community more aggressively than these kinds of patterns.

2 I finally determined that I would not come to you again for yet another agonizing visit. [2]If my visits create such *pain and* sorrow for you, who can cheer me up except for those I've caused such grief? [3]This is exactly what I was writing to you about earlier so that when we are face-to-face I will not have to wallow in sadness in the presence of friends who should bring me the utmost joy. For I felt sure that my delight would also become your delight. [4]My last letter to you was covered with tears, composed with great difficulty, and *frankly,* a broken heart. It wasn't my intention to depress you *or cause you pain*; rather, I had hoped you would see it for what it was—a demonstration of the overwhelming love I have for all of you.

V

Interpersonal relationships are often filled with disagreements and tensions. It's common to hear someone long for the "good old days" of the New Testament when things were simpler and people were holier. But Paul's ministry proves the first-century churches were no different. They were just as full of fights, tensions, and power plays as modern churches are. We should seek to be loving but also firm when the situation demands it. We should be quick to offer forgiveness to and seek

reconciliation with those who turn back from their divisive actions. That's what Paul did.

---

[5]But if anyone has caused harm, he has not so much harmed me as he has—and I don't think I'm exaggerating here—harmed all of you. [6]*In my view,* the majority of you have punished him well enough. [7]So instead of continuing to ostracize him, I encourage you to offer him *the grace of* forgiveness and the comfort *of your acceptance.* Otherwise, *if he finds no welcome back to the community,* I'm afraid he will be overwhelmed with extreme sorrow and lose all hope. [8]So I urge you to demonstrate your love for him once again. [9]I wrote these things to you with a clear purpose in mind: to test whether you are willing to live and abide by all *my counsel.* [10]If you forgive anyone, I forgive that one as well. Have no doubt, anything that I have forgiven—when I do forgive—is done ultimately for you in the presence of the Anointed One. [11]*It's my duty* to make sure that Satan does not win even a small victory over us, for we don't want to be naïve *and then fall prey to* his schemes.

[12]When I arrived at Troas, bringing the good news of the Anointed, the Lord opened a door there for me. [13]Yet my spirit was restless because I could not find my brother Titus. Eventually I told them good-bye and set out for Macedonia.

[14]Yet I am so thankful to God, who always marches us to victory under the banner of the Anointed One; and through us He spreads the beautiful fragrance of His knowledge to every corner of the earth. [15]*In a turbulent world* where people are either dying or being rescued, we are the sweet smell of the Anointed to God *our Father.* [16]To those who are dying, they smell the stench of death in us. And to those being rescued, we are the unmistakable scent of life. Who is worthy of this calling? [17]For we are nothing like the others who sell the word of God like a commodity. *Do not be mistaken;* our words come from God with the utmost sincerity, always spoken through the Anointed in the presence of God.

3 Are we back to page one? Do we need to gather some recommendations *to prove our validity* to you? Or do we need to take your letter of commendation to

others *to gain credibility?* ²You are our letter, every word burned onto our* hearts to be read by everyone. ³You are the living letter of the Anointed One, *the Liberating King,* nurtured by us and inscribed, not with ink, but with the Spirit of the living God—*a letter too passionate* to be chiseled onto stone tablets, but *emblazoned* upon the human heart.

⁴This is the kind of confidence we have in and through the Anointed toward our God. ⁵*Don't be mistaken;* in and of ourselves we know we have little to offer, but any competence *or value* we have comes from God. ⁶Now God has equipped us to be capable servants of the new covenant, not by authority of the written law which only brings death, but by the Spirit who brings life.

Apparently Paul is responding to repeated questions from the church in Corinth requiring him to justify his actions and explain his words. But instead of addressing each separately, Paul suggests a new course of action: let my record be based on the fruit in your lives. The Corinthians had experienced the promised effects of the new covenant—transformed hearts through the Spirit—as prophesied by Jeremiah (31) and Ezekiel (36–37). If the Corinthians agree the Spirit is working in them, then they have to agree that Paul's ministry to them is productive.

How do we stand up to the same test? If our lives were judged based on the fruit of the seeds we have planted and nurtured in the lives of others, would we be proud or mortified?

⁷Now *consider this:* if the ministry of death, which was chiseled in stone, came with so much glory that the Israelites could not bear to look at Moses' face even as that glory was fading, ⁸imagine the kind of greater glory that will accompany the ministry of the Spirit. ⁹If glory ushered in the ministry that offers condemnation, how much more glory will attend the ministry that promises to restore and set the world right? ¹⁰In fact, what seemed to have great glory will appear entirely inglorious in the light of the greater

glory *of the new covenant.* ¹¹If something that fades away possesses glory, how much more intense is the glory of what remains?

¹²In light of this hope that we have, we act with great confidence and speak *with great courage.* ¹³We do not act like Moses who covered his face with a veil so the children of Israel would not stare as the glory *of God* faded *from his face.** ¹⁴Their minds became as hard *as stones;* for up to this day when they read the old covenant, the same veil continues *to hide that glory*; this veil is lifted only through the Anointed One. ¹⁵Even today a veil covers their hearts when the words of Moses are read; ¹⁶but in the moment when one turns toward the Lord, the veil is removed. ¹⁷*By* "the Lord" *what I mean* is the Spirit, and *in any heart* where the Spirit of the Lord is present, there is liberty. ¹⁸Now all of us, with our faces unveiled, reflect the glory of the Lord as if we are mirrors; and so we are being transformed, *metamorphosed,* into His same image from one radiance of glory to another, just as the Spirit of the Lord accomplishes it.

Drawing from Exodus 32–34, Paul uses Moses as a model of one who has been transformed by God's glory, but in a limited way. Moses encountered God (the Lord) through the Spirit on that mountain, but the Spirit now—as a fulfillment of the new covenant—dwells in the hearts of believers and continually transforms them. This transformation is based on a new way of understanding God's revelation: Jesus Himself, the One who reveals God's glory, is the very image of God. Through this Spirit-enabled encounter, believers experience a new way of living and therefore come to resemble the Anointed One as they reflect His glory.

4 Since we are *joined together* in this ministry as a result of the mercy *shown to all of us* by God, we do not become discouraged. ²Instead, we have renounced all the things that hide in shame; we refuse

* 3:2 Other manuscripts read "your hearts."   *3:13 Exodus 34:33-35

to live deceptively or use trickery; we do not pollute God's Word *with any other agenda.* Instead, we aim to tell the truth plainly, appealing to the conscience of every person under God's watchful eye. ³Now if our gospel remains veiled, it is only veiled from those who are *lost and* dying, ⁴because the *evil god* of this age has blinded the minds of unbelievers. As a result the light of the good news, the radiant glory of the Anointed—who is the very image of God—cannot shine down on them. ⁵We do not preach about ourselves. The subject of all our sermons is Jesus, the Anointed One. He is Lord *and Master* of all. For Jesus' sake we are here to serve you. ⁶The God who spoke *light into existence,* saying, "Let light shine from the darkness,"* is the very One who sets our hearts ablaze to shed light on the knowledge of God's glory *revealed* in the face of Jesus, the Anointed One.

⁷But this beautiful treasure is contained in us—*cracked* pots made of earth and clay—so that the transcendent character of this power will be clearly seen as coming from God and not from us. ⁸We are cracked and chipped from our afflictions on all sides, but we are not crushed by them. We are bewildered at times, but we do not give in to despair. ⁹We are persecuted, but we have not been abandoned. We have been knocked down, but we are not destroyed. ¹⁰We always carry around in our bodies the reality of the brutal death *and suffering* of Jesus. As a result, His *resurrection* life *rises and* reveals its wondrous power in our bodies as well. ¹¹For while we live, we are constantly handed over to death on account of Jesus so that His life may be revealed even in our mortal bodies of flesh. ¹²So death is constantly at work in us, but life is working in you.

Jesus' death is the means to new life for others. Similarly when believers suffer for others as Jesus did, their suffering is an avenue for God's life to transform situations.

¹³We share the same spirit of faith as the one who wrote *the psalm,* "I believed; therefore I spoke."* We also believe, and that belief leads us to acknowledge ¹⁴that the same God who resurrected the Lord Jesus will raise us with Jesus and will usher us all together into His presence. ¹⁵All of this is happening for your good. As grace is spread to the multitudes, there is a growing sound of thanks being uttered by those relishing in the glory of God.

¹⁶So we have no reason to despair. Despite the fact that our outer humanity is falling apart and decaying, our inner humanity is breathing in new life every day. ¹⁷You see, the short-lived pains of this life are creating for us an eternal glory that does not compare to anything we know here. ¹⁸So we do not set our sights on the things we can see *with our eyes.* All of that is fleeting; *it will eventually fade away.* Instead, we focus on the things we cannot see, which live on and on.

V

In chapter 3, Paul explains how the Spirit transforms believers so they are conformed to the image of Jesus. He now clarifies that this change means believers embody Jesus' death through suffering and participate in His present, risen life. This life is ultimately experienced through the resurrection of the body in the future, but it also consists of an inward renewal in the midst of the challenges and troubles of daily existence. Our hope is, therefore, not a release from our bodies but a resurrection of our bodies so that the life inside us now will show outside as well. While we still suffer, this hope of bodily resurrection is a matter of faith.

---

5 We know that if our earthly house—a mere tent *that can easily be taken down*—is destroyed, we will then live in an eternal home in the heavens, a building crafted by divine—not human—hands. ²Currently, in this tent of a house, we continue to groan *and ache* with a deep desire to be sheltered in our permanent home ³because then we will be truly clothed *and comfortable,* protected by a covering for our *current* nakedness. ⁴The fact is that in this tent we anxiously moan, *fearing the naked truth of our reality.* What we crave above all is to be clothed so that what is *temporary and* mortal can be wrapped completely in life. ⁵The One who has worked *and tailored* us for this is

* 4:6 Genesis 1:3   * 4:13 Psalm 116:10

God Himself, who has gifted His Spirit to us as a pledge *toward our permanent home.*

⁶In light of this, we live with a daring passion and know that our time spent in this body is also time we are not present with the Lord. ⁷The path we walk is charted by faith, not by what we see with our eyes. ⁸There is no doubt that we live with a daring passion, but in the end we prefer to be gone from this body so that we can be at home with the Lord. ⁹Ultimately it does not matter whether we are here or gone; our purpose stays fixed, and that is to please Him. ¹⁰*In time* we will all stand in judgment before the throne of the Anointed, *the Liberating King,* to receive what is just for our conduct (whether it be good or bad) while we lived in this temporary body.

¹¹So because we stand in awe of the *one true* Lord, we make it our aim to convince all people *of the truth of the gospel;* God sees who we really are, and I hope *in some way* that you'll look deeply into your consciences to see us as well. ¹²*But we hope you understand that* we are not trying to prove ourselves to you *or pull together a résumé that will impress you.* We are simply hoping that you will find a sense of joy in connecting with us. And when you are approached by others (who may value appearances more than the heart) *asking questions about us,* you will be able to offer an answer for them. ¹³If we *seem out of control or* act like fanatics, it is for God. But if we act in a coherent and reasonable way, it is for you. ¹⁴You see, the controlling force in our lives is the love of the Anointed One. And our confession is this: One died for all; therefore, all have died. ¹⁵He died for us so that we will all live, not for ourselves, but for Him who died and rose from the dead. ¹⁶*Because of all that God has done,* we now have a new perspective. We used to show regard for people based on worldly standards and interests. No longer. We used to think of the Anointed the same way. No longer. ¹⁷Therefore, if anyone is united with the Anointed One, that person is a new creation. The old life is gone—and see—a new life has begun! ¹⁸All of this is *a gift* from *our Creator* God, who has *pursued us and* brought us into a restored *and healthy* relationship with Him through the Anointed. And He has given us *the same mission,* the ministry of reconciliation, *to bring others back to Him.* ¹⁹*It is central to our good news that* God was in the Anointed making things right between Himself and the world. This

means He does not hold their sins against them. But it also means He charges us to proclaim the message that heals and restores our broken relationships *with God and each other.*

²⁰So we are now representatives of the Anointed One, *the Liberating King;* God has given us a charge to carry through our lives—urging all people on behalf of the Anointed to become reconciled to *the Creator* God. ²¹He orchestrated this: the *Anointed* One, who had never experienced sin, became sin for us so that in Him we might embody the very righteousness of God.

These simple verses capture the heart of the good news. Lowering Himself, the sinless Jesus took our sin upon Himself and canceled its power through His death and resurrection. As believers are united with Him, they are raised up with Him and embody God's righteousness, experiencing forgiveness, reconciliation, and new life. This righteousness is a new creation gift that can never be separated from the Giver, and so believers only experience it because they are "in Him."

---

6 As for those of us working as His emissaries,* we beg you not to take the grace of God lightly. ²For God says *through Isaiah,*

> When the time was right, I listened to you;
>   and that day you were delivered, I was your help.*

Look, now the time is right! See, your day of deliverance is here! ³*We are careful in what we teach* so that our words won't be a stumbling block and so that no one will discredit our ministry. ⁴But as God's servants, we commend ourselves in every situation. So that with great endurance we persevere even in anguish and hardship. We have been cornered *by the enemy* ⁵suffering beatings, imprisonments, uproars, toil, sleeplessness, and starvation.⁶And by the Holy Spirit with

* 6:1 Literally, apostles   * 6:2 Isaiah 49:8

purity, understanding, patience, kindness, and sincerest love we have proved ourselves. [7]Now with the voice of truth and power of God—armed on the right and armed on the left with righteousness *from God*—we continue. [8]Whether respected or loathed, praised or criticized as frauds, yet true, [9]as unknown *to this world*, and yet well known *to God*, we serve Him. We are treated as dying and yet we live, as punished and yet we are not executed. [10]Though we are sorrowful, we continually rejoice. As *the poorest of* the poor, we bring richness to all, and though we have nothing, we possess all things.

[11]Corinthians, we have been completely open to you. *We've exposed the truth,* holding nothing back while our hearts open wide *to take you in.* [12]We have revealed our affection toward you—though *it's obvious* you have a hard time showing your affection toward us. [13]If I could offer some fatherly advice: open yourselves up as children; share your hearts with us as we have done for you.

[14]Don't develop partnerships with those who are not followers of Jesus' teachings. For what real connection can exist between righteousness and rebellion? How can light participate in darkness? [15]What harmony can exist between the Anointed and Satan?* Do the faithful and the faithless have anything in common? [16]Can the temple of God find common ground with idols? Don't you see that we house the temple of the living God within us? *Remember when* He said,

> "I will make My home with them and walk
>   among them.
> I will be their God,
>   and they will be My people.*
> [17]So then turn away from them,
>   turn away and leave *without looking
>   back*,"* says the Lord.
> "Stay away from anything unclean,
>   *anything impure,*
> and I will welcome you.*
> [18]And I will be for you as a father,
>   and you will be for Me as sons and
>   daughters,"*
> Says the Lord Almighty!

The most important partnership in life is marriage. There are other kinds of union, but the union of husband and wife transcends any other. God created sexual intimacy as a unique gift to marriage. Its purpose goes beyond pleasure and procreation. As a man and a woman join their bodies together, the Spirit does a unique work of binding these two individuals as one person. But the involvement of the Spirit is not possible when a believer is intimate with a nonbeliever. They are not filled with the same Spirit and cannot experience the fullness God intends. Paul's instructions are practical, simple, and clear.

---

7 Because we have these promises, dearly loved ones, out of respect for God we should scour the filth from our flesh and spirit and move toward perfect *beauty and* holiness.

[2]Take us into your hearts; *love us as we love you. You have nothing to fear.* We have hurt no one, ruined no one, swindled no one. [3]I am not writing these things to condemn you, as I said before. Our hearts embrace you, so we stand beside you whether facing life or death. [4]I am completely confident and incredibly proud of you. Even in all this turbulence I am at peace—I am overflowing with joy.

[5]When we came into Macedonia, we were completely worn out—under attack from every angle—nagging opposition on the outside, *our own nagging* fears from the inside. [6]But God, who comforts the downcast, brought us comfort when Titus arrived *from Corinth.* [7]We were relieved, not just to see him, but because he told us how he was encouraged to learn about your longing, your grieving, and your continued enthusiasm for me. So these were all more reasons for me to rejoice!

Jesus said blessings come out of mourning (Matthew 5:4). The very thought is ridiculous to some; but from Paul's perspective, God uses weaknesses and is present in pain. This truth is revolutionary. In the midst of suffering, the mourner abandons pretense and self-consciousness. There we meet

* 6:15 Literally, Belial   * 6:16 Leviticus 26:12; Ezekiel 37:27
* 6:17 Isaiah 52:11   * 6:17 Ezekiel 20:34,41   * 6:18 2 Samuel 7:14

God chose a people for Himself—a people that make up a body, bound together in a covenant. The forces of this world seek to divide and isolate, but God seeks to unite and reconcile. We must all learn to serve one another and hold our self-interests in abeyance to find a greater good in community.

The believers in Corinth were struggling to find unity and harmony in their local church. Some were living selfishly by eating all the food at their common meals or emphasizing issues that create division in the community. For Paul it was not enough that they learn to live well with one another, although that was important. They had to know they were part of a larger body—they belonged to the churches in Jerusalem, Ephesus, Philippi, and the new frontier of Christianity. We are also part of a global church. What would happen if the church would begin to live this simple truth and generously share all it has with our brothers and sisters across the globe?

God and one another in honest ways that open the doors to redemption when we are willing.

---

⁸I knew you would be upset with my last letter, but I do not regret sending it. If there were times I did have second thoughts, it was because I could see that the letter did hurt you, even if only for a while. ⁹Now I am glad—not because it caused you grief but because you were moved to make a permanent change* that can happen only with the realization that your actions have gone against God—I'm glad to know you suffered no long-term loss because of what we did. ¹⁰Now *this type of deep sorrow,* godly sorrow, is not so much about regret; but it is about producing a change of mind and behavior* that ultimately leads to salvation. But *the other type of sorrow,* worldly sorrow, *often is fleeting and* only brings death. ¹¹*Look at what is happening among you!* Notice how authentic and diligent you have become because this godly sorrow has been at work *in your community. But there's more:* your desire to clear your name, your *righteous* anger, your respect, your longing, your zeal, and your *concern for* justice. All these demonstrate how you have been made clean. ¹²So when I wrote my *last difficult* letter, it was not to comfort the victim or confront the perpetrator—it was to stir up your sincere devotion for us under God's watchful eye. ¹³In the midst of all that has happened, *though it has been difficult,* we are comforted *and encouraged.* When we saw the *relief and* joy on Titus's face, we celebrated even more because his spirit had been totally refreshed by you. ¹⁴Now if I have bragged *in the past* about you to Titus, I have nothing to be ashamed of. Just as we've spoken the whole truth to you, I'm glad to know that our boasts to Titus *about you* have proven true as well. ¹⁵His love for you overflows even more as he recalls your obedience and how you *respectfully and somewhat nervously,* with fear and trembling, took him in. ¹⁶I have great joy *now* because I have great confidence in you.

8 Now, brothers and sisters, let me tell you about the *amazing* gift of God's grace that's happening throughout the churches in Macedonia. ²Even in the face of severe anguish *and hard times,* their elation and poverty have overflowed into a wealth of generosity. ³I watched as they willingly gave what they could afford and then went beyond to give even more. ⁴They came to us *on their own,* begging to take part in this work *of grace* to support the *poor* saints *in Judea.* ⁵*We were so overwhelmed*—none of us expected their reaction—that they truly turned their lives over to the Lord and then gave themselves to support us in our work as we answer the call of God. ⁶That's why we asked Titus to finish what he started among you regarding this gracious work of charity. ⁷Just as you are rich in everything—in faith and speech, in knowledge and all sincerity, and in the love we have shown among you*—now I ask you to invest richly in this gracious work too. ⁸I am not going to command you, but I am going to offer you the chance to prove your love genuine in the same way others have done. ⁹You know the grace *that has come to us* through our Lord Jesus the Anointed. He set aside His infinite riches and was born into the lowest circumstance so that you may gain great riches

---

* 7:9 Literally, repent   * 7:10 Literally, repentance   * 8:7 Other manuscripts read "you have shown us."

through His humble poverty. [10-11]Listen, it's been a year *since we called your attention to this opportunity to demonstrate God's grace,* so here's my advice: pull together your resources and finish what you started.

Remember how excited you were at first; it's time to complete this task in the same spirit. [12]Now if there is a willingness to help, give within your means. That's perfectly acceptable. No one expects you to go without or borrow to give. [13-14]The objective is not to go under so others will have some relief; the objective is to use this opportunity today to supply their needs out of your abundance. *One day it may be the other way around,* and they will need to supply your needs from what they have. That's equality. [15]As it is written, "The one who gathered plenty didn't have more than he needed; the one who gathered little didn't have less."*

[16]I praise God who lovingly burdened Titus's heart for you just as He did mine. [17]You see, when we approached him about you, he eagerly stepped up, not only because of our request but because of his own desire to help. [18]We're also sending with him a brother who is well known among the gatherings of believers because of how well he proclaims the good news. [19]And there's more *you should know*: he has been handpicked by the churches to accompany us as we carry on this work of grace. *All this is being done* for the glory of the Lord and to show our own good will. [20]We're being careful so that no one can claim that we are mishandling the funds we've collected. [21]For we are taking every precaution to remain aboveboard—not only in the Lord's eyes, but in the eyes of the people too. [22]So we are also sending another brother who's proven himself time and again. He's certainly *trustworthy and enthusiastic for the gospel; and after hearing about all you are doing,* he's even more excited because he has confidence in you. [23]If anyone asks about Titus, he's my partner and coworker in this ministry to you. If there's any question about who the other brothers and sisters are, they are emissaries* of the churches, traveling to bring glory to the Anointed One, *our Liberating King.* [24]So welcome them before the community in love; show the churches *they represent* that I have not exaggerated your charity and kindness.

9 There's nothing further I could add about your efforts for God's people in Judea. [2]I know you are ready. I bragged on you throughout Macedonia, telling them how the people in Achaia have been prepared since last year; and your passion has been contagious. [3]Still I thought it would be best to send these brothers and sisters ahead to help you finish the final details so all my bragging wouldn't be for nothing. [4]If some of the Macedonians decide to travel with me, all of us would be more than embarrassed if we arrived and you weren't ready to give after the way we've been going on about you. [5]So to help you get your previously promised gift ready, it made sense to me to ask the brothers and sisters to go on ahead so you will have *all the time you need to* put it together as planned and so it doesn't look *thrown together or* coerced.

[6]But I will say this *to encourage your generosity*: the one who plants little harvests little, and the one who plants plenty harvests plenty. [7]Giving grows out of the heart—otherwise, you've reluctantly grumbled "yes" because you felt you had to or because you couldn't say "no," *but this isn't the way God wants it.* For *we know that* "God loves a cheerful giver."* [8]God is ready to overwhelm you with more blessings than you could ever imagine so that you'll always be taken care of in every way and you'll have more than enough to share. [9]Remember what is written *about the One who trusts in the Lord*:

* 8:15 Exodus 16:18   * 8:23 Literally, apostles   * 9:7 Proverbs 22:8 (Septuagint)

He scattered abroad; He gave *freely* to the poor;

His righteousness endures throughout the ages.*

¹⁰The same One who has put seed into the hands of the sower and brought bread to fill our stomachs will provide and multiply the resources you invest and produce an abundant harvest from your righteous actions. ¹¹You will be made rich in everything so that your generosity *will spill over in every direction. Through us* your generosity is at work inspiring praise and thanksgiving to God. ¹²For this mission will do more than bring food and water to fellow believers in need—it will overflow in a cascade of *praises and thanksgivings for our God.* ¹³When this mission *reaches Jerusalem and* meets with the approval *of God's people there,* they will give glory to God because your confession of the gospel of the Anointed One led to obedient action and your generous sharing with them and with all exhibited your sincere concern. ¹⁴Because of the extraordinary grace of God at work in you, they will pray for you and long for you. ¹⁵Praise God for this *incredible, unbelievable,* indescribable gift!

10 I, Paul, appeal to you in the same gentle and loving spirit of the Anointed—*yes,* I who am humble when I'm face-to-face with you but audacious to you *in these letters* when I'm away (*I know what they say*). ²If it were up to me, I'd rather not have to be so bold when I'm with you, especially with the kind of forceful confidence I can work up when I confront those who have accused us of walking in a worldly way. ³For though we walk in the world, we do not fight according to this world's rules of warfare. ⁴The weapons of the war we're fighting are not of this world but are powered by God and effective at tearing down the strongholds *erected against His truth.* ⁵We are demolishing arguments and ideas, every high-and-mighty philosophy that pits itself against the knowledge of *the one true* God. We are taking prisoners of every thought, *every emotion,* and subduing them into obedience to the Anointed One. ⁶As soon as you choose obedience, we stand ready to punish every act of disobedience.

⁷Look at what is going on right in front of you. If anyone is convinced that he belongs to the Anointed, then he should think again; even if he belongs to Him, so do we. ⁸I'm not embarrassed, even if it seems to others I have gone overboard in speaking about the power the Lord has given us to edify and encourage you and not to destroy anyone who strays. ⁹I don't want it to seem as if I'm simply trying to scare you with my letters; *they are not hollow.* ¹⁰For some people are saying, "Paul's letters sound authoritative and strong, but in person he just doesn't measure up—even his speeches don't deliver." ¹¹They need to understand this: whatever we say through our letters when we are away, that is exactly what we will do when we are looking you in the eye.

¹²For we would never dare to compare ourselves with people who have based their worth on self-commendation. They check themselves against and compare themselves with one another. *It just shows that* they don't have any sense! ¹³So we will carefully limit our boasting to the extent only of what God has done in and through us, a reach that extends as far as you. ¹⁴For it wasn't as if we were overreaching *into someone else's territory* by reaching out to you. Weren't we the first ones to bring you the good news of the Anointed One? ¹⁵We carefully put limits on our boasting and avoid taking credit for what others do. But we do hope to see your faith grow so that we can watch our mission really expand all the way to the limits *God has set for us.* ¹⁶*The plan includes* taking the good news to people and lands beyond you. We've no interest in or intention of staking claim to other people's accomplishments in their arenas. *As the Scripture says,* ¹⁷"The one who boasts must boast in the Lord."* ¹⁸Now *let's be clear:* it's not the one who commends himself who is approved; it's the one whom the Lord commends.

Paul's tone changes. Some believe chapters 10–13 may be from his second letter "covered with tears" (2:4). His rebuke and strong warning are meant to lead the Corinthians lovingly to repentance.

11 Please endure a little foolishness on my part; you have come so far with me already. ²*To be completely honest,* I am extremely jealous for you; but it's the same kind of jealousy God has for you. You see, *like an attentive father,* I have pledged your hand in marriage and promised to present

* 9:9 Psalm 112:9   * 10:17 Jeremiah 9:24

you as a pure virgin to *the One who would be your husband,* the Anointed One. [3]But now I'm afraid that as that serpent tricked Eve with his wiles, so your *hearts and* minds will be tricked and you will stray from the single-minded love and pure devotion to Him. [4]So then, if someone comes along and presents you with a Jesus different from the one we told you about, or if you receive a spirit different from the one gifted *through our Lord Jesus,* or even if you hear a gospel different from the one you heard *through us;* then you're ready to go with it.

[5]I consider myself in league with the *so-called* great emissaries; I lack nothing. [6]Even if I'm not the greatest speaker, I make up for it by what I know *of God* and have proved it time and again to you. [7]Was it a sin to humble myself *and serve* you so that you might be lifted up? *Did I wrong you somehow* by instructing you in the good news of God without charge? [8]*In a sense,* I robbed other churches by accepting their support just so I could serve you. [9]If any need arose while I was with you, I didn't trouble anyone. When the brothers and sisters arrived from Macedonia, they covered all my needs so that I didn't become a burden to any of you; and I plan on keeping it that way. [10]For I tell you, as the truth of the Anointed One lives in me, I will continue to boast about this all throughout Achaia. [11]Why am I doing this? It's not because I don't love you—God knows I do—[12-13]but I will continue doing what I am doing to cut off any opportunity—*clearly* some are looking for one—for these false emissaries, these *low-down,* untrustworthy preachers, these posers who act as emissaries of the Anointed, to claim that they work under the same terms that we do. [14]No wonder *they are so good at it.* Satan himself poses as a messenger of heavenly light, [15]so why should we expect less from his servants—*plodding over the earth,* pretending to be ministers of righteousness—but in the end, they'll get what's coming to them.

[16]So as I said before, please don't mark me a fool; but if you must, then please accept me even as that and give me a little more room to boast. [17]What I am saying now is not in character with our Lord but is the bragging of a self-assured fool. [18]Just as other fools brag according to their worldly accomplishments, so I, too, will have to boast; [19]meanwhile, you—so wise, so tolerant—gladly bear this *kind of* foolishness. [20]How easily you tolerate becoming another's slave,

having them consume you, letting them rob you *blind,* or allowing them to edge their way past you or slap you in the face. [21]Embarrassingly I admit that next to them we must look very weak!

But in whatever way they dare to boast—*remember,* I'm speaking *in character* as a fool—I dare to boast *even more!* [22]Are they Hebrews, *God's chosen?* So am I. Are they true Israelites? So am I. Are they descendants of Abraham? So am I. [23]Are they servants to the Anointed One, *the Liberating King?* I am even more so! (I can't believe how foolish I sound.) I have worked harder *for God's kingdom,* taken more beatings, been dragged in and out of prisons, and have been eye-to-eye with death. [24]Five times I have withstood thirty-nine lashes from Jewish authorities, [25]three times I was battered with rods, once I was almost stoned to death, three times I was shipwrecked, and I spent one day and night adrift on the sea. [26]I have been on many journeys *and faced the most extreme circumstances*: perilous rivers, violent thieves, and threats by my own people and by the Gentile outsiders alike. I have faced dangers in the city, in the wilderness, and at sea; and danger from spies among our brothers and sisters. [27]I have survived toil and hardships, sleepless nights, hunger and thirst without a crumb in sight, bare to the cold. [28]As if these external trials weren't enough, there is the daily stress I feel and anxiety I carry for all the churches *under my care.* [29]Who is weak without *this arousing* my empathy? Who gets hurt and offended without *this inciting* my burning anger?

[30]*So as you can see,* if I have to boast, I will, but only in my own weaknesses. [31]The God and Father of our Lord Jesus, He who is worthy of eternal blessing, can confirm that I am telling you the truth. [32]Once, in Damascus, the governor under King Aretas had his people in the city looking for me in order to arrest me. [33]But I crouched in a basket and was lowered out of a window in the city wall, and I narrowly escaped his tight grip.

Paul is speaking of himself in verses 2–5 in an odd, third-person way. He writes cryptically for a purpose: to distract from the fact that, at least for the moment, he is boasting of something other than weakness. In heavenly journeys, Paul has seen amazing sights and heard amazing sounds—sights and sounds no human can or should ever speak of.

But God adds something to keep Paul from being carried away by such ecstasies: He gives His emissary "a thorn in the flesh." Perhaps it is a chronic physical or emotional illness he suffers. Perhaps it is the steady stream of opponents who follow Paul wherever he goes. In God's wisdom, Paul doesn't say because his listeners would likely fixate on whatever problem he has in unhealthy ways. That's what humans do. Still Paul believes that God sent this unwelcome messenger, so he pleads with God three times to remove it. Why just three times? Why doesn't he bombard heaven daily with his pleas? Well, it may be because he knows Jesus prayed three times in the garden for the cup of suffering to be removed. Ultimately Jesus surrendered to the will of the Father, and Paul does too: "Grace is enough, Paul. Grace is enough."

equal. If the cause of Jesus were a fleeting interest or a halfhearted pursuit, then he would have given up after his first beating. But Paul's compassion for those who did not know the beauty of the gospel was stubborn and unyielding. This persecutor-turned-emissary always had his critics. But who could call him insincere?

12 Boasting like this is necessary, but it's *unbecoming and probably unavailing. Since you won't hear me any other way,* let me tell you about visions and revelations I received of the Lord.

²Fourteen years ago, there was this man I knew—a believer in the Anointed who was caught up to the third heaven. (Whether this was an in- or out-of-body experience I don't know; only God knows.) ³⁻⁴This man was caught up into paradise (*let me say it again,* whether this was an in- or out-of-body experience I don't know; only God knows), and he heard inexpressible words—words a mortal man is forbidden to utter. ⁵I could brag about such a man; but as for me, I have nothing to brag about outside my own shortcomings. ⁶So if I want to boast, I won't do so as a fool because I will be speaking the truth. But I will stop there, since I don't want to be credited with anything except exactly what people see and hear from me. ⁷To *keep me grounded and* stop me from becoming too high and mighty due to the extraordinary character of these revelations, I was given a thorn in the flesh—a nagging nuisance of Satan, a messenger to plague me! ⁸I begged

the Lord three times to liberate me *from its anguish;* ⁹and *finally* He said to me, "My grace is enough to cover and sustain you. My power is made perfect in weakness." *So ask me about my thorn,* inquire about my weaknesses, and I will gladly go on and on—*I would rather stake my claim in these* and have the power of the Anointed One at home within me. ¹⁰I am at peace *and even take pleasure* in any weaknesses, insults, hardships, persecutions, and afflictions for the sake of the Anointed because when I am at my weakest, He makes me strong.

¹¹I have become a fool, but you drove me to it. Why didn't you stick up for me? I may not be much, but you could have shown me the same respect as you did the other *so-called* great emissaries.* I am not inferior to them in the least. ¹²Miracles, wonders, and signs were all performed right before your eyes, proving I am who I say, a true emissary *of Jesus.* ¹³With the exception of not asking you to shoulder the burden of my care, I have treated you no differently from any other churches. Forgive me for wronging you *by not charging for my services*!

¹⁴Now listen, for the third time I am ready to travel to you, and *once again* I will not burden you because there's nothing of yours that I want: the only thing I want is you. You see, it's not right for children to have to save up for their parents because it's the parents' job to care for their children. ¹⁵I would happily spend until I had nothing left if it was for you. But just because I love you more, should you love me less? ¹⁶Because even though you didn't have to lift a finger for me, *lies abound that* I deceived you by

* 12:11 Literally, apostles

some clever act. [17]Did I cheat you somehow through one of the coworkers I sent your way? *If any of them defrauded you, I'd like to see it.* [18]I was the one who insisted Titus come to you with the brother I sent along. Did Titus take advantage of you in some way? Didn't we work in the same spirit and follow the same direction?

[19]I hope you don't think that all this time we've been defending ourselves to you. We come as the voice of the Anointed; God will judge whether all our work has been useful in building you up, beloved. [20]*And quite honestly,* I am afraid that when I come, we may both be disappointed with what we find; in my fear, *my thoughts go from bad to worse—into a drama of* friction, rivalry, fevered tempers and fists, selfishness, slander, defamation, pride, and complete chaos. [21]I am worried that when I come to visit that my God will humble me *somehow* before you, that I will have to grieve over all those who have sinned before and then refused to turn away* from their addictions to impure practices, immoral sex, and reckless perversions.

13

This is my third trip to your city and community. *As the Scripture says,* "Every charge must be confirmed by two or three witnesses."* [2]As I said before on my second visit, I say now again while absent. Consider this an advance warning, *if you wish,* to those of you still caught up in your old sins and to all the rest as well: when I come the next time, I will not spare anyone *who is out of order.* [3]You asked to see evidence that *the power of* the Anointed One, *the Liberating King,* is at work in me. *Well, you will see it* because He won't be weak in dealing with you. Instead, He will do great things in you. [4]Now it's true that He was crucified in weakness, but *it's also true that* He lives by God's power. For we *who belong to Him* are weak in Him, but we will live with Him by God's power for you.

Weakness looks like failure in the eyes of the world, but for Paul weakness is an avenue to share in Jesus' death and, therefore, in His life as well. The challenge is to remain faithful even in the difficult times, even when there is no one left to provide support. It is in these times that God's power and comfort are most evident. This call to embrace weakness and suffering is difficult. It is normal to run from pain. But the examples of Jesus in the Gospels, of Paul in his letters, and of David in the psalms are of finding God's strength in times of weakness.

[5]Examine yourselves. Check your faith! Are you really in the faith? Do you still not know that Jesus the Anointed is in you?—unless, of course, you have failed the test. [6]Surely you will realize we have not failed the test, [7]but we pray to God that you will stay away from evil. *What's important is* not whether we appear to have passed the test, but that you do what is right *and act honorably,* even if it appears that we have failed. [8]For there's nothing we can do to oppose the truth; all we can do is align ourselves with it. [9]You see, we celebrate when we are weak but you are strong. Our prayer is *simple*: that you may be *whole and* complete. [10]*How I hope* I am saving you by writing this to you in advance; this letter will spare me from using the Lord's authority to come down on you when I arrive. His intention in giving me this authority is to build you up, not tear you down.

[11]Finally, brothers and sisters, keep rejoicing and repair whatever is broken. Encourage each other, think as one, and live at peace; and God, *the Author* of love and peace, will remain with you. [12]Greet each other with a holy kiss, *as brothers and sisters.* [13]All the saints *here with me* send you their greeting.

[14]May the grace of the Lord Jesus the Anointed, the love of God *the Father,* and the fellowship of the Holy Spirit remain with you all. [Amen.]*

Paul ends his letters as he begins them, praying that grace be with those who read this letter. From first to last, the life of faith is framed by grace.

* 12:21 Literally, repent   * 13:1 Deuteronomy 19:15   * 13:14 The earliest manuscripts omit this word.

GALATIANS

Letter to the churches of Galatia

From Paul, the apostle to the Gentiles

In the decades following Jesus' death and resurrection, the churches were locked in an extremely difficult dispute that had far-reaching implications. The earliest followers of Jesus were mostly Jews who recognized Him as the Liberator for Israel. Some of them taught that all believers—both Jews and non-Jews—had to observe Jewish law in order to enter into the benefits and community created through God's actions in Jesus. These people were called "Judaizers" because they insisted that non-Jews live like Jews. Paul writes Galatians to counter this threat to Christian liberty. The tone of this letter is harsh because Paul believes the very truth of the gospel and his ministry are in jeopardy. Since circumcision is the act that initiated non-Jews into Jewish faith, it becomes a symbol for the whole controversy. In this brief book, Paul lays the groundwork for what becomes the orthodox understanding of salvation; namely, that Jews and non-Jews alike enter into a positive relationship with God by grace through faith, not through observing the law.

Paul begins the letter by insisting that his call as an emissary came directly from Jesus, not any human institution. Apparently some were criticizing him, not only for what they thought was a deficient gospel, but also for lacking credentials. So Paul responds by recounting his own story of how he persecuted the church until he experienced a revelation of Jesus. He sees his call largely in prophetic terms and begins his ministry without any kind of human blessing or instruction. When Paul does present his understanding of the good news years later to the Jerusalem leaders, they affirm his message and confirm his call as the apostle to the Gentiles. But this does not put an end to the controversy. As this letter shows, it is played out again and again in the churches.

Paul argues his case from both the experience of the Galatians and the Hebrew Scriptures. The Galatians have received the Spirit, not because they kept the law, but because they have received the gospel in faith. Likewise he explains that in Scripture faith has always been the way Abraham and his spiritual children have related to God and entered into His promises. Therefore those who put their faith in Jesus as Lord and Savior become the true sons and daughters of Abraham.

1 Paul, an emissary* commissioned directly by Jesus the Anointed One and God the Father (who raised Him from the dead)—not *(as some claim)* an agent of men or any person—²and all the brothers and sisters with me to you, the churches of Galatia.

³May the grace and peace of God the Father and the Lord Jesus the Anointed live in you; ⁴*He is the very Savior* who rescues us from this present, *perverse* age dominated by evil by giving His life according to our Father's will to deal with our sins. ⁵May God's glorious name forever receive honor. Amen.

V

From the opening address, it is clear that Paul is angry with what is going on among the churches of Galatia. He feels compelled to defend himself from opponents who are attacking his call as Jesus' emissary. Paul counters the attack by distancing himself from any human institution: he was not called by any church or committee. God the Father and the Lord Jesus commissioned Paul directly to be the emissary to the nations.

---

⁶*Frankly* I am stunned. I cannot believe that you have abandoned God so quickly—even after He called you through the grace of the Anointed One—and have fallen for a different gospel. ⁷Actually there is only one true gospel of the Anointed, and you—because of divisive prodding by others—are accepting a distorted version which is not the gospel at all!

People are being deceived with an imitation of the true gospel, and they have bought into it. The words are nothing but twisted lies.

⁸No matter the source of the false gospel, even if it is preached by us or a heavenly messenger, *ignore it.* May those *who add to or subtract from the gospel of Jesus* be *eternally* cursed! ⁹Listen again: if anyone preaches to you a gospel other than what you have accepted, may he find himself cursed!

¹⁰Do you think I care about the approval of men or about the approval of God? Do you think I am on a mission to please people? If I am still *spinning my wheels* trying to please men, then there is no way I can be a servant of the Anointed One, *the Liberating King.*

¹¹Know this, dear brothers and sisters: the good news I brought to you isn't *the latest in fiction* or the product of some creative mind. ¹²It is not a legend I learned or one that has been passed down from person to person, *ear to ear*. I was gifted with this message as Jesus the Anointed revealed Himself *miraculously to me.* ¹³Surely you are familiar with my personal history, with my dedication to the teachings and traditions of Judaism. I persecuted the church of God—in fact, I meant to destroy it. ¹⁴I excelled in the teachings of Judaism far above other Jewish leaders, and I was zealous to practice the ways of our ancestors. ¹⁵But God—who set me apart even before birth and called me by His grace—chose, to His great delight, ¹⁶to reveal His Son in me so I could tell His story among the outsider nations. I didn't confer with anyone right away, ¹⁷nor did I go to those who were already emissaries* in Jerusalem. I went straight to Arabia and later returned to Damascus.

¹⁸After *living this adventurous mission for* three years, I made my way to Jerusalem and spent 15 days with Cephas, *whom you know as Peter.* ¹⁹But I didn't see any emissary* other than James, our Lord's brother. ²⁰(You can be certain that what I am offering you *is an authentic account.* Before God, it's the whole truth—I wouldn't lie.) ²¹Later I journeyed to Syria and Cilicia; ²²and *since I had spent so little time in* Judea among the churches of the Anointed One, no one there could pick me out of a crowd. ²³But stories of my call and mission preceded me: "The very man who wanted to kill us all is now preaching the faith he once labored to destroy." ²⁴And so they praised God for the miracle He did in my life.

2 ¹⁻²As a result of a revelation, I returned to Jerusalem 14 years later; and *this time* Barnabas and Titus accompanied me. *When I arrived,* I shared the *exact* gospel that I preach to the outsiders. I first shared God's truth privately with those who were people of influence and leadership because I thought *if they did not embrace the freedom of my good news, then* any work *I had done for Jesus here* and any in the past would be spoiled.

* 1:1 Literally, apostle   * 1:17 Literally, apostles   * 1:19 Literally, apostle

One of the great stories in the Bible is the transformation of Saul, the Pharisee, from a persecutor of the church to the greatest missionary that history has ever witnessed. Seldom does Paul relate that story in his letters. He doesn't need to because he usually does that in person when he is planting a church. But on this occasion, as he defends his call and the gospel, he retells a bit of his personal history to underscore the complete metamorphosis that has taken place in his life. In his former life, Paul admits—quite painfully, no doubt—that he tried to destroy this movement. Borrowing language from the prophets, Paul narrates how God unveiled to him the truth about Jesus. At just the right moment, even while Paul was an active enemy, God revealed His Son to Paul and called him to be heaven's emissary to the nations. Paul immediately stopped his campaign against the church, which was just beginning to emerge from its Jewish roots and spread to the Gentile nations.

³*Listen carefully.* None of the Jerusalem leaders insisted that Titus be circumcised, although he is Greek. ⁴Some people who were pretending to be our brothers and sisters were brought in to spy on the freedom we enjoy in the Anointed One, Jesus—*their agenda was clear:* they wanted to enslave us. ⁵But we didn't give in to them. We didn't entertain their thoughts for a minute! We resisted them so the true gospel—*and not some counterfeit*—would continue to be available to you.

⁶It makes no difference to me (or to God for that matter) if people have power or influence. God doesn't choose favorites *among His children.* Even the so-called pillars *of the church* didn't contribute anything new to my understanding *of the good news.* ⁷But it quickly became obvious to them *what God was doing:* He had entrusted me to carry the good news to the uncircumcised, just as Peter was called to preach to those who were circumcised. ⁸God was at work in the ministry of Peter, as emissary* to the Jews, and was also *moving and* working with me in my ministry to the outsider nations.

⁹When James, Cephas (*whom you know as Peter*), and John—three men purported to be pillars *among the Jewish believers*—saw that God's favor was upon me *to fulfill this calling,* they welcomed and endorsed* both Barnabas and me. *They agreed that our ministries would work as two hands,* theirs *advancing the mission of God* among the Jews and ours toward the outsider nations, *all with the same message of redemption.* ¹⁰In parting, they requested we always remember to care for the poor *among us,* which was something I was eager to do.

¹¹But when Cephas came to Antioch, *there was a problem.* I got in his face and exposed him *in front of everyone.* He was clearly wrong. ¹²*Here's what was going on:* before certain people from James arrived, Cephas used to share meals with the Gentile outsiders. And then, after they showed up, Cephas suddenly became aloof and distanced himself from the outsiders because he was afraid of those believers who thought circumcision was necessary.

V

Since Christianity arises from Judaism, some traveling preachers from Jerusalem think that Jewish believers must remain true to Jewish rules regarding circumcision, Sabbath observance, and kosher food. If they rigorously follow the food rules, then Jewish believers are not supposed to share a meal with "unclean" Gentile outsiders, as Peter has been doing in Antioch. They advocate that Gentile outsiders need to follow Jewish ways and practices to become full members of the family of God. Paul—and the Jerusalem council (Acts 15)—strongly reject this. The apostle argues that it is only the faithfulness of Jesus and the presence of the Spirit that serve as the foundation of the new covenant and as the entrance into the people of God.

¹³The rest of the Jewish believers followed his lead, including Barnabas! Their

* 2:8 Literally, apostle   * 2:9 Literally, gave the right hand of fellowship

hypocritical behavior was so obvious—[14]their actions were not at all consistent with everything the good news *of our Lord* represents. So I approached Cephas and told him in plain sight of everyone: "If you, a Jew, have lived like the Gentile outsiders and not like the Jews, then how can you turn around and urge the outsiders to start living like Jews?" [15]We are natural-born Jews, not sinners from the godless nations. [16]But we know that no one is made right *with God* by meeting the demands of the law. It is only through the faithfulness of Jesus* the Anointed *that salvation is even possible*. This is why we put faith in Jesus the Anointed: so we will be put right with God. It's His faithfulness—not works prescribed by the law—that puts us in right standing with God because no one will be acquitted and declared "right" for doing what the law demands. [17]Even though we are seeking a right relationship *with God* through the Anointed, *the fact is* we have been found out. We are sinners. But does that mean the Anointed is the one responsible for our sins? Absolutely not! [18]If I reconstruct something I have worked so hard to destroy, then I prove myself a sinner.

longer alive—but the Anointed is living in me; and whatever life I have left in this failing body I live by the faithfulness of God's Son, the One who loves me and gave His body *on the cross* for me. [21]I can't dismiss God's grace, *and I won't*. If being right *with God* depends on how we measure up to the law, then the Anointed's sacrifice *on the cross* was the most tragic waste in all of history!

3 Galatians, don't act like fools! Has someone cast a spell over you? Did you miss the crucifixion of Jesus the Anointed that was reenacted right in front of your eyes? [2]Tell me this: Did the Holy Spirit come upon you because you lived according to the law? Or was it because you heard *His message of grace* through faith? [3]Are you so foolish? Do you think you can perfect something God's Spirit started with any human effort? [4]Have you suffered so greatly for nothing—if it was indeed for nothing? [5]You have experienced the Spirit He gave you *in powerful ways*. Miracle after miracle has occurred *right before your eyes* in this community, so tell me: did all this happen because you have kept certain provisions of God's law, or was it because you heard *the gospel* and accepted it by faith?

So why all this personal history? Paul thinks it is useful because the people preaching the false gospel in Galatia claim to be operating under the authority of some of the followers of Jesus from Jerusalem, the mother church. Paul doesn't have their pedigree and, according to them, doesn't deserve the rank he claims as the emissary to the nations. They say that not only is Paul deficient, but his message is, too, because it doesn't bring outsiders to follow the law. So Paul goes toe-to-toe with them, defending not only his call but also his message. The good news he preaches comes directly from the risen Jesus and is confirmed by the Jerusalem leaders.

Paul primarily focuses on the efficacy of the death and resurrection of Jesus as the foundation of the church and of a right relationship with God, but he also correlates this with the presence of the Spirit. If the Spirit is working among the outsiders, it shows that they aren't really "outsiders" when it comes to membership in the people of God. Paul supports this by showing how the presence of the Spirit is none other than the fulfillment of the promises to Abraham. However, the Spirit only came through Abraham's descendant, that is, the new covenant with God is mediated by Jesus and the Spirit, not the law.

---

[19]The law has provided the means *to end my dependence on it for righteousness,* and so I died to the law. Now I *have found the freedom to* truly live for God. [20]I have been crucified with the Anointed One—I am no

[6]*You remember Abraham.* Scripture tells us, "Abraham believed God *and trusted in His promises,* so God counted it to his favor as

* 2:16 Often translated "faith in Jesus."

righteousness."* ⁷Know this: people who trust in God are the true sons and daughters of Abraham. ⁸For it was foretold to us in the Scriptures that God would set the Gentile nations right by faith when He told Abraham, "I will bless all nations through you."* ⁹So those who have faith *in Him* are blessed along with Abraham, our faithful ancestor.

¹⁰*Listen,* whoever seeks *to be righteous* by following *certain* works of the law actually falls under the law's curse. I'm giving it to you straight from Scripture *because it is as true now as when it was written:* "Cursed is everyone who doesn't live by and do all that is written in the law."* ¹¹Now it is absolutely clear that no one is made right with God through the law because *the prophet Habakkuk told us,* "By faith the just will obtain life."* ¹²The law is not *the same thing as life* formed by faith. In fact, *you are warned against this when God says,* "The one who observes My laws will live by them."* *I am trying to tell you that* ¹³the Anointed One, *the Liberating King,* has redeemed us from the curse of the law by becoming a curse for us. It was stated *in the Scriptures,* "Everyone who hangs on a tree is cursed *by God.*"* ¹⁴*This is what God had in mind all along:* the blessing He gave to Abraham might extend to all nations through the Anointed One, Jesus; and we are the beneficiaries of this promise of the Spirit that comes *only* through faith.

¹⁵My dear brothers and sisters, here's a real-life example I can give you: *With a last will and testament, when all the property is accounted for,* the document is signed, witnessed, and notarized; and afterward no one can make changes to it. ¹⁶*In a similar way,* God's promises established *a binding agreement* with Abraham and his offspring. *In the Scriptures,* it is carefully stated, "and to your descendant" (meaning one), not "and to your descendants"* (meaning many). Therefore, *in these covenant promises, God was* not *referring* to every son and daughter *born into Abraham's family* but to the Anointed One *to come.* ¹⁷What this all means is that the law given *to Israel* comes along some 430 years after the promise *made to Abraham;* so it does not invalidate the covenant God previously agreed to *or in any way* do away with His promise. ¹⁸You see, if the law became the sole basis for the inheritance, then it would put God in the position of breaking a covenant because He had promised it to Abraham.

Throughout this argument, one critical question remains: why would God give the law if it would not bring His people into a right standing with Him? Couldn't God have found a better way of doing this? It isn't as if the law is a bad thing or a mistake that God needs to correct. It has a good purpose, but a limited one. It never supplants God's promise to Abraham. Rather, the law keeps sin in check until the time is right for the saving justice that comes through faith in Jesus. The law serves as a tutor or a schoolmaster, revealing our great need for salvation and pointing everyone toward Jesus.

¹⁹*Now you're asking yourselves,* "So why *did* God give *us* the law?" God commanded His heavenly messengers to deliver it into the hand of a mediator for this reason: to help us rein in our sins until the Offspring, about whom the promise was made *in the first place,* would come. ²⁰A mediator represents more than one, but God is *only* one. ²¹*"So,"* you ask, "does the law contradict God's promise?" Absolutely not! Never was there written a law that could lead to *resurrection and* life; if there had been, then surely we could have experienced saving righteousness through keeping the law. *But we haven't.* ²²Scripture has subjected the whole world to sin's power so that the faithful obedience of Jesus the Anointed might extend God's promises to everyone who has faith. ²³Before faith came on the scene, the law did its best to keep us in line, restraining us until the faith that was to come was fully revealed. ²⁴So then, the law was like a tutor, assigned to *train us and* point us to the Anointed, so that we will be acquitted *of all wrong* and made right by faith. ²⁵But now that *true* faith has come, we have no need for a tutor. ²⁶It is your faith in the Anointed Jesus that makes all of you children of God ²⁷because all of you who have been initiated into the Anointed One through the ceremonial washing of baptism* have put Him on. ²⁸It makes no difference whether you are a Jew or a Greek,

* 3:6 Genesis 15:6   * 3:8 Genesis 12:3; 18:18; 22:18; 26:4; 28:14
* 3:10 Deuteronomy 27:26   * 3:11 Habakkuk 2:4   * 3:12 Leviticus
18:5   * 3:13 Deuteronomy 21:23   * 3:16 Genesis 12:7; 13:15; 24:7
* 3:27 Literally, immersion, in a rite of initiation and purification

a slave or a freeman, a man or a woman, because in Jesus the Anointed, *the Liberating King,* you are all one. ²⁹Since you belong to Him *and are now subject to His power,* you are the descendant of Abraham and the heir *of God's glory* according to the promise.

4 Listen. I am going to explain *how this all works:* When a minor inherits an estate *from his parents,* although he is the owner of everything, he is the same as a slave. ²Until the day set by his father, the minor is subject to the authorities or guardians *whom his father put in charge.* ³It is like that with us; there was a time when we were like children held under the elemental powers of this world. ⁴When the right time arrived, God sent His Son into this world (born of a woman, subject to the law) ⁵to free those who, *just like Him,* were subject to the law. Ultimately He wanted us all to be adopted as sons and daughters. ⁶Because you are now part of God's family, He sent the Spirit of His Son into our hearts; *and the Spirit* calls out, "Abba, Father." ⁷You no longer have to live as a slave because you are a child *of God.* And since you are His child, God guarantees an inheritance *is waiting* for you.

"Abba" is an address spoken by children to their fathers expressing intimacy and respect. It would not be out-of-the-question to think of it as "Dad," or "Daddy."

⁸During the time before you knew God, you were slaves to powers that are not gods at all. ⁹But now, when you are just beginning to know *the one True* God—actually, *He is showing how completely* He knows you—how can you turn back to weak and worthless *idols made by men, icons of these* spiritual powers? Haven't you endured enough bondage to these *breathless* idols? ¹⁰You are observing particular days, months, *festival* seasons, and years; ¹¹you have me worried that I may have wasted my time laboring among you.

¹²Brothers and sisters, I have become one of you. Now *it's your turn*—become as I am. You have never wronged me. ¹³Do you remember the first time I preached the good news to you? I was sick, and ¹⁴I know my illness was a hardship to you, but you never drew back from me or scorned me. You cared for me as if I were a heavenly messenger of God, possibly as well as if I were the Anointed Jesus Himself! *Don't you remember?* ¹⁵What has happened to your *joy and* blessing? I tell you, *the place was so thick with love that* if it were possible, you would have plucked out your eyes and handed them to me. ¹⁶And now, do I stand as your enemy because I tried to bless you with the truth? ¹⁷*I'll tell you what these false brothers and sisters are counting on:* your attention. They are ravenous for it. They are not acting *honorably or* in your best interests. They want to keep you away *from the good news we proclaim* so they can have you all to themselves. ¹⁸Listen, there's nothing wrong with zeal when you're zealous for *God's* good purpose. And what's more, you don't have to wait for me to be with you to seek the good. ¹⁹My dear children, I feel the pains of birth upon me again, and I will continue in labor for you until the Anointed One is formed completely in you. ²⁰I wish I were there. This letter is really harsh, yet I am really perplexed by you.

²¹*Now it's your turn to* instruct me. All of you who want to live by the rules of the law, are you really listening to and heeding what the law teaches? *Listen to this:* ²²it's recorded *in the Scripture* that Abraham was the father of two sons. One son was born to a slave woman, *Hagar,* and the other son was born to a free woman, *Abraham's wife, Sarah.* ²³The slave woman's son was born through only natural means, but the free woman's son was born through a promise *from God.* ²⁴I'm using an allegory. *Here's the picture:* these two women stand for two covenants. The first *represents the covenant God made* on Mount Sinai—this is Hagar, who gives birth to children of slavery. ²⁵Hagar is Mount Sinai in Arabia, and she stands for the Jerusalem *we know* now. She has lived in slavery along with her children. ²⁶But there is a Jerusalem *we know* above. She is free, and she is our mother. ²⁷*Isaiah* wrote,

> Be glad, you who feel sterile and never gave birth!
> Raise a joyful shout, childless woman, who never went into labor!
> For the barren woman produces many children,
> more than the one who has a husband.*

* 4:27 Isaiah 54:1

²⁸So you *see now,* brothers and sisters, you are children of the promise like Isaac. ²⁹The *slave's* son, born through only what flesh could conceive, *resented and* persecuted the one born *into the freedom* of the Spirit. *The slave's son picked at Isaac,* just as you are being picked at now. ³⁰So what does the Scripture say? "Throw out the slave and her son, for the slave's son will never have a share of the inheritance coming to the son of the free woman."* ³¹So, brothers and sisters, we are not children of the slave woman, but *sons and daughters* of the free.

5 So stand strong for our freedom! The Anointed One freed us so we wouldn't spend one more day under the yoke of slavery, *trapped under the law.*

²Listen because I, Paul, am going to make this message very clear *so it cannot be misunderstood:* if you undergo the rite of circumcision, then all that the Anointed accomplished will be lost on you. ³And understand this: if you choose to be circumcised, then you will oblige yourself to do every single rule of the law *for the rest of your life.* ⁴You, *and anyone else* who seeks to be on the right side of God through the law, have effectively been cut off from the Anointed, *circumcised from grace,* and cast off from the favor of God. ⁵We, on the other hand, *continue to live* through the Spirit's power and wait confidently in the hope that things will be put right through faith. ⁶Here's the thing: in Jesus the Anointed whether you are circumcised or not makes no difference. What makes a difference is faith energized by love.

⁷Who has impeded your progress and kept you from obeying the truth? You were off to such a good start. ⁸*I know for certain* the pressure isn't coming from God. He keeps calling you *to the truth.* ⁹*You know what they say,* "Just a little yeast causes all the dough to rise," *so even the slightest detour from the truth will take you to a destination you do not desire.* ¹⁰*Despite this,* I'm confident because the Lord *reassures me that* you will *truly hear and* take my message to heart. Besides, *I also know that* these troublemakers, whoever they are, will answer to God and be judged accordingly. ¹¹As for me, brothers and sisters, if I continue to preach circumcision—*as these agitators claim*—then why do I still face persecution? *If I were to preach a compromised version of the good news,* then the scandal of the cross would come to an end. ¹²I really wish that these

people who weigh you down with corrupt counsel would mutilate themselves!

¹³Brothers and sisters, God has called you to freedom! *Hear the call,* and do not *spoil this gift by* using your liberty to engage in what your flesh desires; instead, use it to serve each other *as Jesus taught* through love. ¹⁴For the whole law comes down to this one instruction: "Love your neighbor as yourself,"* so ¹⁵why all this vicious gnawing on each other? If you are not careful, you will find you've eaten each other alive!

¹⁶Here's my instruction: walk in the Spirit, and let the Spirit bring order to your life. If you do, you will never give in to your selfish and sinful cravings. ¹⁷For everything the flesh desires goes against the Spirit, and everything the Spirit desires goes against the flesh. There is a constant battle raging between them that prevents you from doing *the good* you want to do. ¹⁸But when you are led by the Spirit, you are no longer subject to the law.

¹⁹It's clear that our flesh entices us into practicing some of its most heinous acts: participating in corrupt sexual relationships, impurity, unbridled lust, ²⁰idolatry, witchcraft, hatred, arguing, jealousy, anger, selfishness, contentiousness, division, ²¹envy *of others' good fortune,* drunkenness, drunken revelry, and other shameful vices *that plague humankind.* I told you this clearly before, and I only tell you again *so there is no room for confusion:* those who give in to these ways will not inherit the kingdom of God.

Paul has been preaching about the call of God to freedom, and so he now spells it out: we are done with the demands of the law; now we are free to live in the Spirit and to be truly right with God. As free people, the Spirit gives us the characteristics of Jesus; we, too, can freely love in joy and peace. We can have patience along with kindness and faithfulness that can only come from the Father. We can reflect the goodness of God while being gentle in operating with self-control. For those who follow Him and live in the Spirit, these characteristics or fruits are a gift from God. As we grow in the faith, we

* 4:30 Genesis 21:10   * 5:14 Leviticus 19:18; Matthew 7:12; 22:39-40

find that we belong to God and can walk daily in the Spirit.

22The Holy Spirit produces a different kind of fruit: *unconditional* love, joy, peace, patience, kindheartedness, goodness, faithfulness, 23gentleness, and self-control. You won't find any law opposed to fruit like this. 24Those of us who belong to the Anointed One have crucified our old lives and put to death the flesh and all the lusts and desires that plague us. 25*Now* since we have chosen to walk with the Spirit, let's keep each step in perfect sync with God's Spirit. 26This will happen when we set aside our self-interests *and work together to create true community* instead of a culture consumed by provocation, *pride,* and envy.

6 My spiritual brothers and sisters, if one *of our faithful* has fallen into a trap and is snared by sin, *don't stand idle and watch his demise.* Gently restore him, being careful not to step into your own snare. 2Shoulder each other's burdens, and then you will live as the law of the Anointed teaches us. 3Don't *take this opportunity to* think you are better than those who slip because you aren't; then you *become the fool and* deceive even yourself. 4Examine your own works so that if you are proud, it will be because of your own accomplishments and not someone else's. 5Each person has his or her own burden to bear *and story to write.* 6Remember to share what you have with your mentor in the Word. 7Make no mistake: God can't be mocked. *What you give is what you get.* What you sow, you harvest. 8Those who sow *seeds* into their flesh will only harvest destruction *from their*

sinful nature. But those who sow *seeds* into the Spirit shall harvest everlasting life from the Spirit. 9May we never tire of doing what is good and right before our Lord because in His season we shall bring in a great harvest if we can just persist. 10So seize any opportunity *the Lord gives you* to do good things *and be a blessing* to everyone, especially those within our faithful family.

Following in the path of the Spirit is not a chore; instead it opens us up to experiencing the life God has for us.

11Look at how giant these letters are now that I am writing with my own hand! 12The troublemakers who are putting pressure on you to be circumcised are trying to impress the flesh. They want to avoid the persecution that comes from preaching the cross of the Anointed One, *the Liberating King.* 13But even those who receive circumcision can't keep the law—*although they think they can*—and they hope to influence which way you go with your own skin so they can have bragging rights over your flesh. 14May I never put anything above the cross of our Lord Jesus the Anointed. Through Him, the world has been crucified to me and I to this world. 15Let me be clear: circumcision *won't save you*—uncircumcision won't either *for that matter*—for both amount to nothing. God's new creation *is what counts, and it* counts for everything. 16May peace and mercy come to all of you who live by this rule and to the Israel of God. 17In the future, don't let anyone cause trouble for me because I bear in my body the marks that wounded Jesus. 18May the grace of our Lord Jesus, the Anointed One, infuse your spirit *with His,* brothers and sisters. Amen.

EPHESIANS

Letter to the church in Ephesus

From Paul, the apostle to the Gentiles

During Paul's time, Ephesus was one of the great cities of the world. It was a wealthy commercial seaport on the Cayster River, not far from the Aegean Sea in what is western Turkey today. The Ephesians were a proud people; their city was home of the ancient temple of Diana (a goddess known to the Greeks as Artemis), one of the Seven Wonders of the World. The city was immersed in the magical arts, a kind of religion that promised people protection from fate, demons, curses, and incantations. This is why Paul's letter is filled with powerful language and promises that Jesus has defeated them through His death and resurrection.

According to Luke, Paul spent nearly three years in Ephesus planting and nurturing a church there, so it seems a bit odd that the letter itself is so generic. Unlike most of Paul's other letters, Ephesians lacks a personal touch, a personal message to specific members of the church at Ephesus. There's good evidence to suggest that Paul intended this letter to be circulated among a number of churches in Asia, but eventually it came to rest in and was identified with the city of Ephesus. It seems clear from the themes and content that Ephesians is not a letter for any particular church; it's a letter for every church in every age.

Writing from his prison cell, possibly in Rome, Paul pictures all liberated believers occupying a new spiritual location he calls "the heavenly realms." In this place, they enjoy all the spiritual blessings God has prearranged for them, but they also wait for the next act in the drama of redemption. They have already been raised to live in this new reality, but the world is still not yet what it will be when the Anointed One, the Liberating King, comes again. Even now Jesus is positioned at God's right hand, reigning over the spiritual powers the Ephesians fear most; so Paul assures them that as they belong to Jesus and take up the full armor of God, they have nothing to fear.

1 Paul, an emissary* of Jesus the Anointed, *directly commissioned as His representative* by the will of God, to the saints [in Ephesus]* faithful in Jesus the Anointed.

2May God the Father and the Lord Jesus the Anointed surround you with grace and peace.

This letter begins with praise and thanksgiving to

God the Father, who blesses us
Jesus the Anointed, who redeems us
the Holy Spirit, who seals us.

3Blessed be God, the Father of our Lord Jesus the Anointed One, who grants us every spiritual blessing in these heavenly realms *where we live* in the Anointed—*not because of anything we have done, but because of what He has done for us.* 4God chose us to be in a relationship with Him even before He laid out plans for this world; He wanted us to live holy lives characterized by love, *free from sin,* and blameless before Him. 5He destined us to be adopted as His children through *the covenant* Jesus the Anointed *inaugurated in His sacrificial life.* This was His pleasure and His will *for us.* 6Ultimately God is the one worthy of praise for showing us His grace; *He is merciful and marvelous,* freely giving us these gifts in His Beloved. 7*Visualize this:* His blood *freely flowing down the cross,* setting us free! We are forgiven for our sinful ways by the richness of His grace, 8which He has poured all over us. With all wisdom and insight, 9He has enlightened us to the great mystery *at the center* of His will. With immense pleasure, He laid out His intentions *through Jesus,* 10a plan that will climax when the time is right *as He returns to create order and unity*—both in heaven and on earth—when all things are brought together under the Anointed's *royal rule.* In Him 11we stand to inherit even more. As His heirs, we are predestined *to play a key role* in His *unfolding* purpose that is energizing everything to conform to His will. 12As a result, we—the first to place our hope in the Anointed One—will live in a way to bring Him glory and praise. 13Because you, too, have heard the word of truth—the good news of your salvation—and because you believed *in the One who is truth,* your lives are marked with His seal. This is *none other than* the Holy Spirit who was promised 14as

the guarantee toward the inheritance we are to receive when He frees and rescues all who belong to Him. To God be all praise and glory!

This letter begins with praise and thanksgiving offered to God. Paul celebrates all the spiritual "blessings" available to all believers in Jesus, the Anointed One. This means that He is the one through whom God has acted to rescue the world. But more than that, He is the Lord to whom we belong and the spiritual place where all believers are presently located. In God's purpose, heaven has come down to where we live so that we now occupy this wonderful realm where salvation is at work, where God's truth and beauty are a reality, and where we wait as the rest of His plan is worked out.

15This is why, when I heard of the faith in the Lord Jesus that is present in your community and of your great love for all God's people, 16I haven't stopped thanking Him for you. I am continually speaking to Him on your behalf in my prayers. *Here's what I say:*

17God of our Lord Jesus the Anointed, Father of Glory: *I call out to You on behalf of Your people.* Give them minds ready to receive wisdom and revelation so they will truly know You. 18Open the eyes of their hearts, *and let the light of Your truth flood in.* Shine Your light on the hope You are calling them to embrace. Reveal to them the glorious riches You are preparing as their inheritance. 19Let them see the full extent of Your power that is at work in those of us who believe, and may it be done according to Your might and power.

Friends, it is this same might and *resurrection* power that 20He used in the Anointed One to raise Him from the dead and to position Him at His right hand in heaven. *There is nothing over Him.* 21He's above all rule, authority, power, and dominion; over every

* 1:1 Literally, apostle   * 1:1 Some early manuscripts omit this portion.

name invoked, *over every title bestowed* in this age and the next. ²²God has placed all things beneath His feet and anointed Him as the head over all things for His church. ²³This church is His body, the fullness of the One who fills all in all.

V

Often in his letters, Paul records his prayers for his churches. He is constantly talking with God about those he considers his spiritual children. He prays that God will grant them wisdom, knowledge, and great power. This is the same power that was at work when God raised Jesus from the dead and seated Him in heaven. Ultimately Paul knows all powers have been subjected to Jesus, the God-man, and He is destined to be head over all creation. In the resurrection of Jesus, the ultimate redemption of the cosmos has begun, and the church is the first act of God's glorious drama.

---

2 As for you, *don't you remember how you used to just exist? Corpses,* dead *in life,* buried by transgressions, ²wandering the course of this *perverse* world. *You were the offspring* of the prince of the power of air—*oh, how he owned you,* just as he still controls those living in disobedience. *I'm not talking about the outsiders alone;* ³we were all guilty of falling headlong for the persuasive passions of this world; we all have had our fill of indulging the flesh and mind, *obeying impulses to follow perverse thoughts motivated by dark powers.* As a result, our natural inclinations led us to be children of wrath, just like the rest of humankind.

⁴But God, with the *unfathomable* richness of His love and mercy focused on us, ⁵united us with the Anointed One and infused our lifeless souls with life—even though we were buried under mountains of sin—and saved us by His grace. ⁶He raised us up with Him and seated us in the heavenly realms with *our beloved* Jesus the Anointed, *the Liberating King.* ⁷*He did this for a reason:* so that for all eternity we will stand as a living testimony to the incredible riches of His grace and kindness that He freely gives to us

by uniting us with Jesus the Anointed. ⁸⁻⁹For it's by God's grace that you have been saved. You receive it through faith. It was not *our plan or* our effort. It is God's gift, *pure and simple.* You didn't earn it, *not one of us did,* so don't go around bragging *that you must have done something amazing.* ¹⁰For we are the product of His hand, *heaven's poetry etched on lives,* created in the Anointed, Jesus, to accomplish the good works God arranged long ago.

V

The relationship between faith and works is often misunderstood. Some think that salvation is God's reward for good deeds. If that's true, then it can't possibly be a gift. If it were a reward, then heaven would be a place where people might compare notes on what they did to make it through the gates. But Paul is confident in the truth of the gospel. The truth is that salvation is God's gift through Jesus. Grace and faith make salvation real in us. When we are transformed by grace, then we become His new creation and begin to live out the good works He has planned for us. Works, then, aren't the cause of salvation; they are its result. To put it another way, works aren't the means of salvation; they are its presence.

---

¹¹So never forget how you used to be. Those of you born as outsiders *to Israel* were *outcasts,* branded "the uncircumcised" by those who bore the sign of the covenant in their flesh, a sign made with human hands. ¹²You had absolutely no connection to the Anointed; you were strangers, separated from God's people. You were aliens to the covenant they had with God; you were hopelessly stranded without God in a *fractured* world. ¹³But now, because of Jesus the Anointed *and His sacrifice, all of that has changed.* God gathered you who were so far away and brought you near to Him by the *royal* blood of the Anointed, *our Liberating King.*

¹⁴He is the embodiment of our peace, *sent once and for all* to take down the great barrier of hatred and hostility that

has divided us so that we can be one. ¹⁵He offered His body *on the sacrificial altar* to bring an end to the law's ordinances and dictations *that separated Jews from the outside nations. His desire was* to create in His body one new humanity from the two *opposing groups,* thus creating peace. ¹⁶*Effectively* the cross becomes God's means to kill off the hostility *once and for all* so that He is able to reconcile them both to God in this one new body.

¹⁷The Great Preacher of peace *and love* came for you, and *His voice* found those of you who were near and those who were far away. ¹⁸By Him both have access to the Father in one Spirit. ¹⁹And so you are no longer called outcasts and wanderers but citizens with God's people, *members of God's holy family,* and residents of His household. ²⁰You are being built on a *solid* foundation: *the message* of the prophets and *the voices* of God's chosen emissaries* with Jesus, the Anointed Himself, the *precious* cornerstone. ²¹The building is joined together *stone by stone—all of us chosen and sealed* in Him, rising up to become a holy temple in the Lord. ²²In Him you are being built together, creating a *sacred* dwelling place *among you* where God can live in the Spirit.

V

For Paul there are two kinds of people: Jews and Gentiles, or to put it another way, insiders and outsiders. The Prince of Peace is establishing peace where division and hostility once ruled unchallenged. In the Jerusalem temple, a stone wall separated Jewish from non-Jewish worshipers. According to Paul, the cross is God's instrument to dismantle the wall, end the segregation, and make the two into one. God wants one people of God. That has been His plan all along.

Today walls continue to exist, erected strategically to separate people by race, religion, class, culture, and sex. Those who erect these walls, protect them, and maintain them will find that they are enemies of the gospel that brings all together into one worshiping family.

---

3 All this is exactly why I, Paul, am a prisoner of Jesus the Anointed, His representative to the outsider nations. ²You have heard, haven't you, how God appointed me to bring you His message of grace? ³And how the mystery was made known to me in a revelation? I briefly wrote about it earlier. ⁴When you read what I have written, you will be better able to understand *the depth of* my insight into the mystery of the Anointed One, ⁵a mystery that has never before been shown to past generations. Only now are *these secrets* being revealed to God's chosen emissaries* and prophets through the *Holy* Spirit. ⁶Specifically, *the mystery* is this: by trusting in the good news, the Gentile outsiders are becoming *fully enfranchised* members of the same body, heirs alongside *Israel,* and beneficiaries of the promise *that has been fulfilled* through Jesus the Anointed.

⁷I became a servant *and preacher* of this gospel by the gift of God's grace as He exercised His *amazing* power over me. ⁸I cannot think of anyone more unworthy to this cause than I, the least of the least of the saints. *But here I am,* a grace-made man, privileged to be *an echo of His voice and* a preacher to all the nations of the riches of the Anointed One, riches that no one ever imagined. ⁹*I am privileged* to enlighten all *of Adam's descendants* to the mystery concealed from previous ages by God, the Creator of all, through Jesus the Anointed. ¹⁰*Here's His objective*: through the church, He intends now to make known His infinite and boundless wisdom to all rulers and authorities in heavenly realms. ¹¹This has been His plan from the beginning, one that He has now accomplished through the Anointed One, Jesus our Lord. ¹²His faithfulness* *to God* has made it possible for us to have the courage we need and the ability to approach the Father confidently. ¹³So I ask you not to become discouraged because *I am jailed for speaking out* on your behalf. *In fact,* my suffering is something that brings you glory.

¹⁴It is for this reason that I bow my knees before the Father, ¹⁵after whom all families in heaven above and on earth below receive their names, *and pray*:

¹⁶*Father,* out of Your *honorable and* glorious riches, strengthen Your people. Fill their souls with the power of Your Spirit ¹⁷so that through faith the Anointed One

---

* 2:20 Literally, apostles   * 3:5 Literally, apostles   * 3:12 Often translated "faith in Him."

will reside in their hearts. May love be *the rich soil* where their lives take root. May it be the bedrock where their lives are founded *so that together* [18-19]with all of Your people they will have the power to understand that the love of the Anointed is infinitely long, wide, high, and deep, surpassing everything anyone previously experienced. God, may Your fullness flood through their entire beings.

This is a doxology of praise to the One with power that is beyond understanding.

[20]Now to the God who can do so many *awe-inspiring things, immeasurable things,* things greater than we ever could ask or imagine through the power at work in us, [21]to Him be all glory in the church and in Jesus the Anointed from this generation to the next, forever and ever. Amen.

4 As a prisoner of the Lord, I urge you: Live a life that is worthy of the calling He has *graciously* extended to you. [2]Be humble. Be gentle. Be patient. Tolerate one another in *an atmosphere thick with* love. [3]Make every effort to preserve the unity the Spirit has already created, with peace binding you together.

Now that Paul has described the new world as God would have it, he urges believers to live out their callings with humility, patience, and love: to walk as Jesus walked. These are the ways of Jesus. Paul encourages them to do whatever it takes to hold onto the unity that binds people together in peace. He does not ask them to create that unity; this has already been accomplished through the work of the Rescuer and His Spirit. Rather, he calls believers to guard that unity— a more modest but no less significant task—because that unity is founded on God's oneness and work in the world.

[4]There is one body and one Spirit, just as you were all called to pursue one hope.

[5]There is one Lord *Jesus,* one *living* faith, one ceremonial washing through baptism,* and [6]one God—the Father over all who is above all, through all, and in all. [7]*This God* has given to each of us grace in full measure according to the Anointed's gift [8]as *the Scripture* says,

When He ascended to the heights,
    He put captivity in chains;
And *in His triumph,* He gave gifts to the
    people.*

[9](Well, when it says "He ascended," then that must mean that He had descended earlier to the lower levels, that is, to the earth. [10]The One who descended is the same One *who rose from the dead* to ascend far above all the heavens so that He could fill all things.)

[11]It was the *risen* One who handed down *to us such gifted leaders*—some emissaries,* some prophets, some evangelists, as well as some pastor-teachers—[12]so that God's people would be *thoroughly* equipped to minister and build up the body of the Anointed One. [13]*These ministries will continue* until we are unified in faith and filled with the knowledge of the Son of God, until we stand mature *in His teachings* and fully formed in the likeness of the Anointed, *our Liberating King.* [14]Then we will no longer be like children, tossed around here and there upon ocean waves, picked up by every gust of religious teaching spoken by liars or swindlers or deceivers. [15]Instead, by truth spoken in love, we are to grow in every way into Him— the Anointed One, the head. [16]He joins and holds together the whole body with its ligaments providing the support needed so each part works to its proper design to form a healthy, *growing, and mature* body that builds itself up in love.

[17]Therefore, as a witness of the Lord, I insist on this: that you no longer walk in the outsiders' ways—with minds devoted to worthless pursuits. [18]They are blind to *true* understanding. They are strangers and aliens to the kind of life God has for them because they live in ignorance *and immorality* and because their hearts are *cold,* hard stones. [19]And now, since they've lost all *natural* feelings, they have given themselves over to sensual, greedy, and reckless living. They stop at nothing to satisfy their impure appetites.

* 4:5 Literally, immersion, in a rite of initiation and purification
* 4:8 Psalm 68:18   * 4:11 Literally, apostles

[20]But this is not *the path of* the Anointed One, which you have learned. [21]If you have heard Jesus and have been taught by Him according to the truth that is in Him, [22]then you know to take off your former way of life, your *crumpled* old self—*that dark blot of a soul* corrupted by deceitful desire and lust— [23]to take *a fresh breath* and to let God renew your attitude and spirit. [24]Then *you are ready to* put on your new self, modeled after the very likeness of God: truthful, righteous, and holy.

[25]So put away your lies and speak the truth to one another because we are all part of one another. [26]When you are angry, don't let it carry you into sin.* Don't let the sun set with anger in your heart or [27]give the devil room to work. [28]If you have been stealing, stop. Thieves must go to work *like everyone else* and work honestly with their hands so that they can share with anyone who has a need. [29]Don't let even one rotten word seep out of your mouths. Instead, offer only fresh words that build others up when they need it most. That way your good words will communicate grace to those who hear them. [30]It's time to stop bringing grief to God's Holy Spirit; you have been sealed with the Spirit, marked as His own for the day of rescue. [31]Banish bitterness, rage and anger, shouting and slander, and any and all malicious thoughts—*these are poison.* [32]Instead, be kind and compassionate. *Graciously* forgive one another just as God has forgiven you through the Anointed, *our Liberating King.*

We come to God as sinners; but He wants to transform our habits, attitudes, and practices into the ways of Jesus: to live, forgive, and love as He did.

5 So imitate God. *Follow Him* like adored children, [2]and live in love as the Anointed One loved you—so much that He gave Himself as a fragrant sacrifice, pleasing God.

[3]*Listen,* don't let any kind of immorality be breathed among you. Any demoralizing behaviors (*perverse sexual acts, uncleanliness, greediness, and the like*) are inappropriate topics of conversation for those set apart as God's people. [4]Don't swear or spurt nonsense. Don't make harsh jokes *or clown around.* Make proper use of your words, and offer them thankfully in praise. [5]This is what we know for certain: no one who engages in loose sex, impure actions, and greed—which is just a form of idolatry—has any inheritance in the kingdom of God and His Anointed.

[6]Don't be fooled by people whose sentences are compounded with *useless words,* empty words—*they just show they are empty souls.* For, in His wrath, God will judge all the children of disobedience for these kinds *of sins.* [7]So don't *be persuaded into their ignorance; and don't* cast your lot with them [8]because, although you were once the personification of darkness, you are now light in the Lord. So act like children of the light. [9]For the fruit of the light is all that is good, right, and true. [10]Make it your aim to learn what pleases our Lord. [11]Don't get involved with the fruitless works of darkness; instead, expose them *to the light of God.* [12]You see, it's a disgrace to speak of their secrets (so don't even talk about what they do when no one is looking). [13-14]When the light shines, it exposes *even the dark and shadowy* things and turns them into *pure reflections of* light. This is why they sing,

> Awake, you sleeper!
>   Rise from your grave,
>   And the Anointed One will shine on you.

[15]So be careful how you live; *be mindful of your steps.* Don't run around like idiots *as the rest of the world does.* Instead, walk as the wise! [16]Make the most of every *living and breathing* moment because these are evil times. [17]So understand *and be confident in* God's will, and don't live thoughtlessly. [18]Don't drink wine excessively. The drunken path *is a reckless path. It* leads nowhere. Instead, let God fill you with the Holy Spirit. [19]*When you are filled with the Spirit, you are empowered to* speak to each other in *the soulful words of* pious songs, hymns, and spiritual songs; to sing and make music with your hearts attuned to God; [20]and to give thanks to God the Father every day through the name of our Lord Jesus the Anointed for all He has done.

Wisdom is a rare commodity. Paul urges believers, then and now, to walk wisely. It involves living well every day. Time itself seems to be co-opted by dark forces. But when believers understand God's will,

* 4:26 Psalm 4:4

avoid drunkenness, and allow God to fill them with His Spirit, they are able to walk wisely and live well. The Spirit-filled life is not just for a special few; it is the normal Christian life, and it affects everything, including how we live in community and how we treat others at home.

---

²¹*And the Spirit makes it possible to* submit *humbly* to one another out of respect for the Anointed. ²²Wives, *it should be no different* with your husbands. Submit to them as you do to the Lord, ²³for God has given husbands a *sacred* duty to lead as the Anointed leads the church and serves as the head. (The church is His body; He is her Savior.) ²⁴So wives should submit to their husbands, *respectfully,* in all things, just as the church yields to the Anointed One.

²⁵⁻²⁶Husbands, you must love your wives so *deeply, purely, and sacrificially that we can understand it only when we* compare it to the love the Anointed One has for *His bride,* the church. *We know* He gave Himself up completely to make her His own, washing her clean of all her impurity with water and *the powerful presence of* His word. ²⁷*He has given Himself* so that He can present the church as His radiant bride, unstained, unwrinkled, and unblemished—*completely free from all impurity*—holy and innocent before Him. ²⁸So husbands should care for their wives *as if their lives depended on it,* the same way they care for their own bodies. As you love her, you ultimately are loving *part of* yourself *(remember, you are one flesh)*. ²⁹No one really hates his own body; he takes care to feed and love it, just as the Anointed takes care of His church, ³⁰because we are *living* members of His body. ³¹"And this is the reason a man leaves his father and his mother and is united with his wife; the two come together as one flesh."* ³²There is a great mystery *reflected* in this *Scripture,* and I say that it has to do with *the marriage of* the Anointed One and the church. ³³Nevertheless, each husband is to love *and protect* his own wife as if she were his very heart, and each wife is to respect her own husband.

6 *Now to you,* children, obey your parents in the Lord because this is right *in God's eyes.* ²This is the first commandment onto which He added a promise: "Honor your father and your mother, and ³if you do, you will live long and well in this land."*

⁴And, fathers, do not drive your children mad, but nurture them in the discipline and teaching *that come* from the Lord.

⁵Slaves, respect and fear your earthly masters. Obey and serve them with the same sincerity of heart as you serve the Anointed One. ⁶Don't put on a show just because they are looking (as if you were a people pleaser); but as a slave of the Anointed, do the will of God from your heart. ⁷Serve them in good faith as if you were serving the Lord, not men, ⁸because all good deeds are gifted back from the Lord, and they are yours whether you are a slave or not.

⁹Masters, hear this: act in kind to your slaves. Stop *terrorizing and* threatening them. Don't forget that you have a Master in heaven who does not take sides or pick favorites.

¹⁰Finally, *brothers and sisters,* draw your strength and might from God. ¹¹Put on the full armor of God to protect yourselves from the devil and his evil schemes. ¹²We're not waging war against enemies of flesh and blood alone. No, this fight is against tyrants, against authorities, against *supernatural* powers *and demon princes that slither* in the darkness of this world, and against wicked *spiritual armies* that lurk about in heavenly places.

¹³And this is why you need *to be head-to-toe in* the full armor of God: so you can resist during these evil days and be fully prepared to hold your ground. ¹⁴Yes, stand—truth banded around your waist, righteousness as your chest plate, ¹⁵and feet protected in preparation to proclaim the good news of peace. ¹⁶Don't forget to raise the shield of faith above all else, so you will be able to extinguish flaming spears hurled at you from the wicked one. ¹⁷Take also the helmet of salvation and the sword of the Spirit, which is the word of God.

Paul knows that the real battles and dangers we face are not against flesh and blood. The enemies we see are real enough, but they are animated by spiritual forces of darkness that stay

* 5:31 Genesis 2:24   * 6:2-3 Exodus 20:12; Deuteronomy 5:16

strategically hidden from view. These powers often reveal themselves in institutional evils—genocide, terror, tyranny, and oppression—but the weapons needed to combat them are not earthly weapons at all. What is needed, Paul advises, is to stand firm in God's power and to suit up in the full armor of God. Although the devil and his demon armies are destined for destruction, they are serious threats now and must be resisted and beaten back. For Paul, the best offensive weapons we have are the word of God and prayer.

---

[18]Pray always. Pray in the Spirit. Pray about everything in every way you know how! And keeping all this in mind, pray on behalf of God's people. Keep on praying feverishly, and be on the lookout *until evil has been stayed.* [19]And please pray for me. Pray that truth will be with me before I even open my mouth. *Ask the Spirit to guide me* while I boldly defend the mystery that is the good news—[20]for which I am an ambassador in chains—so pray that I can bravely pronounce the truth, as I should do.

[21]I am sending to you Tychicus, my dear brother and faithful minister in the Lord. He will tell you everything that has been going on here with me [22]so you will know how I am and what I am doing. He's coming with news that will hopefully comfort your hearts. [23]Brothers and sisters, *let me leave you with a blessing:*

May peace and love with faith be yours from God the Father and the Lord Jesus the Anointed. [24]May His grace surround all who love our Lord Jesus the Anointed with a never-ending love.

PHILIPPIANS

Letter to the church in Philippi

From Paul, the apostle to the Gentiles

This little letter has had a big impact on the church in Paul's day and ours. At the heart of it is Paul's consistent plea that the Philippians "rejoice in the Lord." For Paul, joy is not a good feeling based on favorable happenings; it is a decision, a deliberate choice to celebrate God's work through Jesus in any and every circumstance. Ironically Paul writes this letter from a prison probably in Rome or Caesarea; no one knows for certain. What is certain is that, despite his chains, Paul is content where he is, in part, because he sees the gospel progressing. As a servant and prisoner of the Lord Jesus, that thrills and satisfies him.

Paul writes this letter to thank the Philippians for a gift he just received and to announce some travel plans, assuming he'd be freed from prison. For years he has enjoyed a warm and intimate friendship with the believers of this little Roman colony, the first church in Europe. From the moment he first preached Jesus' message in Philippi, the church there has supported and encouraged Paul in ways no other church has. Now they have renewed their concern for him with another act of generosity. No wonder the emissary feels closer to them than to any other church he has founded!

One of the most beautiful moments in this letter is a hymn to the Anointed, the Liberating King, in 2:6-11. Whether Paul has composed this hymn himself or quotes it from another source, no one knows. Nevertheless this hymn recounts a beautiful story of love and humility as Jesus descends into the world to serve humanity and face the horrors of the cross; then He is exalted by God, given a unique name, and declared "Lord" by all creatures to the glory of God. Paul makes Jesus the lordly example of humility and urges others to follow Him and adopt His attitude. As disciples of Jesus, Paul, Timothy, and Epaphroditus demonstrate that same spirit of service as they pour themselves out for the gospel and for the Philippians.

1 Paul and Timothy, slaves of Jesus the Anointed One, greet you, *our friends* in Philippi—those set apart by Jesus the Anointed—*and we greet the* elders and deacons *who serve* with you. [2]Grace and peace be with you from God our Father and the Lord Jesus the Anointed.

[3]Whenever you cross my mind, I thank my God for you *and for the gift of knowing you.* [4]My spirit is lightened with joy whenever I pray for you (and I do constantly) [5]because you have partnered with me to spread the gospel since the first day *I preached to you.*

[6]I am confident that the Creator, who has begun such a great work among you, will *not stop in mid-design but will* keep perfecting you until the day Jesus the Anointed, *our Liberating King, returns to redeem the world.* [7]It is only right that I should feel such admiration for you all—you hold me close to your hearts. And, since we are partners in *this great work of* grace, you have never failed to stand with me as I have defended and stood firm for the gospel—even from this prison cell. [8]Before God I want you to know how much I long to see you and love you with the affection of the Anointed One, Jesus.

[9]Here's what I pray for you:

Father, may their love grow more and more in wisdom and insight—[10]so they will be able to *examine and* determine the best *from everything else.* And on the day of the Anointed One, *the day of His judgment,* let them stand pure and blameless, [11]filled with the fruit of righteousness that ripens through Jesus the Anointed.

All this I pray, with a view to God's ultimate praise and glory.

Many come to visit Paul in his imprisonment and listen to him tell the story of Jesus' life, death, and resurrection.

[12]*I have good news,* brothers and sisters; and I want to share it. *Believe it or not,* my imprisonment has actually helped spread the good news *to new places and populations.* [13]Word has spread through the ranks of the imperial guard and to everyone else *around me* that I am in prison because of my faith in the Anointed One. [14]My imprisonment has instilled courage in most of our brothers and

sisters, so they *are trusting God more and* have been even more daring as they speak the good news without fear.

[15-17]*I am well aware that* some people out there are preaching the message of the Anointed One because of jealousies and rivalries. Their motives aren't pure. They're driven by selfish ambitions and personal agendas, hoping somehow to add to my pain here in prison. *And I also know* there are others who are preaching the Anointed from true goodness, motivated by love. *They wish me the best because* they know I'm here in prison in defense of the gospel.

V

Even in difficult times, Paul remains faithful because he realizes that the kingdom and the message of the Anointed One are more important than any one messenger. Paul uses his own willingness to sacrifice himself as a model for believers to follow. He directs them to be good and faithful citizens of the heavenly kingdom, no matter what opposition they receive.

[18]So what *do we do* then? *Listen. What matters is* that in every way, *regardless of the motives*—whether pure or shady—the great story of the Anointed is a cause for joy. I will continue to rejoice [19]because I know that through your *encouragement and* prayers and through the help of the Spirit of Jesus the Anointed, I will soon be released from this dark place. [20]I don't expect that dishonor and shame will plague me in any way, but I do hope that I will continue to be able to speak freely and courageously *about Jesus,* and that now and forever the Anointed One will be glorified and placed above all else through this body of mine—whether I live or die. [21]For my life is about the Anointed *and Him* alone. And my death, *when that comes,* will mean great gain for me. [22]So, if it's His will that I go on serving here, my work will be fruitful *for the message.* I honestly wouldn't know how or what to choose; [23]I would be hard-pressed to decide. I lean toward leaving this world to be with the Anointed One because I can only think that would be much better. [24]To stay in this body of flesh—*even with all its pains and weaknesses*—would best serve your needs. [25]Now that I think of it, I am sure of this: I

would prefer to remain to share in the progress and joy of your growing belief. [26]When I return to you, we will celebrate Jesus the Anointed even more.

[27]*So here is what I want you to do*: conduct yourselves as *true and* worthy citizens of the Anointed's gospel, so that whether I make it or don't make it to see you, I will *at least* hear that you continue to stand, united in one spirit, single-minded *in purpose* as you struggle together for the faith in the gospel. [28]Don't be paralyzed in any way by what your opponents are doing. Your steadfast faith in the face of opposition is a sign that they are doomed and that you have been graced with God's salvation. [29]And now, you have been given the privilege of not only believing in *Jesus* the Anointed, *our Liberating King,* but *being chosen* to suffer for Him as well. [30]You have seen me suffer for Him. *Since I've been away*, you've heard of the other agonizing conflicts I've had to face. Now you know firsthand the pains of this battle.

2 If you find any comfort from being in the Anointed, if His love brings you some encouragement, if you experience true companionship with the Spirit, if His tenderness and mercy fill your heart; *then, brothers and sisters,* [2]*here is one thing that would* complete my joy—come together as one in mind and spirit and purpose, sharing in the same love. [3]Don't let selfishness and prideful agendas take over. Embrace true humility, and lift your heads to extend love to others. [4]Get beyond yourselves and protecting your own interests; *be sincere,* and secure your neighbors' interests first.

[5]*In other words,* adopt the mind-set of Jesus the Anointed. *Live with His attitude in your hearts. Remember:*

[6]Though He was in the form of God,
    He chose not to cling to equality with God;
[7]But He poured Himself out *to fill a vessel brand new;*
    a servant in form
    and a man indeed.
The very likeness of humanity,
[8]He humbled Himself,
    obedient to death—
    a merciless death on the cross!
[9]So God raised Him up to the highest place
    and gave Him the name above all.

[10]So when His name is called,
    every knee will bow,*
    in heaven, on earth, and below.
[11]And every tongue will confess*
    "Jesus, the Anointed One, is Lord,"
    to the glory of God our Father!

V

Paul describes a community where every person considers the needs of others first and does nothing from selfishness; it pulls together rather than pulls apart, and it is a body that knows its purpose and lets nothing interfere with it. It is an extended spiritual family where others line up to become part of this sacred assembly and to make it their home because they feel encouragement and know they are truly loved. So Paul urges the Philippians to strive for this radical unity and fulfill his joy by having the mind of Jesus who humbled Himself, became a servant, and suffered the death of the cross. Jesus becomes the example of humility and service, leading to the kind of unity Paul imagines.

---

[12]So now, my beloved, obey as you have always done, not only when I am with you, but even more so when I can't be. Continue to work out your salvation, with great fear and trembling, [13]because God is energizing you so that you will desire and do what always pleases Him.

[14]Do all things without complaining or bickering with each other, [15]so you will be found innocent and blameless; *you are* God's children called to live without a single stain on your reputations among this perverted and crooked generation. Shine like stars across the land. [16]Cling to the word of life so that on the day of judgment when the Anointed One returns I may have reason to rejoice, because it will be plain that I didn't turn from His mission nor did I work in vain. [17]Even if my lifeblood is to be poured out like wine as a sacrifice of your faith, I have great reason to celebrate with all of you. [18]And for the same reason, you can be glad and celebrate with me.

* 2:10 Isaiah 45:23   * 2:11 Isaiah 45:23

¹⁹I hope in the Lord Jesus to send Timothy your way. He will visit soon *so that he may report to me how you are doing.* To hear all that is going on with you will truly encourage my heart. ²⁰There is no one like Timothy. What sets him apart from others is his deep concern for you *and your spiritual journey. This is rare, my friends,* ²¹for most people only care about themselves, not about what is *dear to the heart* of Jesus the Anointed. ²²You know Timothy is genuine *in the Lord's ways.* He has been a faithful partner to me as we express the good news, as much as my own flesh and blood would have been. ²³I expect to send him soon, and I will as soon as I see how things turn out here. ²⁴I trust in the Lord that it won't be very long before I can come *and be with you in person.*

²⁵But for now, I think it is best to send Epaphroditus home to you. *He has become* my dear brother in the Lord. We have worked well together and fought great battles together, and he was an encouraging minister to me in my time of need. ²⁶He could not wait to see you all. He was concerned for you when he found out you knew how sick he really was. ²⁷In fact, he nearly died. But once again, God *was exceedingly kind and* covered him with His mercy. And I, too, by His mercy, have been spared sorrow on top of sorrow.

²⁸I am so excited to be sending him back to you! I can picture the joy on your faces when he arrives; I can feel my worries falling away. ²⁹Welcome him joyfully in the Lord. Esteem all *spiritual leaders* like Epaphroditus ³⁰because he placed his life in grave danger for the work of the Anointed; he risked his life to serve me when you couldn't.

3 It is time that I wrap up these thoughts to you, my brothers and sisters. Rejoice in the Lord! (I don't mind writing these things over and over to you, as I know it keeps you safe.)

²Watch out for the dogs—wicked workers who *run in packs* looking for someone to maul with their false circumcision.

dietary regulations, keeping weekly and annual holy days, and other Jewish practices. Since the time of Abraham, circumcision has been the mark of the covenant with Abraham's spiritual children. Things are changing: outsiders, non-Jews, are entering into the new covenant.

Do they enter by faith alone, or is it faith plus following God's law for Israel? Paul's answer is clear: it is faith alone that makes Jews and outsiders right with God. So he cautions the Philippians to watch out for those who would chastise them into a false circumcision. Real followers of Jesus know that salvation doesn't come from the blade of a knife but from His cross.

---

³We are the true circumcision—those who worship God in Spirit and make our boast in Jesus the Anointed, *the Liberating King*—so we do not rely on *what we have accomplished in* the flesh.

⁴If any try to throw around their pedigrees to you, remember my résumé—which is more impressive than theirs. ⁵I was circumcised on the eighth day—*as the law prescribes*—born of the nation of Israel, descended from the tribe of Benjamin. I am a Hebrew born of Hebrews; I have observed the law according to *the strict piety of* the Pharisees, *separate from those embracing a less rigorous kind of Judaism.* ⁶Zealous? *Yes.* I ruthlessly *pursued and* persecuted the church. And when it comes to the righteousness required by the law, my record is spotless.

⁷But whatever I used to count as my greatest accomplishments, I've written them off as a loss because of the Anointed One. ⁸And more so, I now realize that all I gained *and thought was important* was nothing but yesterday's garbage compared to knowing the Anointed Jesus my Lord. For Him I have thrown everything aside—*it's nothing but a pile of waste*—so that I may gain Him. ⁹*When it counts,* I want to be found belonging to Him, not clinging to my own righteousness based on law, but actively relying on the faithfulness of the Anointed One. *This is true* righteousness, supplied by God, acquired by faith. ¹⁰I want

Circumcision has become a flash point for the early church. Some are teaching that non-Jews have to become Jews to follow Jesus completely, including circumcision, to know Him *inside and out*. I want to experience the power of His resurrection and join in His suffering, shaped by His death, [11]so that I may arrive *safely* at the resurrection from the dead.

The crucified and risen Jesus is the model that Paul desires to embody by walking deep in His pathway of death and life—suffering and resurrection.

[12]I'm not there yet, nor have I become perfect; but I am charging on to gain anything *and everything* the Anointed One, Jesus, has in store for me—*and nothing will stand in my way* because He has grabbed me *and won't let me go.* [13]Brothers and sisters, *as I said,* I know I have not arrived; but there's one thing I am doing: I'm leaving my old life behind, putting everything on the line for this mission. [14]I am sprinting toward the only goal that counts: *to cross the line,* to win the prize, and to hear God's call *to resurrection life found exclusively* in Jesus the Anointed. [15]All of us who are mature ought to think the same way about these matters. If you have a different attitude, then God will reveal this to you as well. [16]For now, let's hold on to what we have been shown *and keep in step with these teachings.*

[17]Imitate me, brothers and sisters, and look around to those already following the example we have set. [18]I have warned you before (and now say again through my tears) that we have many enemies—people who reject the cross of the Anointed. [19]They are ruled by their bellies, their glory comes by shame, and their minds are fixed on the things of this world. They are doomed. [20]But we are citizens of heaven, *exiles on earth* waiting eagerly for a Liberator, our Lord Jesus the Anointed, to come and [21]transform these humble, *earthly* bodies into the form of His glorious body by the same power that brings all things under His control.

4 For this reason, brothers and sisters, my joy and crown whom I dearly love, I cannot wait to see you again. Continue to stand firm in the Lord, *and follow my instructions in this letter,* beloved. [2]Euodia and Syntyche, I urge you to *put aside your differences,* agree, and work together in the Lord. [3]Yes, *Syzygus,* loyal friend, I enlist you to please help these women. They, along with brother Clement and many others,

have worked by my side to spread the good news of the gospel. They have their names recorded in the book of life. [4]*Most of all, friends,* always rejoice in the Lord! I never tire of saying it: Rejoice! [5]Keep your gentle nature so that all people will know *what it looks like to walk in His footsteps.* The Lord is ever present with us. [6]Don't be anxious about things; instead, pray. Pray about everything. *He longs to hear your requests,* so talk to God about your needs and be thankful *for what has come.* [7]And know that the peace of God (*a peace* that is beyond any and all of our *human* understanding) will stand watch over your hearts and minds in Jesus, the Anointed One.

[8]Finally, brothers and sisters, fill your minds with *beauty and* truth. Meditate on whatever is honorable, whatever is right, whatever is pure, whatever is lovely, whatever is good, whatever is virtuous and praiseworthy. [9]Keep to the script: whatever you learned and received and heard and saw in me—do it—and the God of peace will walk with you.

[10]I could hardly contain my joy in the Lord when I realized you have started to show your care for me once again. Since you have not had the opportunity to show how much you cared until now, *I want you to know how it touched me.* [11]I am not saying this because I am in need. I have learned to be content in whatever circumstances. [12]I know how to survive in tight situations, and I know how to enjoy having plenty. In fact, I have learned how to face any circumstances: fed or hungry, with or without. [13]I can be content in any and every situation through the Anointed One who is my power and strength. [14]Nevertheless, it was admirable of you to participate in my affliction.

V

True contentment is the result of a heart committed to the risen Lord. Think of all the sins, pain, and brokenness that come from coveting. Adultery, murder, stealing, and lying can all be traced directly to a prior condition when hearts and minds are frustrated and discontent.

Notice what Paul says doesn't come naturally; it is learned. The normal, natural state of humanity is discontent and quiet desperation.

It takes a powerful, spiritual presence to transform anxiety into joyous satisfaction. Ironically, it may be the shackles more than his freedom that schools Paul in the art of contentment. Despite the chains, Paul discovers this beautiful state of inner peace through the power of Jesus residing in him.

15You remember, Philippians, at the beginning of my gospel journey after I left Macedonia, no church offered me the financial assistance I needed to do the Lord's work, except you alone. 16Even when I took the message to Thessalonica, you sent provisions to me. Twice even! 17Not that I am looking for a gift—I am just looking toward your reward that comes from your gift.

18With what Epaphroditus delivered to me from your generous pockets, I have even been blessed in excess. I am fully satisfied. I know God is pleased with your dedication and accepts this gift as a fragrant offering, a holy sacrifice, on His behalf. 19*Know this:* my God will also fill every need you have according to His glorious riches in Jesus the Anointed, *our Liberating King.* 20So may our God and Father be glorified forever and ever. Amen.

21Greet every saint there in Jesus the Anointed One, for my brothers and sisters and I send our greetings to you. 22All of the saints, especially those serving in Caesar's household, also send salutations to you. 23May you all continue *the journey* with your spirits strengthened by the grace of the Lord Jesus, the Anointed One. [Amen.]*

* 4:23 Some manuscripts omit this word.

COLOSSIANS

Letter to the church in Colossae

From Paul, the apostle to the Gentiles

Paul wrote this letter about 25 years after his call to be an emissary for Jesus. The head-strong Paul who had planted churches and pioneered the gospel had now become an elder statesman for the growing movement. His reputation was so great that he could send a letter to a church he had neither planted nor even visited and expect to be received as a voice that must be heard.

When Paul wrote this letter, he was in prison. The people in Colossae would have known where, so there was no need to put it in the letter, but that important detail is lost today. It is often said that he wrote it from prison in Rome, although Ephesus or Caesarea cannot be ruled out. The fact is that the Lord's emissary often found himself in prison because his message clashed with the local political, economic, and religious powers. But even as a prisoner, Paul was able to find a secretary or urge a coworker to help him craft and dispatch a letter.

Colossae was an important city located about 100 miles east of Ephesus. There were many religious options in Colossae, Jewish and pagan; and apparently some in Colossae thought that Jesus should simply be added into the mix. But for Paul, Jesus is no add-on. As the Creator and Sustainer, as the head of the church, Jesus deserves their full and undivided attention. According to Paul, Jesus came to liberate not only individuals but all of creation from the powers of darkness.

Paul prays that God will encourage the believers in Colossae to live with a spiritual perspective and that their lives will reflect the transforming power of Jesus (1:9-10). One of the best-known passages in this letter is the wonderful hymn about Jesus found in 1:15-20; it celebrates not only His role as the Creator and Sustainer of the world, but also as the Reconciler and head of the church, which is His body. He then challenges the believers in Colossae to turn from their past, as if their old selves were dead, and to keep their eyes fixed on the goal of new life hidden in Jesus (3:2-4). Paul speaks individually to wives, husbands, children, slaves, and masters and finally asks them to pray with him that "we can go on telling the mystery of the Anointed One." Paul truly sees all believers as sharing in his ministry and his imprisonment.

1 Paul, an emissary* of Jesus the Anointed *serving* at God's pleasure, along with our brother Timothy [2]to you, *dear* holy and faithful brothers and sisters in *the family of* the Anointed who live in Colossae. May grace and peace from God our Father [and the Lord Jesus, the Anointed One]* envelop you.

[3]As always, we've been praying for you, thanking God, the Father of our Lord Jesus the Anointed, [4]ever since we heard of your faith in Jesus the Anointed and your love for His holy ones—[5]*a faith and love* that emerge from the hope you have heard about in the word of truth—the gospel—the very hope that awaits you in heaven. [6-7]The same gospel that was brought to you is growing and bearing fruit all over the world, just as it has been growing among you since the day you heard and took in the truth of God's grace from our beloved fellow servant Epaphras. (He is a faithful minister of the Anointed on our* behalf.) [8]He was the one who told us how you demonstrate your love in *the power of* the Spirit. [9]Since the day we got this good news about you, we have not stopped praying for you. We ask:

This is a prayer for knowledge and insight that only can come from God.

Father, may they clearly know Your will and achieve *the height and depth of* spiritual wisdom and understanding. [10]May their lives be a credit to You, Lord; and *what's more,* may they continue to delight You by doing every good work and growing in the true knowledge that comes from being close to You. [11]Strengthen them with Your infinite power, according to Your glorious might, so that they will have everything they need to hold on and endure hardship patiently and joyfully. [12]Thank You, Father, as You have made us* eligible to receive our portion of the inheritance given to all those set apart by the light. [13]You have rescued us from dark powers and brought us safely into the kingdom of Your Son, whom You love [14]and in whom we are redeemed and forgiven of our sins [through His blood].*

[15]He is the *exact* image of the invisible God, the firstborn of creation, *the eternal.* [16]It was by Him that everything was created: the heavens, the earth, all things within and upon them, all things seen and unseen, thrones and dominions, *spiritual* powers and authorities. Every detail was crafted through His design, *by His own hands,* and for His purposes. [17]He has always been! *It is His hand* that holds everything together. [18]He is the head of this body, the church. He is the beginning, the first of those to be reborn from the dead, so that *in every aspect, at every view,* in everything—He is first. [19]God was pleased that all His fullness should *forever* dwell in the Son [20]who, *as predetermined by God,* bled peace into the world by His death on the cross as God's means of reconciling to Himself the whole creation—all things in heaven and all things on earth.

As Paul gives thanks to God—a normal thing to do in a letter—he remembers a hymn he heard in the churches. The Colossian hymn (verses 15-20), as we call it, is all about Jesus. It celebrates His reign, first as the Creator and Sustainer of the cosmos and second as the head of the church and the One who reconciles every broken thing to God by what He accomplished on the cross. In this hymn, the story of redemption is a witness to God's love. Paul wants the Colossians to understand who they are; but to do that, they must first know to whom they belong.

[21]You were once at odds *with God,* wicked in your ways and evil in your minds; [22]but now He has reconciled you in His body—in His flesh through His death—so that He can present you to God holy, blameless, and *totally* free of imperfection [23]as long as you stay planted in the faith. So don't venture away from what you have heard *and taken to heart*: the *living* hope of the good news that has been announced to all creation under heaven and has captured me, Paul, as its servant.

[24]Now I rejoice in what I've suffered on your behalf, *but even more suffering is ahead for me* as I *take on and* complete what remains of the Anointed's suffering for the

* 1:1 Literally, apostle   * 1:2 Some manuscripts omit this portion.
* 1:6-7 Some manuscripts read "your."   * 1:12 Other manuscripts read "you."   * 1:14 Early manuscripts omit this portion.

sake of His body, the church. [25]I am a servant appointed by God to preach the Word of God until it is known to you and all over— *what I am talking about is nothing less than* [26]the mystery *of the ages*! What was hidden for ages, generations and generations, is now being revealed to His holy ones. [27]He decided to make known to them His blessing to the nations; the glorious riches of this mystery is the indwelling of the Anointed in you! The very hope of glory.

[28]We are preaching Him—spreading the Word to all with *equal amounts of* wise warning and instruction—so that, *at the final judgment,* we will be able to present everyone *to the Creator* fully mature because of what Jesus the Anointed, *our Liberating King,* has done. [29]This is why I continue to toil and struggle—because His amazing power and energy surge within me.

V

At the heart of the good news is a mystery hidden in ancient Scriptures but now exposed to the world through the lives of the church's holy ones. Paul never refers to just one "holy one"; he always uses the plural. He knows that holiness is too difficult for us to accomplish on our own. Each of us has to be called and equipped by God, but we also have to be accompanied by others who've answered the call. Those who say "yes" to Jesus become the church, the company of those rescued from darkness and ultimately from death. Paul is fond of calling the church the body of the risen Jesus. Our own hopes and dreams for the future are concentrated in Him. Not only do we dwell in Him, but He also dwells in us.

---

2 This battle I am facing is huge. And I want you to know I do it for you, for all those at Laodicea, and for everyone else (even those who have never seen my face). [2]I'm working hard to *comfort and* encourage them so *that they will be knit together*—that many hearts would become one through His love. I do it so they will be rich in understanding and have full knowledge of God's mystery, which is the Anointed One

Himself—[3]in Him all the treasures of wisdom and knowledge are concealed. [4]I only tell you this to warn you about those who would try and deceive you with their arguments. They seem plausible enough; *but in the end, they are false.* [5]Even though I cannot be there in the body, my spirit is with you; and I'm happy to know of your good order and your solid commitment to the Anointed One, *our Liberating King.*

Paul calls the believers in Colossae to remain steadfast in their faith.

[6]Now that you have welcomed the Anointed One, Jesus the Lord, into your lives, continue to journey with Him *and allow Him to shape your lives.* [7]Let your roots grow down deeply in Him, and let Him build you up on a firm foundation. Be strong in the faith, just as you were taught, and always spill over with thankfulness. [8]Make sure no predator makes you his prey through some *misleading* philosophy and empty deception based on traditions fabricated by mere mortals. These are sourced in the elementary principles originating in this world and not in the Anointed One (*so don't let their talks capture you*). [9]You see, all that is God, all His fullness, resides in His body. [10]You, too, are being completed in Him, the One who has dominion over all rule, all authority. [11]In Him you were also circumcised, set apart by a spiritual act performed without hands. The Anointed One's circumcision cut you off from the sinfulness of your flesh. [12]You were buried with Him beneath the waters of the ceremonial washing called baptism* and then were raised up with Him by faith in the *resurrection* power of God, who brought Him back from the dead. [13]And when your flesh was still uncircumcised—dead in transgression *and swathed in its sinful nature*—it was God who brought us* to life with Him, forgave all our sins, and [14]eliminated the massive debt we incurred by the law that stood against us. He took it all away; He nailed it to the cross. *But that's not all.* [15]He disarmed those who once ruled over us—those who had overpowered us. *Like captives of war,* He put them on display to the world to show His victory over them *by means of the cross.*

[16]So don't let anyone stand in judgment over you and dictate what you should eat or drink, what festivals you should celebrate,

---

* 2:12 Literally, immersion, a rite of initiation and purification
* 2:13 Some manuscripts read "you."

or how you should observe a new moon or Sabbath days—[17]all these are only a shadow of what shall come. The reality, *the core, the import*, is found in the Anointed One. [18]Don't be cheated out of the prize by others who are peddling the worship of heavenly beings and *false* humility. People like this run about telling *whoever will listen* what they claim to have seen; but in reality they testify only to an inflated mind, saturated in conceit—*not in the Spirit.* [19]They are detached from the very head that nourishes and connects the whole body with all of its nerves and ligaments, a body that grows by the kind of growth that can only come from God.

[20]Listen, if you have died with the Anointed One to the elemental spirits of the cosmos, then why are you submitting yourselves to its rules as if you still belonged to this world? [21]*You hear,* "Don't handle this! Don't taste that! Don't even touch it!" [22]but everything they are obsessed about will eventually decay with use. These rules are just human commands and teachings. [23]*Here's what they are promoting:* fabricated religion, self-humiliation, and bodily abuse. No matter which way they try to tether their bodies, they cannot harness their desires.

V

Paul knows the people in Colossae are facing many religious and philosophical options, none of which are neutral. Notice Paul doesn't say, "Just add Jesus to what you already believe," or, "Factor Jesus into your philosophy," or, "Include Jesus in this or that ritual." The claim that "Jesus is Lord" does not allow that. If Jesus is Creator, Sustainer, and Redeemer of all creation, then all other teachings must give way. All people must bow before Him and only Him.

---

3 So *it comes down to this:* since you have been raised with the Anointed One, *the Liberating King,* set your mind on heaven above. The Anointed is there, seated at God's right hand. [2]Stay focused on what's above, not on earthly things, [3]because your *old* life is dead and gone. Your *new* life is now hidden, enmeshed with the Anointed who is in God. [4]On that day when the Anointed One—who is our* very life—is

revealed, you will be revealed with Him in glory! [5]So kill your earthly impulses: loose sex, impure actions, unbridled sensuality, wicked thoughts, and greed (which is *essentially* idolatry). [6]It's because of these that God's wrath is coming [upon the sons and daughters of disobedience],* *so avoid them at all costs.* [7]These are the same things you once pursued, and together you spawned a life of evil. [8]But now make sure you shed such things: anger, rage, spite, slander, and abusive language. [9]And don't go on lying to each other since you have sloughed away your old skin along with its evil practices [10]for a fresh new you, which is continually renewed in knowledge according to the image of the One who created you. [11]In this re-creation there is no distinction between Greek and Jew, circumcised and uncircumcised, barbarian and conqueror,* or slave and free because the Anointed is the whole and dwells in us all.

Paul tells them the key to remain unified is to show compassion and forgiveness toward one another.

[12]Since you are all set apart by God, made holy and dearly loved, clothe yourselves with *a holy way of life:* compassion, kindness, humility, gentleness, and patience. [13]Put up with one another. Forgive. Pardon any offenses against one another, as the Lord has pardoned you, because you should act in kind. [14]But above all these, put on love! Love is the perfect tie to bind these together. [15]Let your hearts fall under the rule of the Anointed's peace (the peace you were called to as one body), and be thankful. [16]Let the word of the Anointed One richly inhabit your lives. With all wisdom teach, *counsel,* and instruct one another. Sing the psalms, *compose* hymns and songs inspired by the Spirit, and keep on singing— *sing to God* from hearts *full and spilling over* with thankfulness. [17]Surely, no matter what you are doing (speaking, *writing,* or working), do it all in the name of Jesus our Master, sending thanks through Him to God our Father.

V

For Paul it isn't enough just to believe the right things. Right

---

* 3:4 Some manuscripts read "your."   * 3:6 Some early manuscripts omit this portion.   * 3:11 Literally, Scythian

belief always produces right living. The gift of salvation demands that we put into practice the character of our King. Just as we take off and throw away old, worn-out clothes, we must strip off certain attitudes and actions of our old selves. Since our lives have been made new in Him, things like sexual immorality, greed, anger, lies, and the rest must find no place in us. But it is not enough to strip off the old; we must put on the new. And that new creation has many qualities of Jesus: compassion, gentleness, and humility; putting up with each other, forgiving each other, and above all, loving each other. These are the ways of Jesus, so they must be our ways too.

---

consisted of a husband, a wife, lots of children, servants, grandparents, aunts, uncles, and others. So when Paul addresses the family, he does not envision the modern version of it. He addresses the main family members: wives, husbands, children, fathers, and then slaves. The family reflects the order God desires in the church. Each member is to be responsible to the whole, and love and respect are to serve as the guiding principles within family relationships. Paul and Peter both use the term "submission" within family and church relationships as a description of order and support.

---

[18]Wives: be submitted to your husbands as is appropriate in the Lord. [19]Husbands: love your wives, and don't treat them harshly *or respond with bitterness toward them.*

[20]Children: obey your parents in every way. The Lord is well pleased by it. [21]Fathers: don't infuriate your children, so their hearts won't *harbor resentment and* become discouraged. [22]Slaves: obey your earthly masters in all things. Don't just act earnest in your service only when they are watching. Serve with a sincere heart *(even when others aren't watching)*, fearing the Lord *who is always watching!* [23]So no matter what your task is, work hard. *Always do your best* as the Lord's servant, not as man's, [24]because you know your reward is the Lord's inheritance. You serve the Lord, the Anointed One, and [25]anyone who does wrong will be paid his due because He doesn't play favorites.

4 And to you masters: treat your slaves fairly and do what is right, knowing that you, too, have a Master in heaven.

V
Family life has changed since Paul's day. Today, sociologists talk about modern families as "nuclear": two parents with one or two children. In Colossae, as elsewhere in Paul's world, families were extended by nature: they

---

[2]Pray, *and keep praying.* Be alert and thankful when you pray. [3]And while you are at it, add us to your prayers. Pray that God would open doors *and windows and minds and eyes and hearts* for the word so we can go on telling the mystery of the Anointed, for this is exactly why I am currently imprisoned. [4]Pray that I will proclaim this message clearly and *fearlessly* as I should.

[5]Be wise when you engage with those outside *the faith community*; make the most of every moment *and every encounter.* [6]When you speak the word, speak it gracefully (as if seasoned with salt), so you will know how to respond to everyone rightly.

[7-9]I am sending this letter by Tychicus and Onesimus, both dear brothers. Tychicus has been a faithful minister and fellow servant in the Lord. He will update you on me and my* situation here, and he will no doubt be an encouragement to you. Onesimus is one of you; and he, too, has been faithful. You will get the whole story from them.

[10]My cellmate Aristarchus sends his love, as does Mark, Barnabas's cousin. (You've been sent instructions about him, so if he comes to you, welcome him.) [11]Jesus, also called Justus, also sends greetings. These are the only workers in God's kingdom here who are of the circumcision, and they are a great comfort to me.

[12]Epaphras, another one of your hometown fellows and a servant of Jesus the Anointed sends his regards and wants you to know how passionately and sincerely he

* 4:7-9 Some manuscripts read "so he may know about your."

speaks to the Lord about you. He prays *for your spiritual journey,* that you will continue to mature and stand tall in the kind of confidence that comes from knowing God's will. [13]I can testify to his zeal for you and those in Laodicea and Hierapolis.

[14]Luke, the beloved doctor, says hello; and so does Demas. [15]Send my well wishes to the brothers and sisters of Laodicea, especially Nympha and the church that meets in her house. [16]After this letter has been read among you, see that it is also read to the church of Laodicea, and make sure you publicly share the letter I am sending to them. [17]Tell Archippus, "Take care that you complete the service you received in the Lord."

[18]I, Paul, am signing this letter in my own hand. Remember that I am chained. Grace be with you all.

1 THESSALONIANS

Letter to the church in Thessalonica

From Paul, the apostle to the Gentiles

Not long after Paul first went to Europe, he arrived in Thessalonica. After only three weeks of ministering in the local synagogue, the Jews rebelled and started a riot. In their indictment of Paul and his coworkers before the local judge, they said, "These people—they're *political agitators* turning the world upside down!" (Acts 17:5-6). Paul had spent just a few short weeks with the believers in Thessalonica, but he was greatly blessed by them.

In this warm, fatherly letter which is one of his first, he recalls their true faith, tireless love, and enduring spirit. They truly touched his heart. One can sense the instant affection between these new believers and their spiritual parent. He describes himself as a nursing mother caring for her children and as a father soothing his own children. After encouraging them to continue to grow in the faith and telling how word of their response to the good news has spread throughout the regions of Macedonia and Achaia, Paul pleads with them to avoid sexual defilement because their bodies are the dwelling places of the Holy Spirit and should be kept in holiness and purity. He reminds them of the riches that belong to them, warning them of Satan's activities. He then writes of Timothy's report about their faith. Timothy had been left behind when Paul was forced to move out of the area; later Paul's spirit was buoyed when Timothy spoke of their growth in the faith in the midst of a period of stressful days for Paul.

At this stage in the development of the young church, they were not as greatly hindered by false teachers as were the churches in Asia Minor. But there were some who came from Judea sowing seeds of unrest. Still Paul reminds them of his message of grace to the Gentiles. He then turns to one particular issue about those believers who have died and of their standing before God on the coming day of the Lord. Paul tells them that all believers should have confidence whether they die before the return of the Lord or they are present at the time of His return. All have obtained salvation and should not fear that they will miss out on the joy of the King's return. He concludes by emphasizing the importance of encouraging and caring for one another while guarding the truth.

1 Paul, Silvanus,* and Timothy to the church gathering in Thessalonica, *those living* in God the Father and in the Lord Jesus the Anointed.

May grace and peace be yours [from God our Father and the Lord Jesus the Anointed].*

²We always thank God for all of you in our prayers. ³Your actions on behalf of the *true* faith, your *tireless* toil of love, and your unfailing, unwavering, unending hope in our Lord Jesus the Anointed before God our Father have put you consistently at the forefront of our thoughts. ⁴O brothers and sisters loved by God, we know He has chosen you. ⁵*And here is why: what you experienced in* the good news we brought you was more than words *channeling down your ears;* it came to you as a *life*-empowering, Spirit-infused message that offers complete *hope and* assurance! *We lived transparently before you so that* you would know what sort of people we *truly* are. *We did it* for your sake, ⁶and you have modeled your lives after ours just as we are modeling ours after the Lord. You took *to heart* the word *we taught* with joy inspired by the Holy Spirit, even in the face of trouble. ⁷As a result, you have turned into a model *of faith* yourselves for all the believers in Macedonia and Achaia. ⁸In fact, not only has the message of our Lord thundered from your gathering into Macedonia and Achaia, but everywhere *we go,* your faith in God is talked about so we don't even have to say a thing! ⁹You see, they go on and on telling us *the story of* how you welcomed us *when we were introduced to you;* how you turned toward God and realigned your life to serve the one true living God—leaving your idols *to crumble in the dust*—¹⁰and how you now await *the return* from heaven of His Son, whom He raised from the dead—namely, Jesus—our rescuer from the wrath to come.

It's only by the leading of the Spirit that these first-generation church planters find themselves in this most disagreeable city (although it seems there's no place Paul can go without causing a commotion). Likewise, it is neither by chance nor by any human power that these people are drawn out of their comfy old habits into a radical new way of living. A miracle really takes shape when, by trading in their old ways of living, believers take to heart the message of Jesus, and their unshakable faith shakes up conversations everywhere.

Kingdom work begins at the surrender of life, by giving yourself away and expecting nothing in return. Real change is then ushered in by the loving touch of the Spirit, moving out from people living transparently faithful lives even in the middle of commotion.

---

2 Brothers and sisters, you yourselves know that our coming to you was not a waste of time. ²You remember how we had just suffered through brutal and insulting attacks in Philippi; but because of God, we boldly *stepped into the open to* tell you His good news, even though it would likely mean more conflict for us. ³For we haven't approached you—*or anyone else for that matter*—with some error or impure motives or deceitful agenda; ⁴but as we have been approved by God and entrusted with the good news, that's how we are telling the world. We aren't trying to please everybody, but God, the only One who can truly examine our motives. ⁵As you know, we didn't sandwich the truth between cunning compliments—*we told it straight*—and before the eye of God, we never conspired to make a single cent *off of you.* ⁶We didn't come seeking respect from people—not from you or anyone else—although we could have leveraged our position as emissaries* of the Anointed One, *the Liberating King.* ⁷Instead, we proved to be gentle among you, like a nursing mother caring for her own children. ⁸We were so taken by you that we not only eagerly shared with you God's good news, but we also shared with you our own lives. That's how much you've come to mean to us.

⁹Don't you remember, my brothers and sisters, how hard we worked and struggled? We worked day and night so that we wouldn't be a burden to any of you and so that we could *continue to* proclaim to you the good news of God. ¹⁰Both you and God can confirm how well we treated the believers: we were always holy, just, and blameless. ¹¹⁻¹²As you know, we comforted and consoled

---

* 1:1 Silvanus is better known in Acts as Silas.   * 1:1 Some early manuscripts omit this portion.   * 2:6 Literally, apostles

each of you as a father soothes his own children, encouraging you to live lives worthy of God—of the One calling you into His own kingdom and into His glory.

Unlike the Corinthians who struggled to break their old religious and cultural ties when they came to faith, the Thessalonians followed Jesus wholeheartedly and thus faced persecution for their devotion.

[13]So we have good reason to give thanks to God without pausing. For you have taken into yourselves the word of God we brought to you and received it as a message from God—not just something whipped up by someone like you or us—and that word is at work in you who believe. [14]And, brothers and sisters, you even became imitators of the churches of God in Jesus the Anointed that gather in Judea because you were willing to suffer at the hands of your own countrymen as they suffered from the *unbelieving* Judeans. [15]*These are the same people* who killed the Lord Jesus, as well as the prophets, and *continued attacking until they* drove all of us out. They don't just offend God; they are *clearly* hostile to the rest of the people [16]because they are trying to silence our life-saving message to the nations; and as a result, their sins are always filling up *and overflowing*. But in the end, they will face God's wrath.

[17]Brothers and sisters, we are like orphans, separated from you for a short time (in presence, yes, but not in heart); and we desperately desire to see your faces *again*. [18]However, as much as we wanted to come to you—I, Paul, assure you we tried again and again—Satan thwarted our plans. [19]For what is our *true* hope, our *true* joy, our victor's crown in all this? It is nothing if it isn't you standing before our Lord Jesus the Anointed at His arrival. [20]You are our glory! You are our joy!

3 But after all our attempts *to come to you* were frustrated, we decided it was best for Silvanus* and me to stay behind in Athens by ourselves [2]and to send Timothy (our dear brother [and servant of God],* our partner in the good news of the Anointed One) to strengthen, *comfort,* and encourage you in your faith [3]so that you won't be shaken by the sufferings *and wither under this stress* that we know lies

ahead. [4]*Certainly you remember that* when we were with you, we warned you of the suffering we would have to endure; now, as you well know, it has happened. [5]This is why I couldn't stand it anymore and sent *Timothy* to report on *the state of* your faith: because I was worried the tempter had tested you and, if so, all of our hard work would have come to nothing.

[6]*You can imagine my relief and joy* when Timothy returned to us with such good news about you, about your faith and love *for us,* about how you have such good memories of us and long to see us as much as we long to see you. [7]Hearing this *about your faith,* brothers and sisters, brought comfort to us in our *stress-filled* days of trouble and suffering. [8]For if you are set firmly in the Lord, then we can truly live. [9]What thanks would ever be enough to offer God about you for all the jubilant celebration we'll feel before our God because of you? [10]We remain vigilant in our prayers, night and day praying to *once again* see your faces and to help complete whatever may be lacking in your faith.

V

It is obvious Paul loves Jesus, and His Spirit reinforces Paul in every way. How else is he able to walk away from beating after beating or endure trials of the heart and mind? He must constantly be praying for those he can and can't reach, for those he is with and for those he has to leave behind. Paul loves Jesus, and so he cannot help but embrace the world as passionately as he does.

---

[11]May God Himself, our Father, along with our Lord Jesus, [the Anointed One,]* navigate our way to you. [12]May the Lord flood you with an *unending, undying* love for one another and for all humanity, like our love for you, [13]so that your hearts will be reinforced *with His strength,* held blameless and holy before God, our Father, when our Lord Jesus, [the Anointed, *the Liberating King,*]* appears along with all His holy ones. [Amen.]*

* 3:1 Silvanus is better known in Acts as Silas.   * 3:2 Some manuscripts omit this portion.   * 3:11 The earliest manuscripts omit this portion.   * 3:13 The earliest manuscripts omit this portion.
* 3:13 Most manuscripts omit this word.

4 So finally, brothers and sisters, in the *name of our* Lord Jesus, we ask you, we beg you to remember what we have taught you: live a life that is pleasing to God as you are already doing. Yes, we urge you to keep living and thriving in that life! [2]For you know the instructions we gave you, instructions that came through the Lord Jesus. [3]Now this is God's will *for you*: set yourselves apart and live holy lives; avoid *polluting yourselves with* sexual defilement. [4]Learn how to take charge over your own body, maintaining purity and honor. [5]Don't let the swells of lustful passion run your life as they do the outsiders who don't know God. [6]Don't violate or take advantage of a fellow believer in such matters. As we told you before and warned you: the Lord will settle the score with anyone who does these things. [7]Here's why: God does not call us to live impure, *adulterous, scandalous* lives, but to seek holiness *and purity.* [8]If you ignore this message, then you're not only rejecting us but you're rejecting God, the One who has given His Holy Spirit to *live in* you.

Paul uses the language of a loving faith family reaching out to others.

[9]Now there's no need for us to send you instructions on caring for your faith family because God Himself has already taught you how to love outside yourselves. [10]And it's evident *you learned that lesson well* by the way you love all the people of Macedonia. Brothers and sisters, we urge you to love even more [11]and make it your goal to lead a peaceful life, mind your own business, and keep your hands busy in your work, as we have instructed you. [12]That way you will live peacefully with those on the outside, and all your needs will be met without depending on others.

What a beautiful, dramatic transformation! This is Paul's progression from spoon-feeding people better moral choices to trusting them to live by love according to the conviction of the Spirit, their guide to becoming active participants in the kingdom of God. Paul is acknowledging that there is a power at work that is much greater than his pen. In fact, the same

Spirit that inspires Paul's words in these letters is teaching the believers in Thessalonica to live as true believers and teaches us still today.

[13]Brothers and sisters, we want you to be fully informed about those who have fallen asleep in death so that you will not be overwhelmed with grief like those who live outside of the *true* hope. [14]Here's what we believe: since Jesus died and rose again, in the same way, God will bring with Jesus all who have died through Him. [15]For we can say all this to you *confidently* because it is the word of the Lord: we who are still alive and left behind when the Lord comes will not precede those who have fallen asleep in death. [16]*On that day,* with a command *that thunders into the world,* with a voice of a chief heavenly messenger, and with a blast of God's trumpet, the Lord Himself will descend from heaven; and all those who died in the Anointed One, *our Liberating King,* will rise *from the dead* first. [17]Then we who are alive and left behind will be snatched up together with them into the clouds to meet the Lord in the air. This is how *we, the resurrected and the living,* will be with Him forever. [18]So comfort one another *with this hope, and encourage one another* with these words.

Many people fear death; perhaps it's the idea of the unknown that stirs the imagination. Death is the great enemy that stands before believers; but through Jesus' own death and resurrection, the power of death is broken. Paul uses the gentle image of the faithful being asleep as a new perspective on the finality of death. One minute you close your eyes to this world; the next you are celebrating with Jesus and experiencing the resurrection of the body. Those sleeping will not even miss a moment; it will all happen in the blink of an eye.

5 Now, brothers and sisters, you don't need further instruction *from us or anyone else for that matter* regarding how the seasons and times *will play out.* [2]That's

because you know *the truth* well enough. The day of the Lord will *race onto the scene and* surprise us like a thief in the night. [3]People will be going about their business chanting, "All is well! All is at peace!" and in the next moment, *ruin and* destruction will suddenly seize them as labor pains grip a woman about to give birth; for them there will be no escape. [4]My brothers and sisters, *it will be different for you.* You do not dwell in the darkness, so that day will not surprise you like a thief. [5]For you are all children of light. You are sons and daughters of the day. We are not *created* of night, nor are we *owned by* darkness. [6]So then let's not *give in to* sleep *or wander around in a stupor* as some do, but let's stay awake and in control. [7]You see, sleepers sleep through the night, and drunkards drink the night away; [8]but since we belong to the day, we should stay sober *and in control,* covered with a breastplate of faith and love and a helmet of the hope of salvation. [9]For God has not destined us, *His chosen,* to face His wrath but to be the heirs of salvation through our Lord Jesus the Anointed, *the Liberating King,* [10]who died for us. So regardless of whether we are awake or asleep, we will live together with Him. [11]So support one another. Keep building each other up as you have been doing.

[12]Brothers and sisters, we ask you to show appreciation to those who are working hard among you and those who are your leaders as they guide and instruct you in the Lord—*they are priceless.* [13]When you think about them, let it be with great love in your heart because of all the work they have done. Let peace live *and reign* among you.

[14]Brothers and sisters, we strongly advise you to scold the rebels *who devote their lives to wreaking havoc,* to encourage the downcast, to help the *sick and* weak, and to be patient with all of them. [15]Make sure no one returns evil for evil, but always pursue what is good as it affects one another *in the church* but also all people. [16]Celebrate always, [17]pray constantly, and [18]give thanks *to God* no matter what circumstances you find yourself in. (This is God's will for all of you in Jesus the Anointed.) [19]Don't suppress the Spirit. [20]Don't downplay prophecies. [21]Take a close look at everything, *test it,* then cling to what is good. [22]Put away every form of evil.

[23]So now, may the God of peace *make you His own* completely *and* set you apart from the rest. May your spirit, soul, and body be preserved, kept intact and wholly free from any sort of blame at the coming of our Lord Jesus the Anointed. [24]For the God who calls you is faithful, and He can *be trusted to* make it so.

[25]Brothers and sisters, *we ask you to* pray for us. [26]Greet one another *warmly* with a holy kiss. [27]Here is my charge to you before the Lord: have this letter read to all our brothers and sisters [in the faith].* [28]May the grace of our Lord Jesus, *God's* Anointed, be with *all of* you.

Paul knows the healing power of touch. When members of a loving community embrace, the hardest days are easier and no one feels alone.

* 5:27 Some early manuscripts omit this portion.

2 THESSALONIANS

Letter to the church in Thessalonica

From Paul, the apostle to the Gentiles

Compared to the gentle, pastoral tone in Paul's first letter to the Thessalonians, in this letter he seems anxious over what is going on in this robust capital of Macedonia. First, the intensity of persecution against the gatherings of believers is clearly on the rise in and around Thessalonica. But we cannot know exactly who is bringing the pressure on this young community of faith or why they are doing it. What we do know is that it is increasingly dangerous to be a follower of Jesus in this area. Paul assures these new believers that relief is coming when the Lord returns. God's justice will be satisfied when He punishes those who bring such misery on His people.

Second, apparently someone has forged a letter in Paul's name. In that letter, Paul is said to have written that the day of the Lord has already arrived. He is quick to point out that the letter is not from him and to assure the Thessalonians that the day has not arrived. In fact, it won't come, he says, until restraints are removed and "the rebellious one" is unleashed to start a "great rebellion." But as awful as this sounds, Paul again assures them that almost as soon as it begins, the rebellion will be over when the Lord Jesus returns to annihilate the enemy and his minions.

Third, for reasons not altogether clear, a number of people in the community have quit their jobs and are no longer working. As a result, they have become a nuisance and a burden on the rest. Paul confronts them: "Anyone not willing to work shouldn't get to eat!" As he often does, Paul points to his own example. Although as a traveling mission-ary he had the right to live off of the hospitality of others, he didn't exercise that right; instead he went to work daily to take care of his own needs. So he urges the lazy Thessalonians to follow his example. With all these issues going on in the church, no wonder Paul is a bit nervous.

The themes that dominate both 1 and 2 Thessalonians have much to do with matters of last or ultimate things: death, the afterlife, the second coming, judgment, and eternity. Paul addresses these subjects not long after he planted the church. They are clearly salient issues facing the church in Thessalonica, and they continue to interest believers today. Still Paul doesn't answer every question about what will happen next as the story of redemption unfolds.

1 Paul, Silvanus,* and Timothy to the church of the Thessalonians *that gathers in God our Father* and in the Lord Jesus the Anointed. ²May grace and peace from God our Father and from the Lord Jesus the Anointed be with you.

³Brothers and sisters, we cannot help but thank God for you, which is only appropriate because your faith is growing and expanding and because the love *demonstrated by* each and every one of you is overflowing for one another. ⁴So, *of course,* we've proudly bragged about you *within circles of God's people* at other churches *near and far* because, even in *the grip of* much persecution and affliction, you've stood firm in your faith and have persevered. ⁵Your sufferings prove that God's judgment is right! The result: your sufferings have made you worthy—worthy of the kingdom of God, which is the very reason why you are suffering *in the first place!* ⁶It is only right that God would repay with trouble those who have troubled you ⁷⁻⁸and give relief to all of you still bandaging your wounds, as well as to all the rest of us. On that day—when *the clouds draw back displaying* His powerful heavenly messengers in a fiery blaze, Jesus the Lord will appear from heaven dealing out perfect justice to anyone who doesn't know God and anyone who disobeys the good news of our Lord Jesus. ⁹*And what's to become of them?* They'll pay for what they've done; their punishment will be eternal destruction. *And what's worse?* They'll be banished from the Lord's presence and glorious power. ¹⁰On that day when He comes, all the saints *in heaven and on earth* will celebrate the glory *of His power,* and all who believe will *stand and* be amazed—*this includes you* because you believed us when we testified *on His behalf.* ¹¹All this is why we are constantly praying for you, so God will make you worthy of the *great* calling *you have received from Him* and will give you the power to accomplish every good intention and work of faith. ¹²Then the *great* name of our Lord Jesus will be glorified through your lives, and you will be glorified in Him according to the grace of our God and the Lord Jesus, the Anointed One, *our Liberating King.*

On that day—though men and women have spent lifetimes scanning the skies hoping that "perhaps today" is the day of salvation—on that day, the confessed lovers of God and Jesus will glow with all the wonder of children at Christmas.

There are clear premonitions in the Bible about what we can expect on that day; but can anyone, with our rudimentary human knowledge, know what to expect? Jesus confessed that even He did not know the day or the hour when these final moments will play out, so how can we truly know? Likely this fear of the unknown is what took root and began to spread like weeds within the Thessalonians' community. Where fear takes root, faith withers; and people who once focused on the bright hope of the Son turn away.

2 Since, brothers and sisters, we are on the topic of the coming of our Lord Jesus the Anointed and how we will all gather together to meet Him, we ask ²that you don't let your minds get quickly rattled or become anxious because of someone else's so-called "spiritual revelation" or because someone gave you a message or claimed to know of a letter allegedly from us reporting that the day of the Lord has already come! ³Don't be deceived by anyone! That day, *that amazing day,* won't come until after the *great* rebellion and the unveiling of the rebellious one.* *As the spawn of death,* he delights in destruction. ⁴He sets himself up as the *great* adversary *of God* and vies for a place above all other so-called gods or objects of worship. *If it were possible,* he would even take a seat—*yes, exalt himself*—in the temple of *the one true* God, declaring that he himself is God! ⁵Don't you remember me telling you all this the last time we were together? ⁶You know what restrains him now *and what will hold him* until the exact time when he will be revealed. ⁷For the mystery of sin is already working *its way through the world;* He who holds him back now *will continue to suppress him only until*

He is pulled out of the way. [8]It is then that this rebellious one will be *finally* unleashed. But the Lord will slay him with the breath of His mouth; and with the splendor of His coming, He will bring him to his *predetermined* end. [9]Still the rebellious one arrives with all sorts of power, performing signs and fake miracles sanctioned by Satan; [10]he employs every manner of wicked deception to wile away those who are destined for *eternal* death because they reject the love of the truth that leads to salvation. [11]Because of this, God sends a deceptive influence over them so they will wander from the truth and believe the lie. [12]As a result, God will judge all of those who did not entrust themselves to the truth *when it faced them* but instead reveled in wickedness.

[13]*But this is not you,* dearly beloved brothers and sisters of the Lord. We cannot help but thank God for you at all times, because from the beginning He handpicked you for salvation through the Spirit's sanctifying work and your belief in the truth. [14]He called you to this when we shared our good news with you. Now you can take part in the glory of our Lord Jesus the Anointed, *our Liberating King.* [15]So, brothers and sisters, *all you need to do now is* stand firm and hold tight to the line of teachings we have passed on to you, whether in person or in a letter. [16-17]Now may our Lord Jesus (the Anointed One Himself) and God our Father (who has loved us, comforted us eternally, and given us a good hope by His grace) bring comfort to your hearts and strengthen *your wills to accomplish* every good work and word.

taking place in the church; so remain diligent and faithful in service of the Lord.

3 Brothers and sisters, having shared all this, let me ask you to pray for us. Pray that this message of the Lord will spread quickly and receive the praise and respect *it deserves* from others as it has with you. [2]Pray also that we would all be rescued from *the snares of* harmful, wicked people—after all, not all people are believing. [3]Still, the Lord is true to His promises; He will hold you up and guard you against the evil one. [4]We do not doubt the Lord's intentions for you; we are confident that you are carrying out, and will continue to carry out, the commands we are sending your way. [5]May the Lord guide your hearts into God's *pure* love and keep you headed straight into the strong and sure grip of the Anointed One.

[6]*For the sake of the church,* brothers and sisters, we insist in the name of our Lord Jesus the Anointed that you withdraw from any brother or sister who is out of order and unwilling to work, who is straying from the line of teaching we passed on to all of you. [7]You know how essential it is to imitate us *in the way we live life.* We were never undisciplined [8]nor did we take charity from anyone *while we were with you.* Instead, *you saw* how we worked very hard day and night so we wouldn't be a burden to even one person in the community. [9]We had the right *to depend on your help and hospitality, as you know;* but we wanted to give you a model you could follow, *to lay a path of footprints for you to walk in.* [10]This is exactly why, while with you, we commanded you: "Anyone not willing to work shouldn't get to eat!" [11]You see, we are hearing that some folks in the community are out of step *with our teaching;* they are idle, not working, but really busy doing nothing—*and yet still expect to be fed!* [12]If this is you or someone else in the community, we insist and urge you in the Lord Jesus the Anointed that you go to work quietly, *earn your keep, put food on your own table,* and supply your own necessities. [13]And to the rest of you, brothers and sisters, never grow tired of doing good.

[14]If someone disregards the instructions of this letter, make a note of who it is and don't have anything to do with that person

---

Paul brings the situation to life for them: on one side, the rebellious one opposes God by corrupting God's world, telling lies, and instigating fear; but on the other side, there's Jesus, who comes from above and rains mercy over the world with His blood. He stands ready to return to face these enemies. Paul is trying to explain this epic battle with eternal consequences to his friends who have been led astray by false revelations. While this spiritual battle will occur in the future, skirmishes representing the two sides are already so that this one may be shamed. [15]Don't consider someone like this an enemy *(he is an enemy only to himself)* but warn him as *if you were redirecting* your own brother.

Work is part of the ongoing work of creation, an aspect of God's image in us. Those who do not work will be unfulfilled and a burden to those around them.

[16]And now, *dear friends*, may the Lord of peace Himself grace you with peace always and in everything. May the Lord be present with all of you.

[17]This *final* greeting is by me, Paul, *written* by my own hand. This is my signature, *letting you know that* this is a *genuine* letter from me, and so I write to you:

[18]May the grace of our Lord Jesus the Anointed be with all of you.

1 TIMOTHY

Personal letter to Timothy

From Paul, the apostle to the Gentiles

In the first three decades after Jesus launched the Christian movement, no one was more influential than Paul, the former Jewish zealot. Many of the early churches were begun through his ministry or were strengthened by the teaching of the emissaries, by Paul or his associates. Because misunderstandings and false teachings were enormous problems in those early years of the church, Paul traveled throughout the eastern Mediterranean basin bringing authoritative teaching, church order, and a strong apologetic to control heresy and divisive elements. Paul mentored a select group of apprentices as they traveled together. Those dedicated coworkers included Barnabas, Silas, Luke, John Mark, and Apollos. Although many others are also mentioned in his letters, possibly those closest to him were two young men he called his sons: Timothy and Titus.

Several of Paul's letters have survived, most of which are addressed to groups of believers at various locations. Four of his letters are addressed to individuals: Philemon, 1 and 2 Timothy, and Titus. While each letter is uniquely personal, it's clear that Paul intends that these letters be read in the churches.

In this first letter to Timothy, there is conversational warmth that is not found in the church letters Paul wrote. When Paul moved into Macedonia, he had Timothy remain behind in Ephesus for the purpose of confronting false teaching and bringing order to this influential church through qualified elders and deacons. Timothy is encouraged, despite his young age, to handle difficult problems with authority and maturity. He is told to confront elders, to silence overbearing women, and to avoid activities that will call into question his position and standing in the church. In some ways, Timothy is being thrown into the fire; but he is gifted, called, and well equipped. He will make mistakes; but God is with him, and his spiritual father, Paul, shows great confidence in his young son.

It has become traditional to refer to 1 Timothy, 2 Timothy, and Titus as the Pastoral Epistles because they share a number of common features and themes Paul considered useful to those who lead churches.

1 Paul, an emissary* of Jesus the Anointed commissioned by order of God our Savior and Jesus the Anointed, our *living and certain* hope), [2]to you, Timothy, my true son in the faith.

May the grace, mercy, and peace *that come only* from God the Father and our Lord Jesus the Anointed *mark your life.*

[3]As I said that day I left for Macedonia, stay in Ephesus and instruct the *unruly* people *in the church, once and for all,* to stop teaching a different doctrine. [4]*Tell them* to turn away from fables and endless genealogies. These activities just cause more arguments and confusion. Instead, they should concern themselves with *welcoming in and bringing about* the reign of God, which is all about faith. [5]Our teaching *about this journey* is intended to bring us to *a single destination—a place where self-giving* love *reigns* from a pure heart, a clean conscience, and a genuine faith. [6]*Yes,* some have walked away from these traits and have fallen into *a life of endless* blabber and nonsense—[7]they wish to become scholars of the law, but they don't know what they are talking about, and they make these *grand* pronouncements *but clearly don't understand what they just said.*

[8]You and I know the law is good (if used in the right way), and [9]we also know the law was not designed for law-abiding people but for lawbreakers and criminals, the ungodly and sin-filled, the unholy and worldly, the father killers and mother killers, the murderers, [10]the sexually immoral and homosexuals, slave dealers, liars, perjurers, and anyone else who acts against the sound doctrine [11]laid out in the glorious, *holy, and pure* good news of the blessed God that has been entrusted to me.

[12]I thank our Lord Jesus the Anointed who empowers me, because He saw me as faithful and appointed me to this ministry. [13]Despite the fact that at one time I was slandering the things of God, persecuting and attacking *His people,* He was still merciful to me because I acted in ignorance apart from faith. [14]But He poured His grace over me, *and I was flooded* in an abundance of the grace and faith and love that can only be found in Jesus the Anointed.

[15]Here's a statement worthy of trust: Jesus the Anointed, *the Liberating King,* came into the world to save sinners, and I am the worst of them all. [16]But it is for this reason I was given mercy: by displaying His perfect patience in me, the very worst of all sinners, Jesus the Anointed could show that patience to all who would believe in Him and gain eternal life. [17]May the King eternal, immortal, and invisible—the one and only God—now be honored and glorified forever and ever. Amen.

V

It is fair to say that Paul never got over the fact that he violently persecuted the church. Even though his rampage against the first followers of Jesus had ended over 20 years earlier, he still grieved because of what he had done. But when Paul was older, he was moved to celebration and praise because God's mercy is always greater than sin. The Lord Jesus called Paul in the midst of his campaign against Him so that he became a public display of Jesus' patient love. So, if we think somehow we are too far from God's mercy, then we should think again.

---

[18]Timothy, my dear child, I am placing before you a charge *for the mission ahead.* It is in total agreement with the prophecies once spoken over you. *Here it is: with God's message* stirring and directing you, fight the good fight, [19]armed with faith and a good conscience. Some have tried to silence their consciences, wrecking their *lives and ruining their* faiths. [20]Hymenaeus and Alexander are among these; I have had to hand them over to Satan so they might learn not to speak against God.

2 So, first and foremost, I urge *God's people to pray.* They should make their requests, petitions, and thanksgivings on behalf of all humanity. [2]*Teach them* to pray for kings (or anyone in high places *for that matter*) so that we can lead quiet, peaceful lives—reverent, godly, *and holy*—[3]all of which is good and acceptable before the eyes of God our Savior [4]who desires for everyone to be saved and know the truth. [5]Because

There is one God and one Mediator between God and us—
the man Jesus, *God's* Anointed,
[6]Who gave His life as a ransom for all
so that we might have freedom.

---

* 1:1 Literally, apostle

The testimony was given *to me* at just the right time. [7]This is exactly what I was appointed *to do*—*tell everyone His story*—as a herald, an emissary,* a teacher of the outsiders in faith and the truth. (*Listen, I promise it's all true. I'm not lying.*)

[8]*So here's what you tell them;* here's what I want to see: Men, pray wherever you are. Reach your holy hands *to heaven*—without rage or conflict—*completely open.* [9]Women, the same goes for you: dress properly, modestly, and appropriately. Don't get carried away in grooming your hair or *seek beauty in* glittering gold, pearls, or expensive clothes. [10]Instead, as is fitting, let good works *decorate your true beauty and* show that you are a woman who claims reverence for God. [11]*It's best if* a woman learns quietly and orderly in complete submission.

[12]*Now, Timothy,* it's not my habit to allow women to teach in a way that wrenches authority from a man. *As I said, it's best if* a woman learns quietly and orderly. [13]*This is* because Adam was formed first *by God,* then Eve. [14]Plus, it wasn't Adam who was tricked; it was she—the woman was the one who was fooled and disobeyed *God's command first.* [15]Still, God, in His faithfulness, will deliver her through childbearing as long as she* remains in faith and love and holiness with self-restraint.

People are more concerned about their outward appearance than their inner beauty. Paul wants women to pursue the right kind of beauty, the beauty of an inner life fashioned after godliness. That includes proper respect for their husbands, a willingness to learn the truth, and—unlike Eve—avoiding enticing claims. Paul then turns to childbirth. Childbirth is a particularly precarious time in the life of a woman; in that day, many women died trying to deliver their babies. While Paul is not promising lack of pain or assurance of safety in childbirth, he is speaking of God's faithfulness and spiritual rewards to those women who live in faith, love, and holiness, supporting the family and the church in which God places them.

3 *Here's another* statement you may trust: if anyone is seeking a position as overseer *in the church,* he desires an honorable and important work. [2]*Here are the qualifications to look for in* an overseer: a spotless reputation, the husband of one wife, sober-minded, sensible, respectable, welcoming to strangers (*allowing them into his home*), and gifted to teach. [3]Disqualify any drunk or violent man. Look for a gentle man; no belligerent fellow can follow this calling. And he should be free from money lust. [4]He should exert good control over his own household, and his children should obey and honor him. [5](If someone can't manage his own household, then how can he take care of God's family?) [6]He mustn't be someone recently converted; otherwise, he may become arrogant and fall into the devil's condemnation. [7]He should also be respected *for his character and known as an honorable person* by people outside *of the church* so as to avoid the *trips,* traps, *and pitfalls* of the devil.

[8]The same standards apply to deacons: they should be dignified. Double-talking *hypocrites,* heavy drinkers, and those greedy for ill-gotten gain *should* not *be considered.* [9]They should be people who hold tight to the great mystery of faith with a clear conscience. [10]Put these deacon-candidates to the test first; and if they come through without stumbling, then send them out to serve.

[11]Again the same applies to women *in key positions;* they should also be dignified, not *backstabbing* gossips but self-controlled and faithful to the core.

[12]Now deacons should live faithfully as the husband of one wife and be in control of their households, including their children. [13]Those deacons who serve well will achieve a good standing for themselves *in the community* and have great confidence to walk in the faith that is in Jesus the Anointed, *our Liberating King.*

If the church lacks qualified, positive leaders, then it will not succeed in its mission. Paul never provides a job description for "overseers" and "deacons." What he does offer is a list of character traits or qualifications that challenge even the most outstanding

* 2:7 Literally, apostle   * 2:15 Literally, they

disciple. Essentially they are servant-leaders of the church. They give themselves to the church's well-being by teaching the truth, living a life in imitation of Jesus, and defending the church from false teaching. Paul knows firsthand how important it is to discover, train, and empower capable leaders. Everywhere he goes, he invests a lot of himself in coworkers like Timothy. Now it is Timothy's turn to train the next generation.

---

[14]I am writing all this to you, hoping I can come to you before too long; [15]but in case I am delayed, you will know how one ought to behave as a member of God's family—the assembly of the living God, the pillar and foundation that support the truth—[16]and I think you will agree that the mystery of godliness is great:

> He* was revealed in the flesh,
> proven right in the Spirit;
> He was seen by the heavenly messengers,
> preached to outsider nations.
> He was believed in the world,
> taken up *to the heavens* in glory.

4 But even so, the Spirit very clearly tells us that in the last times some will abandon the *true* faith because of their devotion to spirits *sent to* deceive *and sabotage,* and *mistakenly they will end up* following the doctrine of demons. [2]*They will be carried away* through the hypocrisy of liars whose consciences have been branded with a red-hot iron, [3]saying, "Don't marry. Don't eat *such-and-such* foods." But God created all these to be received with gratitude by people who hold fast to the faith and really comprehend the truth. [4]For everything God made is good. *That means* nothing should be rejected as long as it's received with a grateful heart, [5]for by God's word and prayer, it is made holy.

Paul turns from moral character to solid doctrine. People were believing strange doctrines and passing rumors. Timothy is expected to confront legalism and immorality with truth and right thinking.

[6]Place these *truths* before the brothers and sisters. If *you do,* you will be a good servant of Jesus the Anointed, raised and fed on words of true belief, trained in the good instruction you have so clearly followed. [7]Reject worldly fables. Refuse old wives' tales. Instead, train yourself toward godliness. [8]Although training your body has certain payoffs, godliness benefits all things—holding promise for life here and now and promise for the life that is coming. [9]This statement is worthy of trust and our full acceptance. [10]This is what we work so hard for! This is why we are constantly struggling: because we have an assured hope fixed upon a living God who is the Savior of all humankind—especially all of us who believe.

[11]So go out and insist on these things. Teach them. [12]Don't let anyone belittle you because you are young. Instead, show the faithful, *young and old,* an example of how to live: set the standard for how to talk, act, love, and be faithful and pure. [13]Until I get there, make sure to devote yourself to the public reading of Scripture, to exhortation, and to teaching. [14]Don't neglect the gift that was given to you through the prophecy spoken when the company of the elders laid their hands on you. [15]Cultivate *all* these practices; live by them so that all will see *how* you are advancing *and growing.* [16]Take care of yourself, concentrate on your teaching, and stick with these things. If you do, then you will be effective in bringing salvation to yourself and all who hear you.

Paul instructs Timothy not to let his youth cause distraction: meet this objection with loving speech, faithful conduct, pure action, and transparent living as an example for all.

5 Respect an elderly man. Don't speak to him sharply; appeal to him as you would a father. Treat younger men as brothers, [2]elderly women as mothers, and younger women as sisters in all purity.

[3]Honor widows, *but be discerning about* which ones are truly widows. [4]If any widow has children or grandchildren, then go to the descendants first and teach them that it is their spiritual responsibility to care for their own family, to repay their parents *and grandparents* because this is what pleases God.

---

* 3:16 Some manuscripts read "God."

⁵*Here's how you know* if she is a true widow: she is all alone with her hope fixed in God, crying her pleas, prayers, and appeals to God day and night. ⁶But the woman who is living for pleasure is dead as she stands. ⁷You should command these things to everyone to keep them free of blame. ⁸And listen, if someone is not providing for his own relatives and especially his own household, then he is denying the faith and is worse off than an unbeliever.

V

Family members have a duty before God to support their relatives. But when a widow has no family to support her, the church must step in to be her surrogate family. Paul, of course, is thinking of those widows who have served faithfully in the ministry of the church. The elderly are easily forgotten, especially those without caring families. The church is called to honor those who have been faithful servants by maintaining relationships with them and helping them when they are in need.

---

⁹Now only these should be put on the widow registry: a woman who is at least 60 years old, was a faithful wife to one husband, ¹⁰is well thought of for her good works, has raised children, was hospitable, has washed the feet of the saints, has tended to the sick and suffering, and has devoted herself to do good wherever possible. ¹¹Don't add younger women *to the widow roll* because when their desires for pleasure overtake them, they get careless in their devotion to the Anointed One. Their constant thoughts become, "I want to get married," ¹²and such thoughts disqualify them because they have tossed aside their first commitment *to Him*. ¹³Plus, they get into the habit of being idle. Not only are they idle, but they *band together and* roam from house to house, gossiping about and meddling into other people's business; they talk about all sorts of things that should never be spoken of. ¹⁴That's why I think it's best to have the younger widows remarry, have children, and take care of their households so that the enemy gains no opportunity to come with accusations.

¹⁵(*Unfortunately* some have already lined up behind Satan!) ¹⁶Tell any woman of faith: if you have a widow in your family, help her so the church is unencumbered and is free to extend aid to the widows who are truly in need of its help.

¹⁷Elders who are leading well *should be admired and valued.* Double up on the honor shown them; *care for them well*—especially those *constantly and consistently* teaching the word and preaching. ¹⁸For the Scripture agrees, "Don't muzzle the ox while it is treading out *your* grain,"* and, "The worker deserves his wages."*

¹⁹Listen, when or if a charge comes against an elder, don't even acknowledge the accusation unless there are two or more witnesses. ²⁰*Bring any believers* who persist in sinning before the community and publicly scold them so that all the rest will know to fear *sin and its consequences.* ²¹I challenge you—in front of God, Jesus His Anointed, and His select heavenly messengers—to keep these instructions. And don't do anything out of favoritism. ²²Don't be too quick to lay hands *upon anyone* or share in the sins of others—stay clean.

²³*Concerning your health, Timothy,* don't just drink water; drink a little wine. It is good for your stomach and will help with your frequent ailments.

²⁴Some people's sins are clearly on display *before the world.* They lead the way to the *final* judgment. *But it's not so easy* with other people because their sins trail behind *and don't catch up to them until later.* ²⁵The same is true regarding good works; some are there for all to see. Other people's works can be inconspicuous; but *at the final judgment,* they cannot remain hidden.

6 Tell all who labor under the yoke of slavery to treat their masters with honor *and respect, whether or not their masters deserve it.* This will keep God's name and doctrine from being smeared. ²If their masters are believers, then they should not be insolent toward them just because they are your brothers and sisters. Actually they should be even more determined to serve them because the gains from their good works benefit those who are faithful and loved.

Timothy, teach these *instructions,* and appeal *to those under your ministry to live*

---

* 5:18 Deuteronomy 25:4   * 5:18 Compare Luke 10:7

by them. ³If others are teaching otherwise and bringing unhealthy conversations to the community, if they are not sticking to the sound words in the teaching of our Lord Jesus the Anointed, if they are not teaching godly principles—⁴then they are swollen with conceit, *filled with self-importance,* and without any proper understanding. They probably have a gross infatuation with controversy and will endlessly debate meanings of words. That kind of talk leads to envy, discord, slander, and evil mistrust; ⁵and these people constantly bicker because they are depraved in their minds and bereft of the truth. They think somehow that godliness is the way to get ahead. ⁶This is ironic because godliness, along with contentment, does put us ahead *but not in the ways some imagine.* ⁷You see we came into this world with nothing, and nothing is going with us on the way out! ⁸So as long as we are clothed and fed, we should be happy. ⁹But those who chase riches are constantly falling into temptation and snares. They are regularly caught by their own stupid and harmful desires, dragged down and pulled under into ruin and destruction. ¹⁰For the love of money—*and what it can buy*—is the root of all sorts of evil. Some already have wandered away from the true faith because they craved what it had to offer; *but when reaching for the prize,* they found their *hands and* hearts pierced with many sorrows.

¹¹*Timothy, don't let this happen to you*—run away from these things! You are a man of God. Your quest is for justice, godliness, faithfulness, love, perseverance, and gentleness.

Paul asks this young leader to shepherd a divided congregation through one problem after another.

He points to a time when Jesus will arrive to set this world straight.

¹²Fight the good fight of the faith! Cling to the eternal life you were called to when you confessed the good confession before witnesses. ¹³Before God—the life-giving Creator of all things—and Jesus the Anointed, *our Liberating King,* who made the good confession to Pontius Pilate, I urge you: ¹⁴keep His commandment. Have a spotless, indisputable record until our Lord Jesus the Anointed appears *to set this world straight.* ¹⁵In His own perfect time, He will come—blessed is the only Sovereign, the King of kings, and the Lord of lords. ¹⁶He alone possesses immortality; He makes His home in matchless, blinding, brilliant light that no one can approach—no mortal has ever even seen Him, and no human can. So let it be that all honor and eternal power are His. Amen.

¹⁷Here's what you say to those wealthy in regard to this age: "Don't become high and mighty or place all your hope on a gamble for riches; instead, fix your hope on God, the One who richly provides everything for our enjoyment." ¹⁸Tell them to use their wealth for good things; be rich in good works! If they are willing to give generously and share everything, ¹⁹then they will send ahead a great treasure for themselves and build their futures on a solid foundation. As a result, they will surely take hold of eternal life.

²⁰O Timothy, protect what was entrusted to you! Walk away from all the godless, empty voices *out there,* and turn aside from objections and arguments that arise from false knowledge. ²¹(By professing such knowledge, some are missing the mark when it comes to *true* faith.)

May God's grace be with you.

2 TIMOTHY

Personal letter to Timothy

From Paul, the apostle to the Gentiles

This is probably the last letter Paul ever writes. His tone is different in this letter as he writes from his prison in Rome, not long before dying a martyr's death. Gone is his typical optimism that he will soon be released; now he is all but certain that he has come to the end of his life. Yet, while there is an air of acceptance of what is to come, there is also a triumphant tone to this last of the letters from Paul to individuals because Paul will face whatever may come with a clean conscience and a clear sense that he has fulfilled the work God had for him to do. He has run the race of faith and run it well. He will cross the finish line a winner ready to receive the welcome, the accolades, and the crown from his King, Jesus. But Paul knows he is not in this race alone. What awaits him is the same victorious destiny that awaits all who love God and long for His kingdom. For Paul, no one longs more and loves greater than Timothy.

In writing to his younger colleague in Ephesus, Paul effectively deputizes him to carry on proclaiming the gospel. As the apostle passes from this world to the next, he wants to be certain that the good news is in good hands. With Timothy he knows that is the case. Paul encourages Timothy to become a leader and teacher who stands above the pettiness that threatens to tear the church apart. But before the martyr's blade severs Paul's head from his body, Paul wants to see Timothy one last time. So Paul asks Timothy to come to Rome before winter sets in to bring a cloak to keep Paul warm in his prison cell and to collect some books and papers for him.

In this letter, Paul reminds Timothy of his rich spiritual heritage and the need to center his attention on the truth that Paul himself taught. False teachers surround the church, upsetting many and harming the whole community. Jewish legalists are trying to divide the believers; Gentile pagans are introducing immorality into the church fellowships; Rome is seeking to destroy their leaders. Timothy is Paul's last and best hope to counter their negative influences. To protect the church, the young leader must avoid their deceptions, follow Paul's example, and be ready to pass the faith along to the next generation of faithful witnesses.

1 Paul, an emissary* of Jesus the Anointed *commissioned* by God's will according to the promise of life *found only* in Jesus the Anointed, ²to *you,* my dear child Timothy.

May grace, mercy, and peace from God our Father and our Lord Jesus the Anointed be yours.

³-⁴*Timothy,* you are constantly in my prayers. Day and night I remember you before God and give thanks to Him whom I serve with a clean conscience, as did my ancestors. I really want to see you, especially when I remember how you cried *the last time we were together.* Yes, I know it would make me joyful *to see you again.* ⁵What strikes me most is how *natural and* sincere your faith is. I am convinced that the same faith that dwelt in your grandmother, Lois, and your mother, Eunice, abides in you as well. ⁶This is why I *write to* remind you to stir up the gift of God that *was conveyed* to you when I laid my hands upon you. ⁷You see, God did not give us a cowardly spirit but a powerful, loving, and disciplined spirit.

God's gift of faith is like a flame, and when the embers of the fire have cooled you must fan them again and keep them ablaze.

⁸So don't be embarrassed to testify about our Lord or for me, His prisoner. Join us in suffering for the good news by the *strength and* power of God. ⁹God has *already* saved us and called us to this holy calling—not because of any good works we may have done, but because of His own intention and because eons and eons ago (*before time itself existed*), He gave us this grace in Jesus the Anointed, *the Liberating King.* ¹⁰And now, *the time has come!* That grace was revealed when our Savior, Jesus the Anointed, appeared; and *through His resurrection* He has wiped out death and brought to light life and immortality by way of this good news. ¹¹I was appointed a preacher, emissary,* and teacher of this message. ¹²This is exactly why I am suffering. But I am not ashamed because I know Him and I have put my trust in Him. And I am fully certain that He has the ability to protect what I have placed in His care until that day. ¹³Remember the words that you heard from me. Retain them as the model for *healthy and* sound teaching in the faith and love that are *available* in Jesus the Anointed. ¹⁴*As for* the precious thing entrusted to you,

protect it with the help of the Holy Spirit who dwells within us.

V

Paul singles out several individuals in this letter, some for praise, others for harsh criticism. Timothy is an example of one who stayed true to Jesus and His emissary, the imprisoned Paul. Later Paul mentions Hymenaeus and Philetus as victims of a cancer within the church who have turned from the truth. Demas, too, is drawn into the attractions of the world, while Alexander the coppersmith opposes their message. With so many who have abandoned and opposed Paul, it's refreshing to hear of Onesiphorus, who—against all odds—has stayed true to Paul and often visits him in prison to keep up his spirits. Clearly the message is that many may fall away, but a few will continue to be strong for the Lord.

¹⁵You may know *by now* that all those in Asia have turned their backs on me, including Phygelus and Hermogenes. ¹⁶-¹⁷But Onesiphorus was not ashamed of my chains. So when he arrived in Rome, he searched for me and found me. May the Lord show mercy to his house because he has often *stopped by to* refresh my *weary* soul. ¹⁸And may the Lord shower him with divine mercy on the last day. You are well aware of all he did to serve me in Ephesus.

2 But as for you, my child, be empowered by the grace that is in Jesus, the Anointed One. ²Whatever you heard me teach before an audience of witnesses, I want you to pass along to trustworthy people who have the ability to teach others too. ³As a good soldier of Jesus the Anointed, *be ready to* suffer with me. ⁴*Remember that* soldiers on active duty don't get wrapped up in civilian matters because they want to satisfy those who recruited them. ⁵*Look at it another way*: if someone competes as an athlete, he won't *win the race and* be crowned with the wreath if he breaks the rules. ⁶And

* 1:1 Literally, apostle   * 1:11 Literally, apostle

the farmer who exhausts himself *in the field* should be the first to taste his harvest. [7]Think about what I am telling you, and let the Lord give you clarity on all of it.

Paul has mentored no one more privately and successfully than Timothy. Now he charges Timothy to pass the faith along to the next generation. Training leaders is priority one.

[8]Remember Jesus the Anointed, raised from the dead, descended from David's *royal* line. This is *the crux of* my good news! [9]This is why I suffer and why I am *bound and* chained like a lawbreaker. But God's word is not in chains! [10]That's why I endure everything for the sake of God's chosen: so that they might experience salvation with lasting, eternal glory through Jesus the Anointed, *our Liberating King.* [11]Here's a statement you can trust:

If we died with Him,
  we will live with Him.
[12]If we remain *with Him,*
  we will reign alongside Him.
If we deny Him,
  we will be denied by Him.
[13]If we are unfaithful,
  He remains faithful,
For He is not able to deny Himself.

[14]Remind others about these things *that I'm telling you.* Warn them before God to stop their useless bickering over words. *After all, splitting hairs* does no good; it only ruins those *forced to* listen *to their meritless arguments.* [15]Timothy, do everything you can to present yourself to God as *a man who is fully* genuine, a worker unashamed *of your mission,* a guide capable of leading others *along the correct path defined* by the word of truth. [16]Stay away from ungodly babbling because it will only lead deeper into a godless lifestyle. [17]Once these empty voices start to speak, *Timothy,* they infect and spread; and soon the body is consumed with its cancer.* Hymenaeus and Philetus fell victim to it, [18]and they walked away from the truth by claiming that the day of resurrection has already arrived. They are clearly disrupting the faith of some *who are not well grounded.* [19]Regardless *of what they do or say,* God's foundation is strong and firmly in place, etched with this seal: "The

Lord knows the ones who belong to Him,"* and, "Everyone who invokes the name of the Lord ought to stop doing what they know to be wrong."

[20]*Look,* in the mansions *of the rich and powerful* you will find everything from silver and gold serving bowls to wooden containers and clay jars; some are used for special occasions—*where honor is important*—others are used for more mundane tasks. [21]So *tell them,* if they will clean up their lives and purify themselves from dishonorable teachings *that lead people astray,* then they can become honorable vessels, consecrated and useful to the Master, made ready for every good work *He has in store.*

[22]*Timothy,* run away from youthful desires. Instead, *direct your passion to* chasing after righteousness, faithfulness, love, and peace, along with those who call upon the Lord with pure hearts. [23]Excuse yourself from any *conversations that turn into* foolish and uninformed debates because you know they only provoke fights. [24]As the Lord's slave, you shouldn't *exhaust yourself in* bickering; instead, be gentle—no matter who you are dealing with—*ready and* able to teach, tolerant without resentment, [25]gently instructing those who stand up against you. Besides, the time may come when God grants them a change of heart* so that they can arrive at the full knowledge of truth. [26]And if they come to their senses, they can escape the devil's snare and walk freed from his captivity and evil bidding.

3 And know this: in the last days, times will be hard. [2]You see, the world will be filled with narcissistic, money-grubbing, pretentious, arrogant, and abusive people. They will rebel against their parents and will be ungrateful, unholy, [3]uncaring, coldhearted, accusing, without restraint, savage, and haters of anything good. [4]*Expect them to be* treacherous, reckless, swollen with self-importance, and given to loving pleasure more than they love God. [5]Even though they may look or act like godly people, they're not. They deny His power. *I tell you:* Stay away from the likes of these. [6]They're *snakes* slithering into the houses of vulnerable women, women gaudy with sin, to seduce them. *These reptiles can* capture them because these women are weak and

* 2:17 Literally, gangrene   * 2:19 Numbers 16:5   * 2:25 Literally, repentance easily swayed by their desires. [7]They seem always to be learning, but they never seem to gain the full measure of the truth. [8]And, just as Jannes and Jambres rose up against Moses,* these *ungodly* people defy the truth. Their minds are corrupt, and their faith is *absolutely* worthless. [9]But they won't get too far because their stupidity will be noticed by everyone, just as it was with Jannes and Jambres.

> V
>
> Paul challenges Timothy to be prepared. Hard times are coming. Things will go from bad to worse, he warns, because pretentious, hostile, hateful, and betraying people are out there. He tells Timothy to stay away from them and to continue to look to Paul's example, enduring in love and recalling how Paul himself has followed Jesus. For if Jesus was persecuted, then what should His followers expect for themselves? In the midst of this warning, Paul encourages Timothy.

[10]*You have been a good student.* You have closely observed how I have lived. You've followed my instructions, my habits, my purpose, my faith, my patience. You've watched how I love and have seen how I endure. *You have been with me* [11]through persecutions and sufferings—remember what they did to me in Antioch? in Iconium and Lystra? I endured all of it, and the Lord rescued me from it all! [12]Anyone wishing to live a godly life in Jesus the Anointed will be *hunted down and* persecuted. [13]But as for the wicked and the imposters, they will keep leading and following each other further and further away from the truth. [14]So surely you ought to stick to what you know is certain. All you have learned comes from people you know and trust [15]because since childhood you have known the holy Scriptures, which enable you to be wise *and lead* to salvation through faith in Jesus the Anointed. [16]All of Scripture is God-breathed; *in its* inspired *voice, we hear* useful teaching, rebuke, correction, instruction, *and* training for a life that is right [17]so that God's people may be up to the task ahead and have all they need to accomplish every good work.

[4] *And now* I bring you this charge before God and Jesus the Anointed, the one *destined* to judge the living and the dead, at His *glorious* appearance and His kingdom: [2]*go out and* preach the word! Go whether it's an opportune time or not! Reprove, warn, and encourage; *but do so* with all the patience and instruction *needed to fulfill your calling* [3]because a time will come when some will no longer tolerate sound teaching. Instead, they will live by their own desires; they'll scratch their itching ears by surrounding themselves with teachers who *approve of their lifestyles and* tell them what they want to hear. [4]They will turn away from the real truth *you have to offer* because they prefer the sound of *fables and* myths. [5]But you *must stay focused and* be alert at all times. Tolerate suffering. Accomplish the *good* work of an evangelist, and complete the ministry to which you have been called.

> Paul's message: stay focused, suffer hardships, be confident, do the work. The church has always progressed by faithfulness of her saints.

[6]For I am already being poured out, *and the last drops* of this drink offering *are all that remain*; it's almost time for me to leave. [7]I have fought the good fight, I have *stayed on course and* finished the race, and *through it all,* I have kept believing. [8]I look forward to what's in store for me: a crown of righteousness that the Lord—the always right *and just* judge—will give me that day (but it is not only for me, but for all those who love *and long for* His appearing).

[9]Come to me, *Timothy,* as soon as you can. [10]You see, Demas has fallen for this world, abandoned me, and headed off to Thessalonica. Crescens took off for Galatia. Titus has gone to Dalmatia. [11]Luke is the only one left. Bring Mark with you because he is useful in this work and will help look after me. [12]I sent Tychicus to Ephesus. [13]On your way here, pick up the cloak I left with Carpus in Troas, and bring the scrolls—especially the parchments.

[14]*Keep your eye out for* Alexander the coppersmith! He came against me with all sorts of evil—may the Lord pay him back accordingly—[15]so watch your back because

* 3:8 Exodus 7:11,22

he has gone overboard to oppose our message.

16*When it was time* for my first defense, no one showed up to support me. Everyone abandoned me (may it not be held against them) 17except the Lord. He stood by me, strengthened me, and backed the truth I proclaimed with power so it may be heard by all the non-Jews. He rescued me, pried open the lion's jaw, *and snatched me from its teeth.* 18And *I know* the Lord will continue to rescue me from every *trip, trap, snare, and pitfall of* evil and carry me safely to His heavenly kingdom. May He be glorified throughout eternity. Amen.

19Give my regards to Prisca, Aquila, and everyone over at Onesiphorus's house. 20Erastus stayed in Corinth, and I left Trophimus in Miletus because he was sick. 21Try your best to come before winter blows in. Eubulus says hello and so do Pudens, Linus, Claudia, and all the brothers and sisters. 22May the Lord be with your spirit, and may His grace be with you. [Amen.]*

* 4:22 The earliest manuscripts omit this word.

TITUS

Personal letter to Titus

From Paul, the apostle to the Gentiles

Titus was a young coworker with Paul, a part of the emissary's mission team as he planted churches in Asia Minor and Greece. Because of his affection for and trust in Titus, whom Paul described as his "dear son birthed through our shared faith," Paul often delegated to Titus sensitive and difficult situations. One such situation was in Crete, an island in the Mediterranean with a reputation for dishonesty and thievery that was a haven for pirates. We can infer from this letter that the church on Crete was in its infancy and needed to be taught the basics about church leadership and foundational doctrine. The primary message of this letter is that good works come from sound doctrine, the shared faith of believers, and the resulting character that reflects a life lived serving God. In spite of the serious nature of the subject matter and the Cretans' situation, Paul managed to convey his teachings on leadership, sound teaching, and church order in a warm, conversational style.

Titus is the only book in Scripture where Jesus is specifically addressed as "our great God and Savior, Jesus the Anointed." Three times God is identified as the source of salvation, and three times Jesus is referred to as the instrument of salvation. It is one of the few places where the role that each Person in the Trinity has in salvation is isolated: "God our Savior . . . came to save us . . . made us completely new through the Holy Spirit . . . through Jesus the Anointed."

Paul makes it abundantly clear that we are each in need of redemption, but we cannot achieve it by anything that we do on our own. Rather, it is the work that only God can do that brings us salvation. Then Paul comes back and commands Titus to remind believers to "be constant in doing the right things." The last imperative in the book is for all believers to learn to "do what is good."

Paul trusted Titus to appoint elders, to sort out unfinished business, and to set a good example for everyone; the future of the church on Crete rested on Titus's shoulders. In this personal look into the work of a young church planter, we find courage, wisdom, and a zeal for serving God. We see what Jesus was looking for when He called a few to follow Him. Here in Titus we find what a truly devoted follower of Jesus looks like.

1 Paul, servant of God and emissary* of Jesus, the Anointed One, on behalf of the faith *that is accepted* by God's chosen people and the knowledge of the *undeniable* truth that leads to godliness.

V

Paul is ready to defend the truth. He knows it is pure and honorable. He knows that it comes from and leads back to God. In contrast, Paul perceives the constant threat of false teaching that produces chaos, overturns entire families, and is filled with myths and instructions taught by those outside the faith. This counter-truth is filled with lusts and passions that tear down others, and it results in petty debates over family trees with fights and disagreements over the law. The line is clearly drawn between them. Paul leaves no room to sit on the fence; there is no partial truth—the future of the church is at stake.

---

²*We rest in this hope we've been given*—the hope that we will live forever with our God—*the hope that* He proclaimed *ages and* ages ago (even before time began). And our God *is no liar; He* is not even capable of uttering lies. ³*So we can be sure that* it is in His exact right time that He released His word *into the world*—through the preaching that God our Savior has commanded into my care.

His word brings into the world the absolute clarity of God's perspective and life-saving knowledge.

⁴To you, Titus, my dear son birthed through our shared faith: may grace and peace rest upon you from God the Father and Jesus the Anointed, our Savior.

⁵I left you on Crete so you could sort out the chaos and the unfinished business and appoint elders *over communities* in each and every city according to my earlier orders. ⁶*Here's what you should look for in an elder:* he should be above suspicion; *if he is married, he should* be the husband of one wife, raise children who believe, and be a person who can't be accused of rough and raucous

living. ⁷It is necessary that any overseer *you appoint* be blameless, as he is entrusted with God's mission. *Look for someone who* isn't pompous or quick to anger, who is not a drunkard, violent, or chasing after seedy gain *or worldly fame.* ⁸*Find a person who* lovingly opens his home to others; who honors goodness; who is thoughtful, fair, devout, self-controlled; and ⁹who clings to the faithful word that was taught because he must be able, not only to encourage people with sound teaching, but also to challenge those who are against it.

¹⁰You see antagonists everywhere; they are rebellious, loose-lipped, and deceitful (especially those who are from the circumcised lot). ¹¹*Their talk must be quashed*—their mouths sealed up because impure teaching is *flying out of their lips and* overturning entire families for the sake of their own squalid gain. ¹²*I'll tell you,* even their own prophet was heard saying, "Chronic liars, foul beasts, and lazy gluttons—that's who you'll meet in Crete." ¹³And he's right! This is why we have to scold them, sometimes severely, so they will be sound in the faith ¹⁴and be able to ignore Jewish myths as well as any commandments given by those who turn away from the truth.

¹⁵*Listen:* to those who are pure, all things are pure. But to those who are tainted, *stained,* and unbelieving, nothing is pure because their minds and their consciences are polluted. ¹⁶They claim, "I know God," but their actions are a slap to His face. They are wretched, disobedient, and useless to any worthwhile cause.

2 As to you, *Titus:* talk to them; give them a good, healthy diet of solid teaching *so they will know the right way to live.* ²*Here's what I want you to* teach the older men: enjoy everything in moderation, respect yourselves *and others,* be sensible, and dedicate yourselves to *living an unbroken* faith demonstrated by your love and perseverance.

³*And here's what I want you to* teach the older women: Be respectful. Steer clear of gossip or drinking too much so that you can teach what is good ⁴to young women. *Be a positive example,* showing them what it is to love their husbands and children, and teaching them to ⁵control themselves *in every way* and to be pure. *Train them* to manage the

household, to be kind, and to be submissive to their husbands, all of which honor the word of God.

[6]Encourage the young men in the same way: *in every situation,* they should learn to control themselves.

[7-8]*Titus, you have to* set a good example for everyone. Go out of your way to do what is right, speak the truth with the weight and authority that come from an honest and pure life. No one can argue with that. Then your enemies will cower in shame because they have nothing bad to say against us.

[9]Advise all the servants: Work hard for your masters, and be loyal to them. Strive to please. Don't be rude or sarcastic. [10]Don't steal or embezzle *your masters' property.* Show them you are trustworthy, and all the credit will go to the teaching of God our Savior.

[11]*We have cause to celebrate* because the grace of God has appeared, offering *the gift of* salvation to all people. [12]*Grace arrives* with its own instruction: run away from anything that leads us away from God; abandon the lusts and passions of this world; live life now in this age *with awareness* and self-control, doing the right thing and keeping yourselves holy. [13]*Watch for His return;* expect the blessed hope *we all will share* when our great God and Savior, Jesus the Anointed, appears again. [14]He gave His body for our sakes and will not only break us free from *the chains of* wickedness, but He will also prepare a community uncorrupted by the world that He would call His own—people who are passionate about doing the right thing.

V

At times Paul can be unrelenting. As he challenged Timothy in the two letters he addressed to him, Paul also challenges Titus to live the truth he teaches. People are drawn toward God, not through bold arguments, but by passionate godliness. We must be passionate about doing the right thing. Our actions tell the story. Our lives are living parables, shouting the mystery of godliness. Paul tells Titus to be bold, to teach with authority, and not to let anyone belittle him. We get a clear picture of a strong, courageous giant of a man. Titus is sent to the people of Crete—

a people short on virtue and long on vice—to fashion a church of loving disciples.

---

[15]*So, Titus,* tell them all these things. Encourage and teach them with all authority—and rebuke them with the same. *You are a man called to serve, so* don't let anyone belittle you.

3 And remind them of this: respect the rulers and the courts. Obey them. Be ready to do what is good and honorable. [2]Don't tear down another person with your words. Instead, keep the peace, and be considerate. Be truly humble toward everyone [3]because there was a time when we, too, were foolish, rebellious, and deceived—we were slaves to sensual cravings and pleasures; and we spent our lives being spiteful, envious, hated by many, and hating one another. [4]But then *something happened:* God our Savior and His overpowering love and kindness for humankind entered our world; [5]He came to save us. It's not that *we earned it* by doing good works or righteous deeds; He came because He is merciful. He brought us *out of our old ways of living* to a new beginning through the washing of regeneration; and He made us completely new through the Holy Spirit, [6]who was poured out in abundance through Jesus the Anointed, our Savior. [7]*All of this happened* so that through His grace we would be accepted *into God's covenant family* and appointed to be His heirs, full of the hope that comes from *knowing you have* eternal life. [8]This is a faithful statement *of what we believe.*

Concerning this, I want you to put it out there boldly so that those who believe in God will be constant in doing the right things, which will benefit all of us. [9]*Listen,* don't get trapped in brainless debates; avoid competition over family trees *or pedigrees;* stay away from fights and disagreements over the law. They are a waste of your time. [10]If a person is causing divisions *in the community,* warn him once; and if necessary, warn him twice. After that, avoid him completely [11]because by then you are sure that you are dealing with a corrupt, sinful person. He is determined to condemn himself.

A problem ignored is a growing problem. Paul's advice: deal with it.

Don't ignore division. For the church to be strong and honor God, the church is to be one.

[12]I am sending either Artemas or Tychicus to you. When one of them arrives, try your best to make your way to me at Nicopolis (I plan to spend the winter there). [13]Do what you can to get Zenas (the lawyer) and Apollos on their way; make sure they have everything they need. [14]Our people must learn to get involved when a need arises, particularly when the need is urgent. Teach them to do what is good so they won't become unproductive *members of the community.*

[15]Everyone with me sends his greetings. Greet all our friends in the faith. May grace be with all of you. [Amen.]*

* 3:15 Some manuscripts omit this word.

PHILEMON

Personal letter to Philemon of Colossae

From Paul, the apostle to the Gentiles

There's a story behind every letter Paul writes, and this is an especially vivid one. While Paul is in prison, he writes to his friend Philemon, a Christian leader in Colossae, about this man's slave Onesimus. Philemon is apparently a well-to-do follower of Jesus, having a house large enough for a church to gather there. He has a good reputation as a man of faith and love. Somewhere he met Paul, and they became good friends and coworkers in Kingdom causes. Onesimus is Philemon's slave who encounters Paul in prison—tradition says that Onesimus is a runaway slave who happens to meet Paul when he is under house arrest—and becomes a believer. For a time, the Lord's imprisoned emissary finds Onesimus to be a useful assistant; but eventually he sends Onesimus back to Philemon with an appeal rather than a command: Paul asks Philemon to receive Onesimus back as more than a slave—as a beloved brother.

Surprisingly, Paul addresses this letter to Philemon and the entire church that gathers in his home. What seems at first to be a private letter is meant for public reading. Perhaps Paul hopes to bring a bit of social pressure on Philemon, or perhaps Paul wants to address the issue of slave treatment to all Christian slave owners. Paul uses the story of the runaway slave to discuss the larger issues of forgiveness and equality. In the kingdom of God, all relationships must exhibit forgiveness and acceptance of each other; and everyone is an equal participant in salvation, regardless of his or her station in life. The history of humankind is stained by the guilt and pain of slavery. May the words of Paul the emissary echo into modern culture so that believers treat all human beings as brothers and sisters in Jesus.

¹Paul, a prisoner of Jesus the Anointed One, with our brother Timothy, to you, beloved Philemon, our fellow worker; and ²to Apphia our sister, to Archippus our fellow soldier, and to the church that gathers in your house. ³May grace and peace from God our Father and the Lord Jesus the Anointed surround you.

⁴I am constantly thanking God for you in my prayers ⁵because I keep hearing about your love and faith toward our Lord Jesus and all those set apart for His purposes. *Here's what I've been praying on your behalf:*

> ⁶*Thank You, Father, for Philemon.* I pray that as he goes and tells his story of faith, *he would tell everyone so that* they will know for certain all the good that comes *to those who put their trust* in the Anointed One.

⁷My brother, because you are out there encouraging and reviving the hearts of fellow saints with such love, this brings great joy and comfort to me.

⁸Although I am bold enough in the Anointed, *our Liberating King,* to insist you do the right thing, ⁹instead I choose to appeal to you on account of love. I do this for my own sake since I, Paul, am an old man and am held prisoner because of *my service to* Jesus the Anointed. ¹⁰I make this request on behalf of my child, Onesimus,* whom I brought to faith during my time in prison. ¹¹Before, he was useless to you; but now he is useful to both you and me. ¹²Listen, I am sending my heart back to you as I send him to stand before you, *although truly* ¹³I wished to keep him at my side to take your place as my helper while I am bound for the good news. ¹⁴But I didn't want to make this decision without *asking for* your permission.

This way, any goodwill on your part wouldn't be *seen as* forced, but as your *true and* free desire.

¹⁵Maybe this is the reason why he was supposed to be away from you for this time: so that now you will have him back forever— ¹⁶no longer as a slave, but as more than a slave—as a dear brother. Yes, he is dear to me, but I suspect he will come to mean even more to you, both in the flesh *as a servant* and in the Lord *as a brother.*

The gospel is a powerful social force for good, capable of making rich and poor, slave and free into beloved brothers.

¹⁷So if you look upon me as your partner *in this mission,* then I ask you to open your heart to him as you would welcome me. ¹⁸And if he has wronged you or owes you anything, charge it to me. ¹⁹*Look,* I'll put it here in my own handwriting: I, Paul, promise to repay you everything. (Should I remind you that you owe me your life?) ²⁰Indeed, brother, I want you to do me this favor out of obedience to our Lord. It will refresh my heart in Him. ²¹This letter comes, written with the confidence that you will not only do what I ask, but will also go beyond all I have asked.

²²One more thing: you should get a room ready for me as I hope to be released to you soon in answer to your prayers. ²³Epaphras (my fellow prisoner in Jesus, the Anointed One) greets you, ²⁴as well as my fellow workers Mark, Aristarchus, Demas, and Luke.

²⁵May the grace of the Lord Jesus the Anointed be with your spirit. [Amen.]*

* Verse 10 Literally, useful one   * Verse 25 Some early manuscripts omit this word.

HEBREWS

Instruction to Jewish believers

From a leader in the early church

This letter is addressed to Christian believers of Jewish descent in the last half of the first century A.D. Possibly the original audience lived in Rome, since it was written by an unknown leader residing in Italy. For years it was thought that Paul wrote it, but the letter lacks his typical letter-writing features. Still, the themes of the letter, its style, and the reference to Timothy (13:23) suggest that Hebrews comes from somewhere within Paul's circle of friends and coworkers. Because of its tone and structure, some have wondered whether this magnificent epistle may have originally been a sermon that was written down and later circulated as a letter. As Origen said, only God knows who wrote it.

The Jewish Christians faced severe persecution, so severe that some were ready to abandon the faith. The frequent warnings that punctuate the letter indicate that the danger of drifting away is real and imminent. So the author pulls out every argument he can think of to persuade them not to drift away from Jesus. Throughout the letter, he compares the person and work of Jesus to the institutions of the Jewish faith. It may well be that those who are in danger of walking away from faith in Him are going back to their Jewish roots. While it is clear that the writer has appreciation for the Hebrew prophets, the mediation of heavenly messengers, Moses, Joshua, the priesthood, and the temple, he argues that in every way the new covenant brought by Jesus is better than, more than, greater than the old covenant.

Throughout the letter, the author appeals to Scripture itself to demonstrate how Jesus fulfills the Old Testament promises. At the heart of the letter, he presents Jesus as the Great High Priest, offering Himself as the perfect sacrifice once and for all. Although Jesus' death as a sacrifice is discussed in other New Testament writings, it is central in Hebrews. Further, according to this author, all the earlier promises of God are concentrated in His person and work, particularly in His work on the cross. Jeremiah prophesies that God will one day establish a new covenant, creating a permanent relationship with people of faith and erasing completely the guilt of their sins. As a fulfillment of the earlier promises, God's work in reconciling the world through Him is not a temporary measure because Jesus is the final, full, definitive revelation of God.

1 Long ago, at different times and in various ways, God's voice came to our ancestors through the *Hebrew* prophets. [2]But in these last days, it has come to us through His Son, the One who has been given dominion over all things and through whom all worlds were made.

[3]This is the One who—imprinted with God's image, shimmering with His glory—sustains all that exists through the power of His word. He was seated at the right hand of God once He Himself had made the offering that purified *us from* all our sins. [4]This Son of God is elevated as far above the heavenly messengers as His holy name is elevated above theirs.

V

Most images of angels are influenced by art and pop culture—and are far removed from the Bible. The word "angel" literally means "messenger," and it can refer to either a human being or a heavenly being. The Hebrews author is writing about heavenly messengers.

In the Bible, heavenly messengers have several functions—executors of God's judgment, guardians of God's people, heralds of God's plans. They appear at critical moments to chosen people who play important roles in God's salvation, such as arriving to announce the birth and resurrection of Jesus and to transmit God's law to Moses. They are no more than messengers, created beings, who serve the will of God and His Son. Recognizing their place, they bow before the Son in loving adoration.

---

[5]For no heavenly messengers have ever heard God address them with these words *of the psalms*:

You are My Son.
Today I have become Your Father.*

Or *heard Him promise*,

I will be to You a Father,
and You will be My Son.*

[6]Now, when the Son, the firstborn *of God*, was brought into the world, God said,

Let all My heavenly messengers worship Him.*

[7]Concerning the heavenly messengers, God said,

I make My heavenly messengers like the winds,
and My servants like a flame.*

[8]But to the Son He said,

God, Your throne is eternal;
You will rule Your kingdom with the scepter of justice.
[9]You have loved what is right
and hated what is evil;
That is why God, Your God, has anointed You
with the oil of gladness and lifted You above Your companions.*

[10]And *God continues*,

In the beginning, You, Lord, laid the foundation of the earth
and set the skies above us with Your own hands.
[11]*But while* they will someday pass away,
You remain *forever*;
when they wear out like old clothes,
[12]You will roll them up
and change them into something new.
But You will never change;
Your years will never come to an end.*

[13]Did God ever say to any of the heavenly messengers,

Sit here, at My right hand, *in the seat of honor*;
and I'll put all Your enemies under Your feet?*

[14]*No, of course not.* The heavenly messengers are only spirits and servants, sent out to minister to those who will certainly inherit salvation.

2 That is why we ought to pay even closer attention to the voice that has been speaking so that we will never drift away from it. [2]For if the words *of instruction and inspiration* brought by

* 1:5 Psalm 2:7   * 1:5 2 Samuel 7:14   * 1:6 Deuteronomy 32:43
(Septuagint and DSS only)   * 1:7 Psalm 104:4   * 1:8-9 Psalm 45:6-7
* 1:10-12 Psalm 102:25-27   * 1:13 Psalm 110:1

heaven's messengers were valid, and *if we live in a universe where* sin and disobedience receive their just rewards, ³then how will we escape *destruction* if we ignore this great salvation? We heard it first from our Lord Jesus, then from those who passed on His teaching. ⁴God also testifies to this truth by signs and wonders and miracles and the gifts of the Holy Spirit lighting on those He chooses.

V

This letter is punctuated with passages that sound an alarm: danger, both imminent and eternal, is at hand. The real danger is the gentle erosion of rock-solid commitments.

How often it happens! A person makes a decision to follow Jesus. He practically explodes with joy. Then life happens and the invisible forces that shape culture in our world—the idols of consumerism, relativism, and materialism—begin their exacting work to shape us into an image that no longer reflects our Savior. Over and over again, the writer warns us to be careful. Don't neglect this great salvation. Make sure the anchor holds.

---

⁵Now clearly God didn't set up the heavenly messengers *to bring the final word or* to rule over the world that is coming. ⁶I have read something somewhere:

> I can't help but wonder why You care
> about mortals
> or choose to love the son of man.
> ⁷⁻⁸Though he was born below the heavenly
> messengers,
> You honored the son of man like
> royalty,
> crowning him with glory and honor,
> Raising him above all earthly things,
> placing everything under his feet.*

When God placed everything under the son of man, He didn't leave out anything. Maybe we don't see all that happening yet; ⁹but what we do see is Jesus, born a little lower than the heavenly messengers, who is now crowned with glory and honor because He *willingly* suffered and died. *And He did that*

so that through God's grace, He might taste death on behalf of everyone.

Here is God's Son: Creator, Sustainer, Great High Priest. Jesus has to take on our feeble flesh and suffer a violent death. He suffers for what we need.

¹⁰It only makes sense that God, by whom and for whom everything exists, would choose to bring many of us to His side by using suffering to perfect Jesus, *the founder of our faith,* the pioneer of our salvation. ¹¹*As I will show you,* it's important that the One who brings us to God and those who are brought to God become one, *since we are all from one Father.* This is why Jesus was not ashamed to call us His family, ¹²saying, *in the words of the psalmist,*

> I will speak Your Name to My brothers
> and sisters
> when I praise You in the midst of the
> community.*

¹³And *in the words of Isaiah,*

> I will wait for the Eternal One.*

And again,

> Look, here I am with the children God
> has given Me.*

¹⁴Since we, the children, are all creatures of flesh and blood, Jesus took on flesh and blood, so that by dying He could destroy the one who held power over death—the devil—¹⁵and destroy the fear of death that has always held people captive. ¹⁶So notice—His concern here is not for the welfare of the heavenly messengers, but for the children of Abraham. ¹⁷He had to become as human as His sisters and brothers *so that when the time came,* He could become a merciful and faithful high priest of God, called to reconcile a sinful people. ¹⁸Since He has also been tested by suffering, He can help us when we are tested.

3 So all of you who are holy partners in a heavenly calling, let's turn our attention to Jesus, the Emissary *of God* and High Priest, who brought us the faith we profess; ²and compare Him to Moses, *who*

* 2:6-8 Psalm 8:4-6 * 2:12 Psalm 22:22 * 2:13 Isaiah 8:17
* 2:13 Isaiah 8:18

also brought words from God. Both of them were faithful to their missions, to the One who called them. ³But we value Jesus more than Moses, in the same way that we value a builder more than the house he builds. ⁴Every house is built by someone, but the builder of all things is God. ⁵Moses *brought healing and redemption to his people* as a faithful servant in God's house, and he was a witness to the things that would be spoken later. ⁶But *Jesus* the Anointed was faithful as a Son of that house. (We become that house, if we're able to hold on to the confident hope we have *in God* until the end.)

For the first-century Jewish-Christian audience, Moses is the rescuer of Hebrew slaves out of bondage in Egypt—the receiver of God's law and the covenant. They remember how he shepherded the children of Israel safely through the desert for 40 years and led them to the brink of the promised land. He was indeed a remarkable man. Yet what Jesus has accomplished for everyone—not just the Jews—is on a totally different level. Moses was indeed faithful to God and accomplished a great deal as God's servant. Jesus, too, is faithful to God, but He has accomplished what Moses could not because He is God's very own Son.

⁷Listen now, to the voice of the Holy Spirit *through what the psalmist wrote:*

Today, if you listen to His voice,
⁸Don't harden your hearts the way they did
in the bitter uprising *at Meribah*
⁹Where your ancestors tested Me
though they had seen My marvelous
power.
¹⁰For the 40 years *they traveled on*
to the land that I had promised them,
That generation *broke My heart.*
Grieving and angry, I said, "Their hearts
are unfaithful;
they don't know what I want from
them."
¹¹That is why I swore in anger
they would never enter *salvation's*
rest.*

¹²Brothers and sisters, pay close attention so you won't develop an evil and unbelieving heart that causes you to abandon the living God. ¹³Encourage each other every day—for as long as we can still say "today"—so none of you let the deceitfulness of sin harden your hearts. ¹⁴For we have become partners with the Anointed One—if we can just hold on to our confidence until the end.

¹⁵Look at the lines *from the psalm* again:

Today, if you listen to His voice,
Don't harden your hearts the way they did
in the bitter uprising *at Meribah*.

¹⁶Now who, *exactly, was God talking to then?* Who heard and rebelled? Wasn't it all of those whom Moses led out of Egypt? ¹⁷And who made God angry for an entire generation? Wasn't it those who sinned *against Him*, those whose bodies are still buried in the wilderness, *the site of that uprising?* ¹⁸It was those disobedient ones who God swore would never enter into salvation's rest. ¹⁹And we can see that they couldn't enter because they did not believe.

4 That's why, as long as that promise of entering God's rest remains open to us, we should be careful that none of us seem to fall short ourselves. ²Those people in the wilderness heard *God's* good news, just as we have heard it, but the message they heard didn't do them any good since it wasn't combined with faith. ³We who believe are entering into salvation's rest, as He said,

That is why I swore in anger
they would never enter *salvation's*
rest,*

even though God's works were finished from the very creation of the world. ⁴(For didn't God say that on the seventh day *of creation* He rested from all His works?* ⁵And doesn't God say in the psalm that they would never enter into *salvation's* rest?*)

There is much discussion of "rest" in what we are calling the First Testament of Scripture. God rests on the seventh day after creation. In the Ten Commandments God

* 3:7-11 Psalm 95:7-11   * 4:3 Psalm 95:11   * 4:4 Genesis 2:2
* 4:5 Psalm 95:11

commands His people to remember the Sabbath day, keep it holy, and do no work. By letting go of daily work, they declared their absolute dependence on God to meet their needs. We do not live by the work of our hands, but by the bread and Word that God supplies.

But a greater rest is yet to come when we will be released from all suffering, and when we will inherit the earth. Jesus embodies this greater rest that still awaits the people of God, a people fashioned through obedience and faith. If some of us fail to enter that rest, it is because we fail to answer the call.

---

[6]So *if God prepared a place of rest, and* those who were given the good news didn't enter because they chose disobedience *over faith,* then it remains open for us to enter. [7]Once again, God has fixed a day; and that day is "today," as David said so much later when he wrote *in the psalm* quoted earlier:

Today, if you listen to His voice,
Don't harden your hearts.*

[8]Now if Joshua had been able to lead those who followed him into God's rest, would God then have spoken this way? [9]There still remains a place of rest, a true Sabbath, for the people of God [10]because those who enter into salvation's rest lay down their labors in the same way that God entered into a Sabbath rest from His.

[11]So let us move forward to enter this rest, so that none of us fall into the kind of faithless disobedience that prevented them from entering. [12]The word of God, *you see,* is alive and moving; sharper than a double-edged sword; piercing the divide between soul and spirit, joints and marrow; able to judge the thoughts and will of the heart. [13]No creature can hide from God: God sees all. Everyone and everything is exposed, opened for His inspection; and He's the One we will have to explain ourselves to.

By God's word, everything finds a rhythm, a place. It fills, empowers, enlivens, and redeems us. But it also divides and destroys. It pierces

and exposes our disobedience and unfaithfulness.

[14]Since we have a great High Priest, Jesus, the Son of God who has passed through the heavens *from death into new life with God,* let us hold tightly to our faith. [15]For Jesus is not some high priest who has no sympathy for our weaknesses *and flaws.* He has already been tested in every way that we are tested; but He emerged victorious, without failing God. [16]So let us step boldly to the throne of grace, where we can find mercy and grace to help when we need it most.

5 *Remember what I said earlier about the role of the high priest,* even the ones chosen by human beings? The job of every high priest is reconciliation: approaching God on behalf of others and offering Him gifts and sacrifices to repair the damage caused by our sins *against God and each other.* [2]The high priest should have compassion for those who are ignorant of the faith and those who fall out of the faith because he also has wrestled with human weakness, [3]and so the priest must offer sacrifices both for his sins and for those of the people. [4]*The office of high priest and* the honor that goes along with it isn't one that someone just takes. One must be set aside, called by God, just as God called Aaron, *the brother of Moses.*

[5]In the same way, the Anointed One, *our Liberating King,* didn't call Himself but was appointed to His priestly office by God, who said to Him,

You are My Son.
Today I have become Your Father,*

[6]and who also says elsewhere,

You are a priest forever—
in the *honored* order of Melchizedek.*

V

Jesus is the Great High Priest because He serves as the ultimate mediator between God and humanity. In this role He serves as both the priest and the sacrifice that atones for sins once and for all. But we are still called to be

* 4:7 Psalm 95:7-8   * 5:5 Psalm 2:7   * 5:6 Psalm 110:4

priests for each other. These are not mutually exclusive ideas.

Whenever you share a cup of cold water in Jesus' name or pray for someone, you're a priest. You're communicating the grace of God. There are times that we need a priest, too, right? If we are to be like Him, we must allow someone else to be a priest for us. There are problems so great and pains so deep and sins so intractable that we need a person of flesh and blood to join us in carrying our concerns to God.

7When Jesus was *on the earth, a man of* flesh *and blood,* He offered up prayers and pleas, groans and tears to the One who could save Him from death. He was heard because He approached God with reverence. 8Although He was a Son, Jesus learned obedience through the things He suffered. 9And once He was perfected *through that suffering* He became the way of eternal salvation for all those who hear and follow Him, 10for God appointed Him to be a High Priest in the order of Melchizedek.

11I have a lot more to say about this, but it may be hard for you to follow since you've become dull in your understanding. 12By this time, you ought to be teachers yourselves, yet I feel like you want me to reteach you the most basic things that God wants you to know. It's almost like you're *a baby again, coddled at your mother's breast,* nursing, not ready for solid food. 13No one who lives on milk alone can know the ins and outs of what it means to be righteous *and pursue justice;* that's because he is only a baby. 14But solid food is for those who have come of age, for those who have learned through practice to distinguish good from evil.

6 So let's push on toward a more perfect understanding and move beyond just the basic teachings of the Anointed One. There's no reason to rehash the fundamentals: repenting from *what you loved in* your old dead lives, believing in God *as our Creator and Redeemer,* 2teaching about baptism,* *setting aside those called to service through the ritual* laying on of hands, the coming resurrection of those who have died, and God's final judgment *of all people for all*

time. 3No, we will move on toward perfection, if God wills it.

V

It's clear that Jesus wanted His people to grow and mature in faith. Those who don't move beyond the basics—tasting the gifts and powers of the new creation, partaking in the Spirit and the word of God—and then fall away bring shame to Jesus and produce nothing but briars and brambles. There is no stagnant life in the Kingdom. Either you grow and produce a blessing or you languish and descend into a curse. Be warned.

4-6It is impossible to restore the changed heart of the one who has fallen from faith—who has already been enlightened, has tasted the gift of new life from God, has shared in the power of the Holy Spirit, and has known the goodness of God's revelation and the powers of the coming age. If such a person falls away, it's as though that one were crucifying the Son of God all over again and holding Him up to ridicule. 7*You see,* God blesses the ground that drinks of the rain and then produces a bountiful crop for those who cultivate it. 8But land that produces nothing but thorns and brambles? That land is worthless and in danger of being cursed, burned to the bare earth.

9But *listen,* my friends—we don't mean to discourage you completely with such talk. We are convinced that you are made for better things, the things of salvation, 10because God is not unjust *or unfair.* He won't overlook the work you have done or the love you have carried to each other in His name while doing His work, as you are still doing. 11We want you all to continue working until the end so that you'll realize the certainty that comes with hope 12and not grow lazy. We want you to walk in the footsteps of the faithful *who came before you,* from whom you can learn to be steadfast in pursuing the promises *of God.*

13Remember when God made His promise to Abraham? He had to swear by Himself, there being no one greater: 14"Surely I will bless you and multiply your

---

* 6:2 Literally, immersion, in a rite of initiation and purification

Melchizedek is perhaps one of the most mysterious figures in Scripture. He appears for the first time in Genesis 14:17-20 as Abraham returns from battle against Chedorlaomer and his allies. The name "Melchizedek" shows up again in Psalm 110, a song of David that is widely used to celebrate the coronation of the Davidic kings in Jerusalem. When God installs His king upon the throne of Jerusalem, He promises to vanquish his enemies and establish him as an eternal priest according to the honored order of Melchizedek.

But who was Melchizedek? Here Jesus is often referred to as "a priest forever in the order of Melchizedek." This mysterious Melchizedek, king of righteousness and peace, is a precursor to the Prince of Peace. In his brief appearances in Genesis and in Psalm 110, he opens a window into the mystery of God and His plan to redeem the world. The tradition about Melchizedek helps the early church understand Jesus' role as priest and king even if He doesn't seem to fit the traditional categories.

descendants."* ¹⁵And after Abraham had endured with patience, he obtained the promise he had hoped for. ¹⁶When swearing an oath to confirm what they are saying, humans swear by someone greater than themselves and so bring their arguments to an end. ¹⁷In the same way, when God wanted to confirm His promise as true and unchangeable, He swore an oath to the heirs of that promise. ¹⁸So God has given us two unchanging things: *His promise and His oath.* These prove that it is impossible for God to lie. As a result, we who come to God for refuge might be encouraged to seize that hope that is set before us. ¹⁹That hope is real and true, an anchor to steady our *restless souls,* a hope that leads us back behind the curtain *to where God is (as the high priests did in the days when reconciliation flowed from sacrifices in the temple)* ²⁰and back into the place where Jesus, who went ahead on our behalf, has entered since He has become a High Priest forever in the order of Melchizedek.

7 In the Book of Genesis, *we read about when* Melchizedek, the king of Salem and priest of the Most High God, met Abraham as he returned from defeating King *Chedorlaomer* and his allies. Melchizedek blessed our ancestor, and ²Abraham gave him a tenth of everything captured in the battle.*

Let's look more closely at Melchizedek. First, his name means "king of righteousness"; and *his title,* king of Salem, means "king of peace." ³The Scriptures don't name his mother or father or descendants, and they don't record his birth or his death. We could say he's like the Son of God: eternal, a priest forever.

⁴And just imagine how great this man was, that even our *great and honorable* patriarch Abraham gave him a tenth of the spoils. ⁵Compare him to the priests *who serve in our temple,* the descendants of Levi, who were given a commandment in the law *of Moses to collect one-tenth of the income of the tribes of Israel.* The priests took that tithe from their own people, even though they were also descended from Abraham. ⁶But this man, *Melchizedek,* who did not belong to that Levite ancestry, collected a tenth part of Abraham's income; and although Abraham had received the promises, it was Melchizedek who blessed Abraham. ⁷Now I don't have to tell you that it is the lesser one who receives a blessing from the greater. ⁸*In the case of the priests descended from Levi,* they are mortal men who receive a tithe *of one-tenth*; but the Scriptures record no death of *Melchizedek,* the one who received Abraham's tithe. ⁹I guess you could even say that Levi, who receives our tithes, originally paid tithes through Abraham ¹⁰because he was still unborn and only a part of his ancestor when Abraham met Melchizedek.

So Melchizedek must be considered superior even to the patriarch Abraham.

¹¹If a perfect method *of reconciling with God*—a perfect priesthood—had been found in the sons of Levi (a priesthood that communicated God's law to the people), then why *would the Scriptures* speak of another priest, a priest according to the order of Melchizedek, instead of, say, from the order of Aaron? What would be the need for it?

* 6:14 Genesis 22:17 * 7:2 Genesis 14:17-20

It would reflect a new way of relating to God [12]because when there is a change in the priesthood there must be a corresponding change in the law as well. [13]We're talking about someone who comes from another tribe, from which no member has ever served at God's altar. [14]It's clear that *Jesus,* our Lord, descended from the tribe of Judah; but Moses never spoke about priests from that tribe. [15]Doesn't it seem obvious? *Jesus is* a priest who resembles Melchizedek *in so many ways;* [16] He is someone who has become a priest, not because of some requirement about human lineage, but because of the power of a life without end. [17]*Remember, the psalmist* says,

You are a priest forever—
in the *honored* order of Melchizedek.*

[18]Because the earlier commandment was weak and did not reconcile us to God effectively, it was set aside—[19]after all, the law could not make anyone or anything perfect. God has now introduced a new and better hope, through which we may draw near to Him, [20]and confirmed it by swearing to it. [21]The *Levite order of* priests took office without an oath, but this man *Jesus* became a priest through God's oath:

The Eternal One has sworn an oath
and cannot change His mind:
You are a priest forever.*

[22]So we can see that Jesus has become the guarantee of a *new and* better covenant. [23]Further, the prior priesthood *of the sons of Levi* has included many priests because death cut short their service, [24]but Jesus holds His priesthood permanently because He lives His resurrected life forever. [25]From such a vantage, He is able to save those who approach God through Him for all time because He will forever live to be their advocate *in the presence of God.*

[26]It is only fitting that we should have a High Priest who is devoted to God, blameless, pure, *compassionate toward but* separate from sinners, and exalted by God to the highest place of honor. [27]Unlike other high priests, He does not first need to make atonement every day for His own sins, and only then for His people's, because He already made atonement, reconciling us with God once and forever when He offered Himself as a sacrifice. [28]The law made imperfect men

high priests; but after that law was given, God swore an oath that made His perfected Son a high priest for all time.

8 So let me sum up what we've covered so far, *for there is much we have said:* we have a High Priest, *a perfect Priest* who sits *in the place of honor* in the highest heavens, at the right hand of the throne of the Majestic One, [2]a Minister within the *heavenly* sanctuary set up by the Lord, not by human hands.

[3]*As I have said,* it is the role of every high priest to offer gifts and sacrifices *to God,* so clearly this Priest of ours must have something to offer as well. [4]If He were on earth, then He would not be a priest at all because there are already priests who can offer gifts according to the law *of Moses* [5]in a sanctuary that is only a copy and shadow of the heavenly sanctuary. *We know this because* God admonished Moses as he set up the tent for the Lord's sanctuary: "Be sure that you make everything according to the pattern I showed you on the mountain."* [6]But now Jesus has taken on a new and improved priestly ministry; and in that respect, He has been made the Mediator of a better covenant established on better promises. [7]Remember, if the first covenant had been able to reconcile everyone to God, there would be no reason for a second covenant. [8]God found fault with the priests when He said *through the prophet Jeremiah,*

"Look! The time is coming," the Eternal
Lord says,
"when I will bring about a new
covenant with the people of Israel
and Judah.
[9]It will not be like the covenant I made
with their ancestors
when I took them by the hand
and led them out of *slavery in* the land
of Egypt.
They did not remain faithful to that
covenant,
so," the Eternal One says, "I turned
away from them.
[10]But when those days are over," the Eternal
One says, "I will make
this *kind of* covenant with the people
of Israel:
I will put My laws on their minds
and write them upon their hearts.
I will be their God,
and they will be My people.

* 7:17 Psalm 110:4   * 7:21 Psalm 110:4   * 8:5 Exodus 25:40

[11]*In those days*, they won't need to teach
each other *My ways*
or to say to each other, 'Know the
Eternal.'
In those days, all will know Me,
from the least to the greatest.
[12]I will be merciful when they fail,
and I will erase their sins *and wicked
acts* out of My memory
as though they had never existed."*

[13]With the words "a new covenant," God
made the first covenant old, and what is old
and no longer effective will soon fade away
completely.

V

Jeremiah is known as the prophet
of the new covenant. Hundreds
of years before the birth of Jesus,
Jeremiah heard the voice of God
and saw what God had planned:
a new day. A new law inscribed in
the mind and written on the heart.
A new and abiding knowledge of
God. A new covenant where mercy
runs deep and sins are forgiven
and forgotten.

This hope of a new heart is
found even in the midst of the
Mosaic Covenant. Moses foretells
the unfaithfulness of the people
and also tells them of God's promise to restore their hearts (Deuteronomy 30:1-10).

9 Even that *first* covenant had *rules and
regulations* about how to worship and
how to set up an earthly sanctuary *for
God*. [2]*In the Book of Exodus,** we read how the
first tent was set aside for worship—we call
it the holy place—how inside it they placed
an oil lamp, a table, and the bread that was
consecrated *to God*. [3]Behind a second *dividing* curtain, there was another tent which
is called the most holy place. [4]In there they
placed the golden incense altar and the
golden ark of the covenant. Inside the ark
were the golden urn that contained manna
(*the miraculous food God gave our ancestors in the desert*), Aaron's rod that budded,*
and the tablets of the covenant *that Moses
brought down from the mountain*. [5]Above
the ark were the *golden images of* heavenly

beings* of glory who shadowed the mercy
seat.

I cannot go into any greater detail about
this now. [6]When all is prepared as it is supposed to be, the priests go back and forth
daily into the first tent to carry out the duties
described in the law. [7]But once a year, the
high priest goes alone into that second tent,
the most holy place, with blood to offer for
himself and the unwitting errors of the people. [8]As long as that first tent is standing, the
Holy Spirit shows us, the way into the most
holy place has not yet been revealed to us.
[9]That first tent symbolizes the present time,
when gifts and sacrifices can be offered; but
it can't change the *heart and* conscience of
the worshiper. [10]These gifts and sacrifices
deal only with regulations for the body—food
and drink and various kinds of *ritual* cleansings necessary until the time comes to make
things truly right.

[11]When the Anointed One arrived as
High Priest of the good things that are to
come, *He entered* through a greater and
more perfect sanctuary that was not part
of the earthly creation or made by human
hands. [12]He entered once for all time into
the most holy place—entering, not with
the blood of goats or calves *or some other
prescribed animal*, but offering His own
blood and thus obtaining redemption for us
for all time. [13]*Think about it:* if the blood of
bulls or of goats, or the sprinkling of ashes
from a heifer, restores the defiled to bodily
cleanliness *and wholeness*; [14]then how much
more powerful is the blood of the Anointed
One, who through the eternal Spirit offered
Himself *as a* spotless *sacrifice* to God, purifying your conscience from the dead things
of the world to the service of the living
God?

[15]This is why Jesus is the mediator of
the new covenant: through His death, He
delivered us from the sins that we had built
up under the first covenant, and His death
has made it possible for all who are called
to receive God's promised inheritance. [16]For
whenever there is a testament—a will—the
death of the one who made it must be confirmed [17]because a will takes effect only at
the death of its maker; it has no validity as
long as the maker is still alive. [18]Even the
first *testament—the first covenant*—required
blood to be put into action. [19]When Moses
had given all the laws of God to the people,

* 8:8-12 Jeremiah 31:31-34 * 9:2 Exodus 25-26 * 9:4 Numbers
17:1-13 * 9:5 Greek *cheroubin*

In chapter 9 we are reminded that what is most real, what is most true, is the unseen reality. The writer tells us that the temple in Jerusalem, the holiest place on earth, was merely a copy or shadow of another place, the heavenly temple. Whatever took place in this shadowy temple could not change the realities of alienation from God, sin, and death.

Every year on the Day of Atonement, the high priest would don his priestly garb and enter the most holy place in the temple. His task was profound, his duty dangerous: he must appear before God carrying the sins of his people. All the sins of Israel were concentrated in him as he carried the blood of the sacrifice into the divine presence. But there was another day, a Day of Atonement unlike any other, when Jesus concentrated in Himself the sins of the world, hanging on a cross not far from the temple's holiest chamber. Indeed, for a time, He became sin (2 Corinthians 5:21). But unlike the high priest, the crucified and risen Jesus entered the true temple of heaven and was ushered into the divine presence. At that moment, everything changed.

---

he took the blood of calves and of goats, water, hyssop, and scarlet wool; and he sprinkled the scroll and all the people, [20]telling them, "This is the blood of the covenant that God has commanded for us."* [21]In the same way, he also sprinkled blood upon the sanctuary and upon the vessels used in worship. [22]Under the law, it's almost the case that everything is purified in connection with blood; without the shedding of blood, sin cannot be forgiven.

[23]*Since what was given in the old covenant was* the earthly sketch of the heavenly reality, this was sufficient to cleanse the earthly sanctuary; but in heaven, a more perfect sacrifice was needed. [24]The Anointed One did not enter into handcrafted sacred spaces—imperfect copies of heavenly originals—but into heaven itself, where He stands in the presence of God on our behalf. [25]There He does not offer Himself over and over as a sacrifice (as the high priest on earth does when he enters the most holy place each year with blood other than his own) [26]because that would require His repeated suffering since the beginning of the world. No, He has appeared once now, at the end of the age, to put away sin forever by offering Himself as a sacrifice.

[27]Just as mortals are appointed to die once and then to experience a judgment, [28]so the Anointed One, *our Liberating King,* was offered once *in death* to bear the sins of many and will appear a second time, not to deal again with sin, but to rescue those who eagerly await His return.

He who embodied the sins of the world carries His own blood into the holy presence.

10

We have seen how the law is simply a shadow of the good things to come. Since it is not the perfect form of these ultimate realities, the offering year after year of these imperfect sacrifices cannot bring perfection to those who come forward to worship. [2]If they had served this purpose, wouldn't the repetition of these sacrifices have become unnecessary? If they had worked—and cleansed the worshipers—then one sacrifice would have taken away their consciousness of sin. [3]But these sacrifices actually remind us that we sin *again and again,* year after year. [4]In the end, the blood of bulls and of goats is powerless to take away sins. [5]So when Jesus came into the world, He said,

Sacrifices and offerings were not what
    You wanted,
    but instead a body that You prepared
        for Me.
[6]Burnt offerings and sin offerings
    were not what pleased You.
[7]Then I said, "See, I have come to do Your
    will, God,
    as it is inscribed of Me in the scroll of
        the book."*

[8]Now when it says that God doesn't want and takes no real pleasure in sacrifices, burnt offerings, and sin offerings (even though the law calls for them), [9]and follows this with "See, I have come to do Your will,"* He effectively takes away the first—*animal sacrifice*—in order to establish the second, *more perfect sacrifice.* [10]By God's will, we are made holy through the offering of the body of Jesus the Anointed once and for all time.

* 9:20 Exodus 24:8   * 10:5-7 Psalm 40:6-8   * 10:9 Psalm 40:7

[11]*In the first covenant,* every day every *officiating* priest stands at his post serving, offering over and over those same sacrifices that can never take away sin. [12]But after He stepped up to offer His single sacrifice for sins for all time, He sat down *in the position of honor* at the right hand of God. [13]Since then, He has been waiting for the day when He rests His feet on His enemies' backs,* *as the psalm says.* [14]With one *perfect* offering, Jesus has perfected forever those who are being made holy, [15]as the Holy Spirit keeps testifying to us *through the prophet Jeremiah.* After he says,

[16]"But when those days are over," says the Eternal One, "I will make
this *kind of* covenant with the people *of Israel*:
I will put My laws in their hearts
and write them upon their minds,"*

then He adds,

[17]I will erase their sins and wicked acts out of My memory
*as though they had never existed.**

[18]When there is forgiveness such as this, there is no longer any need to make an offering for sin.

[19]So, my friends, Jesus by His blood gives us courage to enter the most holy place. [20]He has created for us a new and living way through the curtain, that is, through His flesh. [21]Since we have a great High Priest who presides over the house of God, [22]let us draw near with true hearts full of faith, with hearts rinsed clean of any evil conscience, and with bodies cleansed with pure water. [23]Let us hold strong to the confession of our hope, never wavering, since the One who promised it to us is faithful. [24]Let us consider how to inspire each other to greater love and to righteous deeds, [25]not forgetting to gather as a community, as some have forgotten, but encouraging each other, especially as the day *of His return* approaches.

The word translated "church" in English Bibles means literally "assembly of the called"; it implies that members have said "yes" to God's call in their lives. We assemble because we are called into being by God Himself. Some people, for reasons only they know, choose to live their Christian faiths in isolation. When they do, they cut themselves off from the gifts, encouragement, and vitality of others. And perhaps, just as tragically, they deprive the church of the grace and life God has invested in them.

---

[26]Now if we willfully persist in sin after receiving such knowledge of the truth, then there is no sacrifice left for those sins—[27]only the fearful prospect of judgment and a fierce fire that will consume God's adversaries. [28]*Remember that* those who depart from the law of Moses are put to death without mercy based on the testimony of two or three witnesses.* [29]Just think how much more severe the punishment will be for those who have turned their backs on the Son of God, trampled on the blood of the covenant by which He made them holy, and outraged the Spirit of grace *with their contempt.* [30]For we know the God who said, "Vengeance belongs to Me—I will repay,"* also said, "The Eternal One will judge His people."* [31]It is truly a frightening thing to be on the wrong side of the living God.

[32]Instead, think back to the days after you were first enlightened *and understood who Jesus was*: when you endured all sorts of suffering *in the name of the Lord,* [33]when people held you up for public scorn and ridicule, or when they abused your partners and companions in the faith. [34]Remember how you had compassion for those in prison and how you cheerfully accepted the seizure of your possessions, knowing that you have a far greater and more enduring possession. [35]Remember this, and do not abandon your confidence, which will lead to rich rewards. [36]Simply endure, for when you have done as God requires of you, you will receive the promise. [37]*As the prophet Habakkuk said,*

In a little while, *only a little longer,*
the One who is coming will come
without delay.
[38]But My righteous one must live by faith,
for if he gives up his commitment,
My soul will have no pleasure in him.*

* 10:13 Psalm 110:1 * 10:16 Jeremiah 31:33 * 10:17 Jeremiah 31:34 * 10:28 Deuteronomy 17:6 * 10:30 Deuteronomy 32:35
* 10:30 Deuteronomy 32:36 * 10:37-38 Habakkuk 2:3-4

[39]My friends, we are not those who give up hope and so are lost; but we are of the company who live by faith and so are saved.

11 Faith is the assurance of things you have hoped for, the absolute conviction that there are realities you've never seen. [2]It was by faith that our forebears were approved. [3]Through faith we understand that the universe was created by the word of God; everything we now see was fashioned from that which is invisible.

Faith begins as hope and indeed is unseen; so many doubt that it is real. What follows is the proof that faith is a reality that can be trusted.

[4]By faith Abel presented to God a sacrifice more acceptable than *his brother* Cain's. *By faith* Abel learned he was righteous, as God Himself testified by approving his offering. And by faith he still speaks, although his voice was silenced by death.

[5]By faith Enoch was carried up *into heaven* so that he did not see death; no one could find him because God had taken him. Before he was taken up, it was said of him that he had pleased God. [6]Without faith no one can please God because the one coming to God must believe He exists, and He rewards those who come seeking.

[7]By faith Noah respected God's warning regarding *the flood—the likes of* which no one had ever seen—and built an ark that saved his family. In this he condemned the world and inherited the righteousness that comes by faith.

[8]By faith Abraham heard God's call to travel to a place he would one day receive as an inheritance; and he obeyed, not knowing where God's call would take him. [9]By faith he journeyed to the land of the promise as a foreigner; he lived in tents, as did Isaac and Jacob, his fellow heirs to the promise [10]because Abraham looked ahead to a city with foundations, a city laid out and built by God.

[11]By faith *Abraham's wife* Sarah became fertile long after menopause because she believed God would be faithful to His promise. [12]So from this man, who was almost at death's door, God brought forth descendants, as many as the stars in the sky and as impossible to count as the sands of the shore.

[13]All these I have mentioned died in faith without receiving the full promises, although they saw the fulfillment as though from a distance. These people accepted and confessed that they were strangers and foreigners on this earth [14]because people who speak like this make it plain that they are still seeking a homeland. [15]If this was only a bit of nostalgia for a time and place they left behind, then certainly they might have turned around and returned. [16]But such saints as these look forward to a far better place, a heavenly country. So God is not ashamed to be called their God because He has prepared a *heavenly* city for them.

[17]By faith Abraham, when he endured God's testing, offered *his beloved son* Isaac *as a sacrifice.* The one who had received God's promise was willing to offer his only son; [18]God had told him, "It is through Isaac that your descendants will bear your name,"* [19]and he concluded that God was capable of raising him from the dead, which, figuratively, is indeed what happened.

[20]By faith Isaac spoke blessings upon his sons, Jacob and Esau, concerning things yet to come.

[21]By faith Jacob, when he was dying, blessed the sons of *his son* Joseph, bowing in worship as he leaned upon his staff.*

[22]By faith Joseph, at his life's end, predicted that the children of Israel would make an exodus from Egypt; and he gave instructions that his bones *be buried in the land they would someday reach.*

[23]By faith Moses' parents hid him for three months after he was born because they saw that he was handsome; and they did not fear Pharaoh's directive *that all male Hebrew children were to be slain.*

[24]By faith Moses, when he was grown, refused to be identified solely as the son of Pharaoh's daughter [25]and chose instead to share the sufferings of the people of God, not just living in sin and ease for a time. [26]He considered the abuse *that he and the people of God had* suffered in anticipation of the Anointed One more valuable than all the riches of Egypt because he looked ahead to the coming reward.

[27]By faith Moses left Egypt, unafraid of Pharaoh's wrath and moving forward as though he could see the invisible God. [28]Through faith, he instituted the Passover and the sprinkling of blood *on the doorposts among the Hebrews* so that the destroyer of the firstborn would pass over their homes without harming them. [29]By faith the people

* 11:18 Genesis 21:12 * 11:21 Genesis 47:31

crossed through the Red Sea as if they were walking on dry land, although the pursuing Egyptian *soldiers* were drowned when they tried to follow.

[30]By faith the walls of Jericho toppled after the people had circled them for seven days. [31]By faith the prostitute Rahab welcomed the *Hebrew* spies *into her home* so that she did not perish with the unbelievers.

[32]I could speak more *of faith*; I could talk until time itself ran out. If I continued, I could speak *of the examples* of Gideon, Barak, Samson, and Jephthah, of David and Samuel and all the prophets. [33]*I could give accounts of* people alive with faith who conquered kingdoms, brought justice, obtained promises, and closed the mouths of hungry lions. [34]*I could tell you how people of faith* doused raging fires, escaped the edge of the sword, made the weak strong, and—stoking great valor among the champions of God—sent opposing armies into panicked flight.

[35]I could speak of faith bringing women their loved ones back from death and how the faithful accepted torture instead of earthly deliverance because they believed they would obtain a better *life in the* resurrection. [36]Others suffered mockery and whippings; they were placed in chains and in prisons. [37]The faithful were stoned, sawn in two,* killed by the sword, clothed only in sheepskins and goatskins; they were penniless, afflicted, and tormented. [38]The world was not worthy of these saints. They wandered across deserts, crossed mountains, and lived in the caves, cracks, and crevasses of the earth.

Stories of faith and faithfulness are central to the First Testament. The writer of Hebrews recalls some of the most memorable examples of how people of faith lived their lives. But what is faith? Faith is more than belief; it is trust, assurance, and firm conviction. Ironically most of those who lived by faith never fully realized the promises God had made. Like us they journeyed as strangers and exiles, longing for another country. We should remember their patient faith when we face prolonged hardships and allow the trials we

face to strengthen our faith rather than destroy it. If we are comfortable here and don't face suffering for our faith, perhaps we aren't fully living by faith and looking forward to a future hope.

---

[39]These, though commended by God for their great faith, did not receive what was promised. [40]That promise has awaited us, who receive the better thing that God has provided *in these last days*, so that with us, our forebears might finally see the promise completed.

12 So since we stand surrounded by *all those who have gone before,* an enormous cloud of witnesses, let us drop every extra weight, every sin that clings to us *and slackens our pace,* and let us run with endurance the long race set before us.

We may feel alone, but we aren't. We are surrounded by an army of witnesses. They have run the race of faith and finished well. It is now our turn.

[2]Now stay focused on Jesus, who designed and perfected our faith. He endured the cross and ignored the shame *of that death* because He focused on the joy that was set before Him; and now He is seated beside God on the throne, *a place of honor.*

[3]Consider *the life of* the One who endured such *personal attacks and* hostility from sinners so that you will not grow weary or lose heart. [4]Among you, in your striving against sin, none has resisted *the pressure* to the point of death, as He did.

God "disciplines" His "disciples." God is training us not just to live here and now, but to have life in the age to come, to share His life and holiness.

[5]Indeed, you seem to have forgotten the proverb directed to you as children:

My child, do not ignore the instruction that comes from the Lord,
or lose heart when He steps in to correct you;

---

* 11:37 Some early manuscripts read "sawn in two." Other early manuscripts read "tempted." Later manuscripts have both.

⁶For the Lord disciplines those He loves,
    and He corrects each one He takes as
    His own.*

⁷Endure hardship as God's discipline *and
rejoice* that He is treating you as His children, for what child doesn't experience
discipline from a parent? ⁸But if you are not
experiencing the correction that all true children receive, then it may be that you are not
His children after all. ⁹Remember, when our
human parents disciplined us, we respected
them. *If that was true,* shouldn't we respect
and live under the correction of the Father
of all spirits even more? ¹⁰Our parents cor-
rected us for a time as seemed good to them,
but God only corrects us to our good so that
we may share in His holiness.

¹¹When punishment is happening, it
never seems pleasant, only painful. Later,
though, it yields the peaceful fruit called
righteousness to everyone who has been
trained by it. ¹²So lift up your hands that are
dangling and brace your weakened knees.
¹³Make straight paths for your feet so that
what is lame *in you* won't be put out of joint,
but will heal.

¹⁴Pursue peace with everyone, and holiness, since no one will see God without it.
¹⁵Watch carefully that no one falls short of
God's favor, that no well of bitterness springs
up to trouble you and throw many others
off the path. ¹⁶Watch that no one becomes
wicked and vile like Esau, *the son of Isaac,*
who for a single meal sold his invaluable
birthright. ¹⁷You know *from the stories of
the patriarchs* that later, when he wished to
claim his blessing, he was turned away. He
could not reverse his action even though he
shed bitter tears over it.

V

The Bible is a brutally honest book.
It contains stories of liars, murderers, and adulterers; and these are
the good guys. If we read the Bible
looking only for positive role models, we'll be quickly disappointed.
But if we are honest with ourselves and confess our own faults,
we will find in Scripture, particularly in the First Testament, that we
have much in common with many
broken saints of the past. But we
must not stay broken. We must follow their path to transformation

through repentance and faith.
Repentance means a change of
heart, a change of mind, and ultimately a change of how we live.
God's grace comes to us and
enables us to turn away from sin
and to turn back to Him.

---

¹⁸You have not come to the place that can be
touched (*as Israel did at Mount Sinai*)—*to a
mountain crowned* with blazing fire, darkness, gloom, and a windstorm—¹⁹or to the
blast of a trumpet and the sound of a voice—
a voice and message so harsh that the people
begged not to hear another word. ²⁰(They
could not bear the command that was given:
that if even a beast touches the mountain, it
must be stoned. ²¹The sight was so terrible
that even Moses said, "I am trembling with
fear.")*

²²No, instead you have come to Mount
Zion, to the city of the living God, to the
heavenly Jerusalem, to heavenly messengers unnumbered, *to a joyful feast,* ²³to
the assembly of the firstborn registered
as heaven's citizens, to God the righteous
Judge of all, and to the spirits of all the
righteous who have been perfected. ²⁴You
have come to Jesus, the mediator of a new
covenant *between God and humanity,* and to
His sprinkled blood, which speaks a greater
word than the blood of Abel *crying out from
the earth.*

²⁵See that you don't turn away from the
One who is speaking; for if the ones who
heard and refused the One who spoke on
earth faced punishment, then how much
more will we suffer if we turn away from
the One speaking from heaven—²⁶the One
whose voice in earlier times shook the earth
now makes another promise: "Yet once more
I will shake not only the earth, but also the
heavens"?* ²⁷The phrase, "Yet once more,"
means that those things that can be shaken
will be removed and taken away, namely,
the *first* creation. As a result, those things
that remain cannot be shaken. ²⁸Therefore,
let us all be thankful that we are a part of an
unshakable Kingdom and offer to God worship that pleases Him and reflects the awe
and reverence we have toward Him, ²⁹for
He is like a fierce fire that consumes everything.*

* 12:5-6 Proverbs 3:11-12   * 12:20-21 Exodus 19:12-13; Deuteronomy
9:19   * 12:26 Haggai 2:6,21   * 12:29 Deuteronomy 4:24

13 Let love continue among you. ²Don't forget to extend your hospitality to all—even to strangers—for *as you know,* some have unknowingly shown kindness to heavenly messengers in this way. ³Remember those imprisoned *for their beliefs* as if you were their cellmate; and care for any who suffer harsh treatment, as you are all one body.

⁴Hold marriage in high esteem, all of you, and keep the marriage bed pure because God will judge those who commit sexual sins.

⁵Keep your lives free from the love of money, and be content with what you have because He has said, "I will never leave you; I will always be by your side."* ⁶Because of this promise, we may boldly say,

The Lord is my help—
   I won't be afraid of anything.
How can anyone harm me?*

⁷Listen to your leaders, who have spoken God's word to you. Notice the fruits of their lives and mirror their faith.

⁸Jesus the Anointed One is always the same: yesterday, today, and forever. ⁹Do not be carried away by diverse and strange ways of believing or worshiping. It is good for the heart to be strengthened by grace, not by *regulations about* what you can eat (which do no good even for those who observe them). ¹⁰We approach an altar from which those who stand before the altar in the tent have no right to eat. ¹¹*In the past,* the bodies of those animals whose blood was carried into the sanctuary by the high priest to take away sin were all burned outside the camp. ¹²(In the same way, Jesus suffered and bled outside the city walls *of Jerusalem* to sanctify the people.)

V

If we are honest, we have to admit that coming to Jesus and entering into His church ruins us—at least as far as this world is concerned. If we identify with Him in His suffering and rejection, we become a reproachful irritation to the powers that rule this culture. If we ever felt at home in this world—if we ever sensed that we belonged—then we would wake up one day to discover that we will never be at home again until we enter the city of God. By entering through Jesus, we become citizens of another city, subjects of another king. As long as we are here, we should live as resident aliens longing to go home.

---

¹³Let's then go out to Him and resolve to bear the insult and abuse that He endured. ¹⁴For as long as we are here, we do not live in any permanent city, but are looking for the city that is to come.

¹⁵Through Jesus, then, let us keep offering to God our own sacrifice, the praise of lips that confess His name without ceasing. ¹⁶Let's not neglect what is good and share what we have, for these sacrifices also please God.

¹⁷Listen to your leaders and submit to their authority *over the community,* for they are on constant watch to protect your souls and someday they must give account. Give them reason to be joyful and not to regret their duty, for that will be of no good to you.

¹⁸⁻¹⁹Pray for us, for we have no doubt that our consciences are clean and that we seek to live honestly in all things. ⁹But please pray for me that I may be restored to you even more quickly.

²⁰Now may the God of peace, who brought the great Shepherd of the sheep, our Lord Jesus, back from the dead through the blood of the new everlasting covenant, ²¹perfect you in every good work as you work God's will. May God do in you *only* those things that are pleasing in His sight through Jesus the Anointed, *our Liberating King,* to whom we give glory always and forever. Amen.

²²Please, brothers and sisters, pay attention to this word of exhortation, for I have written only a few words to you.

²³I want to tell you that our brother Timothy has been set free; and if he arrives soon, he will come with me when I see you next.

²⁴Give my greetings to your leaders and to all of God's people. Those of Italy greet you.

²⁵May grace always be with you.

* 13:5 Deuteronomy 31:6   * 13:6 Psalm 118:6

JAMES

Letter to Jewish believers

From James, the brother of Jesus

What must it have been like to grow up with Jesus as a brother? Now there's a reason for some serious sibling rivalry! In a devout Jewish home during the first century, the Scriptures are recited from memory, and the faith is celebrated in festivals that provide a rhythm to life. Then one day at the synagogue Jesus, a lay person, gets up and starts preaching, healing the sick, and casting out demons. Some people in the community are calling Him a lunatic. Others think He has made a deal with the devil. Even Jesus' own family tries to interrupt His public displays on several occasions because they want to protect Him and guard the family from shame.

As an adult son, it is James's responsibility to defend the family honor. At first, James is not convinced that his brother is the Savior. So what turns this skeptic into a passionate believer and the prominent leader of the Jerusalem church? After the cruci- fixion, when he sees the risen Jesus with his own eyes, James's doubts disappear. Later, at a time when the church is divided over how to incorporate Gentile believers into the formerly all-Jewish group, James steps forward and shows great leadership. He boldly says, "So here is my counsel: we should not burden these outsiders who are turning to God" (Acts 15:19). Thus James endorses Paul's ministry, and with his leadership the brother of Jesus enables the spread of Christianity to the world.

In this letter, James is writing to his fellow Jewish Christians scattered throughout the world in the first century. He is concerned with preserving a connection between his Jewish heritage and the movement begun by Jesus. James does not see himself as a leader of a new religion, but as a Jew who follows the Jesus the Anointed, the Liberat- ing King. Like Peter and Paul, James views the gospel as the fulfillment of promises in the Hebrew Scriptures. But now, through the work of Jesus, outsiders are invited to fol- low as well. James takes honoring the law very seriously; in this letter, he encourages all believers to simply practice what they preach.

1 James, a servant of God and the Lord Jesus, the Anointed One, to the twelve tribes *of Israel* who are spread across the earth: I send you my warmest welcome!

²⁻⁴Don't run from tests and hardships, brothers and sisters. *As difficult as they are, you will ultimately* find joy in them; if you embrace them, your faith will blossom under pressure *and teach you true patience* as you endure. *And true patience brought on by* endurance will equip you to complete the long journey *and cross the finish line—* mature, complete, and wanting nothing. ⁵If you don't have all the wisdom needed *for this journey,* then all you have to do is ask God for it; and God will grant all that you need. He gives lavishly and never scolds you for asking.

Wisdom, as James understands it, is the ability to live life well and make good decisions. Wisdom doesn't come from old age or hard knocks. Wisdom begins with knowing and depending absolutely on God, who is never stingy when it comes to wisdom for those who seek it. He supplies all the wisdom we need when we ask. But when we try to go it alone— without God—trouble is around the corner.

⁶The key is that your request be anchored by your single-minded commitment *to God.* Those who depend only on their own judgment are like *those lost on* the seas, carried away by any wave or picked up by any wind. ⁷Those *adrift on their own wisdom* shouldn't assume the Lord will *rescue them or* bring them anything. ⁸*The splinter of* divided loyalty *shatters your compass and* leaves you dizzy and confused.

⁹If you are a brother of humble means, celebrate the fact that God has raised you up. ¹⁰If you are rich *and seemingly invincible,* savor the humble reality that you are a mere mortal who will vanish like a flower that withers in the field. ¹¹The sun rises with a blazing heat that *dries the earth and* causes the flower to wither and fall to the ground and its beauty to fade and die. In the same way, the rich will fall and die in the midst of their busy lives.

¹²Happy is the person who can hold up under the trials of life. *At the right time,* he'll know God's sweet approval and will be crowned with life. As God has promised, the crown awaits all who love Him.

¹³No one who is tempted should *ever be confused and* say that God is testing him. The One who created us is free from evil and can't be tempted, so He doesn't tempt anyone. ¹⁴⁻¹⁵When a person is carried away with desire, lured by lust, and when desire becomes the focus and takes control, it gives birth to sin. *When* sin becomes fully grown, it produces death.

If you give in to temptation and desire, then sin is born. If you give in to sin long enough, it overpowers you and costs you your life.

¹⁶My dearly loved brothers and sisters, don't be misled. ¹⁷Every good gift bestowed, every perfect gift received comes *to us* from above, courtesy of the Father of lights. He *is consistent.* He won't change His mind or play tricks in the shadows. ¹⁸We have a special role in His plan. He calls us to life by His message of truth so that we will show the rest of His creatures *His goodness and love.*

¹⁹ Listen, open your ears, harness your desire to speak, and don't get worked up into a rage so easily, my brothers and sisters. ²⁰Human anger *is a futile exercise that* will never produce God's kind of justice *in this world.* ²¹So walk out on your corrupt liaison with smut and depraved living, and humbly welcome the word *of truth that will blossom like the seed* of salvation planted in your souls.

²²Put the word into action. If you think hearing is what matters most, you are going to find you have been deceived.

God the Father is the giver of all things and is looking for every opportunity to bless us. But many people have difficulty trusting and receiving good things, even when those things come from God. The problem is that we not only have trouble trusting God's work in our lives, but we also don't always respond to God's voice. People often hear the Scriptures but don't really listen. People store truths in their brains but never put them to use. For James, the only good religion is religion lived out every day.

We are often mesmerized by the rich, powerful, and beautiful people of the world. We dream of associating with them; but when we focus our attention on the fashionable people of this world, it is often at the expense of those who need it the most.

Ignoring the needy and favoring the wealthy is completely contrary to the example Jesus modeled for us while walking on earth. God often chooses those who are the poorest materially to be the richest spiritually. We should welcome everyone equally into God's kingdom, even if it means upsetting boundaries like class and race. The rule is simple: we should treat others in the same way we want to be treated. God does not play favorites, and neither should we.

23-24If some fail to do what God requires, it's as if they forget the word as soon as they hear it. One minute they look in the mirror, and the next they forget who they are and what they look like. 25However, it is possible to open your eyes and take in the beautiful, perfect truth found in God's law of liberty *and live by it.* If you pursue that path and actually do what God has commanded, then you will avoid *the many distractions that lead to* an amnesia of all true things and you will be blessed.

26If you *put yourself on a pedestal,* thinking you have become a role model in all things religious, but you can't control your mouth, then think again. Your mouth exposes your heart, and your religion is useless. 27Real, true religion from God the Father's perspective is about caring for the orphans and widows who suffer needlessly and resisting the evil influence of the world.

2 My brothers and sisters, *I know you've heard this before, but* stop playing favorites! Do not try to blend the genuine faith of our glorious Lord Jesus, the Anointed One, *with your silly pretentiousness.* 2If an affluent gentleman enters your gathering wearing the finest clothes and priceless jewelry, *don't trip over each other trying to welcome him.* And if a penniless bum crawls in with his shabby clothes *and a stench fills the room,* don't look away or pretend you didn't notice—*offer him a seat up front, next to you.* 3-4If you tell the wealthy man, "Come sit by me; there's plenty of room," but tell the vagrant, "Oh, these seats are saved. Go over there," then you'll be judging *God's children* out of evil motives.

5My dear brothers and sisters, listen: God has picked the poor of this world to become *unfathomably* rich in faith and ultimately to inherit the Kingdom, which He has pledged to those who love Him. 6*By favoring the rich,* you have mocked the poor. *And, correct me if I'm wrong,* but isn't it the rich who step on you while climbing the ladder of success? And isn't it the rich who *take advantage of you and* drag you into court? 7Aren't they the ones mocking the noble name *of our God,* the One calling us?

8*Remember His call, and* live by the royal law found in Scripture: love others as you love yourself.* You'll be doing very well if you can get this down. 9But if you show favoritism—*paying attention to those who can help you in some way, while ignoring those who seem to need all the help*—you'll be sinning and condemned by the law. 10For if a person could keep all of the laws and yet break just one; it would be like breaking them all. 11The same God who said, "Do not commit adultery,"* also says, "Do not murder."* If you break either of these commands, you're a lawbreaker, *no matter how you look at it.* 12So live your life in such a way that acknowledges that one day you will be judged. But the law that judges also gives freedom, 13although you can't expect to be shown mercy if you refuse to show mercy. *But hear this:* mercy always wins against judgment! *Thank God!*

14Brothers and sisters, it doesn't make any sense to say you have faith and act in a way that denies that faith. *Mere talk never gets you very far, and* a commitment to Jesus only in words will not save you. 15It would be like seeing a brother or sister without any clothes *out in the cold* and begging for food, and 16saying, "Shalom, *friend,* you should get

* 2:8 Leviticus 19:18   * 2:11 Exodus 20:14   * 2:11 Exodus 20:13

James' focus on works is frequently cited as a contradiction to other messages in the Bible. On the one hand, it appears James is saying that salvation is achieved by works; on the other, writers such as Paul emphasize that salvation comes by faith alone, not works of the law (Galatians 2).

Look carefully and you'll see that Paul and James are talking about different issues. Paul is in the middle of a debate with Jewish Christians over whether Gentiles must live like Jews to enter the family of faith. He says that no one is made right with God by performing the works of the law. Instead, all people are made right by faith, thanks to God's grace. For James the situation is entirely different. The works he is talking about refer to God's people helping the poor, not whether non-Jews must live like Jews. He's concerned about a shallow, insincere, and hypocritical faith.

Paul describes the root of salvation; a person is saved by God's grace received through faith. James is explaining the fruit of salvation; saving faith is a faith that works.

---

inside where it's warm and eat something," but doing nothing about his needs—*leaving him cold and alone on the street.* What good would your words alone do? [17]The same is true with faith. Without actions, *faith is useless. By itself,* it's *as good as* dead. [18]I know what you're thinking: "OK, you have faith. And I have actions. Now let's see your faith without works, and I'll show you a faith that works."

Don't you realize that faith without works is useless, like a glove without a hand or a hat without a head?

[19]Do you think that just believing there's one God is going to get you anywhere? The demons believe that, too, and it terrifies them! [20]*The fact is,* faith has to show itself through works performed in faith. If you don't recognize that, then you're an empty soul. [21]Wasn't our father Abraham made right with God by laying his son Isaac on the altar? [22]The faith *in his heart* was made known in his behavior. In fact, his commitment was perfected by his obedience. [23]That's what Scripture means when it says, "Abraham entrusted himself to God, and God credited him with righteousness."* *And living a faithful life* earned Abraham the title of "God's friend."* [24]*Just like our father in the faith,* we are made right with God through good works, not simply by what we believe or think. [25]Even Rahab the prostitute was made right with God by hiding the spies and aiding in their escape.* [26]Removing action from faith is like removing breath from a body. All you have left is a corpse.

3 My brothers and sisters, do not encourage a large number of you to become teachers because teachers will be held to a higher standard. [2]We all stumble along the way. If a person never speaks hurtful words *or shouts in anger or profanity,* then he has achieved perfection. The one who can control his tongue can also control the rest of his body. [3]It's like when we place a metal bit into a horse's mouth to ride it; we can control its entire body *with the slightest movement of our hands.* [4]Have you ever seen a massive ship *sailing effortlessly across the water? Despite its immense size* and the fact that it is propelled by mighty winds, a small rudder directs the ship in any direction the pilot chooses. [5]It's just the same with our tongues! It's a small muscle, capable of marvelous undertakings.

And do you know how many forest fires begin *with a single ember* from a small campfire? [6]The tongue is a *blazing* fire seeking to ignite an entire world of vices. The tongue is unique among all parts of the body because it is capable of corrupting the whole body. *If that were not enough,* it ignites *and consumes* the course of creation with a fuel that originates in hell itself. [7]Humanity is capable of taming every bird and beast in existence, even reptiles and sea creatures *great and small.* [8]But no man has ever demonstrated the ability to tame his own tongue! It is a spring of restless evil, brimming with toxic poisons. [9]*Ironically* this same tongue can be *both an instrument* of blessing to our Lord and Father and *a weapon* that hurls curses upon others who are created in God's own

* 2:23 Genesis 15:6   * 2:23 2 Chronicles 20:7; Isaiah 41:8
* 2:25 Joshua 2:1-16

image. ¹⁰One mouth streams forth both blessings and curses. My brothers and sisters, this is not how it should be. ¹¹Does a spring gush crystal clear freshwater and moments later spurt out bitter salt water? ¹²My brothers and sisters, does a fig tree produce olives? Is there a grapevine capable of growing figs? Can salt water give way to freshwater?

¹³Who in your community is understanding and wise? Let his example, which is marked by wisdom and gentleness, blaze a trail for others. ¹⁴If your heart is one that bleeds dark streams of jealousy and selfishness, do not be so proud that you ignore your depraved state. ¹⁵The wisdom of this world should never be mistaken for heavenly wisdom; it originates below in the earthly realms, with the demons. ¹⁶Any place where you find jealousy and selfish ambition, you will discover chaos and evil thriving under its rule. ¹⁷Heavenly wisdom centers on purity, peace, gentleness, deference, mercy, and other good fruits untainted by hypocrisy. ¹⁸The seed that flowers into righteousness will always be planted in peace by those who embrace peace.

Worldly wisdom may promise the good life, but it leads to chaos and destruction every time. Ultimately true wisdom comes from God.

4 Where do you think your fighting and *endless* conflict come from? Don't you think that they originate in the *constant pursuit of* gratification that rages inside each of you *like an uncontrolled militia*? ²You crave something that you do not possess, so you murder to get it. You desire the things you cannot earn, so you *sue others and* fight for what you want. You do not have because you have chosen not to ask. ³And when you do ask, you still do not get what you want because your motives are all wrong—because you continually focus on self-indulgence. ⁴You are adulterers. Don't you know that making friends with this corrupt world order is open aggression toward God? So anyone who aligns with this bogus world system is declaring war against the one true God. ⁵Do you think it is empty rhetoric when the Scriptures say, "The spirit that lives in us is addicted to envy and jealousy"?* ⁶*You may think that the situation is hopeless,* but God gives us more grace *when we turn away from our own interests.* That's why Scripture says,

God opposes the proud,
    but He pours out grace on the
        humble.*

⁷So submit yourselves to the one true God and fight against the devil *and his schemes.* If you do, he will run away *in failure.* ⁸Come close to the one true God, and He will draw close to you. Wash your hands; you have dirtied them in sin. Cleanse your heart, because your mind is split down the middle, *your love for God on one side and selfish pursuits on the other.*

Since the beginning, our loving Creator has been pursuing us, drawing us closer to Him. He invites us to move closer to Him so we can be fully His.

⁹Now is the time to lament, to grieve, and to cry. Dissolve your laughter into sobbing, and exchange your joy for depression. ¹⁰Lay yourself *bare, facedown to the ground,* in humility before the Lord; and He will lift your head *so you can stand tall.* ¹¹My brothers and sisters, do not assault each other with criticism. If you decide your job is to accuse and judge another believer, then you are a self-appointed critic and judge of the law; if so, then you are no longer a doer of the law *and subject to its rule*; you stand over it as a judge. ¹²*Know this*—there is One who stands supreme as Judge and Lawgiver. He alone is able to save and to destroy, so who are you *to step in and try* to judge another?

¹³Listen carefully, those of you who *make your plans and* say, "We are traveling to this city in the next few days. We'll stay there for one year while our business explodes and revenue is up." ¹⁴The reality is you have no idea where your life will take you tomorrow. You are like a mist that appears one moment and then vanishes another. ¹⁵It would be best to say, "If it is the Lord's will and we live long enough, we hope to do this project or pursue that dream." ¹⁶But your current speech indicates an arrogance *that does not acknowledge the One who controls the universe,* and this kind of big talking is the epitome of evil. ¹⁷So if you know the right way to live and ignore it, it is sin—*plain and simple.*

5 Hey, you rich folk, misery is on its way; so cry and moan ²*because* you will watch your riches rot before your eyes as the moths devour your fine clothes.

* 4:5 Genesis 6:5   * 4:6 Proverbs 3:34

³Your stockpile of silver and gold is tarnished and corroded, and this rust will stand up in the final judgment and testify against you. It will eat your flesh like fire *and become a permanent and painful reminder that* you have hoarded your wealth through these last days. ⁴Listen. You held back a just wage from the laborers who mowed your fields, and that money is crying out against you, *demanding that justice be done.* The cries of the people who harvested your crops *and made you a profit* have fallen upon the ears of the supreme Lord of heavenly armies. ⁵Your life on the earth has been one of luxury, pleasure, and endless consumption; you have feasted to your hearts' content *on animals you slaughtered, but now* the day of slaughter comes *for you.* ⁶You have condemned and murdered the righteous man, and he did not defend himself.

⁷For this reason, my brothers and sisters, be patient as you wait for the return of the Lord. Look! The farmer knows how to wait patiently for the land to produce *vegetables and fruits. He cannot harvest a freshly planted seed.* Instead, he waits for the early and the late showers *to nourish the soil.* ⁸You need this same kind of patience, *so in the meantime,* strengthen your resolve because the Lord will be coming soon.

⁹Brothers and sisters, don't waste your breath complaining about one another. If you judge others, you will be judged yourself. Be very careful! *You will face* the one true Judge who is right outside the door. ¹⁰The prophets who declared the word of the Lord are your role models, my brothers and sisters, for what it means to live patiently in the face of suffering. ¹¹Look, we bless and honor the memory of those who persevered *under hardship.* Remember how Job endured and how the Lord orchestrated the triumph of his final circumstances as a grand display of His mercy and compassion.

¹²It is even more important, my brothers and sisters, that you remember not to make a vow by the heavens or the earth or by anything. When you say "yes," it should always mean "yes," and "no" should always mean "no." *If you can keep your word,* you will avoid judgment.

¹³Are any in your community suffering? They should pray. Are any celebrating? They should sing praises *to God.* ¹⁴Are any sick? They should call the elders of your church and ask them to pray. They will *gather around and* anoint them with oil in the name of the Lord. ¹⁵Prayers offered in faith will restore them from sickness *and bring them to health.* The Lord will lift them up *from the floor of despair;* and if the sickness is due to sin, then God will forgive their sins. ¹⁶So own up to your sins to one another and pray for one another. In the end, you may be healed. Your prayers are powerful when they are rooted in a righteous life. ¹⁷*Remember* Elijah? He was a man, no different from us. He prayed with great intensity asking God to withhold the rain; God *answered his prayers and* did not allow a single drop of rain to fall for three and a half years. ¹⁸It did not rain until Elijah prayed again *for God to open the skies,* when the rain came down and the earth produced a great crop.

Why should we bother to pray if God already knows what we are going to ask for? Prayer involves so much more than making personal requests. It connects us with God and works to bring our wills into conformity with His.

How, then, should we pray? First, James tells us to pray in community, not just by ourselves and for ourselves. When we pray together, life is shared and community is born. We also confess our sins, not just to God, but to each other. Through this vulnerable transparency, God knits souls together in authentic community, and we discover the true benefit of prayer.

---

¹⁹Brothers and sisters, if someone you know loses his way and rebels *against God, pursue him in love and* bring him back to the truth. ²⁰Know this: If you turn a sinner back from the error of his ways, then you will rescue him from the grips of death and cover *the pain and consequences of* untold sins.

1 PETER

Instruction to the church scattered

From Peter, the apostle to Jewish Christians

This letter is written by Peter, a fisherman from Galilee who became one of the most prominent leaders of the early church. Though his name is Simon, Jesus gave him the nickname "Peter," which means "rock." Jesus said Peter would be the rock or foundation the church would be built on. Although Peter knows he is a key leader in the movement, he is humble enough to understand that Jesus is actually the cornerstone, the One who holds the church together. That's why the image of a temple, crafted from stone, touches Peter so deeply. As the "rock," Peter urges his listeners to come to Jesus, the cornerstone, and join Him in building a new temple and forming a new priesthood where spiritual sacrifices are offered to God.

Peter addresses Christians scattered throughout Asia Minor (modern Turkey). Whether he knows these churches personally, it is impossible to determine. But as one of Jesus' original disciples, a member of "the twelve," his stature and reputation are such that he can gain a hearing as the churches gather. He says they are "living as aliens" because he knows they are having a difficult time relating to the pagan world around them. Like strangers on a journey in a culture and land not their own, these early Christians feel out of step with everyone else. In times of persecution, these Christians come to identify themselves as aliens and sojourners even among their own people.

Writing this letter to encourage believers who were going through intense persecution, Peter shares the lessons he learned from his own oppression. Peter writes this letter "from Babylon," probably a cryptic designation for Rome, the imperial capital where the fires of persecution burn the hottest. According to him, followers of Jesus should not be surprised by the fiery ordeals that come their way. In fact, when they experience social ostracism, imprisonment, torture, and even death, they are participating in the ongoing sufferings of Jesus. So Peter calls them to entrust themselves to God and to have courage in the face of persecution. Suffering that lacks meaning or purpose is suffering without hope, so Peter tries to infuse them with hope by reminding them of who they are and urging them to imitate the One who calls them.

1 Peter, an emissary* of Jesus the Anointed One, to God's chosen people living as aliens scattered *among the unbelievers* in Pontus, Galatia, Cappadocia, Asia, and Bithynia. ²*I am sending this letter to those* who have been selected and destined by God the Father and made holy by *God* the Spirit that you may be obedient to Jesus the Anointed and *purified* by the sprinkling of His blood. May grace and peace beyond all reckoning be yours.

³Blessed is God, the Father of our Lord Jesus, the Anointed One! Because He has raised Jesus the Anointed from death, through His great mercy we have been reborn into a living hope—⁴reborn for an eternal inheritance, held in reserve in heaven, that will never fade or fail. ⁵Through faith, God's power is *standing watch,* protecting you for a salvation that you will see completely at the end of things. ⁶You should greatly rejoice *in what is waiting for you,* even if now for a little while you have to suffer various trials. ⁷*Suffering tests* your faith which is more valuable than gold (remember that gold, although it is perishable, is tested by fire) so that if it is found genuine, you can receive praise, honor, and glory when Jesus the Anointed, *our Liberating King,* is revealed at last.

Early Christians stand apart from the culture and suffer social stigmas and physical persecution at times. Peter challenges them to remain faithful to Jesus who also suffered for not conforming.

⁸Although you haven't seen Jesus, you *still* love Him. Although you don't yet see Him, you do believe in Him and celebrate with a joy that is glorious and beyond words. ⁹You are receiving the salvation of your souls as the result of your faith.

¹⁰The prophets who spoke of this *outpouring of* grace upon you diligently searched and inquired *of the Lord* about this salvation: ¹¹to whom and to what time was the indwelling Spirit of the Anointed referring when He told them about the suffering of the Anointed and the honor that would follow it? ¹²The Spirit revealed to them they were not serving themselves but you. And you have learned from those who told you the good news by the Spirit that was sent down from heaven. Even the heavenly messengers would like to explore this news.

¹³So *get yourselves ready,* prepare your minds to act, control yourselves, and look forward in hope as you focus on the grace that comes when Jesus the Anointed *returns and* is completely revealed to you. ¹⁴Be like obedient children as you put aside the desires you used to pursue when you didn't know better. ¹⁵Since the One who called you is holy, be holy in all you do. ¹⁶For the Scripture says, "You are to be holy, for I am holy."* ¹⁷If you call on the Father who judges everyone without partiality according to their actions, then you should live in reverence and awe while you live out the days of your exile.

¹⁸You know that a price was paid to redeem you from following the empty ways handed on to you by your ancestors; it was not paid with things that perish (like silver and gold), ¹⁹but with the precious blood of the Anointed, who was like a perfect and unblemished sacrificial lamb. ²⁰God determined to send Him before the world began, but He came *into the world* in these last days for your sake. ²¹Through Him, you've been brought to trust in God, who raised Him from the dead and glorified Him for the very reason that your faith and hope are in Him.

²²Now that you have *taken care to* purify your souls through your submission to the truth, you can experience real love for each other. So love each other deeply from a [pure]* heart. ²³You have been reborn—not from seed that eventually dies but from seed that is eternal—through the word of God that lives and endures forever. ²⁴For *as Isaiah said,*

All life is like the grass,
    and its glory like a flower;
The grass will wither *and die,*
    and the flower falls,
²⁵But the word of the Lord will endure
    forever.*

This is the word that has been preached to you.

2 So get rid of hatefulness and deception, of insincerity and jealousy and slander. ²Be like newborn babies, crying out for spiritual milk that will help you grow into salvation ³if you have tasted *and found* the Lord to be good.

* 1:1 Literally, apostle   * 1:16 Leviticus 11:44-45; 19:2; 20:7
* 1:22 Some manuscripts omit "pure."   * 1:24-25 Isaiah 40:6b-8

⁴Come to Him—the living stone—who was rejected by people but *accepted* by God as chosen and precious. ⁵Like living stones, let yourselves be assembled into a spiritual house, a holy order of priests who offer up spiritual sacrifices that will be acceptable to God through Jesus the Anointed. ⁶For it says in the words *of the prophet Isaiah,*

See here—I am laying in Zion a stone,
    a cornerstone, chosen and precious;
Whoever depends upon Him will never
    be disgraced.*

⁷To you who believe *and depend on Him,* He is precious; but to you who don't, *remember the words of the psalmist:*

The stone that the builders rejected
    has been laid as the cornerstone—the
        very stone *that holds together the
        entire foundation,*

⁸and of *Isaiah:*

A stone that blocks their way,
    a rock that trips them.*

They stumble because they don't follow the word of God, as they were destined to do. ⁹But you are a chosen people, *set aside to be* a royal order of priests, a holy nation, God's own; so that you may proclaim the wondrous acts of the One who called you out of *inky* darkness into shimmering light. ¹⁰Once you were not a people, but now you are God's people; once you had not received mercy, but now you have received it.

¹¹Beloved, remember *you don't belong in this world.* You are resident aliens living in exile, so resist those desires of the flesh that battle against the soul. ¹²Live honorably among the outsiders so that, even when some may be inclined to call you criminals, when they see your good works, they might give glory to God when He returns in judgment. ¹³For the Lord's sake, accept the decrees and laws of all the various human institutions, whether they come from the highest human ruler ¹⁴or agents he sends to punish those who do wrong and to reward those who do well. ¹⁵You see, it is God's will that by doing what is right *and good* you should hush the gabbing ignorance of the foolish. ¹⁶Live as those who are free and not as those who use their freedom as a pretext for evil,

but live as God's servants. ¹⁷Respect everyone. Love the community of believers. Reverence God. Honor your ruler.

¹⁸*If you are a* slave, submit yourself to the master who has authority over you, whether he is kind and gentle or harsh *as he deals with you.* ¹⁹For grace is clearly at work when a person accepts undeserved pain and suffering and does so because he is mindful of God. ²⁰For what credit is there in enduring punishment you deserve? But if you do what is right and yet are punished and endure it patiently, God will be pleased with you. ²¹⁻²²For you were called to this *kind of life, as* Isaiah said,

He did no wrong deed,
    and no evil word came from His
        mouth.*

Many believers face intense persecution, but western Christians tend not to experience anything beyond social pressure. Are we merely pursuing comfort, or are we willing to swim against culture?

The Anointed One suffered for us and left us His example so that we could follow in His steps. ²³When He was verbally abused, He didn't return the abuse; when He suffered, He didn't make threats *to cause suffering in*

* 2:6 Isaiah 28:16   * 2:7 Psalm 118:22   * 2:8 Isaiah 8:14
* 2:21-22 Isaiah 53:9

return; instead, He trusted that all would be put right by the One who is just when He judges. ²⁴He took on our sins in His body *when He died* on the cross* so that we, being dead to sin, can live for righteousness. *As the Scripture says,* "Through His wounds, you were healed."* ²⁵For there was a time when you were like sheep that wandered from the fold, but now you have returned to the Shepherd and Guardian of your lives.

Peter calls all believers to humility, submission, and service: everyone to God, citizens to rulers, slaves to masters, wives to husbands, and younger to elders.

3 ¹⁻²In the same way, wives, you should patiently accept the authority of your husbands. This is so that even if they don't obey God's word, as they observe your pure respectful behavior, they may be persuaded without a word by the way you live. ³Don't focus on decorating your exterior by doing your hair or putting on fancy jewelry or wearing fashionable clothes; ⁴let your adornment be what's inside—*the real you,* the lasting beauty of a gracious and quiet spirit, in which God delights. ⁵This is how, long ago, holy women who put their hope in God made themselves beautiful: by respecting the authority of their husbands. ⁶Consider how Sarah, *our mother,* obeyed *her husband,* Abraham, and called him "lord," and you will be her daughters as long as you boldly do what is right without fear *and without anxiety.*

⁷In the same way, husbands, as you live with your wives, understand *the situations* women *face* as the weaker vessel. *Each of you should respect your wife* and value her as an equal heir in the gracious gift of life. Do this so that nothing will get in the way of your prayers.

⁸Finally, all of you, be like-minded and show sympathy, love, compassion, and humility to and for each other—⁹not paying back evil with evil or insult with insult, but repaying the bad with a blessing. It was this you were called to do, so that you might inherit a blessing. ¹⁰*It is written in the psalms,*

If you love life
and want to live a good, long time,
Then be careful what you say.
Don't tell lies or spread gossip or talk
about improper things.

¹¹Walk away from the evil *things in the world—just leave them behind,* and do what is right,
and *always* seek peace and pursue it.
¹²For the Lord watches over the righteous,
and His ears are attuned to their prayers.

But His face is set against *His enemies;*
He will punish evildoers.*

¹³Why would anyone harm you if you eagerly do good? ¹⁴Even if you should suffer for doing what is right, you will receive a blessing. Don't let them frighten you. Don't be intimidated, ¹⁵⁻¹⁶but exalt Him as Lord in your heart. Always be ready to offer a defense, humbly and respectfully, when someone asks why you live in hope. Keep your conscience clear so that those who ridicule your good conduct in the Anointed and say bad things about you will be put to shame.

V

Peter urges us always to be ready to give a reason for the hope that lives within us. But it is important that it be done not with arrogance and contempt, but with gentleness and love—the same virtues that should guide our responses to any hostile challenge. This is one way we can glorify Jesus as King over all our lives—by exalting Him with both our emotions and our intellect.

---

¹⁷For if it is the will of God that you suffer, then it is better to suffer for doing what is right than for doing what is wrong. ¹⁸The Anointed One suffered for sins once for all time—the righteous *suffering* for the unrighteous—so that He might bring us to God. Though He died in the flesh, He was made alive again through the Spirit. ¹⁹And in the Spirit, He went and preached to those spirits held captive. ²⁰*It was these* who long ago lived in disobedience while God waited patiently as Noah was building the ark. At that time, only a tiny band—eight people—was spared from the flood.

²¹The water *through which the ark safely passed* symbolizes now the ceremonial washing through baptism* *that initiates* you into salvation. You are saved not because it

* 2:24 Literally, tree   * 2:24 Isaiah 53:5   * 3:10-12 Psalm 34:12-16
* 3:21 Literally, immersion, in a rite of initiation and purification

cleanses your body of filth but because of your appeal to God from a good conscience, through the resurrection of Jesus the Anointed, *our Liberating King.* ²²Now He has entered heaven and sits at the right hand of God as heavenly messengers and authorities and powers submit to His supremacy.

4 Since the Anointed suffered in the flesh, prepare yourselves to do the same—anyone who has suffered in the flesh *for the Lord* is no longer in the grip of sin—²so that you may live the rest of your life on earth *controlled* not by earthly desires but by the will of God.

V

The reality of suffering in the world causes many to question the existence of an all-powerful and all-loving God. A God of power and love is expected to be both able and willing to remove suffering from our lives. Ultimately, God will make all things new and end suffering, but for now God allows it and calls us to rejoice in the midst of it. Though we may not understand it, pain and suffering have a purpose in God's plan, and our Creator is not immune to it. Through Jesus God enters into our suffering; now we are called to enter into His.

---

³You have already wasted enough time living like those outsiders in the society around you: losing yourselves in sex, in addictions and desires, in drinking and lawless idolatry, in *giving your time and* allegiance to things that are not godly. ⁴When you don't play the same games they do, they notice that you are living by different rules. That's why they say such terrible things about you. ⁵Someday they, too, will have to give an account *of themselves* to the One who judges the living and the dead. ⁶(This is why the good news had to be brought to those who are dead so that although they are judged in the flesh, they might live in the spirit in the way that pleases God.)

⁷We are coming to the end of all things, so be serious and keep your wits about you in order to pray *more forcefully.* ⁸Most of all, love each other steadily and unselfishly, because love makes up for many faults.

⁹Show hospitality to each other without complaint. ¹⁰Use whatever gift you've received for *the good of* one another so that you can show yourselves to be good stewards of God's grace in all its varieties. ¹¹If you're called upon to talk, speak as though God put the words in your mouth; if you're called upon to serve others, serve as though you had the strength of God behind you. In these ways, God may be glorified in all you do through Jesus the Anointed, to whom belongs glory and power, now and forever. Amen.

¹²Dear ones, don't be surprised when you experience your trial by fire. It is not something strange and unusual, ¹³but it is something you should rejoice in. In it you share the Anointed's sufferings, and you will be that much more joyful when His glory is revealed. ¹⁴If anyone condemns you for following *Jesus as* the Anointed One, consider yourself blessed. The glorious Spirit of God rests on you. ¹⁵But none of you should ever merit suffering like those who have murdered or stolen, meddled in the affairs of others or done evil things. ¹⁶But if you should suffer for being a Christian, don't think of it as a disgrace, *as it would be if you had done wrong.* Praise God that you're permitted to carry this name.

People often suffer because of poor decisions that result in shame, but the people of God face persecution for their faithfulness that leads to honor and glory.

¹⁷For the time for judgment has come, and it is beginning with the household of God. If it is starting with us, what will happen to those who have rejected God's good news? ¹⁸*It is written in Proverbs,*

If it is hard for the righteous ones to be saved,
> what will happen to the ungodly and the sinners?*

¹⁹So even if you should suffer now for doing God's will, continue doing good and trust your futures to the judgment and mercy of a faithful Creator.

5 Now for the elders *of the church.* I want to encourage you. *As you know,* I am an elder, too, like you. I have witnessed

* 4:18 Proverbs 11:31

firsthand the sufferings of the Anointed One as well as shared in the glories which are soon to be revealed. [2]*When you* shepherd the flock God has given you, watch over them not because you have to but because you want to. For this is how God would want it not because you're being compensated somehow but because you are eager to watch over them. [3]Don't lead them as if you were a dictator, but lead your flock by example; [4]and when the Chief Shepherd appears, you will be crowned with honor that will shine brightly forever. [5]You who are younger *in the faith*: do as your elders *and leaders* ask. All of you should treat each other with humility, *for as it says in Proverbs,*

God opposes the proud
    but offers grace to the humble.*

[6]So bow down under God's strong hand; then when the time comes, God will lift you up. [7]Since God cares for you, let Him carry all your burdens and worries.

Humility is rarely a virtue that our culture values. We're trained from an early age to show our strengths and hide our weaknesses. This type of thinking also spills over into our models of leadership, as we learn to dictate to others how they should perform. Peter, however, says that we should be humble in our relationships with one another and not lead as dictators. In fact, this humility before one another and God is actually the position of the greatest strength. Our enemy desires to consume us, but we find strength to resist him when we are dependent upon God for His strength.

---

[8]*Most importantly,* be disciplined and stay on guard. Your enemy the devil is prowling around outside like a roaring lion, just waiting *and hoping for the chance* to devour someone. [9]Resist him and be strong in your faith, knowing that your brothers and sisters throughout the world are fellow sufferers with you. [10]After you have suffered for a little while, the God of grace who has called you [to His everlasting presence]* through Jesus the Anointed will restore you, support you, strengthen you, and ground you. [11]For all power belongs to God, now and forever. Amen.

[12]Silvanus,* whom I consider a trustworthy and faithful brother, is carrying this brief letter to encourage you and to testify that here is the true grace of God. Hold on to it.

[13]The church *here* in Babylon* chosen *by God* together with you, sends you greetings. So does my son *in the faith* Mark.

[14]Greet each other with a kiss of love, and may peace come to all who follow *Jesus* the Anointed.

* 5:5 Proverbs 3:34   * 5:10 Early manuscripts omit this portion.
* 5:12 Silvanus is better known in Acts as Silas.   * 5:13 A cryptic designation for Rome

2 PETER

Instruction to the church scattered

From Peter, the apostle to Jewish Christians

Later tradition credits this letter to Peter—one of "the twelve," an eyewitness to much of Jesus' public ministry, and the same disciple who (according to tradition) when sentenced to die requested to be crucified upside down because he felt unworthy to die in the same way his Lord did. Initially there were questions about this letter, so it was one of the last letters accepted and made part of the New Testament canon. Peter writes this second letter to the same churches he addresses in 1 Peter. But the address here is more generic, which suggests that he expects this letter to be read broadly to anyone who shares his faith in Jesus.

Peter begins by celebrating God's power and the true knowledge of God, which leads to salvation. For him salvation consists of escaping the corruption that characterizes this world and sharing in God's very nature. But believers must cooperate with God's work in them in order to live fully into the promises God has for those who believe. Virtue, knowledge, self-control, godliness, and love: these are the characteristics that form the life of any true believer.

At the heart of the letter is a warning against the growing influence of false teachers who have infiltrated the churches. With their greed, sensuality, arrogance, and hatred for authority, these false believers are undermining the church. Peter looks back over Jewish history and notices that God did not spare the disobedient in the past, so God's judgment on the present false teachers is sure. Some of the false teachers are mocking the hope that Jesus will return again, but Peter assures his audience that any delay in Jesus' return has to do with God's patience: He wishes for all to change their ways and enter the Kingdom. The day of the Lord will come, he writes, like a thief in the night, and the old world will give way to a new world as only God can create it.

1 Simon Peter, a servant and emissary* of Jesus the Anointed One, to those who have received the same precious faith we share through the righteousness of our God and Savior, Jesus the Anointed. ²I wish you a full measure of grace and peace *as you grow* in the knowledge of God and of Jesus our Lord.

³His divine power has given us everything we need to experience life and to reflect God's true nature through the knowledge of the One who called us by His glory and virtue. ⁴Through these things, we have received God's great and valuable promises, so we might escape the corruption of worldly desires and share in the divine nature.

V

God took the first step to rescue us from this corrupt world. He has granted us His power, revealed to us true knowledge, and spoken to us great promises. He has done all this for a reason: that we might participate in His own nature and reflect His own life. But we are not passive observers of God's saving actions. We must receive His grace, grow in knowledge, and join Him in this work of redemption.

⁵To achieve this, you will need to add virtue to your faith, and then knowledge to your virtue; ⁶to knowledge, add discipline; to discipline, add endurance; to endurance, add godliness; ⁷to godliness, add affection for others as sisters and brothers; and to affection, *at last,* add love. ⁸For if you possess these traits and multiply them, then you will never be ineffective or unproductive in your relationship with our Lord Jesus the Anointed; ⁹but if you don't have these qualities, then you will be nearsighted and blind, forgetting that your past sins have been washed away. ¹⁰Therefore, brothers and sisters, work that much harder to confirm that God has called you and claimed you. If you do this, then you will never fall along the way; ¹¹and you can be sure that you will be richly welcomed into the eternal kingdom of our Lord and Savior Jesus the Anointed, *our Liberating King.*

¹²That is why I will keep reminding you of these things, even though I know that you believe them and have made these truths a part of your lives; ¹³as long as I draw breath, I know it is right for me to keep on stirring you up with these reminders. ¹⁴I know that soon I must *die and* lay down this *old* body that's been my home—our Lord Jesus the Anointed has told me so. ¹⁵*But before my exodus from this life,* I want to be certain you will be able to call these things to mind anytime you need them even after I am gone.

Faith does not rest upon cleverly devised fables invented by creative minds; it rests upon the testimonies of eyewitnesses who faithfully pass down what they see and hear to others.

¹⁶For *I want to remind you that* when we told you about the power and coming of our Lord Jesus the Anointed, we were relying on what our eyes had seen of His *glorious* majesty, not on cleverly told fables. ¹⁷You see, God the Father lavished honor and glory upon Jesus when the voice of the Majestic Glory echoed *from heaven* and said, "This is My beloved Son, and My favor rests on Him."* ¹⁸*We witnessed this*—we ourselves heard this voice from heaven—when we were with Jesus on that holy mountain. ¹⁹We have a fuller confirmation of the message of the prophets. You would do well to pay close attention to this word; it is like a light that shines for you in the darkness of night until the day dawns when the morning star rises in your own hearts.

Peter and two other disciples see Jesus transfigured. This event and the heavenly voice confirm Jesus' true identity and are a prelude to the greatest miracle of all—the resurrection.

²⁰But notice first that no prophecy found in Scripture is a matter of the prophet's own interpretation. ²¹Prophecy has never been a product of human initiative, but it comes when men *and women* are moved to speak on behalf of God by the Holy Spirit.

2 Just as false prophets rose up *in the past* among *God's* people, false teachers will rise up *in the future* among you. They will slip in with their destructive opinions, denying the very Master who bought their freedom and dooming themselves to

destruction swiftly, [2]but not before they attract others by their unbridled and immoral behavior. Because of them *and their ways*, others will criticize *and condemn* the path of truth *we walk as seedy and disreputable*. [3]These *false teachers* will follow their greed and exploit you with their fabrications, but *be assured that* their judgment was pronounced long ago and their destruction does not sleep.

New Testament writers warn the church to watch out for false teachers. Peter faults them primarily for their immoral lifestyles rather than for doctrinal differences.

[4]For God did not spare the heavenly beings who sinned, but He cast them into the dark pits* of hell* to be kept until the time of judgment; [5]and He did not spare the ancient world, but He sent a flood swirling over the ungodly (although He did save Noah, God's herald for what is right, with seven other *members of his family*); [6]and God condemned the cities of Sodom and Gomorrah, reducing them to ash as a lesson of what He will do with the ungodly in the days to come [7-8](although again He did rescue Lot, a person who did what was right in God's eyes and who was distressed by the immorality *and the lawlessness* of the society around him. Day after day, the sights and sounds of their lawlessness were like daggers into that good man's soul). [9]*If all this happened in the past,* it shows clearly the Lord knows how to rescue the godly from their trials and how to hold the wicked in punishment until the day of judgment.

V

Is God different in the New Testament from what He is in the First Testament? In the First Testament, God seems prone to judgment; but some feel God is more concerned about love in the New Testament. However, the central and most repeated affirmation about God's character in the First Testament is that He is gracious and compassionate (Exodus 34:6-7). And the New Testament clearly does not ignore the idea of God's judgment, as this text shows. His judgment will come, but it is delayed by God's patient mercy.

[10]And above all, it shows He will punish those who let the desires of their bodies rule them and who have no respect for authority. People like this are so bold and willful that they aren't even afraid of offending heavenly beings, [11]although the heavenly messengers—in spite of the fact that they have greater strength and power—make no such accusations against these people before the Lord. [12]These people who speak ill of what they do not understand are no different from animals—without sense, operating only on their instincts, born to be captured and killed—and they will be destroyed just like those animals, [13]receiving the penalty for their evil acts. They waste their days in *parties and* carousing. As they feast with you, these stains and blemishes *on your community* are feasting on their deceptions.* [14]Their eyes are always looking for their next adulterous conquests; their appetites for sin cannot be satisfied. They seduce the unwary soul, and greed is the only lesson they have learned by heart. God's curse lies upon them. [15]They have veered off the right road and gotten lost, following in the steps of Balaam, the son of Beor, *the false prophet*. Balaam loved the reward he could get by doing evil, [16]but he was rebuked for crossing the line into sin; his own speechless donkey scolded him in a human voice, *an amazing miracle* that reined in the prophet's insanity.*

[17]These *people I'm talking about* are *nothing but* dried-up springs, mists driven by fierce winds; the deepest darkness has been set aside for them. [18]They speak *in loud voices* empty and arrogant. They exploit the desires of the flesh, *take advantage of* sensual natures, to entangle people who have just escaped from those who live by deception. [19]They claim to offer them freedom, but they themselves are enslaved by corruption because whatever a person gives in to soon becomes his master. [20]Those who have been pulled out of the cesspool of worldly desires through the knowledge of our Lord and Savior Jesus, the Anointed One, yet have found themselves mired in it again are worse off than they were before. [21]They would have been better off never knowing the way of righteousness than to have known it and then abandoned the sacred commandment they had previously received *and dived back into the muck!* [22]In their cases, the words

from Proverbs hold true: "The dog goes back to his own vomit,"* and *as the Greeks say,* "The sow is washed to wallow in the mud."

3 This is now, my dear friends, my second letter to you. In both of them, I *have tried to* inspire you to a sincere *and pure* way of thinking by reminding you *of what you already know.* ²Remember the words spoken earlier by God's holy prophets and the commandment that our Lord and Savior *gave to you* through your emissaries.* ³Above all, be sure to remember that in the last days mockers will come, following their own desires and taunting you, ⁴saying, "So what happened to the promised *second* coming of Jesus? For everything keeps going just the way it has since our ancestors fell asleep *in death*; since the beginning of creation, nothing's changed."

These believers face persecution every day and eagerly await the day when Jesus will return and judge their enemies. But what is taking so long?

⁵*When they make fun of you,* it's as if the scoffers are deliberately forgetting that long ago when God spoke the word, the heavens came into existence and the earth formed from water and by water. ⁶The waters *later* flooded and destroyed that world. ⁷By that same word, the heavens and earth *we see* now are being reserved for *destruction by* fire, preserved until the time comes for the godless on the day of judgment.

⁸Don't imagine, dear friends, *that God's timetable is the same as ours; as the psalm says,* for with the Lord, one day is like a thousand years, and a thousand years is like one day.*

Scoffers use the delay in His second coming to question if He is going to return at all. Peter responds by saying that God's perspective on time is not like ours. What seems long from a finite, human perspective is incredibly short from an eternal one. Peter also describes how God is not slow, but patient. God wants to allow the time needed for as many sinners as possible to turn from their sinful ways. Unlike some depictions

of God as vindictive and enjoying inflicting punishment on people, the God we see here desires that all be saved and not destroyed. If we had true spiritual insight, we would not be amazed by the severity of eternal judgment but by the intensity of God's mercy.

---

⁹*Now* the Lord is not slow about enacting His promise—slow is how some people want to characterize it—*no, He is not slow* but patient *and merciful* to you, not wanting anyone to be destroyed, but wanting everyone to turn away from following his own path and to turn toward God's.*

¹⁰The day of the Lord will come *unexpectedly* like a thief in the night; and on that day, the sky will vanish with a roar, the elements will melt with intense heat, and the earth and all the works done on it will be seen as they truly are.* ¹¹Knowing that one day all this will come to pass, think what sort of people you ought to be—how you should be living faithful and godly lives, ¹²waiting *hopefully* for and hastening the coming of God's day when the heavens will vanish in flames and the elements melt away with intense heat. ¹³*What will happen next,* and what we hope for, is what God promised: a new heaven and a new earth where justice reigns.

¹⁴So, my friends, while we wait for the day of the Lord, work hard to live in peace, without flaw or blemish; ¹⁵and look at the patience of the Lord as your salvation. Our dearly loved brother Paul, according to the wisdom given him, has written about this. ¹⁶He says *essentially* the same in all of his letters, although uneducated and unstable readers misinterpret the difficult passages, just as they always misread Scripture, to their *spiritual* ruin.

¹⁷So *hear my final words,* my friends. Now that I have warned you about what's ahead, keep up your guard and don't let unprincipled people pull you away from the sure ground *of the truth* with their lies and misunderstandings. ¹⁸Instead, grow in grace and in the *true* knowledge of our Lord and Savior Jesus, the Anointed, to whom be glory, now and until the coming of the new age. Amen.

* 2:22 Proverbs 26:11 * 3:2 Literally, apostles * 3:8 An allusion to Psalm 90:4 * 3:9 Literally, repent * 3:10 Other manuscripts read "be burned up."

1 JOHN

Instructions to believers everywhere

From John, the apostle

This letter was written by John the emissary, one of Jesus' earliest followers. Before he became a disciple, John worked as a fisherman with his father Zebedee and his brother James on the Sea of Galilee. Once he joined Jesus, John became one of Jesus' closest friends, part of an inner circle within "the twelve" that included Peter, Andrew, and James. But out of all the disciples, it seems that John had the closest relationship with Jesus. He was known as "the disciple loved by Jesus" (John 19:26; 21:7,20).

John writes this letter from Ephesus, a bustling seaside city whose ruins are now found in Western Turkey. Although 1 John is classified as a letter, it doesn't have all the elements of a letter written in its day. It has no typical opening or closing. In fact, it is not written to one person or church in particular, but is directed to several different churches made up mainly of non-Jews. He writes this letter as an old man, after serving in ministry for a very long time. He uses a tender, fatherly tone toward people he views as his spiritual "little children"—the new generation of Christians who have not seen Jesus with their own eyes as John did.

John begins this letter much as he does his Gospel. In both writings, he opens by stressing the eternal nature of Jesus. He explains how Jesus was with the Father from the beginning, before the creation of the world and before He was revealed to the world in human flesh. John then describes God as light and encourages believers to walk in the light by stepping away from the darkness of sin. Like other New Testament writers, he also warns believers to beware of false teachers who deny the true identity of Jesus. But most of all, John focuses on love—how God lavishes His love on His children and how they are to do the same to one another. The love of God must overwhelm the believer's desire for the material things of this life. John goes so far as to say, "Don't fall in love with this *corrupt* world or *worship* the things it can offer. Those who love its corrupt ways don't have the Father's love living within them" (2:15).

1 We want to tell you about the One who was from the beginning. We have seen Him with our own eyes, heard Him with our own ears, and touched Him with our own hands. This One is *the manifestation of* the life-giving Voice, [2] and He showed us real life, *eternal life.* We have seen it *all, and we can't keep what* we witnessed *quiet*—we have to share it with you. *We are inviting you to experience* eternal life through the One who was with the Father and came down to us. [3]What we saw and heard we pass on to you so that you, too, will be connected with us intimately *and become family.* Our family is united by our connection with the Father and His Son Jesus, the Anointed One; [4]and we write all this because retelling this story fulfills our* joy.

[5]What we are telling you now is the very message we heard from Him: God is *pure* light, undimmed by darkness of any kind. [6]If we say we have an intimate connection with the Father but we continue stumbling around in darkness, then we are lying because we do not live according to truth. [7]If we walk *step by step* in the light, where the Father is, then we are ultimately connected to each other *through the sacrifice of* Jesus His Son. His blood purifies us from all our sins. [8]If we go around bragging, "We have no sin," then we are fooling ourselves and are strangers to the truth. [9]But if we own up to our sins, God shows that He is faithful and just by forgiving us of our sins and purifying us from the pollution of all the bad things we have done. [10]If we say, "We have not sinned," then we depict God as a liar and *show that* we have not let His word find its way into our hearts.

The word "sin" has virtually disappeared from modern conversation. Afraid of sounding judgmental, we call sin something else—a mistake, an addiction, a tendency, a bad decision—and ignore it as normal and natural behavior. But John is calling the church to a radical holiness where those in the church will regularly remember their sins and seek God's forgiveness. Each sin, small and large, injures us or someone else; it imprints on our soul, makes us imperfect, and separates us from the perfect God. If we

confess our sins to God each day, then He will purify our hearts and draw us closer to Him.

---

2 *You are* my little children, so I am writing these things to help you avoid sin. If, however, any believer does sin, we have a *high-powered* defense lawyer—Jesus the Anointed, the righteous—*arguing on our behalf* before the Father. [2]It was through His sacrificial death that our sins were atoned. But He did not stop there—He died for the sins of the whole world.

John is affectionately addressing this letter to his "little children," and he is writing to help them avoid sin and the pain and guilt that come with it. The glamour of decadent lifestyles devoid of God is often advertised as the epitome of joy and freedom. But what are often conveniently left out of these portrayals are the agonizing consequences of such destructive lifestyles. Meaningful pleasure comes not when we are enslaved by the empty promises of the world, but when we are living in loving obedience to God.

---

[3]We know we have joined Him in an intimate relationship because we live out His commands. [4]If someone claims, "I am in an intimate relationship with Him," but this big talker doesn't live out His commands, then this individual is a liar and a stranger to the truth. [5]But if someone *responds to and* obeys His word, then God's love has truly taken root and filled him. This is how we know we are in an intimate relationship with Him: [6]anyone who says, "I live in intimacy with Him," should walk the path Jesus walked.

[7]My loved ones, *in one sense,* I am not writing a new command for you. I am only reminding you of the old command. It's a word you already know, a word that has existed from the beginning. [8]However, in another sense, I am writing a new command for you. The new command is the truth that He lived; and now you are living it, too,

* 1:4 Other manuscripts read "your."

because the darkness is fading and the true light is already shining *among you.*

⁹Anyone who says, "I live in the light," but hates his brother or sister is still living in the shadows. ¹⁰Anyone who loves his brother or sister lives in the light and will not trip *because his conscience is clear.* ¹¹But anyone who hates his brother is in the darkness, stumbling around with no idea where he is going, blinded by the darkness.

We are deeply loved by God. When we turn and love those members of our faith family whom God loves, we are set apart and different from the world.

¹²I am writing to you, my children, because your sins have been forgiven by the authority of His name.

¹³I am writing to you, fathers *and mothers,* because you have known Him *as the Creator,* as the One who started everything.

I am writing to you, young people, because *He has given* you *the power to* conquer the evil one.

¹⁴I have written to you, my children, because you have known the Father.

I have written to you, fathers *and mothers,* because you have known Him, the Creator.

I have written to you, young people, because the voice of God remains *and is heard* among you. *Remember that* you have conquered the evil one.

¹⁵Don't fall in love with this *corrupt* world or *worship* the things it can offer. Those who love its corrupt ways don't have the Father's love living within them. ¹⁶All the things the world can offer to you—the allure of pleasure, the passion to have things, and the pompous sense of superiority—do not come from the Father. These are *the rotten fruits* of this world. ¹⁷This *corrupt* world is already wasting away, as are its selfish desires. But the person really doing God's will—*that person* will never cease to be.

¹⁸My children, this is the final hour. You have heard that the antiChrist, *the greatest enemy to His kingdom,* is coming, but in fact, many antiChrists are already here. This development tells us how late it really is. ¹⁹A group has left us, but they were not part of our family. If they were truly our brothers and sisters, they would have remained *for the duration* with us. When they left, they made it *ever so* obvious that they were not part of us.

²⁰You have been given an anointing, *a special touch* from the Holy One. You know *the truth.** ²¹I am not writing to you because you do not know the truth, but because you do know it. You know that no lie belongs to the truth. ²²The liar is the one who says, "Jesus is not really the Anointed One." This is the antiChrist, the one denying both the Father and the Son. ²³Anyone who denies the Son does not know the Father. The one affirming the Son enjoys an intimate relationship with the Father as well.

²⁴Let *the good news,* the story you have heard from the beginning of your journey, live in *and take hold of* you. If that happens *and you focus on the good news,* then you will always remain in a relationship with the Son and the Father. ²⁵This is what He promised us: eternal life.

²⁶I also am writing to warn you about some who are attempting to deceive you. ²⁷You have an anointing. You received it from Him, and His anointing remains on you. You do not need any other teacher. But as His anointing instructs you in all *the essentials* (all the truth uncontaminated by darkness and lies), it teaches you this: "Remain connected to Him."

²⁸So now, my little children, live in Him, so that whenever He is revealed, we will have confidence and not have *to hang our heads in* shame before Him when He comes. ²⁹If you know that He is just *and faithful,* then you also know that everyone who lives *faithfully* and acts justly has been born into a new life through Him.

3 Consider the kind of extravagant love the Father has lavished on us—He calls us children of God! It's true; we are His *beloved* children. And in the same way the world didn't recognize Him, the world does not recognize us either.

When we feel like we are not good enough to be loved by God, we should remember that God's love is greater than our doubts. We must silence the sounds of condemnation so we can hear the voice of God's loving assurance and

* 2:20 Other manuscripts read "all things."

remember that He has selected us to be part of His family.

---

²My loved ones, *we have been adopted into God's family; and* we are officially His children now. The full picture of our destiny is not yet clear, but we know this much: when Jesus appears, we will be like Him because we will see Him just as He is. ³All those who focus their hopes on Him *and His coming* seek to purify themselves just as He is pure. ⁴Everyone who lives a life of habitual sin is living in moral anarchy. That's what sin is. ⁵You realize that He came to eradicate sins, that there is not the slightest bit of sin in Him. ⁶The ones who live in *an intimate relationship with* Him do not persist in sin, but anyone who persists in sin has not seen and does not know the real Jesus.

⁷Children, don't let anyone pull one over on you. The one doing the right thing is just imitating Jesus, the Righteous One.

If you are wondering if your faith is authentic, take a look at your life. Are you doing what is right?

⁸The one persisting in sin belongs to the diabolical one, who has been all about sin from the beginning. That is why the Son of God came into our world: to destroy the plague of destruction inflicted *on the world* by the diabolical one. ⁹Everyone who has been born into God's family avoids sin *as a lifestyle* because the genes of God's children come from God Himself. Therefore, a child of God can't live a life of persistent sin. ¹⁰So it is not hard to figure out who are the children of God and who are the children of the diabolical one: those who lack right standing and those who don't show love for one another do not belong to God.

¹¹The central truth—the one you have heard since the beginning *of your faith*—is that we must love one another. ¹²Please do not act like Cain, who was of the evil one. He *brutally* murdered his own brother.* Why would he do something so despicable? Because his life was devoted to evil *and selfishness,* and his brother chose to do what is right.

¹³Brothers and sisters, don't be shocked if the *corrupt* world despises you. ¹⁴We know that we have crossed over from death to real life because we are devoted to true love for our brothers and sisters. Anyone who does not love lives among corpses.

Do you ever wonder if you are just silently sleeping through days, months, and years? There is one indicator of real life: true love for others.

¹⁵Everyone who hates other members of God's family is a murderer. Does a murderer possess the *beautiful* life that never ends? No. ¹⁶We know what true love looks like because of Jesus. He gave His life for us, and He calls us to give our lives for our brothers and sisters.

¹⁷If a person owns the kinds of things we need to make it in the world but refuses to share with those in need, is it even possible that God's love lives in him? ¹⁸My little children, don't just talk about love as an idea or a theory. Make it your true way of life, and live in *the pattern of gracious* love.

¹⁹⁻²⁰There is a sure way for us to know that we belong to the truth. Even though our inner thoughts may condemn us *with storms of guilt and constant reminders of our failures,* we can know in our hearts that in His presence God Himself is greater than any accusation. He knows all things. ²¹My loved ones, if our hearts cannot condemn us, then we can stand with confidence before God. ²²Whatever we may ask, we receive it from Him because we follow His commands and take the path that pleases Him. ²³His command is clear: believe in the name of His Son, Jesus the Anointed, and love one another as He commanded. ²⁴The one who follows His teaching and walks this path lives in an intimate relationship with God. How do we know that He lives in us? By the gift of His Spirit.

4 My loved ones, *I warn you*: do not trust every spirit. Instead, examine them carefully to determine if they come from God, because the *corrupt* world is filled with *the voices of* many false prophets. ²Here is how you know God's Spirit: if a spirit affirms *the truth* that Jesus the Anointed, *our Liberating King,* has come in human flesh, then that spirit is from God. ³If a spirit does not affirm *the true nature of* Jesus the

* 3:12 Genesis 4:8

How can the words of prophets be tested to discover the truth? The most important question is whether they acknowledge that Jesus is fully God and fully human. In the first century, many people were so convinced that this material world was corrupt and evil that they couldn't imagine how a perfect God could wrap Himself in imperfect skin. Many today still function as if the physical world is a bad thing; this understanding is demonstrated when they downplay the hope of bodily resurrection and emphasize the heavenly destination of souls. Implicitly, this belittles Jesus' own incarnation and resurrection.

On the other hand, many people accept Jesus' humanity but deny His divinity. He may have been a great teacher, they say, but certainly not the incarnation of God. However, Jesus made bold claims about who He was and what He came to do. These are not the things a great teacher would have said or done if they had not been true. It is fair to say that no other life has drawn so much scrutiny, and no other life has ever elicited such praise.

Anointed, then that spirit does not come from God and is, in fact, the spirit of the antiChrist.* You have heard about its coming; in fact it is already active in the world. [4]My children, you have come from God and have conquered these spirits because the One who lives within you is greater than the one in this world. [5]But they are of this world, and they articulate the views of the *corrupt* world, which the world understands. [6]We come from God, and those who know God hear us. Whoever is not from God will not listen to us. This is the way we discern the difference between the spirit of truth and the spirit of deception.

[7]My loved ones, let us devote ourselves to loving one another. Love comes straight from God, and everyone who loves is born of God and truly knows God. [8]Anyone who does not love does not know God, because God is love.

[9]Because of this, the love of God is a reality among us: God sent His only Son into the world so that we could find *true* life through Him. [10]This is *the embodiment of true* love: not that we have loved God *first,* but that He loved us and sent His *unique* Son *on a special mission* to become an atoning sacrifice for our sins. [11]So, my loved ones, if God loved us so *sacrificially,* surely we should love one another. [12]No one has ever seen God *with human eyes*; but if we love one another, God *truly* lives in us. Consequently God's love has accomplished its mission among us.

[13]How can we be sure that He *truly* lives in us and that we *truly* live in Him? *By one fact:* He has given us His Spirit. [14]We have watched *what God has done,* and we stand ready to provide eyewitness testimonies to the reality that the Father sent the Son to be the Savior of the world. [15]If anyone unites with our confession that Jesus is God's own Son, then God truly lives in that person and that person lives in God. [16]We have experienced and we have entrusted our lives to the love of God in us.

God is love. Anyone who lives *faithfully* in love also lives *faithfully* in God, and God lives in him. [17]This love is fulfilled with us, so that on the day of judgment we have confidence based on our identification with Jesus in this world. [18]Love will never invoke fear. Perfect love expels fear, particularly the fear of punishment. The one who fears *punishment* has not been completed through love.

[19]We love because He has first loved us. [20]If someone claims, "I love God," but hates his brother or sister, then he is a liar. Anyone who does not love a brother or sister, whom he has seen, cannot possibly love God, whom he has never seen. [21]He gave us a *clear* command, that all who love God must also love their brothers and sisters.

> It's easy to say "I love God," but genuine love reflects God's love. If we belong to God, then we will love each other regardless of how hard love is.

5 Everyone who trusts Jesus as the *long-awaited* Anointed One is a child of God, and everyone who loves the Father cannot help but love the child fathered by Him. [2]Then how do we know if we truly love God's children? We love them if we love God and keep His commands. [3]You see, to love

* 4:3 Literally, one who opposes the Anointed One and His kingdom

God means that we keep His commands, and His commands don't weigh us down. [4]Everything that has been fathered by God overcomes the *corrupt* world. This is the victory that has conquered the world: our faith.

[5-6]Who is the person conquering the world? It is the one who truly trusts that Jesus is the Son of God, that Jesus the Anointed is the One who came by water and blood—not by the water only, but by the water and the blood.

V

Just as we do not get to choose our biological brothers and sisters, we do not get to choose our spiritual brothers and sisters either. But what comes along with loving the Father is loving all His other children—even the really annoying ones! While it might seem to be easier to go off and live in isolation rather than put up with those we are not naturally attracted to, there are responsibilities that come with living in a spiritual family. We reflect our worship of God by living in respect with our Christian brothers and sisters. How we treat the people around us on a daily basis is the real test of our love for God.

The Spirit of God testifies to this truth because the Spirit is the truth. [7]So there are three testifying witnesses: [8]the Spirit, the water, and the blood. All three are in total agreement. [9]If we accept the testimonies of people, then we must realize the testimony of God is greater *than that of any person.* God certified *the truth* about His own Son. [10]Anyone who trusts the Son of God has this truthful testimony at the core of his being. Anyone who does not trust God calls God a liar because he ignores God's truthful testimony regarding His own Son. [11]And this is the truth: God has given us *the gift of* eternal life, and this life is in His Son. [12]If you have the Son, you have eternal life. If you do not have the Son of God, you are not acquainted with *true* life.

[13]I am writing all of this to you who have entrusted your lives to the Son of God—so you will realize eternal life already is yours. [14]We live in the bold confidence that God hears our voices when we ask for things that fit His plan. [15]And if we have no doubt that He hears our voices, we can be assured that He moves in response to our call.

[16]*In this regard,* if you notice a brother or sister *in faith* making moral missteps and blunders, disregarding and disobeying God *even to the point of God* removing this one *from the body* by death, then pray for that person; and God will grant him life on this journey. *But to be clear,* there is a sin that is ultimately fatal *and leads to death.* I am not talking about praying for that fatal sin, [17]but I am talking about all those wrongs and sins that plague God's family that don't lead to death.

[18]We all know that everyone fathered by God will not make sin *a way of life* because God protects His children *from the evil one,* and the evil one can't touch them. [19]Have confidence in the fact that we belong to God, but also know that the world around us is in the grips of the evil one. [20]We also can be sure of the fact that the Son of God has come and given us a mind so that we may know Him as *the embodiment of all that is* true. We live in this truth, in His Son Jesus, the Anointed One. He is the True God and eternal life.

[21]My little children, keep away from idols.

V

John's final bit of pastoral advice sounds an alarm against idolatry. If we look carefully at our culture and into our own hearts, we will find we are ultimately concerned about ourselves, our entertainment, our comforts, and our wallets. None of these are worthy of our highest devotion; but we put more time, energy, money, and emotion into these than we do into the one true God. So John's warning should be heeded: watch out for the steady impulse to love other things more than God.

2 JOHN

Letter to a lady and her children

From John, the apostle

John, the emissary of Jesus, writes this second letter shortly after his first. But unlike his first letter, where he jumps into the heart of the matter with a direct witness about Jesus, John begins this brief letter in the customary way by stating who is writing the letter and to whom it is written. He describes himself as "the elder." This is probably an affectionate title his readers know him by, referring both to his old age and to his authority as an eyewitness to the life of Jesus. As with his first letter, the recipients are not completely disclosed. John is writing to "a lady . . . along with her children." Since he doesn't list any of their names, it is possible that he is using the phrase to signify a church and its members. Regardless of the specific recipient, this letter addresses the concerns of all believers, not just a few individuals, just as his first letter did.

Two major themes stand out in the letter: love and truth. Even though John emphasized love in his first letter, he proves its importance by expounding on it in this one. He describes love as measurable action—not sentimental emotion or academic theory. He says love is accomplished when we obey the teachings of Jesus. Next he warns of the danger of false teachers, as he did in his first letter. False teachers who deny that Jesus is both fully God and fully human are not to be tolerated. Welcoming them in any way, especially with hospitality, promotes their deceptive plans.

John sees love and truth embodied flawlessly in the person of Jesus. He wants to encourage his readers to reflect the true love of God by knowing who Jesus is, resisting false teachers, and serving each other selflessly.

[1]I, the elder, to *you*, a lady chosen *by God* along with her children. I truly love *all of you* and *am confident that* all who know the truth share in my love for you. [2]The truth, which lives *faithfully* within all of us and will be with us for all eternity, is the basis *for our abounding love.* [3]May grace, mercy, and peace from God the Father and Jesus the Anointed, the Father's own Son, surround you *and be with you always* in truth and love.

[4]I was so filled with joy to hear stories about your children walking in truth, in the very way the Father called us to live. [5]So now, dear lady, I am asking you to live by the command that we love one another. I'm not writing to you some new commandment; it's one we received in the beginning *from our Lord.* [6]Love is defined by our obedience to His commands. This is the same command you have known about from the very beginning; you must live by it. [7]The *corrupt* world is filled with liars and frauds who deny the reality that Jesus the Anointed has come *into the world* as a man of flesh *and blood.* These people are deceivers and anti-Christs.* [8]Ensure that you do not lose what we have worked for so that you will be fully rewarded.

[9]Any person who drifts away and fails to live in the teachings of the Anointed One, *our Liberating King,* does not have God. But the person who lives in this teaching will have both the Father and the Son. [10]If any person comes to you with a teaching that does not align with the true message *of Jesus,* do not welcome that person into your house or greet him *as you would a true brother.* [11]Anyone who welcomes this person has become a partner in advancing his wicked agenda.

[12]I have so much more to tell you, but I would rather meet with you personally than try to capture these sentiments by ink on paper. I hope to come and see you so that our joy will be complete.

[13]The children of your chosen sister send you warm greetings.

* Verse 7 Literally, those who oppose the Anointed One and His kingdom

3 JOHN

Letter to believers in the first century

From John, the apostle

The elder John writes this third letter specifically to a dear friend of his named Gaius. John wants to commend Gaius for his outstanding Christian lifestyle, so John sends this uplifting personal word to Gaius and his community. What most impresses John about Gaius is how this church leader regularly opens up his home to house, feed, and encourage traveling ministers. At this time, many prophets, missionaries, and teachers travel from place to place to serve new congregations. Given the Christian perspective on love, it is appropriate for them to rely on the generosity of their fellow believers. While John's second letter stresses the importance of refusing hospitality to false teachers, John's third emphasizes the importance of showing hospitality to true ones.

John contrasts the hospitable behavior of Gaius with the selfish behavior of a man named Diotrephes. Diotrephes is a controlling leader within the church who refuses to welcome ministers into his home and forces out any members of the church who are caught helping them. John urges Gaius to avoid being influenced by the bad example of Diotrephes. He explains that welcoming ministers into believers' homes is about more than just hospitality—it is about reflecting the goodness of God.

John closes his letter by praising another man named Demetrius; it is likely that he carries the letter to Gaius from the elder. John assures Gaius that unlike Diotrephes, Demetrius is a man of truth who may be trusted. Just like John's two previous letters, this letter focuses on living the truth found in Jesus by serving others in love. We don't have to travel full-time to spread the message of Jesus. Being generous with our time, money, and energy from our very own homes is a powerful way to serve God and fellow believers.

[1]I, the elder, to Gaius, who is much loved *by all and loved* in truth by me.

[2]My beloved friend, I pray that everything is going well for you and that your body is as healthy as your soul is prosperous. [3]I was thrilled when the brothers and sisters came and told me stories of your faithfulness as you continue to walk in the truth. [4]The greatest joy in my life is hearing how my children are walking in the truth.

[5]My friend, you demonstrate your faithfulness in all the things you do for the brothers and sisters; even when they are strangers to you, *you treat them as family*. [6]These *friends* tell the *entire* church how you have extended your hand to them in love. You will do well to send them on in a way that is in keeping with God. [7]They have gone out to serve under the banner of the Name, and they do not accept gifts from those outside our faith community. [8]We should give people like this our full support so that we can share in this work for the truth.

[9]I wrote some things specifically to the church, but Diotrephes, who loves to be the one up front, rejects us. [10]If I come, you can be sure that I will call him out and draw attention to his actions. He assails us with lies and deceit. As if that were not enough, he does not welcome the traveling missionaries *into his home*. Instead, he hinders any who do so and expels them from the church.

[11]Dear friend, don't follow his evil ways. Instead, imitate the good *and righteous* life. The one doing what is good belongs to God, but those who pursue evil have never even laid eyes on God.

[12]Demetrius has a good reputation with everyone *we know*. The truth stands on his side, and we add our unreserved recommendation *to the long list of accounts on his behalf*. You can rest assured that we are telling the truth.

[13]There is so much I would like to say to you, but I do not want to say it with ink and pen. [14]I expect us to be together soon and talk about these things face-to-face.

[15]May you experience true peace. I send you greetings from the fellow believers here. Greet all our friends there personally.

JUDE

Letter to Christians everywhere

From Jude, a Christian leader

Although this letter is named for its author rather than for its recipients, identifying this "Jude" is a bit of a challenge since Jude (or Judas) was a common name at the time. Because the hero of the Maccabean wars bore the name Judas, Jewish parents often named their boys Judas during this period. The author describes himself as a servant of the Anointed Jesus and the brother of James. But which James? That, too, was a common name. Church tradition suggests that he was James, the brother of Jesus, the head of the Jerusalem church, and the author of the letter James. If so, this makes Jude the second New Testament letter written by a family member of Jesus. During Jesus' public ministry, Jude was not a disciple of Jesus. As with other members of His family, Jude likely became a follower of Jesus after the resurrection when the crucified and risen Jesus appeared to His followers and family.

Jude writes this letter in the last half of the first century A.D. to an audience facing critical problems related to the influx of false teachers in their church. These false teachers are not out in the world where they may be easily avoided; they have infiltrated the church and are making inroads into the leadership of the young and vulnerable community. He writes this letter to encourage believers to keep up the struggle for the true faith. Some things are worth fighting for, and the truth of the gospel is one of them. Jude has often seen God's grace perverted by those who want to turn freedom into a license to sin. This was a common problem then, and it remains one now. If God is loving and forgiving, and if God's grace is free, then it is easy to take His goodness for granted. Jude counters that to do so denies our central confession: Jesus is Lord and Master.

After urging his audience to fight for the true faith, Jude looks back over a number of stories from the Bible and Jewish tradition that demonstrate how God's judgment has fallen upon those who disobey Him. In the same way, vile characters have slithered into Christian congregations in various places and are dismantling the spiritual communities by grumbling, faultfinding, and promoting sexual perversion. Yet Jude is hopeful that if true believers will pray in the Spirit and continue in God's love, these defectors will be judged and defeated.

A careful comparison of this letter and Peter's second letter demonstrates a lot of common ideas and themes. Clearly the audiences for both letters were facing similar troubles. The problem of false teaching in the church was not just an ancient problem. Even today, Jude's authoritative counsel holds.

¹Jude, a slave of Jesus the Anointed and a brother of James, to *you*, the ones whom God our Father loves and has called and whom Jesus, the Anointed One, has kept. ²Kindness, peace, love—may they never stop blooming in you and from you.

³Friends, I have been trying to write you about our common salvation. *But these days my heart is troubled,* and I am compelled to write to you and encourage you to continue struggling for the faith that was entrusted to the saints once and for all. ⁴Vile men have slithered in among us. Depraved souls who stand condemned have made a mockery of the grace given to us, using it as a pretext for a life of excess, lived without any thought of God. These *poor fools* have denied Jesus the Anointed, our one Lord and Master.

⁵You have heard the stories many times, *and the Spirit has enlightened you about their meaning,* but you still need to be reminded. Remember when the Lord saved our ancestors from the land in Egypt? *He breathed life into their earthen lungs* and took back the life from those who did not believe. ⁶And God has kept the *rebellious* heavenly messengers bound and chained in utter darkness—*shadowy gloom*—until the time when His judgment arrives, because they failed to keep their rightful positions and abandoned their appointed realms. ⁷Sodom and Gomorrah and all their neighbors were defeated by their own sexual perversions as they pursued the strange and unnatural impulses of the flesh. Let these who *went their own way and* are experiencing the eternal heat *of God's vengeance*—a punishment by fire—be a warning to you.

⁸*These stories are examples to help you understand the fate of* those dreamers who have *slipped in and* defiled your community, rejected those in charge, and insulted the glorious majesty of the heavenly messengers. ⁹Even their chief, Michael, when disputing with the devil over Moses' body, did not offer his own taunting judgment against him. Michael simply said, "May the Lord's rebuke fall on you."*

¹⁰The deceivers among you despise what they do not understand; they live without reason like animals, reacting only with primal instincts; and their ways are corrupting them. ¹¹Woe to these *deceivers! They are doomed!* They have followed in the footsteps of *their father* Cain, sold their souls for profit into Balaam's deceit, and suffered the devastation of Korah's rebellion.

¹²These men are cold stones on the warm hearth of your love feasts as they glut themselves without fear, thinking only of their own benefit. They are waterless clouds, carried away by the wind; autumn's lonely and barren trees, twice dead, uprooted; ¹³violent waves of the sea *breaking over the bow*, foaming with shame; *lost and wandering stars* destined to live forever in gloomy darkness.

¹⁴During the seventh generation after Adam, the prophet Enoch said, "Look! The Lord came, and with Him tens of thousands of His holy messengers ¹⁵to judge wicked men and convict the impious and ungodly for all they have said and all the hard things they have done against the Holy One." ¹⁶These men are complainers who look long and hard to find the faults of other men. They are led by their own lustful desires *like fools down the path of destruction*. They are arrogant liars who want only to get ahead of others.

¹⁷But you, friends, remember the words of the emissaries* of our Lord Jesus the Anointed, *the Liberating King*: ¹⁸"At the end of time, some will ridicule *the faithful* and follow their lusts *to the grave*." ¹⁹These are the men among you—those who divide friends, those concerned ultimately with this world, those without the Spirit. ²⁰⁻²¹You, however, should stand firm in the love of God, constructing a life within the holy faith, praying the Spirit's prayer, as you wait eagerly for the mercy of our Lord Jesus the Anointed, which *leads* to eternal life.

²²Keep being kind to those who waver *in this faith*. ²³Pursue those who are singed by the flames *of God's wrath*, and bring them safely *to Him*. Show mercy to others with fear, despising every garment soiled by the *weakness of human flesh*.

²⁴Now to the One who can keep you upright and plant you firmly in His presence—clean, unmarked, and joyful in the light of His glory—²⁵to the *one and* only God, our Savior, through Jesus the Anointed our Lord, be glory and greatness and might and authority; just as it has been since before He created time, may it continue now and into eternity. Amen.

* Verse 9 Zechariah 3:2   * Verse 17 Literally, apostles

REVELATION

Letter to the seven churches

From John, the apostle

On the island of Patmos in the Aegean Sea, a prophet named John writes to congregations of faithful but frightened Christians in Asia Minor. Under the dim light of an oil lamp, John paints a picture of the vision he was given of the world that is and that is to come. This book of letters and visions is to be sent to the hardy churches that have stood strong through persecutions, heresies, and many temptations. However, knocking at the door are Satan and his forces. They are encroaching on the domain of God's kingdom.

Satan's minions, led by the beast and the false prophet, are ready to battle the armies of heaven. This war that begins in the celestial realm spills over to the world below. While the nations of earth rally around the banner of the evil one, heavenly messengers prepare for a battle that has all of creation at stake.

Still, as John knows, the Lamb-King has already vanquished evil in the world. John's ink-stained hands write of the One who is renewing all of creation and establishing an everlasting order. God has Rome and all the powers that rule the earth on a short leash. Soon the nations of the earth will see the All Powerful, the One who has given His life for the many. This is the future as it has been unveiled to John.

John writes of what he sees and hears in his vision. Sometimes he hears one thing but turns to see something altogether different. Sometimes he sees multiple images of the same event as if he is viewing it from different perspectives. These visions are dynamic; they far exceed contemporary imagery and are far superior to what can be produced on film or through television. John's apocalyptic images challenge the imagination. The imagery in Revelation involves numbers, word pictures, and symbols that held religious and political significance for the churches in Asia Minor. Many of the images come from the Hebrew prophetic literature of Isaiah, Ezekiel, and Daniel, as well as other non-ancient Jewish texts. John's audience did not need a guide to interpret the ciphers; each image was relevant to them. However, those living in a twenty-first-century context must decipher these images to understand what they meant for John's world and what they mean today.

Prologue

1 This is the revelation of Jesus the Anointed, *the Liberating King: an account of visions and a heavenly journey.* God granted this to Him so He would show His followers the realities that *are already breaking into the world and* soon will be fulfilled. Through His heavenly messenger, He revealed to His servant John *signs and insight into these mysteries.* 2John, *in turn,* gave witness to the word of God and to the *glorious* truth revealed about Jesus, the Anointed One, *the Chosen Ruler,* by *carefully* describing everything he saw.

3Blessings come to those who read *and proclaim* these words aloud; blessings come to those who listen closely and put the prophetic words recorded here into practice. The finale is approaching.

4*I,* John, to the seven churches in Asia:

May you experience God's favor *and rest* in the peace that comes from the One who is, the One who was, and the One who is coming; from the seven Spirits, *the Perfect Spirit,* constantly before God's throne; 5and from Jesus the Anointed, the Witness who is *true and* faithful, the first to emerge from death's cold womb, the *chosen* Ruler over all the kings *and rulers* of the earth.

To the One who loves us and liberated us from *the grip of* our evil deeds through His very own blood 6and who established us to be *His* kingdom and priests for God, His Father. May glory and power be His throughout all the ages. Amen.

7Look! He is coming with the clouds, *in glory.*
    He will capture every eye,
    Even of those who pierced Him through.
    All the nations of the earth will
        be pierced with grief when He
        appears.

Yes, may all this be *done according to His plan.* Amen.

Lord God: 8I am the Alpha and the Omega, [the very beginning and the very end,]* the One who is, the One who was, and the One who is coming: the All Powerful.

9I, John, your brother who shares with you *this journey* in persecution and the *establishment of the* Kingdom and endurance in Jesus, was on the island called Patmos because *of the ministry* of the word of God and my testimony about Jesus. 10I was in the Spirit on the Lord's Day *(the first day of the week),* and I heard a voice behind me. It sounded like the blast of a trumpet.

A Voice: 11[I am the Alpha and the Omega, the very beginning and the very end.]* Make a book of what you see, write it down, and send it to the seven churches [which are in Asia]*: Ephesus, Smyrna, Pergamum, Thyatira, Sardis, Philadelphia, and Laodicea.

12When I turned around to see what sort of voice this was that was addressing me, I saw seven golden lampstands. 13And among the lampstands, I saw One like the Son of Man *right in front of me* dressed in a long robe. Across His chest was draped a golden sash. 14His head and hair were pure white, white as wool and white as snow; His eyes blazed like a fiery flame; 15His feet gleamed like brightly polished bronze, purified *to perfection* in a furnace; His voice *filled the air and* sounded like a roaring waterfall. 16He held seven stars in His right hand, from His mouth darted a sharp double-edged sword, and His face shone a brilliant light, like the blinding sun.

The Son of Man is none other than the risen Jesus shining in glory, moving among the lampstands.

17When I saw Him, I fell at His feet. It was as though I were dead. But He *reached down and* placed His right hand on me.

The One: This is not the time for fear; I am the First and the Last, 18and *I am* the living One. I entered the realm of the dead; but see, I am alive now and for all the ages—even ages to come. [Amen.]* I possess the keys *to open the prison* of death and hades. 19Now write down all you have seen—all that is and all that will be. 20Regarding the mystery of the seven stars you saw in My right hand and of the seven golden lampstands: the seven stars are the *heavenly* messengers who preside over the seven churches, and the seven lampstands are the seven churches *themselves.*

* 1:8 Most manuscripts omit this portion.   * 1:11 Early manuscripts omit this portion.   * 1:11 Most manuscripts omit this portion.
* 1:18 The earliest manuscripts omit "Amen."

As the story unfolds, we're told that the lampstands signify the churches. During harsh times of persecution, the faithful often wonder where their Master is. Is He even aware of what they are experiencing? John's vision confirms what the gospel already teaches: Jesus is present with them even in their suffering, moving among those who dare to bear the light. Lampstands, of course, are not the light. They only carry the light. The true Light that has come into the world is none other than Jesus, the Son of Man (John 8:28).

Letter to Ephesus

2 The One: Write *down My words, and send them* to the messenger of the church in Ephesus. "These are the words of the One who holds the seven stars in His right hand, the One who walks *and moves* among the golden lampstands:

²"I know your deeds, your *tireless* labor, and your patient endurance. I know you do not tolerate those who do evil. Furthermore, you have *diligently* tested those who claim to be emissaries,* and *you have found that they* are not *true witnesses.* You have *correctly* found them to be false. ³*I know* you are patiently enduring and holding firm on behalf of My name. You have not become faint.

⁴"However, I have this against you: you have abandoned your first love. ⁵Do you remember what it was like before you fell? *It's time to* rethink and change your ways;* go back to how you first acted. *However,* if you do not return,* I will come quickly* and *personally* remove your lampstand from its place. ⁶But you do have this to your credit: you despise the deeds of the Nicolaitans *and how they concede to evil.* I also hate what they do.

⁷"Let the person who is able to hear, listen to *and follow* what the Spirit proclaims to all the churches. I will allow the one who conquers *through faithfulness even unto death* to eat from the tree of life found in God's *lush* paradise."

Letter to Smyrna

⁸Write *down My words, and send them* to the messenger of the church in Smyrna. "These are the words of the First and the Last, the One who was dead and returned to life:

⁹"I know [your deeds and]* the difficult ordeal you are enduring and your poverty, although you are actually rich. I am aware of the offensive accusations preached by those who call themselves 'Jews.' But these people are not the Jews *they pretend to be*; they are actually the congregation of Satan. ¹⁰In the face of suffering, do not fear. Watch; the devil will throw some of you into prison shortly so that you might be tested, and you will endure great affliction for 10 days. Be faithful throughout your life, until the day you die, and I will give you the *victor's* wreath of life.

¹¹"Let the person who is able to hear, listen to *and follow* what the Spirit proclaims to all the churches. The one who conquers *through faithfulness even unto death* will escape the second death."

Letter to Pergamum

¹²Write *down My words, and send them* to the messenger of the church in Pergamum. "These are the words of the One with the sharp double-edged sword:

¹³"I know [your deeds and]* where you live. It is where Satan, *the adversary,* has established his throne. You have stayed true to My name, and you did not deny your trust in Me even in the *eventful* days of My faithful witness, Antipas. He was killed among you *in that place* where Satan dwells.

¹⁴"However, I have a few matters against you: some *who live* among you hold to the teaching of Balaam, who instructed Balak to set up a stumbling block before the people of Israel.* *As a result,* some among you are eating food prepared for idol worship and committing immoral sexual acts. ¹⁵You have others who are holding firm to the teaching of the Nicolaitans. ¹⁶Therefore, change your ways and turn to Me.* If you do not, I will quickly come to where you live and will battle them with the sword of My mouth.

---

* 2:2 Literally, apostles   * 2:5 Literally, repent   * 2:5 Literally, repent   * 2:5 Some manuscripts omit "quickly."   * 2:9 The earliest manuscripts omit this portion.   * 2:13 The earliest manuscripts omit this portion.   * 2:14 Numbers 22–24   * 2:16 Literally, repent

¹⁷"Let the person who is able to hear, listen to *and follow* what the Spirit proclaims to all the churches. To the one who conquers *through faithfulness even unto death,* I will feed you with hidden manna and give you a white stone. Upon this stone, a new name is engraved. No one knows this name except for its recipient."

Letter to Thyatira

¹⁸Write *down My words, and send them* to the messenger of the church in Thyatira. "These are the words of the Son of God, the One whose eyes blaze like flames of fire and whose feet gleam like brightly polished bronze:

¹⁹"I know your deeds, love, faithfulness, service, and endurance. Your labors greatly increase *in quality* as you travel along this journey.

²⁰"However, I have this against you: you have tolerated that woman Jezebel, who is a self-anointed prophetess and who misleads My followers to commit immoral sexual acts and to eat food prepared for idol worship. ²¹I have provided her enough time to turn away* *from her indecency,* but she refuses to turn from these immoral acts. ²²Watch; I will throw her back into her sickbed with those who committed adultery with her, and I will make *them a bed of great affliction* if they do not abandon her indiscretions and turn* *to follow Me.* ²³I will *punish her by* striking her children dead. Through this all the churches will know I am the One who *relentlessly* explores the mind and heart, and I will deal with each of you as you deserve according to your acts.

²⁴"I say to the rest of you in Thyatira, those who have not held to the teachings *of Jezebel* and who remain ignorant of *the real meaning of what is called* the deep things of Satan, I will not burden you with anything more. ²⁵Just keep on task, and keep the faith until I return.

²⁶"And as for those who conquer *through faithfulness even unto death* and continue to labor with Me until the *close of the* final curtain,

I will give them authority over the
    nations.
²⁷And they will rule the nations with an
    iron scepter,
        as fragile clay jars are shattered to
        pieces.*

As I received this authority from My Father, ²⁸I will bestow the morning star to the victor.

²⁹"Let the person who is able to hear, listen to *and follow* what the Spirit proclaims to *all* the churches."

V

For centuries many Jews had been scattered throughout the known world, exiled to the lands east of the Jordan River from the promised land by powerful invading nations. After Jerusalem fell in A.D. 70, even more Jews left Judea, this time crossing the Mediterranean looking for some place far from Roman cruelty. That's why, as John writes these letters to churches in Asia Minor, he recalls some of the most infamous characters from Israel's past—Balaam, Balak, and Jezebel. The ordeals facing John's churches are not all that different from those Israel faced hundreds of years before. Many of the same struggles plague churches in the West to this day. The names may change, but the problems confronting God's faithful do not.

Letter to Sardis

3 **The One:** Write *down My words, and send them* to the messenger of the church in Sardis. "These are the words of the One who has the seven Spirits of God, *the Perfect Spirit,* and the One who holds the seven stars:

"I know the things you do—you've claimed a reputation of life, but you are actually dead. ²Wake up *from your death-sleep,* and strengthen what remains *of the life you have been given* that is in danger of death. I have judged your deeds as far from complete in the sight of My God. ³Therefore, remember what you have received and heard; *it's time to* keep these instructions and turn back from your ways.* If you do not wake up *from this sleep, I will come in judgment.* I will creep up on you like a thief—you will have no way of knowing when I will come. ⁴But there are a few

---

* 2:21 Literally, repent   * 2:22 Literally, repent   * 2:26-27 Psalm 2:8-9   * 3:3 Literally, repent

in Sardis who don't have the stain *of evil works* on their clothes. They will walk alongside Me in white, *spotless garments* because they have been proven worthy.

5"The one who conquers *through faithfulness even unto death* will be clothed in white garments, and I will *certainly* not erase that person's name from the book of life. I will acknowledge this person's name before My Father and before His heavenly messengers.

6"Let the person who is able to hear, listen to *and follow* what the Spirit proclaims to all the churches."

Letter to Philadelphia

7Write *down My words, and send them* to the messenger of the church in Philadelphia. "These are the words of the holy One, the true One, and the One who possesses the key of David, which opens *the possibilities* so that no one can shut them. The One who closes *all options* so that no one can open:

8"I know your deeds. See, I have placed before you an open door, which no one can shut. *I have done this* because you have limited strength, yet you have obeyed My word and have not denied My name. 9Watch, and I will make those of the congregation of Satan—those who call themselves 'Jews' but are not because they lie—come before you penitent, falling at your feet. Then they will know how much I have loved you. 10Because you have obeyed My instructions to endure and be patient, I will protect you from the time of trial which will come upon the whole earth and put everyone in it to the test. 11I will soon return. Hold tight to what you have so that no one can take away your *victor's* wreath.

12"As for the one who conquers *through faithfulness even unto death*, I will plant that person as a pillar in the temple of My God, and that person will never have to leave *the presence of God. Moreover,* I will inscribe this person with the name of My God and the name of the city of My God, New Jerusalem—which descends out of heaven from My God—and My own new name.

God's intention for the world is this: "I will be your God, and you will be my people." This is fulfilled by those who are faithful to Him.

13"Let the person who is able to hear, listen to *and follow* what the Spirit proclaims to all the churches."

Letter to Laodicea

14Write *down My words, and send them* to the messenger of the church in Laodicea. "These are the words of the Amen, the Faithful and True Witness, the Beginning of God's creation:

15"I know your works. You are neither cold *with apathy* nor hot *with passion.* It would be better if you were one or the other, *but you are neither.* 16So because you are lukewarm, neither cold nor hot, I will vomit you out of My mouth. 17You claim, 'I am rich, I have accumulated riches, and I need nothing'; but you do not realize that you are miserable, pathetic, poor, blind, and naked. 18So here is what I suggest you do: buy *true gold* from Me (gold refined by fire so that you can be *truly* rich), white garments (to cover you so that you can keep the shame of your nakedness from showing), and eye ointment (to treat your eyes so that you may see clearly).

19"Those I love I also correct and discipline. Therefore, be shamelessly committed *to Me,* and turn back.* 20Now pay attention; I am standing at the door and knocking. If any of you hear My voice and open the door, then I will come in to *visit with* you and to share a meal at your table, and you will be with Me.

21"The one who conquers *through faithfulness even unto death* I will place next to Me on My throne, just as I Myself conquered and took a place *of honor* with My Father on His throne.

22"Let the person who is able to hear, listen to *and follow* what the Spirit proclaims to all the churches."

4 After I wrote down these messages, I saw a door standing open in heaven and heard again the first voice that sounded like a trumpet.

A Voice: Come up here, and I will show you what must happen after this.

John's next vision begins when he sees an open door in heaven. What happens next would be impossible for John to imagine.

* 3:19 Literally, repent

²Immediately I was *caught up* in the Spirit, and I saw a throne that stood in heaven and One seated on the throne. ³The One enthroned gleamed like jasper and carnelian, and a rainbow encircled the throne with an emerald glow. ⁴Encircling that *great* throne were twenty-four *smaller* thrones with twenty-four elders clothed in white robes with wreaths fashioned of gold on their heads. ⁵Out of the *great* throne came flashes of lightning, sounds of voices, and peals of thunder. In front of the great throne, seven torches were ablaze, which are the seven Spirits of God. ⁶Also in front of the throne was a glassy sea of shimmering crystal.

In the midst of the throne and encircling the throne were four living creatures, covered all over with eyes, front to back. ⁷The first living creature was like a lion, the second creature was like an ox, the third creature had a face like the face of a human, and the fourth creature was like an eagle in full flight. ⁸These four living creatures, each of which had six wings and was covered with eyes—eyes on the outside and on the inside—did not cease chanting. All day and night *they were singing*.

Four Living Creatures: Holy, holy, holy
Is the Lord God who is the All Powerful,
    who was, and who is, and who is
        coming.

⁹And when the living creatures declared glory and honor and thanksgiving to the One seated on the throne, the One who lives throughout all the ages, ¹⁰the twenty-four elders fell prostrate before the One seated on the throne, worshiped the One who lives throughout all the ages, cast their *golden* wreaths before the throne, and chanted *to Him*.

24 Elders: ¹¹Worthy are You, O Lord; worthy are You, O God,
    to receive glory and honor and power.
You *alone* created all things,
    and through Your will *and by Your design,* they exist and were created.

Man moves among seven lampstands and holds seven stars in His right hand because the number "seven" represents perfection and completeness. Another important number is "twelve" because it represents the people of God. The children of Israel consisted of twelve tribes, and Jesus called "the twelve" to follow Him and embody the new covenant. The number "twelve" and multiples of "twelve" recur throughout the book to signify the people of God, so here the twenty-four elders (12 + 12) signify the people of God, both the old and new covenants.

5 And then I saw a scroll in the right hand of the One seated upon the throne, a scroll written both on the inside and on the outside. It had been sealed with seven seals. ²Then a mighty heavenly messenger proclaimed with a loud voice,

Mighty Messenger: Who is worthy to break the seals and open the scroll?

³No creature *of creation* in all heaven, on all the earth, or even under the earth could open the scroll or look into its *mysteries*. ⁴Then I began to *mourn and* weep bitterly because no creature *of creation* was found who was worthy to open the scroll or to look into its *mysteries*. ⁵Then one of the elders consoled me.

One of the 24 Elders: Stop weeping. Look there—the Lion of the tribe of Judah, the Root of David. He has conquered and is able to break its seven seals and open the scroll.

⁶I looked, and between the throne and the four living creatures and the *twenty-four* elders stood a Lamb who appeared to have been slaughtered. The Lamb had seven horns and seven eyes (the eyes are the seven Spirits of God sent out over all the earth).

Throughout this book of letters and visions, numbers play an important role. Numbers and their multiples are signs of great mysterious realities. The Son of

John hears that the Lion of the tribe of Judah, the Root of David, has arrived and will open the seals to reveal the scroll's mysteries. But when he turns to see the Lion, he sees a Lamb instead. Not everything is as it appears. The Lamb stands, even though He has been slaughtered as a sacrifice, because He has been resurrected from the dead. And now in his vision, John sees things as they truly are: the Lamb-King has seven horns and seven eyes, signifying the perfect power and perfect sight He possesses to rule the world.

---

[7]The Lamb came and took the scroll from the right hand of the One seated upon the throne. [8]And when He took it, the four living creatures and twenty-four elders fell prostrate before the Lamb. *They worshiped Him, and* each one held a harp and golden bowls filled with incense (the prayers of God's holy people). [9]Then they sang a new song.

Four Living Creatures and 24 Elders:
You are worthy to receive the scroll,
　to break its seals,
Because You were slain. With Your blood,
　You redeemed for God
　people from every tribe and language,
　　people from every race and
　　nation.
[10]You have made them a kingdom; You have
　appointed them priests to serve our
　God,
and they* will rule upon the earth.

[11]When I looked *again,* I heard the voices of heavenly messengers (numbering myriads of myriads and thousands of thousands). They surrounded the throne, the living creatures, and the elders.

Thousands of Messengers (*with a great voice*):
[12]Worthy is the Lamb who was slain.
Worthy is the Lamb to receive authority
　and wealth and wisdom and
　greatness
And honor and glory and praise.

[13]Then I heard every creature in heaven and on earth and beneath the earth and in the sea and all things in them echoing *the messengers.*

Every Creature: To the One who sits on the throne and to the Lamb

Be blessing and honor and glory and power
Throughout the ages.

[14]And the four living creatures kept on repeating:

Four Living Creatures: Amen. *Amen.*

And the elders fell down and worshiped [Him who lives forever].*

6 Then I saw the Lamb break the first of the seven seals, and I heard one of the four living creatures call out with a thundering voice.

First Living Creature: Come!

[2]Then I looked, and what a sight! There was a white horse carrying a rider with a bow. He wore a wreath and came riding like a conqueror, intent on complete victory.
　[3]The Lamb broke the second seal, and the second living creature called out.

Second Living Creature: Come!

[4]Then another horse, fiery red, sped forth. Its rider was granted the power to steal peace from the earth and received a large sword so that people would slaughter each other.
　[5]The Lamb broke the third seal, and the third living creature called out.

Third Living Creature: Come!

Then I looked; and behold, there was a black horse! Its rider held in his hand a balance scale. [6]And I heard a voice emanating from the middle of the four living creatures.

A Voice: A quart* of wheat for a whole day's wage,* three quarts of barley for a whole day's wage, but do not harm the olive oil and the wine!

[7]And when the Lamb broke the fourth seal, the fourth living creature called out.

Fourth Living Creature: Come!

[8]I looked; and behold, there was a pale green horse! Its rider's name was Death, and Hades

* 5:10 Other manuscripts read "we."   * 5:14 Some manuscripts omit this portion.   * 6:6 Greek, *choinix*, a Roman unit of measure
* 6:6 Literally, denarius

accompanied him. Together they were granted authority over one-fourth of the earth to kill with weapons, with famine, with disease, and with wild animals that roamed the earth.

V

The breaking of the seals releases the four riders and a series of disasters and plagues. Even though what follows appears to be extreme violence unleashed against the earth and its inhabitants, there is a limitation to what follows. Death and Hades have the authority to kill, but their authority extends only to one-fourth of the earth. The slaughtered souls cry out for vengeance, but they will have to wait a little longer until more martyrs are killed for their testimony.

9When the Lamb broke the fifth seal, I saw under the *heavenly* altar the souls of those murdered for holding fast to the word of God and their testimony. 10They cried out in a great, *singular* voice.

Murder Victims: How much longer, O Lord, the holy One, the true One, until You pronounce judgment on the inhabitants of the earth? Until You avenge our blood?

11Then they were each given a white robe and told to rest for a little while longer—soon their number would be complete. In a little while, more of their fellow servants, brothers, *and sisters* would be murdered as they had been.
12When the Lamb broke the sixth seal, a great earthquake shook the earth and the sun *grew dark and* became black (like mourning sackcloth) and the full moon became red like blood. 13The stars of heaven fell to earth as a fig tree drops its fruit during a *winter* storm. 14The sky snapped back as a scroll when it is rolled up. Every mountain was shaken off its foundation, and every island melted into the sea. 15The rulers of the earth, the important and the great, the generals, the wealthy and the powerful, the slave and the free person, all hid themselves in the caves and among the mountains' rocks. 16They pleaded

with loud *suicidal* requests to the rocks and mountains.

People of the Earth: Fall on us. Hide us from the *fierce* presence of the One who sits on the throne, from the wrath of the Lamb. 17The great day of their* wrath has come. Who can withstand it?

7 After this *vision*, I saw four heavenly messengers standing at the four corners of the earth. They were holding back the four winds so that the earth would not be *overcome by violent, rushing* winds blowing over the land or over the sea or blowing down any tree. 2Then I saw a *fifth* messenger, coming up with the sun as it was rising *in the east*, carrying the seal of the living God. He called with a *great and* loud voice to the four messengers who had authority to harm the earth and its seas.

Fifth Messenger: 3Do not harm the land or the sea or the trees until we seal the servants of our God *with a mark of ownership* on their foreheads.

4-8Then I heard that 144,000 would receive the seal, that is 12,000 from every tribe of Israel: Judah, Reuben, Gad, Asher, Naphtali, Manasseh, Simeon, Levi, Issachar, Zebulun, Joseph, and Benjamin.
9After *I heard about* these *who would be sealed*, I looked and saw a huge crowd of people, which no one could *even begin to* count, representing every nation and tribe, people and language, standing before the throne and before the Lamb, wearing white robes and waving palm branches. 10They cried out with one loud voice.

Crowd: Salvation comes only from our God, who sits upon the throne, and from the Lamb.

V

John hears that 144,000 people out of Israel are destined to be sealed, but then he turns to see an innumerable multitude from every people group in the world. What he sees reveals the truth of what he hears: the number "144,000" is not an exact count of who will be saved but is a symbolic number

* 6:17 Other manuscripts read "His."

(12 x 12 x 1000). "Twelve" is a number that signifies all the people of God, from both the Old and New Testaments. In reality, between the sixth and seventh seal, there is an interlude, an opportunity for people from every nation to enter into the people of God, to receive God's mark, and to take their places among the redeemed.

---

[11]All the heavenly messengers stood up, encircling the throne and the elders and the four living creatures, and they fell prostrate before the throne and worshiped God.

Heavenly Messengers, Elders, and Living Creatures: [12]Amen! Praise and glory and wisdom
And thanksgiving and honor
And power and might
Be to our God on and on throughout all the ages. Amen.

One of the Elders (to me): [13]Who are these people clothed in white robes, and where have they come from?

John: [14]Sir, surely you know *the answer to your own questions.*

One of the Elders: These are coming from the *time of* great suffering and affliction. They have washed their robes in the blood of the Lamb, cleansing them *pure* white.

[15]Responding *out of a heart filled with praise,* they congregate before the throne of God
and constantly worship Him day and night in His temple.
The One seated on the throne will *always* live among them.
[16]They will never be hungry or thirsty again.
The sun or blazing heat will never scorch them,
[17]Because the Lamb *who stands* at the center of the throne is their shepherd *and they are His sheep,*
and He will lead them to the water of life.
And God will dry every tear from their eyes.

8 When the Lamb cracked open the seventh *and final* seal, *a great* silence filled all heaven *penetrating everything* for about half an hour. [2]Then I saw seven heavenly messengers, the ones who stand before God, receive seven trumpets.

[3]An *eighth* messenger came and stood before the altar carrying a golden censer. He received a large portion of incense to complement the prayers of all the saints on the golden altar *that sits* in front of the throne. [4]From the hand of the *eighth* messenger, the smoke of the incense mixed with the prayers of God's people and billowed up before God. [5]The messenger filled the censer with fiery *coals* from the altar and cast it upon the earth, causing *a great commotion of* thunder, rumblings, flashes of lightning, and an earthquake.

Throughout the ages God's people have been asking Him for justice in their prayers and laments. Now, in response to these, God pours out His judgment.

[6]The seven heavenly messengers raised the seven trumpets and prepared to sound them.

[7]The first messenger sounded *his trumpet,* and a blast of hail and fire mixed with blood was cast down to the earth. *As a result,* one-third of the land was set ablaze, one-third of the trees were burned, and all the green grass was scorched.

[8]The second messenger sounded *his trumpet,* and something like a great mountain, *with bright flames of* burning fire, was cast into the sea. *As a result,* one-third of the sea turned into blood, [9]one-third of the living sea creatures died, and one-third of the ships were obliterated.

[10-11]The third messenger sounded *his trumpet,* and a great star called Wormwood dropped out of heaven, flaming like a torch as it fell on one-third of the rivers and the springs. *As a result,* one-third of the waters turned *bitter like the herb* wormwood so that many people died from the *poisonous* bitter waters.

[12]The fourth messenger sounded *his trumpet,* and one-third of the sun, one-third of the moon, and one-third of the stars were darkened. *As a result,* one-third of their light *flickered and* failed. For one-third of the day, *the sun* did not shine; and likewise for one-third of the night, *the moon and stars* did not give their light.

[13]Then I saw an eagle flying through midheaven, and I heard it cry with a loud voice.

Eagle: Woe, woe, woe—*horror, disaster, and calamity*—to the earth dwellers! The rest of the trumpet blasts from the last three messengers are about to sound.

When the trumpets blast, another cycle of disasters begin. Each calamity affects one-third of the earth, its inhabitants, and the heavenly lights. Time flies as the disasters intensify.

9 Then the fifth messenger sounded *his trumpet.* I saw a star that had dropped out of heaven to earth. He received the key *that unlocks the shaft leading* to the abyss, *the pit that falls away to nothingness;* and [2]he opened *the shaft to* the abyss. *Huge columns of* smoke rose from the depths of the cavern—*a black, ugly* smoke as if from a great furnace so that the sun was darkened and the air was thickened by the *blanket of* smoke from the shaft. [3]From the smoke, locusts appeared *and swarmed* upon the earth. They were given power, like the power of scorpions on the earth. [4-5]However, they were instructed not to damage any grasses, plants, or trees that grow from the earth. Instead, they were given power for five months to torture, but not to kill, the people without the seal of God upon their foreheads. The torment they inflicted was like the sting of a scorpion when it strikes. [6]During those days, people will seek any way possible to kill themselves, but death will not befriend them. They will long to die *and end their miseries,* but death will elude them.

[7]The locusts looked like horses *clad in armor,* ready for battle. They wore golden wreaths on their heads, and their faces appeared human [8]with hair as *long as* women's hair, but they had teeth as *sharp as* lions' teeth. [9]They had armor that appeared to be iron plated; and when their wings flapped, they sounded like an army of horse-drawn chariots rushing into battle. [10]They have tails like scorpions with stingers, and the power invested in them to inflict torture on people for five months lies in their tails. [11]They were ruled by the messenger of the abyss, whose Hebrew name is Abaddon and whose Greek name is Apollyon, *both meaning "the Destroyer."*

[12]The first disaster has occurred; there are two more disasters to come.

[13]Then the sixth messenger sounded *his trumpet;* and I heard a voice from the four corners of the golden altar that is before God, [14]commanding the sixth messenger with the trumpet.

A Voice: Set loose the four messengers who are bound *in chains* at the great river Euphrates.

[15]Then the four messengers, who had been held *in chains* until the hour and the day and the month and the year when they would kill one-third of humanity, were released.

[16]I heard that 200 million soldiers rode in the cavalry. [17]This is how these horses and their riders appeared in my vision: the riders wore breastplates of fiery red, smoky blue,* and sulfur yellow. The heads of the horses seemed to be like the heads of lions; they breathed fire and smoke and sulfur from their mouths, [18]killing one-third of humanity with the three plagues coming out of their mouths. [19]The *lethal* power of these horses was not only in their mouths but also in their tails because their tails, which resembled snakes, had heads that inflicted injury.

[20]The rest of humanity, those not killed by these plagues, did not rethink their course and turn away* from the devices of their own making. *Despite all these calamities,* they continued worshiping demons and idols crafted in gold, silver, bronze, stone, and wood. *They bowed down to images* which cannot see or hear or walk. [21]They failed to turn away* from their murders, their sorceries, their sexual immoralities, and their thefts.

God's judgment is not only to punish. He wants people to turn to Him for all their needs, but they often look anywhere else for aid and remain in rebellion.

10 Then I saw another extremely powerful messenger descending out of heaven. He wore a cloud wrapped around him, and a rainbow was covering his head. His face *shone* like the sun, and his legs *blazed* like columns of fire. [2]In his hand, he held a little scroll that had been unrolled. He placed his right foot on

* 9:17 Literally, jacinth, a semiprecious blue stone   * 9:20 Literally, repent   * 9:21 Literally, repent

the sea and his left foot on dry land; [3]then he shouted with a voice that sounded like a roaring lion. When he cried out, the seven thunders answered with their own rumbling voices. [4]As I was about to record the thunders' answer, a voice from heaven stopped me.

A Voice: Seal up all the seven thunders have spoken; do not write it down!

[5]Then the messenger, whom I saw standing on the sea and on the dry land, raised his right hand into heaven [6]and swore *an oath* to the Eternal One—who always lives, who created heaven, earth, the sea, and all that is in them.

Heavenly Messenger: Time has run out. [7]Whenever the days arrive and the seventh messenger sounds his trumpet, the mystery of God will be accomplished just as He announced to His servants, the prophets.

[8]Again, the voice I heard from heaven addressed me.

A Voice: Go. Take the *little* scroll that is unrolled in the hand of the messenger standing both on the sea and on the dry land.

[9]I then went to the messenger and asked him to give me the little scroll.

Heavenly Messenger: Take it, and eat it. Although in your mouth it will be sweet to taste, sweet as honey, it will become bitter when it reaches your stomach.

[10]I took the little scroll from the hand of the messenger and ate it. In my mouth, it was sweet like honey, but my stomach became bitter after I swallowed it.

Heavenly Messengers *(repeating)*: [11]Once again, you are to prophesy about many peoples, nations, languages, and kings.

The scroll John eats is taken from the hand of the powerful messenger who announces the fulfillment of all the prophecies. Just as it did for the Old Testament prophet Ezekiel (2:8–3:4),

---

the scroll represents the message John is required to proclaim; but first he must take it in and it must become a part of him. Initially it tastes sweet, but as it settles deep within him, it becomes bitter. God's message is always bittersweet. It is sweet joy for those who turn to God, but bitter sadness for those who do not accept it.

---

11 Then I received a measuring rod. It resembled a staff, and I was commanded *to take measurements.*

A Voice: Get up, and measure the temple of God, the altar, and those who worship in it. [2]However, do not measure the court outside of the temple. Separate that area out because it has been handed over to the nations. They will trample over the holy city for 42 months. [3]I will authorize my two witnesses to prophesy for 1,260 days dressed in sackcloth, *the clothes that mourners wear.*

[4]These *two witnesses* are the two olive trees and two lampstands standing in front of the Lord of the earth. [5]If anyone wishes to harm the witnesses, fire spews out of the witnesses' mouths and consumes their foe *in flames.* Anyone who wishes to harm them is *destined* to die this way. [6]They have the authority to shut up the sky so that no rain may fall during the time of their prophecies. They also have authority to turn the waters into blood and to strike the earth with any plague whenever they desire.

The two witnesses bear a striking resemblance to the faithful prophets of Israel and the faithful martyrs of the churches. Together they stand speaking God's message as the nations rant and rave and trample the holy city. The lampstands, which signify the churches, are not the light, but they welcome the light and present it to the world. The olive tree, even today, is a symbol of Israel. Olive trees supply the oil for the lamps so that they may burn brightly in the darkness. For a season, the two witnesses enjoy God's protection, but a time is coming when they will fall victim to the nations and then lie silent.

---

[7]On the day they finish their testimony, the beast from the abyss will declare war on them and win victory by killing them. [8]Their dead bodies will lie in the street of the great city (which, spiritually speaking, is called Sodom and Egypt) where their Lord was crucified. [9]For three and a half days, representatives of the peoples and ethnicities, languages and nations stare down at their lifeless bodies and refuse them a proper burial. [10]Because these two prophets tormented the earth dwellers *by speaking God's message*, the people will rejoice over their dead bodies and celebrate their deaths by exchanging gifts with one another.

[11]At the end of the three and a half days, the spirit of life that comes from God entered their corpses, *raising them,* and they stood *again* on their feet. Those who looked on were terrified by what they saw. [12]Then they heard a great voice from heaven.

A Voice: Come up here!

Their enemies watched *the spectacle* as the witnesses ascended into heaven in a cloud. [13]In that same hour, a great earthquake shook *the earth* causing one-tenth of the city to crumble *into dust,* and 7,000 people were killed in the earthquake. Then the rest *who were left alive,* quaking in fear, *turned and* glorified the God of heaven.

[14]The second disaster has passed; watch as the third disaster comes quickly. [15]The seventh messenger sounded *his trumpet,* and great voices in heaven confessed:

Voices from Heaven: The kingdom of
    the world has given way to the
       kingdom of our Lord
    and of His Anointed One.
    He will reign throughout the ages.

When the seventh messenger blows his trumpet, the kingdom of this world comes to an end. The rule and reign of God and His Anointed has arrived in full to eclipse the rogue kings who rebelled against the Creator and mocked His good name. God's kingdom entered our world in the incarnation, death, and resurrection of Jesus. It slipped in almost unnoticed beneath the noses of the powers that be. It grows silently as a seed in the earth until it fills the cosmos.

Today Christians live between the times: we live as aliens and strangers rescued from this present darkness, but we also live as citizens who long for the Kingdom that is to come. Until then we are to seek His kingdom and help carve out the territories for Him.

---

[16]Then the twenty-four elders, who sit before God on their thrones, fell prostrate and worshiped God.

24 Elders: [17]We give You thanks, Lord God,
    the All Powerful,
  who is and who was.
For You have wielded Your great power
    and have begun Your reign.
[18]The nations have raged *against You,*
  but Your wrath has *finally* come.
It is now time to judge *all of* the dead,
To give a just reward to Your servants, the
    prophets,
  and to the saints and all who honor
    Your name,
both the small and the great,
And to destroy those who cause
    destruction to the earth.

[19]Then God's temple in heaven was opened up, and His covenant chest could be seen within His temple. Lightning flashed *all around.* Noises and thunder rumbled. The earth trembled. Heavy hailstones fell *from the sky.*

12 *As I looked,* a great sign appeared in heaven: a woman *came into view* clothed in *the radiance of* the sun, *standing* with the moon under her feet, and she was crowned with a wreath of twelve stars on her head. [2]She was *painfully* pregnant and was crying out in the agony of labor. [3]Then a second sign appeared in heaven, *ominous, foreboding*: a great red dragon, with seven crowned heads and ten

horns. ⁴The dragon's tail brushed one-third of the stars from the sky and hurled them down to the earth. The dragon crouched in front of the laboring woman, waiting to devour her child the moment it was born.

⁵She gave birth to a male child, who is *destined* to rule the nations with an iron scepter. *Before the dragon could bite and devour her son,* the child was whisked away and brought to God and His throne. ⁶The woman fled into the wilderness, where God had prepared a place *of refuge and safety* where she could find sustenance for 1,260 days.

V

The sign that appears in the vision is of a celestial woman who gives birth to a son. While it's possible this could refer to Mary, the mother of Jesus, it is also possible this is a symbol of God's chosen people. The faithful remnant of Israel is the womb that carried the Lord and delivered Him to the world. While the great red dragon does his best to destroy and devour Him, God has another plan. Since then, the dragon and his minions have done their best to harangue and persecute the woman's children. But again he does not have the final word.

⁷A battle broke out in heaven. Michael, along with his heavenly messengers, clashed against the dragon. The dragon and his messengers returned the fight, ⁸but they did not prevail and were defeated. *As a result,* there was no place left for them in heaven. ⁹So the great dragon, that ancient serpent who is called the devil and Satan, the deceiver of the whole world, was cast down to the earth along with his messengers. ¹⁰Then I heard a great voice in heaven.

A Voice: Now the salvation and the power
and the kingdom of our God
and the authority of His Anointed One
have come.
For the accuser of our brothers and
sisters,
who relentlessly accuses them day and
night before our God,
has been cast down *and silenced.*

¹¹By the blood of the Lamb
and the word of their witnesses,
they have become victorious over him,
For they did not hold on to their lives,
even under threat of death.
¹²Therefore, rejoice, all you heavens;
celebrate, all you who live in them.
But disaster will befall the earth and the
sea,
for the devil has come down to your
spheres,
And he is incredibly angry
because he knows his time is nearly
over.

¹³When the dragon realized he had been cast down to the earth, he pursued the mother of the male infant. ¹⁴In order to escape the serpent, she was given the two wings of the great eagle to fly *deeper* into the wilderness to her own special place where she would find sustenance for a time, and times, and half a time. ¹⁵Then from his mouth the serpent spewed water like a *raging* river that chased after the woman, *trying to sweep* her away in the flood. ¹⁶But the earth came to her rescue. It opened its *gaping* mouth and swallowed the river that spewed from the dragon's mouth. ¹⁷*As a result,* the dragon was enraged at the woman and went away to make war on the rest of her children—those who keep the commandments of God and hold fast to the testimony of Jesus.

¹⁸And [the dragon]* stood *waiting* on the sand of the seashore.

13 I saw a beast with ten horns and seven heads rising out of the *blackness of the sea.* On its horns hung ten crowns, and on its heads were inscribed blasphemous names. ²This beast was like a leopard, its feet were like the claws of a bear, and its mouth was like the jaws of a lion. The dragon bestowed it with his power and his throne and his great authority. ³One of the beast's heads appeared to have suffered a fatal blow, but its mortal wound had *somehow* been healed. Amazed *at the miracle and its power,* all the earth followed the beast. ⁴People worshiped the dragon because he had given his authority to the beast, and they worshiped the beast *because of its power.*

Earth: Who can match the beast? Who can fight against it?

* 12:18 Some late manuscripts read "I."

V

The beast emerges from the murky waters resembling the dragon; but it has other features, too, that resemble the four beasts as described in Daniel 7. Daniel, in his visions, learns that the beasts represent the empires that terrorized Israel and the rest of the world: the Babylonians, Persians, Medes, and Greeks. Prophetic images are difficult to identify. The beast in John's vision could be none other than the Roman Empire or another empire to come later. Rome has its own beastly authority, the Caesar, who demands worship. "Caesar is Lord," they dare to claim. But John knows better. In every generation, powerful people and institutions arise—political predators that demand loyalty, sometimes even worship.

V

The second beast, which later becomes "the false prophet," has horns like the lamb; but its true nature is revealed in its dragon-like voice. Many pretenders and posers exist in the spiritual world. This new beast wants the world to believe it represents the True God, the only King worthy of worship. But it's a deceiver, a counterfeit of the true King; it steals devotion away from the one true God, producing signs to dazzle the inhabitants of the earth.

5And the beast was given a mouth that bellowed arrogant boasts and uttered great blasphemies, and it was permitted to do what it willed for 42 months. 6Its mouth opened with a stream of insults against God, blaspheming His name, cursing His dwelling and those who live in heaven. 7Also it received permission to declare war against the saints and conquer them. Not a single nation, people, language, or ethnicity could escape its dominion. 8The inhabitants of the earth will worship it, *that is,* all those whose names have not been recorded before the foundation of the world in the book of life of the Lamb who was slaughtered.

9Let the person who is able to hear, listen *carefully*.

10If someone is destined for captivity,
   a captive he will be.
If someone is destined [to die]* by the
      sword,
   by the sword he will die.

The endurance and faithfulness of the saints will be *tested* here.
   11As I watched, I saw a second beast, *this one* rising up from the earth. It had two horns like a lamb, but it was speaking with the voice of a dragon.

12This earth-beast exercises all of the authority given to it by the first beast, and it forces the earth and all its inhabitants to *bow down and* worship the first beast, whose mortal wound had been healed. 13And the earth-beast performs fantastic miracles. *Like Elijah on Mount Carmel,* it even causes fire to blaze down from heaven to earth for all to see. 14Since it is allowed to perform these miracles in the presence of the first beast, the earth-beast deceives the inhabitants of the earth, commanding them to make an image of the first beast that had survived the mortal wound inflicted by the sword. 15And the earth-beast was granted permission to breathe into the image *and to animate it* so that it could even speak. It decreed that those who refuse to worship the image of the *first* beast must be killed, 16and the earth-beast mandates that all humans must carry a mark on their right hands or foreheads: both great and small, both rich and poor, both free and slave.

The beast demands worship and requires all to carry its mark. Those who don't face severe punishment.

17Those who do not carry this mark, that is, *those who do not have* the name of the *first* beast or the number representing its name *inscribed on them*, are not allowed to sell *their wares* or buy *in the market.*
   18Here is *divine* wisdom: let anyone who understands *these mysteries* figure out the number of the beast because it is the number of a person. Its number is 666.*

* 13:10 Other manuscripts read "to kill." * 13:18 Some manuscripts read 616.

V

The number "666" stands in contrast to the perfection of the Lamb and the Spirit. Because this number is "the number of a person," readers have tried to pin down the identity of this person throughout history. In John's day, the name and title "Nero Caesar" was a likely candidate for the beast because Nero persecuted and executed believers, demanding obedience and even worship. Every era seems to have its Neros, those beastly characters who occupy seats of power and yet use their power to oppress God's people. The speculation continues as to this person's identity, but what has not changed is the message of hope in the midst of extreme persecution; that is the beauty proclaimed in this vision given to John.

14 *The scene changed.* I looked and saw the Lamb standing on top of Mount Zion, and with Him were the 144,000 who had His name and His Father's name inscribed on their foreheads. ²And I heard a voice from heaven roaring like a waterfall and clapping like thunder. The voice I heard was like a symphony of harpists playing their instruments. ³*As I watched,* they began to sing a new song before the throne, the four living creatures, and the *twenty-four* elders. The only ones with the ability to learn this song were the 144,000 who had been rescued from the earth, ⁴virgins who had not given themselves to sexual relations. They follow the Lamb wherever He goes. They have been purchased from among humanity as the firstfruits, *set apart* for God and the Lamb. ⁵In their mouths, no lie was found; no blemish marred them.

⁶I saw another messenger flying through midheaven. He carried an eternal gospel, bringing good news to all the citizens of the earth—every ethnicity, nation, language, and people.

Heavenly Messenger (*with a loud voice*): ⁷Fear God. Give Him glory, for the time of judgment has arrived. Worship the One who fashioned heaven and earth and created the seas and the springs.

⁸Another messenger, a second, came along.

Second Messenger: Fallen, fallen is Babylon, the great city! She has intoxicated all the nations with the wine of the wrath of her sexual perversion.

⁹Another messenger, a third, followed.

Third Messenger (*with a loud voice*): Those who worship the beast and its image, and all who receive its mark on their foreheads or on their hands, ¹⁰will *be forced to* drink the wine of God's wrath, poured out undiluted into the cup of God's anger. And they will face the torment of fire and *the agony of* sulfurous flames before the holy messengers and the Lamb. ¹¹The smoke of their torment will rise throughout the ages for eternity. Day and night will come and go without pause or cessation. There will be no end to the torture experienced by those who worship the beast and its image and by those who receive the mark of its name.

¹²Here is the patient endurance of the saints, those who keep the commandments of God and remain faithful to Jesus.

¹³Then I heard a voice call out from heaven.

A Voice: Record this: "Blessed are the dead who have died in the Lord from now until the end."

Spirit: Yes, they will rest from their labors because their deeds remain with them.

¹⁴Then I saw a white cloud, and seated on the cloud was one like the Son of Man, a golden wreath atop His head and a sharp sickle in His hand. ¹⁵Another messenger proceeded from the temple and called with a loud voice to the One who sat on the cloud.

Heavenly Messenger: Take Your sickle and reap *the harvest,* because the harvest of the earth is full and ripe and because the time to harvest has come.

¹⁶Then the One seated on the cloud swung His sickle over the earth, and the earth gave up its harvest.

¹⁷Just then another messenger proceeded out of the heavenly temple. He also had a sharp sickle. ¹⁸Then another messenger (the one with authority over fire) came out

from the altar, and he called with a loud voice to the one who had the sharp sickle.

Messenger of Fire: Take your sharp sickle and gather together the clusters *of grapes* from the vines of the earth, for the grapes are ripe *and ready for harvest.*

19So the heavenly messenger swung his sickle over the earth, gathered the fruit of the vine from the earth, and threw it into the great winepress, which is the wrath of God. 20And the winepress was trampled outside of the city, and blood flowed from the winepress. *The blood ran deep.* It reached as high as the bridle on a horse and ran for the distance of about 185 miles.

The New Testament God is not a God of fluffy love as some suppose. His judgment, while difficult to comprehend, is real; and fear of it should motivate repentance now.

15 Then I saw another sign in heaven, great and amazing: seven messengers with seven plagues—plagues that marked the end. With these the wrath of God reached its end.

2And then I saw something like a sea made of glass mixed with fire *flashing through it.* Those who had been victorious over the beast, its image, and the number of its name were standing on the sea of glass, holding the harps of God in their hands. 3As *they stand and play their harps,* they sing the song of Moses, the servant of God, and the song of the Lamb.

Victors: Great and amazing are Your works, Lord God, the All Powerful.
  Right and true are Your ways,
    King of all nations.
4Who will not fear You, Lord?
    Who will not glorify Your name?
  Because You alone are holy,
    all the nations will come
    and worship before You,
  For Your righteous judgments have been revealed.

5After I had taken all this in, I looked *again;* and the inner part of the tabernacle of witness opened in heaven. 6Out of the temple came seven messengers, clothed in pure linen, bright *and shining,* their chests clad in a golden sash, carrying seven plagues. 7Then

one of the four living creatures *stepped over to* give to the seven messengers seven golden bowls brimming with the wrath of God who lives throughout the ages. 8The temple was full of the smoke *billowing* from the *magnificent* glory of God and from His power, and no one could enter the temple until the seven plagues of the seven messengers accomplished their *God-ordained* end.

Just as God used the plagues to judge the Egyptians and deliver His people from bondage (Exodus 7–12), these plagues will help rescue God's faithful servants.

16 Then I heard a great voice coming from the temple ordering the seven heavenly messengers.

A Voice: Go and pour out the seven bowls of the wrath of God upon the earth.

2So the first messenger poured out his bowl onto the earth. *When he did,* a foul-*smelling,* painful sore broke out on each person who bore the mark of the beast and who worshiped its image.
  3The second messenger poured out his bowl into the sea. *When he did,* the waters became like the blood *that spills* from a dead body, and every living creature in the sea died.
  4The third messenger poured out his bowl into the rivers and springs of *fresh* water. *When he did,* they, too, became blood. 5And I heard the messenger over the waters speak.

Messenger over the Waters: You are just,
    O holy One who is and who was,
  for You have judged these things
    rightly.
6Because people shed the blood of the saints and prophets,
    You have given them blood to quench their thirst.
  They are deserving of these punishments.

God's judgment is true and just. Violent people are thirsty for blood, so God gives it to them. Sometimes judgment means receiving what you desire.

7And I heard *a voice from* the altar agree.

A Voice: Yes, Lord God, the All Powerful, true and right are Your judgments!

[8]The fourth messenger poured out his bowl on the sun. *When he did,* the sun was permitted to blister people with its fire. [9]The incredible heat *of the sun* burned their skin; but instead of rethinking their actions* and glorifying God, they cursed God's name because He had the power to carry out these plagues. [10]The fifth messenger poured out his bowl on the throne of the beast. *When he did,* its kingdom was blanketed in darkness. People chewed on their tongues out of *the depth of* their agony. [11]Still they refused to change their wicked ways,* so they cursed the God of heaven because of their painful afflictions and *ulcerous* sores.

[12]The sixth messenger poured out his bowl on the great river Euphrates. *When he did,* the river dried up and became a road so that the kings from the east *and their armies* could make their way. [13]What I saw next *troubled me deeply*: three foul spirits like frogs appeared, belched from the mouth of the dragon, the mouth of the beast, and the mouth of the earth-beast. [14]These frogs are demonic spirits. *As they go into the world,* they perform miracles persuading the kings of the world to gather for the *last* battle on the great day of God, the All Powerful.

The dragon, beast, and earth-beast are an unholy trinity who send out demonic spirits. These spirits resemble frogs and remind the reader of the plague of frogs that invaded Egypt before the exodus. These foul spirits roam the world, persuading the kings of the earth to assemble together to do battle against God and His chosen.

A Voice: [15]See, I am coming like a thief! Blessed is the person who watches and waits, dressed and ready to go, so as not to wander about naked, exposed to disgrace.

[16]And the kings gathered at the place called Har-Magedon in Hebrew.

Har-Magedon means Mount Megiddo and is sometimes transliterated "Armageddon." This refers to the battleground where the armies of the earth, led by the forces of evil, will assemble to mount their final attack against God. This place is often associated with the plain of Megiddo in northern Israel because the fertile land there has often been turned into fields of blood during gruesome battles. In a place like this, for one last time, evil will raise its ugly head against good.

---

[17]*Finally,* the seventh messenger poured out his bowl into the air. *When he did,* a great voice came out of the temple, from the throne.

A Voice: It is accomplished!

[18]*At the sound of the voice,* there were flashes of lightning, sounds *of voices,* rumblings of thunder, and tremors of an earthquake. In all of human history, there had never been an earthquake of this magnitude. [19]The great city was torn into three parts, and the cities of all the nations fell. God remembered the great city, Babylon, and made her drink the cup of His fury and wrath. [20]Every island sank *into the ocean,* and no mountains were left to be discovered. [21]And great hailstones, each weighing nearly 100 pounds, fell from the sky onto the people until they cursed God because the plague of hail was so severe.

17 And then one of the seven messengers entrusted with the seven bowls came over to me.

Guide: Come, and I will show you the *true nature and God's* judgment of the great whore who is sitting on the many waters. [2]She has seduced all the kings of the earth into committing lewd, sexual acts; and *most* earth dwellers have become intoxicated with the wine of her harlotry.

[3]*Immediately* I was in the Spirit, and the guide picked me up and carried me off. In the middle of a *vast* desert, I saw a woman sitting on a scarlet-colored beast covered with blasphemous names. The beast had

* 16:9 Literally, *repenting*   * 16:11 Literally, *repent*

seven heads and ten horns *like the beast I had seen earlier rising out of the sea.* ⁴The woman was dressed in purple and scarlet fabrics; she shimmered with gold and jewels and pearls. *I looked closer and saw that* her hand held a golden cup brimming with abominations, *bubbling over* with the impurities of her sexual exploits. ⁵On her forehead was inscribed a name, a mystery: "Babylon the great, the mother of whores and the abominations that defile the earth." ⁶I looked and saw that the woman was drunk because she had gorged herself on the blood of the saints and the blood of those people who refused to deny Jesus *even to save their own lives.* When I saw her, I was filled with wonder.

Guide: ⁷Why are you so amazed? I will reveal to you the mystery of this woman and of the beast with seven heads and ten horns that carries her. ⁸The beast you saw was, and is not, and is about to come up out of the abyss and go away into *eternal* destruction. And the earth dwellers, whose names have not been inscribed in the book of life from the foundation of the world, will be astonished when they see the beast because it was and is not and is to come.

⁹Here is the mind possessing wisdom: The seven heads signify the seven mountains where the woman is seated. They also stand for seven kings. ¹⁰Five have fallen, one is alive, and the last has not yet come *to reign.* But when he does come, he will be allowed to reign only a short time. ¹¹Regarding the beast that was and is not, it is *actually* an eighth *ruler* that springs from the seven and goes away into *eternal* destruction. ¹²The ten horns you saw stand for ten kings who have not yet ascended to power, but they will be invested with royal authority for a single hour *and will reign* together with the beast. ¹³These come together for one purpose *and one purpose alone*: to yield their power and authority to the beast. ¹⁴Together they will make war on the Lamb, and the Lamb will be victorious over them because He is the Lord over all lords and the King over all kings; and those who stand with Him are called, elect, and faithful.

¹⁵(continuing to speak to me) The waters you saw, where the whore is seated, represent the peoples and multitudes, ethnicities and languages. ¹⁶The beast and the ten horns you saw will despise the whore; they will make her a wasteland and strip her naked. They will gorge themselves on her flesh and incinerate her with fire. ¹⁷For God has placed in their hearts to do what He has purposed, *that is,* to become one in mind and to surrender their kingdoms over to the beast until the words of God accomplish their end. ¹⁸And the woman you saw—she is the great city that rules over the kings of the earth.

V

Because Babylon is the city responsible for the destruction of Jerusalem's first temple in 586 B.C., John uses this ominous symbol to describe the Babylon of his day— Rome, the city on seven hills. In A.D. 70, the Roman armies march against Jerusalem, destroy the second temple, and scatter the Jewish people.

The whore, who is identified as Babylon, is a symbol to readers in John's day of Rome and its allure. Its beauty and power are legendary, but beneath the surface lies the truth of its nature. People who ally themselves with Rome and all that it represents are partners with ruin. In the years since John's Revelation was first written, the whore has been seen as many different world forces. What Rome represents in John's day has been replicated by many different world powers and their material attractions.

18 Next I saw another messenger descending from heaven. *I knew he* possessed great authority because his glory illuminated the earth.

Heavenly Messenger (*with a powerful voice*): ²Fallen, fallen, is Babylon the great *city*! It has become a habitat for demons, A haunt for every kind of foul spirit, a prison for every sort of unclean and hateful bird. ³For all the nations have drunk *deeply* from the wine of the wrath of her immorality,

And the kings of the earth have *disgraced
themselves by* engaging in *gross*
sexual acts with her,
and the merchants of the earth have
grown fat and rich, profiting off
the power *purchased with* her
luxury.

⁴Then I heard another voice from heaven
urge,

A Voice: My people, get away from her—
fast.
Make sure you do not get caught up in
her sins.
Put some distance between you so that you
do not share in her plagues.
⁵For her sins *are higher than the highest
mountain*. They reach far into the
heavens,
and God has not forgotten even one of
her missteps.
⁶Deal out to her what she has dealt out *to
others*,
and repay her double according to her
deeds.
In the cup where she mixed her drink,
mix her a double.
⁷Whatever glory she demanded and
whatever luxury she lived,
give back to her the same measure in
torment and sorrow.
Secretly she says in her heart:
"I rule as queen;
I am not like a widow;
I will never experience grief."
⁸Because of this *arrogance*, in a single day,
plagues will overwhelm her.
Her portion will be death and sorrow
and famine,
And she will be incinerated with fire,
for mighty is the Lord God who exacts
judgment on her.

⁹And the kings of the earth, who committed lewd, sexual acts and lived lavishly
off of her, will weep and wail over their loss
when they see the smoke from her burning
body rise into the sky. ¹⁰They will stand at a
distance, fearing they, too, might fall victim
to her torment. They will moan,

Woe to you, our great city!
Babylon, the *most* powerful city *in the
world*.
In a single hour, your day of judgment has
come.

**Since greed and seeking unjust gain
are two of Babylon's greatest sins,
economic collapse becomes the basis
of God's judgment.**

¹¹And the merchants *and the magnates*
of the earth weep and mourn over her
demise because no one is buying their
goods any longer: ¹²*warehouses remain
full* of gold, silver, jewels, and pearls; fine
fabrics, purple, silk, and scarlet *cloth*;
fragrant woods, items made of ivory, and
items finely crafted out of expensive wood;
bronze, iron, and marble; ¹³cinnamon,
spices, incense, myrrh, and frankincense;
wine, olive oil, rich flour, and wheat; cattle,
sheep, horses, chariots, and human cargo
(the *trafficked* souls of humanity).

¹⁴Everything your heart desired
has gone away;
All the glitz and glitter
are lost to you forever;
you'll never have them again!

¹⁵The sellers of these goods, who made
a fine profit from her, will stand at a distance. *Like the kings*, they will fear her punishment *might fall on them too*. They will
weep and mourn *their loss*.

¹⁶Woe to you, our great city,
dressed in finest linens, in purple and
scarlet *fabrics*,
dazzling in gold and jewels and pearls.
¹⁷In a single hour, all this wealth is gone.

And all the sea captains, all those who
sail the seas, sailors, and those who make
a living by the sea, stood at a distance.
¹⁸*Strong men* were reduced to tears as they
gazed on the smoke that rose from her
ruins. "Was there ever any city like her?"
they asked. ¹⁹They threw dust in the air
covering their heads. They wept *bitterly*
and mourned *their loss*.

Woe to you, our great city;
all who had ships at sea
became rich off your wealth!
In a single hour, you have been utterly
ruined.

²⁰Rejoice over her *torment*, O heaven.
Join in the celebration, you saints, emissaries,* and prophets because God has judged
in your favor and against her.

* 18:20 Literally, apostles

²¹Then a mighty messenger picked up a huge stone—it looked like a great millstone—and he cast it into the sea.

Mighty Messenger: *Watch and see.* This is
    how Babylon, the great city,
    will be thrown down; violently *will she
      go down,*
    and they will search for her in vain.
²²Never again will the sound of *music* grace
      your streets.
    The melodies and harmonies of the
      harpists and musicians and flutists
      and trumpeters
    will never be heard again.
And never again will an artisan of any craft
    be found *in your markets,*
And never again will the grinding of the
      millstone
    provide rhythm to your city,
²³And never again will the light of a lamp
    bring warm light *to your houses,*
And never again will the voices of the
      bridegroom and bride
    bring joy *to your festivities.*
For the merchants were the magnates of
      the earth,
    and all the nations fell prey to your
      sorceries.
²⁴And in her *streets* the blood of the
      prophets, saints,
    and all who have been slaughtered
      upon the earth, ran freely.

19 *The scene changed.* After this, I heard the great sound of a multitude *echoing* in heaven.

Multitude: Praise the Lord!
    Salvation and glory and power *truly*
      belong to our God,
     ²for true and just are His judgments.
He has judged the great whore
    who polluted the *entire* earth with her
      sexual immorality,
And He has vindicated the blood of His
      servants, which she shed.

³Again praise *spilled from heaven.*

Multitude: Praise the Lord!
    The smoke rises up from her *ruins* forever
      and ever.

⁴And the twenty-four elders and four living creatures fell on their faces and worshiped God who reigns on the throne.

Four Living Creatures and 24 Elders:
    Amen, Praise the Lord!

A Voice from the Throne: ⁵Give praise to
      our God,
    all of you, God's servants,
All who reverence Him,
    small and great.

⁶And I heard what seemed to be an immense crowd speaking with one voice—it was like the sound of a roaring waterfall, like the sound of clashing thunder.

Multitude *(in unison)*: Praise the Lord!
    For the Lord our God,
      the All Powerful, reigns *supreme.*
    ⁷Now is the time for joy and happiness.
    He deserves all the glory we can give
      Him.
    For the wedding feast has begun; the
      marriage of the Lamb to His bride
      has commenced,
    and His bride has prepared herself *for
      this glorious day.*

V

The church that suffered and remained pure is now prepared for a time of glorious celebration. As Israel has been the bride of God, now the church—the bride of the Anointed One—will be intimately united with the Lamb. God and His people are about to become one. The marriage feast has been arranged at great expense, and the festivities are about to begin. But before the wedding, some things need to be put in order.

---

⁸She had been given the finest linens to
      wear,
    linens bright and pure,
    woven from the righteous deeds of the
      saints.

Guide: ⁹Write this down: "Blessed are those who are invited to the marriage feast of the Lamb." What I am telling you are the true words of God.

¹⁰At that, I fell down at his feet to worship him, *but he refused my praise.*

Guide: Stop it. Don't you see? I am a servant like you and your brothers and sisters, all who hold fast to the testimony of Jesus. Address your worship to God, *not to me!* For the testimony about Jesus is *essentially* the prophetic spirit.

[11]I looked up and saw that heaven had opened. Suddenly, a white horse appeared. Its rider is called Faithful and True, and with righteousness He exercises judgment and wages war. [12]His eyes burn like a flaming fire, and on His head are many crowns. His name was written *before the creation of the world,* and no one knew it except He Himself. [13]He is dressed in a robe dipped in blood, *and* the name He was known by is The Word of God. [14]And the armies of heaven, outfitted in fine linen, white and pure, were following behind Him on white steeds. [15]From His mouth darts a sharp sword with which to strike down the nations. He will rule over them with a scepter made of iron. He will trample the winepress of the fury of the wrath of God, the All Powerful. [16]And there on His robe and on His thigh was written His name: King of kings and Lord of lords.

[17]Then I *looked up and* saw a messenger standing in the sun; and with a loud voice, he called to all the birds that fly through midheaven.

Heavenly Messenger: Come. Gather for the great feast God is preparing *for you* [18]where you will feast on the flesh of kings, the flesh of captains, the flesh of the *rich and* powerful, the flesh of horses and their riders—all flesh—both free and slave, both small and great.

[19]I *looked down,* and I saw the beast *I had seen earlier* and the kings of the earth with their armies gathered together to wage war against the One riding the white horse and His *heavenly* army. [20]The beast was soon captured along with the false prophet, *the earth-beast I had seen earlier* who performed signs to deceive those who had agreed to receive the mark of the beast and those who worshiped its *detestable* image. Both of them were thrown alive into the lake of fire that burns with sulfur. [21]And all who remained met death at the blade of the sword that proceeded from the mouth of the One riding on the *white* horse. All the birds feasted fully on their flesh.

In one of the final, decisive battles, the rider on the white horse leads the armies of heaven against the enemy armies of the beast and the false prophet. His enemies are easily defeated, and the beast and the false prophet are thrown into the lake of fire. When the battle is over, the rider known as "King of kings and Lord of lords" turns His attention to the dragon.

20 Then I saw a messenger coming from heaven. In his hand was a key to the abyss and a great chain *that had been forged in heaven.* [2]He seized the dragon, that ancient serpent who is the devil and Satan, and bound him for 1,000 years *with the great chain.* [3]The messenger cast him into the abyss and locked it and sealed him in it so that he could not go about deceiving the nations until the 1,000 years had come to completion. Afterward he must be released for a short time.

[4]Then I saw some thrones, and those seated in judgment were given the right to judge. Standing there were the souls of those who were beheaded because of their testimony of Jesus and the word of God. They had refused to worship the beast or its *detestable* image and had not received the mark upon their foreheads or upon their hands. They had come back to life and reigned with the Anointed One, *our Liberating King,* for 1,000 years. [5]Now as for the rest of the dead, they were not given life until the 1,000 years were completed. This is the first resurrection.

[6]Blessed and holy are the ones who take part in the first resurrection. Over these, the second death has no power; they will serve as priests of God and His Anointed, and they will reign with Him for 1,000 years.

[7]When the 1,000 years are completed, Satan will be released from his prison. [8]And he will crawl out *of the abyss* in order to deceive the nations located at the four corners of the earth, Gog and Magog* *as Ezekiel described them,* in order to rally them together for *one final* battle. They are in number as the grains of sand on the shore. [9]They marched *in unholy array* over the expanse of the earth and surrounded the

* 20:8 Ezekiel 38–39

camp of the saints and the beloved city. *As they laid siege to the city,* fire rained down from heaven and incinerated them. ¹⁰And the devil who had deceived them was cast into the lake of fire and sulfur, where the beast and the false prophet had already been thrown; and the *unholy* trio will be tortured day and night throughout the ages.

Since the beginning, Satan, the dragon, has brought trouble on all the sons and daughters of Adam. Now John sees the truth of his destiny. Ultimately the one who brings such pain and sorrow upon the world will be bound and thrown into the lake of fire. But evil is not easily defeated; John watches as he mounts one last, futile attack against God's people and His beloved. Never again will he raise his ugly head against those who remain faithful to the One who sits on the throne and to the Lamb.

¹¹*The scene changed.* I saw a great white throne, and One was seated upon it. The earth and heaven receded from His presence; there was no place for them. ¹²And I saw the dead, great and small, standing in front of the throne. Some books were opened. Then another book was opened; it was called the book of life. And the dead were judged according to what had been recorded in the *first* books; *these were the records* of everything they had done. ¹³And the sea surrendered its dead. Death and Hades gave up their dead as well. And all were judged according to their works. ¹⁴Then Death and Hades were cast into the lake of fire. This is the second death, the lake of fire. ¹⁵And everyone whose name could not be found *among the names* written in the book of life was thrown into the lake of fire.

21 I looked again *and could hardly believe my eyes.* Everything above me was new. Everything below me was new. *Everything around me was new* because the heaven and earth that had been passed away, and the sea was gone, completely. ²And I saw the holy city, the new Jerusalem, descending out of heaven from God, prepared like a bride *on her wedding day,* adorned for her husband *and for His eyes only.* ³And I heard a great voice, coming from the throne.

A Voice: See, the home of God is with *His* people.
He will live among them;
They will be His people,
And God Himself will be with them.
⁴*The prophecies are fulfilled:*
He will wipe away every tear from their eyes.*
Death will be no more;
Mourning no more, crying no more, pain no more,
For the first things have gone away.

⁵And the One who sat on the throne announced *to His creation,*

The One: See, I am making all things new. (turning to me) Write *what you hear and see,* for these words are faithful and true. ⁶It is done! I am the Alpha and the Omega, the beginning and the end. I will see to it that the thirsty drink freely from the fountain of the water of life. ⁷To the victors will go this inheritance: I will be their God, and they will be My children. ⁸*It will not be so* for the cowards, the faithless, the sacrilegious, the murderers, the sexually immoral, the sorcerers, the idolaters, and all those who deal in deception. They will inherit *an eternity in* the lake that burns with fire and sulfur, which is the second death.

John sees an amazing sight. It is something no one had ever seen nor will ever see until that day arrives. Scene by blessed scene passes before the prophet. Finally he is transported to the end of history only to discover it is no end at all; it is a new beginning. The prophecies—every last one of them—are coming true. God's plan will be accomplished on earth as it is in heaven when the new Jerusalem comes down and He lives among His people. All things will become new.

* 21:4 Isaiah 25:8

9And then one of the seven messengers in charge of the seven bowls filled with the seven last plagues came over to me.

Heavenly Messenger: Come *with me, and* I will show you the bride, the wife of the Lamb.

10He took me away in the Spirit and set me on top of a great, high mountain. *As I waited for what I thought was a bride,* he showed me the holy city, Jerusalem, descending out of heaven from God. 11It gleamed *and shined* with the glory of God; its radiance was like the most precious of jewels, like jasper, and it was as clear as crystal. 12It was surrounded with a wall, great and high. There were twelve gates. Assigned to each gate was a messenger, twelve in all. And on the gates were inscribed the names of the twelve tribes of Israel's sons. 13On the east *wall were* three gates. On the north *wall were* three gates. On the south *wall were* three gates. On the west *wall were* three gates. 14And the city wall sat *perfectly* on twelve foundation stones, and on them were *inscribed* the names of the twelve emissaries* of the Lamb.

15My guide held a golden measuring rod. With it he measured the city and the gates and the walls. 16And the city is laid out with four corners in a *perfect* square, the length the same as its width. He measured the city with his measuring rod, and *the result was that* its length and width and height are equal: 1,444 miles, *a perfect cube.* 17And my guide measured the wall; it was nearly 72 yards *high,* in human measurements, which was the instrument the guide was using. 18The wall was made of jasper, while the city itself was made of pure gold, yet it was as clear as glass. 19The foundation stones of the wall of the city were decorated with every kind of jewel: the first was jasper, the second sapphire, the third agate, the fourth emerald, 20the fifth onyx, the sixth carnelian, the seventh chrysolite, the eighth beryl, the ninth topaz, the tenth chrysoprase, the eleventh jacinth, the twelfth amethyst. 21The twelve gates were twelve pearls, each gate *expertly* crafted from a single *beautiful* pearl. And the city street was pure gold, yet it was as transparent as glass.

22And in the city, I found no temple because the Lord God, the All Powerful, and the Lamb are the temple. 23And in the city, there is no need for the sun to light *the day* or moon *the night* because the resplendent glory of the Lord provides the city with *warm, beautiful* light and the Lamb illumines every corner *of the new Jerusalem.* 24And *all peoples of* all the nations will walk by its *unfailing* light, and the rulers of the earth will stream into the city bringing with them the symbols of their grandeur and power. 25During the day, its gates will not be closed; the darkness of night will never settle in. 26The glory and grandeur of the nations will be *on display there,* carried to the holy city by people *from every corner of the world.* 27Nothing that defiles or is defiled can enter into its *glorious gates.* Those who practice sacrilege or deception will never walk its streets. Only those whose names are written in the Lamb's book of life *can enter.*

V

John had never seen a city without a temple. In fact, every city John ever entered had many temples dedicated to many gods—all, of course, except Jerusalem, which only had one temple. But now in his vision, he sees a different kind of city, the holy city, the new Jerusalem. As he looks around its streets of gold and magnificent buildings, he sees no temple reaching into the sky. No temple is needed in this city because God and the Lamb live with them, constantly in view. Their throne sits prominently in the city. Their light forever illumines its streets and citizens.

---

22 My heavenly guide brought me to the river of *pure* living waters, *shimmering as* brilliantly as crystal. It flowed out from the throne of God and of the Lamb, 2flowing down the middle and dividing the street of the holy city. On each bank of the river stood the tree of life, *firmly planted,* bearing twelve kinds of fruit and producing its sweet crop every month *throughout the year.* And the *soothing* leaves that grew on the tree *of life* provided precious healing for the nations.

V

Fed by a crystal clear river is the tree of life. In the beginning, Adam

* 21:14 Literally, apostles

and Eve were prevented from eating from the tree once they were expelled from the garden of Eden. Divine creatures and a flaming sword then stood guard at the entrance to the garden (Genesis 3:24). Now the tree of life returns to the story, a single tree situated on both sides of the river. No one is denied access to its luscious fruit and healing leaves.

³No one or nothing will labor under any curse any longer. And the throne of God and of the Lamb will sit *prominently* in the city. God's servants will *continually* serve *and worship* Him. ⁴They will be able to look upon His face, and His name will be written on their foreheads. ⁵Darkness will never again fall *on this city*. They will not require the light of a lamp or of the sun because the Lord God will be their illumination. *By His light*, they will reign throughout the ages.

Guide *(speaking to me):* ⁶These words are faithful and true.

And the Lord, the God who inspired the prophets, has sent His heavenly messenger to show to His servants what must soon take place.

The Anointed One: ⁷Look now, I am coming soon! The one who remains true to the prophetic words contained in this book will truly be blessed.

⁸I, John, am the one who heard and witnessed these visions. And when I heard and witnessed them, I fell prostrate at the feet of the heavenly guide who showed them to me. ⁹But he refused.

Guide: You must not do that! I am a servant with you, with your brothers and sisters the prophets, and with those who keep the words contained in this book. Worship God instead!
¹⁰(continuing) Do not seal up the prophetic words contained in this book *for another day*, for the finale is near. ¹¹Let the one given to evil continue down evil's path and the one addicted to filth continue to be its servant. But let the one who is righteous

journey along the righteous road, and let the holy continue in holy ways.

The Anointed One: ¹²See, I am coming soon, and I will bring My reward with Me. I will pay back every person according to the deeds he has done. ¹³I am the Alpha and Omega, the First One and the Last One, the beginning and the end.

¹⁴Blessed are those who wash their garments. *In the end,* they have rightful access to the tree of life and will enter the city through its gates. ¹⁵The dogs, the sorcerers, those who commit immoral acts, the murderers, the idolaters, and all who love and practice deception must remain outside *the gates for all eternity.*

Jesus: ¹⁶I, Jesus, have sent My messenger to *show you and guide* you so that you in turn would share this testimony with the churches. I am the Root and the Descendant of David, the Bright Morning Star.

The Spirit and the Bride: ¹⁷Come.

And let everyone who hears these words say, "Come."

And let those who thirst come.
All who desire *to drink,* let them take *and drink* freely from the water of life.

John closes his book with a warning to safeguard the integrity of his prophecy.

¹⁸Beware, everyone who hears the prophetic words of this book. *Know this for certain:* if anyone adds to these words, God will add to that person the plagues described in this book. ¹⁹And if anyone subtracts from the prophetic words of this book, God will remove that person's access to the tree of life and to the holy city which are described in this book.
²⁰The One who testifies to these realities makes this promise:

The Anointed One: Yes. I am coming soon.

To which we say, "Amen. Come, Lord Jesus."
²¹May the grace of the Lord Jesus [the Anointed One]* be with all [the saints].* Amen.

* 22:21 Some manuscripts omit this portion.   * 22:21 The earliest manuscripts omit this portion.

Topical Guide to the Notes

The references below are to the larger notes found on the pages of Bible text. Those references that are in bold type are to the notes that span both columns of text and are always at the top of the page. The references that are not bold refer to the verse immediately preceding the appropriate note. These notes are always within the column of Bible text below the solid gold line ending in "V."

Abbreviations used in the Guide

Matthew	Ma	Ephesians	Ep	Hebrews	He		
Mark	Mk	Philippians	Ph	James	Jam		
Luke	Lk	Colossians	Col	1 Peter	1 Pe		
John	Jo	1 Thessalonians	1 Th	2 Peter	2 Pe		
Acts	Ac	2 Thessalonians	2 Th	1 John	1 Jo		
Romans	Ro	1 Timothy	1 Ti	2 John	2 Jo		
1 Corinthians	1 Co	2 Timothy	2 Ti	3 John	3 Jo		
2 Corinthians	2 Co	Titus	Tit	Jude	Jude		
Galatians	Ga	Philemon	Phile	Revelation	Re		

Key	Comment	Reference	
adultery	David and Bathsheba	Ma	1:6
Anointed One	Jesus is the one Jews have waited for	**Ma**	**1:1**
Anointed One	Jesus teaches, preaches, and heals	Ma	9:38
Anointed One	Jesus is not what is expected	Ma	11:2
Anointed One	Pilate recognizes Jesus	Ma	27:17
Anointed One	return date is a mystery	Mk	13:37
Anointed One	John doubts if Jesus is He	**Lk**	**7:20**
authorship	Luke is educated	**Lk**	**1:1**
authorship	Paul is sincere	**2 Co**	**12:5**
baptism	John washes Jesus	Lk	3:22
battle	fight darkness with God's word and prayer	Ep	6:17
battle	Jesus and the rebellious one	2 Th	2:17
battle	in Megiddo	Re	16:16
blessing	comes from living faith in community	He	10:25
capital punishment	crucifixion	**Lk**	**23:23**

Key	Comment	Reference	
disobedience	church quickly loses its way	Ac	2:47
disobedience	is the problem and the punishment	Ro	1:32
disobedience	new creations can't return to old behavior	Col	3:17
disobedience	daily confession brings us closer to Him	Jam	1:10
divination	disciples draw lots until Spirit enters	**Ac**	**1:26**
emissaries	disciples whom Jesus sends into the field	Ma	10:1
faithfulness	necessary in trying times	Jo	10:42
faithfulness	of Paul	**Ac**	**21:14**
faithfulness	makes anyone a member of God's family	Ro	9:29
faithfulness	changes circumstances	1 Co	7:19
faithfulness	during suffering	2 Co	4:18
faithfulness	during opposition	Ph	1:17
faithfulness	love of Jesus produces endurance	1 Th	3:10
faithfulness	during persecution	2 Ti	3:9
faithfulness	the world can erode commitments	He	2:4
faithfulness	when promises aren't fully realized	He	11:38
faithfulness	produces works	**Jam**	**2:20**
false prophet	looks like a lamb to steal devotion from God	Re	13:11
false prophet	thrown into lake of fire with beast	Re	19:21
fame	people hear of Jesus' words and deeds	Ma	4:25
fame	Jesus is popular for His demeanor	**Mk**	**1:1**
fame	Jesus' family dislikes His popularity	Mk	3:30
family	all believers in Jesus are siblings	Ma	8:22
family	Jesus' family forgets Him at the temple	Lk	2:49
family	all believers in Jesus are siblings	Jo	19:27
favoritism	all are welcome in the Kingdom	Jam	2:7
fear	of Pharisees and Sadducees about Jesus	Ma	16:1
fear	of Jesus just before death	Mk	14:42
fear	remedied by depending on Jesus	Jo	3:21
fear	unnecessary because God is among His people	Jo	7:39
fear	of Peter	Jo	13:38
fear	unnecessary because God is among His people	Jo	15:27
fear	pulls the Thessalonians away from Jesus	2 Th	1:12
focus	determines your choices	Ma	6:23
focus	on Jesus' will, not those who preach it	1 Co	1:13
forgiveness	better than vengeance	Ma	18:22
forgiveness	characterizes the kingdom of God	**Lk**	**4:43**

Key	Comment	Reference	
format	poetry	Lk	1:45
format	Book of Acts is Luke's second volume	**Lk**	**24:33**
format	use of "voice"	**Jo**	**1:1**
format	John's invitation	Jo	21:25
format	Luke's second volume emphasizes work of the Spirit	**Ac**	**1:1**
format	Luke's focus switches from Peter to Paul	Ac	12:25
format	Luke ends as the good news is spreading freely	**Ac**	**28:31**
foundation	Jesus is cornerstone of the church	Ma	16:19
genealogy	Jesus fulfills prophecies of the Anointed	Ma	1:17
genealogy	Jesus is a new Adam	Lk	3:38
generosity	God gives to the undeserving	Ma	20:16
generosity	God's people should all work together	1 Co	16:9
generosity	God's people should sacrifice for each other	**2 Co**	**8:9**
generosity	have less to give more	2 Co	9:5
God's glory	seen at Jesus' resurrection	Jo	12:18
God's glory	seen when encountering Jesus through the Spirit	2 Co	3:18
God's people	Paul goes to the Jews first	Ac	13:52
God's people	not all Jews will be saved	Ro	11:32
God's people	are one	Ep	4:3
God's people	follow Jesus, a humble servant	Ph	2:11
God's people	anyone may join	Re	7:10
grace	Paul's testimony	**Ga**	**2:3**
grace	beginning of change	He	12:17
greatness	disciples wonder who is the best	Mk	9:34
greatness	requires humility	Mk	10:45
greed	absent in God's kingdom	Ac	19:41
growth	Spirit brings maturity	1 Th	4:12
growth	necessary to stay in the Kingdom	He	6:3
heavenly messenger	serves God's will	He	1:4
history	Romans are cruel governors	Lk	3:1
history	Paul goes to Rome as a prisoner	Ro	15:33
hope	fulfilled when Jesus is resurrected	Jo	20:18
humility	generosity should have no ulterior motive	Ac	5:11
humility	gives leaders great strength	1 Pe	5:7
identity	Who is Jesus?	Jo	1:27
idols	rejecting Jesus is like worshiping idols	Ac	7:50
idols	anything loved more than God	1 Jo	5:21

Key	Comment	Reference
imagery	Jesus is sheep, shepherd, and sacrifice	Jo 10:18
imagery	washing feet represents opportunities for service	Jo 13:10
imagery	the Kingdom is like a vineyard	Jo 15:8
imagery	disciples must fish in a new way	Jo 21:3
imagery	caught fish represent the new faith community	Jo 21:12
imagery	receiving grace is like being adopted	Ro 8:17
imagery	a cultivated olive tree is like God's family	Ro 11:24
imagery	lampstands are the churches, but Jesus is light	Re 1:20
imagery	the beast is a political predator	Re 13:4
imagery	Babylonia represents evil world power	Re 17:18
immorality	incest and other sins cannot be ignored	1 Co 5:8
immutable	God's mercy delays His judgment	2 Pe 2:9
indwelling	followers of Jesus are His body	Col 1:29
infanticide	Herod questions wise men	Ma 2:6
infanticide	Herod kills boys under 2 years old	Ma 2:16
intercession	Paul prays for those he teaches	Ep 1:23
judgment	of everyone	Ma 7:2
judgment	Paul's trial in Rome	Ac 24:27
judgment	of sin when Jesus was on the cross	Ro 8:8
judgment	success is apparent in the result	2 Co 3:6
justice	the cross frees the world from sin	Ro 3:18
king	Jesus' claim is treasonous	**Jo 18:33**
kingdom	here now, established after the seventh trumpet	Re 11:15
kosher	healthy food not as important as healthy spirit	Mk 7:23
laws	Levirate marriage	Ma 22:28
laws	Pharisees demand strict observance	Lk 5:29
laws	deeper purpose of Sabbath	Lk 6:2
laws	are good, but it's better to serve others	Jo 5:17
laws	expose sin but don't free from death	Ro 7:14
laws	unnecessary when grace is accepted	1 Co 6:11
laws	prepared God's people to have faith in Jesus	Ga 3:18
laws	unnecessary after the Spirit	Ga 5:21
leadership	emissaries appoint seven food managers	Ac 6:4
leadership	comes from God, not humans	Ac 14:18
leadership	Christianity doesn't threaten Roman rule	Ac 26:32
leadership	qualifications for elders	1 Ti 3:13
leadership	passionately follow God	Tit 2:14

Key	Comment	Reference
lion of Judah	is Lamb-king	Re 5:6
Lord's Supper	Jesus' body is bread and blood is wine	Mk 14:25
Lord's Supper	gives a glimpse of the Kingdom	Lk 22:14
Lord's Supper	affirms Jesus' life and sacrifice	**Jo 6:62**
love	how gifts work together	1 Co 12:31
love	more important than religious practices	1 Co 13:3
love	should permeate our witness to Jesus	1 Pe 3:16
love	greater than doubt	1 Jo 3:1
loyalty	few stay on God's path	2 Ti 1:14
marginalized	all should help them	Ma 18:14
marginalized	shepherds visit Jesus first	Lk 2:20
marginalized	the good Samaritan	Lk 10:37
marginalized	church is to support faithful widows and elders	1 Ti 5:8
marriage	ended by adultery	Ma 19:9
marriage	more may be accomplished by singles	**1 Co 7:8**
marriage	Spirit binds believers together but not nonbelievers	2 Co 6:18
marriage	the Anointed and the church are united	Re 19:7
mercy	God forgave Saul's persecution of Christians	1 Ti 1:17
miracle	Mary was a virgin	Ma 1:19
miracle	used to meet needs and reveal the Kingdom	Ma 4:4
miracle	caused by faith	Ma 21:21
miracle	at the Jordan River	Mk 1:8
miracle	Jesus has power over nature	Mk 4:41
miracle	caused by woman's faith	Mk 5:34
miracle	Jesus raises the dead	Mk 5:43
miracle	disciples help with loaves and fishes	Mk 6:44
miracle	caused by faith	Mk 6:52
miracle	Jesus heals the blind man in stages	Mk 8:26
miracle	disciples can't heal the boy	Mk 9:29
miracle	Jesus heals blind Bartimaeus	Mk 10:52
miracle	Jesus curses the fig tree	Mk 11:14
miracle	Jesus' signs and wonders announce the Kingdom	**Lk 4:43**
miracle	healed man is questioned by Jewish leaders	Jo 5:9
miracle	Jesus raises Lazarus	Jo 11:44
miracle	Paul's first puts him and Silas in prision	Ac 16:40
miracle	Paul raises the boy who fell from the window	Ac 20:12
mother	dragon attacks the infant	Re 12:6

Key	Comment	Reference	
mourning	suffering requires dependence on God	2 Co	7:7
name	Jesus is Immanuel	Ma	1:23
name	what God's people do reflects on Him	Ro	2:29
numbers	meanings of seven and twelve	Re	4:11
numbers	meaning of 666	Re	13:18
obedience	seeks love and truth over worldly desires	1 Co	4:13
obedience	Paul was called by God and Jesus to his work	Ga	1:5
obedience	honor Jesus' supremacy and God's grace	1 Pe	2:17
obedience	yields pleasure	1 Jo	2:2
order	church is like family	Col	4:1
outsiders	God cares for the Gentiles	Lk	4:19
outsiders	welcome in the Kingdom	Lk	13:30
outsiders	Jesus' message is for everyone	Ac	10:43
outsiders	Spirit enters them	Ac	11:18
outsiders	grace is for everyone	**Ac**	**22:24**
passion	Peter is driven by emotion	Mk	8:32
patience	allows many to come to Him before judgment	2 Pe	3:8
peace	Sabbath is the day to recognize God's provision	Ma	12:1
peace	comes in the presence of God	Jo	16:18
peace	comes from commitment to the Anointed	Ph	4:14
peace	awaits God's people	He	4:5
Pentecost	Spirit enters the disciples	Ac	2:13
persecution	in the first century and now	Ac	5:42
persecution	spreads Jesus' message	Ac	8:3
persecution	God sustains His followers	Ac	18:11
persecution	struggles have stayed the same	Re	2:29
position	expected by James' and John's mother	Ma	20:21
position	place on earth is reversed in the Kingdom	Lk	14:24
power	scares community of demon-possessed man	Mk	5:20
power	leaders ask where His comes from	Mk	11:33
power	good news reveals how God restores His people	**Ro**	**1:16**
power	of God cannot be understood as a philosophy	1 Co	2:5
praise	God redeemed the world through the Anointed	Ep	1:14
prayer	Jesus seeks solitude	Mk	1:37
prayer	Jesus asks for God's will	**Lk**	**22:39**
prayer	personal and corporate	Jam	5:18
preparation	John the Baptist precedes Jesus	Ma	3:4

Key	Comment	Reference
preparation	John the Baptist precedes Jesus	Jo 1:18
pride	rich man doesn't follow Jesus	Mk 10:31
pride	Paul's pain keeps him humble	**2 Co 12:5**
priesthood	perform daily rituals in temple	**Lk 1:5**
priesthood	corrupted under Roman rule	Jo 18:28
priesthood	Jesus mediates between humans and God	He 5:6
priesthood	Order of Melchizedek	**He 7:3**
promise	love is the only obligation	Ro 13:10
prophecy	kingdom of heaven	Ma 25:13
prophecy	Jesus enters Jerusalem on a donkey	Mk 11:10
prophecy	Jesus enters Jerusalem on a donkey	Lk 19:44
prophecy	all are coming true	Re 21:8
prophets	Moses wanted the Hebrews to listen to the next one	Ma 17:5
prophets	not usually priests	Lk 1:13
prophets	John abandons the priesthood of his family	**Lk 3:7**
prophets	Paul explains Jesus' restoration	Ro 1:4
reconcile	begins with God's gift of grace and salvation	Ro 5:12
redemption	Jesus is sanctifying everyone	Mk 7:30
redemption	God's people must exemplify it	Jo 14:21
redemption	resurrection begins God's work saving all	1 Co 15:28
redemption	freedom from death	1 Co 15:49
redemption	righteousness is God and comes to those "in Him"	2 Co 5:21
redemption	accepting God's grace, then growing in it	2 Pe 1:4
remnant	those who survived God's judgment	Ro 11:6
rescue	results from faith not works	Ep 2:10
rescue	Jesus completed what Moses began	He 3:6
respect	wise men bring Jesus gifts	Ma 2:11
respect	woman douses Jesus in perfume	Mk 14:9
respect	should be shown to governing authorities	Ro 13:4
restoration	believers are able to fulfill God's will	Jo 21:18
restoration	comes from the justice of Jesus' actions	Ro 3:26
restoration	happens when Jesus is resurrected	Ro 10:4
revolution	peace with Jesus, violence with Barabbas	Mk 15:14
revolution	must be spiritual	Jo 16:28
sacrifice	giving results in receiving God's rewards	Ma 16:28
sacrifice	Jesus is the innocent substitutionary sacrifice	Mk 14:61
sacrifice	actions are offerings to God	Ro 12:2

Key	Comment	Reference	
sacrifice	surrender rights for the love of another	1 Co	10:26
sacrifice	life to enter the Kingdom	1 Th	1:10
Samaritans	tainted religion by marrying outsiders	Jo	4:4
Satan	dragon makes a final attack before being bound	Re	20:10
servitude	our master must be chosen	Ro	6:23
suffering	has a place in God's plan	1 Pe	4:2
supremacy	Jesus is Lord	Col	2:23
teaching	Sermon on the Mount	Ma	5:1
teaching	kingdom of heaven	Ma	18:1
teaching	judgment	Ma	24:3
teaching	parables apply truth to everyday life	Mk	4:20
teaching	parables encourage reflection	Lk	8:4
teaching	Jesus trains the disciples	Lk	9:27
teaching	parable of the returning son is an invitation	Lk	15:32
teaching	Kingdom is here now	**Lk**	**19:27**
teaching	Paul uses culture to explain the good news	Ac	17:34
teaching	emulate Paul's life, not just his words	Ac	20:38
temple	made up of believers	Ma	17:25
temple	Jesus expels the merchants	**Ma**	**21:11**
temple	Jesus expels the merchants	Mk	11:17
temple	veil to most holy place tears when Jesus dies	Mk	15:38
temple	veil to most holy place tears when Jesus dies	Lk	23:45
temple	unnecessary when God and Lamb are present	Re	21:27
thanksgiving	Colossian hymn	Col	1:20
transfiguration	confirms Peter's identification of the Anointed	Mk	9:10
tree	of life	Re	22:2
trinity	the Spirit chooses where to give gifts	1 Co	12:6
trinity	dragon, beast, earth-beast are unholy	Re	16:14
trust	leaders must choose to believe in Jesus or not	Ma	21:44
trust	Peter knows God is in control	Ac	12:17
trust	suffering requires dependence on God	2 Co	1:11
trust	weakness leads to dependence on God	2 Co	13:4
trust	should lead to action	Jam	1:22
truth	Pharisees are hypocritical	Ma	23:1
truth	Pharisees are blind to it	Jo	9:41
truth	is never complete	Ac	19:7
truth	Paul's message is from God and Jerusalem	Ga	2:18

Key	Comment	Reference	
truth	only one	Tit	1:1
truth	Jesus is fully God and fully human	**1 Jo**	**4:6**
victory	Anointed suffers and dies to win Kingdom	**Lk**	**24:7**
victory	comes from God's love	Ro	8:39
vision	scroll is bittersweet like God's judgment	Re	10:11
vision	God's witnesses have temporary protection	Re	11:6
wandering	Kingdom members are resident aliens on earth	He	13:12
wealth	best used to care for the poor	Lk	16:31
wealth	early church had greedy and generous members	Ac	4:37
wisdom	is following God's way	Ep	5:20
wisdom	dependence on God	Jam	1:5
women	first to hear Jesus is resurrected	Mk	16:8
work	Paul earns a wage and donates his teaching time	1 Co	9:14
worship	treatment of others reflects love of God	1 Jo	5:6

The Titles of Jesus

Early Christians looked for language to do justice to who Jesus is and what He has accomplished. They told stories, used titles, composed hymns, formed new rituals, and adapted earlier traditions in order to convey something true and meaningful about what they had come to believe about the role Jesus of Nazareth is playing in the unfolding drama of redemption. Of all these ways of expressing His significance, it was the titles attributed to Jesus—perhaps more than any other element—that helped to shape early Christian beliefs and devotion to Jesus.

We want to examine a few of His most significant titles, but first we must consider the role Jesus Himself played in using these titles. A casual glance at the Gospels reveals that Jesus used only one title when speaking of Himself: "Son of Man." He never referred to Himself as the Anointed One, the Lord, the Savior, or the Son of God. He reluctantly accepted certain claims about His identity, but He did not make them of Himself. However, many christological titles—as they are called—in one way or another go back to Jesus. The kinds of things Jesus said and did during His public ministry—especially those which landed Him in trouble with the authorities—are the raw materials for later Christian reflections on His significance and the titles they employ. When, for example, Jesus claimed to forgive sins, His opponents accused Him of blasphemy for usurping a role that properly belongs to God (Luke 5:21). When He stilled the storm on the Sea of Galilee with a word, His disciples wondered who He was since the storm appeared to obey Him (Matthew 8:27). When asked directly by Jewish leaders whether He was the Anointed One, Jesus responded with a cryptic answer about the Son of Man seated at the right hand of Power and coming on the clouds (Matthew 26:64; Mark 14:62; Luke 22:69). In the looming crisis after Jesus' death and resurrection, His followers considered all He had said and done so they could answer once and for all the question, who is this Jesus? Answers to ultimate questions never come quickly. Over time the early followers of Jesus constructed a coherent story of His life, adorned with these titles drawn from tradition, experience, and Scripture. We turn now to consider a few of those titles.

Rabbi

At first, the earliest followers of Jesus thought of Him primarily as a teacher because He exuded an authority no other teacher of their day appeared to have. For that reason, some called Him *rabbi,* which means, "teacher." A rabbi was expected to know the Hebrew Scriptures—which we call the Old Testament—teach them, and help people apply them to their lives. People came to Jesus with Scripture-based questions such as, What is the greatest commandment? Who is my neighbor? How should we pray? He answered sometimes directly and at other times indirectly in parables, but His answer was always consistent with the Scripture. Jesus developed a reputation as a master storyteller and purveyor of God's wisdom, and in the first century, teaching and wisdom went hand in hand.

Son of Man

Jesus spoke of Himself consistently and cryptically as the "Son of Man." This title, more than any other, has stirred a great deal of debate: Where did it come from? What does it mean? Is it really a title at all? While scholars disagree over answers to these questions, we can shed some light on the significance of this phrase to Jesus and His earliest followers. It likely comes from Daniel's vision of someone like the "Son of Man" who comes with the clouds and is presented to the Ancient of Days (God). In this heavenly scene, God grants him a kingdom that includes every nation and lasts forever (Daniel 7:13-14). Although Daniel may not have intended "Son of Man" as a title, it became associated with Jesus because it hints at His heavenly origin, makes Him a representative of God's people, and foreshadows the universal rule He will exercise forever. If Daniel's vision is the background of Jesus' title, then Jesus' use of it to refer to Himself represents a bold claim about who He is and what He has come to do.

Anointed One

At some point it became clear to His followers that Jesus is the *Messiah* or "Anointed One" (other translations simply transliterate this title from the Greek as "Christ"). According to their conviction, God has anointed Jesus and set Him apart for a special mission, namely, to restore God's people, repair the brokenness that has overtaken the world, and establish true and lasting peace. Since their hope of such a leader was rooted in God's covenant with King David (2 Samuel 7:12-16), the title "Son of David" is a related title referring to Jesus' role as an ideal king who comes to rule in the place of His exalted ancestor.

In *The Voice* translation, we have often used the phrase "Liberating King" in conjunction with "Anointed One" to express both the royal and the saving aspects of the One who has been set apart. Jesus is truly a king who comes to liberate the world from sin, death, disease, evil, and oppression.

Son of God

The title "Son" or "Son of God" underscores both Jesus' intimate relationship with God and His exalted status. It is used in a variety of ways, depending on the context. On one level, "Son" describes Jesus' role as the "Anointed One" (Matthew 16:16), God's select agent to restore the world after the damage done by sin and death. To put it another way, this title is a way of expressing the claim that Jesus is the long-awaited Messiah. On another level, "Son" reflects Jesus' exalted status as Lord and Master. Paul writes that Jesus is designated the Son of God with power upon His resurrection from the dead (Romans 1:3-4). And on a third level, the New Testament teaches that the Son's coming makes it possible for those who believe to also become children of God. If Jesus is the natural born Son, then those who trust in God have been adopted into His eternal family and are fully enfranchised members of God's people.

Lord

Christians must be identified not only by what they believe but by what they do. As we read the New Testament, it becomes clear that Christians are those who gather together and call upon the name of the Lord Jesus (1 Corinthians 1:2). They direct prayers to Him, compose hymns in His honor, baptize in His name, and gather around the Lord's table for a sacred meal. These practices define the Christian faith and are associated with the title "Lord." This title was applied to Jesus not long after His resurrection. Early Christians understood He was "master," which ranked His followers as "servants," a typical Christian self-designation. Since "Lord" is also used to translate God's divine name in the Greek Scripture, this title links Jesus with the divine name, character, and actions. In relationship with God the Father who is the source and goal of creation, the Lord Jesus is the agent of creation and the means of its ultimate redemption (1 Corinthians 8:6). Perhaps more than any, the title "Lord" situates Jesus in close association with God, so close that Jesus is included within the divine identity.

Savior

The title "Savior" occurs 24 times in the New Testament. Roughly half of those refer to God; the others refer to Jesus. The title emphasizes the close bond between God the Father and Jesus the Son and the similar functions shared by them in establishing peace and justice in the world. The title literally describes someone who provides salvation—deliverance from enemies and protection from harm. This salvation could be temporal and physical or eternal and spiritual.

Confessing Jesus as "Savior" or "Lord" was risky in an empire dominated by powerful political figures who insisted they be hailed with the same titles. To be considered loyal to Rome, citizens were required publicly to praise and honor the emperor as "Lord" and "Savior." Christians refused to do so because they knew only Jesus was worthy of those honors. As a result, Roman officials distrusted the Christians and subjected them to persecution.

Logos (Voice)

As we have discussed on page 140, early Christians referred to Jesus as the *Logos*. By doing so, they were adopting and adapting an accepted religious and philosophical category to express select aspects of Jesus' nature and work (see especially John 1 and Hebrews 1). Recognizing that no one English word or category adequately conveys the meaning of *Logos,* we have elected to translate the word as "Voice." Some early Christian theologians employ the title to emphasize Jesus' existence prior to His entrance into our world, to underscore His unique role as mediator and sustainer of creation, to highlight His function as one who reveals the truth of God, and to express Jesus' divinity while at the same time distinguishing Him from God the Father. The title is closely associated with the claim that Jesus embodies the wisdom of God.

Many other titles in the New Testament express Jesus' significance: the Prophet like Moses, the Second Adam, the Image of God, the Wisdom of God, the High Priest, and the Alpha and Omega, just to name a few. No title completely captures the truth of who Jesus is and what He has and will accomplish in redeeming the world. Still, early Christians tried—with the language and traditions available to them—to express key elements of Jesus' significance as they understood them. They went back to Scripture, mined their traditions, and discovered how various images, prophecies, hopes, dreams, and aspirations converged around Jesus whose remarkable life, death, and resurrection became for them, and for us, the center of life.